WAXAHACHIE

ARCHITECTURE GUIDEBOOK

WAXAHACHIE

ARCHITECTURE GUIDEBOOK

MARGARET CULBERTSON
ELLEN BEASLEY

TCU Press
Fort Worth, Texas

Library of Congress Cataloging-in-Publication Data

Names: Beasley, Ellen, author. | Culbertson, Margaret, author.
Title: Waxahachie architecture guidebook / Ellen Beasley and Margaret Culbertson.
Description: Fort Worth, Texas : TCU Press, [2020] | Includes bibliographical references and index. | Summary: "This fully illustrated volume explores the exceptional architectural legacy of Waxahachie, Texas. Beginning with the landmark Ellis County Courthouse designed by James Riely Gordon, the guidebook documents residential, commercial, and institutional buildings-both large and small-as well as the individuals who designed, built, and owned them. Styles, forms, architects, builders, owners, and occupants are identified and described, giving insight not only into the town's architectural riches and building culture, but also into its economic and social history. The authors offer new documentation for many buildings through their use of original sources, including early newspapers and mechanics' liens, and an extensive knowledge of the period design books that were so popular with Waxahachie lumberyards. Concentrating on the downtown and the older neighborhoods, the Waxahachie Architecture Guidebook is an invaluable resource for visitors, curious residents, and anyone studying the buildings and architecture of Texas"-- Provided by publisher.
Identifiers: LCCN 2020025989 | ISBN 9780875657448 (paperback)
Subjects: LCSH: Architecture--Texas--Waxahachie--Guidebooks. | Waxahachie (Tex.)--Buildings, structures, etc.--Guidebooks. | LCGFT: Guidebooks.
Classification: LCC NA735.W39 B43 2020 | DDC 720.9764/2815--dc23
LC record available at https://lccn.loc.gov/2020025989

TCU Press

TCU Box 298300
Fort Worth, Texas 76129
817.257.7822
www.prs.tcu.edu

To order books: 1.800.826.8911

Design by Bill Brammer

For

Burke Evans

a.k.a.

Ernest Burke

when growing up in Waxahachie

and

Dr. E. Burke Evans, Galveston resident.

Physician, teacher, preservationist, artist,

and

benefactor and friend to many.

(Burke loved it all.)

Ellis County Courthouse.

CONTENTS

PREFACE

The Ellis County Museum was established in 1968 by a group of fifty citizens who recognized the need to preserve artifacts, encourage historical study, and promote public interest. To further those goals, in the first year of the museum's existence several homeowners opened their historical homes to the public for a tour. Named the Gingerbread Tour for the town's many Victorian-era homes with their ornate porch and eve ornamentation, the tour continues annually on the first weekend in June.

At the time of his death, Dr. Ernest Burke Evans, a pioneer of historical preservation in Galveston who had spent his early years in Waxahachie, was sponsoring a project through the Ellis County Museum to research and document the historical buildings of Waxahachie. Having worked with architectural historian Ellen Beasley at the Galveston Historical Foundation, he reached out to her to produce an architectural guidebook for the city where he grew up.

Ms. Beasley enlisted Margaret Culbertson, who also published in the field of architectural history, to share the research and writing. They both spent many hours in the Ellis County Clerk's office, Sims Library, and the Ellis County Museum, among other collections and resources, searching for information about Waxahachie's residential and downtown areas.

As Waxahachie grows, the historical area will become more important, and this documentation of its historic buildings and their early owners will be invaluable.

The Ellis County Museum is proud to have facilitated this work and will always be indebted to Dr. Evans, Ms. Beasley, and Ms. Culbertson for the legacy Waxahachie is gaining from the *Waxahachie Architecture Guidebook.*

Glinda Felty

President, Ellis County Museum Board

ACKNOWLEDGMENTS

Both of us were well aware of Waxahachie's extraordinary architectural resources long before beginning the guidebook project. Margaret grew up visiting grandparents in Waxahachie and then moved there with her family when she was twelve. Ellen, like all of Burke Evans's friends in Galveston, often heard him reference the buildings and architecture of his boyhood home. It was Burke who, with a copy in hand of the *Galveston Architecture Guidebook* as a model, initiated the Waxahachie project in association with a receptive Ellis County Museum.

To borrow a phrase, "it takes a village" to write an architecture guidebook for a special place—and writing one for Waxahachie is no exception. This publication reflects the interest, help, and encouragement of many people beginning, of course, with the primary benefactor, Burke Evans. We are grateful to Burke for his generosity and unfailing enthusiasm, and to the museum board and staff for their in-kind support, most especially curator Shannon Simpson for his many hours of proofreading, technical assistance, and his familiarity with the museum's extensive photograph collection. A special thank you to museum volunteer and genealogy enthusiast Judy Seibert, who spent countless hours researching the genealogy-related facts that enrich many of the individual entries in the book.

One of the most pleasant aspects of the project was having the excuse to meet so many Waxahachie property owners and residents, and for Margaret, becoming reacquainted with many of them. There are too many to list here, but sincere thanks to all those who talked and corresponded with us, responded to our inquiries, shared their histories, documents, and observations, and welcomed us into their homes. Waxahachie definitely has an abundance of those who take pride in place!

We extend our appreciation to the following who helped in a variety of ways: Nancy Adrian, Harold Barnard, Wayne Bell, Mattie Borders, Mary Sue Britton, Steve and Hilda Chapman, Billinelle Currie, Carroll Davis, Joal and John Donovan, Samantha Estey, Glinda and Larry Felty, Stephen Fox, Billy Ray Hancock, John and Roblyn Herndon, David Hudgins, Kirk Hunter and Maureen Moore, Joe Jenkins, Becky and Jim Kauffman, Rafael Longoria, *Waxahachie Daily Light*'s Jim Perry, Cindy Polley, Nancy Post, Andy Sias, Anita Simpson, Daniel and Leah Lawless Smith, David and Pat Smith, city parks director John Smith, Sylvia Smith, Michael Scott, Paul Stevens, Amber Villarreal, Fred Weldon, Judy Wells, county engineer Joe White, and Sandra and Ron Wilkinson.

Staff members of the following institutions were generous with their expertise and time, and making materials and records available to us: Nicholas P. Sims Library, Reference Department; Waxahachie Independent School District, Office of the Superintendent; City of Waxahachie, multiple offices; Ellis County Clerk's Office; and Ellis County District Clerk's Office. Nor could we have accomplished this without having access to the records as well as the knowledgeable staff of the Ellis County Abstract & Title Company, Inc.

TCU Press and its staff provided outstanding support and understanding of this project, including Dan Williams, director, Melinda Esco, production manager, Kathy Walton, editor, and Molly Spain, assistant editor. Special thanks also to Bill Brammer, of FUSION29, for the book design and to Jim Parsons, of Preservation Houston, for creating the maps that grace each section.

We also must include a shout-out to members of the Waxahachie High School Interact Club and their faculty sponsor Megan Mills for their help at the library.

Ellen Beasley and Margaret Culbertson
May 2020

Since Ellen moved to Waxahachie for several years to work on the guidebook, and Margaret was returning to a place where she had lived, we each have a few individual acknowledgments to make.

To Max and Earlane Simpson for being so welcoming when I arrived in Waxahachie; to John and Marie Chiles for being so supportive and such good friends while I was there; and to Glinda Felty for her steady hand and good humor.

Ellen Beasley

I would like to thank the family and friends who shared the journey that led to this book, beginning with my parents, Dale and Warren Culbertson. They grew up in Waxahachie, and contributed their knowledge of the town and its history, encouraged my interest, and aided my research. My sister Kaye Fuller's encouragement and interest were invaluable, and brother-in-law Roger Fuller donated the camera that Ellen and I used to take most of the photographs in the book. Sydney Barr assisted with her own family history and Waxahachie memories, as well as providing a welcome home-away-from-home during the continuing research trips after my father's death in 2008. Kerry Goelzer gave wise counsel regarding text and images. Through this long process, my partner Sims McCutchan provided unfailing love and support, which enabled the completion of the work.

Margaret Culbertson

USING THE GUIDEBOOK

The *Waxahachie Architecture Guidebook* consists of seven geographic sections. Each section is designated by a letter and a subheading. The letters indicate the order of the sections, beginning with *A: Downtown* and following a counter-clockwise spiral through the city ending with *G: University and Williams Additions*. The subheadings incorporate the name or names of major historic neighborhoods and subdivisions in the section. Not all of the subdivisions within a section are included in the section titles, and a subdivision's borders sometimes extend beyond those of the section that nominally includes it.

Each of the seven sections begins with a brief introduction, followed by a map marked with numbers for each of the buildings or sites described in the section.

Individual entries are identified by a heading that includes street address, the historic name of the building (if there is one), the date of construction, and the name of the original architect and/or builder, if documented. If a year is preceded by a "c." (c. 1885), documentary evidence places construction within three years before or after that date. If the *c.* precedes two years joined by a hyphen (as in c. 1885-1890), construction occurred at some point within that range of years. If a range of years is not preceded by *c.*, then construction continued throughout those years. Later alterations are described in the text. If more than one building is illustrated and discussed in an entry, the addresses in the heading are listed from left to right as the buildings appear in the photograph.

A description and history of the building or site follows the entry heading. Some entries include references to other buildings, and the addresses of those buildings are in bold type if there are separate entries for them. Most buildings listed in the guide are not open to the public, and, except for commercial, institutional, and government buildings, should be viewed only from the street or sidewalk.

The following sources are mentioned with such frequency that abbreviated titles (given in italics below) are used in the text. Full titles and bibliographical information are included in the selected bibliography at the end of the book.

■ ***1876 bird's-eye view* and *1886 bird's-eye view:*** Two nineteenth century lithographic bird's-eye views provide documentation of streetscapes as well as individual buildings, one published in 1876 and the other in 1886.

■ ***Sanborn maps:*** The Sanborn Map Company produced detailed maps of Waxahachie, and thousands of other cities around the country, to assist fire insurance companies and underwriters in determining risk. They provide building footprints and color-coded information about building materials. Sanborn maps for Waxahachie date from 1885, 1890, 1893, 1898, 1904, 1909, 1914, 1925, and 1959, but early maps primarily cover only the downtown area and industrial sites. The company expanded coverage in later years to include many residential areas, but certain parts of town were never included in the maps.

■ ***Deed records* and *mechanics' liens:*** Records in the Ellis County Clerk's Office, primarily deed records and mechanics' liens, also were key in the research process. Deed records document the ownership changes of properties and can sometimes help to estimate construction dates when the cost of the property changes significantly. Mechanics' liens, which were contracts between property owners and their builders, describe the structures to be built and specify payments and completion dates. In addition, if an architect provided plans for the building, the name of the architect was sometimes included in the document. Although the mechanics' liens often refer to "attached plans," those are no longer extant. Unfortunately for historians, a mechanic's lien was not filed for every building.

■ **The *Daily Light* and the *Enterprise:*** The local newspapers, the *Waxahachie Daily Light* and the *Waxahachie Enterprise*, used in combination with the Sanborn maps and deed records, have enabled the dating of many buildings and provided useful information about owners, builders, and architects.

This guidebook is by no means a comprehensive listing of all the significant buildings in Waxahachie. Time and space have limited the number of buildings that could be included. Many worthy buildings remain to be explored and enjoyed. The authors have tried to include examples of notable design, representative examples of building types, and buildings designed, owned, or used by persons of interest. We also have included multiple examples of the same building type to document the range of years when specific types were constructed and the variety of designs and details that were used. Preference has been given to buildings that have retained their physical integrity, but exceptions have been made when a building is particularly significant or few other examples of the type have survived.

The authors have endeavored to present accurate listings, but guidebooks are always a work in progress. Readers who are aware of inaccuracies or who know of or discover additional documents or information are encouraged to report them to the Ellis County Museum.

Section Name —— **SECTION B** **TOWN ADDITION** —— Geographic Section

Map Code —— **B-1**
Building Address —— **308 North Monroe Street**
St. Paul's Episcopal Church
[now Francesca Chapel]
Date —— *1887*

Description —— This tiny gem of unadorned Gothic Revival design is the oldest surviving church building in Waxahachie, and it still stands on its original site. Its cruciform plan was unusual for a small church of the time. Most Gothic Revival churches of this size followed the English Gothic parish church model with a nave attached directly to the smaller space of the chancel...

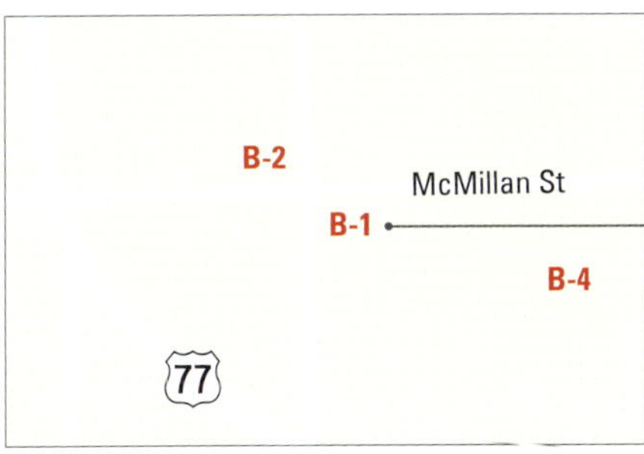

Building Location

Introduction

Waxahachie's unusually extensive collection of well-preserved buildings of the late nineteenth and early twentieth centuries can tell us much about the history of the town and region. The economic, social, and cultural forces of the time all played a part in the form and appearance of the structures that line the streets. Agriculture, railroads, cotton, commerce, education, and religion all have left their traces. Exploring these buildings enables us to meet the men and women who designed, built, inhabited, and preserved them and to admire their creativity, adaptability, and craftsmanship.

The buildings we see today, however, tell us almost nothing about Waxahachie's earliest years, for none of the 1850s buildings survive. The fertile Blackland Prairie drew settlers in the mid-nineteenth century, and in 1847, Emory W. (E. W.) Rogers claimed a headright of 640 acres near Waxahachie Creek and built a cabin where the Rogers Hotel now stands. The land was then part of Navarro County, but in 1849 became part of the newly established Ellis County. Rogers offered sixty acres of land close to the creek to successfully secure the county seat, and additional settlers soon followed. The only physical remnant of that era is the tilt off true north in the orientation of downtown streets, which aligned with the placement of Rogers's cabin, according to the 1892 *Memorial and Biographical History of Ellis County*.

Growth was slow through the 1850s and 1860s, for the area's economy was based on diversified agriculture, and slow wagons drawn by oxen or mules on bad roads were the only means of getting crops to urban markets. Most of the town's buildings from these years have been lost to fire or the even more destructive force of progress, but land agent Robert M. Wyatt's diminutive two-room office avoided these dangers and remains as the oldest commercial building in town and a rare example of vernacular Greek Revival architecture in this part of Texas.

Bird's Eye View of Waxahachie, 1876. *Courtesy Ellis County Museum.*

With the arrival of its first railroad in 1879 the city that we admire today began to take shape. The railroads provided an efficient and affordable means of transport, and farmers began to convert their fields from diversified crops to income-producing cotton. Waxahachie became a regional commercial center as bankers, lawyers, and merchants prospered, serving the needs of the farmers. The railroads not only carried cotton to market, but also brought in lumber and other building materials that enabled more, and better, construction.

A comparison of the 1876 and 1886 bird's-eye views of the town shows the transformation enabled by railroads and cotton production. In 1876, many of the commercial buildings surrounding the courthouse were only one story, and most were built of wood. The residential structures were all built of wood, mainly one-story gable-roofed structures, and most stood within two blocks of the square. Marvin College stood in isolation at the town's northern edge. By 1886, two story brick structures lined the square, and the city had visibly grown in density. Larger, more complex houses lined streets, which had been extended in all directions. To the north, the Marvin College building

Bird's-eye view of Waxahachie, 1886. *Courtesy Ellis County Museum.*

had been acquired by the city for use as a public school and no longer stood alone. Houses lined the streets to its east, west, and south. Substantial residences also lined streets west of the square. To the east, across a small bridge, can be seen two churches, a school, and multiple small houses that constituted the African American area, then known as Freedman Town.

Growth continued into the 1890s with the Ellis County Courthouse serving as the most spectacular example. Local developers platted and promoted new residential subdivisions, with the West End Addition, platted in 1889, being the largest and most carefully planned. The principles of the late nineteenth-century garden suburb movement are evident in the design of its streets, two parks, and streetcar line to the square.

Between 1900 and 1905 new public and institutional structures marked major developments in the city that would provide long-term benefits. Community leaders worked on many fronts to develop economic, educational, and cultural assets, with outstanding success. The cotton mill of 1901, the Chautauqua auditorium of 1902, the three-story Park School building of 1904, and the Sims Library of 1905 are evidence of a flurry of activity aimed at diversifying the city's economy

Trinity University's decision to move to Waxahachie in 1901 had a major impact on the city's growth and reputation. The community donated the ten-acre campus and funded construction of the 1902 Main Building, by Dallas architects Hubbell & Greene, shown here in a c. 1910 photograph. *Courtesy of the Dr. Charles W. Simpson Family and the Ellis County Museum.*

and improving its educational resources. But the successful 1901 campaign to bring Trinity University to Waxahachie surpassed them all in significance for the city's growth. The university not only brought students and faculty to town, it served as an educational and social resource for the community. Families moved here from the surrounding countryside and region so that their children could live at home and attend the university. Trinity increased Waxahachie's reputation throughout the state. Its athletic fields even served as the site of an air show in 1925 by the world-famous African American pilot Bessie Coleman, who had grown up in Waxahachie.

Waxahachie gained national recognition through the sports pages in 1916, when the Detroit Tigers baseball team selected the city for their spring training site. They returned in 1917, and in subsequent years they were followed by the Cincinnati Reds, Chicago White Sox, and Kansas City Blues. After floods damaged the ballpark in 1922, Waxahachie dropped from the national sports scene until 1945, when Paul Richards, a local boy, became a star with the Detroit Tigers in the World Series. His long and successful career in baseball as player and manager led to a national familiarity with the city's name, at least among baseball fans. The baseball park where the Detroit Tigers played is long gone, but its replacement bears the name of Paul Richards.

This c. 1931 panorama, taken from the courthouse, shows the west side of the square (on the left) as completely rebuilt after fires in 1912 and 1913 and the north side (center and right) before the nineteenth-century façades were altered and updated to appeal to the twentieth-century public. The four-story Rogers Hotel (far right) stands on the site of E. W. Rogers's 1847 cabin. From Chamber of Commerce brochure *Waxahachie: Queen City of the Cotton Belt. Private Collection.*

The Great Depression of the 1930s dealt a serious blow to Waxahachie's growth, as did World War II, and Trinity University's departure for San Antonio in 1942. The Southwestern Bible Institute, later to become the Southwestern Assemblies of God University, bought the campus in 1943, returning activity to the buildings and, eventually, expanding the campus.

After the war, new manufacturing concerns began to locate in town, providing employment and bringing new residents. Among the earliest was Tyler Refrigeration, which moved into the old cotton mill buildings in 1945. Southome Furniture Industries arrived in 1951, and Larkin Packer Company in 1955. Highway construction in the 1950s and 1960s facilitated these developments and enabled more Waxahachie residents to commute to work in Dallas and Fort Worth.

Waxahachie has served as a location for numerous films, and though their economic impact cannot equal the city's other industries, they have shared the rich resources of the city's historic architecture with viewers around the world. Major movies filmed here that won Academy Awards include *Bonnie and Clyde* (1967), *Tender Mercies* (1983), *Places in the Heart* (1984), and *Trip to Bountiful* (1986). Waxahachie native Robert Benton won the Oscar for best original screenplay for *Places in the Heart*, which he also directed. Horton Foote, who wrote the screenplay for *Trip to Bountiful*, also wrote and directed two other movies that were filmed in Waxahachie, *1918* (1985) and *On Valentine's Day* (1986).

Postcard view of a Waxahachie cotton yard, c. 1914. *Private Collection.*

The historic architecture that draws filmmakers, visitors, and new residents to Waxahachie would not have survived in its current state without the efforts of multiple organizations and individuals. Ellis County Museum, founded in 1968, helped to support Waxahachie's preservation movement from its inception, and it continues to do so today. It sponsored the first Gingerbread Trail tour of homes in 1969, and the tours have continued annually since then. Historic Waxahachie, Inc., founded in 1977, has encouraged and enabled preservation in a multitude of ways, including local oversight of the 1985 historic resources survey, creation of printed tours, and saving and moving the Wyatt Real Estate Office and the Calaboose. The City of Waxahachie's Heritage Preservation Commission has coordinated, enabled, and promoted architectural preservation and appreciation through a variety of programs and initiatives. Finally, the citizens of Waxahachie have made this progress possible through their support of these organizations and programs, and through purchasing, restoring, maintaining, and using historic buildings.

Even with the extensive work of these organizations, governmental entities, and individuals, significant buildings have been lost in recent years, and others are threatened. The area's continuing major growth will present even more challenges in the future. By presenting and documenting the history of representative examples of Waxahachie's surviving buildings, the authors hope to increase awareness and understanding of the many factors involved in their design and construction and demonstrate the benefits of preserving them. We invite readers to enjoy these buildings and their stories, whether walking on the sidewalks, driving the streets, or touring through these pages from the comfort of home.

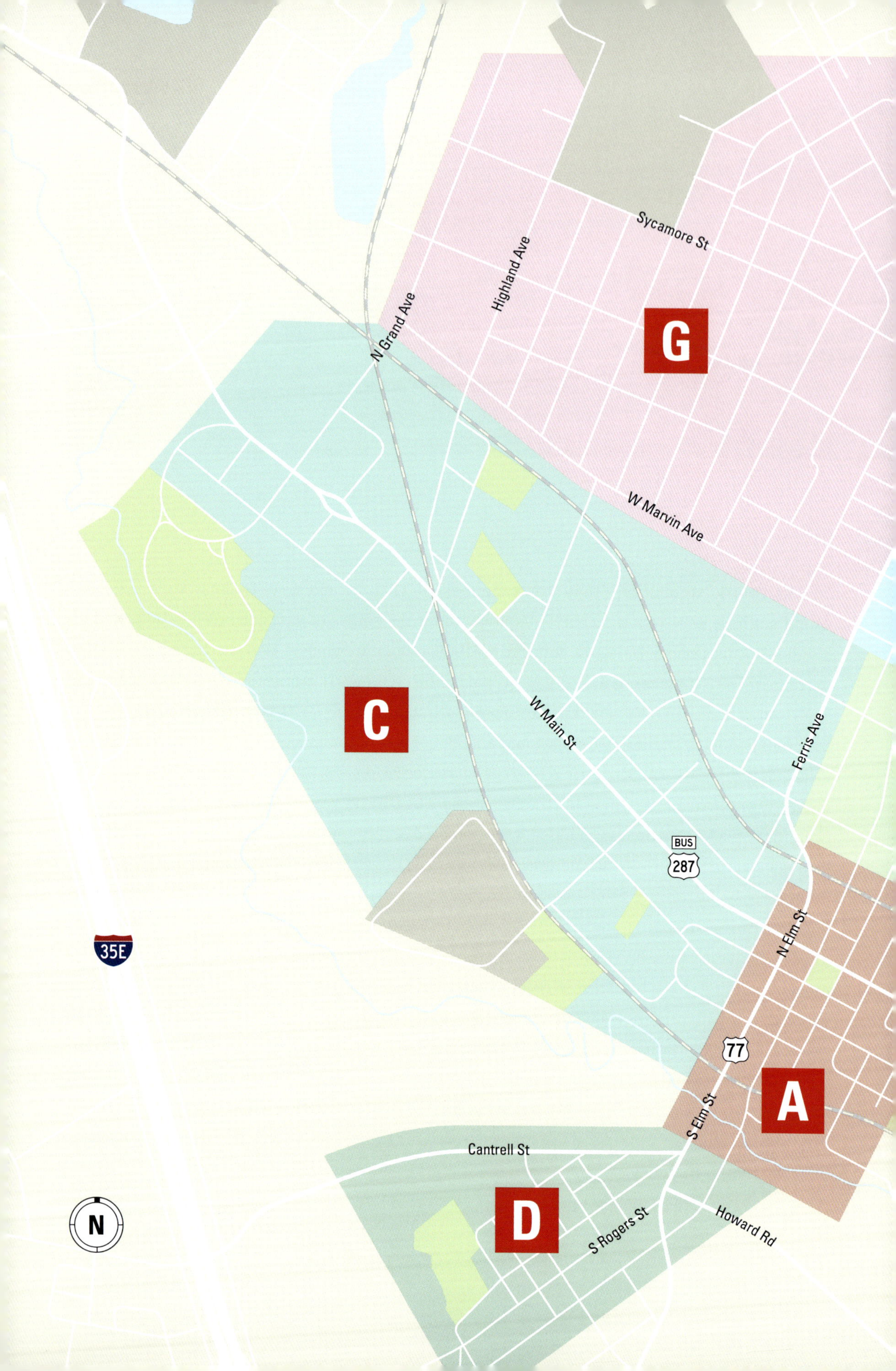

Sycamore St
Highland Ave
N Grand Ave
G
W Marvin Ave
C
W Main St
Ferris Ave
BUS
287
N Elm St
35E
77
A
S Elm St
Cantrell St
D
N
S Rogers St
Howard Rd

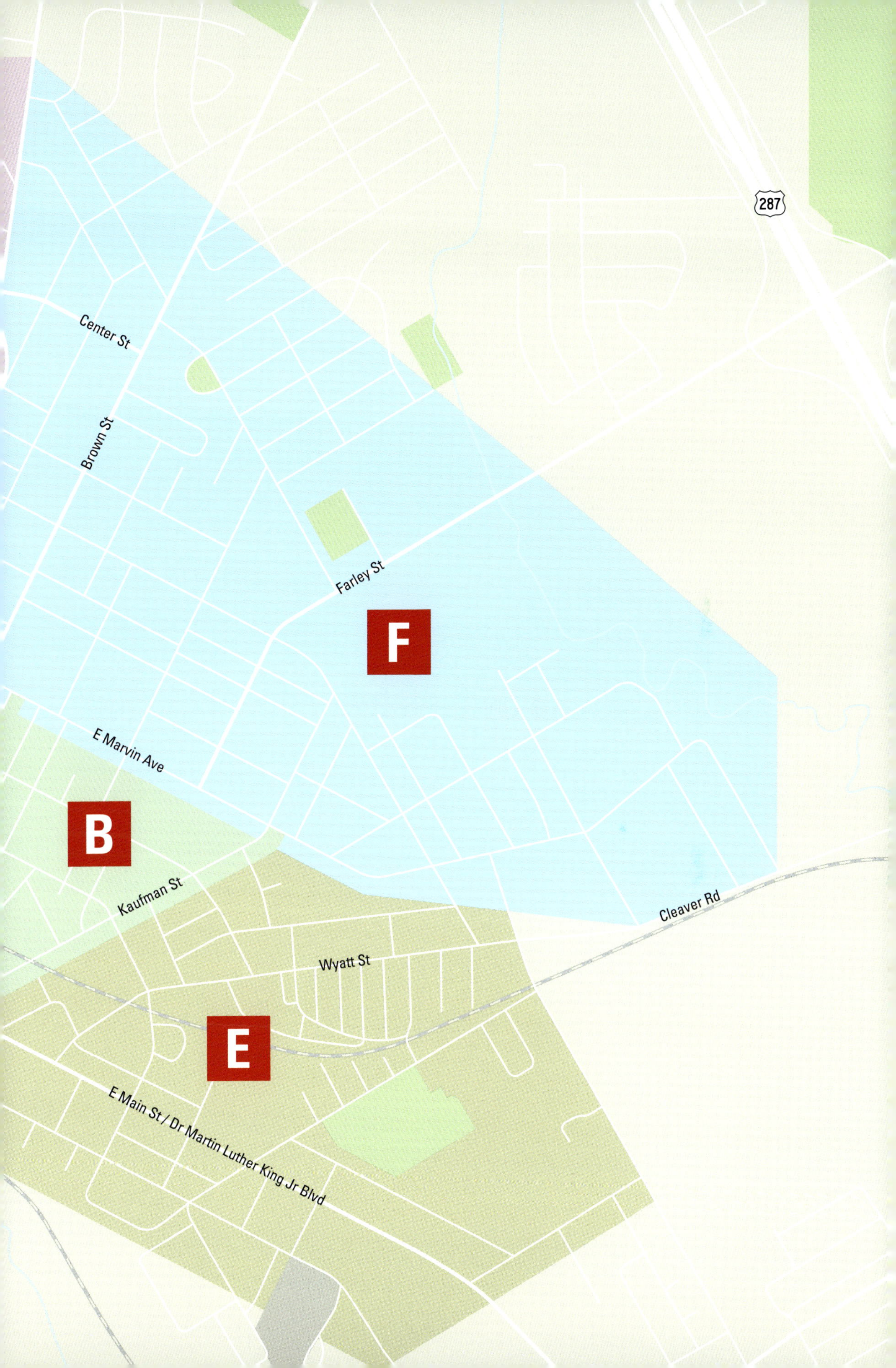
287
Center St
Brown St
Farley St
F
E Marvin Ave
B
Kaufman St
Cleaver Rd
Wyatt St
E
E Main St / Dr Martin Luther King Jr Blvd

SECTION A

Downtown

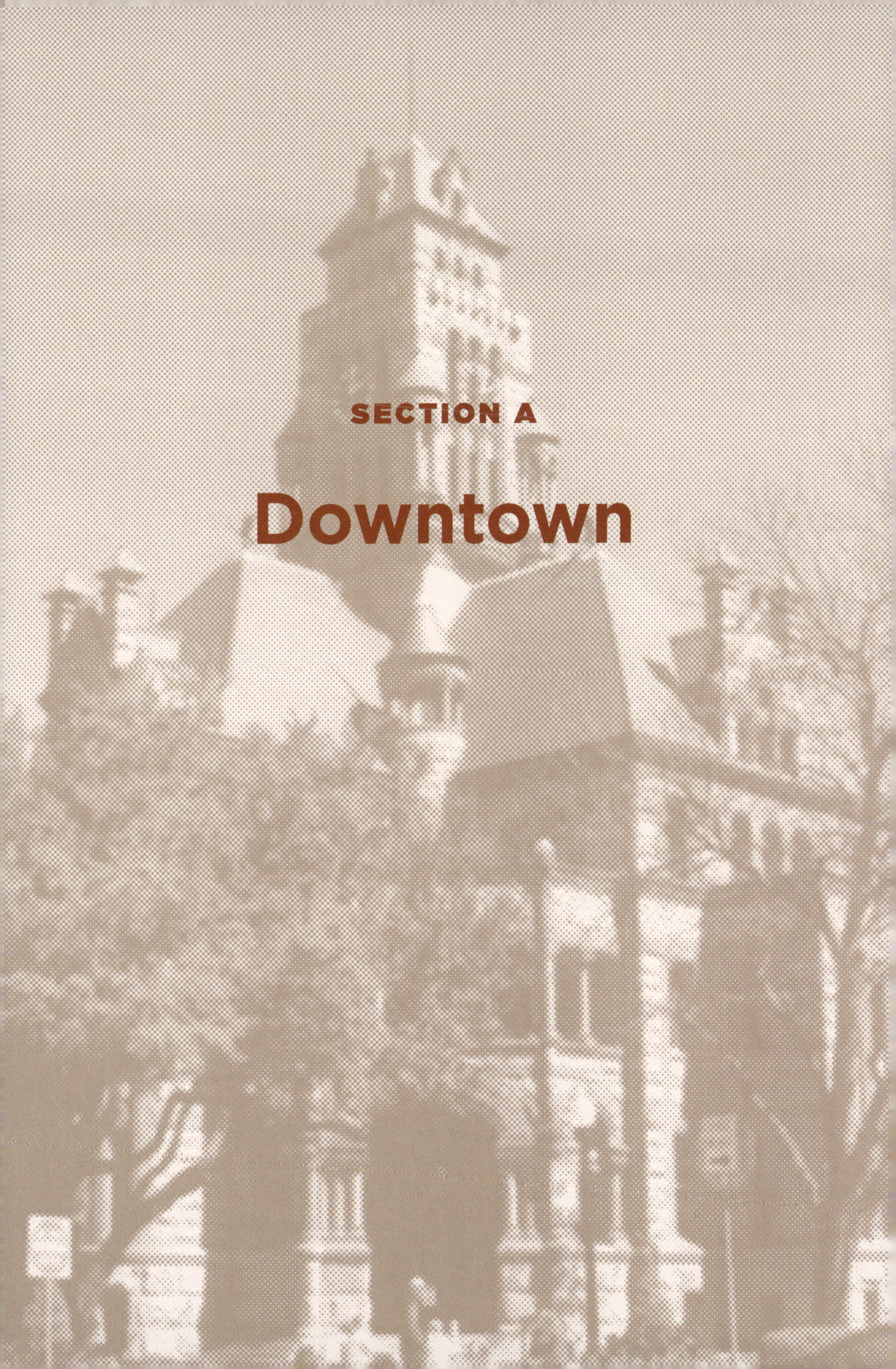

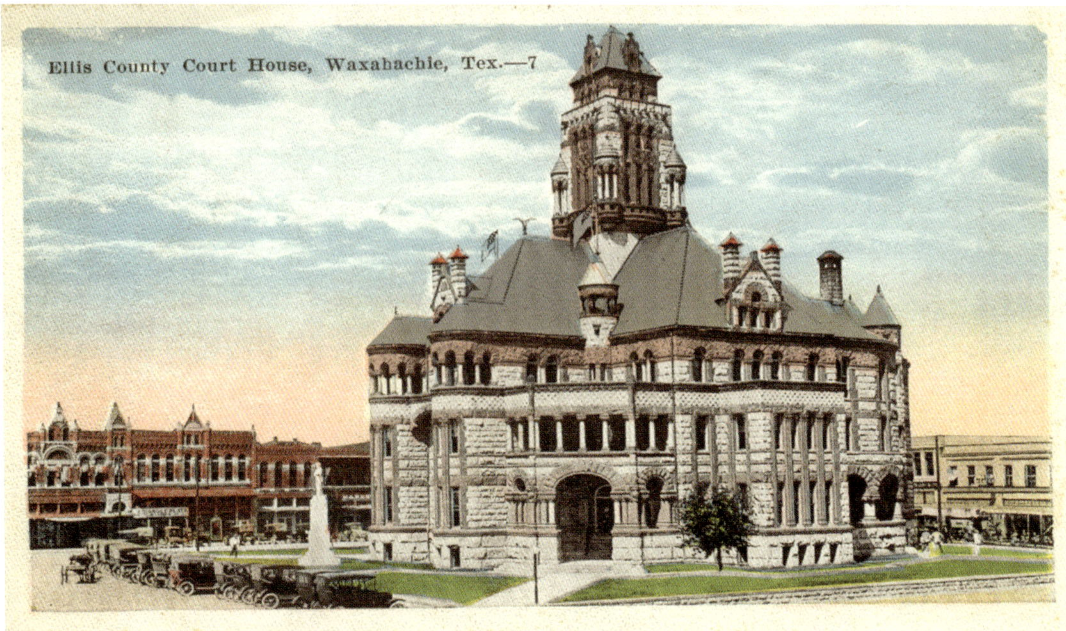

Ellis County Courthouse with north side of the square in the background.
Partially tinted postcard, c. 1915. *Courtesy Ellis County Museum.*

INTRODUCTION

Since Waxahachie was established in 1850 and a forty-block town plan adopted, Courthouse Square has always been where it is today—and where it will always be. Its history is one of constant flux as it has spent a lifetime accommodating and embracing an ever-changing community. Now dominated by what many call *the* premier Texas courthouse, it is easy to forget that the Waxahachie square began with a scattering of frame buildings, some not much more than sheds. Each side of the square evolved at its own pace, as illustrated in 1876 and 1886 bird's-eye views.

In the center of the square in both views is the prim two-story square-shaped limestone structure which, when built in 1873, seemed adequate for a county population of about 7,500 and a county seat of about 1,350. In the 1876 view, the north side is a row of stone and brick two-story iron fronts; the east and south sides are an assortment of frame buildings; and the west side is split with a one-story frame row on the south half and a two-story row on the north half.

By the late 1880s, Ellis County had become a major cotton-producing county and Waxahachie a commercial center with populations approaching 30,000 and 3,000 respectively. The square shown in the 1886 view reflects that shifting status, as the courthouse was then surrounded by up-to-date two-story masonry buildings with cast-iron fronts and canopies, molded cornices, and plate-glass store windows. The 1873 courthouse is clearly out of step, especially compared with other courthouses being built across the state since 1881, when the Texas state legislature authorized bonds to build new county seats.

West side of Waxahachie square, c. 1871. *Courtesy Ellis County Museum.*

During the years 1888-1895, Waxahachie set the stage for its architectural icon. An impressive number of major buildings were either completed or well underway in and around the square long before construction began on James Riely Gordon's courthouse. Those included, to name a few, the Masonic Temple (the first three-story building on the square), Citizens National Bank, City Hall and Fire Station, the north side of the square, and the Ellis County Jail.

Postcard street scene showing three-story Masonic Temple overlooking south side of the square on an early fall day when farmers brought their cotton to town to be ginned, c. 1905. *Courtesy Webb Gallery Collection.*

Fires were often the prelude to new construction, with the worst of these on December 21, 1893, when the block north of the square was totally destroyed. By midsummer 1894, the entire block had been rebuilt and the businesses reopened. There were more fires to come, the most recent in December 2011 on the east side of the square, but post-fire stories have changed. After those early fires, clearing and rebuilding began immediately, but that was when the square was the most valuable real estate in town. That is no longer the case.

Entering the twentieth century, Waxahachie was in a good place. It was a thriving regional economic center, its population 4,215 in 1900, a number that grew to 6,205 in 1910. Within the original town boundaries, industrial and commercial uses were pushing out residential properties which, in turn, were moving into platted neighborhoods. It was a shift that defined the Waxahachie downtown, bordered by Houston and Texas Central tracks on the north, Waxahachie Creek on the south, Jackson Street on the east, and Elm Street on the west.

Ellis County Jail (back section) and jailor's residence (front section), corner of Rogers and Water Streets. Photograph probably taken not long after construction in 1888. *Courtesy Ellis County Museum.*

There were notable additions within these boundaries in the early twentieth century. Between 1902 and 1908, three railroad companies built passenger depots, an indication of Waxahachie's importance as a destination. The year 1913 saw the opening of two instant landmarks: the Rogers Hotel and the United States Post Office and Federal Building. Fires in 1912-1914 also left their mark on the south and the west sides of the square.

A substory hovers in the background throughout this post-1900 period. On October 16, 1903, the *Daily Light* reported that liveryman and wagonyard owner Conde Mosley had bought the first automobile in Waxahachie. At the time, no one understood nor could anyone have predicted the profound impact that the automobile would have on squares and downtowns in communities across the country.

It took several decades in Waxahachie before the inevitable changes began to emerge with the opening of auto-oriented shopping centers that not only attracted new businesses but also drew businesses out of downtown. The year 1964 saw the first demolition of a building on the square to make way for a parking lot. Conversely, Citizens National Bank, in 1966, moved from its corner to another downtown location where automobiles could be accommodated without destroying the historic fabric of the square. It was a decision that probably saved the square as a square. Some business owners stayed and modernized their downtown buildings in hopes of competing with their newer shopping-center counterparts. It was the classic struggle between old and new. Most importantly, the largest downtown employer, the county, also stayed, governing from the Gordon courthouse and, in 1982, buying several vacant buildings on the square for needed office space.

The early 1970s was a time of uncertainty for historic downtowns across America, but Americans, including Waxahachians, were beginning to respond in multiple ways. Preservation was emerging as a small but passionate movement; the Bicentennial was creating a greater appreciation for local and national historic resources; and more and more people were realizing that it was a "do or die" moment for many places like Waxahachie's downtown if they were to survive. In April 1975, the twenty-five-block Ellis County Courthouse Historic District was listed on the National Register of Historic Places. In 1977, Historic Waxahachie, Inc. was founded. The city established the Heritage Preservation Commission to provide protection and guidance for preserving and renovating structures in the downtown historic district. It also became an award-winning participant in the Main Street Program in the 1980s.

Revitalizing a downtown is a long and arduous process, one that demands a sustained and steady commitment by a community. Waxahachie has made that commitment, but it does get tested. In 2006, the county considered building new facilities on the north side of town. Fortunately, city and county officials, working together, developed, and voters approved, an alternative plan that kept the county offices downtown. As of this writing, the downtown has been infused for several years with the energy brought by a developer whose program encourages second-story living quarters on the square. Not a new idea, but one to be tested for the first time in Waxahachie. Keeping it all in check is Gordon's Ellis County Courthouse.

West side of Waxahachie square, mid-1940s.
Courtesy Ellis County Museum.

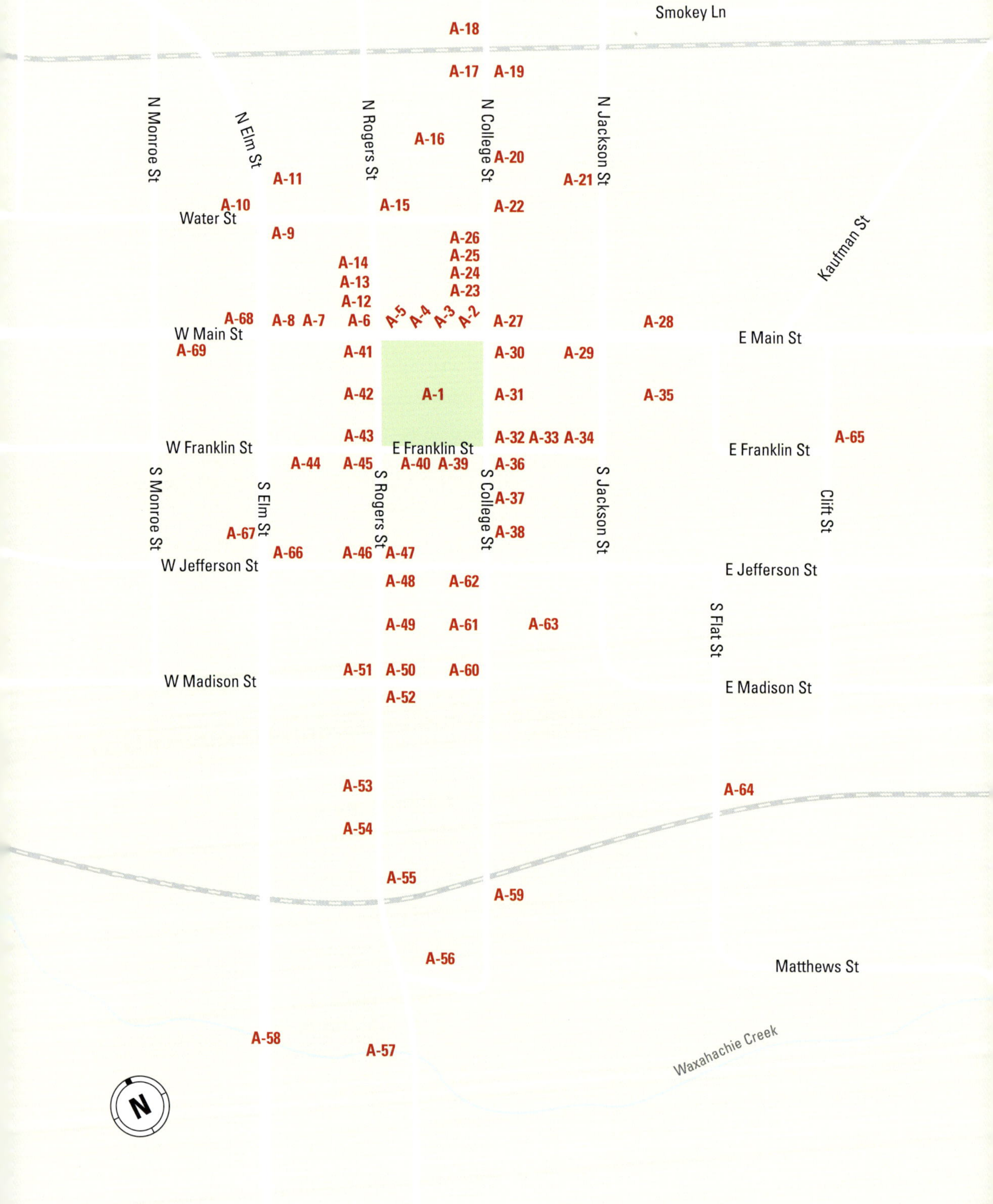

Smokey Ln
A-18
A-17 A-19
N Monroe St
N Elm St
N Rogers St
N College St
N Jackson St
A-16
A-20
A-11
A-21
A-10
Water St
A-15
A-22
A-9
A-26
A-25
A-24
A-23
A-14
A-13
A-12
Kaufman St
A-68 A-8 A-7 A-6 A-5 A-4 A-3 A-2 A-27
A-28
W Main St
E Main St
A-69
A-41
A-30
A-29
A-42
A-1
A-31
A-35
A-43
A-32 A-33 A-34
A-65
W Franklin St
E Franklin St
E Franklin St
A-44 A-45 A-40 A-39 A-36
S Monroe St
S Elm St
S Rogers St
S College St
S Jackson St
Clift St
A-37
A-38
A-67
A-66 A-46 A-47
W Jefferson St
E Jefferson St
A-48 A-62
S Flat St
A-49 A-61 A-63
A-51 A-50 A-60
W Madison St
E Madison St
A-52
A-53
A-64
A-54
A-55
A-59
A-56
Matthews St
A-58
A-57
Waxahachie Creek
N

A-1 Ellis County Courthouse

A-2 100 W. Main St.
Getzendaner Building

A-3 108 W. Main St.

A-4 110 W. Main St.
Texas Theater

A-5 114 W. Main St.
Ferris Building

A-6 200 W. Main St.
Citizens National Bank

A-7 208-210 W. Main St.
Trippet-Ferris Building

A-8 212 W. Main
Site of City Hall and Fire Station Building

A-9 104 North Elm St.
Municipal Building

A-10 300 Water St.
Gulf Service Station

A-11 200 North Elm St.
Citizens National Bank

A-12 105 N. Rogers St.

A-13 107 N. Rogers St.

A-14 109 N. Rogers St.

A-15 200 N. Rogers St.
Ellis County Jail

A-16 Singleton Plaza

A-17 Waxahachie Calaboose and Wyatt Real Estate Office

A-18 301 N. College St.
Waxahachie Medicine Company

A-19 228 N. College St.
Site of Houston and Texas Central Depot

A-20 210, 212, 214 N. College St.

A-21 209 N. Jackson St.
George Brown Plaza

A-22 200-202 N. College St.
Waxahachie Steam Laundry

A-23 109 N. College St.

A-24 111 N. College St.

A-25 113 N. College St.

A-26 115 N. College St.

A-27 100 N. College St.
Rogers Hotel

A-28 201-217 E. Main St.

A-29 110-114 E. Main St.

A-30 101 S. College St.
Durham Building

A-31 Site of 105, 107, 109, 111 S. College St.

A-32 115 S. College St.
Courthouse Park

A-33 109 E. Franklin St.

A-34 113, 115 E. Franklin St.

A-35 109 S. Jackson St.
- Ellis County Courts and Administration Building
- City Parking Garage

A-36 201 S. College St.
Masonic Temple Building (now Ellis County Museum)

A-37 203-207 S. College St.
Lewis-Templeton Building

A-38 209, 211, 213, 215 S. College St.

A-39 107 W. Franklin St.
Levy Building

A-40 109-113 W. Franklin St.

A-41 100 S. Rogers St.
Chapman & Chapman Building

A-42 104-112 S. Rogers St.

A-43 114 S. Rogers St.
Waxahachie National Bank Building

A-44 209-211 W. Franklin St.
E. S. Campbell Building

213-215 W. Franklin St.
C. W. Gibson Building

A-45 200 S. Rogers St.
Williams Block

A-46 208 S. Rogers St.
Texas Mortgage & Banking Co. Building

A-47 217 S. Rogers St.
Edens Building

A-48 301 S. Rogers St.
Walker Building

A-49 307 S. Rogers St.
Cook Building

A-50 315 S. Rogers St.
Peters Block

A-51 306 S. Rogers St.
Moffett Building

A-52 401 S. Rogers St.
United States Post Office/Federal Building (now Waxahachie City Hall)

A-53 408 S. Rogers St.
Waxahachie Livery & Transfer Building

A-54 410 S. Rogers St.
Wm. Cameron & Company Lumber Yard (now Downtown Farmers Market)

A-55 423 S. College St.
Trinity and Brazos Valley Depot; Rock Island Depot

A-56 501 S. Rogers St.
Missouri-Kansas-Texas Depot

A-57 S. Rogers St. at Waxahachie Creek
Rogers St. Bridge

A-58 Waxahachie Viaduct

A-59 441 S. College St.
Shive & Keys

A-60 310 S. College St.
Will Moore & Sons Building

A-61 308 S. College St.
Byers Building

A-62 105 W. Jefferson St.
Will Moore Building

A-63 300 block S. College St.
Ellis County Detention Center (now Wayne McCollum Detention Center)

A-64 503 S. Flat St.
National Compress Co. Building

A-65 109 Clift St.
El-Co Creamery

A-66 212 W. Jefferson St.
Maybin Service Station

A-67 204 S. Elm St.
Sinclair Service Station

A-68 300 W. Main St.
Sims-Thomson Garage

A-69 315 W. Main St.
Highway Garage

A-1
Ellis County Courthouse
1895-97; James Riely Gordon, architect

Every architecture guide to Waxahachie has to begin on Courthouse Square with the Ellis County Courthouse. The majestic Richardsonian Romanesque-style courthouse was designed by San Antonio-based James Riely Gordon who, without question, was one of the most accomplished regional practitioners of both the architectural style and the courthouse building type—and this, the Ellis County Courthouse, is universally considered his finest example.

Gordon's design is the fourth Ellis County Courthouse, its predecessor a two-story square-shaped limestone structure built in 1873. Twenty years later, there were those ready to build a new courthouse to reflect the now-established importance of both city and county as a major cotton-producing, commercial center. But the populace was divided into two courthouse factions— those clamoring for a new one and those opposed for financial reasons. The deciding body, the five-member Ellis County Commissioners Court, was also split. Following the 1894 fall election, a lame-duck court voted to build a new courthouse according to Gordon's plans and specifications submitted by Otto P. Kroeger, a San Antonio contractor and frequent Gordon collaborator. The lame-duck court accepted Kroeger's proposal without competitive bidding, and quickly maneuvered for the demolition of the 1873 courthouse, which left the incoming court, which took office November 30, 1894, with no choice but to build a new courthouse according to Gordon's design. The new court hired the Fort Worth architectural firm Messer, Sanguinet & Messer, and most particularly Marshall Sanguinet, who was already known to Waxahachians, to resolve contractual and specification issues and then to serve as "on-site architect."

Once construction was fully underway in March 1895, citizens had two years to become well versed in the Richardsonian Romanesque style as they watched the new courthouse transform their downtown square. The first clue of things to come was the three-foot-thick twisted steel and concrete foundation, an indication that this building was going to be massive. The building footprint, with its straight planes, curves and rounded shapes, recessed spaces, squared corners, and angled surfaces, not only reflects characteristics of the style but also the complexity of Gordon's plan. Texas stone of contrasting colors and textures, including gray and rose-pink granites, Burnett County limestone, and Pecos red sandstone, delineate floor levels, frame openings and arches, and embellish surfaces. The richly detailed clock tower—a frequent feature of public buildings in the style—raises the structure to a "loftiness" not present in previous Gordon courthouses, according to author Chris Meister in his book, *James Riely Gordon: His Courthouses and Other Public Architecture*. Today, the tower remains a familiar skyline landmark from many vantage points both in town and around the countryside.

Gordon's brilliance as an architect would have meant very little without exceptionally skilled artisans and craftsmen to execute his designs. It is the stonework that distinguishes this courthouse from other Gordon examples. Although the carved faces decorating the building draw the greatest attention, most especially the twelve faces on the north or main entrance, the precision-cut stonework on every façade also deserves acknowledgment. Local historian Fred Weldon, in his study "Carved Ornament of the Ellis County Courthouse," credits Sanguinet with ensuring that adequate funds were budgeted for quality stonework and encouraging the county to subcontract the work to the Dallas stone yard of German-born stonemason Theodore Beilharz. According to Weldon, stone was probably prepared and carved in Dallas, then transported to the building site, where carver Harry Herley served as Beilhartz's on-site supervisor.

Walking into the Ellis County Courthouse can be something of a surprise to those unfamiliar with Gordon's innovative and copyrighted interior "Signature Plan." There is no lofty space or atrium as expected; rather, one enters a wainscoted hallway that encircles the floor with doorways along the perimeter leading into offices, courtrooms, and services, which is a plan repeated on all three floors. At the center is a cast-iron staircase, its placement and openness serving as an air shaft, an ingenious plan for pre-air-conditioning days when windows were kept open. It is an interior, writes Meister, that "exudes controlled nobility." (At the same time, it was an impossible plan for those with disabilities, as was true for most staircases of the period.)

When built, the Gordon courthouse was the community centerpiece, not only because it was a spectacular building and the county seat, but also because it anchored what was the economic heart of Waxahachie and the surrounding area. Although the square gradually lost its hold on commercial activity, the courthouse remained a commanding presence on the landscape. Generally, it was treated with more reverence than not as alterations, mostly interior, were necessary to accommodate an expanding county staff and services as well as technological changes in mechanical and business systems.

In May 2000, the Ellis County Courthouse was among the first courthouses in Texas to receive funds from the ongoing Texas Historic Courthouse Preservation Program, established by the Texas legislature and Gov. George W. Bush in June 1999 and administered through the Texas Historical Commission. Stone restoration and, in some instances, replacement were the major issues of the project, which cost between $10 to $12 million with $3.5 million from the state and the remaining sum from the county. The architectural firm ARCHITEXAS was responsible for the restoration project. The restored building was rededicated in October 2002.

Standing on the west side of the courthouse lawn is the Confederate Monument installed by the local chapter of the Daughters of the Confederacy and dedicated on November 2, 1912. On the south side lawn is the bronze statue of Richard Ellis, president of Texas's first constitutional convention and the person for whom the county is named. Dedicated on November 12, 1936, it was a Centennial gift from the State of Texas to Ellis County. The sculptor was Attillio Piccirille.

A-2
100 West Main Street
Getzendaner Building

1894; attributed to Marshall Sanguinet, architect, and to M. E. Kerrigan & Co., contractor

After the 1893 fire that destroyed the entire block north of the courthouse, Capt. W. H. Getzendaner probably turned to Fort Worth architect Marshall Sanguinet and Dallas contractor M. E. Kerrigan to design and construct his new building on the northwest corner of Main and College Streets. At a cost of $10,000, it was the most expensive of the new structures going up on the block. The choice of Sanguinet and Kerrigan would have been a logical choice for Getzendaner, given that they were already working together on the nearly completed Citizens National Bank building (**200 West Main**) at the corner of Main and Rogers Streets. Kerrigan had to move his crew and equipment only one block to the east to begin another project. For Sanguinet, it meant adapting plans and elevations from previous projects built in Fort Worth in the early 1890s to the Waxahachie site.

The Getzendaner Building firmly anchored the corner site with a square tower. Unfortunately, the tower was removed after a fire in 1924, but fortunately, other features that make the second-story façade unique have survived. The tri-parte Palladian window groupings draped with double brick pilasters and corbelling and decorated with carefully placed cast-iron garlands and medallions are truly extraordinary. The façade has a delicacy and design akin to refined cabinet furniture and is clearly the creation of a person with a sophisticated eye and an understanding of classical motifs—and a love of fiddling with them. It was a professional trait that began early with Sanguinet, whose studies at Washington University in St. Louis in the 1870s emphasized architecture (architectural degrees were not given) and who chose to serve apprenticeships in both architecture and cabinetmaking. The secondary façade on College Street also displays exceptional brickwork, as was typical of corner buildings dating from the 1880s and later.

Originally, the lower floor of this building was partitioned into two commercial spaces with offices above. The central stepped parapet and single window at the second level marked the office entrance and stairwell. When druggist Lemuel C. (Lem) Curlin signed a five-year lease in 1912, the building experienced its first "remodeling"—most notably, removal of the first-floor partition to create a 9,000 square foot space, which necessitated moving the stairway entrance to the west wall. He also installed large display windows. Curlin was already a highly successful twenty-seven-year-old businessman with drugstores on the north and west sides of the square when, in spring 1913, he opened his new store. It featured twelve departments, mahogany fixtures trimmed in gold work, marble, and art glass, and a soda fountain with stools and tables to seat sixty. When Waxahachie adopted its present street numbering system in 1921, this location was assigned the first number—100 West Main Street.

Curlin had gained a national reputation in his profession and was still a young man when he died of pneumonia in 1922, and although his own career was cut short, he had cemented this corner as a drugstore location. Following a 1924 fire, the building was converted back to two units on the first floor with the corner location rented to Hamilton-Inabuit Drug Co. (successors to Curlin Drug Co.) and the inside location to Piggly-Wiggly Grocery Store, which remained there for over ten years. In April 1925, Waco-based Curry Brothers Drug Co. negotiated a ten-year lease for the corner spot and opened with a new name, Trinity Pharmacy, and a new slogan, "on the corner where you meet your friends." The Trinity name was used by subsequent owners until the store closed in 2009. The building is still owned by Getzendaner family interests.

A-3
108 West Main Street

1894; attributed to Marshall Sanguinet, architect
1972; David Raney, designer

In 1972, the street-level façades of two buildings on the north side of the square were drastically altered, the entrances repositioned, and a single street number adopted by a new owner and business, Raney Furniture and Carpet Company. The 1894 second-story façades, however, were left intact, so look up—always a good idea anyway when studying historic buildings.

At the upper level the two original structures are easily distinguished. The building on the right was a double storefront separated by a shared, centrally placed street entry and stairwell denoted by the smallest arched window on the second-floor façade. (The 1972 redo moved the entrance to the far left of this building.) Detailing on this building is unmistakably that of architect Marshall Sanguinet, including a variation of the double pilasters on **100 West Main** and, on this building, the low pediment faced with diapered brickwork that appears in photographs of Sanguinet's Dundee Office Building in Fort Worth. The smaller brick building on the left, with two show windows at street level and four original arched windows on the second floor, was incorporated as the west third of the 1972 Raney Furniture façade.

When it was built in 1894, Waxahachie Mayor E. A. DuBose owned the east side of the larger building while Henry and Sarah Cerf owned the west side. It was a very practical, often-used arrangement, as a single staircase gave more space to both sides. DuBose was a druggist who arrived in Waxahachie in the 1870s, bought his property in 1882, and maintained a drugstore at this location with business partner W. G. Lomax until 1901. That year he became general manager of the Waxahachie Cotton Mill factory, a project he championed during his years as mayor, 1884-1889 and 1893-1899.

Henry and Sarah Cerf were among Waxahachie's early Jewish merchant families. They bought the west half of the property in March 1892 from relatives who had owned it since 1882. Around 1900, the couple, "having acquired a comfortable fortune," began selling off their grocery business and real estate investments, and in 1906 they moved their family to New York City.

The smaller building had a typical storefront with display windows and centered entrance at street level. Its elongated arched windows, heightened parapet, and stepped pediment, all still visible on the second story façade, give it a distinct identity in the row of buildings. In 1874, Major G. J. and Susan Penn had bought the property on which there was a two-story stone building, which they rebuilt after *both* the 1882 and the 1893 fires. Penn, who sold books and stationery, was first known as "The Book Man," but like most early residents, he juggled many interests: a grocery partnership, rental properties, selling insurance, and serving as postmaster for ten years. Periodically, his wife Susan sold flowers and plants from her hothouse on their College Street residence. In 1905, the Penns sold this building to baker Reinhold Boehle who, after a year of negotiating space to build ovens and a bakehouse on leased property along the alley, moved into the building in 1906. Boehle's Bakery remained there through the 1930s. Waxahachie native Bill Pitts, who was born in 1920, remembered that one of his favorite childhood treats was buying a five-cent loaf of warm Boehle's "mity-nice" bread, lathering it with butter, and sitting on the curb to eat it with his playmates.

Dorothy and Howard Raney and son David undertook their 1972 renovation project at a time when the preservation movement was in its early stages. There was little in the way of guidelines or guidance on either national or state levels, and it would be almost three decades before the local Heritage Preservation Commission was formed. Prior to moving to this location, their furniture store was at the intersection of North Rogers and Water Streets, and to their credit, the Raneys, unlike many downtown businesses that were moving to new shopping centers along Highway 77, chose to stay in downtown Waxahachie. Raney Furniture remained here until circa 1991.

A-4
110 West Main Street
Texas Theater

1934; Ritz Theater, architect unknown; O. B. Bennett, contractor

1939; Texas Theater, Houston & Smith, architects; O. B. Bennett, contractor

This simplified Art Deco facade obviously indicates a building history that evolved very differently from the rest of the 1894 north side row. Originally, it was a double storefront structure with two commercial units on the first floor and offices on the second, with the exterior a near match to its corner neighbor. Early signs of changes to come began in February 1907 after Frances Moffett Simpson inherited the property that her father, John H. Moffett, had bought in 1905. Renaming it the Simpson Building, Frances and her husband Dr. C. W. Simpson rented one storefront to L. C. Smiley's gentlemen's clothing shop, which offered an "expert clothesologist" to help customers make selections, and the other to the Edison Entertainment Company to show "high class moving pictures." Opening on February 15, the Theatorium was the first Waxahachie business devoted solely to showing "moving pictures," but within two months, a second movie theater, the Empire, opened on the south side of the square. Both theaters would have been simple setups with folding chairs and perhaps a muslin sheet for the screen.

Driven by a rapidly changing technology, intense competition, and an almost manic public response, the theater experienced a succession of makeovers beginning in early 1909, when the Theatorium moved to the west side of the square, and the Majestic Theatre, "a new place of amusement," rented the full first floor of the Simpson Building and offered both moving pictures and vaudeville to an audience of "about 400 seats." In July 1912, the Dixie Theatre replaced the Majestic and reopened with the most up-to-date machine that showed pictures "steady as a rock" and a $2,000 Wurlitzer electric orchestra that was "an entertainment in itself." In August 1918, a refurbished New Dixie opened with a double billing of "Uncle Tom's Cabin" and "Wild Women and Tame Lions." It was probably at this time that the interior was converted into a two-story theater with a balcony. The executors of druggist Lemuel Curlin's estate bought the building in 1925, and leased theater management not to a local amusement company as the Simpsons did, but to Harold B. Robb and Ed. H. Rowley, whose Dallas-based R & R Development Company became one of the largest developers and managers of theater properties in the Texas-Oklahoma region.

The greatest architectural makeover came in September 1934, when the Dixie closed "to be transformed into a new theater" with all but the walls torn down and rebuilt. Reopening in November as the Ritz Theater, the 1894 brick façade was replaced with a white stucco front, "modernistic in design," with green and orange trim, a silver and black marquee, and neon lights. Combined with the "ornate and bizarre designs" of the Egyptian-motif interior, Waxahachie could now boast of having a small-town version of a big-city movie palace. Fire gutted the theater in December 1938, but it reopened in March 1939 as the Texas Theater, with an interior designed by Dallas interior decorator Allen Hamilton. Three years later, in early 1942, the building was "fire-wrecked" again and rebuilt using the same 1938 plans, but with an interior designed by Eugene Gilboe. Photographs taken in 1936 and 1942 show that the façade, as seen today, reflects the 1930s alterations. (Sadly, there are no images of that Egyptian interior.)

The Texas Theatre is the only extant building in Waxahachie that can be described as Art Deco, a style that enjoyed a short-lived popularity in the United States from circa 1925 into the late 1930s. Considered a style of decoration and ornament, it was used for office buildings, apartment houses, and theaters, the latter its most popular building type in small towns. Although the Waxahachie theater never had elaborate Art Deco detailing, it exhibits basic characteristics of the style: smooth-faced walls, pronounced horizontal banding often in the form of parallel straight lines, vertical emphasis as seen in the center panel, straight-headed windows, and a ziggurat or stepped motif repeated here in the ticket window, canopy, and parapet. The look, streamlined and futuristic, was a rejection of historic revival styles—a rejection of what this building was originally.

In 1973, the movie theater, then known as The Picture Show, was given another new look as part of a downtown clean-up campaign. The new front featured Spanish tile on the street level and composition shingles above. The theater, like many other downtown theaters across the country, entered a period of uncertainty that included numerous attempts to develop the property without any long-term success and occasional threats of demolition. Acknowledging the historic importance of the Texas to the square and to the community, the City of Waxahachie purchased the property with Tax Increment Reinvestment Zone monies in May 2009. In 2015, the City of Waxahachie entered into an agreement with Lake-Moreno LLC for the redevelopment of the Texas Theater. That project is still in progress.

A-5
114 West Main Street
Ferris Building

1894; attributed to Marshall Sanguinet, architect; C. M. Sammons, contractor

Originally, this building and its neighbor at **110 West Main** were near-mirror structures that together covered almost eighty-two feet of prime Main Street frontage. Built by two different property owners, this one, built by Judge J. W. Ferris, with its remaining Romanesque Revival characteristics and details, provides an indication of the original appearance of the building next door. Originally, the buildings were anything but flat-roofed. Rather, a heightened attic story with a raised parapet, elaborate brickwork, and peaked gables and pinnacle pediments created a picturesque roofline that was a hint of things soon to come on a new Ellis County Courthouse. Given its corner location, this building had a rounded corner tower with a conical roof that balanced its squared counterpart on the Getzendaner Building at the east end of the block.

Judge Ferris, no doubt in concert with W. H. Getzendaner (one suspects that the absentee owner of 110 West Main had little to say in all this), wanted a building that architecturally was appropriately deferential to but not overshadowed by the newly completed Citizens National Bank at **200 West Main**. Whereas Sanguinet's involvement in the design and rebuilding of this building remains an attribution, the *Enterprise* identified C. M. Sammons as "our home contractor" for the Ferris Building, which means, in all probability, that he was also the original contractor of **110 West Main**. From the outset, the 1894 Ferris Building housed commercial and office space; it was never used for banking purposes. At the time of the 1893 fire, Citizens National Bank was located on this corner in the stone building where it had been for twenty years and was just a few months shy of moving into its new facility across the street.

When Judge Ferris died in 1899, his two sons inherited substantial real estate holdings that were eventually partitioned in 1920 with his younger son Thomas A. (T. A.) Ferris, a director and cashier of the bank, receiving this structure. His first floor tenants were Emily Wagenhauser's hat shop that had been on the corner since spring 1912 and the Palm Sweet Shop in the east side storefront. When those leases expired in 1924, T. A., like several downtown property owners, leased his building (except for the second floor front offices) to a national corporation, the Philadelphia-based F. W. Woolworth Company. Four years later, Ferris, now living in Dallas, sold the property to Charles L. Penn which is when "Penn Building/1894" appeared on the facade. Penn, the son of Major G. J. and Susan Penn, was considered, at the time, one of the South's outstanding inland cotton merchants and, on the local scene, was an active real estate investor. When Woolworth's lease expired in 1934, Penn rented the building to J. C. Penney.

The attic floor and roofline details of the Penn Building were probably removed following a fire in the adjacent theater building in 1938. Romanesque Revival style buildings were high maintenance with their elaborate brickwork and spindly details, but there were other factors contributing to their gradual deterioration: a diminishing number of bricklayers interested in their upkeep if indeed they had the needed skills; a growing preference for simpler, more modern styles; and sometimes, as here, extenuating circumstances such as the fire.

The Penn Building has a long association with the furniture business, specifically Marchman's Home Furnishings and Carpets that opened here in 1953 and then became Happy's Home Furnishings in 1973. In 2013, business and property owner Harris Lee Jenkins received a Texas Treasure Business Award from the Texas Historical Commission in recognition of its "providing employment opportunities and support to the state's economy for at least fifty years."

A-6
200 West Main Street
Citizens National Bank

1893-94; Marshall Sanguinet of Messer, Sanguinet & Messer, architect; M. E. Kerrigan & Co., contractor

When selecting a firm to design their new bank building, the Citizens National Bank (CNB) directors chose Marshall R. Sanguinet, one of the most skilled architects in north Texas at the time. Sanguinet's frequent involvement in this and other major projects in Waxahachie during the 1890s had a tremendous impact on the city's development, but his influence has been overshadowed by the Ellis County Courthouse project and its architect, James Riely Gordon. Early in 1893, CNB directors, having decided that the bank had outgrown its two-story building on the northeast corner of Block Two, acquired this narrow 32 x 100 ft. lot known as "the Pickett corner." It was the site of a free-standing native white rock storehouse built by C. D. Pickett in 1871. Once the bank awarded the $15,000 contract to build Sanguinet's design to Dallas contractor M. E. Kerrigan & Co., the "landmark" was demolished and construction of the formidable three-story building began. The new building was well underway when, on December 20, 1893, their corner bank building across the street burned, along with the other buildings on the block. The bank rescued its safe with *all* its records and "did not lose a minute" in resuming operation the following day in temporary quarters. Three months later, on March 29, 1894, the bank opened for business on the first floor of their new building, with rental offices on the second floor and the Elks Hall on the third. The bank remained here for almost thirty-three years.

An imposing building today, Sanguinet's bank building was even more imposing—as in medieval fortress—when built. Originally, the tower block was finished with an octagonal corner turret capped with a conical roof and yet another floor with narrow dungeon-like windows. A corbelled parapet encased a heightened pyramidal roof with sharply pointed gable dormers and a crested ridge with long dagger lightning rods. With or without the tower roof, Sanguniet's bank building was in the Richardsonian Romanesque style, as would be the future Ellis County Courthouse; for public and large business buildings, that was the most prevalent architectural style at the time. The corner entrance portal with open loggia and chamfered entrance doors follows Texas High Victorian bank typology. Squat columns, rough stone archways, and a stone first floor finish are typical of the style, as is the contrasting brick on the upper facades. Stone stringcourses, window sills, and roof coping provide more contrast and definition of building elements and floors. A balconet on the second story of the Rogers Street façade marks the entrance and stairway to the upper floors, while an arched entrance on Main Street originally led to a rental office space and secondary staircase.

In 1896, two years after the bank was completed, Sanguinet's firm printed a booklet entitled "Some Work from the Office of Sanguinet and Staats Sucessors [sic]To: Messer Sanguinet and Messer Architects Fort Worth Tex" in which the Waxahachie bank building and a strikingly similar City National Bank and National Hotel building in Bowie, Texas, are illustrated. The Bowie building, constructed circa 1890, is no longer extant, but it is obvious that Sanguinet adapted the earlier Bowie design for the Waxahachie bank. Other illustrations of both built and unbuilt projects in the booklet show that the tower block and pyramidal roof were favorite design elements of Sanguinet and his partners.

As part of a modernization program in 1919, the bank replaced the pyramidal roof and turret with a flat roof and pressed metal cornice, a change that ostensibly was in response to the bank's growth over twenty-five years and the need for additional vault space and an updated lobby. No doubt, but the new look was also prompted by competition from two new bank buildings on the square at the Franklin and Rogers Streets intersection—the somewhat folksy Guaranty State Bank built in 1915 and the elegant Waxahachie National Bank built in 1918. Upon completion of its six-month remodeling project, Citizens National Bank advertised that it was moving into "its new, commodious building" on December 22, 1919, where it remained until 1927. Today, the Sanguinet bank building is rental office space. The fact that it no longer serves as a bank does not detract from its being unquestionably one of the most important structures on the square.

A-7
208-210 West Main Street
Trippet-Ferris Building

1890-91; C. J. Griggs, contractor

When built, this double commercial building was situated between two structures that were already considered landmarks: the 1871 "old Pickett store" on the east and the 1867 Cumberland Presbyterian Church on the west. Within three years, both landmarks were gone, and the Trippet-Ferris Building found itself wedged between two of Waxahachie's most exuberant architectural monuments of the late nineteenth century—Citizens National Bank (**200 West Main**) on the east and City Hall on the west. The commercial front, however, held its own, thanks to height, proportions and upper floor detailing, most notably the pressed metal cornice with rosettes, brackets, and finials, the brick corbel table, and the nailhead patterned pressed-metal window transoms. The lower level was a typical cast-iron store front that survives in remarkably original condition along with transom openings above the canopy on the east or Trippet side of the building. The iron front, labeled by Pullis Bros., iron manufacturers in St. Louis, is one of few extant marked iron fronts in Waxahachie *not* labeled by Mosher Ironworks of Dallas. The black tile front on the west side reflects changes probably made in the late 1930s, the alterations partially blocking the outside entry to the very narrow staircase leading to the second floor. One wonders how all the portly businessmen photographed standing on Waxahachie sidewalks in the late nineteenth-early twentieth centuries maneuvered these narrow stairways that were not uncommon in the downtown. This stairway was particularly busy from 1904 until circa 1925, when the Enterprise Publishing Corporation that included both *Enterprise* and *Daily Light* newspaper offices and a job printing business occupied all the west side of the building and the second floor.

Aaron Trippet and Justus W. Ferris were contemporaries, born in 1822 in Missouri and in 1823 in Hudson, New York, respectively. Both were early Waxahachie residents, Ferris arriving in 1854 to begin a law practice and eventually a banking business with W. H. Getzendaner, while Trippet arrived in 1861 and moved from farm to town in 1865 to open a dry goods and groceries business, sometimes in partnership with family members. Trippet's 208 West Main property intersected with his original store building, which fronted North Rogers, thereby giving him a sizable L-shaped space that wrapped around the Citizens National Bank building. In recent years, this exceptional pair of buildings has been overlooked and underappreciated because of its off-square location and the demise of City Hall, its neighbor to the west. It is an important surviving example of the two-story iron-front brick commercial buildings that graced the square area during the 1880s and early 1890s—this one with unusual pressed-metal details.

A-8
212 West Main
Site of City Hall and Fire Station Building (demolished 1964)

1892; Gill, Moad, & Gill, architects;
J. M. Johnson, contractor

There is always one demolition that a community laments more than others, and for white Waxahachie, it was the City Hall and Fire Station building, a brick and stone Late Victorian hunk that anchored this corner for seventy-two years. It was not a subtle building—nor did the architects and city fathers intend for it to be. After voters approved the project and bonds were issued to finance the structure, elected officials engaged in considerable haggling over the city's priorities, some arguing that given the city's growth, the water and school systems should take precedence even though the bond money could not be used for anything but a City Hall. Finally, the contract to build the design of Dallas architects Gill, Moad, & Gill was awarded on April 9, 1892, to local contractor J. M. Johnson for $11,850 with a six-month completion deadline. Johnson did not meet the deadline, but the city was in the building by the end of the year.

With tall arched openings, the lower level of both street facades accommodated teams of horse-drawn fire wagons. The entire second story featured a running arcade of closely spaced arched windows with colored glass transoms. Square cupolas marked the Main Street corners while a taller cupola on the east side held the fire bell. A large auditorium on the second floor was used by the city and other organizations until 1899, when insurance rates became too prohibitive to allow outside groups. Late in 1908, the space was converted into "one of the best-equipped club rooms in the state" for Waxahachie's volunteer fire fighters, complete with sleeping rooms, mission furniture, pool and billiard tables, and portraits of Capt. W. H. Getzendaner, Col. James S. Davis, and Col. R. A. Davis, benefactors of the city's three hook and ladder clubs. In 1922, the volunteer force was replaced by paid firefighters who continued to use the space.

As Waxahachie grew and traffic increased, keeping city offices as well as the fire station at this location became more and more difficult. Preservation and adaptive use were not yet on the horizon when new municipal facilities were built in 1964, and the city demolished the building. The parking lot remains today as a rebuke, but the loss probably helped to inspire the emergence of local preservation efforts a few years later that undoubtedly saved other major buildings and historic neighborhoods.

A-9
104 North Elm Street
Municipal Building
1964; Upshaw & Todd, architects

When Waxahachie replaced the elaborately embellished Victorian building at the corner of West Main and Elm Streets that had served as both City Hall and fire and police stations since 1892, city fathers built this small but boldly modern building, which in the 1960s was equated with a progressive, forward-moving community. The city had long been debating the need for a new City Hall in a new location because the movement of fire trucks in and out of traffic on an increasingly busy Elm Street was approaching intolerable. In 1961, voters approved a $230,000 bond issue that included a municipal building for which the exact location and building program were yet to be determined—most particularly, whether plans should include housing all three services in a single building. By fall, Arlington architect Morris Neel had just started working on the project when he died unexpectedly in late November at age thirty-nine.

Waxahachie-born Forrest Upshaw and partner Stuart Todd were given the job. By late March 1962, the council reviewed three possible downtown locations with several options that either kept all services on one site or separated them on two. The council chose the latter, placing the Municipal Building for city offices and council chamber at this location, and the police and fire departments on back-to-back lots in the 400 block of Water and West Main Streets.

These were not the first buildings that Upshaw or the firm designed for Upshaw's hometown. A 1943 graduate of Waxahachie High School, Upshaw received his bachelor's degree in architecture from the University of Texas in 1951, which means he just missed incoming dean Harwell Hamilton Harris and his group of modernist architect-teachers known as the Texas Rangers. Still, Upshaw left UT a modernist and worked in the Dallas offices of architects Charles Stevens Dilbeck and Adams & Adams before launching his own firm for a brief period, followed by his partnership with Todd in 1958. The two men met at Adams & Adams where Todd, a University of Michigan graduate in architecture, also worked.

The Municipal Building is the most prominently positioned—and the most forceful—of the firm's Waxahachie buildings. According to architectural historian Stephen Fox, it is "pure Wrightian" with its flat roof, minimal coping at the roofline, smooth unornamented wall surfaces, absence of decorative detail around the openings, and most dramatically, the second story cross insertion cantilevered over the wall below. One wonders what the public reaction was to the exterior of the building, given that it was unlike anything in town, but the local newspaper offers no clue or any editorial comment other than calling it "another sign of progress." The newspaper did infer that the public would approve of the floor plan, which placed business offices including the city manager on the first floor and council chambers upstairs.

Within ten years of moving into the new building, City Hall moved again to a larger structure, the refurbished 1913 Post Office building at **401 South Rogers**. Fortunately, the 1964 building at North Elm was not demolished. Rather, it was acquired by Citizens National Bank, which added the three columns to the cantilevered front, perhaps intending to give a visual tie to its primary building across the street. One hopes the bank will continue to appreciate its modernist appendage, which fits comfortably on Elm Street, and Waxahachie will be committed to preserving one of its rare architectural modernist expressions. It represents an experimental period in architecture and a time before communities began their self-conscious discussions about what constitutes compatible infill buildings in historic settings.

A-10
300 Water Street
Gulf Service Station

1948

One of the earliest signs of something "modern" on the north side of downtown was the Gulf Service Station built in 1948. It is a classic example of the canopied version of what was called Gulf's "icebox" station and was built by Clarence H. Lander, the local wholesale distributor for Gulf products and owner of multiple Gulf stations in the downtown. Hometown boy Munsey Bass was named operator of the new station, publicity noting that he was returning to the service station business and bringing with him fifteen years of "auto experience" along with his familiar "fish sign" and slogan, "Gas with Bass." Bass also moved his Frazer-Kaiser car dealership to this location, where he remained until he signed with another oil distributor in mid-1953.

Porcelain enamel tile was a favorite building material for the streamlined Moderne-style service stations dating from the mid-1930s into the 1950s. For starters, the cinder block construction faced with enamel panels was sleek in appearance. It was durable, relatively inexpensive at the time, and easy to maintain or, as noted by more than one observer, it could be hosed off—like a car. An August 1951 photograph in the *Daily Light* Business Review section shows that originally there was a single canopy on the Water Street façade. The Elm Street canopy was probably added not long after the US Highway 77 Extension Project in 1952. Prior to the highway project, Elm Street ended just south of the railroad tracks, and north-and-south-bound traffic through town used Ferris Avenue and Water Street. The project eliminated the Water Street jog by extending Elm Street over the tracks and curving into Ferris Street. Tire Town has been at this location since the mid-1970s.

A-11
200 North Elm Street
Citizens National Bank

1964-66; Thomas E. Stanley, Architects & Engineers; IBE Corporation, general contractors; Naud Burnett Landscape Company, Inc.

Established in 1868, Citizens National Bank had been located on the courthouse square since 1872, but that was no longer an option in the early 1960s when the bank needed to accommodate parking and drive-in services. It simply could not stay on the southwest corner of the square, where it had been since 1927. This Elm Street location—the fifth for the bank—was a good solution for both town and bank: It maintained the bank's commitment to downtown Waxahachie, gave it space to develop, and avoided the demolition of historic buildings.

Bank president Mark E. Singleton Jr. chose Dallas-based Thomas E. Stanley, considered one of the country's premier bank architects, to design the new building. Singleton and his board could rest assured that Stanley would propose no surprises, because the design would follow the "new image of banking" that the architect used in all his bank projects. Characterized by vertical lines, strict symmetry, columnar supports, smooth wall surfaces, quality materials, and flat projecting rooflines, it represented "a concept of classic contemporary architecture," as described in the *Daily Light* but no doubt borrowing Stanley's words. Stanley and other practitioners of formalism, the academic term for this easily recognizable modern style, used the columned façade as the base for huge urban projects such as the fifty-two-story First National Bank of Dallas, his joint venture with fellow Dallas architect George Dahl, which opened in 1965. In smaller projects, however, the columned façade *is* the building, as in Waxahachie, where six white Italian marble columns frame the front exterior in contrast to the recessed gray solar glass wall. On February 18, 1966, the daylong formal opening drew some five thousand people who toured the two-story bank lobby and second floor offices. For an added local touch, female employees were attired in new moss-green uniform-suits designed and made by Semmes Inc. of Waxahachie.

Stanley's CNB building was designed to support two or three additional stories, but fortunately those have not been built to loom over Waxahachie's downtown center. Instead, the mature oak trees and shaded building create a softened streetscape that maintains the scale of historic Waxahachie.

A-12
105 North Rogers Street
1871; 1891

This building and the one to its right, although very different in outward appearance today, were probably built at about the same time in 1871 and of the same "native white rock" used in many downtown buildings at the time. Early Sanborn maps, the first in 1885, show three structures built of stone from Main Street to the alley.

In late May 1891, several months after the Trippet-Ferris Building was completed at **208-210 West Main Street**, the *Enterprise* reported that merchant A. Trippet was now remodeling his "old store house," which was the stone building that he built here after buying the property in 1870. Trippet updated the exterior of the older building with a brick façade, corbelled parapet, and cast-iron storefront, the *Enterprise* describing the building as "practically rebuilt." On the interior, he connected the two buildings and formed a large L-shaped space that wrapped around the corner bank property and dubbed it "The Emporium." It proved to be a popular location for Trippet's annual Christmas sales extravaganza and for occasional local events like the annual flower show of the Sims-Watson Chapter of the United Daughters of the Confederacy, with its "battle of the flowers" in November 1908. Early in 1917, S. P. Spalding moved his furniture store here from its South Rogers location. Scott Furniture operated in this building from the late 1970s to 2011.

A-13
107 North Rogers Street
1871; multiple alterations

The 1871 stone base of this building is more easily detected from the street than its neighbor at **105 North Rogers** due to the "padded" walls that suggest multiple replasterings, the inset windows, and the thick alley wall visible at the basement level. When the property sold in 1880, the deed referred to the "rock storehouse," the same building that brothers and restaurateurs, S. C. and Robert Ash, bought in 1885. At that time, the two-story structure had a double gallery with an elaborate metal cornice that appears in the 1886 bird's-eye view and a circa 1910 photograph. Early Sanborn maps also show a stairway on the alley wall, all of which accommodated the Ashes' residence on the second floor, not a typical arrangement for Waxahachie but one that would not have been unusual for an English family like the Ashes.

The Ashes moved their restaurants to different locations around the square but did not sell this property until July 1913, when it was purchased by S. P. Spalding, a Waxahachie furniture dealer and undertaker whose business on the east side of the square burned in the 1911 Siddons Hotel fire. Spalding moved his funeral business to this location and made several cosmetic changes to the building, i.e., recording his name in tiles that can still be seen on the front step, removing the upper gallery, and replacing the metal cornice with a stepped parapet painted with the letters "Spalding Funeral Directors." Early in 1917, he moved his furniture store from its post-fire location on South Rogers to **105 North Rogers** and kept both businesses in the adjoining buildings through the mid-1920s.

A-14
109 North Rogers Street
1893; C. M. Sammons, contractor

This one-story cast-iron storefront building typifies a number of small commercial structures built just off Courthouse Square, usually in groups of four, and most built during 1893-1894. In this instance, the brick foursome replaced an assortment of wood buildings that burned in 1891. In May 1893, the same four property owners whose buildings had burned contracted C. M. Sammons to construct their new brick buildings. Sammons subcontracted the job to R. J. Harley from Dallas, and the two men, in turn, subcontracted specific work elements to others like J. M. Callens and J. E. Morton, who provided materials and labor for plasterwork, the latter information disclosed in a lien that Callens and Morton filed to collect payment (a frequent occurrence). Three of the buildings were built in summer 1893 while the fourth, on the Water Street corner, was not built until 1896.

N. G. Davis, original owner of this alley-line building, was typical of many property owners in the downtown area in the late nineteenth century. After he arrived in Waxahachie with his family soon after the Civil War, his business interests gradually extended beyond his listed occupation as a carpenter to include rental properties. He bought this property, one of several he owned, in 1876, and when this structure was built, had the threshold cast for posterity with "N. G. DAVIS 1893." The first tenants in the new row are unknown, but when the 1898 Sanborn was drawn all four tenants were food- and drink-related: 109 and 113 were saloons, 111 was a meat market, and 115 a bakery. This building is most closely identified with printer George Bayless who, with C. E. Shuster, rented the building before purchasing it in 1904. They bought 111 in 1907. Their partnership operated under the name Southern Printing Co. until Shuster's death in 1919, after which Bayless—or "Pos," short for Possum—became sole owner. Bayless Printing & Office Supplies remained in the Bayless family and in this building through the late 1980s.

The careful restoration of this building in 2002 by owners Becky and Jim Kauffman for her interior design business, Living Spaces, is an important chapter in the preservation story of downtown Waxahachie. The other three buildings in the row were demolished to make way for a bank parking lot in 1971, and although this building survived, the façade had been drastically defaced and the entrance shifted to one side in the 1960s. However, the exposed cast-iron corner pilasters gave the owners hope for what they *might* find with careful removal of the materials, which did indeed reveal the classic double-door commercial entry with transoms and display windows, corbelled brickwork, and labeled Mosher Ironworks storefront. The project was among the first to be financed through a low-interest loan program promoted by the city and local banks specifically for preservation projects in downtown Waxahachie.

The only visible example of "the paving infection" that struck Waxahachie in 1913 is at the intersection of North Rogers and Water Street. The *Daily Light* reported in April that the streets surrounding Courthouse Square and leading into it were being paved "at a merry clip." Streets on the square itself were paved with creosoted wooden blocks, while those leading into the square, like North Rogers, were paved with brick. This section was uncovered as part of the beautification program initiated for this area in 1973 by Citizens National Bank President Marvin E. Singleton Jr.

A-15
200 North Rogers Street
Ellis County Jail
1888; Pauly Jail Building & Manufacturing Co.

When this structure was completed in September 1888, Ellis County could boast having a rotary jail, one of just seventeen (possibly eighteen) built in the United States, and at the time considered a major innovation in the field of prisoner incarceration. The building when viewed on Rogers Street was a bit deceiving, appearing, as it does today, as a subdued and sturdy dark brick Victorian residence—which it was. Jails were frequently built to double as the residence for the city or county law enforcer, in this case for the Ellis County Sheriff and his family. This front façade definitely presented a residential stateliness with attenuated proportions, a circular bay and conical roof, steeply pitched roof, and long narrow windows. Decorative detailing was restricted to brick corbelling that fringed the metal cornice and to smooth light-colored stone lintels and sills that set the openings.

Although the Water Street façade matched the residential front in height, materials, and brick detailing, it presented a very different, somber impression as a formidable institutional building. (Bars on the windows were a dead giveaway.) The two-story rotary jail that dictated the building footprint was located at the rear in an octagon-shaped cell wing. The connecting midsection housed the jail entry, a processing space for inmates, the sheriff's office, the kitchen that served both residence and jail, and what was called the lunatic asylum. At the time, if a locality provided any facilities for non-dangerous mentally ill individuals, it was the jail.

This was the third jail built on property that the county bought in 1855. The first was a 16 x 16 ft. two-story wood structure that the commissioners replaced in 1874 with a 30 x 20 ft. one-story stone jail to which a second story was added in May 1875. In winter 1877, iron "cells or cages," purchased from P. J. Pauly & Brother of St. Louis, Missouri, for $2,750, were installed on the upper floor. The Pauly firm was founded in 1856 by a family of steamboat blacksmiths who, in their occupational travels, observed that adequate detention facilities were needed to transfer and house prisoners. They began manufacturing small movable cages that served as jails and within three decades had developed a system of cell-work and jails that were sold and built throughout the country.

By the mid-1880s, Ellis County Commissioners, weary of frequent jailbreaks and an undersized jail, once again looked to what was now the Pauly Jail Building & Manufacturing Co., and in November 1887 signed a $35,000 contract for the company to build "a Jail House... according to Plans No 61 & specifications," a reference either to a plan in the firm's catalogue or to one of over six hundred plans and drawings in their architectural office. (Only remnants of these documents have survived; no drawings or specifications have been found for the Waxahachie jail.) Contracting for a Pauly rotary jail meant that a Pauly crew came to Waxahachie to construct the building and install the rotary jail, as it required mechanics and laborers familiar with the apparatus. The commissioners hired local builder and brick mason Dennis Mahoney to oversee the project on behalf of the county, but nothing in the records suggest that it was built by a local work force.

The Ellis County rotary jail was a two-tier circular cell structure, each tier with ten pie-shaped cells that turned on a shaft that was mounted on pilings in the basement and extended through the roof. The outer grated cell was stationary with a single sliding door that opened into a vestibule. The internal circular structure revolved and, by turning a crank, the jailer could line up a single cell with the opening. Individual cells measured eight feet long and approximately four feet at the shaft end and eight feet on the outside with a four-foot door, a space considered adequate for two prisoners if necessary. Walls between cells were solid, but both ends were grated. The jail also had conventional cells as well as death-row and solitary confinement cells with iron rings in the basement.

It was "the massiveness of the much-read-of county jail" that "amazed" a local reporter when he toured the facility soon after it opened. Escapes were reduced, occurring only when prisoners were in areas other than the "squirrel cage." But problems emerged as could be expected when maintaining what had to be a finely-tuned mechanical system. On May 26, 1899, the *Enterprise* cried out that "this old rotary cell outfit is a disgrace to a civilized county and ought to be abolished" after prisoner "old man McCain" was badly hurt and one of his ears almost cut off when he was caught in the rotary cage door. It could have been worse—a prisoner's head was crushed in the rotary jail in Maryville, Missouri, in 1904.

The circular cells in Waxahachie were finally dispensed with in 1929 when the jail was moved to new facilities at Franklin and Jackson Streets. During the Depression, several relief programs including the WPA used this site. In fall 1941, a power machinist bought the metal in the building and in February 1947, the county sold the property at public auction for $10,000. The new owner, auto dealer and repairman Thomas Hipp, lived in the residence while removing the second floor of the jail and replacing the octagon shape with a rectangular garage and office for his business. W. T. Esselman Electric followed in 1955. Citizens National Bank acquired the property in 1973 as part of its beautification project for the block, and among its tenants, provided gratis office space to the newly organized Historic Waxahachie, Inc., in 1978. Bank president Marvin E. Singleton Jr. oversaw restoration of the building in 1980-1983. Since the 2009 closing of Rose Cameron's BBQ Pit Restaurant on the Water and College Streets side, the building has settled into office use only.

A-16
Singleton Plaza

1974; Naud Burnett & Associates, landscape architects; Miller & Norton, general contractors

Singleton Plaza was dedicated on October 5, 1974, to the memory of Col. Marvin E. Singleton, who served as sixth president of Citizens National Bank in 1931-1938. It also reflects the interests in community issues and design that the colonel's son and successor, Marvin E. Singleton Jr., pursued during his tenure as bank president from 1938 to 1987. Providing customer parking was a primary reason for relocating the bank from the square to the corner of Elm and Water Streets in 1966, but Singleton went one step further and hired Naud Burnett to landscape the bank parking lot—something of a novelty in Waxahachie at the time (and still is). Seven years later, amidst the ever-growing search for off-street parking in the downtown, Singleton acquired this full block east of the bank, from Rogers Street to College Street and from Water Street to the railroad right-of-way. Once again he commissioned Burnett, this time to transform the property north of the jail, formerly the site of a lumberyard, into a public parking plaza. Like many landscaping projects, it improves with age.

On the south side of the plaza is a hint of San Antonio, a below-street serpentine walkway along a spring-fed stream of historic Rogers Spring Branch that was uncovered during the project.

Please note: The walkway is not handicap accessible.

A-17
Waxahachie Calaboose and Wyatt Real Estate Office

Calaboose: c. 1888; Wyatt Office: c. 1867-68

The Calaboose, the term derived from the Spanish *calabozo* (dungeon), and the Wyatt office, now located to its right, typify the many small buildings that were part not just of Waxahachie's early years but also of early development in any town. They represent the buildings that usually disappear from the landscape as a town grows. That would have happened here had Historic Waxahachie, Inc. not moved them and Citizens National Bank not offered a resting place on Singleton Plaza.

Life was treacherous for a calaboose. To begin with, they were viewed as temporary structures, cheaply built, and subject to rough treatment, no maintenance, and fire. This survivor has an unusual construction feature that may explain its longevity. Interior partitions are stacked wood slats, which are far denser and slower to burn than the usual single vertical plank walls. Assigning an exact date to this calaboose is difficult. Documents disclose that Waxahachie built a "new" one in 1879 (suggesting it replaced an earlier one), at least two more in 1886 and 1888, and repaired one in 1891 that may have been this structure. The calabooses were placed on the Ellis County jail property at Rogers and Water Streets until the late 1880s, when the city bought property in the 200 block of Jackson Street for a calaboose and a pound. Minor offenders arrested for such things as drunkenness and petty theft populated the calaboose, which tended to be especially crowded on Waxahachie's "First Monday" that began as a horse-trading day but quickly evolved into "a regular fair day" every month. In 1915, the calaboose was put out of commission when the more substantial City Jail was built across the alley from City Hall at Elm and Main Streets. The obsolete building languished on Jackson Street until Historic Waxahachie moved it to Singleton Plaza around 2005.

Robert M. Wyatt's two-room office is not only the oldest commercial building in Waxahachie but is also a rare surviving example of vernacular Greek Revival architecture in this part of Texas. Wyatt, born in Virginia in 1822, grew up surrounded by buildings that looked like Greek temples, as the style was at its height in the East during the 1820s and 1830s, with some of the finest examples found in Richmond, where Wyatt apprenticed as a carpenter. The style spread west and continued to be built for a short time after the Civil War.

Wyatt and his family arrived in Waxahachie in November 1860. He soon replaced the carpentry trade with the job of county assessor followed by his election as county surveyor, an office he held until 1868, after which he devoted full time to the land agency he had been fostering. When Wyatt built his office on the southeast corner of Jackson and East Main Streets, he definitely knew that it had a look and size that other pioneers would associate with banks, lawyers, and physicians. The distinctive temple front was obvious with its pediment gable front, full-width portico with squared columns, and central entry. Construction elements original to the building, i.e., flush siding on the front façade, board and batten construction on the sides, and double-hung wooden sash windows with 6/6 lights on all four facades, are intact. There was only one other building like it in Waxahachie—the first building constructed in 1868 for the newly formed bank that became Citizens National Bank.

After Wyatt's death in April 1889, "Wyatt's old office," as locals were calling it in 1891, periodically served as an office for family members, including his son, John F., and as the polling place for residents of Waxahachie's First Ward, which encompassed property on the south side of Main Street. The building survived an early 1920s move to the center of the block to make way for a filling station on the corner. In 2000, Wyatt descendants, specifically the Frances W. Dillard Trust and trustees DuBose A. Lomax and Susanne L. Rocket, made it possible for Historic Waxahachie, Inc. to preserve the structure.

A-18
301 North College Street
Waxahachie Medicine Company
1913

Courthouse Square was the prime location for retail businesses in Waxahachie, but for businesses that relied on the delivery and/or distribution of products, the coveted spots were on a railroad track or spur, ideally with space for loading docks. Unlike their retail counterparts, they were not designed to attract the passerby.

Originally, this building served as headquarters for the Waxahachie Medicine Company, a business founded in 1905 primarily by druggist and patent medicine man John S. Herring. When building at this new location in 1913, the company was already doing a large wholesale business shipping its "Ideal Remedies," including medicines, extracts, and soaps, all over the country. The local cotton seed oil mill and the medicine company were closely tied, as the mill supplied the components for many of the laboratory's products. As the medicine company expanded its own product line, it also became distributor for other brands. In a November 1935 article about Ellis County's economic recovery efforts, the *Dallas Morning News* cited the company, now also called Ideal Laboratories Inc., as one of Waxahachie's "chief business firms of national scope." The last city directory listing for a related business at this address was in 1958 for Ideal Home Products, manufacturers of flavors, cosmetics, and home remedies, M. E. Singleton Jr., president. Glenn's Carpet Company has been at this location since 2003, the staff occasionally finding medicine bottles and other artifacts dating from the earlier occupants.

Directly behind this building, the warehouse at 300 North Rogers was built in two stages, as marked clearly by a vertical line on the trackside wall. In 1911, Allen Lasswell, a well-known name among Waxahachie grocers, built the west half, or Rogers Street side, of the warehouse, the date documented by a deed of trust between Lasswell and contractor W. W. Edwards. Sometime in the early 1920s, the Boren-Stewart wholesale grocery company, managed by Lee Lasswell (Allen's son), built an addition on the east side that almost doubled the building size. In the early 1930s, the company returned to the Lasswell name and remained here through the 1950s.

A-19
228 North College Street
Site of Houston and Texas Central Depot (demolished 1967)
1902; Olle J. Lorehn, architect; Charlie Jones, contractor

Railroad tracks have defined the northern and southern boundaries of Waxahachie's downtown core since the railroads came to town, in 1879 on the north side and in 1887-1888 on the south side. The Houston and Texas Central, forerunner to what is now Union Pacific, opened tracks and instituted passenger-freight service in 1879 from a depot on the west side of North Rogers Street. In 1902, the railroad built a one-story brick passenger depot at this location. Designed by Houston-based architect Olle J. Lorehn, it was typical of the period except for the stepped gable ends that may have reminded Lorehn of his Swedish birthplace. Built five years before the two depots were built on the south side of downtown, it is the only one that did *not* survive. Southern Pacific discontinued passenger service to Waxahachie in 1948. In 1967, the depot was sold and demolished to make way for a car lot.

The one-story building at 216 North College originally housed an automobile dealership which the city purchased in 1983 and adapted for offices. When renovated in 2000 for use as police headquarters, the city, to its credit, and Rob Hobbs Architects, opted for a low-profile presence on the street. The history of this building and the surrounding area are reminders of just how much the automobile was consuming downtown after World War II.

A-20
210, 212, and 214 North College Street
210: c. 1921
212 & 214: 1926

This brick threesome is typical of one-story vernacular brick commercial structures that filled out secondary streetscapes in larger towns and Main Streets in rural communities from circa 1910 through the 1930s. The building at 210 (on the right in this photograph) was built soon after the property was bought by Jesse Hart in 1921—its first occupant probably a short-lived College Street Market. After new property owners Wayne and Tammy Strickland bought and renovated the building in 2003, it became a local "institution," the popular College Street Pub. The two 14-foot wide buildings that complete the row, 212 and 214, were built in 1926. Even with buildings as unadorned as these, the simple spacing of parapet pilasters calls attention to the separation of the buildings and, in the case of 210, to the organization of the three-bay façade.

A-21
209 North Jackson Street
George Brown Plaza
Plaza: 1998; Splash Pad: 2017

A shaded passageway to the right of **210 North College** leads to the George Brown Plaza, named for Waxahachie's first African American councilman and mayor.

There also is an entrance to the plaza from North Jackson Street. Born in 1925 in the neighboring town of Italy, Brown moved to Waxahachie with his family when he was junior high school age and graduated from Oak Lawn School in 1943. A decorated World War II veteran, he attended Paul Quinn College and worked as a mechanic in the auto department of the local J. C. Penney store from 1968 to 1988, after which he co-owned and operated Brown and Moody Garage on Ennis Street until retiring in 2000. Elected to the council first in 1970, Brown served the city for thirty-two years, including his time as mayor from 1980 to 1983. City Council dedicated the plaza in his honor on June 30, 1998, and in 1999, he was the first African American to receive the Waxahachie Citizen of the Year Award. A joint effort between the Waxahachie Parks Board and the Waxahachie Community Development Corporation resulted in the 2017 addition of a splash pad.

A-22
200-202 North College Street

Waxahachie Steam Laundry

1887-88
(photograph 2009)

Many Waxahachians remember these buildings as home of the Waxahachie Steam Laundry and also remember John E. McWhorter, who became sole owner of the business in 1920. Until 2011, and as shown in this 2009 photograph, the buildings exemplified two-story structures that were built in downtowns everywhere before the "iron-front" with cast-iron columns and elaborate cornices dictated commercial facades. Without mechanics' liens to prove otherwise, this pair, prior to alterations, could have been dated 1870 based on their exterior appearance when, in fact, 200 (right) was built in 1888 and 202 in 1887. Originally, the buildings were used for other purposes, but this property, on a slope with the Rogers Spring Branch cutting across the backside, was ideally positioned to become a steam laundry in the early 1890s. The buildings were *heavily* used, which resulted in numerous interior changes and rear additions over the years, but the early street façades were always maintained. The current multicolor brick walls date from a 2012 rehabilitation that was approved in concept but not in execution by the Heritage Preservation Commission.

The passageway to the right of the laundry building, now a parking lot, was created in early 1918 when the Texas Electric Railway Company purchased, then demolished the buildings on the site and constructed sidings to service a new one-story Interurban passenger station and baggage-express office building that is still extant at 116 North College. It was a very tight squeeze. For pedestrians, it must have been startling to see what looked like railcars crashing through the building facades. The last run of the Waxahachie to Waco route of the Texas Electric Interurban was in 1948.

A-23
109 North College Street

1894

The December 1893 fire destroyed the buildings on this quarter block (109 through 115 North College) as well as those facing the square. In fact, it was believed that the fire started in a millinery shop in the one-story brick row which, at the time, was all rental property. The owners immediately rebuilt, and the shops, like those facing the square, were back in business by mid-summer 1894. The rebuilt row of four near-matching one-story flat-roofed commercial buildings followed the gentle slope of College Street with stepped parapets, decorative corbelled cornices, and cast-iron fronts made by Mosher Ironworks of Dallas. Originally, each shop had a center double-door entrance with transom above and display windows to the sides. Over the years, the buildings have been given varying treatments. In this case at 109, the corbel table and parapet were left in their original state when the street façade was remodeled circa 1955.

A-24
111 North College Street
1894

This building has been identified with the printing business in Waxahachie from 1912, when it was purchased by the Middleton family, to the present. The date appearing on the parapet, 1887, is the year that schoolteacher Thomas J. Middleton purchased the *Ellis County Mirror* and moved his family from Mountain Peak to Waxahachie to become editor and publisher of the weekly newspaper. With the help of four Middleton children, T. J. added job printing to the newspaper business in 1904, and circa 1908 moved the offices from South College to **109 North College**. He disposed of his newspaper properties in fall 1911, but two sons, Marcellus (known as "Sales") and Montgomery, maintained what had become Middleton Printing Company. Upon T. J.'s death in October 1912, his widow Jennie bought this property with the help of friends and moved the print shop to this location (111). Although the Middleton family eventually sold the business, the building remained in continuous use as a print shop, and in 2013, College Street Printing and owner Kenneth Denny received a Texas Treasure Business Award from the Texas Historical Commission.

A-25
113 North College Street
1894

The interior of this building is totally unexpected. At the back is a diminutive version of a "grand staircase" that splits into a narrow open gallery hugging both sides of the interior walls. Sanborn maps show similar staircases in other buildings in downtown Waxahachie, but one is never shown in this building, which means it is a later insertion. Space, or lack of space, could be an issue in these small structures, and galleries added storage space. Sometimes openings were cut in party walls to create larger retail spaces: the 1904 Sanborn map documents that this had been done to connect **113** and **115 North College** for a wallpaper and paint store. In 1909, a furniture warehouse utilized both spaces. The small-pane window modifications on the exterior probably date from the early 1970s.

A-26
115 North College Street
1894; 1913, second floor addition

When built, this was a one-story building like the rest of the row. The name, "Yeager," is cast in the threshold and almost worn away, but the "1894" construction date is very clear. Lawyer Elijah Fisk Yeager had bought this as investment property in 1882, two years after he became owner and editor of the *Waxahachie Enterprise*. Yeager died at age forty-six in 1890 at which time his wife, Minnie Burton Rainey Yeager, assumed her husband's place at the newspaper. Six months before the 1893 fire, Minnie died of consumption.

The property remained in the Yeager family until it was sold in early 1913 to retail merchant and furniture dealer M. T. Knight and his wife Cora, who hired carpenter A. D. Wright to add a second story that would serve as their residence while they operated their business on the first floor. The Knights and Wright signed two very exacting mechanics' liens for the $1,150 project, specifying that first-story walls would be ten feet high and second-story walls eight feet high, even detailing that the second floor would be "canvassed and papered with paper to cost 25c per roll." Living above the store was not a typical arrangement in downtown Waxahachie, but apparently the Knights were quite content, as they never moved to another location and both of them died here, M. T. in 1943 and Cora in 1954.

There is the belief among Waxahachians that this property was a brothel, a deduction based on its having a second story balcony—considered a sure sign of a brothel. It seems to be a badge of honor, not just in Waxahachie but in many places, to own an historic building with that titillating distinction. Waxahachie had its prostitutes, but nothing has been found to substantiate the claim for this building. It was a boarding house at times, as were many buildings and residences in town.

A-27
100 North College Street
Rogers Hotel

1912-13; C. D. Hill & Co., architect; Gross Construction Co., contractor

With the Interurban passenger station and baggage rooms housed in the hotel building and the Interurban as well as local streetcars stopping at the door, the Rogers Hotel typifies a building genre built across America in the late nineteenth-early twentieth centuries—the railroad hotel. Catering primarily to business travelers, the Rogers, like many of its counterparts, can be described as sturdy, solid, functional, and, if buildings are allowed a gender, masculine. Indeed, the clientele was predominantly male, mostly traveling salesmen who stayed in one of the 12 x 12 cubicle rooms and displayed their merchandise in one of the "sample rooms" that were part of the hotel floor plan. Designed in the office of leading Dallas architect C. D. Hill, the four-story structure with full basement and two-story rear wing was built, as stated in promotional materials, "of reinforced concrete, faced with dark mottled brick, trimmed with Bedford stone and is ABSOLUTELY FIRE PROOF." The hotel owner, the Waxahachie Real Estate and Building Association, was especially anxious to assure potential guests that the building was safe given that its predecessor, the 1882 Siddons Hotel, burned in a devastating fire on November 12, 1911.

With an exterior that has changed little since its construction, the Rogers Hotel is a straightforward early twentieth century commercial building that was "a design of extreme simplicity . . . its individuality" depending on the effective placement of well-balanced details and contrasting materials. Exterior elements emphasized horizontality—the flat roof with low parapet and projecting cornice, bands of large windows with contrasting stone detailing and sills, and leaded glass transoms above the storefront windows. Main Street was clearly the primary façade, as denoted by "Rogers" cast in stone above the entrance and placement of the light well that gave both air and light to the upper floors. The roof accommodated a garden on the west side and sleeping tents "for the open air enthusiast" on the east. The hotel opened for business in early April 1913, followed by a formal reception hosted by hotel manager Robert Harrison and his wife on May 1. According to the *Daily Light*, it was "one of the most brilliant social events of the season" and the roof garden, which was lit by Japanese lanterns and where refreshments were served, was one of the most popular places for the two to three thousand people in attendance.

In keeping with the "extreme simplicity" of the exterior, the interior reflected "modest dignity." It was not flamboyant nor was it intended to be; rather, it was serviceable and comfortable. Many interior details remain intact, including the curved wood reception counter faced with dark green tile and the Florentine floor tiling in the "Hom'y Com'fy" lobby. The floor plan is not altered; the mezzanine overlooking the lobby and dining room is still in place, as is the elevator (although updated). All rooms were supplied with hot and cold artesian water, and some rooms had private baths. Other amenities included steam heat, electric lights and fans throughout, telephones in all the rooms, and screens on all the outside openings. Mineral water was piped from the city's well at Flat and East Jefferson Streets to the public water fountain (public to whites) in the lobby, N. W. Pierce's barber shop and baths in the basement, and the swimming pool that was installed in the basement in 1916 to entice major league baseball teams to Waxahachie for spring training. The pool achieved its stated purpose, attracting the Detroit Tigers in 1916-1918, the Cincinnati Reds in 1919, and the Chicago White Sox in 1921. Some said it also gave the hotel an unmistakable odor.

The Rogers Hotel was never just for travelers. From the

outset, it was a center for major civic and social events, a residential hotel for some, and a place to dine or to patronize the storefront businesses at the corner and along North College Street. There was no other space like it in Waxahachie, and at its height, it would be the envy of every modern-day developer of mixed-use projects. As happened nationwide, the Rogers' popularity gradually declined as automobiles became the primary mode of transportation and businesses moved out of downtown—in Waxahachie's case, after Highway 77 was widened in 1952. Beginning in the 1970s, there were several efforts to revitalize the hotel but without any long-term success. In 2000, Tony Cimino restored the structure and opened it as a hotel, but that, too, was unsuccessful and was followed by other rocky attempts. In 2014, the present owners, Lake-Moreno Partners LLC, acquired the property as part of their preservation and development project for the square and surrounding area.

The Rogers Hotel occupies what has always been considered the most historic spot in town, the site where Waxahachie founder E. W. Rogers and his wife Nancy built their log cabin in 1847. The cabin became a stopover for travelers on the old Shawnee Trail leading from the Red River to San Antonio and a meeting place where pioneers shaped the future Ellis County and Waxahachie. In 1856, the couple replaced the cabin with the "large and commodious" two-story hotel they called the Rogers House. John Siddons bought the property in 1871 and eventually changed the name to Siddons Hotel. When the hotel burned in May 1882, the local newspaper lamented the loss of "one of the old landmarks of our town." Another Siddons Hotel was immediately built on the same site; it was replaced by the present Rogers Hotel when it burned in 1911.

A-28
201-217 East Main Street
1920-28

The buildings in this row, simple as they may be, reflect varying stages of original condition, renovation and reconstruction, and collectively add a visual dimension to the gentle slope of East Main Street for people moving in and out of Courthouse Square. W. M. Koger built the row of one-story vernacular brick commercial buildings in the 1920s. Koger gave his occupation as farmer, but like many successful farmers in the area, he also invested in Waxahachie real estate.

After acquiring all the properties in the block that fronted East Main Street, Koger developed the row in two phases by first demolishing the existing buildings on the Jackson Street side and building units 201-207 and 209-211 in 1920. Early businesses at these addresses included Harry Byers's and Joe Katz's dry goods stores and Angelus Kakos's Candy Kitchen. It was not until fall 1927 that Koger began constructing the second phase, only to be interrupted the following February when fire destroyed the building at 209-211. Koger quickly rebuilt that structure and completed the row to Flat Street (now closed off).

When Koger died in 1942, his estate was partitioned among his six surviving children, and gradually parcels were sold to non-family members. A. E. McDonald & Son Produce Company was a longtime occupant on the east end of the row (217). Realtor and insurance agent Lee Lasswell bought the adjacent building (215) in 1949 and rented it to numerous businesses before selling to Building Corporation Local 514 in 1976 who, in turn, sold it to the Democratic Party in 2005.

A-29
110-114 East Main Street
1912

Property owners John F. Wyatt and T. A. Ferris, two of Waxahachie's real estate titans, built this row of commercial rent property as quickly as possible to replace the buildings they lost November 12, 1911, in the Siddons Hotel fire. The *Daily Light* reported on December 31 that Wyatt was "having material placed on the ground" for his two storefronts on the east end of the row at 112 and 114. One of Wyatt's pre-fire tenants, grocer F. J. Devers, returned to his corner spot while a new tenant, grocer Lee Lasswell, replaced bicycle repairman A. D. MacKoy at 112. Furniture dealers and undertakers W. K. and Marvin Rudolph returned to Ferris's new buildings at 108 and

110, where they would remain until selling their furniture business in August 1923. The row exhibits all the basic exterior characteristics of the one-story vernacular storefront building type—parapets, transoms, centered double-door entries, display windows, and kickplates. On the interior, the 1914 Sanborn map noted concrete floors and "steel ceil[ings]," both considered fire retardant features. The uniformity of the row is more pronounced than usual due to few alterations over the years and a precise paint job that contrasts window and door trim with dark brick. Originally, canopies were attached to the row.

A-30
101 South College Street
Durham Building

1912; H. A. Overbeck, architect; J. S. McCanless, contractor
1936 extension, O. B. Bennett, contractor
(photograph 2009)

The history of this building is a little more complicated than the date and name appearing on the escutcheon at the top of the building suggest. Like so much of Waxahachie's courthouse square, the building took shape as the result of a fire, in this instance, the November 12, 1911 Siddons Hotel fire that jumped across Main Street and destroyed the north third of this block including the 1896 Odd Fellows' three-story red-brick and stone headquarters building that anchored this corner. Within two months, the IOOF acquired a new location at **208 South Rogers** and sold their 40 x 90 ft. burned out property on the square to dry goods merchant S. W. Durham, whose store was located in the Masonic Temple building at **201 South College**, just one block to the south. (Truth be known, the Odd Fellows were already in the mood to move before the fire.)

Durham immediately cleared the fire debris (a stipulation of the sale) from his new lot and commissioned Dallas architect H. A. Overbeck to design a two-story building "patterned after the most modern designs and especially adapted to department store needs." Durham's selection of an architect was easy, as Overbeck had recently completed a new residence for Durham and his wife Phoebe at **603 North Rogers**. Like the new "Durham Building" on the square, the residence exhibited influences of the Prairie style, a style for which Overbeck was known and that the Durhams clearly liked.

But the downtown building that Durham built and Overbeck designed is only two-thirds of the building seen today. In 1916, P. A. Chapman acquired the Durham Building and signed a ten-year lease with a new tenant, the New York-based S. H. Kress & Co., a national chain of 5-10-15 Cent Stores established in 1896. When Charles L. Penn, another familiar name in local real estate circles, bought the building in 1926, he extended the lease for ten years. As renewal time for that lease approached in March 1936, Penn acquired twenty-two feet of the adjacent property, which was essentially destroyed in a 1935 fire that did lesser damage to Penn's building. In the subsequent twenty-five-year lease agreement, Penn gave Kress the option of tearing down all or part of the existing building and rebuilding, but whatever Kress chose to do, the front width of the building, now sixty-two feet, had to "conform in design and to appear as one building as near as reasonably possible."

Had Kress chosen to demolish the existing structure and start anew, this corner of the square would probably be the site of an Art Deco building, the corporation's preferred style in the mid-1930s. Instead, the 1912 Overbeck building was skillfully extended and the original detailing adjusted and duplicated to create the graceful building seen today. There was still the low roof and parapet, projecting eaves, ribbon windows, and contrasting narrow bands connecting second story window sill and lintel lines around the building, but the longer, lower proportions of the 1936 building gave greater emphasis and an added elegance to the horizontality of the original design. Ornament was kept to the geometrical stone carving on the capital columns separating the second story windows and piers and to the escutcheon on the re-centered Mission-shaped parapet, the latter a detail that also appears on the front dormer of the Durhams' house on North Rogers.

Who was the architect of the 1936 downtown project? Perhaps Overbeck. He was still practicing, but it also seems plausible that it was one of Kress's own army of in-house architects, since the chain was completing a seven-story structure in Fort Worth at the time. Whoever is responsible, the 1936 structure is an admirable example of architectural respect and restraint that began with a well and carefully designed building in 1912.

In February, 1970, Kress opened a new store in Northgate Shopping Center on Highway 77 and maintained both stores before ending the company's over fifty years on the square in midsummer. Many Waxahachians associate the building with Kress's successor, Cheeves Bros. Department Store, which had been in business in Waxahachie at 300 South Rogers from 1897 until November 1968, when their original store burned. After renting an interim location, Cheeves moved to this building in August 1970 and remained here until the late 1980s.

A-31

Site of 105, 107, 109, 111 South College

(photograph 2009)

On January 18, 2011, Waxahachians experienced a devastating sense of living history when the buildings shown here were either completely destroyed or so heavily damaged by fire that they had to be demolished. The timing and aftermath of the disaster could not have been worse given that Waxahachie, like the rest of the country, was suffering from an economic depression that some residents felt was mirrored in the square being the "shabbiest" they had ever seen. Ironically, prior to the 2011 fire, the east side was the most commercially active side of the square, with a mix of businesses and offices. Architecturally, the buildings exhibited changes and alterations that had taken place over the years, but all maintained their historic late 1870s form and height with shopfronts and display windows at street level and offices on the second floor. Owners of the burned-out properties gave the city permission to use the empty lots for public space until they are sold and redeveloped.

The 1890 Waxahachie National Bank building stood at 115 South College until it was demolished in 1971. *Courtesy Ellis County Museum.*

A-32

115 South College Street

Courthouse Park

2003; Anthony Mottla, architect

Dedicated on September 12, 2003, the Courthouse Park was designed not only to grace a corner on the square but also to fill specific needs: public restrooms for a growing tourist trade, a small gathering and rest area for both tourists and locals, and an aesthetic cover for the courthouse chiller unit and electrical equipment placed on the alley side of the property. The 1890 Waxahachie National Bank building stood at this pivotal corner until it was demolished in 1971 to be replaced by a parking lot. It was a huge loss to the square. Even though the bank was only a sliver of a building—twenty-four-foot frontage on the square, ninety feet along Franklin Street—the three-story red brick and sandstone Romanesque structure was a stately companion to the Masonic Temple across the street. Together, they created an impressive gateway on the southeast side of the square. In 1919, the bank moved across the square to **114 South Rogers** and sold this building, which then housed numerous commercial enterprises including, as advertised, "the only tire store on the Square" before it and the adjoining structure were demolished.

Ellis County acquired the property in the early 1980s. Alluding to the arched openings and chamfered corner of the 1890 bank, architect Anthony Mottla designed a pocket park shaded by a maturing canopy of trees. The project was a community-wide collaboration with participation by both the city and the county along with many organizations and individuals whose names appear on commemorative plaques and paving bricks placed in the park.

A-33
109 East Franklin Street
c. 1894

When the Waxahachie National Bank Building opened in January 1891 at the corner of South College and East Franklin Streets, it meant that every lot fronting the courthouse square was occupied by a two- or three-story brick commercial structure. No longer were there any frame buildings to be replaced or empty lots to be filled (unless, of course, there was another fire), so investors and business owners turned their attention to properties along the streets leading *into* the square. The 1890s saw a flurry of projects of one-story brick buildings that followed a standard form—iron fronts, large plate-glass display windows, centered entrances, and corbelled parapets. Usually built in multiples, most were built as rental property by hopeful investors who anticipated that the land on which the structures sat would become, with time, more valuable for higher development or sale.

Unquestionably, the most notable of these structures is this building, but surprisingly little can definitely be documented for such an extraordinary structure. A few things are definite: the property belonged to Lilly A. Clift and W. B. Clift, whose family had owned this end of Block 9 since the 1850s, but it is uncertain that the building was built by the Clifts. It was built sometime between the April 1893 and the October 1898 Sanborn insurance maps, and it was built by highly skilled brick masons with a whimsical touch. The building follows the standard form for these one-story commercial structures, but detailing and execution are anything but standard, beginning with the inlaid stonework on the pediment and other parapet motifs and on the alley wall. There might be the temptation to date the stonework as a much later detail, but it appears in a 1915 photograph. It could have been added by an early tenant, but occupancy was fluid, which makes that unlikely.

The wide parapet with stepped corbeling and capped brick piers and the large transoms above the canopy create the impression of a building larger than it is. Fanciful brick and stone work on the alley corner and repeated corbeling along the alley roofline are exceptional not just in their precise detailing but also in their placement on an alley wall. The parapet and building silhouette suggest that the post-fire buildings constructed in 1894 on the north side of the square, most especially those on the east end, were the inspiration for 109 East Franklin and that it may have been built by the same brick masons.

The careful renovation of the building in 2013 by attorneys Kent and Constance Smith McGuire for their offices preserved these and other historic features of the unique façade. Canopies were a common feature on most commercial buildings of this period, but few are left and even fewer still have a tin ceiling as does this structure. The labeled Mosher iron front with thresholds is also intact.

A-34
113 and 115 East Franklin Street
1913

Although the corner building at 113-115 East Franklin never had the architectural finesse of its neighbor and has experienced major alterations, its story brings together three of Waxahachie's strongest personalities from the 1890s and early 1900s. In June 1890, Richard Vickery, deemed "one of our liveliest capitalists" by the local paper, bought the Franklin/Jackson Street corner lot. Born in England in 1850, Vickery migrated to America in 1869 and to Waxahachie in 1877 where he exchanged his successful career as merchant for that of "capitalist" (his word) around 1886. Vickery probably built the three-unit frame building that appears on this corner on the 1893 Sanborn map as a temporary structure, but it was still there when he sold the property in 1907 to H. L. and M. M. Wyatt who, in turn, sold it to brother John Wyatt in January 1913. Five months later, Wyatt built the core of what is seen on the corner today, the original plan still evident with two stores fronting Franklin and a third store on Jackson Street.

Beginning in the early 1890s, African American barber Thomas J. (Tom or T. J.) Frierson rented space on this corner property from Vickery and then Wyatt. Born in Tennessee in 1871, Frierson came to Waxahachie around 1890, and in October 1892, announced that he had gotten a "beautiful lot of furniture for his barber shop on Jackson Street." In 1898, Frierson advertised that he was a "Designer of Features and Facial Upholsterer" who trimmed whiskers and hair "in all the Languages" and manufactured "Mediterranean Sea-Foam and Hydralic Shampoo." After Wyatt rebuilt the corner building, Frierson rented **113 East Franklin** and remained here until sometime in the early 1930s when he closed his barber shop to devote full time to the substantial East Waxahachie real estate ventures that he began accumulating in the mid-1890s. Contrary to what many people believe, Frierson never owned property in downtown Waxahachie.

A-35
109 South Jackson Street
Ellis County Courts and Administration Building
City of Waxahachie Parking Garage

2008-2010; HDR Architecture, Inc., architects;
Balfour Beatty, Inc., general contractor;
The Staubach Company, Program Manager

Dedicated on June 2, 2010, this four-block complex was a long time coming to downtown Waxahachie. As early as 1975, the county began acquiring buildings on the courthouse square and in other locations to accommodate expanding offices and services that could no longer be housed in the glorious 1897 Ellis County Courthouse. By the mid-1990s, it was obvious that the county had no choice but to build new facilities, and after a contentious debate as to where they should be located, the county assembled these four blocks.

Construction of a three-story, 49,750 square foot, $6,235,000 justice center fronting East Main Street began in spring 2001. One year later, in April 2002, the new county engineer Joe White issued a stop order because of serious structural issues with the unfinished building. The eventual result was multiple lawsuits lasting several years, and in late 2005-early 2006, demolition of "the pink elephant," the latter a reference to the Exterior Finish Insulation System (EFIS) that symbolized the project's many problems.

County and city citizens again entered into a heated argument as to whether the county facilities should remain downtown or be moved to the north side of town, at which point the city offered to finance and build an adjacent three-hundred-car parking garage, thereby resolving the major concern regarding a downtown location. In May 2007, voters approved a $53.875 million bond package that covered the Ellis County Courts and Administration Building on this site and a jail expansion south of Jefferson Street. The city issued bonds to fund the third component of the project, the parking garage.

A-36
201 South College Street
Masonic Temple Building [now Ellis County Museum]

1889; Alonzo Bostwick Bristol, architect;
H. D. Timmons and Dennis Mahoney, contractors

On Saturday, June 8, 1889—three weeks after ground was broken—the cornerstone at Waxahachie's new Masonic Temple was laid with "Imposing Ceremonies," followed by an estimated crowd of 2,500 local and regional Free Masons, residents, and visitors trooping across the creek for a "Magnificent Barbecue" in Bullard's Park. By late August, the cornice was being placed on the nearly completed building, and by mid-September the first floor was almost ready for occupancy in the first three-story building on the courthouse square.

The rapid-fire construction schedule was typical of Waxahachie's building industry at the time. Overseeing the project were co-contractors H. D. Timmons and Capt. D. (Dennis) Mahoney, an obvious choice since both were lodge members and successful in their respective trades. Timmons owned a major lumber company, while Mahoney was an established brick mason and contractor whose reputation would soon extend far beyond the area. The choice for architect, Alonzo Bostwick Bristol, was less obvious, although there may be a simple explanation: There were lodge members familiar with Bristol's Dallas buildings, most particularly his design for the third Dallas city hall that had just been completed. There is a brief article in the *Enterprise* on August 2, 1889, that ties Bristol to the project; it reports that Bristol, "architect of the Masonic Temple now being erected," stayed with an old schoolmate (not a lodge member) when on a site visit to Waxahachie.

Bristol's design for the Masons' High Victorian Italianate home followed the prescribed fraternal lodge floor plan, with commercial space on the ground floor, offices on the second, and lodge hall on the third. Bristol gave the primary College Street façade a festive look—ornate and richly textured but also orderly, balanced, and elegant. On the street level, recessed double-door entries and a center display window are set behind a row of cast-iron columns and transom windows. Brick piers separate the upper-story paired windows with segmental arches on the second floor and round arches with jigsawn details on the third. Corbeling and dentiling are also part of the mix. A robust pressed metal cornice with console brackets and anthemion pinnacles caps the building on the front façade while small pediments denote principal bays on the less flamboyant side elevation. The only exterior evidence of Mason ownership are their symbols, the compass and the square that are painted along with the building date on the center pediment on Franklin Street. Tucked in the back corner is an arched doorway that gives access to the upper floors. The building is amazingly intact, even surviving the application of black structural glass on the entrance façade in the late 1930s. Fortunately, the cast iron columns were covered and not removed, which meant that restoration with some modification was possible in 1981.

When built, the first floor was the largest retail space on the square and a coveted location for dry goods stores, the first tenant being J. B. Boone and his Tennessee Store that remained here until 1897. The succession of stores included S. W. Durham & Co., which was here before moving one block north in 1912, and K. Wolens Department Store, which rented the space from 1936-1964, the longest period of any business at this location. The second floor attracted an array of tenants, including organizations like the Ladies Social Club and the Waxahachie Commercial Club as well as individual attorneys and physicians. The most notable early tenant was the artist and painting instructor or, as described by the local newspaper, "the well-known Texas artist" Prof. Laurence L. Cohen. From early 1892 into the late 1890s, his corner studio with tall windows on both sides not only gave him great light but also offered the best view in town when the courthouse was built.

The third floor, accessed only by an interior staircase from the second floor, belonged to the Masons and followed their exacting rules regarding arrangement and furnishings. Although their meetings and ceremonies were restricted to members, they periodically offered use of the banquet hall (but not the main lodge hall) to other groups such as the Jewish community, for services in the early 1890s, and the Gathered Brethren, for a revival in spring 1901. The Masons moved to a new temple at **516 West Main** in July 1926. They sold this property in 1929 to Waxahachie businessman D. D. Eastham, whose son, Jack Byrd Eastham, sold the building to the Ellis County Historical Museum and Art Gallery, precursor to the Ellis County Museum, in 1975. The following year, the museum opened to the public.

When the Masonic Temple was under construction in 1889, the local newspaper declared it "will be the most handsome building in the city," not an unreasonable declaration since the courthouse was yet to be built. Even though the Masonic Temple would soon be overshadowed by Gordon's courthouse (as would be every other building subsequently built on the square), Bristol's building maintains its stately, regal position as one of the most important buildings on the courthouse square.

A-37
203-207 South College Street
Lewis-Templeton Building
1890; A. J. Kibler, contractor

The 1889 Masonic Temple and the Lewis-Templeton Building built a year later totally transformed the southeast corner of the square. The Temple replaced a rambling two-story double-galleried frame building known as the City or Ellis Hotel, the name associated with longtime owners and operators Jimmy (J. H.) and Irene Ellis (not related to Richard Ellis for whom the county was named). The Ellises gave this lot and the old Ellis dwelling that was on it to their only son Pierce A. Ellis, who apparently intended to build a structure because he signed a party wall agreement with the Masons just before they began construction. But Pierce changed his mind and sold his lot in June 1890 to William F. Lewis and Judge M. B. Templeton, who immediately had the house hauled away and hired A. J. Kibler to build the Lewis-Templeton Building.

Kibler, an experienced contractor, and Lewis, manager of the local M. T. Jones lumberyard, are probably responsible for the design of the building, which, by the end of July, had evolved from a one to a two-story project. Slender cast-iron columns with acanthus caps defined the four bays on the street level which were divided into two commercial spaces, each having a large window bay and a bay with double doors opening directly onto the sidewalk rather than being recessed. As it is today, the narrow door to the second-floor stairway was placed on the north side of the façade. The second story façade was clearly modeled after the paired windows on the Masonic Temple, but the cornice is simply a raised parapet with stepped corbeling.

It would be impossible to track all the mercantile businesses that rented space in the building, but among the first tenants were W. E. Ward's hardware store and Timmins & Hines fancy and staple grocery stock, while the *Mirror*, one of Waxahachie's three newspapers (described as the "editorial tripod" in one article) and several lawyers were upstairs. In 1899, Judge Templeton, now the sole owner, sold the building, and after several interim owners, attorney Will Hancock bought it in 1907 and refurbished the upper floor, the *Daily Light* reporting in August 1910 that Hancock "has perhaps the most handsome suite of offices in the city." Renamed the Hancock Building, Will practiced here for almost fifty years and was followed by his son Forrest. Businesses associated with the building included John Quarles Department Store at 205 from 1914-1927 and C. E. Youngblood's Grocery at 207 from circa 1909-1925. In the late 1930s to early 1940s, the Ellis County Women's Sewing Room was located on the second floor of 207. The WPA program gave employment to local women and was jointly funded by county and federal governments.

Over the years, first-floor entrances were moderately modified while the second-floor façade was left virtually intact. The Hancock family owned the building until 1982, when Richard D. Redington and Penelope Graves Redington acquired the property and conducted what was, at the time, one of the most extensive restoration projects to be completed in the downtown area. The project architect was Stan Graves, Penelope's brother, who eventually became director of the Texas Historic Courthouse Preservation Program. A succession of owners has followed the initial renovation. In 2013, extensive rebuilding was required on the rear of the structure when the back wall collapsed, fortunately at an hour when the building was empty.

A-38
209, 211, 213, 215 South College Street
1893

There is no better example than these four properties of just how fluid the real estate scene was in Waxahachie in the late nineteenth century. As of late 1883, when Josephine Atkinson bought the property with her separate monies, William Atkinson's livery and stable business occupied this part of the block from the alley to Jefferson Street. With completion of the Masonic Temple and the Lewis-Templeton Building on the north half of the block, the Atkinsons' property took on new significance for Waxahachie and Dallas developers and for the Atkinsons, who had put the property up for sale with an asking price of $5,000. In August 1890, Dallas real estate firm Murphy & Bolanz expressed an interest in building a three-story brick block on the lots and signed an option contract, but this plan never materialized. By May 1891, rumors were flying that Waxahachie capitalist Richard Vickery was buying the property "to build a 2-story brick . . . the lower floor for businesses and the entire upper floor to be fitted up for an Opera house in the most modern style." Instead, in late 1892, Vickery and another local investor, J. W. Manning, opted for something considerably less grandiose. Vickery bought the alley-side lot while Manning acquired the two interior lots, and in late February 1893, the newspaper reported that the two men "were erecting three brick houses" (209, 211, 213 South College). On November 23, Vickery bought the corner lot from the Atkinsons and on December 2 resold it to two other Waxahachie investors, C. J. Harris and W. F. Timmins, who may have completed a partially constructed building or immediately built the corner structure (215 South College).

The four storefronts are classic examples of vernacular one-story commercial buildings, this being one of the most intact rows in downtown Waxahachie. Although uniform in basic form—flat roof, parapet with stepped corbeling, cast-iron front with columns, and large display windows—the corner building is an exception to the centered entrances and is thirty feet wide, about eight feet wider than its neighbors. The 209 iron front bears the name of Mosher Ironworks of Dallas, while the 211-213 iron fronts are from Queen City Iron Works (location unknown), and the 215 iron front is unmarked.

Grocer W. B. Moore was probably one of the earliest merchants to locate in the row, leasing the 211 building soon after it was completed. He remained at this location until he retired in 1942, dying the same year at the age of eighty-six. From the late 1930s into the 1940s, the dimly lit, cigar smoke-filled Gibson's Domino Parlor at 209 was off-limits and therefore the most enticing business in the row for ten and twelve year-old Waxahachie boys like John Chiles. In 1933, the Enterprise Publishing Co., parent company of the *Waxahachie Daily Light*, moved its offices and printing plant to 215, and in 1969 expanded into 213, where the newspaper remained until moving to 200 West Marvin in 1981. Lawyer James R. Jenkins has practiced at 215 since August 1989 and like other lawyers in the downtown—and like many before—is frequently seen walking to and from the county offices.

A-39
107 West Franklin Street
M. Levy Building
c. 1881

Like every side of the square, the south side began with a collection of simple frame buildings. After "another devastating fire" destroyed half of the block on April 30, 1880, the *Enterprise* noted that the eight buildings were "entirely of wood, one and two stories" and encouraged property owners "to cover that side of the square with a handsome uniform block of at least two stories." By the time the March 1885 Sanborn map was drawn, two-story brick and stone structures were on every lot—except for the east corner, where several small frame buildings remained until 1889. A circa 1914 photograph shows that it was not a uniform row of buildings, but rather a mix of second-story Victorian façades with arched windows and pronounced cornices.

The M. Levy building still exhibits some evidence of those 1880s commercial buildings. Although the pronounced decorative cornice is gone, the surviving tall, narrow second-floor windows hint of its earlier proportions and appearance. It gained notoriety in January 1895 when a "gambling den" was discovered in a back room on the second floor, the *Enterprise* telling police that they needed "to keep a keen look-out for the occupants of the seemingly isolated rooms in the rear of some of the upper floors in Waxahachie buildings." By the early 1900s and well into the 1950s, the south side was known for its concentration of cotton buyers and agents in the second-story offices. Marty and Tina Haight renovated the Levy building in 2007 for her Plaid Donkey dress shop on the street level and his roofing-construction offices on the second.

The empty lot to the left once held a two-story structure built in 1889 by Col. R. A. Davis. Margaret Cecile

Curlin, proprietor of the Texas Theater across the square, owned the building when it opened as the Ritz Theater in 1939. Since it was the only movie theater in a corner building on the square, African Americans were allowed to patronize it before desegregation because they could enter through a side door. The Jaycees bought and demolished the Davis building in 1964 to provide off-street parking in downtown.

A-40

109-113 West Franklin Street

109-111: 1916

113: 1915

A fire in December 1914 destroyed the building on the west corner of this block and damaged 109 to 115 enough to require total rebuilding or significant repairs. Although Ralph Getzendaner's two-story brick building, 109-111 West Franklin, received the least damage, he announced plans to "remodel" his building in September 1916. All traces of the earlier elaborate brick cornice and narrow second-floor windows were removed, the new façade displaying the wider windows and geometric decorative brickwork representative of the more up-to-date Prairie style popular at the time. T. J. McDade's building, 113 West Franklin, sustained more damage than Getzendaner's, and consequently McDade began his rebuilding more promptly. By April 22, 1915 the newspaper reported that the building, which housed the McDade and Mackoy Drug Store, was "rapidly nearing completion."

The two buildings to the west, at 115 and 117 West Franklin, were rebuilt in 1915 by their owners to appear as companion buildings, housing the Empire Theater at 115 and Guaranty State Bank at 117. In 1953, the bank, then Waxahachie Bank & Trust Co., purchased the theater building and in 1954, encapsulated the façades of both buildings with what was the most extreme modernization on the square. Ellis County bought the buildings in 1982 and used them for office space until completion of the Justice Center in 2010. The current façades of 115 and 117, a 2016 redo by the Jim Lake Companies, returned red brick walls and a chamfered entrance to this corner of the square, although they lack any of the depth or ornament of the 1915 façades (a trait easily remedied). The scale of the neighboring buildings has been retained, and once again the block is lined with retail space shaded by a succession of suspended canopies. Living units are on the second floor.

A-41

100 South Rogers Street

Chapman & Chapman Building

1914; Ozee & Ozee, contractors

As with other blocks surrounding the square, the west side started with a hodgepodge of frame, often false-front buildings. In June 1879, the *Enterprise* reported that all the west side property owners agreed to replace their assorted frame buildings at one time with brick structures. The contract was awarded to Waxahachie stonemason John Solon, and by late August, "the splendid new block" was underway. By mid-March 1880, nine structures were completed with "open iron fronts for the lower stories . . . a superior quality of brick manufactured at Dallas" for the upper stories and sides, and stone for rear and interior walls. Of special interest was the Opera House on the north corner, which remained a city focal point not just for theatrical events but also for dances, roller skating, and other social events well into the late 1890s. All first-floor storefronts housed retail businesses until 1883, when the building on the south corner became a bank.

Those 1880 buildings survived intact until a fire on July 7, 1912, and another fire and gas explosion on September 9, 1913, caused heavy damage. The buildings at **104-112 South Rogers** were rebuilt immediately following the explosion, but several more months passed before cousins Homer and O. H. Chapman began construction on this, the last of the brick buildings to be built on the west side. The delay was caused by the Chapmans' debating whether they should collaborate with the adjoining property owners or proceed independently. They chose the latter, perhaps because they chose a Fort Worth contractor, Ozee & Ozee. In general appearance, however, the Chapmans' building still took its cue from its newly built neighbors, but a simple architectural detail sets it apart—the parapet crown that gives the roofline a distinct silhouette and raises the building above the rest of the row and, most importantly, emphasizes its corner position.

The Chapmans had no difficulty renting second floor offices, while the first floor proved to be prime retail space in its highly visible location on a Main Street corner. Gough-Davidson Dry Goods Co. was the first business to rent the space, moving from another Chapman-owned building around the corner at 209 West Main. Other local firms at this location included the Waxahachie Dry Goods Co. (c. 1918-28) and Greenwell-Chiles Food Store (1936-41), the latter renting the space before Sears Roebuck & Co. moved in (1942-58).

A-42
104-112 South Rogers Street
1913

After the fires in 1912 and 1913, owners of the five lots numbering 104-112 South Rogers harkened back to 1880 and agreed to build a uniform row of buildings. The resulting two-story brick row is in many ways like two-story commercial buildings built around the square in the late 19th and early 20th centuries. They are similar in height with a flat roof and parapet, paired windows across the second story, and storefronts on the street level, yet the west side buildings have a distinctly different look from their earlier counterparts. They were, as described at the time, "in the modern style," characterized by flatter, plainer wall surfaces and an absence of three-dimensional ornamentation. The parapet, corbeling, and window lintels are simply suggested by a lighter colored brick rather than executed in elaborate brickwork. Documentary photographs show that, originally, framing for second-story windows and the now-covered multi-paned first floor transom row were painted a light color (probably white) that gave the west side buildings a far stronger—and livelier—presence on the square than what they have today.

Three merchants returned to the west side to rent their pre-fire location after the buildings were completed in 1913. William Bismarck Reymuller's paint and wallpaper store had been located at 106 since July 1899, and would remain at this address until he retired in the early 1930s. Duke & Ayers 5 & 10 Cent Store reopened at 108, while druggist Lem Curlin returned to 112. Curlin was one of several merchants who simultaneously operated two stores on different sides of the square, his second and larger location being on the north side.

Cotemporary articles reporting major disasters in a community can be valuable sources of information. For example, the *Daily Light*'s account of the 1912 fire reveals that the 1880 buildings on the west side of the square were constructed primarily of white rock quarried just east of town and that the brick was made in Waxahachie, the lime burned down on the creek. Although it is known that bricks were manufactured in early Waxahachie, few specifics about the industry have surfaced, so any clue is welcome. At the time of both the 1912 and 1913 fires, articles mentioned that a number of men, either renters or employees in a store below, roomed on the second story of the 104-112 properties. When rebuilt, second floor space was devoted entirely to professional offices, a form of gentrification that signaled Waxahachie's growth as a business center.

A-43
114 South Rogers Street
Waxahachie National Bank Building
[later Citizens National Bank Building]
1918; Lang & Witchell, architects;
B. F. & C. M. Davis Co., general contractor

This corner became a bank corner in 1883 when the newly established First National Bank opened its doors in an 1880 stone building that was on the south end of the block. When Citizens National Bank absorbed First National in 1905, another newly established bank, State Bank & Trust Company, moved into the same stone building and remained there until merging with Guaranty State Bank in 1917 and moving across the street to 117 West Franklin. By the end of 1917, Homer N. Chapman had bought both the vacated bank building on this corner and the adjoining Queen Theatre, which gave him forty feet of prime real estate on the west side of the square. The *Daily Light* reported in early January 1918 that the buildings were being demolished to make way for "a handsome new bank building." As construction got underway in March, Chapman and Waxahachie National Bank (WNB) signed a ten-year lease agreement whereby the bank committed to an annual rent of $3,720 for the first floor, mezzanine, and basement vault. The agreement also meant that WNB would be vacating its building across the square at 115 South College.

To design his new building, the aspiring twenty-six-year-old businessman commissioned Otto Lang and Frank Witchell, described by architectural critic David Dillon as "the premier commercial architects" in Dallas at the time. Trained in the Classical Beaux Arts tradition, they were comfortable designing all manner of historic and experimental styles during their partnership, which lasted from 1905 to 1942. Although Dallas is where they "literally shaped the skyline of the city," according to architect Marcel Quimby, their imprint extended to other Texas towns and cities including Waxahachie, where their contribution was this pristine and elegant Neoclassical-style bank building that both architects and owner knew would not go unnoticed in a major cotton-producing and trade center.

Witchell was already familiar with Waxahachie, having apprenticed in the Dallas office of Ellis County Courthouse architect J. Riely Gordon in the late 1890s and worked in the Fort Worth office of Sanguinet and Staats in 1898. In addition, Chapman's choice of architects may have been encouraged by family friend Royal A. Ferris. Ferris, the son of Judge J. W. Ferris, had grown up in Waxahachie but moved north in 1884 to become a Dallas banker and eventually president of the American Exchange National Bank (AENB). It is worth noting that 1918 was not only the year in which Chapman commissioned Lang & Witchell to design the Waxahachie bank, but also the year that AENB commissioned the firm to design its bank and office building for downtown Dallas.

The firm's Neoclassical-style bank assumes a monumental presence on the Waxahachie square if for no other reason than its smooth, light colored stone surface is in sharp contrast to the dark brick facades of surrounding buildings. (A classical revival building was seldom built in anything but a light-colored stone.) The exterior presents an air of self-assurance and wealth while at the same time respecting its older neighbors in height, symmetrical arrangement, and restrained detailing. The arched entry with rounded fanlight and pedimented doorway dominates the front elevation, the same arched shape repeated in the Franklin Street window openings. Detailing includes a Greek Key frieze band that visually divides the façade, egg and dart molding on the cornice and frieze, and round stone medallions cast with American eagles flanking the arches. Classical references also graced the interior, where the Southern Architectural Cement Stone Co. of Dallas provided "All ornaments for the Banking Room and Lobby," according to an October 1918 mechanic's lien between Chapman and the company. The lien, recorded in the Ellis County Clerk's Office, is one of several that make this bank building one of the most thoroughly documented structures on the square.

Waxahachie National Bank opened for business in their new building on January 1, 1919. Less than three months later, bank vice president Lynn D. Lasswell sent a glowing recommendation for Lang & Witchell to an Eastland, Texas, bank that was selecting a firm to design its new building. Lasswell wrote that "we now occupy the building recently built for our use by the Chapmans, and same was designed by Messrs. Lang & Witchell of Dallas. We left the color, design, and finish of the building, entirely with the architects and the effect is very harmonious, and the building comfortable in every respect. Should you see fit to secure their services . . . we feel sure you will make no mistake." The Eastland bank, however, chose San Antonio architect Henry T. Phelps. (The letter is in the Lang & Witchell Collection, Alexander Architectural Archive, University of Texas Libraries.)

In 1927, Citizens National Bank, having acquired both Waxahachie National Bank and this building, moved from the northwest corner of West Main and Rogers (**200 West Main**) to this corner and remained here until 1966. The building did not have another permanent occupant until Ellis County purchased it for the Tax Assessor-Collector's office in early 1975. The staff adapted to the space, making minimal changes during the thirty-five years they were here. The building is now owned by private developer Mutual Pursuits LLC.

A-44

209-211 West Franklin Street

E. S. Campbell Building

1902-03

213-215 West Franklin

C. W. Gibson Building

1902-03

To be precise, construction of these buildings began in September 1902, the *Enterprise* reporting on the nineteenth that four carloads of bricks were unloaded for Charles W. Gibson's and Edgar S. Campbell's buildings. When completed in March 1903 at a cost of $18,000, *Enterprise* editor Col. R. D. Hudson, or "Innocence" as he signed his newspaper columns, toured the interiors of the "modern, up-to-now buildings." The dry goods business of Edgar's brother John S. Campbell filled the first floor of his building at 209-211, "the high walls with light streaming in from bottom to top" making "even an ordinary man look better . . . to say nothing of the thousands of good looking ladies who will now visit this emporium." On the second floor "elegant law offices" overlooked West Franklin Street, while the back side was rented to the Dunlap Rifles, Waxahachie's "crack military company" for an armory and possible drill space. Gibson's business at 213-215 offered groceries, hardware and implements, and occupied both floors of his building, Hudson noting that the electric elevator "whizzing through space" transported Gibson's inventory of wagons, buggies, and implements to the second floor.

Architecturally, the exterior shows many similarities to the Romanesque Revival buildings built on the north side of the square in 1894—i.e., large arched windows, stepped parapet, and decorative brickwork. There are also obvious differences denoting a shift in taste; most especially surface decoration here is more subdued, less intricate, and not as three-dimensional: the Palladian window motif on the Getzendaner Building at **100 West Main** and on this building offer a good comparison. The centrally placed staircase opening onto the sidewalk was common to many two-story double buildings in downtown Waxahachie, but few are in their original state as seen here. The Campbell Building remains remarkably intact with a suspended canopy, multi-paned transom row, and a Dillon Company cast iron storefront manufactured in Dallas and dated 1902. It may be one of the few in existence, since the firm operated for a short two-year period, circa 1902-1904.

J. S. Campbell & Co. stayed in business at 209-211 until J. S. died in 1935, after which Coward's Paint Co. began its long occupancy at this location. Southwestern Telegraph and Telephone Company rented the second floor in summer 1906 and maintained offices there as Southwestern Bell until late summer 1956. In 1994, Bruce and Julia Webb acquired the building for their unique business, Webb Gallery, which features one-of-a-kind art and antiques. The Webbs' national reputation allows them to live anywhere, but they chose to remain in Waxahachie—and to live above their gallery.

In 1908, Gibson rented his second floor at 213-215 to The Benevolent and Protective Order of Elks of Waxahachie who, in turn, hired an architect (unidentified) to draw plans for its lodge hall, which opened with a "brilliant social affair" in September. Gibson retired soon after and began renting his first floor to a series of grocers, pharmacists, and other businesses. In 2006, property owner Dusty Autrey renovated the Gibson Building, a project that involved constructing an historically sympathetic street-level façade.

A-45

200 South Rogers Street

Williams Block

1897; George M. Barnes, architect;
Dennis Mahoney, contractor

In 1893, Cynisca Sweatt Williams received this corner property as part of a much larger estate she inherited from her businessman-investor husband John G. Williams. The existing structure was a two-story brick commercial row known to everyone in town as "the Bradshaw

Block," built in 1883 by lawyer Amzi Bradshaw. John G. Williams and H. H. Dunn purchased the property after Bradshaw died in 1885, with Williams acquiring his partner's interest in 1891. It was a lucrative piece of rental real estate—as was everything on the square—so Cynisca lost little time in rebuilding the block after it was completely destroyed by fire in January 1897. In early May, an advertisement in the *Dallas Morning News* invited contractors to submit proposals "for the erection and completion of one brick business block" according to the plans and specifications of architect George M. Barnes. The contract was let on May 17 to Dennis Mahoney, and by September, the two-story "Williams block" of pressed brick trimmed in stone was ready for tenants. Brickmason and contractor Mahoney's name is well known, whereas little is known about Barnes. Born in Tennessee in 1858 and moving to Texas in the late 1880s, he is listed as an architect living in Ennis in the 1900 census, but by 1910 was a builder in San Jose, California. The Williams Block is his only documented project in Waxahachie.

Barnes looked to the buildings on the north side of the square to frame his design and utilized many of the same elements, the most obvious being the squared corner tower with pyramidal roof. Not only did the tower give a presence to the southwest intersection of the square when it was built, it remains the *only* intact corner tower (minus a few pilaster extensions) on the square today. The building covers a quarter of the block, with four cast-iron storefronts opening onto Rogers Street. On the second floor, the simplified treatment of window surrounds is typical of brick commercial structures built in the late nineteenth-early twentieth centuries, while the checkered brick coursing that defines the parapet is the most distinctive brickwork on the building.

The Williams Block housed two of Waxahachie's most popular department stores, Jolesch and Chaska, and Marchman's. Jolesch and Chaska, who opened their first Waxahachie store in 1875, moved to this newly finished corner storefront in fall 1897. The firm had stores in other towns including Ennis, which may be where the connection was made between Mrs. Williams and Ennis-based architect Barnes. When Jolesch and Chaska closed this store in fall 1928, their business covered three-quarters of the first floor as well as a portion of the second floor.

Ten years later, Riley L. Marchman and his father, Riley G. Marchman brought their mercantile background from Lindale, Texas, to Waxahachie and opened their department store at this location in December 1938, renting from the Williams heirs. During their more than forty years in business, the firm completed two major alterations to the building. In 1948, large plate glass display windows and Travertine marble were installed by Fin Garvin & Sons on the first-floor façade in what was to be the first phase of a modernization plan. The second phase would have wrapped the second story in a windowless smooth-surfaced marble, but that was never done. In 1974-1975, a third generation of Marchmans replaced the 1948 alterations with the present street-level façade. Designed by Dallas architects Peter A. Rivera Associates, it represents a loose interpretation of the original façade. The project was the first major renovation of a downtown building after designation of the Ellis County Courthouse District in 1974.

A-46
208 South Rogers Street
Texas Mortgage & Banking Co. Building
[now I.O.O.F. Building]
1891; C. M. Sammons, contractor

It is hard to imagine, but a drawing published in the September 9, 1892 *Enterprise* and later photographs show that this was the first of the flamboyant brick blocks built in Waxahachie in the 1890s—its flamboyancy intended, perhaps, to compensate for its location near, but not on, the square. To guarantee that the Texas Mortgage & Banking Co. building did not disappear down the South Rogers Street slope, the roofline was marked with a high flag-flying corner cupola, bulbous finials, and a cornice and parapet with extraordinarily intricate brickwork and corbelling. It was unlike anything in town. Although those features have long been obliterated, the original front façade with four commercial spaces and some detailing are still discernible, i.e., the arched entry bay and four commercial spaces on the street level, and the arched windows with colored glass transoms and brick piers on the second floor.

This building was Capt. Charles M. Sammons's first of many contracts in Waxahachie, a fact revealed in the company's announcement that it would close for the funeral of the fifty-eight-year-old New York native on March 28, 1907. Sammons's obituary disclosed that he was trained as an architect and contractor, but during his years in Waxahachie he advertised as a contractor and builder, never an architect, suggesting that he had concluded, like many fellow architects at the time (and since), that contracting was more profitable than an architectural practice. There is no documentation that Sammons was this building's architect, so that remains an open question.

Texas Mortgage & Banking Co. was an expansion of T. J. Cole and R. G. Phillips's partnership as real estate and loan agents, which they started in the late 1880s. Phillips bought this quarter block in July 1890, which means the company was positioned to begin construction shortly after it was chartered. On March 13, 1891, the *Enterprise* reported seeing a draft of the new building (no mention of an architect), and within five months it was completed. The mortgage company set up first floor offices in the south corner. The major tenant, the "Tell-the-Truth Clothiers," the Matthews Bros., rented the north half of the building, which they renamed the Matthews Building for their "immense" 50 x 100 ft. men's clothing store. The Waxahachie I.O.O.F. Lodge acquired the building on December 16, 1911, one month after their building on the square burned in the Siddons Hotel fire. Texas Mortgage and Matthews Bros. continued as tenants, but Joe Cohn Gents' Furnishings store replaced Matthews Bros. in 1914, while Texas Mortgage sold to a new corporation, the Texas Mortgage Loan Co., in 1918.

Exactly when the exuberant cornice and parapet disappeared is not documented, but it was after 1925. The lodge still owns the building and continues to rent the commercial spaces and use the second floor as its lodge hall. To the right of the staircase entry is the cornerstone from the 1896 I.O.O.F. lodge building that burned on the square in 1911.

A-47
217 South Rogers Street
Edens Building
1887-88; H. D. Timmons, contractor; Jack McManus, brick contractor

In 1891, at age nine, Edwina Edens became owner of this property, which at the time was a typical storefront building with a recessed center entrance framed by large display windows. Edwina's father B. F. Edens had built it after he and her mother, Willie Meriwether Edens, moved from Grapeland, Houston County, to Waxahachie in fall 1886. Within an eight-month period in 1890, Edwina's parents and infant sibling died, leaving a considerable estate to be divided between Edwina, who was given the Edens Building as well as other properties, and her older half-sister Luna.

Throughout the 1890s, Edwina's appointed guardian, family friend Judge Anson Rainey, rented the commercial and office spaces to the usual list of businesses and organizations, but in 1899 he secured a five-year lease with the United States Postmaster General to move the Waxahachie post office to the first floor, an arrangement that lasted through July 1913, when the new post office building at **401 South Rogers** was completed. In summer 1908, the fraternal benefit organization, Woodmen of the World (WOW) rented the second floor for their local hall and then bought the building in 1910 from Edwina and her husband Ray Wiess. It then became known as the WOW building (along with dozens of other WOW buildings across the country). There are no Waxahachians who remember seeing movies at The Gem, the moving picture theater that operated at this location in 1913-1914, but there are many who remember voting in this building, an off-and-on use that began as early as 1892 and ended in 2007.

Local contractor Fin Garvin's alterations to the building in 1947 reflected the standard 1940s-1950s treatment for older downtown buildings, i.e., the street level was modernized with large plate glass windows and narrow Roman brick while the historic second-story façade was left relatively intact. The WOW tenant at the time was E. P. Harbin's Firestone tire store. In 1977, WOW sold the property. It was acquired in 2011 by Southwest Data Solutions, LLC, a computer software company that received approval from the Heritage Preservation Commission for its rehabilitation project.

A-48
301 South Rogers Street
Walker Building
1914-15; Frank Compton and Grover Richards, contractors

The first Walker Building on this corner was built in 1895 at a time when commercial development was rapidly replacing early residential properties to the south of Jefferson Street. Contractor Capt. Charles M. Sammons built a two-story two-unit brick building with a sixty-foot frontage on South Rogers Street for prominent Waxahachie physician George W. Walker Sr. who, in turn, had a tenant-in-waiting, F. S. Cronk, hardware merchant, plumber, and machinist, whose on-site shop repaired heavy equipment. It was the type of business that would be long identified with the corner.

The December 29, 1912 fire that destroyed the upper east half of the block heavily damaged the backside of the Walker Building and displaced the renter at the time, Will Moore, another hardware merchant. Moore seized the opportunity, bought the corner lot across the alley, and proceeded to build his own building (**105 West Jefferson**) while the Walkers repaired their 1895 structure and rented to grocer P. P. Smith.

Alas, the Walker Building was destroyed by yet another fire on August 8, 1914, after which the Walkers contracted Frank Compton and Grover Richards to build this solid, minimally adorned building that typifies the early twentieth-century commercial structures built south of Jefferson Street. The suspended canopy, some form of which would have been found on most if not all commercial buildings of the period, has been retained in recent renovations and is placed, in this instance, below the transom windows, which allows light into the interior while shading the display windows. The side elevation, with its generous supply of windows on both floors, is a notable example of an orderly secondary façade that contributes to the streetscape.

A-49
307 South Rogers Street
Cook Building
1937; Bertram C. Hill, architect; O. B. Bennett, contractor

On May 5, 1937, three months after purchasing this property, Waxahachie insurance agent and realtor Herman C. Cook signed a ten-year lease with J. C. Penney Company. Cook obviously viewed it as a long-term investment because he assumed the full cost of major alterations to both the exterior and interior of the building. At the time, the upper floor reflected its original 1893 construction date as part of the Peters Block that extended from 307 to 315 South Rogers. The street level, however, had been altered in 1920 by the lessee, the Oldham Hardware Company, who replaced the original two doors and three display windows with an "up-to-date" centered door with two large show windows. With plans and specifications provided by noted Dallas architect Bertram C. Hill, Cook agreed to "remove existing front and old cast iron columns and construct a typical Penney Company front," and to "change windows as necessary," the latter reflecting a complete overhaul of the interior. The two men were well known to each other, as Hill had designed the "Early American Farmhouse" that Cook and his wife Julia Mae built on the outskirts of Waxahachie in 1934 (demolished).

The challenge for Hill was to expand interior space within the confines of the existing building which, in turn, determined exterior treatment. As explained in the lease agreement, the ground floor was lowered two feet and the ceiling raised three feet, which eliminated the original transom row and allowed the insertion of "a merchandise balcony" or mezzanine level that corresponds to the band of triple windows on the exterior. The floor adjustment can be detected when comparing this façade with its neighbor at **301 South Rogers**. Hill gave the Penney's façade a more contemporary look with slightly raised linear brick detailing on the parapet and a top row of steel windows combining vertical and horizontal panes. Penney's name filled the space between the window rows. As part of the deal, Cook received both an annual rent and a percentage of the department store's sales above a specified amount. The partnership obviously worked, as it lasted through 1964, during which time Cook maintained his insurance office on the second floor. When Penney's opened a new store in a shopping center on Ferris Avenue in 1964, another department store, K. Wolen's, moved into this building.

The black window frames and muntins as well as the first-floor lintel are a post-1985 change. Although the treatment is an historical deviation from a lighter neutral color, it gives Hill's façade a smarter, crisper, even more modernist look.

A-50
315 South Rogers Street

Peters Block

1893; F. L. Stevenson, contractor

When building activity picked up in this area in the early 1890s, gin owner Lemuel H. Peters was among the investors. From late 1892 through May 1893, Peters cobbled together several properties totaling a South Rogers frontage of 133 feet. He then hired Dallas contractor F. L. Stevenson (the same contractor who was building a double brick for V. H. Shelton at 308 South College Street) to build the two-story Peters Block, an ambitious project that extended from this Madison Street corner through what is now **307 South Rogers**. In fact, as the 1893 financial panic was unfolding, Peters so overextended himself with this and other projects (including a corn mill) that he was forced to sell this development in mid-January 1894. His buyer? None other than Waxahachie capitalist Richard Vickery, who paid Peters $5,096.70 and assumed his debt.

Moderately altered on the ground floor, this corner segment of the Peters Block retains ample original features to show that the row was typical of two-story storefront buildings identified with the 1880s. When compared with what was built a year later on the north side of the square, it was a very conservative façade, on the cusp of being out of date, with its narrow windows, brick hood moldings, and simple corbeled parapet. Mosher Bros. of Dallas produced the cast-iron columns and storefront.

Peters's name remained attached to the block for several years, but by the early 1900s it was known as the Vickery Building (one of several in town). Among the businesses identified with this corner were S. P. Spalding's furniture store from 1912 through 1917, followed by S. W. Durham, who moved his two dry goods stores from the square into this building in 1918. Other stores at this location included Jeff North Feed & Seed Store (late 1930s), Katz Department Store (c. 1945-1950), and Levine's Department Store (c. 1950-early 1980s). Common Threads Quilting opened at this address in January 2005.

Next door to the left, at 311 South Rogers, the drastically altered façade still displays the original iron columns that match those on 315. Lynn Reagor, "one of those wide-awake business men," opened his grocery store at 311 around 1910, then bought the building in 1916 from Richard Vickery's estate. When Safeway Grocery & Market moved in across the street in the mid-1930s, Reagor closed his grocery, but his wife maintained her beauty shop at this address and rented space in the front to Nay C. Maxwell, who established Maxwell's Jewelry in 1946. Maxwell's son John purchased the building from Reagor heirs in 1978. In 2014, Maxwell's Jewelry received a Texas Treasure Business Award from the Texas Historical Commission in recognition of three generations of Maxwell family members, including John and his wife Billie and their son Jody, who have continued the business at the same location for over fifty years.

A-51
306 South Rogers Street (previously 314)

Moffett Building

1902; C. J. Griggs, contractor

It is hard to visualize, but when B. R. Moffett built this structure its size and bulk totally dominated the surrounding area. Originally three stories in height, it filled the 60 x 100 ft. lot. With street-level retail space and two open upper floors for displaying heavy equipment, the latter accessible via an elevator, Moffett rented to a succession of businesses like the Ellis County Hardware Company which, in March 1903, advertised its "complete line" of plows, riding corn and cotton planters, blacksmith and mill supplies, and builders' and shelf hardware. In a circa 1912 photograph, the piers that mark the corners and front bays of the building are painted a light color (probably white) that gave the front façade a column effect and created an even more formidable presence on the street. The window sills and lintels were also painted. Exactly when the third floor was removed is not documented, but it was sometime in the early 1930s. The narrow strips near the top of the building were originally third-story windowsills.

This building was one of several locations of Safeway Grocery in downtown Waxahachie. Many residents, however, remember this block because of Cheeves Bros. Dry Goods Store, which was on the northwest corner of the block in a circa 1897 building that burned in November 1968.

A-52
401 South Rogers Street
United States Post Office/Federal Building
[now Waxahachie City Hall]
1913; James Knox Taylor, Supervising Architect of the Treasury; Fred Tarry & Son, contractor

When the United States Post Office opened in 1913, Waxahachie could boast of having not one but two architecturally significant governmental buildings. The other, of course, was the Ellis County Courthouse designed in the exuberant (but dark) Richardsonian Romanesque style of San Antonio-based architect James Riely Gordon and built on the courthouse square in 1895-97. In contrast, this sedate Neoclassical-style post office was designed in the Washington office of James Knox Taylor, Supervising Architect of the Treasury, the department responsible for Federal buildings. The two buildings frame the years in which American institutional and governmental architecture moved from Romanesque to Classical, a move brought about by the belief that America deserved a new, more appropriate style of architecture based on ancient Greek and Roman precedents and given a popular boost by the 1893 Chicago World's Fair. Taylor, schooled in classical design like most architects of the period, was a strong advocate of classical design during his superintendence from 1897 to 1913 and was responsible for the design and construction of literally hundreds of post offices throughout the country. The Waxahachie post office is representative of those built in smaller communities.

Deemed "the lordly pile" by the *Daily Light*, the building imparts a sense of dignity and order with its monumental scale, perfectly symmetrical façade, and smooth-faced stone, all characteristics of the Neoclassical style. Built "entirely of the beautiful Warrensburg sandstone" from Missouri, the two-story building is dominated by a recessed front portico with colossal columns and pilasters in the Doric order. Decorative grillwork covers the primary entrance transom and the second-story portico windows, one of few instances where the term "decorative" can be applied to the exterior. Pedimented window surrounds with kneeling brackets and low-relief pilasters highlight the first-floor openings and bays on all facades. Originally, UNITED STATES POST OFFICE was carved into the entry side of the classical entablature encircling the building.

The post office building was unique in Waxahachie but not unique to Waxahachie, as Taylor's office worked with a vast set of interchangeable designs and specifications that Jay C. Henry discusses in his book, *Architecture in Texas, 1895-1945*. An almost identical post office can be seen in Mineral Wells, whereas examples in Hillsboro and Sulphur Springs follow essentially the same form and floor plan, but the detailing is Renaissance, not Roman. Taylor's office fluctuated between using the two classical design sources, and variations of both abound throughout Texas. It was a design program that gave medium- and small-sized communities like Waxahachie a remarkable architectural legacy—one that will never be repeated.

On the interior, the Waxahachie post office duplicated a standard floor plan with primary first floor space devoted to public and mail services and with offices on the second floor. The interior was finished with materials from multiple sources, including yellow pine from Alabama and Georgia and marble from Tennessee, the first shipment of the latter rejected and requarried because "the eagle-eyed inspector" judged it was not "the desired pink tinge." Some items were produced closer to home, such as the front door frame and threshold, peepholes, and brass grilles and post office screens made by a familiar name, Mosher Manufacturing Company in Dallas. The peepholes were for "watch galleries" that allowed "the chief inspector," coming from his office in Fort Worth, to spy on suspected errant employees, the *Daily Light* commenting that "our pessimistic government concedes no man's honesty until he is dead and his state has gone to probate." The system was not unique to Waxahachie's post office.

Once construction began in spring 1911, the Waxahachie project was not without its complications. Contractual and completion issues became so serious that by early 1913, the *Daily Light* reported that Taylor's office dispatched Paul Rubin to correct the Waxahachie situation, which Rubin described as "the greatest 'hodgepodge' he ever tackled." Rubin's combined skills as both an interior finishings expert of Federal buildings and a project mediator suggest that he had handled this scenario many times before.

Formally opened on July 18, 1913, the post office remained here until moving to **316 North College Street** in March 1967, after which this building became known as the Federal Building and housed various offices. The city bought the property in September 1974 and, taking advantage of its inclusion in the newly designated Downtown Historic District listing on the National Register of Historic Places, obtained matching Federal funds for the exterior restoration, with Gordon W. Wilson the consulting architect. Interior spaces were rearranged for city offices that moved into the building in December 1975—in time for the Bicentennial. City Hall expansion was inevitable as Waxahachie's population grew, and in the late 1990s the council commissioned Garland-based architect Ron Hobbs to prepare plans for refurbishing the older building and constructing a new addition. By matching materials and colors and following the Rogers Street slope, the long, lean addition does not overwhelm the historic structure.

A-53
408 South Rogers Street
Waxahachie Livery & Transfer Building
1913

Solid and serviceable, this two-story brick building was built by blacksmith A. H. Paillet as rent property for a livery and transfer business. The construction year is noteworthy because it was built when Waxahachie, like other cities and towns across the country, was seeing construction of its first automobile garages. Simple as it is, the building represents a pivotal moment in history, when a single technological invention—the automobile—began transforming society not just in Waxahachie but throughout the western world.

Since the mid-1890s, Paillet had operated his successful blacksmith shop on the lot to the immediate north of this property, while a wagon yard occupied the sizeable corner property extending from Rogers to Elm Street, and a carriage and paint shop operated on the Elm Street side of the block. On July 19, 1913, just a day after the new post office opened across the street, the *Daily Light* announced that "progressive citizen" Paillet, having "become inoculated with the building fever," had awarded the building contract. The article also noted that "special attention is to be given the architectural details adaptable to the livery business," which meant that exterior openings and interior spaces were large enough to allow the passage and storage of buggies, carriages, and horses. Paillet leased the building to F. L. Perry, who advertised "The Horse Hotel . . . We Meet All Trains" in the 1913 directory.

By 1916, "The Horse Hotel" had been replaced by the Waxahachie Garage & Repair Co. A documentary photograph taken during this time shows no alterations to the structure, but it does show a brick exterior totally covered with painted advertisements for all things automobile and an early gas pump on the curb. By 1924, R. H. Smellage and B. Morris, automobile dealers who were also cotton-buying partners, added their name to the signs, some of which are still visible on the north wall. Although a blacksmith continued working on this block into the late 1950s, Paillet had sold his Waxahachie real estate and retired to the Rio Grande Valley by 1919. The City of Waxahachie now owns the building and plans to adapt it for offices.

A-54
410 South Rogers Street
Wm. Cameron & Company Lumber Yard
[now Downtown Farmers Market]
c. 1919-20; 1950s, office remodel

This site, identified with numerous lumber dealerships since 1889, was given new life in 2012 and 2013 when the city, using Tax Increment Reinvestment monies, converted the back portion into the Downtown Farmers Market, with Brad Yates as contractor. With vendor spaces replacing lumber racks, the lumberyard quickly became a popular and functional setting for Saturday morning markets. Buoyed by the success of the Farmers Market rehabilitation, the city renovated the interior of the office building in 2014 and began the search for a tenant who would complement the market. FRESH Market and Coffee opened in that space in October 2014. It has proven to be a successful combination for both businesses as well as for the revitalization of the south end of downtown Waxahachie and surrounding properties.

Lumber sheds followed a similar form for decades, which makes determining a specific construction date difficult, but the footprint for this lumberyard, which includes a long, centrally placed shed open on both sides and an attached office on the east end, first appears on the 1925 Sanborn map, suggesting that it was probably laid out in 1919-1920, soon after the property was bought by the Waco-based Wm. Cameron & Company, Inc., one of the largest lumber dealerships in the region. The front office was updated more than once; the narrow Roman brick, display windows, and slanted supports are typical of the 1950s.

With the railroads came the lumberyards to Waxahachie. Coinciding with completion of the Waxahachie Tap Railroad tracks on the north side of town in late fall 1879, the W. J. and T. A. Montgomery and the M. T. Jones lumberyards opened adjacent to the tracks at the Kaufman Street crossing. In 1887, the Missouri, Kansas, and Texas Railway tracks were completed on the south or creek side of town, and in fall 1889 local contractor and builder H. D. Timmons established his lumber and building materials business on this site, soon to be followed by Cleburne-based competitor Conway-Leeper across the street. (Construction was booming!) Timmons remained here until 1900, when he relocated to property abutting the tracks on the north side of the square between Rogers and College Streets. In circa 1905, Waxahachie businessmen Ed Campbell and brothers J. E. and O. B. Dunaway built a new lumberyard complex on this site and stayed here (although there were shifts in owners) until July 1919, when the Cameron enterprise bought the property. The last lumber dealership to operate here was locally owned Waxahachie Building Supply, which closed in 2006. The city has owned the property since 2007.

A-55
423 South College Street
Trinity and Brazos Valley Depot (T & BV);
Rock Island Depot
1907; attributed to Charles H. Page Jr., architect;
Louis Roswell Wright, contractor

By the late nineteenth century a railroad architecture had evolved. Probably the most familiar building type identified with the industry, both historically and now, is the one-story passenger depot with a tower of modest height, usually centrally placed on the trackside façade and flanked by a wing on each side. There were hundreds, thousands really, of variations of this classic depot built across the country, and when you see a building like this, you know exactly what it is. Waxahachie had three built during the years 1902 through 1908. The first of these was the Houston and Texas Central depot built adjacent to the tracks on the north side of the square in 1902 and demolished in 1967. The other two have survived here on the creek side of town, both adapted to other uses.

On Monday, April 9, 1906, Col. Mike Sweeney, vice president and general manager of the Trinity and Brazos Valley railroad (T & BV), rolled into Waxahachie in his private car "Bianca" hitched to a Katy train. Sweeney, who was surveying T & BV track lines under construction between Waxahachie and Houston, stated that crews were working about four miles south of Teague, the junction of the Dallas and Fort Worth lines. He also reported that a two-story depot would be erected in Teague for use as both the railroad's general offices and as a passenger station, while "the depots for Corsicana and Waxahachie will be alike, an octagon style of architecture." Not only are the two smaller depots nearly identical, they also share some similarities with the much larger depot, indicating that all three were designed by Austin-based Charles H. Page Jr., the architect specified in a contract for the Teague project. No such document has been located for the Waxahachie depot, but it seems safe to assume that Page's firm designed it, since it also designed a series of T & BV freight and passenger depots between Mexia and Cleburne.

The Teague depot opened in February 1907. In early April, track crews crossed the corporation line into Waxahachie, where the T & BV and Katy lines would be connected. On July 26, Dallas contractor Louis Roswell Wright, who also built the Corsicana depot, began construction of the Waxahachie depot, promising that it would be completed in ninety days, a deadline he missed, although the building was occupied by the end of the year.

To describe the Waxahachie depot as an "octagon style of architecture" is a bit of a misnomer, since the main body of the structure itself is not octagonal, the usual prerequisite for the term. Instead, the main body is a quirky, almost whimsical combination of three very differently shaped sections which, along with the red brick crenelated detailing and red clay roof, has a storybook look with a touch of the Romanesque. On the south or track side is the two-story octagonal tower (thus, "octagon style") attached near the center of the building where it served as both ticket window and observation lookout. The almost square eastside block with a steep hipped roof and kicked eaves was the waiting room for whites. On the west side, the low spreading block split by an arched passageway was the waiting room for African Americans and the baggage room.

Chartered in 1902, the Trinity and Brazos Valley Railway Company, commonly called the "Boll Weevil," was experiencing financial difficulties even before the Waxahachie connection was made and the depot built. In June 1914, T & BV entered into receivership, and in 1930 was reorganized as the Burlington-Rock Island Railroad Company, at which time the Waxahachie depot became known as the Rock Island Depot. When the railroad moved out in 1963, the newly formed Nay Company leased the property. It initially sold grain elevator and feed mill equipment, eventually expanded into general commercial construction, and in 1999 it purchased the depot. The Nay Company deserves credit for its pivotal role and over fifty-year commitment to the preservation and development of this part of Waxahachie's downtown. One can only imagine what might have happened had the company not stepped forward in 1963.

The long one-story frame building to the east and across South College Street is the T & BV Railway Freight House, which was built at the same time as the depot. Appearing on the 1909 Sanborn Insurance Map, this is the type of simple, vernacular service building that frequently does not survive much less retain detailing such as the stick or carpenter gothic brackets and bargeboard under the eaves. Hopefully, its owner, the City of Waxahachie, will give it an adaptive use that supports its preservation and surroundings.

A-56
501 South Rogers Street
Missouri-Kansas-Texas Depot (MKT)
1908; W. T. Stanberry, contractor

The Missouri-Kansas-Texas Railroad (the Katy) came to Waxahachie in 1887, built its first passenger depot in fall 1889, began talking about building a larger one in 1902, the year the Houston and Texas Central depot was built, and procrastinated another six years before actually doing so. No doubt, the process was speeded up when the Trinity and Brazos Valley Railroad took less than five months to build its depot just across the tracks in 1907.

The delay occurred in part because railroad officials and Waxahachie residents could not agree on how expensive a depot the town warranted. Railroads, not just the MKT, based that decision on passenger and/or freight traffic and not necessarily on a town's population. In February 1907, MKT announced that a new depot, "right up to now in every detail," would open in Waxahachie before

September 1. Come October, however, Waxahachie was sending a delegation to Austin to demand that the Texas Railroad Commission require a depot costing no less than $12,000 to $15,000 be built. The result? The MKT prepared new plans and construction began in summer 1908. In all probability, the new as well as the rejected designs were produced by the railroad's engineering department working with an in-house architect and a set of standardized plans. The contractor was W. T. Stanberry who, after finishing the Waxahachie project in late December, transferred his crew to Lancaster to build another Katy depot.

Waxahachie's Katy depot can be described as horizontal, symmetrical, and disciplined. It shows the assurance of an architect who was definitely "right up to now," familiar with the Prairie style that was introduced in Chicago at the beginning of the twentieth century. Identified with architectural genius Frank Lloyd Wright, the low, horizontal lines were inspired by the open prairies of the Midwest, but there were other sections of the country, like Texas, where the style was right at home. The strong horizontality of the Waxahachie depot begins with the extended slope and projecting eaves of the red tile hipped roof. Exterior wall surfaces, including those of the observation deck on the south façade, are divided into sharply defined horizontal bands of color—yellow-orange brick for the primary wall surfaces, an almost-white limestone stringcourse, red brick for the dado or wainscoting, and finally, a narrow limestone foundation plate.

Katy passenger service through Waxahachie was discontinued in 1964 (one year after Trinity and Brazos Valley ended its passenger service), and freight service stopped in 1988. The city, viewing the depot as essential to redevelopment on the south side of downtown, acquired the land and right-of-way in 2007 and the neglected depot in 2008. Waxahachie-based Anthony Mottla served as project architect for the $1.37 million restoration, which was completed in 2010 primarily with Tax Increment Reinvestment Zone monies. The depot is used as retail space but is also equipped to accommodate a restaurant.

The circa 1976 "Katy Caboose" was added to the setting in 2011 by Historic Waxahachie, Inc. Typical of many railroad cars that travelled through Waxahachie, the caboose was found in St. Louis, Missouri, by David Hudgins, HWI member and railroad buff. As funds permit, HWI is restoring the interior for opening to the public.

A-57
South Rogers Street at Waxahachie Creek
Rogers Street Bridge
1890; Wrought Iron Bridge Company

The Rogers Street Bridge was one of thirteen bridges funded by the Ellis County Commissioners as part of a countywide bridge-building project in the late 1880s-early 1890s. The commissioners were the overseers of early county roads—in fact, that was their primary responsibility—each commissioner responsible for the roads and bridges in his respective precinct. On Friday, February 28, 1890, the *Enterprise* reported that material for "the double iron bridge to be put at the foot of Rogers street came in Monday night on the M. K. & T. road." Construction would begin the following week after "the old bridge that now spans Waxahachie creek at that point [is] taken down and moved to Chambers creek." Within two months, the new bridge was "nearing completion."

The Wrought Iron Bridge Company, one of the largest bridge builders in the country, fabricated the Rogers Street Bridge at its plant in Canton, Ohio. Founded in 1864, the company specialized in relatively short-span iron truss bridges that were often sold to a county entity via the company's printed catalogue of bridge designs and a local agent who, in Waxahachie, was T. R. Anderson, owner of the Waxahachie Machinery Company. Mass produced in Canton and shipped unassembled by train to the station nearest their destination, smaller bridges such as those for Ellis County were assembled by local contractors, whereas the company sent its own crews for larger projects.

The Rogers Street Bridge is an increasingly rare surviving example in Texas of a Pratt through-truss bridge, one of the most common bridge types built in the United States from 1844 (when invented by father and son Thomas and Caleb Pratt) into the early twentieth century. Identified by vertical members and diagonals that slope toward the center on the side panels, it was also one of the types most frequently produced by the Ohio company because the design easily transitioned from wood to iron and steel. The approach to both ends of the bridge was an extended wood decking that abutted the eighteen-foot wide, forty-three-foot long wood roadway of the bridge itself. Guardrails and posts, now iron, were originally wood. A five-foot wide cantilevered pedestrian walkway was attached to the east side of the bridge, probably from the time the bridge was built. It appears in a circa 1910 photograph as does the Bridge Store at the south end of the bridge. Sadly, the cast iron plaques identifying the company and still attached to the top end rails of the truss in 1985 have disappeared.

Although there were other bridges crossing the creek, this bridge was the largest, widest, and most strategically placed for traffic moving in and out of the south side of town. Heavily used from the beginning, maintenance was demanding, as a random sampling of newspaper reports suggests: needed repairs in 1899, condemned in 1902, closed in December 1908 until a new floor was installed, and this was before the automobile! In 1917, Texas was among the last of the states to create a highway department and began, slowly, to develop a system of state highways. The north-south Highway 6 was routed through town over the Rogers Street Bridge, and by the mid-1920s, increased traffic was stressing the bridge even more. Relief came in 1931 when a concrete and steel viaduct (now scheduled for demolition) was built to the west and became the primary carrier for highway and local traffic, at which time the Rogers Street Bridge became an alternate local route. In summer 1952, city council funded a renovation by the Austin Bridge Company, choosing repair over demolition for two reasons: the bridge's value as an emergency route and its convenience for farmers in the large rural area to the south to get into town without facing heavy highway traffic, especially during harvest season.

Recognized in 1981 as a Recorded Texas Historic Landmark, the bridge officially closed in 1990, thereby making the "scary" ride across the bridge as well as a walk on the cantilevered footbridge that was used into the 1980s only a memory for many Waxahachians. In January 2005, the bridge was rededicated following a major restoration that was a joint project of the city, the Texas Department of Transportation, and the Federal Highway Administration. Rogers Street Bridge is now on the southern tip of the Downtown Historic District and a picturesque addition to the Hike and Bike Trail.

A-58
Waxahachie Viaduct

1931; Texas State Highway Department

Bridge Engineers, designers;
Purvis & Bertram, contractors

It is no exaggeration to say that the opening of the Waxahachie Viaduct on December 12, 1931, remains one of the most momentous events in Waxahachie's history. Until that day, most people moving in a north-south direction through Waxahachie, whether they were locals or long-distance travelers, used the narrow and antiquated 1890 Rogers Street Bridge to cross Waxahachie Creek and the railroad tracks. With the opening of the viaduct, Waxahachie entered the era of modern travel.

When the viaduct opened, the *Daily Light* pointed out that the structure measured, with approaches, 1,600 feet from Madison Street to a point south in Bullard Heights. Reinforced concrete piers and beams supported the concrete and steel overpass "proper" or viaduct span that was 1,120 feet long and thirty feet wide with a five-foot sidewalk on the west side. A heavy concrete balustrade formed the railings. According to Joe Jenkins, who was six years old in 1931, the viaduct was called "the White Way" because it was brilliantly illuminated at night with lights at thirty-foot intervals. The White Way term carried over from a civic program launched in 1913 to make Waxahachie "one of the best lighted cities" in Texas, but it originated in New York City around 1900 in reference to the Broadway Theater District. The viaduct may not have been quite as glamorous as Broadway but, says Jenkins, "Waxahachians thought it was a big deal just to go see it and drive across it."

Fort Worth contractors Purvis & Bertam built the viaduct in ten months. The authorized Resident Engineer was native Waxahachian W. A. Spalding, who graduated from the University of Texas with a civil engineering degree in 1896. Built during the Depression, the project attracted an influx of unemployed men looking for work, but townspeople were adamant that the expected one hundred hirees should be only "bona fide residents of Waxahachie and not those who have rushed here at the last minute to claim that they are." To what extent the request was accommodated was not recorded. Planning for the viaduct actually began in the mid-1920s as part of the much larger national Lakes-to-Gulf project that connected a line of highways from Duluth, Minnesota, to Galveston, Texas. The *Daily Light* noted that the viaduct opening marked completion of the "last big project" on the Highway 6 portion of the route.

The Waxahachie Viaduct is listed on the National Register of Historic Places, but after years of debate and minimal maintenance by TX-DOT, the latter determined it has to be replaced.

A-59
441 South College Street
Shive & Keys
c. 1908-12

Grain dealer Walter E. Shive bought this property on June 26, 1908, and on the following day formed a partnership with John D. Keys, a coworker at the Waxahachie Grain Company. The two men were now proprietors of the electric grist mill (electricity powered the machinery) that was on prime property in Waxahachie's industrial section, fronting one hundred feet on College Street, extending east to Flat Street, and abutting the MKT spur track. The partners immediately assumed operation of the mill, which was housed in a long narrow one-and-a-half story frame building with the gable end at right angles to the street and a covered platform on the south façade. Something similar to the current building appears on the October 1909 Sanborn map but without tin cladding. The cladding may have been applied to an existing building or perhaps to a new mill building sometime around June 1912, when Shive & Keys built, according to the *Daily Light*, "one of the largest hay barns in this section of the country . . . a mammoth hay barn [that is] made of corrugated iron and covers 65,000 square feet, is about forty feet high and will store 500 tons of hay."

The November 1914 Sanborn map shows both the hay barn and this building encased in "corrugated iron," which was considered a safer material than frame for storing highly self-combustible grain and feed at any location, but perhaps even more so here. On October 12, 1913, the Texas Electric Railway, known as the Interurban, opened service connecting Waco and Dallas, with the route through Waxahachie following College Street. To cross over the creek and the railroad tracks, the company built what became known as the Waxahachie Trestle, a 1,454-foot-long, 40-foot-high steel overpass with wires and spark-prone cars passing literally within touchable distance of Shive & Keys's grain and feed store before dipping to street level just south of Madison Street and following College Street through downtown. The mill building survived the Interurban, which operated through 1948, but the barn did not.

Shive & Keys operated a highly successful partnership until Keys retired in 1935. Shive continued on his own into the early 1940s. Current owners Dennis and Beverly Horak, working with architect Anthony Mottla, built a sizeable addition in 2009 which they described as "an example of modern recycling," a reference to the aged materials incorporated in the design.

A-60
310 South College Street
Will Moore & Sons Building
1917; R. H. York, contractor

Four years after Will Moore built his hardware and implement store on the northeast corner of this block (**105 West Jefferson**), he financed this building, almost of equal size, to house his growing automobile business. He bought the empty 80 x 95 ft. property in 1917 from William Atkinson, whose one-story brick livery stable had covered the lot from c.1892 to 1913. It was a land-use transition that was taking place on numerous properties at the time. When the railroad came to Waxahachie, the southern end of downtown was prime real estate for such businesses as livery stables, wagon yards, and moving and storage companies, all of which needed large tracts of land and wanted easy access to the railroads. Many of those uses were gradually replaced, as happened on this corner, with auto-related businesses that were looking for the same things—sizeable tracts of land and railroad access.

In mid-October, Moore commenced construction of what was to be a one-story brick warehouse building, but a month later he was installing a "modern service station" and planning to hire a mechanic who knew "the workings" of the three cars he sold—the Mitchell, Oakland, and Dort. Come early December and with the building "almost completed according to original plans," Moore decided to add a second story to give ample room for the service station and accessories departments on the first level and "the storage of several car loads of new cars" on the upper floor. The resulting building was clearly auto-friendly with a four-bay front façade, the bays separated by wide flat pilasters. At street level, bay-width display windows flanked two narrower bays that originally were garage door openings.

When the building opened, Moore's two sons, Stacey and Stewart, had joined the business, now known as Will Moore & Sons. Following Stacey's death in 1923 at age twenty-five, Moore began renting spaces on the street level to auto-related businesses and second-floor spaces to various organizations and businesses. In the late 1920s, American Legion Troop C Armory headquarters were here; it was a "skating hall" and an arena for wrestling matches; and during the 1930s it was the Columbian Club Ballroom with a stage at one end, where entertainers like Lawrence Welk and his orchestra performed in February 1934, followed by Dallas band leader Durward Cline and his "Eleven Piece N.B.C. Orchestra" in April.

In 1945, Moore heirs sold the building to James H. Harbin for a paint and body shop in conjunction with his automobile dealership across the street. After Harbin moved out, the building housed several businesses until 1991, when it was converted into an antiques mall. Harbin's daughter Hilda Harbin Chapman revitalized the mall in 1994, a business venture that evolved into her commitment to downtown Waxahachie and leadership roles in the Downtown Merchants Association, the Waxahachie Partnership Inc., and the Chamber of Commerce.

A-61
308 South College Street
Byers Building
1929

Grocer Harry Byers's pared-down store building was under construction at the time the stock market crashed on October 29, 1929. Byers, who was a first-generation American born in Dallas in 1893 of Russian immigrant parents, opened his first Waxahachie grocery store in rented space on East Main Street in the early 1920s. He bought this lot in March 1929 from widow Katie D. Shelton, and on September 9, the *Dallas Morning News* reported that Byers was building "a new brick store structure on South College street." Although Byers's initial timing was not the best, his grocery business operated at this location into the late 1950s. Later alterations to the façade include the addition of stucco over the brick and replacing the second floor windows.

This lot had significance in Waxahachie history as the site of the Shelton Opera House from 1902 until it burned in the December 1912 fire. Merchant V. H. Shelton had bought the property—a vacant lot—in October 1892, after which he and his wife Katie hired Dallas contractor F. L. Stevenson to build a two-story business house according to plans prepared by architect A. J. Armstrong. In 1902, the Sheltons adapted the building for use as an opera house in response to what many believed was the city's most "pitiable" need—"a place where amusements worthy of an enlightened people's patronage may be had." The Sheltons had a history of investing in the town's cultural life, having created a Music Hall for staging musical events in their music store and making an early attempt to establish a library in their drugstore. After the 1902 and 1903 opera seasons, they concluded that Waxahachie could support "a first class opera house" and hired A. C. Higginson, a Kansas City, Missouri, architect known for his theater design, to prepare plans for a complete overhaul of the building interior. Opening on September 26, 1904, the proclaimed thousand-seat playhouse with balcony was the primary venue for live entertainment in Waxahachie until the 1912 fire.

The Sheltons suffered the greatest loss of the property owners affected by the fire. Times had changed since 1904, and by 1912 they were competing with three moving picture houses on the square and booking wrestling matches to provide live entertainment. Consequently, the Sheltons' replacement structure had only rentable commercial space, but that, too, was no longer standing by 1925, and the lot remained vacant until Byers bought it and built his store in 1929.

A-62
105 West Jefferson Street
Will Moore Building
1913

This building has been a solid anchor to the south side of Waxahachie's downtown since its construction in 1913. Its importance to the landscape is a combination of the building itself and its association with two long-standing businesses that reflect the changing economics of downtown Waxahachie—Moore Hardware Co. and The Dove's Nest Restaurant. Hardware and implement merchant Will Moore bought this property from the estate of Richard Vickery after a fire on December 28, 1912, destroyed this corner of the block and damaged the Rogers Street corner behind it, where Moore was renting space for his business. On May 6, 1913, the *Daily Light* reported that Moore, "after keeping an impatient public waiting," disclosed details about his new two-story 72 x 92 ft. business house that would, of course, be "thoroughly modern in every particular." The façade was faced with pressed vitrified brown brick from the "world famous Coffeyville plant," and the lower floor was finished with glass fronts and "all the 'trimmings' that go to make a first class business house." Moore was in his new building at the corner of Jefferson and College by late fall.

Moore's building typifies commercial structures built during the 1910-1925 period. Horizontality wraps both sides of the flat-roofed two-story building beginning with the metal parapet that doubles as a linear billboard. The molded cornice, evenly spaced second story windows, simple corbel table above the transom windows, extended suspended canopy, and display windows present a tailored façade. The chamfered or angled corner entrance is a simple but welcoming gesture to pedestrians walking along both streets and to people looking down the College Street slope from the square above.

Moore's original plan to rent part of the second story was short-lived, because he needed the space for his own expanding inventory. Heavy implements including tractors and other equipment were transported to the upper floor via an elevator on the alley side of the building, but he was soon storing, repairing, and itching to sell automobiles (like everybody else in town), which prompted him to build another structure on the south end of the block in 1917 (**310 South College Street**). Financial complications in the 1930s forced him to eliminate all but his hardware business, which he maintained until his death in 1946. His family continued the business at this location into the late 1980s.

Whereas Moore's hardware business was the anchor of this corner for almost seventy-five years, The Dove's Nest Restaurant assumed that role in 1994 when owners Cindy Goss Burch and husband Andrew Burch made a long-term commitment to the resurgence of downtown Waxahachie. Their story actually begins in 1986, when Cindy's mother Marilyn Goss Harris opened Marilyn's Art Room, first in the Hancock Building (**203-205 South College**), then acquiring and moving to the Moore Building. When Mrs. Harris retired in 1994, the business evolved into The Dove's Nest Restaurant with an adjacent gift, antiques, and home accents shop. In 1998, architect Anthony Mottla converted the wide-open second floor into a sophisticated above-the-store living space for the couple.

A-63
300 block South College Street,
(photograph shows east or Jackson Street side)
Ellis County Detention Center
[now Wayne McCollum Detention Center]

1990; Maxey & Associates, Inc., architect;
The Cadence Group, general contractor

2001; DCW, Inc., architects;
Roy Anderson Corp., construction

2008-2010; HDR Architecture, Inc.;
Balfour Beatty, Inc., general contractor

Named in honor of Wayne McCollum, Ellis County Sheriff from 1956 to 1977, the detention center was built in three phases. It began in 1990 with construction of a 192-bed, 49,000-square-foot structure that covered the full block from Jefferson to Madison Streets and College to Jackson Streets. This initial structure set the tone for subsequent additions. The height was determined by surrounding commercial buildings while the tan-colored concrete block surfacing was intended to meld the building (as much as possible) into the background. Placement on the southward slope of College Street reduced the overwhelming bulk of the building with the most visible edges softened by rounded or "turret" corners.

The second phase opened in November 2001, with three levels and 52,000 square feet. The third and largest phase, which was part of the Ellis County Justice Center expansion program, extended from College to Flat Streets and opened in 2010 with almost 86,000 additional square feet of space.

A-64
503 South Flat Street
(photograph shows Matthews Street side)
National Compress Co. Building

Even though cotton dominated Waxahachie's economy for decades and placed the small city on the world market for a period, there are few cotton-related industrial sites remaining here today. The National Compress Company Building is one exception. It was one of two compresses built in Waxahachie at a time when a high-density compress was considered essential for any inland locale wanting to compete in the cotton industry. These compresses reduced ginned bales to nearly half their size which, in turn, meant that the railroads could transport many more export-ready bales to Galveston or Houston.

The Waxahachie Compress & Storage Company, a local enterprise, built Waxahachie's first compress on the south side of Waxahachie Creek on acreage bought from David and Margaret Bullard in May 1892. Compress machinery began arriving in June, and by mid-August the compress was operating. In January 1895, George H. McFadden of McFadden & Bro. of Philadelphia, one of the largest cotton merchants in the country, bought this property on the north side of the creek and four months later sold it to the National Compress Company of New Jersey. Both compresses are shown on the September 1896 Waxahachie map—one on each side of the creek and both on railroad spurs—but the locally owned compress, lacking the resources of the national company, was sold at public auction in April 1898.

The original National Compress building, first shown on the 1898 Sanborn map and documented in early photographs, was a frame open-sided shed measuring about 240 x 150 ft. with a low-pitched clerestory roof that let light in and air out. On the north façade and under the shed, a brick enclosure housed the cylinders and other mechanical equipment; nearby was a separate iron-clad two-story compressor tower that extended twenty feet above the roof. An uncovered platform with fire hydrants and a hose system surrounded the shed on all but the track side. Fire was always a fear, but the National Compress was fortunate to be located just south of the City Water Works and, according to David Hudgins, Waxahachie Fire Chief from 1986-2012, would have had its own fire brigade before the city established a paid fire department in 1922. Period photographs taken during cotton season show cotton bales stacked on the compress platform and on the adjoining separately owned cotton yards.

The New Jersey company sold the Waxahachie complex to a newly incorporated National Compress Company of Texas in March 1906 for $150,000. In 1917, company management described Ellis County as "the banner cotton county of the world" and the company itself as "the banner press of the country," predicting that it would press 75,000 bales of "the fleecy staple product" that year.

The building's jagged roof line and concrete fire walls indicate multiple additions built over the years, but the expanse of the industrial structure is not understood until driving its length on Matthews Street. When the 1985 historic resource survey was conducted, it was still operating as a compress (although then as the Waxahachie Compress Co.) which, along with its condition and appearance, was the basis for its inclusion on the National Register of Historic Places. Since that time, compress operations were gradually discontinued and the building converted to warehouse use. The compress tower can still be seen from Madison and Clift Streets.

A-65
109 Clift Street
El-Co Creamery
1910

In basic form, this small commercial building is nondescript—a simple rectangular structure with a pitched roof and gable end to the street. What makes it unusual and distinctive is the building material—concrete blocks molded to look like rough stones for the walls and smooth stone for the lintels and quoins. Built in 1910 for the El-Co Creamery, there is little doubt that the blocks were produced by another local enterprise, the Waxahachie Cement Stone Manufacturing Company. It is one of two existing concrete block structures—the other being the 1906 Cotton Mill office (**821 Circle Street**)—built during the short period that the company was in operation from 1906 to circa 1914.

Prior to the creamery opening on October 25, 1910, the *Enterprise* expressed some interest in the "handsome structure," noting the concrete blocks, cement floor, and machinery from U. Gault & Co., of Chicago. The readership, however, was more interested in reading that "the sanitation of the building is perfect and the machinery is of the most modern design," since Waxahachians were in step with many Americans who were becoming more aware of health and sanitation issues. The El-Co stockholders planned to produce butter and milk, then add an ice cream factory. Area farmers were solicited to supply the raw milk materials and instructed "to purchase [their] own separator . . . from any of the hardware stores." Production got underway, but there were obviously problems, as the *Daily Light* reported in December 1912 that El-Co Creamery was "to be rejuvenated throughout" with new machinery, new paint, and a new general manager, Charles A. Grant, a graduate of Cornell University. Under Grant's "more vigorous and scientific management," greater attention would be given to "the famous pasteurized system of purity and hygiene," while farmers would be encouraged "to pay more attention in the future than at present, to the care of cows and their products."

El-Co's market covered a hundred-mile radius in every direction from Waxahachie and also included butter shipments via parcel post to within 160 miles of the city. Management changed in the early 1920s when J. A. Hurley moved from Dallas, where he was a manufacturer's agent (business unspecified), and became the new owner. He concentrated solely on making ice cream and changed the name to Arctic Ice Cream with the slogan "Made in Waxahachie for Waxahachie People." Arctic Ice Cream operated until the late 1930s. Elco Dairy (a different corporation from El-Co Creamery), producers of milk and cream under management of J. P. Wakeland, was listed on Bell Branch Road in the 1936 directory.

One block to the south, at the southeast corner of Clift and East Jefferson, stood the 1908 Hot Wells Natatorium. Built by five local entrepreneurs after mineral water was discovered nearby, a vaguely Greek Revival-inspired two-story frame structure enclosed a 20 x 70 ft. swimming pool. Patrons (white only) paid an entrance fee to use the hot well waters in the pool and baths in the Natatorium, but access to a fountain and trellis pavilion in Hot Well Park on the east side of the building was free. Repeated mechanical problems and the drowning of a Trinity University student in May 1911 contributed to the Natatorium's failure and the sale of the property in 1912. The building was used for storage before it was demolished in 1928, but the park fountain, with segregated outlets for the white and the black populations, remained publicly available until 1955.

A-66
212 West Jefferson Street
Maybin Service Station
c. 1927

John Margolies writes in his book *Pump and Circumstances: Glory Days of the Gas Station* that Americans saw an explosion of the new building type in the 1920s, the numbers jumping from some 12,000 drive-in stations in 1921 to 143,000 in 1929. Olin Maybin's service station, built during that period, is a good example of stations designed to blend into their surroundings, in this case duplicating the size, scale, and outline of one-story flat-roof commercial buildings that sat squarely on several Waxahachie downtown street corners (see the northeast corner of Elm and Madison). The service station version is distinguished by a triangular cut under the parapet and roof, held firmly in place by solid corner columns and creating a space wide enough for two vehicles and a narrow service island. The same parapet detailing—rectangular shapes outlined with soldier bricks (bricks laid with the long, narrow side exposed) and accented with granite diamonds and squares is seen on other buildings in downtown Waxahachie dating from the mid-to-late 1920s. Directly across Jefferson Street, Carlisle Chevrolet also had a triangular gas station at the corner of its first dealership, built in 1926.

Maybin, who was born in Waxahachie in 1894, operated a station at this location for about ten years before moving across the street to **204 Elm** in July 1937. Other businesses have located here. The Rogelio Aguilar family opened their Two Amigos Taqueria in one of the small retail spaces on the Elm Street side of this building in 2003 and ten years later expanded into the service station.

A-67
204 South Elm Street
Sinclair Service Station
1937

As the filling station developed into a specific building type, major oil companies experimented with different designs, and eventually most adopted an identifiable corporate style for their outlets and supplied plans and specifications for local contractors. Waxahachie did not want for examples, especially on Elm Street. By 1930, Sinclair had introduced its distinctive Spanish "castle" design with cream colored stucco walls and green tile roofing. Stations like this were duplicated hundreds of times across the country, even to the number and placement of decorative inset tiles on the broken pediments of the canopy. However, 1937 is a late construction date for this particular design because the growing popularity of trailer caravans had made the canopy an outmoded feature for obvious reasons. That fact did not dampen Olin Maybin's enthusiasm when he announced in mid-July that he was moving from his old location across the street at **212 West Jefferson** into "our new Sinclair Station" and invited friends and customers to get their cars "Sinclairized." Maybin remained at this address until October 1959, six months before he died.

The station to the south at 306-308 South Elm was built according to Texaco plans in 1936 by owners Weldon Tucker and Tom Whipple.

A-68
300 West Main Street
Sims-Thomson Garage
1913; E. S. Boze, designer and builder

When this "Monument to Motordom" opened on March 5, 1913, the "20,000 Feet of Floor Space" supposedly made it the "Largest Garage in the South," with room for 120 automobiles. Investors Clarence Thomson and Dabney Sims, ages thirty-five and twenty-nine respectively, and both from neighboring Italy, entered the rapidly evolving world of automobiles when they established a motor repair shop on Water Street in 1909. Three years later, Sims acquired this half block (two lots, each 100 feet square) and after removal of the City's skating rink from the site, the partners contracted E. S. Boze to design and build a one-story brick garage measuring one hundred feet on West Main and two hundred feet along Elm Street. In late January 1913 and after the brickwork was completed, they added a partial second story fronting one hundred feet on Main Street. The change was probably prompted by inquiries from potential tenants looking for office space like Waxahachie Gas Company and photographer Mrs. Claudia Devenport.

No doubt Sims and Thomson were anxious to have their garage and "complete machine shop" ready for the Rogers Hotel reopening in early April and for the spring touring season. By early May, the *Daily Light* reported that it was already "a powerful puller of outside business," having attracted auto enthusiasts on cross-country tours from more than twenty states, including New York and Wyoming. The garage would have been a welcome sight for automobile owners and clubs whose primary interest was a structurally sound, covered place to park their vehicles and get them serviced overnight. Like all Boze buildings, function and sturdiness compensated for what might have been lacking in aesthetics—the only hint of trim being the parapet corbeling on the flat-roofed structure. Entries into the garage were on Water and Elm Streets and a drive-through entry on Main Street. As shown on the 1914 Sanborn map, the interior of the one-story section was one large space with small areas sectioned off for "oil," vulcanizing, repairs, etc., the remaining space for car storage. There was no elevator. The only gas pump, with a 280-gallon underground tank, was just outside the Elm Street entrance.

Local automobile owners also stored their cars here for a fee. Most cars were still recreational vehicles, designed and equipped to be used in good weather and stored when not, and as yet, few Waxahachie residents had their own garage.

By 1918, Thomson had moved to Dallas, and the garage was known as the Central Texas Auto Garage, suggesting that the men had sold their garage business, but Sims continued leasing the building until selling it in 1919. Keeping track of all the car dealers and garage owners and/or managers who conducted business in this building over the next twenty years and whether they were owners or renters is a challenge. Among the dealerships advertised at this location were Grimland's Cadillac, Waxahachie Nash, Jarvis Motor, Worsham Buick, and others. In the late 1930s, the Sawyer-Graham Motor Co. dealership moved here before buying the Highway Garage across the street in 1955.

Originally, there was not a drive-in gasoline station at the Main/Elm Street corner of the building. One probably appeared around 1918, but the first to be documented is the Blue Front Filling Station, owned and managed by J. H. and J. L. Kimball, according to the city directory of 1922—the same year that Cecil Counts bought the business. In the early 1930s, Counts sold to Ike Teague, who owned several service stations at different locations during his lifetime and who is remembered for his motorcycle with side car and his motto, "Don't cuss, call us." The building took on a different look when painted all white in the 1940s, which is also when the longtime renter, the Waxahachie Gas Company, filled in the corner space for offices (the change clearly visible). As in the past, the building houses a variety of uses.

The Sims-Thomson Garage building is one of the most underappreciated structures in downtown Waxahachie. Over the years, it has done a yeoman's service as it accommodated a multitude of owners and inhabitants and while doing so, managed to hold its shape with minimal defacement, the latter a reflection of both its owners and its adaptability. Although some alterations have occurred, the basic core and footprint of the original building remain intact. Its contributions to the Waxahachie streetscape are twofold: it anchors the northwest corner of downtown and gives a solid edge to the Elm Street route while it also frames movement in and out of Courthouse Square on West Main Street, one of Waxahachie's busiest thoroughfares.

A-69
315 West Main Street

Highway Garage

1916-17; Richards & Few, contractors

On August 30, 1916, the *Daily Light* announced that O. H. Chapman had contracted Richards & Few to build a garage and "a home for the Buick" at this location for W. E. Hipp. Occupancy by the end of November was delayed when Hipp decided to add a full second floor to the 90 x 140 ft. building for "a paint shop and finishing department." About to open in late January, it was again delayed but this time for a unique reason: it became "the Brown tabernacle" for evangelist John E. Brown's month-long Union Gospel Revival in March. Seats were brought from Chautauqua Auditorium with evening and weekend audiences expected to number as many as two thousand worshipers in "the mammoth tabernacle." Brown held his closing sessions in a tent so Hipp could prepare for the opening of his Quick Service Garage and Buick-Hudson dealership on Monday, April 2.

The Chapman family had owned the property since 1912, and given their history with other building projects, it is probable that O. H. Chapman and an architect were responsible for the initial garage design, with Hipp assuming the role of client once the project was underway. The simple yet polished building exterior seen today does not differ substantially from the 1917 structure. The Main Street façade was divided into six bays, all with storefront windows, with the exception of one garage-door opening (the exact bay remains unclear) on the street level and triple one-over-one window groupings on the second story. There was a second garage opening at the Monroe Street alley corner near the interior elevator. The floor plan was not complicated—large open spaces on both floors with storefront units along Main Street and, according to the 1925 Sanborn map, a sixty-five-car capacity garage.

When the garage opened, Hipp handled all car sales and his "competent" mechanic Jack Wilson directed "the repairing, service, storage and washing of cars." Three separately owned auto-related businesses rented space including the Douglass Auto Supply Co., which offered "accessories including gasoline, oils and greases, tires and tire repairing and quick tire service."

Frequent changes in the building's occupants reflected the fluidity of the automobile business in these early years. By early January 1919, Paul Douglass had assumed Hipp's lease (Hipp was back on Water Street) and added a Chevrolet agency to his garage/auto supply business, the cars displayed in "a beautiful new show room with Main street entrance." When C. B. (Cleve) Youngblood bought the garage business in early 1922, he changed the name to the Highway Garage & Repair Company. In March 1923, J. W. N. O'Bannion and R. I. Owen from Bardwell bought both the "Highway Garage" (their quotation marks) and car agency but sold the garage business to Harry Shores in February 1924, Shores noting that he had "employed 'Buster' Hays, young colored man, well known to the motoring public."

By the late 1920s, the dealership space was replaced with a clothing manufacturer, but in the late 1930s a car agency returned to a Main Street unit when James H. Harbin opened his Plymouth and DeSoto showroom. The Chapmans sold the property in the mid-1940s to Zweig-Olian, a Dallas-based clothing manufacturing company that occupied most of the building but rented space to a Hudson dealership. It appears the Highway Garage closed at this time. Beginning in the early 1950s and lasting through the mid-1980s, the building housed a succession of dealerships or "motor companies."

In 1999, Karl Goss, Jack DuFon, and Dean Gray, partners in the Waxahachie Restoration Group, acquired the deteriorating property and contracted architect Anthony Mottla to adapt the building for twelve apartments on the second floor (still an open space) with tenant parking on the backside of the lower level and commercial units on West Main Street. The award-winning certified tax project was listed on the National Register of Historic Places in 2003.

The Elm Street side of this block is the site of one of Waxahachie's earliest detached filling stations, another new building type that evolved with the automobile. Thus far, the first person documented at this location is W. C. Biggers in 1920 but there was doubtless a station here before that. Exactly when it opened and what it looked like is not documented, but the Chapmans, who owned the property at the time, probably built and leased it. Eventually the service station was sold as a separate property and among its later owners were Paul Richards, Waxahachie's retired major league baseball player, and his wife Mattie, who bought it in December 1954.

SECTION B

Town Addition

Detail from the 1886 Waxahachie Bird's Eye View showing the section northeast of the square, with College being the wide street in the middle, ending at Marvin College; Kaufman the street at an angle on the right; and Rogers (then called Dallas) to the left of College Street. *Courtesy Ellis County Museum.*

INTRODUCTION

The 1876 bird's-eye view of Waxahachie shows that early residential growth, beyond the blocks surrounding the square, moved north on Kaufman, College, Rogers (Lafayette at that time), and Monroe Streets. With the barrier of Waxahachie Creek on the south, the lure of Marvin College to the north, and the planned route of the town's first railroad just north of the square, development to the north made perfect sense. Ten years later the 1886 bird's-eye view confirmed continued growth and increased density along the same streets heading north. Kaufman, College, and Rogers (Dallas Street in 1886) could boast the highest concentrations of substantial dwellings, with Monroe and Williams (then Marshall) not far behind, and a surge moving northward from Marvin along what is now Brown Street.

This section includes those streets north of downtown but south of Marvin College, and the blocks east of downtown to Kaufman Street, all of which were part of the Town Addition. (The Addition also included blocks west of downtown that are covered in Section C.) The name Town Addition might lead one to expect orderly, consistently sized blocks and lots, but these blocks are anything but consistent. The original town plan embodied the perfect geometry possible on a plot of land owned by a single person in an area with few settlers. When the city limits were expanded in 1871, the Town Addition plat had to accommodate roads and a patchwork of varied ownership

The 1899 Baptist church building stood at the corner of North Rogers and MacMillan Streets until the 1950s, when it was demolished to make room for a larger structure. This tinted postcard was published by E. C. Kropp Co., Milwaukee, c. 1918. *Courtesy Ellis County Museum.*

Built in 1905, this Prairie style Methodist church building stood at 308 North College until it was demolished in 1950. The congregation built a new church at 505 West Marvin. *Courtesy Ellis County Museum.*

that had evolved as the town grew, and the result was an assortment of oddly shaped blocks.

Several of Waxahachie's oldest remaining houses can be found in this section, along with excellent, well-preserved examples of domestic architecture of the late nineteenth and early twentieth centuries. Two-story houses belonging to leading merchants and businessmen were interspersed with one-story cottages and, later, bungalows. Religious buildings include the city's oldest, St. Paul's Episcopal Church (now Francesca Chapel), and one of its most architecturally notable, Central Presbyterian Church.

Major church buildings in the section that have not survived include the 1899 Gothic Revival Baptist church that faced North Rogers Street and the 1905 Prairie style Methodist church on North College.

College Street had the potential to be Waxahachie's one grand avenue. It linked the square with Marvin College, was wider than the other early north-south streets, and the college buildings punctuated the vista from the square and the railroad depot with a major architectural and cultural landmark. The first wave of houses were rectangular cottages with attached porches, similar to many others in town, but soon prominent citizens began building substantial two-story dwellings in the latest styles. By the mid-1880s, it had become one of the most prestigious streets in town. The development of new subdivisions in the 1890s challenged that status, but several of the major families remained on College Street, and in 1904, the new Park School building provided a more up-to-date and impressive structure at the end of the avenue. In the first two decades of the

This postcard from c. 1910 shows the view north from the square, looking down North Rogers (on the left) and North College (on the right). The roofs of the jail and railroad depots are in the foreground, and the 1904 Park School building is visible at the end of North College. *Private Collection.*

twentieth century, some of the existing dwellings were updated to reflect the Colonial Revival and Prairie styles popular at the time, and new houses and bungalows in those same styles were also constructed.

College Street lost much of its luster in the ensuing years. Commercial buildings crept further north of the square, replacing residential structures. A large barren church parking lot on the west side of the street interrupts the progression of buildings and landscaped yards. In contrast is the new construction on the southwest corner of Marvin, where a branch office of Edward Jones Investments was built both in a scale and with a set-back consistent with neighboring buildings and respectful of its location as a gateway to the downtown.

Kaufman Street originally started at the northeast edge of Waxahachie's original town site, at the point where Main Street crossed Rogers Spring Branch. Kaufman ran at a northeasterly diagonal from Main Street to what became East Marvin. Proximity to the town's core and connection to outlying areas meant that Kaufman Street was a busy thoroughfare, and with its incline—if newspaper reports are any indication—a regular temptation for those wanting a fast ride into town. With the opening of the Waxahachie Tap Railroad in 1879 (later the Houston and Texas Central Railroad), the Kaufman Street crossing became the center of Waxahachie's lumber business, and the street became a residential choice for many in the building trades.

The McDade family in front of their newly remodeled house at 408 Oldham Avenue, c. 1904. *Courtesy Ellis County Museum.*

This passenger depot for the Fort Worth and New Orleans and the Central Texas and Northwestern railways, built in 1886, also served as the residence of the local manager and stood at the corner of Parks and Williams Streets. *Courtesy Ellis County Museum.*

Postcard showing a Lake Park mule-drawn streetcar and an electric interurban car on College Street, just north of the square, c. 1912. *Courtesy Ellis County Museum.*

Time has not been generous to Kaufman Street. The street as a residential location could not compete with the West End and other suburban developments, although some chose to stay in their family homes. More properties became rental in the early twentieth century with two of Waxahachie's major landlords, John F. Wyatt and Mark Smith, buying properties along the street. More recently, the Catholic Church's development has significantly altered the Kaufman Street neighborhood behind it. The long-term effects of the looming Ellis County Justice Center remain uncertain.

In contrast, Oldham Avenue survived the twentieth century in good form. Now connecting Kaufman and North College Streets, it originally was interrupted by the Oldham Branch, which ran south into the Rogers Branch. It first bore the rather inauspicious name of Mill Street, due to the presence of a grain mill where the street intersected the branch. Wooden bridges crossed the branch for many years, but when the 1890 Sanborn map was drawn, only a narrow footbridge is shown, which would have left the street essentially in two parts—two blocks west of the branch, accessible from North College, and four blocks on the east side, accessible from Kaufman Street. Planning for the Lake Park street railway signaled a change, and on July 1, 1891, the *Enterprise* reported that the railway "broke dirt on Oldham Avenue." By the time of the 1896 Phillips & Hawkins map, the mill was gone, the branch had been bridged, and the streetcar ran the length of the avenue from College to Kaufman, where it then headed north to Marvin and Vickery Streets. With the streetcar came some of the grandest houses on the avenue, including the homes of street-railway investors E. H. Griffin and J. F. Strickland.

The street railway tracks on Oldham were not the first to run through this part of town. One block north of Oldham passenger trains rumbled east and west along Parks Avenue beginning in July of 1886. Serving the Fort Worth and New Orleans and the Central Texas and Northwestern railways, the depot stood at the corner of Parks and Williams streets. In 1901 the track was closed, but the depot building remained for several years and was used as a residence. A few years after the Parks Avenue tracks were gone, new tracks were being laid on North College for the interurban from Dallas, which began service to Waxahachie in 1912.

The significance of the concentration of well-preserved noteworthy structures in this section was confirmed when the Oldham Avenue Historic District and the North Rogers Historic District were listed on the National Register of Historic Places in 1986, as were many houses on North College, Williams, and Kaufman streets as part of the Multiple Resource Area Thematic Group that was listed the same year. Even more structures have been recognized and restored in the ensuing years.

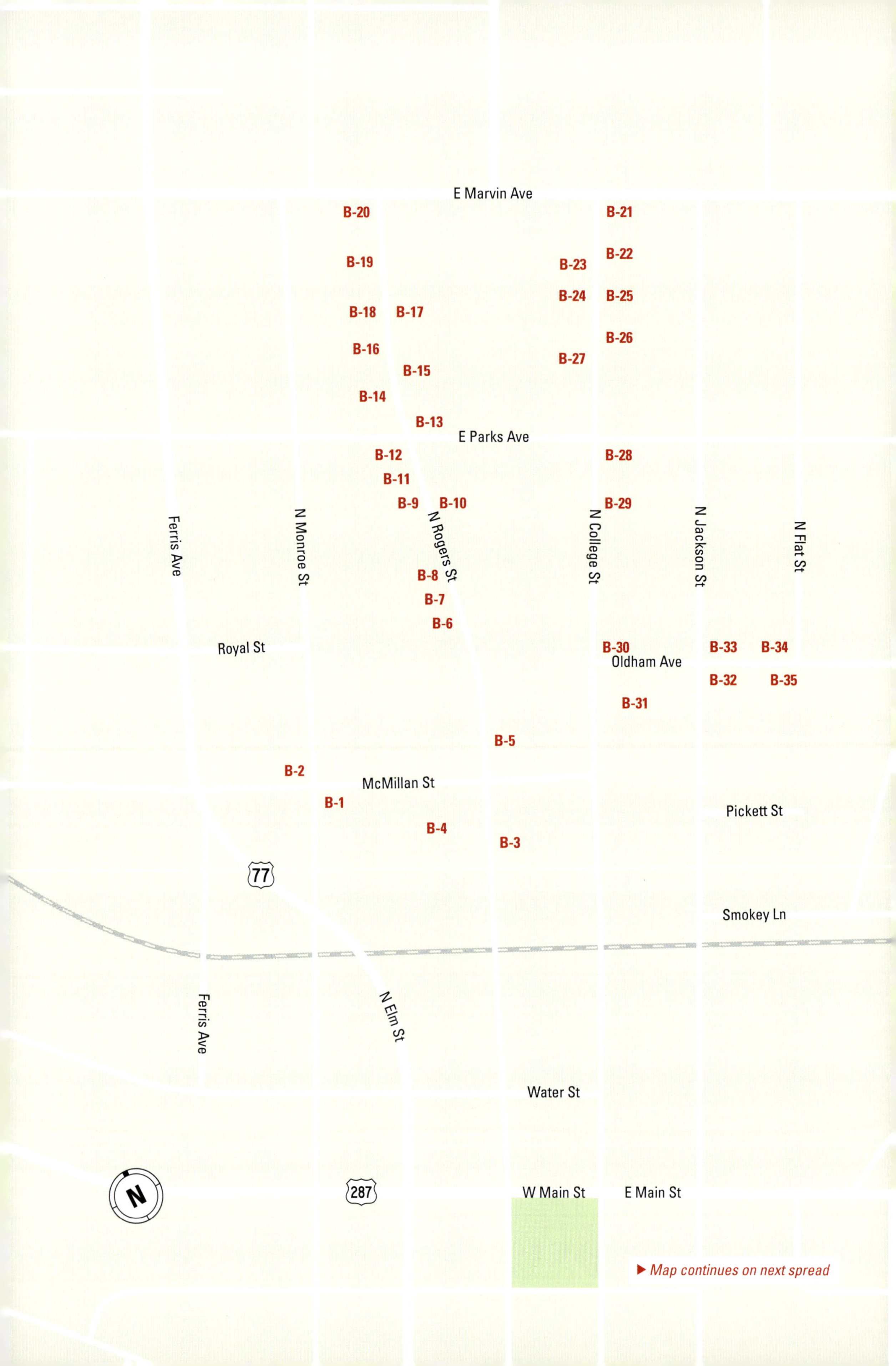

▶ Map continues on next spread

B-1 308 N. Monroe St.
St. Paul's Episcopal Church (now Francesca Chapel)

B-2 401 N. Monroe St.

B-3 306 N. Rogers St.
Southwestern Bell Telephone Building

B-4 315 N. Rogers St.
First Baptist Church

B-5 400, 402, 404 N. Rogers St.

B-6 503 N. Rogers St.

B-7 507 N. Rogers St.

B-8 509 N. Rogers St.

B-9 515 N. Rogers St.

B-10 514 N. Rogers St.

B-11 519 N. Rogers St.

B-12 523 N. Rogers St.

B-13 600 N. Rogers St.

B-14 603 N. Rogers St.

B-15 604 N. Rogers St.

B-16 607 N. Rogers St.

B-17 610 N. Rogers St.

B-18 611 N. Rogers St.

B-19 615 N. Rogers St.

B-20 619 N. Rogers St.

B-21 520 N. College St.

B-22 516 N. College St.

B-23 515 N. College St.

B-24 513 N. College St.

B-25 512 N. College St.

B-26 508 N. College St.

B-27 503-505, 507, 509-511 N. College St.

B-28 418 N. College St.

B-29 414 N. College St.

B-30 402 N. College St.
Central Presbyterian Church

B-31 316 N. College St.
United States Post Office

B-32 200 Oldham Ave.

B-33 201 Oldham Ave.

B-34 205 Oldham Ave.

B-35 208 Oldham Ave.

◆ *B-36-B-72 on pp.78-79*

◀ Map continues from previous spread

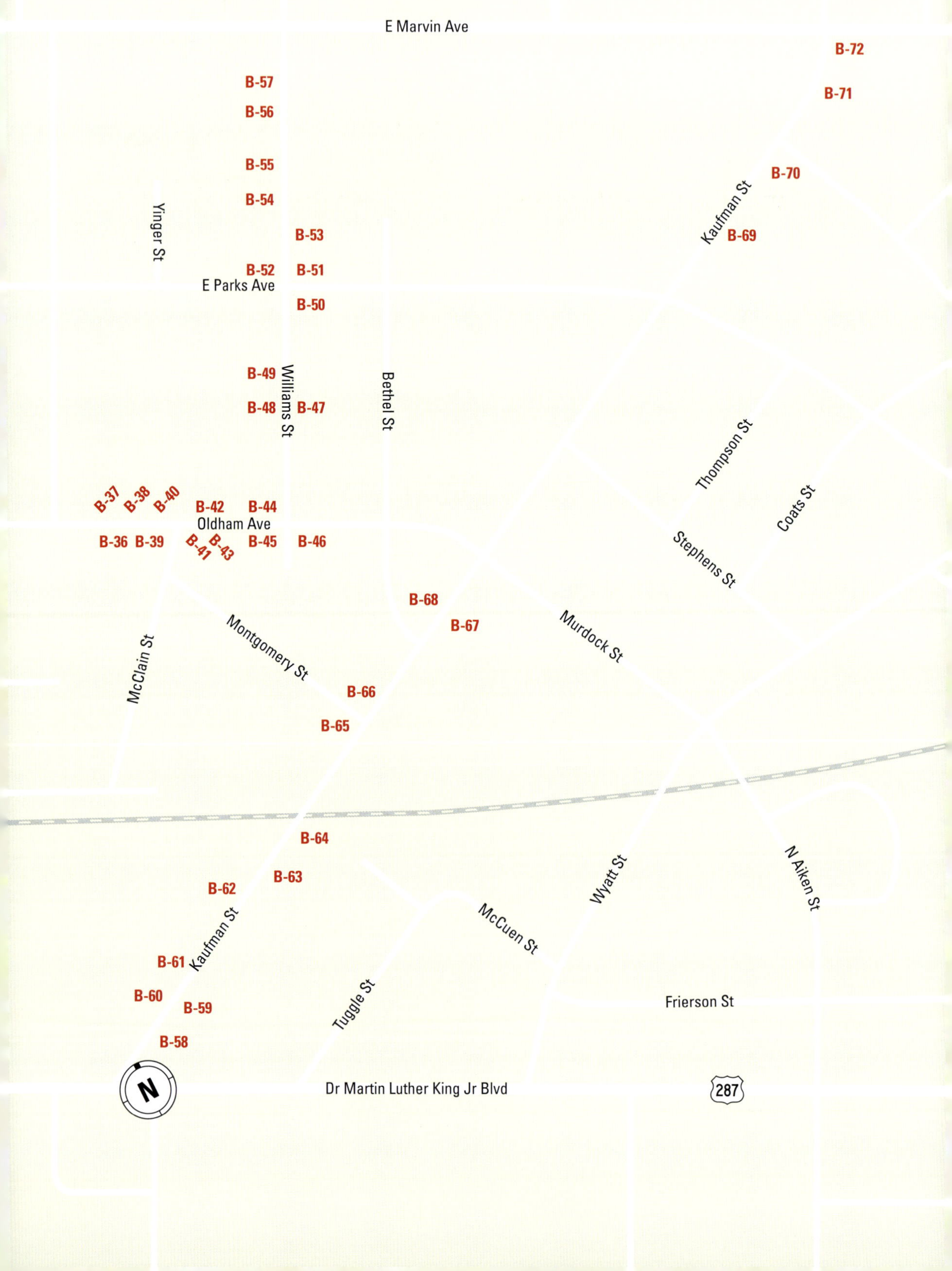

◆ *B-1-B-35 on pp.76-77*

B-1
308 North Monroe Street
St. Paul's Episcopal Church
[now Francesca Chapel]
1887

This tiny gem of unadorned Gothic Revival design is the oldest surviving church building in Waxahachie, and it still stands on its original site. Its cruciform plan was unusual for a small church of the time. Most Gothic Revival churches of this size followed the English Gothic parish church model with a nave attached directly to the smaller space of the chancel. In St. Paul's the primary exterior Gothic Revival elements are the steeply pitched roofs and the lancet windows. Tall single lancet windows along the nave and transept walls provide a strong vertical emphasis, and triple lancet groupings mark the east end, transept ends, and the entrance porch, or narthex. The interior is dominated by the original collar-braced open timber roof of stained, varnished pine. Regular Episcopal church services in Waxahachie began in 1876, but the congregations remained small, and it was more than ten years before a church building was constructed. There were only twelve registered communicants in 1887, when the building was consecrated. Bishop Alexander Charles Garrett of the Northern Texas Diocese encouraged church building across his territory and probably was involved in the design of St. Paul's. His journal entry for July 21, 1887, read, "Inspected St. Paul's church which is a very pretty and substantial structure, churchly in design and well constructed." St. Paul's congregation moved to a new building on Ovilla Road in 2002.

The bulk of the First Baptist Church rising behind emphasizes St. Paul's diminutive size. A smaller wood-frame Baptist church stood there when St. Paul's was built, but it still would have exceeded St. Paul's in size.

B-2
401 North Monroe Street
1896; C. J. Griggs, builder

This well-preserved L-plan house still displays its original delicate decorative millwork in the gable eaves and between the porch columns. In a mechanic's lien dated September 22, 1896, local contractor C. J. Griggs agreed to build for Fount Ray and his wife Johnie [sic] this "one-story frame building of five rooms," according to plans and specifications "furnished by the owners as architects" for the sum of $1,500. The Rays might have found their design inspiration in a similar plan by Abilene builder J. M. Archer that was published in the April 1893 issue of the periodical *National Builder*. On October 9, 1896, the *Enterprise* noted that the "new cottage" was nearly complete and would be "quite handsome when finished." But the Rays never spent much time in their fine new home. In early January 1897, they temporarily relocated to Austin while Fount served as calendar clerk of the state senate during the twenty-fifth session of the Texas legislature, having been nominated by fellow Waxahachie resident, Senator Jack Beall. In 1898, they moved to Dallas and eventually settled in El Paso, where Fount became district manager of Texas Employers Insurance Company. The house remained in the family, however. Fount's brother Melville (M. B.) Ray and wife Ola lived here for many years while he worked as a liveryman and then operated Ray's Garage on North Rogers. The lot originally adjoined the property of their father, pioneer Texas Methodist Episcopal preacher, Rev. Fountain Pitts Ray.

B-3
306 North Rogers Street
Southwestern Bell Telephone Building
1956; Hinger Construction Company, contractors
1966 addition; James T. Taylor & Son, Inc., contractors

The construction of this building in 1956 enabled a major step forward in Waxahachie's communication technology—the installation of a dial system for the local telephone exchange. In fact, in its early years it was called the "Dial Building" in the *Daily Light* even though it housed offices and switchboard operators along with the new switching equipment. When construction started, there were 4,279 telephones in the Waxahachie exchange, and callers had to talk to an operator to make a connection. At the groundbreaking ceremony, Southwestern Bell's district manager stated that only four other Texas cities had buildings like Waxahachie's. (Many others soon appeared across the state.) The switch to dial telephone service occurred on October 6, 1957, when Mayor Maxon Graham placed the first call. Most operators did not immediately lose their jobs with the switchover, for they were still needed for person-to-person and collect calls, but change was on its way. The paper noted that thirty-five operators would continue to be employed "for the present." A two-day open house was scheduled to give the public a chance to see the "dial switchers at work, accurately and rapidly completing your telephone calls."

The building originally consisted of two parts, a one-story section on the right that contained the business office, and the larger two-story section on the left with the distinctive narrow vertical panels of cast stone connecting the first and second floor windows. In 1966 a second floor was added on top of the office, transforming the building into a unified two-story block. A slight variation of brick color at the second floor above the entrance provides visual evidence of the change.

B-4

315 North Rogers Street

First Baptist Church

1957-59; Easterwood & Easterwood, architects; C. L. Henrick & Sons, contractors

The current beige brick sanctuary building designed by Waco and Fort Worth architects Easterwood & Easterwood was the final piece of a complete rebuilding campaign of the First Baptist campus that began in 1948 with an education building designed by Joseph H. Gaylord and Company. This was followed in 1951 by an additional education building with a large assembly room that could be used for services when the 1899 red brick sanctuary building was demolished in preparation for the new sanctuary. When Easterwood & Easterwood were selected for the sanctuary building's design, the firm had strong Baptist connections, since the founder Birch D. Easterwood (1885-1969) designed several buildings on Baylor University's Waco campus, including Pat Neff Hall. In the 1950s, the firm designed multiple Baptist churches for Texas cities, including Galveston, Wichita Falls, and Dallas. The sanctuary's orientation was changed from that of the previous two buildings. The main entrance faces McMillan Street, rather than North Rogers, but a secondary entrance from North Rogers at the base of the dominant corner tower acknowledged the previous orientation. In 2017, First Baptist Church began construction of a new larger campus at US 287 and Broadhead Road.

B-5

400, 402, and 404 North Rogers Street

1911-12

Construction of these pert speculation houses was started in May 1911 by then Dallas County residents and owners of the property, L. R. and Minnie Campbell, and completed in 1912 by Waxahachie cotton dealer and real estate investor Charles L. Penn. A deed of trust between the Campbells and the Waxahachie Lumber Company, and assumed by Penn when he purchased the property in May 1912, provides construction dates. Although one-story pyramidal houses were not unusual in Waxahachie at the time, including a projecting hipped-roof wing was very unusual. Penn and his wife Mayme sold the houses to three separate buyers in late 1912 to early 1913. The owners of 404, Samuel M. Rudolph, furniture store proprietor, and his wife Eula, acquired the other two properties in late 1917 and early 1918, and rented all three houses.

B-6

503 North Rogers Street

c. 1898-1904

The side-gabled, one-story I-house with attached front porch and back wing that appears on the 1898 Sanborn map was, in all likelihood, essentially the house that was on this property when druggist Warren G. Lomax bought it in 1886. By the time the 1904 Sanborn map was completed, the structure had evolved into the current modified L-plan structure with central hipped roof and cross gables. The earlier house may have been demolished and totally replaced, but the gable-roofed back extension suggests that it was remodeled by one of two couples who owned the property between 1898 and 1904. Austin residents B. M. and Maggie Worsham were owners from February 1897 to October 1901, when they sold it to meat market owner David M. Belt and his wife Alice who, in turn, sold it in 1907 to William G. and Zula Johnson. A deacon in the First Baptist Church, Johnson was manager of the Waxahachie Steam Laundry, a "home industry" in operation since the early 1890s. In the late teens, the Johnsons moved this house to the northern edge of their lot, built and moved into the bungalow at 501 North Rogers, and then rented the older house. By the mid-1920s, the Johnsons were living in Los Angeles, California, and renting their Waxahachie properties, which they eventually sold.

B-7
507 North Rogers Street
1903; George Rousseau, "superintending architect"; E. S. Boze, builder

In May 1898, two years after moving from Houston to Waxahachie, grocer Junius E. Leigh and his wife Anna E. purchased this property and lived in an existing three-room L-plan house until late 1903. On December 7, the couple signed a very detailed mechanic's lien with local contractor E. S. Boze "to erect, build and construct . . . a two room addition to a three room cottage, changing and remodeling the three old rooms, making two new rooms, one new hall and two new porches, putting in a new brick foundation under the new addition and the old part of the house, [and] a new stack chimney with two new Cabinet mantels." Boze provided plans and specifications and also named George Rousseau as "superintending architect." Financed by the Standard Savings and Loan Association of Detroit, the $800 job was to be "ready for use and occupancy" by January 1, 1904. The transformation or remodeling of the Leighs' house was not unusual. What is unusual, however, is the detailed documentation that describes what was done to the residence.

The Leighs' new look was a modified L-plan one-story frame dwelling with a front porch that wrapped around the southeast corner façade. The new design incorporated the original front gable, including fish-scale (or imbricated) shingles that also survived a 1912 remodel by contractor H. D. Rankin, which is probably when the Doric porch columns appeared. In a more recent remodel, the nineteenth-century decorative bargeboard in the front gable was lost and the front door replaced.

After moving to Dallas in 1915 for both Leighs to work at Sanger Bros. department store, they sold this property in 1918. As in Waxahachie, Mrs. Leigh pursued her extensive commitment to women's professional clubs and Baptist groups. At the time of her death in April 1941, she was cited as one of few women to have served on the executive board of the Southern Baptist Convention.

B-8
509 North Rogers Street
1898

This house, which like its neighbor at **507 North Rogers** began life in the mid-1880s as a basic L-plan dwelling, has been enlarged, remodeled, and renovated numerous times. In fact, in September 1898, five months after neighborhood resident and investor George C. (and Helen) Groce bought the property in March, the *Dallas Morning News* reported that he was "remodeling cottage on North Rogers street." The footprint of the one-and-a-half story house shown on this lot on the October 1898 Sanborn map was the largest dwelling on the block at that time and is a near-match to the current hipped-roof, cross-gabled structure. The Groces remained in their house at **519 North Rogers**, eventually selling this rental property in 1905. It was either owner-occupied or rented by four subsequent owners until 1920, when railroad engineer John B. Fulton bought the house and lived here with his wife Jane for fifty-one years. A major renovation project begun in 1979 by new owners John and Donna Bailey included removing aluminum siding and reproducing the gingerbread trim found on neighboring houses.

B-9
515 North Rogers Street
c. 1893

This house and its neighbor at 513 North Rogers were once identical twins. Later owners of that house added the gable and dormer windows, but this house retains its original form and much of the original trim. During the 1890s, cottages such as these with a central projecting gable wing were a popular house type for investors building rental property in Waxahachie. Early Sanborn maps for Waxahachie show that there were far more examples of the house type than are extant today. In fact the type, which is usually referred to as a T-plan, was so popular in and identified with Waxahachie that it was called the "Waxahachie cottage" in a period plan book published by the St. Louis architect Herbert C. Chivers in 1901 and subsequent editions.

The popularity of the type was probably due primarily to two characteristics, the first of which was a practical one. The perpendicular orientation of the house to the street required less land than many houses where the plan ran parallel to the street—the replacement of an earlier L-plan house with two "Waxahachie cottages" on this lot being a good example. The second characteristic was an aesthetic one. With its projecting front gable, bay front, and receding sides shaded by an attached porch, the cottage enabled some of the same decorative flourishes found on larger, more flamboyant Queen Anne style houses.

The 1886 bird's-eye view shows this side of North Rogers lined with I-and L-plan houses. Over the years, these structures were either remodeled, as was done at **503** and **507 North Rogers**, or completely replaced, as was done at this location. When bachelor P. N. Gray bought this lot for rental purposes in 1893, he bought one lot with one house for $1,500. When Gray's heirs sold the same piece of property for $2,800 to G. C. Groce in 1897, it was described in the deed as "now divided into two lots" and was shown on the 1898 Sanborn map with a "Waxahachie cottage" on each. The Groces, who lived at **519 North Rogers**, rented the cottages.

B-10
514 North Rogers Street
1901

This house, the last to be built and the only one of six left standing on the east side of North Rogers Street south of Parks Street, has a sad story. It was built in fall 1901 by Alex Sweatt and his wife Fannie Belle Price Sweatt, whose mother, widow Mrs. M. E. Price lived in a two-story house on the corner. In April 1901, Mrs. Price gave her daughter "the garden lot of the place on which I now reside" and which had a seventy-five-foot frontage on Rogers Street. In September, the Sweatts signed a $1,200 mortgage "for making certain improvements" and built their house immediately. On December 21, twenty-year-old Fannie Belle died several days after giving birth to Lynn Alexander, the couple's only child. Less than one year later, on October 6, 1902, twenty-six-year-old Alex died of Bright's disease in his mother-in-law's house; his own house had been rented in August. Lynn Alexander grew up in his grandmother's house surrounded by aunts and uncles. He received the rental income from his parents' house and once the estate was settled, became the owner.

The house is an intact, unaltered example of a modified L-plan house, but of an unusual type that can almost pass as an L-plan to a casual passerby. Only a slight jog in the roof line and in the porch reflect the central hipped roof section of a modified L-plan. When built in September 1901, the house duplicated one in the next block north at **604 North Rogers** that had been constructed in May of that year. The Sanborn maps of 1909 show that this was more than just copying the façade. Both houses shared a very distinctive footprint, particularly in the back, with an L-shaped porch, a tiny projecting room (perhaps a bathroom) on one side, and a traditional rear wing on the other, but—with a jog in it. The turned columns, scalloped brackets, and trim on the front porch are original. A recent renovation included a major addition to the rear.

B-11
519 North Rogers Street
1887; 1934

During the years 1887-1902, attorney G. C. Groce and his Corsicana bride Helen M. Halbert bought and sold the properties now numbered 507 through 523 North Rogers. Married in December 1886, the couple's first homestead was at this location in an L-plan cottage that they built in summer 1887 and sold in 1901. Although the house has been extensively remodeled, the basic L-plan, with a front-facing gable and side wing, is clearly discernible. The present façade dates from 1934, when Waxahachie merchant D. S. Roth owned the property. An article appearing in the August 8 issue of the *Daily Light* noted that the house was "one of the most attractive places that has been remodeled and repainted . . . Mr. Roth has shown what can be done with modern architecture and improvements."

B-12
523 North Rogers Street
c. 1895

This is one of those structures for which documents offer only clues, not a specific construction date, but which, when combined with the house type and decorative details (even though some are replacements), lead to the conclusion that this is another example where a smaller house evolved into a larger modified L-plan cottage. When businessman B. R. Moffett bought the property as an investment in 1888, there was a house on the lot, probably the one shown on the 1886 bird's-eye view. In 1893, Moffett sold the property to adjacent property owners G. C. and Helen Groce who, one year later, sold it to Dr. Charles W. Simpson. The young doctor and his wife E. Frances Moffatt Simpson relocated from Ferris to Waxahachie in spring 1892, the local paper noting that Dr. Simpson "has just returned from taking special lectures in New York." Within two years, he became county health inspector, a position he held for several years. The Simpsons were a very social couple, and it was probably during the early years of their ownership that this house assumed much of its present appearance. By 1900, they were renting the property and living on West Main Street.

The Simpsons sold the property in 1905 to W. D. and Byrdee Anderson. It was a convenient location for Mr. Anderson, who had only a short walk along Monroe Street to the Waxahachie Ice Company, where he was manager. In 1909, the Andersons traded convenience for a more fashionable address by selling their North Rogers house to traveling salesman Early W. and Myrtle Rice, and moving to the West End. Mr. Rice was noted for his horticultural hobby which, in 1929, featured 350 rose bushes in the yard.

The modified L-plan structure is distinguished with bays on both the front and south sides and a wraparound porch that extends the full length of the south façade. Decorative details including fish-scale shingles on the gables, jig-sawn corner brackets under the gable ends, and cornice dentils and jig sawn brackets reflect late-nineteenth century construction. The porch was restored circa 1980.

B-13
600 North Rogers Street
1923

When widow Ada B. King bought this property in 1913, she also acquired a U-shaped house built in 1887 by the previous owner, Emma B. Davis. For Miss Davis, one of the most independent and business-minded women in Waxahachie at the time (as documented by local newspaper articles), the sale of this property signaled her eventual move to Dallas. For Mrs. King, the purchase also signified a major change in her life—moving from a dispersed rural district into town with her three children just a few months after her physician husband Harry King died. Ten years later, in May 1923, Mrs. King contracted Fort Worth builder H. H. Harbin to supply building materials costing $3,000 that were needed to replace the older structure with this six-room house "of standard construction." Indeed, the house has all the characteristics of a modest plan-book bungalow with its double-front gables, tapered porch columns on brick piers, paired windows, triangular brackets under the eaves, and exposed roof rafters. In February 1925, Mrs. King took out a second loan, presumably to build the similar bungalow at 602 North Rogers. Both houses are shown on the October 1925 Sanborn map.

Various sources indicate that Mrs. King struggled financially. In addition to her rental properties, Mrs. King worked as a private family nurse and hearing aid agent, the latter her occupation in 1930 when she was rooming in a house in Ennis. In February 1931, the Waxahachie paper reported that she had moved back from Ennis and once again was living at this address. County records document that Mrs. King did not make it through the Depression with her property: it was sold at public auction in 1937.

B-14
603 North Rogers Street
1909-10; H. A. Overbeck, architect

This house is known to many locals as the "Durham House," which was the name of both the family that built the house and the popular restaurant that was located here in the 1970s and 1980s. The restaurant received national attention with a commendation in *Esquire Magazine*. When dry goods merchant S. W. Durham and his wife Phoebe bought the sizeable corner lot in 1904, they moved into an earlier residence to which they "made some substantial improvements." The 1909 Sanborn map (the first to record this area) shows a vacant lot at this location, while the 1910 census lists the Durhams as renters on Monroe Street, indicating that they had relocated temporarily so the older residence could be demolished (or moved) and their new house built.

The one-and-a-half-story pyramidal structure that the Durhams built was a sophisticated architect-designed version of what was considered Waxahachie's most fashionable house type at the time. Graced with a covered porch on three sides, the most distinguishing feature of the house was the Mission style parapet on the front dormer, a detail that was repeated on Durham's downtown store built on the east side of the square in early 1912. Not surprisingly, both buildings were designed by Dallas architect H. A. Overbeck. To get a sense of how the house would have appeared with its original porch, view the house at **716 West Main**, also designed by Overbeck with similar massing, a pyramidal roof, and its porch still wrapped around three sides. In 1919, the Durhams moved to Virginia Avenue and sold this property to bank president Ben C. Kelly and his wife Ella, who moved in with six children according to the 1920 census. Over the years, the house was converted into three apartments before being adapted for restaurant use. Karl and Annette Goss purchased it in 1991 and restored it back to a single-family residence.

B-15
604 North Rogers Street
1901

Twenty-six-year-old Mary Browning, feme sole, received this parcel as part of her inheritance from the estates of her grandmother Mary Paulina Davis and her mother Fidelia Davis Browning in 1901. The Davises were one of Waxahachie's pioneer families, with major land and business investments that extended far beyond Ellis County. Since she was living with her widowed grandfather Robert A. Davis on West Jefferson Street, and since it was considered improper for a young, single woman to live in a house alone, she built this house on the lot as a rental property. The *Enterprise* noted on May 24, 1901, that Mr. and Mrs. Fletcher Norton had moved into the "cottage erected for them by Miss Mary Browning." In February 1906, Miss Browning married lumberyard manager Eli Hastings Ackley. Early in their marriage, the couple moved to Canyon City, where Eli was president of a lumber company. Widowed in 1914, Mrs. Ackley and her two sons moved back to Waxahachie in fall 1920 and lived in this house while building a more modern house—the double-gable bungalow next door at 608 North Rogers. The family's first listing at the new address was in the 1924-25 city directory. Mrs. Ackley stayed there until the late 1930s when she moved into another, larger house that she built on Ferris Avenue. Mrs. Ackley served as a trustee of the Waxahachie Independent School District and president of the local PTA, and she organized the first African American PTA in Waxahachie. She died in 1961 of injuries from an automobile accident. The tree with twisted trunks in the front yard is a fruitless mulberry, but the patient person who trained the trunks to grow in their sinuous path is unknown. The house at **514 N. Rogers**, built four months after this one, duplicated its form and footprint.

B-16
607 North Rogers Street
1901

On October 4, 1901, the weekly *Enterprise* reported that the surprise party held at "the elegant new home" of George C. Newton on September 27 not only celebrated his daughter Nell's birthday but also formally opened "the hospitable mansion . . . to the social circle." (There was a mother, but the mother, as was often the case, was not referenced in the article.) Newton was a Kentucky-born, well-established forty-seven-year-old jeweler with a shop on the square when he bought this property in 1893. He lived in an existing house with his wife Ella, their five children, and his mother before replacing it in 1901 with this two-story modified L-plan dwelling. Queen Anne detailing and trim on the curved two-story front porch and fish-scale shingles on the gable fronts and porch divide seem appropriate for a house that enjoyed an active social life—if newspaper reports are any indication. The Newton heirs sold the house in 1918 to meat market owner Sam Nycum.

B-17
610 North Rogers Street
1923; Ramsey Brothers, builder

On August 23, 1923, the *Daily Light* noted that this "handsome eight room brick veneer residence" was nearing completion. Built for Ed Gentsch and his wife Lillie Mae, the bungalow is distinguished by a generous front gable with dentil detailing, an unusual brick-veneer rather than a standard frame façade, and a porte-cochère. Gentsch moved to Waxahachie around 1910 and opened the "Airdome" theater in 1913. He continued in the motion picture business as president of the Waxahachie Amusement Company through the 1920s. The couple moved to Vernon, Texas, in 1933.

B-18
611 North Rogers Street
1914

On June 16, 1914, Sarah Wyatt Thompson and the Waxahachie Lumber Co. signed a Deed of Trust whereby the latter agreed to finance this house for an initial cost of $3,000 that eventually totaled $4,800. (Mrs. Thompson was identified as feme sole in the document, since she was divorced.) Construction obviously began immediately, because the footprint of her new residence is shown on the October 14, 1914 Sanborn map. It replaced the mid-1880s L-plan house where she had lived since acquiring the property in 1897 from her brother John F. Wyatt.

Mrs. Thompson's bungalow—a classic example of a modest one-story frame bungalow with intersecting gable roofs—is virtually unchanged. The gable roof running parallel to the street extends from the south-side porte cochère to the north-side porch, and gives the house a sense of generous proportions. The front gable with overhanging eaves and triangular brackets frames the primary single-door entrance, while a recessed intersecting gable marks the roof peak of the rear extension on the house. Unfortunately, Mrs. Thompson's agreement with the lumber company does not name either a contractor or an architect. Family members say that the same contractor built this house and John Wyatt's house on the corner at **619 North Rogers**. The design most likely came from one of the many plan books that the lumber company kept on hand.

Mrs. Thompson was an important and very active member of the First Baptist Church located just a few short blocks away. Newspaper clippings in her scrapbook document that she frequently interacted with visiting ministers and their families, so it was probably no surprise to the community when she married a pioneer minister and formidable figure in the Baptist Church, the Rev. B. W. N. Simms, on January 27, 1920. The Simmses lived here throughout their married life. He died at age eighty-five in 1934 and she at age eighty-one in 1938. A 1921 photograph showing the couple and Lucile, their African American employee, in front of the house illustrates how little the house has changed. However, what is most noticeable in the picture, an impressive cedar arbor arched over the sidewalk leading up to the house, no longer exists.

B-19
615 North Rogers Street
1885; A. J. Kibler, builder
c. 1910-20 alterations

Educator Presley J. Herndon and his wife, Eva May Wyatt Herndon, purchased this property on November 10, 1897, just five days after Mrs. Herndon's sister, Sarah Wyatt Thompson, bought the property at **611 North Rogers**. However, unlike Mrs. Thompson, who eventually replaced her 1880s dwelling with a more fashionable bungalow, the Herndon family chose to periodically update and enlarge the picturesque cottage that A. J. Kibler built in 1885 for newspaperman E. C. Huckabee and his wife Kate. Originally, the Huckabee-Herndon dwelling was a basic L-plan house with an ample supply of Victorian trim on the gable front, the three-bay porch that curved around the south corner of the building, and the roofline cresting. The 1914 Sanborn map documents several changes. The side porch had been enclosed, which is probably when turned porch posts were replaced with heavier Doric columns, and a small addition that would become larger was attached to the northeast corner.

Married in December 1895, Presley and Eva May lived their entire married life, with the exception of those first two years, in this house. Eva May, daughter of Robert M. and Amanda Wyatt, was born in Waxahachie in 1873 and attended Baylor Female College at Belton. Presley J. Herndon, born in Kentucky in 1865, came to Texas in 1891 to visit his grandparents and while here, accepted a position to teach sixth grade, met Eva May, and never left. (Most likely, he met Eva May before accepting the job.) He remained with city schools, including twenty-six years as principal of Waxahachie High School, until retiring in 1933. Two daughters, Evelyn and Rosabel, were also lifetime teachers and lifetime residents of this house. A 1903 Herndon family photograph shows what was still essentially the Huckabee façade and a cedar arch over the sidewalk that may be a Herndon-Wyatt touch, as one appears in a later photograph taken in front of Mrs. Thompson's house at **611 South Rogers**.

Across the street, 614 and 616 North Rogers were built in the 1880s by J. E. Prince for rental houses. Subsequent owners over the years have altered the once identical L-plan houses. At 616, a hipped roof appears to have been built over the L-crossing of the two gable roofs, giving the appearance of the modified L-plan cottages that were popular in the late nineteenth and early twentieth centuries.

B-20
619 North Rogers Street

1915-16; Brickey & Brickey, architects

John F. Wyatt's decision to build this substantial two-story Prairie style residence capped a three-year period of major change in his life. In February 1912, at the age of fifty-one, he married for the first time. In August 1913 his first and only child was born, and he retired from business soon after. In March 1914 he bought this lot next to his sisters' houses at **615** and **611 North Rogers**. By November 1915 ground was broken for the new house, the first and only house Wyatt would build for himself after a long, successful career in real estate and loans. As a bachelor businessman, he lived in boarding houses after his father, pioneer Waxahachie surveyor and land agent Robert M. Wyatt, died in 1889. In fact, he probably became acquainted with his future wife Emma Cumby when he lived in a boarding house owned by her husband J. M. Cumby. When their romance began is unknown, but in 1910, while keeping a boarding house in Dallas, Emma filed for divorce. Two years later, on Valentine's Day, she and Wyatt were married in Dallas. The newly married couple settled in Waxahachie on Kaufman Street and kept a fairly low profile, at least judging from the newspapers, until after her first husband, who had remained in Waxahachie, died of a heart attack in May 1913.

Since this corner lot faces West Marvin and North Rogers Streets, the new house joined a series of architect-designed Prairie style show places that had been built on West Marvin, beginning with **415 West Marvin** in 1906. Prime among those was **603 West Marvin**, built by another successful real estate businessman, E. C. McCartney, in 1913. That house, designed by C. D. Hill, inevitably would have influenced the Wyatts, as they planned their new home with Dallas architects Brickey & Brickey two years later. (Silas Brickey and his sons designed many homes in Oak Cliff around this time.) Although the Wyatt house used wood siding rather than brick, as in the McCartney house, other details are duplicated, such as the dark brick porch supports and balustrades, and the urns resting on the entrance bay supports. The house may have lacked the fine details and expensive materials of McCartney's house, but it would have impressed visitors with its visible pride and exuberance, due to its placement on the lot and its scale, as well as its expansive double entrances, ready to welcome both family and community. John and Emma both stayed in the house until their deaths in 1932 and 1957, respectively. It remained in the family until 1998, when Louis and Linda Brown began a major restoration.

520 North College Street before the Neoclassical makeover.

B-21
520 North College Street
1920

A major Neoclassical-style remodeling in 1920 almost completely hides the 1894 Queen Anne style house that banker John J. Metcalfe had D. A. Cook build for him according to plans by mail-order architect George F. Barber. Metcalfe sold the house to T. O. Cheatham in 1904. On February 21, 1920, the *Daily Light* reported that alderman T. O. Cheatham contemplated remodeling his College Street home so that it would be "converted into a modern home." Newspapers of the time tended to credit male homeowners with any building or remodeling plans, but it is very possible that Cheatham's daughter Ivy was the mastermind behind these plans. After obtaining an MA in history from Columbia University in New York in June 1919, she was back in Texas and could well have felt that the house her family had purchased in 1904 was hopelessly old-fashioned. The makeover moved the entrance door to the center and regularized the window openings for proper classical symmetry. It also removed as many traces of the Queen Anne style as possible, including two dormers, decorative turned woodwork on the second-floor balcony, an entire second-floor balcony on the north side, the first-floor wraparound porch, and the octagonal porch extension. The slight projection of the current entrance and the screened balcony above incorporate what was a first-floor bay window and second-floor balcony, minus its turned wood decoration. Ivy and her father both actively pursued public service. Mr. Cheatham served as alderman for thirteen years and mayor for four years, while Ivy was the high school's assistant principal and Dean of Women. Ivy continued to live in the house until her death in 1963 at the age of seventy-seven.

B-22
516 North College Street
1920

Although new Victorian ornaments on the current front porch disguise the fact, this house was built in the Prairie style and probably originally had square columns with sloping sides similar to those next door at **512 North College**. The dormer may be a later addition also. The house was probably built in fall 1920, for on December 11 of that year the *Daily Light* reported a party in "the handsome new home of Mrs. C. M. Supple on College street." City Attorney Charles M. Supple bought the property from the Yeager estate in July 1898, several months before his marriage to Maud Burk. According to the newspaper, he made improvements to the house at that time, but after twenty years, the couple rebuilt in a more up-to-date style. Supple, who was born in Milledgeville, Georgia, in 1863, came to Texas in the late 1880s and taught school and studied law in Waco and Austin before coming to Waxahachie in late summer 1889. In addition to two terms as Waxahachie's city attorney, he served as a special district judge on several occasions and as president of the Ellis County Bar Association.

B-23
515 North College Street
1905

W. G. and Maggie Reagor, along with their daughter, lived on rented farm property outside Waxahachie before buying this lot for $700 in May 1905 and building this cottage, which was the couple's maiden venture into Waxahachie real estate. A comparison with its next-door neighbor at **513 North College** shows this house to be a simpler version of the popular modified L-plan house. According to the 1907 directory, W. G. was working as an oil company agent while living at this address. The following year, the couple sold the property for $2,100—not a bad return on their initial investment—and moved to a house on Williams Street.

B-24
513 North College Street
1901; E. S. Boze, builder

The *Enterprise* reported in November 1901 that E. S. Boze was building this "handsome cottage" for sisters Mrs. Sammie (S. M.) Sharp and Miss Annie Ransom. Built on a half-acre lot that the Ransom family had owned since the late 1880s, the house was a modified L-plan residence distinguished by two front-facing gables on each side of the hipped roof dormer. At the time of the 1900 census, Sammie, a widow with two young children ages three and one, and Annie, who worked as a stenographer, comprised the household. No question that Ransom women were resourceful individuals. Both Sammie and a third sister Helen were working for the telephone company in the late 1880s. In 1890, Sammie married telegraph operator Theodore M. Sharp in McKinney. In 1892, Helen opened her own insurance agency in Waxahachie and was still in business when she died in November 1896, her obituary stating that she had been "thrown upon her own resources . . . to make her own way." The same was true for Sammie, who returned to Waxahachie after her husband died, probably in early 1899. Once her house was completed, Sammie supported her family by renting rooms and selling women's specialty clothing, while also investing in US bonds, General Mills and Westinghouse stock, and local real estate. When she died in 1950, her son Ransom Sharp inherited her estate.

B-25
512 North College Street
1922; H. H. Hardin, builder

Given the history of other houses on North College, there might be a temptation to assume that this is another remodel, but it is not. A front-page article in the *Daily Light* on July 24, 1922, reported that the previous house on this property, bought by George F. and Henrietta Smith in 1912, "had been wrecked" and that a new two-story residence would replace it. On the same day, July 24, the Smiths contracted Fort Worth builder H. H. Hardin to construct a "new house to have wood shingle roof; fourteen rooms, and the necessary porches and windows" for $5,000, to be paid in one note due in sixty days. With its straightforward Prairie style, the house breaks with its neighbors at **508** and **418 North College** by avoiding any Neoclassical elements.

The Smiths had been living in Waxahachie since late 1905, with George first working as a cotton buyer and then a tax collector. The 1920 census lists him as an oil company salesman, and that job evidently financed the new construction that replaced the previous house at this address, where the Smiths had been living since 1912. George switched to selling real estate in the late 1920s, a risky occupation when the Depression hit. In late 1934, George was working in Wichita County, but the couple was still claiming this house as their homestead. The 1936 city directory shows Henrietta, but not George, at this address, which is listed as apartments. George reappears here in the 1939 directory, working as a watchman, but that year marked the end of their struggle to maintain ownership of the house. It was sold by a loan corporation, and the Smiths moved to Wichita Falls.

B-26
508 North College Street
1919-20

In August 1919, Herbert L. Crosby and his wife Anna bought a one-story house on this property, referred to as the "Reagor house." The *Daily Light* reported in early December that they were remodeling. In February 1920 it noted that the "modern home of H. L. Crosby . . . is nearing completion" and when finished it would be "one of the most attractive residences in the city." The expanded and remodeled result blends two popular styles of the time, with the Prairie style represented in the wide overhanging eaves. Their neighbors' remodeling of **418** and **520 North College** in a Neoclassical style probably influenced the Crosbys' decision to include a full-height porch with the Neoclassical columns shown here. The Crosbys moved from Winnsboro (north of Tyler) to Waxahachie in mid-summer 1919 for Herbert to take over as owner and manager of a retail hardware store. All did not go smoothly for the family. In March 1921, Mrs. Crosby applied to have her husband declared insane, and in 1925, he died at the North Texas Insane Asylum in Terrell. Herbert's brother took over as owner and manager of Crosby Hardware Company, while Mrs. Crosby continued living here and, like many people (often widows), rented out part of her house. The 1936 city directory listed the Crosby Apartment House at this address. She died in 1949.

B-27
503-505, 507, and 509-511 North College Street
1924-28, Ye Planry Corp., architect

This unusual threesome of brick residential structures was built for dentist Dr. D. M. Colquitt and his wife Mossie. They built the duplex at 503-505 North College first, in 1924, and probably lived in half of it while their home at 507 was being built in 1925. In March of that year, they contracted with O. B. Bennett to build for $7,000 "one brick veneer eight room house, with hall, bath room, breakfast room, front and back porches." They must have liked being landlords, for in October 1927, they contracted with Cameron & Co. to build for $2,500 another duplex on the other side of their house, 509-511 North College. The only difference in the duplexes is the design of the small roofs over the entrance doors. All three buildings were based on designs included in a catalogue of house plans published by the Dallas firm Ye Planry Corporation in the early 1920s. Dr. Colquitt graduated from Baylor Dental School in Dallas in 1919, and the couple lived in Italy briefly before settling in Waxahachie. They lived in their brick bungalow throughout their lifetimes—he died in 1957, she in 1965.

B-28
418 North College Street
1887; c. 1910

Blacksmith A. S. Farley and his wife Sonora Wise Farley bought this lot in 1878 and either built a house or moved a house onto the property. Nine years later, on August 19, the *Enterprise* reported that Farley had moved his "old" residence to the rear of his lot in order to build a new two-story one. By mid-December, the new house—"one of the handsomest and most substantially constructed" in the city—was nearing completion at the cost of about $3,500. It is worth noting that when the Farleys built their house, it was adjacent to the Fort Worth & New Orleans railroad tracks that ran along Parks Street. Railroad mania was at its height, and living near—even practically on—the tracks did not discourage upscale real estate development.

The 1887 two-story L-plan house has elaborate bargeboard gable ends. The projecting front gallery with Doric columns replaced the original gallery probably around 1910, definitely in the years framed by the 1909 and 1914 Sanborn insurance maps.

The Farleys, having no children of their own, raised three Farley nephews here—and it was a lively household if the number of events for young people reported in the newspapers is any indication. After A. S. died in 1904, Sonora's sister Laura Wise Bush and her husband, T. C. Bush, an evangelist and pastor of the Gathered Brethern, moved into the house. When Sonora died in 1934, her obituary noted that she had lived at this location for almost fifty-seven years. The family sold the property after Reverend Bush died in 1948.

B-29
414 North College Street
1899

In mid-October 1899, the *Enterprise* reported that "Mrs. Nash's former cottage on College street presents an imposing appearance since its conversion into a two-story building of modern design," which refers to the house as seen today. The "former cottage" was a one-story four-room rectangular house that was like most early houses built along College Street and that Lu Nash and her attorney husband N. J. Nash built after purchasing the property in August 1874. The Nashes and Lu's brother Anson Rainey, also a lawyer, came to Waxahachie in 1873. Both men assumed prominent positions in the community. Anson eventually became a district judge while N. J., after being elected Waxahachie mayor in 1874, resigned in 1879 to become Ellis County Attorney, the position he held when he died in 1881 at age thirty-one.

Mrs. Nash, also thirty-one, was left with a household of three young children (one less than a year old), her mother-in-law, a niece, and a servant. By fall 1883, she had opened a school in her backyard and for the next eighteen years taught either in her private school or a public institution. According to the local paper, in fall 1889 she enlarged the "school room" to accommodate sixty-three pupils. The 1898 Sanborn map shows that, by this time, the school was a one-story rectangular addition about the same size as, and set perpendicular to, the front cottage and connected by a passageway.

Just before classes began in fall 1899, Mrs. Nash made changes to her residence. The front-facing gable extension on the east side and a second story were added to the "front cottage." By October 20, her school enrollment was fifty-three students, while the enlarged front house, according to the 1900 census, accommodated Mrs. Nash, three children, four nieces, and a nephew ranging in ages from fourteen to twenty-three, two of whom were teachers.

Mrs. Nash and her heirs sold the property in 1901, and Mrs. Nash, unable to find an alternative location, closed her school. After two intervening owners and demolition of the school room by 1904, local attorney Mark Smith bought the property in 1906. Smith served several terms as Ellis County Judge and, according to his 1956 obituary, was known as the dean of the Ellis County Bar Association. The Smith family sold the property in 1992. With the exception of minor details, the street façade appears today as it was refashioned in 1899.

B-30
402 North College Street
Central Presbyterian Church
1918-19; C. D. Hill, architect

C. D. Hill's design for Waxahachie's Central Presbyterian Church almost duplicates his Oak Lawn Methodist Church built in Dallas from 1911 to 1915. Waxahachie's version lacks the extensive terracotta on the side towers of the Dallas church (probably a budget issue), but the grand central entrance with unified terracotta door surrounds continuing into the Perpendicular Gothic window tracery above is an almost exact copy. A substantial education wing in the rear, with multiple rectangular double-hung stained-glass windows to provide summer ventilation, contains classrooms, meeting rooms, and offices. Hill had completed a majestic Beaux-Arts city hall for Dallas in 1914, making him one of the most prominent architects in North Texas, but having designed Waxahachie's Rogers Hotel in 1912, he was not a stranger to Waxahachie.

The church that commissioned this building began as the Cumberland Presbyterian Church of Waxahachie in 1853. The congregation worshiped in shared facilities before constructing their first building near the square in 1869-70, although they also shared that building with the Baptists for a few years. In 1892, that site was exchanged for this one on College Street, and the old building was moved to this location. Trinity University's move to Waxahachie in 1902 brought more congregants to the church, and a larger church building was completed in 1905, the same year that Cumberland Presbyterian changed its name to Central Presbyterian. But even that Neoclassical style structure of white pressed brick, costing $18,000, could not keep up with the continued growth and prosperity of the church. In 1914, the church Session began the process of planning for what would become the current building, though they did not pass a resolution to engage architects until late 1916. (There also may have been an unacknowledged competition between Waxahachie's Presbyterian affiliations. The First Presbyterian Church, a Southern Presbyterian church, also was making plans for a new building on West Main around the same time, and they managed to complete their building first.) The Central Presbyterian building eventually cost over $112,000, with $70,000 of that funded by Waxahachie banker and investor P. A. Chapman, whose son Homer Chapman provided $5,000 for the organ. The first service was held on Easter Sunday, 1919.

B-31
316 North College Street
United States Post Office
1966-67; Fincher Construction Co., Dallas

The dual need for more space to process mail and to park cars prompted Waxahachie and the US Postal Service to build a new post office in the mid-1960s. Fortunately, Waxahachie, unlike some communities, chose NOT to demolish its landmark post office building at **401 South Rogers**. Selection of this new site on the corner of College and Oldham Streets did require demolition of the 1896 Major Penn house, but the trade-off kept the facility in downtown Waxahachie and on the north side of downtown, the direction in which the city was growing.

The bidding process took place in spring 1965. Terms of the bid followed the government's "lease plan," whereby the successful bidder bought the land, constructed the building according to postal specifications, and then leased it to the department for twenty years, with an option to purchase the property or extend the lease at the end of that period. The agreement meant that (1) the department's capital investment was limited to postal equipment and (2) the property remained on the tax rolls. Dallas contractor Carlton J. Fincher was awarded the job based on his low bid of a yearly rental of $17,727. Fincher had built other post offices, including one of similar size in Lufkin. The flat-roofed one-story brick post office in Waxahachie opened in late March 1967.

Waxahachie once again debated the pros and cons of keeping the main post office in the downtown area before renovating and expanding the structure in 2008-09. Obviously, the pros won, and in 2011, it became postal property.

B-32
200 Oldham Avenue
1887

In 1873, Major G. J. and Susan Penn bought from E. W. Rogers two lots on the south side of what was then called Mill Street. The lots extended from College Street to the Rogers Spring Branch. Mill Street was renamed Oldham Avenue, but the east-west street was so closely identified with the Penn family that the local newspaper sometimes called it Penn Street. While the Penns lived on the corner lot with College Street frontage, over time they built several houses on the second or back lot—the lot to the east of Jackson Street—for both rental and family use. The *Waxahachie Enterprise* kept track of Major Penn's Oldham-Jackson real estate transactions. In April 1887, he rented one of his existing properties in the neighborhood to Thomas J. Middleton, the new owner and editor of another Waxahachie paper, the *Ellis County Mirror*. In September, Penn built this house for his daughter and son-in-law, Belle and Dick [Clark D.] Pickett. Two years later, in fall 1889, the Picketts moved to Main Street and the Middleton family, in turn, "moved into the place vacated by Pickett." The Penns then sold this corner property to B. R. Moffett, who continued renting to the Middletons until January 1894, when they became the owners.

The residence that the Middletons bought was atypical of most houses built in Waxahachie in the late nineteenth century. Most were built with a center-hall floor plan and centered front entrance. Few were built with a side-hall floor plan, this being one of the exceptions. The offset primary entrance opens into a hallway that runs alongside two rooms and accommodates the staircase to the second-floor hall. With its squared front façade, low hipped roof, wide cornice band (missing the brackets), and off-centered long, narrow front windows, the house had a distinctly Italianate flavor in its early years. The square ridge at the peak of the roof suggests that the house may have had, at one time, a square cupola or a balustrade, also typical Italianate features.

When the 1900 census was taken, Middleton, his wife Jennie Shook Middleton, and their six children, ages ten through twenty-eight, were living here. The Middletons had married in 1871 in their native Tennessee, where he graduated from Cumberland University and taught school, a profession that brought the family to Texas in 1876 and eventually to Mountain Peak. By 1887, Middleton, then a thirty-nine-year-old father with seven children who was apparently looking for a career change, bought the *Ellis County Mirror* and moved his family to Waxahachie. His success as a newspaperman was due in part to his large family, who staffed the paper. In addition to becoming one leg of the city's "editorial tripod" and an officer in the Texas press association, Middleton was politically active—unsuccessfully running for office on the Democratic ticket—and a champion chess player. He died in August 1912. Middleton family members and relatives continued living in the house until 1982.

Originally, the house had a full-width one-story front porch which was replaced, according to Sanborn maps, with a wraparound porch circa 1900. This house is very similar to the O. F. Parks house at **604 West Jefferson** that was also built in 1887.

B-33
201 Oldham Avenue
1901

When Mrs. M. J. Cooke purchased this lot for $825 on September 30, 1901, she apparently had an action plan in mind. Less than four months later, in January 1902, she sold the lot, along with this newly built structure, for $4,500 to Major Penn's son, Jackson Lee Penn, who quickly resold the property for the same amount to the Waxahachie District of the Northwest Texas Conference of the Methodist Episcopal Church South (now the Methodist Church). For over forty years, the ten-room house served as the parsonage for the district presiding elder.

At first glance, the structure appears to be a duplex because of its scale and two front-facing gables. Indeed, similar plans and elevations published in period house-plan books were usually reserved for two-family houses, but this building and Waxahachie's other similar example at **201 East University** were both built as single-family residences. The full-width one-story front porch wrapping around both sides is original to the house, as is the upper balcony extending over the single-door primary entrance.

B-34
205 Oldham Avenue
1904

On February 26, 1904, the *Enterprise* noted that the "Hon. W. H. Fears is having a handsome cottage home erected on Oldham Avenue next to the district parsonage." The Fears's cottage is one of several modified L-plan houses that share the simplified details and classical porch columns found in many of the pyramidal houses popular at the time. It is an exception because it also includes an entrance door flanked by sidelights, which was typical in pyramidal houses, but seldom in modified L-plans.

Lawyer Fears was well known to *Enterprise* readers who had kept abreast of the opinionated and popular attorney's activities since the mid-1880s. Born in Georgia in 1854, Fears migrated to Texas in 1871 but spent the years 1874-1877 living in the far West. He then returned to Texas, was admitted to the bar in 1878, and opened a joint practice in Ennis in 1883. He was active in the Democratic Party, fought prohibition vociferously, was charged for aggravated assault for a shooting in Ennis, and spent considerable time attending county court in Waxahachie. When elected county attorney in 1892—a position he held for four years—Fears and his wife Annie M. Moore bought a house in Waxahachie's West End. In 1896 they built a large two-story house at **1500 West Main**, also in the West End. Being members of the Methodist Church may have influenced their decision to move from west to east Waxahachie (the reverse of what most Waxahachians did) and to build next door to the district parsonage.

B-35
208 Oldham Avenue
1902; McCanless & Ingram, builders

On July 4, 1902, the *Enterprise* reported that "Maj. G. J. Penn and son, Charley, have finished moving into their elegant home on Oldham Avenue which has just been completed." Undoubtedly, the major's wife Susan and Charley's wife Mayme also moved to the new abode but, as was often the case at the time, newspaper reports did not acknowledge the distaff half. Certainly, all the Penns were involved in the family's real estate maneuvers during the six months leading up to the move. In December 1901, the older Penns sold the now-empty lot to the west of this house to their daughter Belle and her husband Clark D. (Dick) Pickett, who built a two-story dwelling. (That structure burned in December 1934.) In July 1902, the Penns sold their imposing 1896 architect-designed house on the corner of College and Oldham to their oldest son, Jackson L. Penn, which suggests that construction of this house began early in the year.

The July 1902 article noted that the house had five rooms plus bath and pantry rooms, sewerage and water connections, three fireplaces with tile hearths and handsome mantels, "conveniently" arranged closets, and a large hall extending through the building. Exterior details were ignored except for the "nicely screened" back gallery. Architecturally, the Penns' new residence on Oldham represents a transitional style. Some features are identified with Victorian or Queen Anne houses of the late nineteenth century, such as the high-pitched hipped roof and twin front gables with decorative fish-scale shingles and pent roofs. Other features, however, are indicators of the early twentieth century, i.e., the single plane of the front façade, the low-slung entry pediment, and the single-door primary entrance with transom and sidelights, found in many pyramidal houses of the period as well as other house forms with Colonial Revival and Neoclassical details.

After Major Penn died in March 1905, Mrs. Penn and their son and daughter-in-law continued living here until March 1909, when they sold the property to Waxahachie postmaster William G. McClain and his wife Pearl. The McClains added to the back of the house, sold a strip of land extending to the creek in 1912 (now the site of 300 Oldham, built in 1985), and sold this house in 1918. The house has a long association with Lula Satterfield, a teacher in the Waxahachie school system for over twenty-five years. Miss Satterfield bought the house in 1923; her estate sold it in 1960, the same year in which she died.

B-36
304 Oldham Avenue
1893; c. 1905

This modified L-plan one story dwelling sits on the site of the Farmers Flour Mill that was built circa 1883, when Oldham Avenue was known as Mill Street. "The Mill property," as it was called in deed records, originally extended from the east side of the creek to McLain Street, but when miller F. A. Maines sold the mill in 1884, he kept his residence on the corner lot. After several sales transactions and unsuccessful attempts to operate the mill, it was demolished in April 1893 and the property was sold in July to confectioner William J. Owen, who built the simple L-plan house shown on the 1898 Sanborn map.

In March 1905, B. L. and Carrie A. Cornwell bought the property for $900 and, in turn, sold it for $1,600 in January 1907, an indication that the house assumed its larger, present form with hipped roof, cross gables, and L-shaped porch during the Cornwells' ownership. Commission merchant Ulysses T. Buckner bought the property on January 28, just two days before his marriage to May Middleton who, as the oldest child of newspaperman Thomas J. Middleton, had lived at the corner of Oldham and Jackson with her family since 1887. Indeed, theirs was a neighborhood romance because Buckner, according to the 1900 census, lived with his sister Sallie and her husband J. F. Strickland at the corner of Oldham and Williams Streets. The *Enterprise* reported that the couple would move to their own residence one month after their wedding, indicating that they also made some changes to the house.

The Buckners, who were active members of Central Presbyterian Church, lived here throughout their lives: Mr. Buckner died in 1937, Mrs. Buckner in 1956. Their only son, Ulysses T. Jr., moved to the Middleton house at **200 Oldham** in the early 1960s, and upon his death in 1982, left a portion of his estate to the Sims Library for children's programs.

B-37
305 Oldham Avenue
1916; Ye Planry Co., architect
D. D. Lawrence, builder

After buying this property in 1911, cement contractor Joe C. Jarrett and his wife Alberta lived in the existing house until it burned in spring 1916. On August 5, the Jarretts contracted Robertson County builder and Joe's step-brother, D. D. Lawrence, to construct in sixty days and for $1,800 "a one story frame house of five rooms" with plans and specifications furnished by Ye Planry Co. of Dallas. (Bathrooms were not usually included in the room count given in mechanics' liens and newspaper accounts, but by this date, they were included in the houses.) The *Daily Light* documented on August 10 and 19 that it was really a joint project, with Joe laying the reinforced concrete foundation for a stucco structure with "a summer sleeping apartment on the top with openings on all four sides."

The Jarrett house introduced a new building type—the Craftsman bungalow—to the Oldham streetscape. It is a classic example with front-facing double gables with knee braces in the eaves, a low-slung roof with exposed rafter ends, and a gable porch and lateral pergola with squared wood supports on brick piers. The house also classifies as an "airplane bungalow," with its second-floor pop-up "cockpit" in the form of the "sleeping apartment" mentioned in the *Daily Light*. Given Jarrett's occupation and that this house was also his business address, it is no surprise that the frame dwelling was stucco veneered, a popular bungalow finish but one not common to Waxahachie bungalows. In 1923, the Jarretts sold the house to the First Methodist Church and moved to Harris County.

B-38
307 Oldham Avenue
1899; E. S. Boze, builder

In September 1899, Horatio Lee Bunkley, a furniture salesman, bought this lot from his mother, who lived next door at **309 Oldham**. One month later he married Kate Leigh. (He was the only one of Mrs. Bunkley's five sons to marry.) On November 1, the couple contracted with E. S. Boze, a leading Waxahachie contractor, to build this modest modified L-plan house. The Bunkleys paid Boze $900 to build the "five-room frame shingle roof dwelling house," plus $100 for materials. Embellishments were minimal: shaped shingles in the gable end, a transom over the single-entry door, and turned porch columns, probably with decorative brackets. In January 1917, three months after Horatio's mother died, the couple sold this house to W. M. Mincey (who lived at **308 Oldham**) and moved their family of seven children to Ross Street. Two years later, they moved to Breckenridge, Texas.

B-39
308 Oldham Avenue
1911; c. 1917, second floor addition

According to a circa 1906 First Baptist Church members directory, William M. and Mabel Mincey were already renters at this location when, in April 1907, they bought the lot and house, an L-plan house that had been part of the old mill property. With the opening of their W. M. Mincey & Co. dry goods store on South Washington Street in fall 1906, the couple focused on their business before building the house that the *Daily Light* reported was "progressing nicely" on June 12, 1911. The footprint for the house on the 1914 Sanborn map appears to be the same house seen today—pyramidal square-shape with a generous covered porch on both street sides—except it is noted as only one story on the map. There are two possible explanations for the discrepancy. First, it could have been an incorrect notation, but mistakes on Sanborn maps are very rare. Or the upper floor may have been a later alteration, perhaps in early 1917, after Mincey bought the house across the street at **307 Oldham** to serve first as a temporary residence for his own family while adding this second floor, and then as home for his parents.

Mincey was typical of many young, ambitious men who moved to Waxahachie in the late nineteenth and early twentieth centuries. Born in Georgia in 1869, he moved first to Sherman, Texas, in 1896, where he connected with dry goods merchant S. W. Durham. When Durham moved his family to Waxahachie in late 1899 to open a branch store, Mincey also moved to Waxahachie where, according to the June 11, 1900 census, he lived in a boarding house on Franklin Street. He married a sister of Durham's wife that summer and worked as a traveling clothing salesman before opening his own dry goods business. Both Minceys were active members of their adopted community—Mrs. Mincey in the Baptist church, while Mr. Mincey served as a councilman and as president of the Chamber of Commerce. They sold this house in 1925, and after living in Dallas for several years, resettled in Ennis near a daughter. Both are buried in the Waxahachie City Cemetery.

B-40
309 Oldham Avenue
1895; post-1985 renovation

The Bunkley property and family are important to the Oldham neighborhood story. When Mrs. Ann H. Bunkley died in 1916 at age seventy-eight, her obituary noted that "one of the most interesting characters of our community" had been a Waxahachie resident for thirty-two years and had always lived on Oldham Avenue in "one of the first houses built on the street." Mrs. Bunkley was born in Georgia in 1838. Her father was a Baptist minister who moved his family to Smith County, Texas, when she was young. Married in 1854 and widowed with nine surviving children in 1876, she moved to Waxahachie in 1884 and bought all of Block 3 ($1,000 for an acre) on the north side of what became Oldham Avenue.

There is no record of Mrs. Bunkley's first residence on the property, but a November 27, 1895 contract between Mrs. Bunkley and lumberyard manager Wm. F. Lewis for materials for improvements offers a description of the building that evolved into the existing structure. It was a "One Story framed house" with six rooms (including two rooms measuring 16 x 16 ft.), two halls, and three galleries. The 1904 Sanborn map shows the three galleries, or porches, one across the front façade and the other two along both sides of the back wing. In all probability, the house was built, enlarged, and maintained over the years by Mrs. Bunkley's five sons, whose mix of skills from carpenter to plumber left little that her boys could not do. They also had other businesses including the Bunkley Bros. Custom and Cotton Gin Mills that were adjacent to the railroad tracks on the west side of College Street, as shown on the 1886 bird's-eye view. Only one of the sons married, and he built the house next door at **307 Oldham**. The four sons and one daughter who never married lived out their lifetimes in this house. The current front façade, including front door, porch supports, and balustrade, reflect a post-1985 renovation.

B-41
400 Oldham Avenue
1909; c. 1912 extension

Not by coincidence, dentist Dr. Clarence C. Cooke bought the vacant lot at this location on November 21, 1905, just thirteen days after his future mother-in-law, Mrs. Lou Green, bought the house next door at **402 Oldham**. After getting married in June 1906, Dr. Cooke and Mary Green either lived with the Greens or rented a house elsewhere until March 1909, when the *Daily Light* reported that they were building a "handsome cottage" on Oldham. The Cookes' house is a variation of most pyramidal houses in Waxahachie. Rather than having the usual single-plane front façade, an outward projection denotes the entrance and narrow windows (rather than sidelights) flank the entrance door. Originally, the house was symmetrical in shape. The east side extension was probably built soon after Mrs. Cooke's mother died in October 1911 and her widowed father moved in with the couple. The family lived here until moving to **201 E. University** in late 1918-early 1919, a move that left them with two rent houses on Oldham Avenue.

Born in Emory, Texas, in 1875, Dr. Cooke graduated from Baylor University, after which he received a dental degree from Vanderbilt University in Nashville. He moved to Waxahachie in time to be included in the early June 1900 census listing and opened what would become a forty-year practice.

B-42
401 Oldham Avenue
1899; c. 1925

This most curious of residential façades in Waxahachie can only be understood when seeing the original high-pitched front gable and draped roofline shown in a documentary photograph taken not long after the house was built. But even with the photograph, the inspiration for this unique architectural statement remains a mystery.

In September 1899, Jack A. Beall, attorney and former Ellis County State Representative, bought this property after fire destroyed the 1894 house on the lot on June 15. No doubt Beall and his wife Patricia Martin Beall were drawn to the location because each of them had a sister living on the block—Emma Beall Griffin and Sally Martin Strickland at **409** and **500 Oldham**, respectively. Construction began at once, and by late December, Waxahachie and Dallas newspapers reported that "Jack Beall's cottage is receiving the finishing touches."

The early photograph along with the 1904 Sanborn map reveal a one-and-a-half story cottage with a complicated multi-hipped-and-gabled roof, a recessed front entrance flanked by projecting bay windows, and a full-width front porch wrapping around both sides. It seems safe to say that it was an architect-designed building but, thus far, no document has surfaced that names either an architect or a builder. Architect Marshall Sanguinet comes to mind, given his penchant for mixing historic styles with a sophisticated and sometimes whimsical imagination, as evidenced by his buildings on the north side of Waxahachie's Courthouse Square and the residential designs produced in his Fort Worth office. The Beall house, designed as the ultimate interpretation of the T-plan cottages that were so popular in Waxahachie, seems in character for Sanguinet.

Business and political interests drew the Bealls to Dallas, and in August 1904, the couple sold the house to compress manager H. W. Parks, who was followed by dentist R. L. Schmitt and his family in 1909. Rancher and prominent cotton seed breeder Delta Dee (Dee Dee) Floyd and his wife, osteopathic physician Dr. Amy May Floyd, bought the property in 1911. "Mrs. Dr. Floyd" (as married female doctors were addressed at the time) specialized in diseases of women and children and officed in the house. According to subsequent owners, it was the Floyds who, around 1925, replaced the draped front gable with a bulky hipped-roof dormer-like extension above the entry and made interior alterations, especially to the second floor. The Rev. Walter Huber and his wife Margaret, who bought the property in 1978, are responsible for converting the oversized dormer into the gable-roofed balcony now on the second floor. Completed in time for the 1980 Gingerbread Trail, the new balcony reintroduced a pediment shape to the front façade.

B-43
402 Oldham Avenue
1903; H. W. Madson and W. B. (Bird) Forrest, builders

In November 1905, Mrs. Lou Green, wife of carpenter William P. Green, bought this property with her "separate monies." The six-room house that she bought for $1,400 had been built in fall 1903 by Waxahachie builders Madson and Forrest for Judge Frank and Mabel Barker. It is another example, like **208 Oldham**, of a transitional center-hall cottage that mixes Queen Anne features with elements of the pyramidal house type that became so popular in Waxahachie by 1910 and that the Greens' daughter Mary and son-in-law Dr. C. C. Cooke built next door at **400 Oldham**.

After his wife died in 1911, Mr. Green moved in with the Cookes and rented this house. He remained a member of the Cookes' household until he died in 1925, by which time the family was living in the West End. In the late 1930s, the Cookes moved back to their old neighborhood, specifically to this house, where Dr. Cooke died in 1947 at age seventy-one. Mrs. Cooke sold the house in 1955 and moved to Baytown to live with her daughter.

B-44
407 Oldham Avenue

1893; E. H. Griffin, contractor

Exactly three months—December 30, 1892, to March 31, 1893—transpired from the time that E. H. Griffin bought this lot, built a house, and moved his family into their new residence, described in the March 3 *Enterprise* as "of the Queen Anne style, conveniently modernized." Moving meant crossing the street from the house that he and his wife Emma Beall Griffin had built at **408 Oldham** in the fourth year of their marriage. In the intervening eleven years, Griffin had expanded his contracting business to include real estate development and had become one of Waxahachie's leading businessmen. It is worth noting that when building this house, Griffin was involved in one of his largest projects, the tandem development of the Lake Park Street Railway and the Park Hill subdivision, but he chose to stay in his old neighborhood.

The placement of this two-story modified L-plan house on a rise, with minimal front yard and fanciful Queen Anne detailing on the two-story wraparound porches, firmly anchored the corner. According to the extensive *Enterprise* article, the trim was the product of Waxahachie planers Musgraves Brasher & Co. Others credited with producing all the interior and exterior work included the M. T. Jones Lumber Co., which presented the "elegant" 265-pound front door to Mrs. Griffin. Although the house was Griffin's fifteen-year wedding anniversary gift to his wife, it also served as an advertisement for his contracting business: in 1894, he received two major residential contracts for architect-designed houses, the H. W. Leeper house on West Main (no longer extant) and the T. J. Cole house at **309 East Marvin** (now altered).

After Griffin died in 1913 and Mrs. Griffin in 1920, the couple's three sons rented the house until 1940, when they sold the property to Ernest and Sovola Bynum Shackelford, who returned it to single-family use. Mrs. Shackelford is well-known in the history of Waxahachie educators, having taught in Waxahachie and surrounding school districts during the 1930s and 1940s. In 1954, she was appointed principal of Ferris Elementary School, a position she held until her retirement in 1975. In 1988, the new Shackelford Elementary School was named in her honor.

B-45
408 Oldham Avenue

1882-83; E. H. Griffin, builder; 1904

When druggist T. J. McDade and his wife Sue bought this property in June 1899, they bought what was known as the "Old Griffin Place," a corner lot with a one hundred-foot Oldham Avenue frontage and a generously proportioned, two-story L-plan house built in 1882-83 by a young, ambitious contractor named E. H. Griffin. By the time the McDades acquired the property, there had been several intervening owners, but the 1886 view and 1898 Sanborn map illustrate that the house remained essentially as built. Its present appearance can be attributed to an extensive remodeling project undertaken by the McDades in 1904 and to Jimmy and Patricia Cox who, after purchasing the property in 1977, restored the house according to a circa 1904 photograph.

On July 4, 1904, the *Daily Light* reported that McDade had moved his family so their house could be "overhauled and remodeled throughout." By August 26, they were back in what was "now one of the most attractive places on Oldham Avenue." The original two-story L-plan form with a front-facing gable-end was still obvious, but several architectural features and details, mostly porch-related, offered a connection with Waxahachie's more up-to-date Queen Anne and Colonial Revival style residences. The earlier one-story inset front porch was extended across the entire façade and wrapped around the east corner, and a second-story balcony and open tower were added. Supported by fluted Doric columns, the porch and balcony are adorned with pediments. The first-floor pediment frames the primary entrance, while the second-floor pediment serves as a decorative filler in the space between the gable and the tower.

Born near Macon, Mississippi, in 1863, T. J. McDade and his parents were living in Grayson County, Texas, when the 1880 census was enumerated. By March 1890, T. J. was working in a Waxahachie drugstore and one year later, opened a drugstore in a short-lived partnership. He established his own business in 1892—the same year in which he returned to Macon to marry Sue Peterson. When the McDades moved to Oldham Avenue in 1899, the oldest of their three children was seven. In the early 1920s, T. J. left the drug business to become vice-president of Guaranty State Bank and Trust and, in 1924, the McDades sold the house and moved to Dallas.

B-46
500 Oldham Avenue
1897; C. W. Thrash, builder; c. 1903

This house, one of the most robust Queen Anne structures remaining in east Waxahachie, is identified with one of the city's most illustrious self-made businessmen, J. F. Strickland. In October 1889 and two months after marrying Sallie Martin, Strickland—grocer, liquor merchant, and real estate investor—bought this property at a sheriff's sale. The couple did not immediately move into an existing 1888 cottage on the property, but they were living there by February 1893, when the *Enterprise* reported that he was "grading and beautifying" his Oldham yard. For the next few years, Strickland concentrated on overseeing his growing real estate investments, dissolving a grocery business in the aftermath of the Panic of 1893, and assuming management of the Waxahachie Electric Company. By May 1897, the Stricklands were ready to make their statement on Waxahachie's architectural scene and contracted C. W. Thrash to build, in sixty days, "a two story frame house of six new rooms, and other improvements on the old building" for $2,500. The rear portion of the house probably constitutes the surviving visible portion of the "old building."

When built, the Stricklands' two-and-a-half story structure was all Queen Anne—asymmetrical, vertical hipped roof with multiple gables, broken wall surfaces, corner tower, and full-width one-story front porch curving around to the east side. The distinctive octagonal corner tower probably was inspired by the tower in mail-order architect George Barber's design "A Southern Villa" that was published in the March 1897 issue of the magazine *American Homes*. A comparison of the 1898 and 1904 Sanborn insurance maps shows that the Stricklands could not resist tweaking their new residence in that six-year period. The first-floor porch was extended around the west corner of the façade, and a second floor balcony was added. The paired Doric columns no doubt replaced Eastlake supports. If Sanborn maps and visible evidence are any clue, the Stricklands and their neighbors, the McDades at **408 Oldham**, were making changes to their properties at exactly the same time. Perhaps there was a little neighborhood competition to see who could have the most up-to-date house on the street.

Business pursuits drew the Stricklands to Dallas. They moved there in summer 1904, but did not sell their Waxahachie house to A. J. Walcott of Midland until August 1905. The Walcotts arrived in time to celebrate, with an elaborate house wedding, the marriage of their oldest daughter Henri Lea to Tom C. Cole on December 27. Following several owners and conversion of the house into apartments, Mary Beth and Billy Lothridge are credited with the initial major renovation in the late 1970s. The house is a popular, frequent address on the Gingerbread Trail.

In the early years of the automobile, the Oldham-Williams intersection became known as "The Corner" to many residents of Waxahachie and a destination point for Sunday afternoon family drives. Until 1933, when the current brick duplex replaced the R. G. Phillips house on the northeast corner of the intersection, four imposing and elaborately detailed dwellings provided a concentration of architectural exuberance unequaled elsewhere in the town. Even with only three of the original four houses, the corner is still impressive.

B-47
110 Williams Street
Early 1870s; moved to this location c. 1907

Until 1909, this lot was empty on Sanborn maps, which means that **110 Williams**, a considerably older house than 1909, was moved to this location. Deed records provide the answer. In 1907, Joseph G. (J. G.) and Sallie Phillips engaged in two real estate transactions. They bought this lot in January and in May sold their residential property on the east side of Kaufman Street, just south of the railroad tracks. And voila! The 1909 Sanborn maps for both locations show the Kaufman Street lot empty and this house on the new Williams Street lot, with a footprint matching their previous house. The main section is a basic two-story I-house, i.e., two rooms wide and one-room deep with a center hall. The back wing exterior and the interior floor arrangement indicate that multiple additions and adjustments were made over the years. The double gallery on the front façade was rebuilt in a recent renovation.

J. G. and Sallie were among a large contingency of Kentucky-born Phillips family members who were early settlers in Ellis and Kaufman Counties. This couple came to Texas in 1855 and to Waxahachie in 1861. J. G. established a profitable trade as a wagon builder, and he and Sallie bought their first piece of Kaufman Street property, the original site of this house, in 1871. Local newspapers kept track of back-and-forth visits between family living in the two counties, and in January 1902 reported that J. G., Sallie, and daughter Kate moved to the town of Kaufman. They rented this house, in its original location, until returning to Waxahachie in 1907. J. G. died here in 1913 and Sallie in 1918. Kate died at a brother's house in Kaufman in 1932; the family sold this house in 1935.

B-48
111 Williams Street
1873

Two characteristics—the steeply pitched gable roof and the side-by-side single-door front entrances—suggest that this is one of the oldest extant residential buildings in Waxahachie. The house is an enlarged version of a side-gable two-room house type without a center hall. Whereas most buildings that fit this vernacular type are only one-story in height and one room deep, this one is one-and-a-half stories and two rooms deep. Some modifications have been made to the structure, but its basic core remains as built by William and Elizabeth Payne, probably in late 1873.

In that year, the Paynes, both in their sixties, migrated from Indiana to Waxahachie and bought three lots fronting Williams Street (then called Marshall Street) from E. W. Rogers for $125. When William died in 1874, his heirs shared interest in this property and an eighty-acre farm located three miles north of Waxahachie. Elizabeth continued living at this address with other family members. In early 1900, at age ninety-one, Elizabeth "sold" her interest in both properties to grandson and farmer Austin J. (A. J.) Charles and grandson-in-law and house painter John D. Keys for ten dollars and the promise that they would furnish half the expense for "her maintenance and support during [her] natural life." Elizabeth died here in June 1909, three months after her one hundredth birthday. A. J., who had moved into town and was working as a carpenter, became sole owner of this house when the other heirs sold him their interests in "the old Payne Homestead lot." The Charles family owned the property into the 1960s.

B-49
113 Williams Street
1908

On May 12, 1908, meat market owner and butcher Sam Nycum and his wife Mamie bought the middle lot of what had been the Payne family's homestead property. It was an instance of a Waxahachie tendency to start construction almost immediately after purchasing a lot, or "buy and build," for the *Daily Light* reported on June 20 that "Sam Nycum has had a neat bungalow erected on Williams street." It is also an example of a house design probably ordered from or inspired by a published plan book, a practice common in Waxahachie and nationally. The same book could have been used a year later for **301 Kaufman** and **909 West Marvin**. A comparison of this house and its near neighbor at 301 Kaufman shows the same house with the same proportions and front façade arrangement, i.e., a full-width front gable, attached front porch, entrance-denoting pediment and columns, and single front door with sidelights and flanking windows. The difference lies in the choice of detailing. Whereas the owners of 301 Kaufman chose Colonial Revival details, the Nycums opted for detailing often interchangeably identified with bungalows and the Craftsman style, such as the triangular knee brackets in the eave overhang and exposed rafter ends under the porch roof. In 1911, the Nycums sold the house. Six different owners followed before it was purchased in 1921 by then Justice of the Peace Lem Wray, who would eventually serve three terms as Ellis County Judge. The addition on the south side with multiple windows was probably built as a sleeping porch and dates to the Wrays' tenure. Judge Wray and his wife Jessie Mae Keeler Wray were both from Milford. The small bungalow next door at 117 Williams dates to c. 1915 and also rests on land that was once part of the original Payne family homestead property.

B-50
116 Williams Street
1901

Built as rental property, this one-story modified L-plan house has changed very little since its construction, which was probably soon after Dr. D. G. Thompson bought the lot in October 1901. Typical of many small houses, the house was built with a front porch and a rear wing which, in this case, is clearly visible on the corner lot. The two-over-two windows in the rear wing suggest that an older building, or, at least, older building materials, were incorporated into the house. A back porch running the length of the wing is on the interior façade.

B-51
200 Williams Street
1906; H. W. Madson, builder

German-born tinner Paul Bauder and his wife Mary, whose parents were also German born, bought this corner lot in mid-July 1906. On August 7, they signed a contract with H. W. Madson to build, in thirty days and for $795, this pyramidal cottage for which they supplied the plans and specifications, which implies they were selected from a published plan book. The Bauders' house is a variation of the pyramidal house type, with a partial front porch under the principal roof, a plan that offered more interior living space than versions with a full front porch. Paul Bauder died in 1908, the 1910 census listing

Mrs. Bauder at this address with four daughters, ages seven to twenty-two. When she died in 1946 at age eighty, this was still her home. Her daughters, all married, were living in Dallas and Houston.

B-52
201 Williams Street
1909

In December 1908 Ellis County Tax Assessor Jack Killebrew bought this property and soon built a new house with all the traits of the Waxahachie version of a larger pyramidal house—full front porch, gracefully sloping roofline, hipped-roof dormer, single-door center entrance with sidelights and transom, and Ionic porch columns. Smaller, simpler examples of the same house type are seen across the street at **200** and **202 Williams**. After Jack Killebrew died in 1930, his wife Martha continued living here with daughter Marie, who was a teacher. According to 1936-1952 city directory listings, Mrs. Killebrew operated "The Community Store," a neighborhood grocery at this location. It was not the only business on the block: the Smith Hobby Shop was located at 206 Williams from 1942 into the mid-seventies.

An existing structure had to be demolished before the Killebrews could build their up-to-date residence in 1909, and that structure was a railroad depot. Today, it is hard to imagine that in the late nineteenth century passenger trains for the Fort Worth and New Orleans and the Central, Texas and Northwestern railways rumbled along Parks Avenue and that the passenger depot sat on this corner. The depot, built in 1886, was originally planned for the corner of Parks and Flat Streets (as shown on the 1886 bird's-eye view) but was shifted to this location because it offered more space for the 36 x 100 ft. building and 150-foot-long platform. In what was a typical arrangement at the time, the depot also served as residence for railroad personnel, in this instance vice-president and local general manager Hans Helland and his family. After the branch track closed in 1901, the Hellands purchased the depot property where they continued living while Hans worked throughout the state as a consulting railroad engineer. In December 1908, they sold the corner to the Killebrews and moved to San Antonio, where Hans became city engineer.

B-53
202 Williams Street
1910

Evangelist Thomas C. Bush built this pyramidal cottage shortly after buying the lot in March 1910. At the time, Rev. Bush was pastor of the Gathered Brethren Church on Bethel Street, one street to the east. The house is one of the most intact examples of the simplest and smallest versions of its type in Waxahachie. It probably served first as an interim residence for Bush's family, including his widowed sister-in-law Sonora Farley, while their permanent, much grander house at **418 College** was given a classical columned facelift. None of the family is listed at either location in the 1910 Census, suggesting they were in transition. By the time the 1913 city directory was published, they were back on College Street and a renter was living at this address.

B-54
207 Williams Street
1911

Although the design of this 1911 house is unique in Waxahachie, similar designs are found in house-plan books of the period, including the 1910 edition of Herbert C. Chivers's *Artistic Homes*. The narrow side of the hipped roof—rather than the long side, which would be more typical—is turned to define the primary street façade. Originally, the paired windows on the front façade were flanked by a narrow, recessed corner porch on each side. The sturdy, squared porch columns and flared brackets are motifs repeated on the pilasters of the projecting dormer. To the rear is a later camel-back addition that is minimally intrusive. The house was built by farmer and sometime furniture dealer W. H. Davis and his wife Margaret Lula, who bought the property in early January 1911. The previous owners' house had burned in August 1910.

B-55
209 Williams Street
c. 1886

The core of this simple side-gable cottage was probably built by railroad employee J. F. Olsen soon after buying the lot in summer 1886. Architecturally, the cottage is far simpler than are the movements of its earliest occupants. In August 1905, Olsen, now a miller, sold the property to another miller, J. T. Williams, whose entrepreneurial ambitions during the twenty-eight months that he owned this house can be followed through the local papers. In September, Williams sold his New Grist Mill (which he built in fall 1902) to Olsen and presumably rented the house when he left with his family in early October for Indian Territory, where he operated a corn sheller until early 1906. He then moved to Paul's Valley, a logging community in east Texas, to build a grist mill and elevator. The family returned to Waxahachie in time to be listed at this location in the 1907 city directory and to open, in February, the "Eatitorium," a confectionary, restaurant, and rooming house on the square. In October, Williams traded that business to C. O. Adkins for a farm, although (no surprise) Williams had "not yet decided upon plans for the future." In mid-December, the Williamses sold this house to Adkins. In 1909, it became the home of realtor Robert H. Connally, his wife Josephine, and their four children when they downsized from their imposing residence at **307 Brown Street** and moved next door to Mr. Connally's business partner, C. O. Adkins on Williams Street. Members of the Connally family lived here into the 1930s.

B-56
215 Williams Street
1922

When in their seventies and their fifty-second year of married life, retired farmer E. A. Bivings and his wife Mattie built this house on a lot they bought in June 1922. They had lived for many years on the far east end of Marvin Street but needed to move closer into town because of Mr. Bivings's failing health. The house they built was this small, classic double-gable bungalow. The couple lived here just two years before Mr. Bivings died on July 2, 1924, the *Daily Light* identifying him as the "Confederate veteran and well-known Waxahachian." Mrs. Bivings, who served as president of the local Sims-Watson Chapter of the United Daughters of the Confederacy, died in 1931 in the Fort Worth home of one of their eight children.

B-57
217 Williams Street
c. 1895; moved to this location 1951

Here is another of Waxahachie's T-plan houses, in this instance one that was moved to this location in 1951. Neither early Sanborn maps nor city directories document anything or anyone at this location. In March 1951, realtor E. E. Griffin bought the lot for $800 and in late April advertised a "semi-duplex" with "6 rooms and bath" at this address. In May he sold the property for $6,500 to Mrs. Cassie Boone. Exactly what was meant by "semi-duplex" is unclear, but there are separate entrances on each side of the cross gable wings, indicating that there were both shared and private spaces. City directories from 1952 through 1958 list two separate occupants, including the owner, at the address.

B-58
104 Kaufman Street (demolished)
c. mid-1880s

This 2007 photograph of the two-room one-story frame dwelling that was at 104 Kaufman is included in the guidebook because it was one of the best and most important surviving examples of a type of small house once common to Waxahachie, especially in its working class and minority neighborhoods. The simple rectangular form with gable roof and integral rear ell had two single-door entrances and wood-sash double-hung windows opening onto the attached three-bay porch. The porch trim—turned supports, jig-sawn brackets, and frieze—is evidence that Waxahachie's fixation with "gingerbread" was not confined to larger structures and that the demise of smaller buildings such as this has been a great loss to the city.

B-59
106 Kaufman Street
c. 1893-94

Determining exact construction dates and placement of all the small houses located at the southern end of Kaufman Street is treacherous because property lines often shifted and buildings were moved, reconfigured, and demolished during the 1880-1915 period. This T-plan house, however, is definitely on its original site. In 1883, Canadian-born Nora Reynolds and John, her New York-born, railroad engineer husband, bought their first Kaufman Street property—the "house and lot" (lot 2) where 110 Kaufman now stands and where the Reynolds probably lived. One year later, they bought this lot (lot 3), which included the seller's 16 x 24 ft. carpenter's shop that both parties agreed would not be moved immediately. What the Reynolds planned for their Kaufman properties is unknown, as Nora was a twenty-five-year-old widow with a child by the end of the year.

With her dressmaking, boarders, and rental property, Nora earned enough to buy, in 1893, part of lot 4 and to build this house shortly thereafter. For her new house, Nora chose the most distinctive and up-to-date small house type being built in Waxahachie at the time. The house, however, differs from other local T-houses in two respects: space was added by extending one side of the "T" rather than building to the rear, and the placement of a second front-facing gable on that extension was an unusual if not unique feature for Waxahachie T-houses. The turned porch supports, jig-sawn brackets with teardrops, and scalloped edging are original details.

The May 13, 1904 issue of the *Enterprise* reported that Mrs. Reynolds had rented this house to insurance agent and City Alderman W. L. P. Leigh and his family. Nora and son T. J. had moved to El Paso County, and in 1906 sold all their Kaufman Street properties. Eventually the Reynolds' properties, along with other properties on the south end of Kaufman, were acquired by Waxahachie's real estate magnate John F. Wyatt. Based on Sanborn maps, the houses at 110 and 112 can be ascribed to changes occurring between 1909 and 1914. The pyramidal house at

110 Kaufman was probably a transformation of an earlier structure, while 112 Kaufman, with its two single-door front entrances, was a new version of an old house type.

B-60
111 Kaufman Street
c. 1885-1900

Although repositioned and altered, the basic forms of the three small late-nineteenth-century houses at 107, 109, and 111 Kaufman are obvious. The most intact is the L-plan house at 111 Kaufman, which was moved to this location circa 1920—not an uncommon activity, because the neighborhood was always full of small houses that could easily be moved as development and changes in ownership occurred. This end of Kaufman Street, which runs into Main Street, will probably always be in flux.

B-61
115 Kaufman Street
1913; Waxahachie Lumber Company, contractor

Although originally built in 1879 as a one-story L-plan cottage and rebuilt after a major fire in 1887, a 1913 renovation has obscured any hints of its earlier appearance from the street. The 1913 contract for materials and labor with the neighboring lumberyard described the work as an "erection or repair of improvements" at a cost of $1,200. The makeover included rear enclosures and additions as well as a total refashioning of the front façade—i.e., converting the gable roof to a hipped roof, boxing in the front-L to create a single-plane front wall, and framing the centered entrance door with small-paned sidelights that match the second story window panes. Although the windows are a Prairie-style touch, it is the porch, with its low, full-width pediment supported by four squared brick columns—all common Prairie-style features—that suggests the owners, Patrick Henry (Pat) Templeton and his wife Nannie, wanted to make an up-to-date architectural statement.

The house stands on property that was part of a twelve-acre tract that lawyer John D. Templeton and his wife Phoebe, former Missourians, bought from Nicholas and Helen Oldham in 1869. The Templetons built their homestead in the middle of the tract and sold off lots to the south. On December 16, 1879, they gave their twenty-three-year-old bachelor son Pat this lot, located between the family homestead and the lumberyard to the north. The *Enterprise* reported on January 9, 1880, that Pat had built "one of the neatest and most tasty cottage residences in town," and noted eleven months later, in February 1881, his marriage to Nannie M. Watson from Italy's Watson Plantation family. The couple lived their forty-year marriage at this location. Other family members lived here, including Pat and Nannie's daughter Brevard, who served as Ellis County treasurer from August 1909 until retiring in January 1964. She was one of the first women to run for public office in the county. Templeton heirs sold the property in 1966.

B-62
123 Kaufman Street
1913; Waxahachie Lumber Company

The arrival of the first railroad in Waxahachie—the Houston and Texas Central Railroad in 1879—also brought Waxahachie's first lumberyards. Indeed, a lengthy article in the *Enterprise* on September 19, 1879, reported that four lumberyards were under consideration. Two actually materialized, both at the Kaufman Street railroad crossing: the W. J. and T. A. Montgomery Lumber Yard and the

M. T. Jones Lumber Yard. Both appear on the 1886 bird's-eye view, but in early 1890, M. T. Jones absorbed its competitor. By spring 1893, the business was known as the William F. Lewis Lumber Yard, named for the Jones manager who was also an original stockholder. When Lewis went bankrupt in fall 1896, M. T. Jones resumed ownership, and in July 1904 sold it to the Waxahachie Lumber Company. Although the name had changed, it was essentially a restructured version of the older business.

The 1910 *Waxahachie Illustrated* publication described the Waxahachie Lumber Company as the oldest lumber company in town and noted that one of its strongest features was allowing people to pay for their new homes in installments. The accompanying photograph showed the "yards and office," the latter a two-story hipped-roof, double-galleried residential structure.

In 1913, the company replaced the outdated office building with a structure that was more in keeping with much of what they and their associates had been building for the past six years. The new office was a commercial adaptation of the bungalow form. According to an article in the May 21 issue of the *Daily Light*, the old building had been sold and moved "to East Main street in Freedman" for use as a restaurant and rooming house while the new building was "one story and twenty by twenty-four feet."

After being vacant for many years, yet surviving in near-original condition, this diminutive building was renovated in 2017. All the windows were shortened, which, in turn, heightened the dado or wainscoting that encircled the building, and the triple-window groupings that flanked the front door were replaced with paired windows. The result is a stockier appearance that lost the light, pavilion-like quality of the earlier structure.

B-63
124 Kaufman Street
1901; J. S. McCanless, builder

Ernest M. Hines built this commodious two-story modified L-plan house fourteen years after he bought the property and, with his widowed mother Nannie J. Hines, moved to Waxahachie from the family farm on Chambers Creek near Forreston. Ernest's father, South Carolinian Thomas Jefferson Hines, bought and sold land in Tennessee and Texas before settling in Ellis County with multiple landholdings and slaves in the early 1850s. Ernest was a child of Thomas's second marriage in 1859 to Nannie J. Young, who also came from a family with large landholdings and who was thirty-five years her husband's junior.

When they moved to town in 1887, the twenty-year-old farmer and landholder and his mother probably first lived in a house already on the two-and-a-half acre parcel. A third person was added to the household in 1895 when Ernest married Laura Whipple, who was eleven years his senior and sister of onetime county attorney Thomas P. Whipple. On September 1, 1901, the *Enterprise* reported that Ernest, having completed an "elegant cottage" on his lot, was "now laying the foundation for a magnificent two-story residence" on the adjoining lot. Sanborn maps and a documentary photograph show that the cottage was a one-story L-plan house.

It is entertaining to speculate what the dynamics were among the three residents-to-be when it came to design and details for the two-story house. Was Ernest the sole decision-maker? Did the women have a say? Regardless of who made the decisions, this is one of the best examples and best preserved of the large-scale two-story modified L-plan dwellings in Waxahachie. The decorative woodwork of the porches, including turned wood posts and balusters, spindle frieze, and jig-sawn brackets, all appear to be original. Only the elaborate bargeboards and gable ornaments visible in an early photograph have been lost over the years. The setback on the lot and generous yard give the house a stately presence; the sight of it probably gave great pleasure to the lumberyard personnel across the street, who might well have had something to do with its construction. The *Enterprise* declared the ten-room house to be "one of the most elegant homes in the city."

The Hines's lifetime in the house had a very sad ending. Ernest and Laura continued living here after Nannie died at age eighty-four in 1919. On April 19, 1925, Ernest was shot and killed on the property by Sam Hardin, a blacksmith and junk dealer who lived and conducted his business in a small building that he rented on the corner of the Hines's lot. Hardin stated at his trial that Ernest had threatened him with an auto pump if he did not clean up his growing stock of junked parts. Five years later, on September 25, 1930, Laura Hines was hit and killed by an automobile as she was crossing the street to visit a neighbor. After Laura's estate was settled, the property became the home of Ernest's nephew, T. Frank Timmins, who carried on the family occupations of farmer and landowner.

B-64
128 Kaufman Street
c. 1912-13; 1939

This simple vernacular commercial structure appeared on the Kaufman Street landscape around 1912, with Homer H. Hinman listing both his residence and "second hand goods" at this address in the 1913 directory. The 1914 Sanborn map shows, for the first time, a rectangular building with the short or gable-end facing the street near the railroad tracks. Although it started out as a junk store—known as "The Curiosity Store" in 1916-1919—by September 1918 proprietor Ed Barshop was also carrying "a Large New Stock of Groceries" while still buying "junk of all kinds." By the mid-1920s, it was a neighborhood grocery store whose clientele also included railroad-related personnel and travelers. The Kaufman Street switch and siding of the Houston and Texas Central Railroad was a busy place for unloading goods, lumber, and even circuses when they came to town. Passengers also could board here. Clayton's Grocery, owned by D. J. Clayton, was here from 1924 to 1939. Mr. and Mrs. J. G. Ferguson purchased the property in spring 1939, and the *Daily Light* noted on March 31 that they "had completely remodeled the building." The Fergusons sold the business in 1952, but retained ownership of the building for several years. The suspended canopy that shaded openings on the front façade was removed in a recent renovation.

B-65
209 Kaufman Street
c. 1885; c. 1889

Although it is clearly visible on the 1886 bird's-eye view—albeit with just a small front porch—records do not offer a clear-cut construction date for this two-story L-plan house located on property that lumberyard owner M. T. Jones bought in fall 1882. Most likely, Jones built the house not long before selling it in June 1885 for $1,375 to railroad conductor William J. McCrabb and his wife, Kate. The *Enterprise* noted in April 1886 that McCrabb and his adjoining neighbor to the south, lumberman William F. Lewis, were both making improvements to Kaufman Street properties that they sold four months later.

Dr. Lewis Meriwether of Houston moved his family to the McCrabb house in late December 1886, and in early January, opened his office in the DuBose & Lomax drug store on the square. Early February 1889, the Meriwethers sold the property to businessman E. L. Huffman in what was the first of five ownership changes during the next ten years. The Huffmans are probably responsible for replacing the original partial front porch shown on the 1886 view with the full-width porch and second-story balcony seen today. That configuration appears on the July 1890 Sanborn map, the first to show this area.

B-66
301 Kaufman Street
1909

The residence at 301 Kaufman, built by John and Ruth Quarles, is closely tied to one other house in Waxahachie—its near-twin at **909 West Marvin**, also built in 1909. As reported by the *Daily Light*, the Quarleses' previous house and contents were "totally destroyed" in an afternoon fire on March 4, 1909. One week later, the newspaper announced that Dr. L. H. Graham and family had moved into their new "handsome home . . . one of the latest types of bungalows" at 909 West Marvin. Less than five weeks later, the Quarleses' new house was "nearing completion," which means that by the end of April, Waxahachie had two very unusual, almost duplicate houses. The Quarleses' six-room house was slightly smaller and with less detailing than the Grahams' house.

It is very possible that the design for both came from a yet-to-be discovered plan book used by a local lumberyard. Although labeled a "bungalow," this house, like 909 West Marvin, does not represent a common building type. The first-floor façade closely resembles those found in standard pyramidal houses, with a central entrance and flanking windows and an attached porch with an entrance-denoting pediment and Ionic columnar supports. Instead of a pyramidal roof, however, the full-width gable roof expands upper story living space.

Dry goods merchant John Quarles and his wife Ruth Montgomery Quarles built this house on property that Ruth's family had owned since 1863. The couple's paths crossed sometime around 1900, when forty-year-old Virginia bachelor John was a dry goods "salesman" living in a Waxahachie boarding house, and nineteen-year-old Ruth was a dry goods clerk living with her parents on Kaufman Street. Whether or not they worked in the same store is unknown, but in 1905 they married. In 1912, the couple opened Quarles Dry Goods Co, which they operated at **205 South College** until John died in 1927; Ruth continued working as a saleslady in another store. Her estate sold this house in 1959.

B-67
312 Kaufman Street

1902; McCanless & Ingram, contractors

Grain dealer D. H. Thompson and his wife Mary Nettie built this house immediately after her parents, H. D. and Hannah Murdock Timmons, gave part of their homestead tract on Kaufman Street to the Thompsons in August 1902. By the end of the year, the Thompsons and three children (three more to come) were living in their new house next door to the grandparents. No doubt the Timmonses' lumberyard in Bullard Heights supplied the materials and architectural details for its construction.

Not only was this the sole Neoclassical residence built on Kaufman Street, it was one of few built on Waxahachie's east side. An *Enterprise* article of mid-November 1902 described the nearly completed ten-room house as "after the style of the old southern homes which were in vogue several generations ago." Subsequent contemporary articles labeled it "colonial," which was their standard term for anything with columns. A photograph in the 1910 *Waxahachie Illustrated* publication shows that the house is basically intact, except for a Palladian-shaped dormer window centered on the hipped roof and other fixable alterations such as siding.

D. H. (for David Henry, which he never used) was another one of Waxahachie's self-made men. Born in Tennessee in 1863, D. H. and his parents came to Texas in 1870 and to Ellis County in 1873. As a young adult, he worked as a bookkeeper in a brother's store, served as city treasurer in 1886, and held other positions while at the same time speculating in grain and cotton seed. When he married Mary Nettie in 1895, he was thirty-two years old and a very wealthy man, his grain dealings extending into Mexico. Called the "Dean of Waxahachie Business Men" in his 1934 obituary, D. H. was an advocate for such causes as the Good Country Roads effort, most specifically macadam surfacing; a public weigher to ensure accuracy when weighing cotton; and African American property ownership. Mary Nettie lived here until her death in 1961.

It is worth noting that the two most imposing houses on Kaufman Street—the Hines house at 124 and the Thompson house at 312—make very different architectural statements but were built within a year of each other and by the same contractor, J. S. McCanless.

B-68
313 Kaufman Street
1904; S. J. Erwin, builder

When built, three sides of this modified L-plan house were in full view on the odd-shaped lot. What distinguishes the house from many others of this type is the attached porch that fills the front L, turns the angled corner, and runs the full length of the original south side. For $1,320, S. J. Erwin built the five-room house for barber shop and bath house proprietor Logan Walker Bateman, his wife Willie, and their two children. The contract was signed on January 6, 1904, and the *Daily Light* reported that the family moved into their recently completed house on February 9.

B-69
608 Kaufman Street
1912; A. N. Guthrie; builder

Built at the tail-end of Waxahachie's pyramidal house era, this structure shows how closely pyramidal and bungalow houses are related. What is basically a pyramidal house assumes a bungalow appearance due to a greater horizontal emphasis achieved by using tapered box porch supports on brick piers rather than the slender classical columns usually found in earlier pyramidal houses, and by not interrupting the horizontal line of the porch roof with an entrance-denoting pediment also commonly used in pyramidals.

According to a mechanic's lien dated September 3, 1912, A. N. Guthrie agreed to build in thirty days and for $1,975 this six-room house for W. J. and Julia Stevenson on what had been their homestead property since 1894. It was a good location for the Stevensons, because it was near the east-side mule barns of the Waxahachie Street Railway Company, where W. J., known as "Uncle Billie," was superintendent for many years. Upon completion of the house, the couple's daughter and son-in-law, Pearl and E. Q. Vestal, immediately bought the property, assumed the note, and moved into the larger, more up-to-date house with the parents. Mrs. Stevenson died in 1915, and two years later, the Vestals sold the property.

B-70
616 Kaufman Street
1893

This two-story L-plan house was probably the house to which farmer and carpenter Albert A. Bradshaw and his wife Harriet moved their large family when they left the farm for town. No doubt, Bradshaw was his own contractor and built the house (with help) shortly after purchasing the property in March 1893. As was true for many farm families, the move was prompted, at least in part, by the educational opportunities that Waxahachie offered, the 1900 census listing six of the Bradshaw children "at school." And to be practical, the parents may have felt that the town setting offered more opportunities for their five daughters to meet future husbands.

The Bradshaws' 1893 L-plan house is basically the same house that was built ten years earlier at **209 Kaufman**. Functional, adaptable, and familiar, the L-plan was one of the most popular house types built throughout the southeast during the years 1880-1910. In its simplest, most unadorned form, period plan books labeled it a "Farmhouse." There is a stateliness to its simplicity, as this house clearly demonstrates.

The Cantrell family on the porch of 622 Kaufman, c. 1890.

B-71
622 Kaufman Street
1888; 1905

On the surface, it seems logical to describe this L-plan house as the house for which laborer David Crockett Cantrell and his wife Millie Grizzle Cantrell signed a material man's lien in March 1888, to buy from the M. T. Jones Lumber Company $400 of "lumber and building material . . . suitable to Erect a dwelling for us." However, a late 1890-early 1891 Cantrell-Tenery family photograph changes part of the story—but also adds to it. The photograph discloses that originally this was a rectangular, gable-end two-room house with a small rear addition. By 1909, when the first Sanborn map documented this part of Kaufman, both the front ell and a rear extension had been built, and one of those, probably the front ell, was the "new room" reported in the *Daily Light* on April 15, 1905. It is likely that all construction phases were built by Mr. Cantrell and his brother-in-law Lucian Grizzle, who was a member of the Cantrell household for most of their married life. (The current photograph of the house reflects a recent renovation.)

As appealing as the documentary photograph is—Mr. Cantrell in his work clothes, Mrs. Cantrell wearing a white eyelet-trimmed apron and holding baby Willie, and daughters Dalton and Leona in white pinafores and each holding a wooden-head doll—it becomes even more appealing upon learning about the family. Both Cantrells were born in Monroe County, Mississippi. They married in Waxahachie in 1886, raised their four daughters (the fourth daughter Rena was born in 1899), and lived out their lifetimes in this house. When Cantrell died a widower at age seventy-eight in 1934, he was working as a truck farmer. The local obituary noted that the "quiet and unassuming" Mr. Cantrell and his "estimable and cultured wife . . . raised their family of four girls who have become outstanding in culture, refinement and in religious attainments." All four daughters had professional lives before marrying, three as teachers and one as a bookkeeper. Their father's funeral service was held at the home of daughter Leona Cantrell Tenery and her husband Dr. William C. Tenery at **905 West Marvin Street**. The obituary concluded by stating that a large crowd was in attendance "just as it all should be, for Crockett Cantrell was a good man."

B-72
626 Kaufman Street
1908-09; 1916

Everyone heading east on East Marvin is treated to a full view of this generously proportioned pyramidal house gracing the southeast corner of Kaufman Street. Its angled positioning on the lot emphasizes the pyramidal features—wraparound porch, gently sloping extension of the primary hipped roof, and hipped-roof dormers. Tax records and residents' observations suggest that this may be another one of those Waxahachie houses where an earlier structure lurks beneath its present appearance.

Bookkeeper Samuel H. Thornhill and his wife Eola bought this property in September 1899 for $850 and may have lived in an existing house for several years before making the major changes, although it is unclear whether they built a new house or extensively altered an older one. One-time resident Dupree Davis Jr.

speculated that the Thornhills began with a center-hall four-room house that they (and their unknown contractor) transformed into one of the most fashionable house types in Waxahachie at the time. Thornhill was an enterprising young man whose purchase of a cotton exchange business in 1906 predated the rise in the assessed value of this property from $600 to $2,500 in the years 1907-1909. Whatever its structural origins, there can be no doubt that the Thornhills are primarily responsible for the house as it appears today, a conclusion substantiated by the property footprint on the 1909 Sanborn map. In January 1910, the Thornhills sold the house, and after two interim owners, Reinhold and Ruby Boehle bought it in July 1913. The Boehles were proprietors of Boehle's Bakery, a Waxahachie institution on the square at **108 West Main** for nearly forty years. The *Daily Light* reported in August 1916 that they were remodeling the house with "extensive improvements" including a sleeping porch, but the 1925 Sanborn map shows that the footprint remained the same. Their son sold the house in 1941. Public school teacher Jewel Davis acquired the property in November 1942 and resided here with her brother, County Clerk A. Dupree Davis Sr., and his family. It remained in the Davis family into the early 1990s.

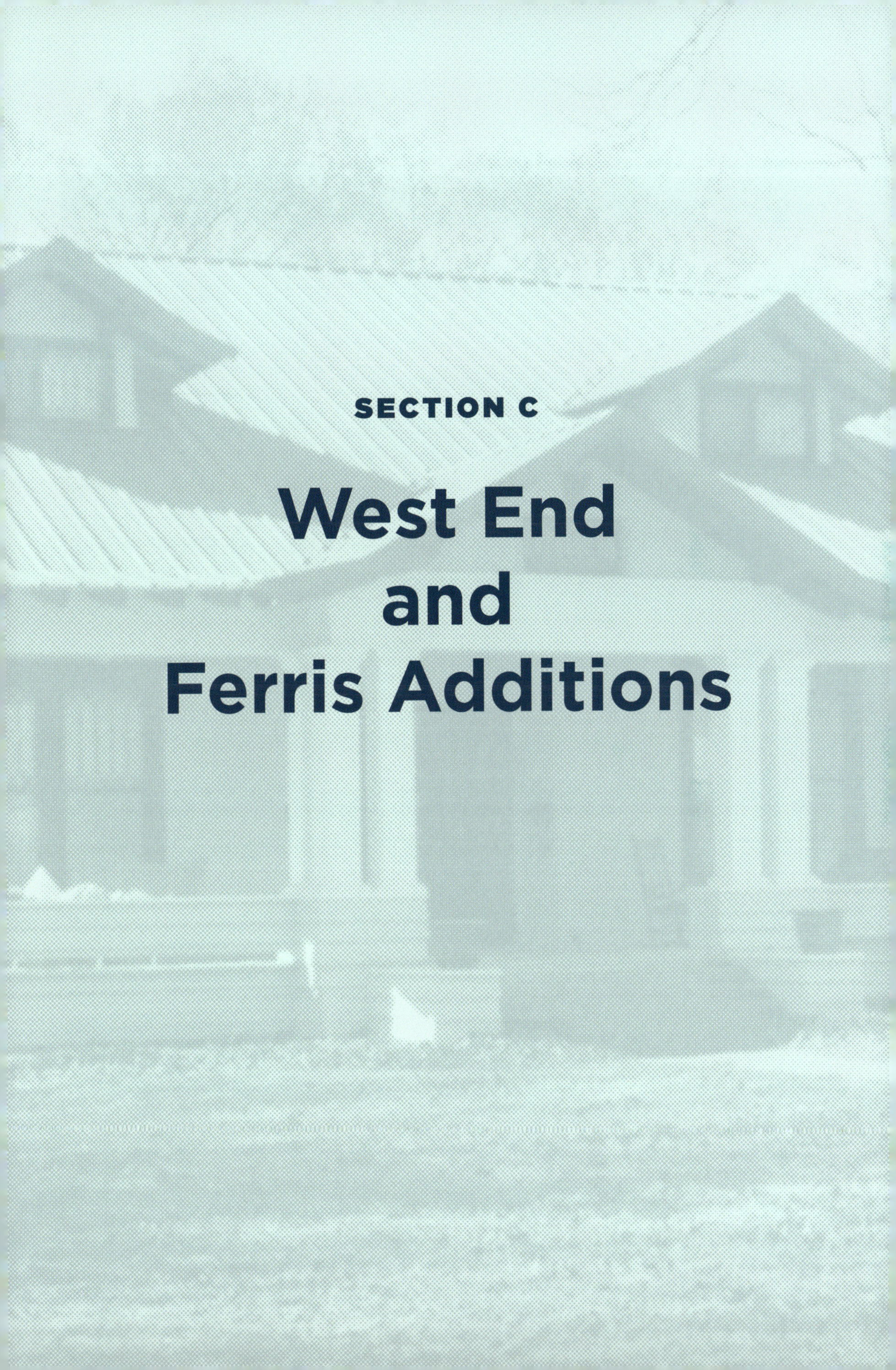

SECTION C

West End and Ferris Additions

Detail from the 1886 bird's-eye view showing the growth west of the square. The J. W. Ferris house can be seen at the top right of the image, with multiple outbuildings and bordered by rows of trees on the north and west. *Courtesy Ellis County Museum.*

INTRODUCTION

This section, west of downtown and south of West Marvin Street, includes some of Waxahachie's finest Queen Anne and Neoclassical style residences along with excellent, well-preserved examples of earlier and later homes. Although it remains primarily residential, a few outstanding early twentieth-century institutional buildings can also be found here. Waxahachie residents embraced a long-standing American tradition of identifying neighborhoods by cardinal directions (with Manhattan's East and West sides perhaps the best known) with their own West and East Ends. "West End Items," a news and gossip column in the *Enterprise*, documents the use of "West End" for the neighborhood west of downtown at least as early as 1882, and in 1889, the West End Addition was platted. The 1876 bird's-eye view shows that Waxahachie had not yet expanded to the west, but the coming of the railroads, beginning with the "Tap" in 1879, sparked new growth, which the 1886 bird's-eye view recorded. Houses lined all the east-west streets that were south of the Rogers Branch (Water, Main, Franklin, and Jefferson). Two large houses stood at the west and north edges: J. C. Gibson's at West Main and Gibson Streets, and J. W. Ferris's at Ferris and McMillan. Continued development soon stretched beyond even those "rural" estates.

View from the courthouse looking west down Main Street, from a c. 1904 fold-out postcard titled "Bird's Eye View of Waxahachie." The large, light-colored building visible in the distance where Main Street curves is the Sims Library. *Private collection.*

J. W. Ferris built this stylish Italianate residence in 1880, just outside the city limits, at the intersection of Ferris Avenue and McMillan Street. It stands out in the 1886 bird's-eye view for its size, numerous outbuildings, and curving drives and walkways. *Courtesy Ellis County Museum.*

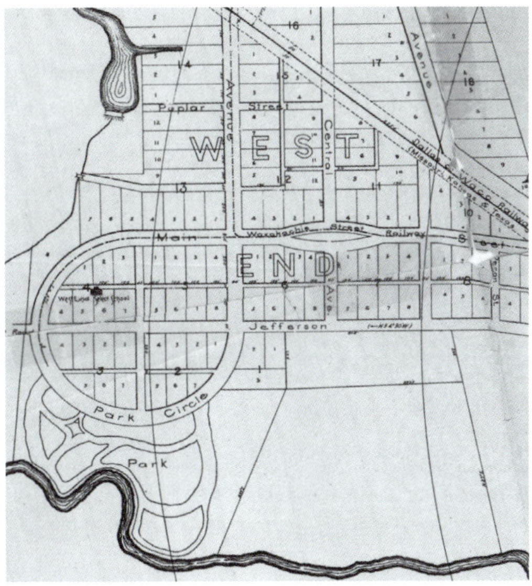

This detail from the 1896 Phillips & Hawkins city map shows the major part of the West End Addition, including the Ellipse in the center and a park by the creek, with landscaped, curving paths, and the circular street named Park Circle, all novel features in Waxahachie at the time. *Courtesy Ellis County Museum.*

Osce Goodwin, general manager of the West End Addition, built this house in 1890 on West Main Street, in the new development. (No longer extant.) *Courtesy Ellis County Museum.*

The West End Addition, platted in 1889, marked a major change in the design and scale of Waxahachie's residential development. Laid out in a picturesque plan with parks and a curving street at its western end, the addition introduced the national trend of garden suburbs made accessible by streetcar systems. Seven of Waxahachie's "young and successful business men," as described in the August 2, 1889 newspaper, formed the Waxahachie Investment Company to create this addition of 125 acres west of the Main Street crossing of the Dallas and Waco Railroad. Osce Goodwin served as general manager and also as trustee with R. G. Phillips and T. A. Ferris. The company's investments in the development included extending the street railway through the addition, planting shade trees along the street, landscaping the small park called the Ellipse in the middle of Main Street, and creating a much larger park near the creek at the southwest corner of the addition. The larger park's design included winding paths, an artificial lake, and a large pavilion.

Getzendaner Memorial Park in the early 1930s, from a Chamber of Commerce brochure *Waxahachie: Queen City of the Cotton Belt. Private Collection.*

The Chautauqua auditorium, built in the West End Park in 1902, drew large crowds from across the state every summer for the Chautauqua Assembly and also served as a municipal auditorium. The red color used for the roof on this tinted postcard probably does not reflect the original wood-shingled roof color. *Courtesy Ellis County Museum.*

The developers were selling lots, not building houses for sale, but several built homes for themselves in the addition, and many of the town's prominent citizens soon joined them. Local newspapers lauded the development's healthful location, free from the "smoke and dust" of neighborhoods near downtown.

The West End Park, though created as part of the West End Addition, became a resource for the entire town almost immediately, and when the Cumberland Presbyterian Chautauqua began holding their summer assemblies in the park in 1900, the Waxahachie Investment Company deeded the property to the Chautauqua Park Association. It finally became an official city park in 1914 when R. W. Getzendaner and his sister acquired the land and donated it in memory of their parents. It is still known as Getzendaner Memorial Park today. The Getzendaner family was also associated with Waxahachie's earlier, smaller park on land where Sims Library now stands (515 West Main). Originally the site of Waxahachie's first Masonic Hall and Academy, it was donated by R. W.'s parents to the city in 1896 to serve as a public park until a library could be built there.

Waxahachie Cotton Mill. The first section of the two-story brick mill building was completed in 1901, and additional wings and buildings were constructed in later years. The concrete brick office building in the foreground, built in 1906, is the only surviving structure of the complex. *Courtesy Ellis County Museum.*

This photograph, probably taken from one of the mill buildings, shows some of the forty-two cottages built for cotton mill workers on the land where the Patrick Street Apartments stand today. The two-story building in the upper right is the M. T. Patrick house. *Courtesy of the Dr. Charles W. Simpson Family and the Ellis County Museum.*

Closer to town, the area north of Water Street and the Rogers Branch remained undeveloped until the city extended its boundaries to incorporate the area in 1890. Justus W. Ferris, who had built his two-story Italianate home there in 1880, objected to the incorporation. When he lost that battle, he responded by platting his land as the Ferris Addition. Construction remained sparse until after Justus's death in 1899, when his son Thomas, who had been involved in the West End Addition, took over the property.

In 1900 over one hundred Ellis County residents invested in a major industrial project that was built on undeveloped land between the Ferris Addition and M. T. Patrick's land on the west. The Waxahachie Cotton Mills eventually grew to encompass two large mill buildings, several warehouses, a power plant, forty-three workers' cottages, and a boarding house. In 1908 it employed 175 workers and processed four thousand bales of cotton annually. The industrial activity and workers' housing did not deter residential growth in the nearby Ferris Addition, which saw much of its growth between 1902 and 1929. Ferris Avenue remained primarily residential through the first half of the twentieth century, but improvements to US Highway 77 in the early 1950s transformed it into the major north-south artery through town. The houses that remain on this once sleepy street have been converted to commercial use.

▲Map continued on next spread

C-1 404 W. Main St.

C-2 408 W. Main and 407 Water St.
Fire-Police Building *(now Fire Station No. 1)*

C-3 410 W. Main St.

C-4 414 W. Main St.

C-5 417 W. Main St.

C-6 500 W. Main St.

C-7 501 W. Main St.
First Presbyterian Church

C-8 503 W. Main St.

C-9 510 W. Main St.

C-10 511 W. Main St.
Waxahachie Masonic Temple *(now Boze Mitchell McKibbin Funeral Home)*

C-11 512 W. Main St.

C-12 515 W. Main St.
Nicholas P. Sims Library

C-13 604 W. Main St.

C-14 605 W. Main St.

C-15 700 W. Main St.

C-16 701 W. Main St.

C-17 705 W. Main St.

C-18 708 W. Main St.

C-19 711 W. Main St.

C-20 712 W. Main St.

C-21 716 W. Main St.

C-22 717 W. Main St.

C-23 802 W. Main St.

C-24 808 W. Main St.

C-25 809 W. Main St.

C-26 813 W. Main St.

C-27 814 W. Main St.

C-28 817 W. Main St.

C-29 818 W. Main St.

C-30 819 W. Main St.

C-31 902 W. Main St.

C-32 903 W. Main St.

C-33 905 W. Main St.

C-34 906 W. Main St.

C-35 912 W. Main St.

C-36 208 Patrick St.

C-37 219 Patrick St.

C-38 221 Patrick St.

C-39 232 Patrick St.

C-40 233 Patrick St.

C-41 239 Patrick St.

C-42 243 Patrick St.

C-43 821 Circle St.
Waxahachie Cotton Mill Office Building

C-44 814 Water St.

C-45 213 Gibson St.

C-46 716 Water St.

C-47 700 Water St.

C-48 213 N. Hawkins St.

C-49 219, 221 N. Hawkins St.

C-50 604 Water St.

C-51 514 Water St.

C-52 511 Water St.

C-53 510 Water St.

C-54 406 Water St.

C-55 210 N. Monroe St.
Waxahachie Bottling Works

C-56 106 S. Monroe St.
Southland Office Building

C-57 414 W. Franklin St.

C-58 415, 417, 419 W. Franklin St.

C-59 420, 422 W. Franklin St.

C-60 407 W. Jefferson St.
Ellis County Woman's Building

C-61 409 W. Jefferson St.

C-62 413, 415 W. Jefferson St.

C-63 417 W. Jefferson St.

C-64 507 W. Jefferson St.

C-65 510 W. Jefferson St.

C-66 513 W. Jefferson St.

C-67 527 W. Jefferson St.

C-68 600 W. Jefferson St.

C-69 601 W. Jefferson St.

C-70 604 W. Jefferson St.

C-71 607 W. Jefferson St.

C-72 106, 108, 110 S. Hawkins St.

C-73 200 S. Hawkins St.

C-74 206 S. Hawkins St.

C-75 207 S. Hawkins St.

C-76 210 S. Hawkins St.

C-77 214 S. Hawkins St.

C-78 300 S. Hawkins St.
Waxahachie City Cemetery

C-79 301 S. Hawkins
Paul Richards Park

C-80 1000 W. Main St.

C-81 1001 W. Main St.

C-82 1008 W. Main St.

C-83 1009 W. Main St.

C-84 1015 W. Main St.

◆ *C-85–C-109 on pp. 124-25*

C-110
301 N. Elm St.
The Appliance House

C-111 500 Royal St.

C-112 503 Ferris Ave.

C-113 507 Ferris Ave.

C-114 512 Ferris Ave.

C-115 519 Ferris Ave.

C-116 609 Ferris Ave.

C-117 617 Ferris Ave.

C-118 407 W. Parks St.

C-119 409 W. Parks St.

C-120 412 W. Parks St.

C-121 502 W. Parks St.

C-122 501 Gibson St.

C-123 411 Gibson
W. Ward School *(now Waxahachie Independent School District Administration Building)*

C-124 408 Gibson St.

C-125 608 Royal St.

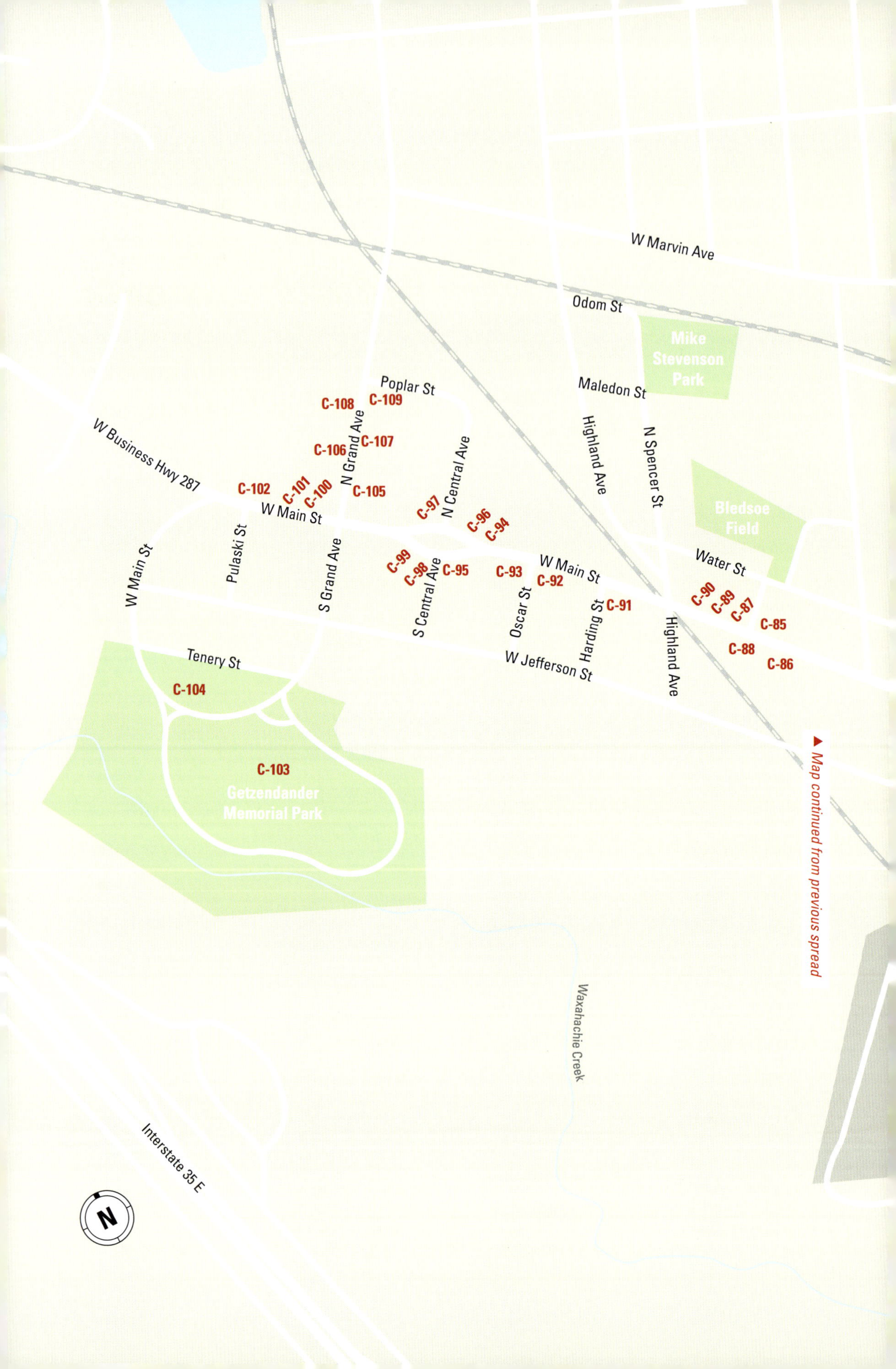

▲ Map continued from previous spread

◆ C-1-C-84 on pp.122-23

C-85 1020 W. Main St.

C-86 1021 W. Main St.

C-87 1022 W. Main St.

C-88 1025 W. Main St.

C-89 1026 W. Main St.

C-90 1030 W. Main St.

C-91 1109 W. Main St.

C-92 1121 W. Main St.

C-93 1203 W. Main St.

C-94 1206 W. Main St.

C-95 1209 W. Main St.

C-96 1210 W. Main St.

C-97 1300 W. Main St.
Coca Cola Bottling Plant

C-98 1303 W. Main St.

C-99 1307 W. Main St.

C-100 1404 W. Main St.

C-101 1408 W. Main St.

C-102 1500 W. Main St.

C-103 W. End Park
(now Getzendaner Memorial Park)

C-104 Chautauqua Auditorium

C-105 202 N. Grand Ave.

C-106 203 N. Grand Ave.

C-107 206 N. Grand Ave.

C-108 209 N. Grand Ave.

C-109 212 N. Grand Ave.

◆ C-110-C-125 on pp.122-23

C-1
404 West Main Street

c. 1893

In the early 1890s this lot was empty and owned by the Christian Church, which stood just to the west, where the fire station is now located. Church member and prominent businessman John C. Gibson purchased the lot in May of 1893. Since the lot extended the full depth of the block, from Main Street to Water Street, he was able to build two almost identical houses back-to-back, this one facing West Main and the other facing Water. City directories indicate that he used both as rental housing, with Wells Fargo agent J. E. Light living here in 1895. In 1907, soon after the death of his wife and a year before his own death, John Gibson provided support for several of his female relations by deeding this property to them. The house is a well-preserved example of a popular Waxahachie house type in the 1890s, the T-plan, although in this and many other cases, it might be called more accurately a cruciform plan, for a rear wing extends from the center of the house in addition to the front wing. A more upscale example of a T-plan house, built as the residence of a dry goods merchant, can be found farther down the street at **1008 West Main**.

C-2
408 West Main and 407 Water Streets
Fire-Police Building
[now Fire Station No. 1]
1963; Upshaw & Todd, architects;
C & L Construction Company, contractor
1999-2002; Anthony Mottla, architect;
Better Build Construction, contractor

When built in 1963, this back-to-back building was Fire Station #1 on Main Street and City Police Station on Water Street. It was part of the 1961 bond package that also funded the new City Hall at **104 North Elm Street** (and Fire Station #2 on John Arden Drive). Designed by Dallas-based partners Forrest Upshaw and Stuart Todd, the original building was minimalist in appearance with the Water Street façade showing similarities to Upshaw's Southland building at **106 Monroe Street**. By the late 1990s, it was used solely as a fire station, and the cramped department offices on the Water Street side prompted Fire Chief David Hudgins to initiate the remodeling project that produced the present façades. On Main Street, the original recessed glazed entry and rock-faced west corner were squared off and bricked while the Water Street side was extended outward to add office and meeting space on the interior and to create a mini-ceremonial plaza on the outside. Images of historic events and the cornerstone from the demolished 1892 City Hall are displayed around the plaza. The large bell displayed on West Main originally hung in the tower of the 1892 city hall and fire station that once stood two blocks to the east.

C-3
410 West Main Street
c. 1915-20

The long section of this L-plan house may date to 1887, when the newspaper reported that J. P. H. Nelson's "new residence near the Christian Church will be completed soon." When the church building burned in 1892, the paper noted that Nelson's house was damaged but not destroyed. The 1898 through 1914 Sanborn maps show a two-story porchless I-plan house on this lot with its narrow gable end oriented to Main Street. By the 1925 Sanborn map, the current reorientation and expansion (or replacement) of the original house had been completed. Nelson served as county surveyor before becoming the city engineer who surveyed the 1889 proposal to extend the city boundaries. After the city council approved the extension in May of 1890, the newspaper reported that Nelson was laying out new streets and establishing lines of old ones. Nelson's sister Madge inherited the house upon his death in 1915, and its current appearance probably dates to that time.

C-4
414 West Main Street
c. 1888, 1896

Large houses close to town, including this one, became ripe for conversion to boarding houses in the 1890s, as prosperous families moved to the more desirable neighborhoods being developed further out West Main and East Marvin. Originally built by dry goods merchant Nathan Brown in the late 1880s, this house was expanded in 1896 by its new owners for just such a purpose. Dr. W. F. and Gertrude West paid contractor H. D. Timmons $915 to "be used in the improvement" of the house, which probably involved adding the gable-front bay on the left and extra rooms to the rear. In the 1900 Census the household included W. F., his second wife Lillian, three children, two black servants, Lillian's parents, and eight boarders. A subsequent owner, widow Mary M. Wyatt, continued to take in boarders. After she married John Beatty in 1916, the couple also ran a boarding house across the street at **417 West Main**. Operating two houses may have been too much, for they sold the other house in 1920.

Originally the house was probably a modified L-plan, with the bay on the right dating from that period. Its narrower windows are typical of the 1880s. The 1898 Sanborn map, which was the earliest to include this part of Main Street, indicates that the bay on the left had been added by then and that the porch wrapped entirely round the right side to the rear of the house. The side portion of the porch has been enclosed since then. Even with such changes and additions made over the years, the overall appearance and proportions of the house are representative of the late nineteenth-century Queen Anne style.

C-5
417 West Main Street
1893

Although built in 1893, the exterior details of this two-story modified L-plan house reflect many changes by its owners over the years. In April 1893 the *Ellis County Mirror* noted that Dr. D. G. Thompson had his "old residence removed and will erect a handsome one in its stead," but by 1917 this stretch of Main Street had declined in desirability for single family residences. John and Mary Beatty, who also owned the house across the street at **414 West Main**, bought this property and turned it into a boarding house. Texas Power and Light foreman Earl Miller and his wife Maude purchased it in 1923 and lived here through the 1920s. Photographer Moreland Herring bought the house in 1948 and lived upstairs with his wife for twenty-six years, using the lower floor as his studio. During Mr. Herring's ownership, much of the original decorative exterior woodwork was removed and replaced by extensive wrought-iron work. The large multi-paned windows on the lower level of the front bay date to that period. In the 1980s, the wrought iron was replaced with antique porch supports and decorative brackets from a house in Mississippi.

C-6
500 West Main Street
c. 1890s

Although this house reflects alterations by many builders over the years, the composition of its three front gables, projecting varying distances from the pyramidal roof, remains the major, and most distinctive, element of its appearance. The gables and pyramidal roof probably date from the late 1890s or early 1900s. The sun porch on the east and the front porch with its plain, slightly tapered supports date to between 1914 and 1925. Dr. R. P. Sweatt built a house on this lot in the 1870s, but it appears on the 1886 bird's-eye view as a side gable cottage with rear ell, set well back from the street. That structure may remain within or behind the current house, but no traces are visible from the street. Benjamin F. Spalding bought the house in 1886 and moved here from Franklin Street with his young wife Mary and their two sons. Benjamin had come to Texas in 1859 with his brother John. He bought John's furniture business in the mid 1870s, and in 1882 surprised his family by marrying his sister-in-law's youngest sister, who was twenty years his junior. Benjamin sold the furniture business to his cousin Sterling Spalding in 1891 and concentrated on his farming interests until his death in 1908. His widow Mary continued to live in the house until her death in 1933.

C-7
501 West Main Street
First Presbyterian Church
1916-17; W. W. Edwards, contractor

When Waxahachie's Southern Presbyterian congregation placed the cornerstone for the town's only Beaux-Arts-Classical-Style church building on January 7, 1917, construction was already well underway. The unknown architect used classical Greek elements to highlight an accomplished façade of depth and variety. Although the projecting Greek temple front dominates the façade, its four columns frame only windows, not an entrance. The entrance bays are recessed to its sides and are approached by long stairways that extend forward to the sidewalk. Landings at the temple base break the ascent and are joined by a balustraded terrace that provided a place for the congregation to mingle after services. The Greek Doric order is used for the columns and pediment, and Greek anthemions, or palmette designs, surmount the entrance doors. The blue and gray tones of the stained glass windows stand out against the beige and cream colors of the brick walls and trim, and windows are liberally distributed on all four sides of the building. When the *Daily Light* announced on July 29, 1916, that W. W. Edwards had won the contract for the church, the reporter avoided any stylistic descriptions of the design, describing the temple façade as a "gable front," but he noted that there were "plenty of windows, for ventilation." The lower level was to house not only Sunday school rooms, but also a public gym. When Waxahachie's two Presbyterian churches merged in the 1970s, this building was sold to the Ellis County Art Association. Recently acquired by Lake Properties, plans for the building have not yet been announced.

C-8
503 West Main Street
c. early 1890s

This one-story modified L-plan cottage originally stood a few feet to the east, but was moved to make room for the new Presbyterian church when owners W. D. and Byrdie Anderson sold the property in 1916. It then served as the manse for the minister. The presence of two hipped roofs between the gabled wings is unusual, but accentuates the asymmetrical corner entrance. Deed records do not provide clear evidence for the builder or date of construction, but the 1895 directory shows merchant S. Y. Matthews living here, and the footprint on the 1898 Sanborn map matches this house. In 1899 Matthews moved farther out Main Street to the new West End addition and built **1121 West Main**. The porch has been filled in for commercial purposes.

C-9
510 West Main Street
1909

The history of this block provides an object lesson on the mobility of buildings in the early twentieth century. The 1886 bird's-eye view and the 1898 Sanborn maps show a small side-gable cottage on this lot that was moved to the rear of the block (513 Water Street) by the time the 1904 Sanborn was produced. Next door to the east, a one-story cottage (no longer extant) was turned around and "redone" for its owner Dr. Leonard Keplinger, according to an April 1907 article in the local newspaper. Keplinger also owned this lot and had this one-story hipped roof bungalow built for rental in early 1909. The March 11 *Daily Light* reported that Dr. and Mrs. G. W. Stone would be occupying the house, which was an "attractive building" with appointments that were "right up to now." Dr. Keplinger was an eye, ear, nose, and throat specialist who practiced in Waxahachie for twenty-nine years.

C-10
511 West Main Street
Waxahachie Masonic Temple
[now Boze Mitchell McKibbin Funeral Home]
1925-26; Westbrook-Crown Co., architects;
O. B. Bennett, contractor

This three-story Neoclassical style Masonic Temple was entirely dedicated to lodge activities when it was constructed. Waxahachie's previous temple, built in 1889 (**201 South College**), included commercial and office rental space below the lodge rooms to provide income and support the building maintenance. This new temple echoed the changing preferences among Masons in the early twentieth century to exclude commercial uses in their buildings. A perspective drawing by the architects, published in the *Dallas Morning News* on November 22, 1925, shows the original entrance, now obscured by later additions. A prominent broken pediment crowned a central entrance door flanked by pedimented windows at ground level. The ground floor contained a game room, banquet hall, and lodge offices. The lodge hall on the second floor included additional seating on a mezzanine level. The multipaned windows on the upper floors of the façade have been filled in, but the remaining windows on the sides indicate the original fenestration patterns.

Depression-era funding shortages led the Masons to lease the first floor to the Spalding-Omohundro Funeral Home in 1935. The Masons moved into a new lodge building in 1992. This building still presents an image of imposing solidity as it rises above the funeral home additions that surround its base. The one-story L-plan cottage that originally stood here was moved to the rear of the lot by the Masons before beginning construction. When James F. Saxon and Thomas H. Champion, both of Tyler, purchased the funeral home in 1937, the *Daily Light* noted that the "residence in the rear" was undergoing extensive repairs before Mr. Champion moved in with his family. Perhaps the addition of brick veneer on the façade of the cottage dates to that time.

C-11
512 West Main Street
c. 1883

O. F. Parks sold this lot in July of 1884 for $1,400 more than the $300 he paid to purchase it two years previously, indicating that he built this house during that interval. Subsequent owners appear to have used the property for rental income until the widowed Mrs. Nora Lamberth purchased the house in 1898. She lived here with her children until 1915, when she sold it to R. J. Gammon, a sales clerk at the Jolesch and Chaska department store. Gammon's wife Mamie continued to live in the house after his death in 1936. Although remodeled over the years and adapted to commercial use, the original character of the house is clear in the forward-projecting gable wing and the L-wing to the right. The steeply pitched gable roofs and the second floor windows extending into the gables are characteristic of the Gothic Revival style, although this simplified version lacks the decorated bargeboards often associated with that style. The tall narrow windows are typical of the 1880s. A house of similar design was pictured in an 1887 St. Louis newspaper article about Waxahachie as an example of the better houses built in the town.

C-12
515 West Main Street
Nicholas P. Sims Library
1903-04; S. Wemyss Smith, architect; Stephenson Contrcting Co., contractors

The City Beautiful movement arrived in Waxahachie with the Sims Library. The movement's supporters aimed to improve society by integrating beautiful architecture and planned environments into America's civic centers. The library's Beaux-Arts Classical building and its placement well back from the street, within a landscaped park setting, embodied those ideals. The building is a gem of compact monumentality, with carefully designed details that emphasize the central entrance bay without destroying the unity of the three-part façade. Its resemblance to Dallas's 1901 Carnegie Library is not surprising, given that architect S. Wemyss-Smith trained with the architect of the Dallas library, Marshall R. Sanguinet. Born in England in 1876, Wemyss-Smith came to America in 1892, apprenticing with Sanguinet & Messer in Fort Worth and studying at Kenyon College in Ohio. He practiced alone and with partners in Fort Worth and Waco before moving to Oklahoma City in 1907 to partner with S. A. Layton and design the state capitol. He obtained the Waxahachie commission after the Library Board issued a public request for plans in May 1903. Wemyss-Smith, in partnership with Stewart Moore, also designed libraries in Corsicana, Cleburne, Belton, and Terrell.

Waxahachie's library was built of Tiffany-Enameled Bricks that were manufactured in Illinois, with contrasting copper panels and cornice. The library's unornamented later additions could have created a jarring contrast with the bold Neoclassical building, but the use of the same glazed-brick facing helps them to recede into a bland, almost supportive background. Waxahachie's first Masonic Hall and Academy originally stood on the site, which was later owned by Mr. and Mrs. W. H. Getzendaner. They donated the land to the city in 1896 for a public park but stated their desire that it would serve as a site for a public library in the future.

Although built during the early period of Carnegie grants for library construction, Waxahachie's library was privately funded. Local landowner Nicholas P. Sims willed the entirety of his estate (around $60,000) for the establishment and maintenance of a public library and lyceum for Ellis County. His stepson-in-law Oscar E. Dunlap suggested the bequest to Mr. Sims and served as chairman of the Board of Trustees, shepherding the project through its planning and execution. The *Enterprise* even noted Dunlap's trip "East" in September 1905 to "secure a librarian." He may have veered a bit north after setting out, for only two weeks later the paper announced the arrival from Fayetteville, Arkansas, of the new librarian, Irene Dabney Gallaway. (The Waxahachie newspapers and city directory consistently spelled her name "Galloway," but she spelled it "Gallaway" in the genealogical books she later wrote.)The paper noted she had "installed a number of Carnegie libraries in Texas, and has considerable experience in library work." She remained in charge of the Sims Library until 1920, and ended her career back in Fayetteville, as head of that public library.

C-13
604 West Main Street
1904; Hubbell & Greene, architects; Dennis Mahoney, contractor

Dennis Mahoney and his wife Mary built this handsome Neoclassical-style house two years after he was awarded the contract to construct the main building for Trinity University when it moved to Waxahachie. (That imposing structure still stands at the center of the former Trinity campus at **1200 Sycamore**.) Mahoney had been active in Waxahachie and the surrounding region since the 1880s, with projects that included the first Waxahachie street railway in 1889, the 1899 east wing of the Old Main Building at the University of Texas at Austin (demolished), and Waxahachie's 1889 Masonic Temple Building (with H. D. Timmons). In his 1904 mechanic's lien with

H. D. Timmons & Sons, Mahoney specified that he would pay Timmons $1,000 for the brick, lime, cement, sand, and lumber to be used in the construction of the house, but that he (Mahoney) would build the house according to plans by the Dallas architects Hubbell & Greene, the same architects who designed Trinity's building. In their design for the Mahoney house, the full-height portico with elaborately detailed pediment and Ionic columns dominates the façade, and large-scale dentils adorn the pediment.

James P. Hubbell and Herbert M. Greene formed their partnership in 1900 and designed a number of homes and prominent buildings in Dallas, including the Parkland Hospital and the Scottish Rite Cathedral, both in 1913, and the Neiman Marcus building of 1914. In 1922, Greene became the university architect of the University of Texas, succeeding Cass Gilbert. Mahoney died only two years after constructing the house, but his wife continued to live here until her death in 1932. Their daughter, Bertie Lee, returned to the house in 1943 with her husband, William Thompson, and remained until her death in 1967, when it became the first home of the Ellis County Museum, now located at the southeast corner of the square.

C-14
605 West Main Street
1896; H. D. Timmons, builder

On March 12, 1896, only seven days after purchasing the lot, deputy tax collector Joe C. Thompson and his wife Minnie contracted to pay H. D. Timmons $1,800 to build this house, described in the mechanic's lien as a "frame, shingle roof house with five rooms, two halls, two galleries, four fire places, one flue, brick piers, bath room, closets, and water connections." By May 8, the *Enterprise* noted that the "cottage" was "nearly ready for occupancy." Timmons was an active Waxahachie builder who also served as a school trustee and city alderman. The Thompsons sold the house to Charles R. Gibson in 1910. Born in Alabama, Gibson came to Waxahachie after the Civil War. He founded the *Enterprise* in 1876, but sold it when he was elected to the state legislature in 1878, where he served as Speaker of the House during the eighteenth session. When Gibson and his wife Emma bought this house, he was sixty-eight years old, retired from politics, and writing a regular column for the newspaper. He was known throughout the area for his "squibs," as he called his writings, and in 1925 Waxahachie's banks and stores closed in honor of his eighty-third birthday. He died later that same year. This modified L-plan house is distinguished by the small angled projection at its northeast corner. A similar angled projection was included in the house at **1002 East Marvin**, built 1893-94, and one owned by T. A. Ferris (no longer extant) that was illustrated in an 1887 St. Louis newspaper article about Waxahachie.

C-15
700 West Main Street
1913

The *Daily Light* on February 16, 1913, noted the recent completion of this house for Mrs. Sara E. Bynum, describing it as her "splendid new residence on Main Street." Sara was a widow in her mid-fifties when she built the house. Although relatively well-off financially, she built a house of this size with the specific intent of taking in lodgers. The February 7 *Daily Light* reported that "Miss Zelma Beachum and sisters" were moving to the "new Bynum residence on West Main street." For much of the 1920s, S. J. Bennett and his wife Eura Lee stayed here. S. J. was a railroad conductor, and Eura Lee ran the Nifty Thrifty Dress Making Shop in the Curlin Building downtown. The wide overhanging eaves, absence of decorative detail, and horizontal emphasis of the porch and roof lines are characteristic of the Prairie style. The closely-placed windows on the second floor at the east side indicate the presence of what originally was a sleeping porch, a popular feature in early twentieth-century houses.

C-16
701 West Main Street
1914; S. E. Hanshaw, contractor

The year before building this one-story brick bungalow Frank C. Rogers was working at Cheeves Department Store on the square and living with his wife Rebecca in a frame cottage at **503 West Main**. When the 1910 Census was taken they also had two lodgers at that address. By 1914 their situation had improved enough to enable the construction of this stylish new house that they did not have to share with lodgers. When the *Daily Light* reported Frank's three-week buying trip to New York and Chicago, his position as manager of Cheeves was also mentioned. Advertising revenue from the store may have influenced journalistic coverage of Frank's activities, for the *Daily Light* also noted when he hired Dallas contractor S. E. Hanshaw for this house in May 1914, as well as when construction was completed. The *Dallas Morning News* even published a photograph of the bungalow in October of 1915. Although the original colors cannot be determined from that black-and-white photograph, it does show the paint tones in the gables to have been the reverse of the current ones, with light-colored decorative woodwork standing out against a dark ground.

C-17
705 West Main Street
c. 1913

Eye, ear, nose, and throat specialist Dr. Edgar F. Gough and his wife Clyde built this substantial two-story house after purchasing the lot in January of 1913. They moved here from an older house further west on Main Street (**912 West Main**). Dr. Gough worked downtown until he built this house with a space for his office. The house also was large enough to allow lodgers, including dentist Charles A. Dahnke and his wife Essie in 1920 and schoolteacher Irene Smith in 1930. The strong symmetry of the central projecting two-story porch with paired windows on either side gives the impression of a foursquare house, but a closer look at the first level reveals that the side porch is inset, and the lower portion of the front porch extends across only the right two-thirds of the façade. In 1939 a goldfish pond in the back yard made the pages of the *Dallas Morning News* when a cardinal was reported to have been seen feeding the fish.

C-18
708 West Main Street
c. 1920

This one-and-a-half story bungalow probably dates to around 1920, when the appraised tax valuation jumped from $1,500 to $2,500. It either replaced the previous one-story 1890s cottage shown on Sanborn maps or involved a major renovation and addition to that structure. Its basic form, horizontal proportions, and decorative details are all representative of the early 1920s rather than the nineteenth century. The broad expanse of the low hipped roof incorporates the deep wraparound porch and dominates the view from the street, distracting attention from the two-story sections toward the rear. Mrs. Alta Taylor Willis built the house when she was in her early sixties. The daughter of Ellis County's first elected sheriff, J. E. Prince, Sr., Alta married R. D. Willis, who died when she was still in her thirties. As a widow with three young children, she entered one of the few occupations open to women in small towns at the time, keeping a boarding house. Census records and city directories document that she continued to rent rooms at this location for most of the next forty years. The three entrances off the porch indicate that this bungalow probably was designed with the renting of separate apartments in mind.

C-19
711 West Main Street
c. 1890, 1908

Originally, this modified L-plan house stood on the lot next door (717 West Main Street) and was the home of merchant Henry Cerf and his family. When the Cerfs moved to New York City in 1906, they sold the property to English-born John Harrison, a prosperous local farmer and businessman. Harrison's failing health had led to his decision to move into town, and he died in September 1907. Only a few months later the *Enterprise* of April 24, 1908, noted that John's son James was converting the cottage on West Main into "a handsome colonial home," and the columns with Ionic capitals and relief ornament in the front gable date from that time. James also married in 1908. A local story claims that James's father arranged the wedding by sending to England for the bride, who arrived with her nanny. However, census records indicate that Fannie Harrison, a cousin, arrived in 1900 at the age of thirty-six and lived for eight years with the Harrison family before marrying James. James was then fifty-one and Fannie in her early forties. When they decided to build a new brick house on their corner lot around 1920, they moved this house to its current location. In the 1920s advertising agent W. H. Grizzard and his wife Hattie owned the house. Their daughter Mabel, principal of the Central Ward School, lived here with them.

C-20
712 West Main Street
1924; Bertram C. Hill, architect; Ramsey Brothers, contractors

Ice was a profitable commodity in the days before air conditioning, and William D. Anderson evidently prospered as the manager of the Waxahachie Ice Works, as well as through investments in varied interests. In August of 1924 the *Texas General Contractors Association Bulletin* recorded Anderson's contract to pay the Ramsey Brothers $25,000 to construct this house, a sizeable sum for the time. Anderson also would have had architect's fees to pay, for he commissioned the prominent Dallas architect Bertram C. Hill to design the house. The resulting design included a double-height, vaulted music room and was significant enough for the *Dallas Morning News* to publish an announcement and picture on September 21, 1924. The multiple steeply pitched gables, arched entrance porch, and patterned brick veneer walls would have been considered in the English Cottage style when the house was built. The substantial servant's house in the rear echoes the materials and style of the main house.

A native of Gonzales, Texas, and a graduate of Texas A&M, Anderson served as a captain in the Spanish American War before moving to Waxahachie. In addition to his position as manager and then president of the Waxahachie Ice Company and his work as a cotton broker, he served as a trustee of Trinity University and president of the Chamber of Commerce, the Guaranty Bank and Trust Company, and the School Board. Anderson continued to live in the house until his death in 1953, and it remained in the family until 1994.

C-21
716 West Main Street

1904; H. A. Overbeck, architect;
B. F. Sargent, contractor

Ed Chaska and his wife Marie built this house after a fire in February 1904 damaged their previous dwelling. The fire evidently did not compromise the structure of the older home, for the *Enterprise* noted that S. P. Skinner bought and moved it to West Jefferson Street for use as rental property. But Chaska and his wife were probably ready for an excuse to build a new house. He was a prominent merchant, co-owner of the Jolesch and Chaska dry goods store on the southwest corner of the square (**200 South Rogers**), and made regular buying trips to the East Coast, often accompanied by his wife. They wanted a stylish new house that would reflect their taste as well as their financial success. Dallas architect H. A. Overbeck provided the plans, and B. F. Sargent was hired to "look after the work," according to the *Enterprise*. In May of 1904, the *Fort Worth Star-Telegram* noted that both Chaska and M. B. Templeton were starting construction of handsome new homes, each to cost the sizable sum of $8,000. Templeton's house, still standing at **203 North Grand**, was more imposing, with its full two stories and massive Ionic columns, but Chaska's was more tightly composed and finely detailed. Its slender Ionic columns and relief ornament in the porch gable give it a Colonial Revival flavor, but the strong horizontal emphasis of the hipped roof and the broad wraparound porch herald the coming of the bungalow, a house type that was just emerging in California at the time. The convex-curved sides of the dominant projecting dormer were also new to Waxahachie at the time and proved to be very popular with the local builders, though usually in a much more modest form. Overbeck also designed the house across the street, at **717 West Main**.

C-22
717 West Main Street

c. 1920; H. A. Overbeck, architect

Although built several years after the house directly across the street (**716 W. Main**), this one-story hipped-roof bungalow shows the same architect, H. A. Overbeck, echoing the form and massing of his previous design, but clothing it in a Mission style rather than Colonial Revival. Cream-colored eaves, corner brackets, and trim highlight and delineate the almost identical brownish-red shades of the brick and the terra cotta roof tiles. Careful design and construction are evident both in the house and servant's house in the rear, but the extent of the actual financial investment is disguised by their relatively modest scale and the conventions of the style. If the $60,000 cost cited in a biographical article about Overbeck in the 1922 *Encyclopedia of Texas* is correct, this was the most expensive house built in Waxahachie at the time. The quality of materials and workmanship undoubtedly contributed to the expense. Several stories relating to the owner's close supervision of the construction and insistence on perfection probably are rooted in truth, and such a close watch would have been easy for him since he was living next door at the time. James W. Harrison and his English wife Fannie moved their previous house to the lot next door (**711 West Main**) and sold it after moving into their new house on the prime corner location. The son of prosperous farmer and businessman John Harrison, James inherited the means to fund this subtle showplace. Tax records indicate that the house was probably built around 1920.

C-23
802 West Main Street
1955; H. H. Harden, contractor

A two-story house built by druggist B. F. Fearis in 1887 stood here until 1954, when the owner Mrs. Dorothy Cosmus offered it for sale "to be moved or torn down," making an empty lot available for construction of West Main Street's second Ranch-style house. (The first was at 704 West Main.) Horace H. Harden, a contractor and builder in Milford (twenty miles south of Waxahachie), bought the property in December 1954. A building permit for this house, described as having six rooms, two baths, and a double garage, was issued to Aubrey Splawn in March 1955, but the property was not officially sold to Aubrey and his wife Leona until June of that year. The house was finished by October 2, when the *Daily Light* noted that Mrs. Splawn hosted the members of the Reagor Springs Home Demonstration Club in her new home. Aubrey was born near Reagor Springs, a few miles east of Waxahachie, but attended Waxahachie schools. He owned and operated the Phillips Weatherstripping Company in Dallas but also farmed in Reagor Springs. He and Leona lived here until his death in 1977.

C-24
808 West Main Street
1889; J. S. Truitt, builder

Beneath and behind several updates, including the brick pillars of the front porch, lies the substantial Queen Anne style house built by merchant and cotton buyer Clark D. Pickett and his wife Belle. They signed the mechanic's lien with J. S. Truitt on July 15, 1889, and on November 8 the newspaper noted that they had moved in. The $4,350 they paid Truitt ensured that the result would be prominent enough to justify the newspaper's description of an "elegant new home" and to stand proudly across the street from city leader John C. Gibson's large two-story house. Pickett sold the house in 1896 to J. H. Miller, president of the Waxahachie National Bank, who remained in the house until he and his family moved farther out to the West End and a house on Grand Street in 1909. George H. Cunningham, a wealthy farmer who was also associated with Miller as vice president of the Waxahachie National Bank, then bought the house. When the 1910 Census was taken the next year, George was eighty-two years old and his wife Tennessee was sixty-nine. Two of their grown children, Jennie and Barzilla, were still single and living at home. George and Jane Hambrich, white servants in their late sixties, lived in a small house at the rear of the property. Daughter Jennie continued to live in the house after her parents died, and her brother Barzilla built the house next door (**814 West Main**). The changes to the front porch were made after 1926, when Dr. M. E. Hastings purchased the property for his family.

C-25
809 West Main Street
c.1888, c. 1930s

The original two-story house that prominent businessman John C. Gibson built on this lot remained at least through 1925, according to the Sanborn maps. An extensive renovation, including the removal of the second floor, took place after that date, but remnants of the earlier house can be seen in the tall narrow windows in the façade, the front doors, and the projecting bay on the east side of the house. Born in Alabama in 1826, Gibson had been an early settler of Waxahachie, arriving in 1863. In addition to varied commercial and agricultural interests, he took such an active part in encouraging the railroads that the first locomotive into Waxahachie was named for him. In 1871 he married Amelia Hines, the widow of John Hines and sister of M. T. Patrick. The house sheltered an extended family for many years, with the 1895 directory showing John's grown son C. W. also living in the house, and the 1900 Census listing John, his wife Amelia, stepdaughter Anna Hines, and niece Kate Burrough. Two years after John's death in 1908, Thomas M. Holland bought the house and lived here with his wife Loula through the 1930s. Holland was with the dry goods firm J. S. Campbell & Co. at **209-211 West Franklin** when he bought the house, but by the 1920s he had moved with the times to become bookkeeper for the Cornwell Motor Company. According to a descendent of the Hollands, the second floor and Victorian-era decorative ornaments were removed in the 1930s after a fire.

C-26
813 West Main Street
1891

The profusion of lacy decorative brackets in the gables and fine spindlework on the porch distinguish this modified L-plan house, along with its balanced, though asymmetrical, composition of multiple triangular gables. On November 27, 1891, the *Enterprise* noted that William A. Gibson was having a "neat residence" built near his father's. It was indeed near, for his father, John C. Gibson, lived next door at **809 West Main**. William later moved to a larger property on Patrick Street and deeded this house to his stepsister, Anna L. Hines, in 1897. Anna continued to live next door with her mother and stepfather, and this house provided rental income. She moved to Dallas in the early 1920s but continued to own the property until her death in 1935.

C-27
814 West Main Street
c. 1914

Barzilla Cunningham built this house for his wife Berta and their infant daughter Leta May in late 1913 or early 1914. He had lived next door at **808 West Main** with his parents for many years and brought his wife to the family home when he finally married in his thirties, but the birth of his child may have provided the impetus for the new house. The *Dallas Morning News* published a photograph of the house in September of 1915 on a page that featured business and development in the North Texas area. The youngest of nine children, Barzilla assisted his aging father, George H. Cunningham, in the management of his affairs, and served as administrator of the substantial estate upon his father's death. When Barzilla died unexpectedly of peritonitis in 1916, Berta moved back to live with her parents, the P. A. Chapmans, across the street at **903 West Main**. This house remained in the Chapman and Cunningham families for many years, with Berta's brother John owning it in the early 1920s, and Barzilla Cunningham's sister, Elizabeth Edmondson, owning it from 1926 until her death in 1941. Elizabeth's daughter, school teacher Betty Kate Edmondson, continued to live in the house for many years. Dallas television weatherman Warren A. Culbertson and his family lived in the house from 1964 to 1999.

The brick veneer and generous dimensions of this side-gable bungalow with shed-roof dormer indicate the prosperity of its builders, although it appears modest between the lighter-colored, taller, more assertive houses on each side. Much of its own substantial size extends to the rear and is less visible from the street. Its basic form is similar to more modest examples in Waxahachie's University neighborhood at **207 University** and **218 Virginia**, but this is the best-preserved, having avoided additions and retaining its original porch supports and windows. The façade features strong symmetry, with triple windows on either side of the entrance door and the central dormer exactly matching the width of the porch entrance bay below it. The symmetry is tempered by the sun porch on the east side and the jog it provides in the roofline. The balanced proportions, details, and plan indicate a skilled designer, but the architect or design source is unknown.

C-28
817 West Main Street
1890; Musgrave, Brasher & Wise, builders

Teacher Kate Burrough was deeded this lot in March of 1890 by her uncle John C. Gibson, and in April of that same year the *Enterprise* noted that carpenters had "commenced erection of a dwelling" for her. The house was complete by June 27, according to the paper. On the twenty-eighth, Kate signed a mechanic's lien to pay Musgrave, Brasher & Wise $1,166 for the construction of the five-room "residence house" on the lot. The residence was intended for rental income, for the 1900 Census shows Kate living with her uncle and aunt at **809 West Main**. Jack Beall, then a state senator, and his wife Patricia were tenants before building their house at **401 Oldham** in 1899. Kate Burrough was born in Winchester, Tennessee and educated at Mary Sharp College in that city before she came to Waxahachie in 1886, when she was eighteen. In 1887 she opened a school in the Academy building on Main, where the Sims Library stands now, but later taught in the public school. She was teaching in Grapevine, Texas, when she married Eugene Kelly in 1907. She and her new husband sold this house in 1908, moved to Mississippi, and eventually moved back to Tennessee. The new owner, Fletcher Norton, used the house for rental income, as did subsequent owners until Jim and Becky Kauffman bought it and began their restoration in 1992.

C-29
818 West Main Street
1924; H. B. Thomson, architect

Farmer and landowner Otis Brack Dunaway replaced his family's nineteenth-century cottage with this Colonial Revival home in 1924. He obtained the plans from Dallas architect Henry B. Thomson in 1923 and advertised in the August 1923 Texas General Contractors Association *Bulletin* for builders to bid on the $11,000 project. Architect Thomson had been born in Texas, but studied at MIT and traveled in Europe before settling in Dallas to practice. He was well-established and busy designing residences in Highland Park as well as commercial projects when he fulfilled this commission for Dunaway. His design for the house de-emphasizes its mass by recessing the east wing behind a corner porch with latticed balustrade on the second floor and by having the west section of the façade project slightly forward.

Dunaway was part owner of Dunaway Brothers Lumber Company and also had farm and land interests. The Dunaways' daughter, Sarah Louise, was fourteen when the house was constructed, and her wedding reception was held here in 1936. After her parents' death, she and her family lived in the house.

C-30
819 West Main Street
1936; O. B. Bennett, builder

In March of 1936 the *Daily Light* reported that the "former McCall home" had been torn down to allow the erection of this "cottage" for Dr. C. R. Wright. The large chimney on the façade and the gable entry with arched door are among the design elements characteristic of Tudor Revival and English cottage style houses of the time, but the bricks patterned like quoins at the corners of the two front wings indicate a French eclectic influence as well. The design closely resembles no. 20459 in *Distinctive Southern Homes*, a catalogue of house designs published by *Holland's Magazine* in February, 1936.

A Methodist minister, Charles R. Wright had served as pastor in several Texas towns and as presiding elder of Waxahachie, Corsicana, Fort Worth, and Waco districts. He also was a member of the board of Fort Worth's Methodist Hospital. It was his wife's family connections that led to the choice of this lot for their new house. Mary Frances Cunningham McCartney Wright was the daughter of wealthy Ellis County farmer and banker George H. Cunningham, who had lived at **808 West Main** for the last few years of his life. In 1936, when Mrs. Wright purchased the lot, two of her nieces lived across the street, Mrs. M. E. Hastings in the old family home at 808 West Main and Betty Kate Edmondson at **814 West Main**. Only a year after the Wrights built their house, Dr. Wright died. Mrs. Wright remained here until her own death in 1948. In early 1949 Dr. Robert Mayo Tenery bought the house and lived here with his family for many years. Dr. Tenery's son, Dr. Rob Tenery, published a memoir, *Dr. Mayo's Boy*, which recounted a history of Waxahachie's health care in the twentieth century through the careers of his father and his grandfather.

C-31
902 West Main Street
1887, 1890

Born in Tennessee in 1830, Robert Pierce Sweatt studied medicine in that state and in Kentucky before moving to Texas in 1852. When he arrived in Waxahachie in 1854, there was only one other physician in the town. After practicing medicine for over thirty years, he had the means to invest in real estate on the western end of Main Street, away from the increasingly busy downtown. The newspaper noted his intent to build on this lot in September of 1887. Two years later, stylish new houses began appearing in the West End Addition, a few blocks away, and they may have inspired Dr. Sweatt or his wife to update their house with a more distinctive look. The polygonal tower and dormers were probably added in March of 1890, when the *Enterprise* noted that Dr. Sweatt "is building a new front that is truly handsome." The renovations were complete by July of that year, when the *Enterprise* reported on the coming out party hosted by the Sweatts for their daughter Julia, "a young rosebud who has just entered the portals of society." The reporter described the house as a "handsome two-story, with wide verandas and large windows, spacious halls and broad staircases that lead to the breezy upper rooms." The distinctive tower and dormers are similar to examples found in the same issue of the magazine *Shoppell's Modern Houses* that included the design used by Mrs. Sweatt's brother, Oscar Dunlap, for his 1890 house at **1203 West Main**. The porch columns with Ionic capitals may date from a later remodeling, perhaps soon after Sweatt's youngest daughter Etta and her husband Muncie L. Campbell inherited the house in 1903. The rear wing that extends out to the east is a more recent addition.

C-32
903 West Main Street

1916; Charles William Bulger, architect; W. W. Huff, contractor

Dallas architect C. W. Bulger designed this Georgian Revival house for P. A. Chapman. When it was completed in December, 1916, the *Daily Light* credited Dallas contractor W. W. Huff as being "in charge of construction." It also declared the house to be "without question the most beautiful residence in this section of the country." Although Chapman began his career as a farmer, he found success in banking and oil investment as well as land and other real estate. By the time he built this house at age sixty-eight, his wealth and reputation reached beyond Waxahachie. The *Dallas Morning News* noted his plans for the house in May of 1916, giving the estimated cost to be from $20,000 to $25,000. The estimated cost rose to over $40,000 by December, according to the Waxahachie paper. Chapman continued to invest in a variety of areas, buying part of the original King Ranch in South Texas in 1919. The *Daily Light* probably was not exaggerating when Chapman was described as a "business genius" in his obituary of 1924.

Architect C. W. Bulger, who also designed the Praetorian Building in Dallas, created an interesting interplay between curving and rectangular elements in this strongly symmetrical façade. Instead of a central entrance door, the curved balustrade of the porch centers above a decorative oval window and below a Palladian dormer. The delicate multiple-mullioned windows of the sunroom and sleeping porch wing on the east side form a contrast to the solidity and balance of the brick façade that would not have been quite as pronounced originally, when two of the first-floor full-length arched windows were surrounded by lacy wood latticework. Chapman's substantial investment is evident in the design, materials, and craftsmanship of the house rather than in its size.

C-33
905 West Main Street

c. 1888, c. 1937

Although significantly altered in the 1930s, this house originally dates to the late 1880s. Businessman John C. Gibson, who lived in a large two-story house a few lots to the east at **809 West Main**, owned the property and probably built this house for rental income. Residents included physician A. B. Small, who lived here in 1895. Gibson sold the house in 1900, but it continued as a rental for many years. The front chimney and west wing were added after 1925, according to Sanborn maps. The current entrance porch with curved roof probably dates to 1937, when Gertrude Davis, the widow of R. H. Davis, bought the property.

C-34
906 West Main Street

1903-04

The *Enterprise* noted that attorney John Thomas Spencer completed this "handsome little cottage" in January 1904. It is possible that some of the materials used in its construction came from the 1870 Cumberland Presbyterian Church, for the *Enterprise* reported three months earlier that Spencer had bought the church building, which was being replaced, and that he would convert it into a "handsome residence." This probably was not a case of moving the church intact and adapting it. (A photograph of the church shows that it was a simple front-gable rectangular structure with a tower above the west entrance.) Spencer was born in Ellis County and educated at Trinity University (before it moved to Waxahachie) and the University of Texas in Austin. He began his law practice in Waxahachie around 1892, went into partnership with O. H. Chapman in 1902, and was elected county judge in 1906, serving in that capacity for four years. His wife, Mamie, continued to live in the house after John died in 1937. The modified L-plan house includes a Colonial Revival pediment above the entry porch. Its exterior design is similar to one by Dallas architect E. H. Silven that was published in an April 1901 issue of the magazine *Farm and Ranch*. The addition to the rear and east dates from the 1990s.

C-35
912 West Main Street
1896

Story E. Fowler and his wife Florence bought this lot in April of 1896, and on May 26, the *Enterprise* noted that "Story E. Fowler will erect a neat one-story residence on his property recently purchased in the West End." The delicate decorative woodwork and the corner entrance add complexity and depth to a modified L-plan cottage. Fowler's choice of location, close to the fashionable new West End Addition, and his investment in elaborate, stylish ornament declared his business and social aspirations. A few years later his real estate and loan business was successful enough to enable him to build a much larger two-story home (no longer extant) two blocks away on Main Street that was pictured in the *Dallas Morning News* in August of 1911. Eye, ear, nose, and throat specialist Edgar F. Gough and his wife Clyde purchased this house from the Fowlers in 1909, living here until 1922, when they moved to the house they built at **705 West Main**. Thomas H. Jones, who owned and managed the Waxahachie Hardware Company, moved here with his wife Lucy and stayed in the house through the 1930s.

C-36
208 Patrick Street
1951; Boese & Harkrider, architects;
McCann Construction Co., contractors

The Fort Worth architectural and engineering firm of Boese & Harkrider designed Waxahachie's first public housing project, consisting of thirty one-story buildings with two apartments in each and one administrative building. Completed in the summer of 1951, the buildings appear similar but are composed of three different models in graduated sizes, with the smallest model having one-bedroom apartments, and the largest three-bedroom apartments. The *Daily Light* of April 8, 1951, noted that each apartment would have metal kitchen cabinets, an electric refrigerator, and a gas range. Flat roofs topped the buildings originally, in keeping with the modern style often utilized in public housing of the period. Design standards published by the Federal Public Housing Authority mandated distances between buildings and minimum room sizes, as well as building materials that were fireproof and low in maintenance costs. The flat roofs, however, led to recurring leakage problems, and they were eventually replaced by the current hipped roofs. Since the project was planned during the era of segregation, a separate African American complex, consisting of twenty-two duplex buildings similar in design to these, was built at **800 North Getzendaner** and opened in 1953. Boese & Harkrider also designed Texas public housing projects in Brownsville (1949-51), Corsicana (1952), and Paris (1952-53).

C-37
219 Patrick Street
c. 1911, 1950

This one-story pyramidal-roofed structure first served as a mule barn behind the house next door at **221 Patrick** for Thomas J. Bullard, after he bought the property in 1911. The only son of Ellis County pioneer D. B. Bullard, Thomas raised and traded livestock and needed a large barn to shelter his sizable herd of mules and other livestock. In the early 1890s he had established a monthly mule market in downtown Waxahachie, known as First Monday, which became a major regional market. Hundreds of buyers and sellers swarmed around the square each First Monday, bringing business to the local stores and saloons, in addition to the trades among themselves. Thomas retired from the livestock business in 1922, but the extra-large barn remained behind the house until 1948-49, when it was donated by the owner Rev. E. S. Bledsoe to the Optimist Club and moved to its current location. Proceeds from an annual carnival held on the square enabled the Optimists to convert the barn into a youth center that opened in 1950 and to build the swimming pool to the south a couple of years later. In 1953, local Baptist minister Herman Rice received attention in the *Dallas Morning News* when he objected to boys and girls swimming together in the pool and dancing together in the center. He also accused the club of financing its activities with the proceeds of gambling, meaning the carnival's fund-raising bingo games. The controversy soon settled, and bingo, mixed bathing, and dancing continued here for many years. From 1989 until 2009 the building served as a community senior center.

C-38
221 Patrick Street
1897, 1922

A major renovation of 1922 hides most traces of the original 1897 house, but this side-gable bungalow displays eccentric variations from a symmetrical form that probably reflect the plan of the earlier structure. William A. Gibson and his wife Electra built the original house a year after he and Marshall T. Patrick bought a twenty-acre plot to divide between them. Gibson was a prominent grocer who only a few years before had built a cottage at **813 West Main**, next to his father's home. Nonetheless, he took the opportunity to share in this investment with his stepmother's brother and built the first house on the block two years before Patrick started construction on his own house. Thomas J. Bullard and his wife Mary bought the Gibsons' house and acreage in 1911. Bullard retired from his livestock business in 1922, and the *Daily Light* noted that they were remodeling and repainting in June of that year. The current exterior probably dates from that remodeling. The large mule barn that Bullard built behind this house was later moved next door and converted to the Optimist Youth Center.

C-39
232 Patrick Street
1906

This lot formed part of a large block set aside in the early 1900s for cotton-mill workers' housing, but Marshall T. Patrick guaranteed a buffer between himself and the workers when he purchased the six lots across the street from his imposing residence at **233 Patrick** in November 1905. He sold this lot to Mrs. Emma Bickley the next day, and she probably built her one-story side-gable cottage with central dormer soon after. She was living here with her two children by the time of the 1907 directory. Although the house appears rather plain at first glance, particularly in comparison to the Patrick house across the street, closer inspection reveals interesting touches, including an entrance gable emerging from the porch shed roof that echoes the dormer gable above. Decorative shingles adorn the gables and the dormer, and the entrance door is slightly recessed. Traveling salesman W. L. McElree and his wife Corinne bought the house from Mrs. Bickley in 1914 and lived here, along with their son W. L. Jr. and his wife Mackie.

C-40
233 Patrick Street

1899-1900

Joseph W. Northrup, architect; C. J. Griggs, builder

It comes as no surprise that the street bears the name of the owner of this imposing two-and-a-half story frame house, Marshall T. Patrick. The house dominates the streetscape, through its size, distinctive design, and generous lot, all of which reflected Patrick's financial presence in the community. At the time the house was built, Patrick owned extensive land and livestock holdings and served as president of Waxahachie's First National Bank, which later merged with Citizens National Bank. Born in Tennessee, he arrived in Waxahachie after the Civil War and established his fortune by operating a freighting business and then a grocery. In 1881 he helped to found the private bank that became the First National Bank. Although Patrick moved with his wife and three daughters to Nashville, Tennessee, in the 1880s for the girls to attend school, he continued to visit Waxahachie regularly to look after his farming and livestock interests. In the late 1890s the family returned to Waxahachie and rented a house while they planned and built this house to provide a suitable setting for the social activities of the three unmarried daughters, all in their twenties. Family legend says that daughter Emma had wanted a brick Colonial design until the builder, C. J. Griggs, convinced her that the land on the site would not properly support its weight. The final design, which came from the pages of the May 1892 issue of the *Scientific American, Architects and Builders Edition*, featured Colonial decorative elements, which must have appealed to Emma, adorning a basic Queen Anne form, with prominent corner tower, asymmetrical façade, shingle siding, and steeply pitched roofs. The side gable roof of the central core provides an interesting variation from the more common hipped roofs of Waxahachie's modified L-plan houses with corner towers. When the editor of the *Enterprise* published his description of the new house on February 9, 1900, he lauded its modern conveniences and the landscaping with its curving graveled driveways and walks. Well water supplied the house and gardens, pumped by the windmill emerging from the picturesque structure, also based on a published design, that still can be seen behind the house. Daughter Annie married lawyer and Deputy District Clerk Edgar P. Kemble in the house three years after its completion, and they both lived here until the house next door (**239 Patrick**) was built for them. Funeral services were held in the house for all five family members, including daughter Emma, who never married and continued to live here until her death in 1969, at the age of ninety-four.

C-41
239 Patrick Street

1907

Symmetry reigns supreme in this charming one-and-a-half story side-gable bungalow. The central front gable of the entrance is flanked by gable dormers in the roof, and on the first-floor façade paired windows flank the entrance door with sidelights. Even the double columns of the porch reinforce the theme of balanced pairs. Although built only a few years later than the large Patrick house next door, this house represents a totally different style and aesthetic. In contrast to the vertical emphasis and asymmetry of the larger house, this one hugs the earth and possesses the horizontal emphasis of an early bungalow. Both, however, display an attention to proportions, details, and style that resulted in distinctive designs. It is therefore not surprising that this house was built for M. T. Patrick's daughter Annie and her husband Edgar P. Kemble a few years after their marriage in 1903. The *Daily Light* reported on July 29, 1907, that the Kembles had moved into their new home, where they entertained Missouri Governor Joseph W. Folk. (Governor Folk was in town to address the Chautauqua Assembly.) The Patrick family involvement in building the house is reflected in the fact that the property was never transferred to Annie and her husband. After Edgar's untimely death in 1911, Annie and her children moved back to the large family house next door, and this house was rented until it was sold in 1919 to garage owner J. T. Cooper.

C-42
243 Patrick Street
c. 1915

Howard W. Wolfe and his wife Maude probably built this one-story side-gable bungalow soon after purchasing the lot from M. T. Patrick's widow, Susan, in April 1915. Wolfe taught foreign languages at Trinity University, and the couple lived on Ferris Avenue before building here. Bungalows more commonly have wide front porches, but the 1925 Sanborn map indicates that the current form, with only a side porch, was original. It still can be classified as a bungalow due to the strong horizontal of the side-gable roof, the deep eaves with decorative supporting brackets, and the band of four windows that reinforce the horizontal emphasis. The design may have been inspired by an example in a catalogue of bungalow plans published by the Los Angeles firm E. W. Stillwell & Co. The catalogue's text described the design as "a splendid example of the "something different" idea," with a corner porch that was "liked by many people because it is so easily screened from public view." A preference for porch privacy truly was "something different" during this period, when sitting on the porch was a social, and generally, public, pastime.

C-43
821 Circle Street
Waxahachie Cotton Mill Office Building
1906

This small concrete-block office building is the lone architectural survivor of an important Waxahachie industrial venture. The Waxahachie Cotton Mills produced a heavy cotton fabric called duck cloth using cotton grown in the area. Construction of the first mill building, a two-story brick structure, began in 1900, with production starting in March 1901. This office building was part of a 1906 expansion project and replaced an earlier wood office. The complex eventually included an additional weaving building and several brick warehouses. Although the economic advantages of producing cotton products in Texas over exporting raw cotton were evident, few successful mills were built before the late nineteenth century. Waxahachie's newspapers and businessmen began advocating a cotton mill in the late 1880s, and in 1898 planning became serious for this locally owned mill. It was evidently a propitious time for such ventures; four other mills were constructed in cotton-producing areas of north Texas the same year as Waxahachie's. When Texas Commissioner of Agriculture Robert T. Milner visited the mill in 1908, the facility contained 204 looms and 9,000 spindles, and consumed 4,000 bales of cotton annually. Of the 175 workers in that year, about 20 percent were children. The mill's boarding house no longer exists, but a few of the forty-two cottages built for the workers remain on the other side of Circle Street and facing Gibson and Water Streets. (Cottages along Textile Street were later replaced by the Patrick Street public housing.)

The mill could not withstand the economic downturn of the Great Depression and the decline of local cotton production. Waxahachie's most important industrial enterprise since 1900 closed in 1934. The buildings served as the winter home for the Clyde Beatty Circus and its animals in 1944, but finally became an active industrial site again when Tyler Refrigeration bought the property in 1945. Tyler was a pioneer in the production of frozen food display cases for grocery stores. Tyler flourished in this location for many years and added buildings to the site before moving operations to a plant outside of town. In 2009, all the buildings on the site were demolished except for this one.

Concrete blocks molded to look like stone were first made in the 1870s, but they did not become widely popular until the early 1900s. Portable molding forms even became available to individuals and contractors to make blocks on building sites. This building's blocks may have been produced at the Waxahachie Cement Stone Manufacturing Company, which built its plant around this time just across Gibson Street from the cotton mill.

C-44
814 Water Street
c. 1897

Mrs. L. E. Green may have been using her own money when she bought this lot in 1897, for she was listed as the sole purchaser in the deed, but her traveling-salesman husband lived in the house with her and two of their children when the Census was taken in 1900. (The census taker noted only the initials of their given names, A. A. for Mr. Green and L. E. for his wife.) In building a modified L-plan Queen Anne style cottage they chose the most popular house type in Waxahachie at the time, but the stepped-back corner entrance porch of their house was less common. The pyramidal-roof rear wing was added after the 1959 Sanborn map, perhaps when the house was converted to a restaurant in the 1980s. Mrs. Green sold the house in 1905 to J. T. and Sarah Richards. Their son Paul was born three years later and lived in the house until the age of seventeen, when he began his long and successful career in baseball. Paul Rapier Richards played in the major leagues with the Brooklyn Dodgers, New York Giants, Philadelphia Athletics, and Detroit Tigers. He managed the Chicago White Sox and the Baltimore Orioles in the 1950s and early 1960s.

C-45
213 Gibson Street
1901

This side gable cottage is probably one of the ten "beautiful and comfortable little cottages" built for cotton mill workers that were mentioned in an April 26, 1901 *Enterprise* article about improvements being made for the mill. Placed on an L-shaped plot carved out of the undeveloped part of the block, seven of these houses faced Circle Street, two faced Water, and this one faced Gibson. Sanborn maps show us that all ten were identical in plan with central rear wings when built, but the surviving cottages show multiple additions and changes made by individual owners after the cotton mill closed and these lots were sold. This one still gives a general idea of the original appearance of a simple, unornamented side-gable front with attached shed-roof porch, but additions to the side and rear are clearly visible. A second entrance door between the surviving door and the window to its left has been closed in. The house at 818 Water Street still has both doors. There is no indication that these houses were intended for two families; two front doors were common at the time in small houses like this that had no interior hallways. Other houses for mill workers were constructed behind the mill and on both sides of Textile Street. Sanborn maps show that some were side-gable plans like these, although without rear wings, but there were also several square hipped-roof cottages with inset corner porches and a few shotgun plans. Although none of these survive in their original location, the hipped roof cottages were photographed by Charles M. Simpson for his *Sanitary Survey of Waxahachie, Texas* (1917).The smaller cottage across the street at 212 Gibson is probably one of two mentioned in the 1901 article as having been built by T. A. Ferris on his property "just east of the cotton mill."

C-46
716 Water Street
1907

The current appearance of this two-story hipped-roof house probably dates to 1907, when the local newspaper noted that William C. Jennings was having improvements made at his home on Water Street. No photographs survive to show the house in its earlier form, and the Sanborn maps do not include this address until 1914, when the current footprint with two stories is shown. The 1907 improvements probably were major, for the square form, one-over-one windows, wide eaves, and porch details all represent the styles current then. In fact, the full-height entry porch with one-story full-width porch behind it closely matches the porch configuration built in March of that year at **1107 West Marvin**. (The one-story portion of that porch was later removed.) Born in Tennessee in 1865, Jennings was associated with the Waxahachie Bottling Works as early as 1894, and he continued as a co-owner and proprietor until the plant was bought by the Coca Cola Company of Dallas in 1917. He lived here with his family until his death in 1937.

C-47
700 Water Street
c. 1880

The small scale of this side-gable house adds to its considerable charm. Since the three front gables are too small to function as the Gothic-Revival dormers they mimic, they assume a purely decorative function. Although the current ornamental bargeboards in the two smaller gables were added in a later renovation, the gables could well have possessed scrollwork or turned-wood decoration originally, judging from other small-scale houses of the period in Waxahachie. Carpenter William H. George probably built the house soon after purchasing the property in July 1880. The 1886 bird's-eye view shows the dwelling with its triple gables and a T-extension to the rear, but without any front porch. William and his wife Bettie lived in the house until 1890, when they sold it to furniture merchant John R. King.

C-48
213 North Hawkins Street
c. 1905

This block of North Hawkins Street served as a site for small-scale rental housing for laborers beginning in the early 1900s. This one-story side-gable cottage appears to be the only survivor of four small houses documented in the 1909 Sanborn map, three on the west side of the street and one on the east. Furniture merchant J. R. King, who lived in the gabled cottage facing Water Street (**700 Water Street**), built it on the rear of his property. In February 1905 the local paper noted that a small fire damaged the roof his "small house" on Hawkins. Many other examples of the form were built, with slight variations in size and proportions, as low-income rental housing in Waxahachie during this period. (You can see the same form nearby, on a larger scale, in the houses built for cotton mill employees at 816 Water Street and **213 Gibson Street**.) The hipped-roof cottage next door (215 North Hawkins), with a later camelback gable-roof addition looming in the rear, may have been built by R. H. Thompson after he bought the property from J. R. King in 1911. A house with its footprint first appears on the 1914 Sanborn map. At the time of the 1910 Census, four households were noted on North Hawkins Street between Water Street and the railroad, all African Americans. By 1913, the city directory shows two houses occupied by whites and two by African Americans. In 1922, all were white.

C-49
219 and 221 North Hawkins Street

These two hipped-roof square cottages with inset corner porches first appear on the 1925 Sanborn map, but probably were built or moved here before 1920. The city directories and Census show a constantly changing array of renters in this block in the 1920s, with varied occupations— furniture refinisher, oil mill machinist, and several house painters. Sanborn maps show that the front-gable bungalow at 217 North Hawkins appeared at this location after 1959, but its form and details indicate that it was probably built in the 1920s and moved here from another location.

C-50
604 Water Street
1880

Early Waxahachie merchant Aaron Trippet built this two-story I-house in 1880, with its substantial size simultaneously demonstrating his financial success and sheltering his large family. The Census of that year records nine children and four grandchildren living with Aaron and his second wife Martha. By the time Aaron and Martha celebrated their fiftieth wedding anniversary in 1898, they had eleven children and forty-two grandchildren, but most no longer lived in the house. A Missouri native, Aaron came to Waxahachie in 1865 and bought this property in 1869. The one-story side-gable wing at the rear of this house may date to that time. The current two-story porch was added sometime after 1914. The 1886 bird's-eye view shows the two-story I-house with a one-story shed-roof porch, and the Sanborn maps from 1898 through 1914 continue to record a one-story porch, with the two-story porch first appearing in the 1925 map. The pedimented door and window frames are typical of the late 1870s and early 1880s in Texas.

Aaron ran a dry goods store on the square for many years, in addition to investing in real estate. He was also involved in the Waxahachie National Bank, serving as vice president when it was organized in 1890. He built the two-story brick business building at **208-210 West Main Street** in partnership with J. W. Ferris. Aaron's granddaughter Myrtle lived in the house in the 1920s with her husband Edward M. Naughton, who cofounded the mail-order nursery Naughton Farms with his brother Joe. They operated the nursery on this property for many years, expanding to additional properties on Water Street and Hawkins Street, until moving it to the outskirts of town around 1940. Descendants of Aaron and Martha continued to live in the house until the 1990s.

C-51
514 Water Street
c. 1895

House carpenter N. G. Davis probably built the core of this one-story cross-gable cottage in the late 1870s or early 1880s, but its current form and details date to c. 1895 and later. Davis purchased the parcel of land including this lot in 1867 from Waxahachie pioneer E. W. Rogers. He was living on this block when the 1880 Census was taken, and although he sold off much of his parcel in the early 1880s, he kept this lot. The 1886 bird's-eye view shows a smaller cottage without a porch in this location. T. R. Anderson bought the lot from Davis's estate in 1895 and probably expanded the house soon after. Anderson ran the Waxahachie Machine Works, located a couple of blocks to the east on Water Street. In 1904 Anderson sold the house to Deputy County Clerk Clint P. Spalding. Spalding's grandson Robert Benton wrote the screenplay and directed the 1984 movie *Places in the Heart*, which was filmed in Waxahachie and the surrounding area. (Benton received the Academy Award for Best Original Screenplay, and Sally Field received the Best Actress Award.)

C-52
511 Water Street
1907; E. S. Boze, builder

When Dr. Leonard Keplinger bought this lot in 1901, it stretched through the block and included two houses, one facing Water Street and the other West Main Street. Keplinger lived in the larger house on Main Street and rented the smaller house. He was struck with a building frenzy a few years later when the April 12, 1907, *Enterprise* recorded that he was having W. W. Walston remodel his Main Street house (no longer extant), turning it around, changing the front, and adding rooms. The newspaper also noted that he was having a different contractor, E. S. Boze, erect a five-room cottage on Water Street. The relatively low-pitched roof, horizontal proportions, and Ionic columns of this modified L-plan cottage are typical for the construction date, but the narrow windows and entrance door look as if they may have been reused from the previous house. It is also possible that the earlier house was updated and expanded by Boze, rather than built from scratch.

C-53
510 Water Street
c. 1899

Later renovations of the front porch have given this two-story modified L-plan house a split personality. Sometime after the 1925 Sanborn map was published, the owners removed the original ornamented wrap-around porch and replaced it with this projecting rectangular porch with brick pillars and an enclosed upper level. But the stripped-down clarity of the earlier bay-windowed wing next to the porch stands its ground and makes the nineteenth-century origin of the house clear. Part of the first floor may date to the early 1880s, for the 1886 bird's-eye view shows a one-story house with wrap-around porch in this location. In 1889 developer and tax collector W. G. Williams sold that one-story house to county treasurer A. J. Baxter. Sterling Price Spalding bought the house in 1894, and it still had only one floor in the 1898 Sanborn map. Spalding may have added the second floor in 1899, perhaps inheriting funds after the death that year of the uncle in Missouri who had raised him. The 1904 Sanborn map shows a two-story house with the current footprint. Although born in California where his father Tom Spalding prospected for gold in the mid-nineteenth century, Sterling's family moved back to Missouri in 1870, where he trained in the furniture business. In 1890 his uncle, Waxahachie's Benjamin F. Spalding, invited Sterling to join him in his furniture and undertaking business. Two years later, Sterling bought out Benjamin and ran the business for several years, first with James McCartney and then with his son Tom. Sterling could easily walk to work, for the store was located only a few blocks away at **103-05 North Rogers Street**.

C-54
406 Water Street
1921; D. H. Thompson Lumber Company, builder

When brick contractor Harvey H. Richards and his wife Jimmie built this "two-story brick veneer house of ten rooms" for $3,000 in 1921, it was on a block in transition. The 1914 Sanborn map shows only late nineteenth-early twentieth century frame houses on both sides of Water Street from Monroe to Hawkins Streets, but when the 1922 city directory was published, the north side included the Richardses at this address, a filling station on the east corner, and a car dealership to the west of the couple, no doubt in the same commercial building that is on the corner today.

Harvey Richards is one of those fleeting figures on Waxahachie's building scene. The 1918 phone directory listed the couple at 302 West Main Street, and the newspaper credited him in 1920 with building a service station at Franklin and Elm Streets and laying the sidewalk at the Orphan's Home. In February 1920, they bought this property, which included a sizeable house, for $3,500. Exactly one year later and after paying off their note, they demolished the existing building and contracted the D. H. Thompson Lumber Company to build this four-square house according to plans and specifications that the couple furnished. The residence is a textbook example of the building type: a solid rectangular block, low-pitched hipped roof with central dormer and wide overhanging eaves, symmetrical front façade with an offset entrance and a full-width one-story porch with a pediment over the entrance bay, and tapered, squared wood porch columns resting on brick piers. The brick veneer is an atypical feature of the building type in Waxahachie—most are frame.

One can only speculate if the Richardses ever intended to permanently settle in Waxahachie because the house was rented according to the 1924-25 directory and labeled "Boarding" on the 1925 Sanborn map. In 1930, the couple was living in Brady, McCulloch County, where he was still a contractor, but deed records indicate recurring financial difficulties with the Waxahachie property until the bank finally sold it to J. A. Finley of Waxahachie for $2,500 in 1936. During the late 1940s and into the 1950s, Finley and his wife Ada operated the Cottage Hotel at this address and the Finley Hotel at 401 West Main.

The small brick commercial structures across the street were built circa 1927 with the largest building at 403 Water originally housing the Supreme Ice Cream Factory. In 1970, Oma and Charles Shaw opened Oma's, their sandwich shop there. Over the years, the building has acquired distinction not for its architecture but as home of Oma's Jiffy Burger, a Waxahachie icon of another kind.

C-55
210 North Monroe Street
Waxahachie Bottling Works
1913; E. S. Boze, builder

The brick Waxahachie Bottling Works was another compact, no-nonsense commercial building that local contractor E. S. Boze added to his builder's resume. When the bottling company was established in 1891, it was part of the Waxahachie Ice Works complex that was located in the curve of Rogers Spring Branch just below the railroad tracks and on what became the west side of Monroe Street. When the street was cut through in the mid-1890s, the considerably larger ice works stayed where it was while the bottling plant was moved to this location on the east side of the street. In early 1913, manager W. C. Jennings cleared "the old wooden buildings" and contracted Boze to erect "a modern plant for the making of soda pop." Four years later, the Coca-Cola company of Dallas bought the business and equipment from co-owners Jennings and W. D. Anderson, and signed a three-year lease that was extended into the mid-1920s. Many Waxahachians identify the structure with the Global Laundry and Dry Cleaning Company that opened here in 1930 and stayed for over sixty years.

C-56
106 South Monroe Street
Southland Office Building
1958; Forrest Upshaw, architect

It is a pity that this small-scale minimalist office building gets overlooked in its off-the-beaten path location—a pity because it is one of few truly modern-style structures built in Waxahachie. Constructed of cinder block and brick veneer, the exterior, including a scalloped metal awning, has escaped major alterations, the most distracting change being the replacement of floor-to-ceiling plate glass window and entrance openings with reflective glass. In mid-March 1958, the Southland Cotton Oil Company moved its general office staff from Paris, Texas, to this building, with the *Daily Light* noting that the Dallas-based architect Forrest Upshaw Jr. was a Waxahachie native. The original interior was classic 1950s in "tones of brown and beige with partitioning walls of walnut paneling and textone [a textured paint] in a harmonizing sandalwood shade." The entire structure was equipped with year-round air-conditioning, still worthy of note at the time. Southland moved out in the mid-1960s, and subsequent tenants have been a series of governmental offices.

C-57
414 West Franklin Street
c. 1899-1903

Built as rental property by Dr. D. G. Thompson, this one-story modified L-plan cottage may contain parts of an older, two-story house shown on the 1898 Sanborn Map. On March 31, 1899, a major fire destroyed three homes across the street and also damaged this one. The newspaper account does not describe the extent of the damage, but since the 1904 Sanborn map shows the same house footprint, but with only one story, the removal of the second floor was likely related to the fire. By the time of the 1909 Sanborn, the rear wing and porch had been extended. The straightforward, no frills façade that we see today probably dates to renovations after the fire. Since Dr. Thompson lived close by, at **414 West Main**, he easily could keep an eye on his renters. The 1910 Census shows dry goods clerk John E. Rogers living here with his wife Vida, along with two lodgers.

C-58
415, 417, and 419 West Franklin Street
1911 (415), 1910 (417 and 419)

These two-story hipped-roof houses all present the horizontal proportions and absence of ornament that would have earned them the label of "Modern" when they were constructed. Today they are considered a vernacular form of the Prairie style. Although they each vary in plan and details, they look alike to the casual observer due to their consistency of form and scale. They were all built after a fire on San Jacinto Day in 1910 burned the houses on this end of the block. Alpheus L. Rogers, city alderman and a clerk at Cheeves Brothers department store, built 415 soon after purchasing the lot in January 1911. The *Daily Light* of January 25 reported the purchase and Mr. Rogers's plan to have an "eight-room, two-story residence" erected. Before the fire, hardware merchant Will Moore had lived next door in a 1905 two-story frame dwelling on a large lot that stretched from 415 to the end of the block. The *Dallas Morning News* reported his loss at $5,000 for house and furniture, but he found a way to profit from the disaster by dividing the lot and building the two houses we see today. He built the house at 419 first and sold it in November 1910 to James D. and Mary MacKoy for $4,000. James co-owned the McDade and MacKoy drug store a few blocks away on East Franklin. As soon as that sale was settled, Moore let a contract to build a new residence at 417, according to a report in the *Daily Light*. Moore sold that house in February 1912 to J. G. Cornwall, who almost immediately sold it to Lucian T. Graham and his wife Jeannetta. The Grahams operated a boarding house at 417 for several years. The 1920 Census lists eight lodgers living in the house along with Lucian, his wife, and his sister-in-law. Among the lodgers were hardware store manager Burton Prince and his wife.

C-59
420 and 422 West Franklin Street
1920

Originally called the Joyce Apartments, after the builder's wife, this pair of two-story brick-veneer apartment buildings heralded a new era in multi-family housing for Waxahachie. The *Daily Light* of September 18, 1920, noted that the "beautiful brick apartments" were the first up-to-date apartments to be built locally and that they "would do credit to a town much larger." Each building contained four apartments, each of which had five rooms and a bath, with a gas fireplace in each living room. The "artistic" ceilings of the living and dining rooms bore "ribbon festoon work in light blue colors." A garage was built in the rear to accommodate the tenants' automobiles. The exterior form of the twin buildings clearly reflected their multi-family identity, in contrast to the boarding houses nearby on the south side of Franklin Street, which masquerade as large single-family dwellings. Four entrance doors on the front porch of each building mark the separate entrances for the four apartments. Flat roofs and brick veneer set the buildings apart from the surrounding frame houses with hipped or gable roofs. Though clearly not bungalows, their plans closely resemble the design for "A Four-Flat Building" (No. 164) in the 1914 book of plans *California Bungalow Homes*, published in Los Angeles by the Bungalowcraft Company.

The apartments were intended for well-to-do couples interested in an up-to-date alternative to the single-family house. Early tenants, including John E. and Mollie Dunaway, fit that description. John was elected chairman of the board of the new Waxahachie sanitarium in 1920, and was listed in the 1924-25 directory as vice president of the local Shamrock Oil Company and vice president of Waxahachie National Bank. The apartments soon became known as the Smith Apartments, after their builder John C. Smith. According to the *Daily Light*, Smith was "an enterprising, public spirited man" who had been instrumental in bringing Trinity University and the Chautauqua to Waxahachie. Smith served as minister of the Cumberland Presbyterian Church from 1898 to 1906, and then became secretary of Trinity, but by 1920 he was investing in these buildings, and the Census listed him as an oil promoter. He left Waxahachie for Houston in 1923 and lived there until his death in 1948. Smith sold the buildings to Will T. Hughes in 1922, but they continued to be known as the Smith Apartments into the 1940s.

C-60
407 West Jefferson Street
Ellis County Woman's Building
1925; Bertram C. Hill, architect; Ramsey Brothers, contractor

Waxahachie reflected national and state trends when in the late nineteenth century its women established literary clubs that rapidly evolved to encompass social concerns. Waxahachie's first women's clubs included the Sappho Chautauqua Literary and Scientific Circle, begun in July 1889, and the Waxahachie Shakespeare Club, established in December of the same year. The connection between studying literature and promoting social welfare may not appear obvious now, but at the time it was considered a logical extension from improving the self to improving the community. In 1899 Waxahachie's Shakespeare Club began campaigning to improve sidewalks and trash pick-up. That same year it sent a delegate to the annual meeting of the Texas Federation of Women's Clubs, which had just changed its name from the Texas Federation of Literary Clubs to signify its growing interest in public affairs and its new affiliation with the national organization, the General Federation of Women's Clubs. One of the Waxahachie Shakespeare Club's first major projects was the establishment of a "rest room," meaning a place for women from the country to wait with their children while their husbands transacted business in town. In 1902 the club rented the "old Wilson place," a block from the square on West Main Street, for that purpose and hired a matron to supervise the facility.

Women's clubs grew in size and number in Waxahachie during the next two decades, and the obvious need for a shared meeting place was satisfied when Mrs. Quincy Davis Getzendaner donated the site of her parents' homestead in their memory to the city in 1924. In a fitting manner, a club woman announced the gift. Mrs. J. M. Alderdice, chairman of the Century Club's civic committee, noted that the facility was to include an auditorium seating 250 and, continuing the earlier concern for rural women visiting town, a "lounge and rest room . . . for the use of all Ellis County women."

Dallas architect Bertram C. Hill designed three Waxahachie houses (**401 East Marvin**, **1004 West Marvin**, and **712 West Main**) before receiving this commission. He followed established custom for such club buildings by creating a structure that looked residential, rather than institutional. Hill took advantage of the corner site by placing a gabled entrance porch facing each street, providing separate entrances for the auditorium and the lounge. The steeply pitched gables, arched entrance porches, patterned brick veneer walls, and multi-paned casement windows flanking the prominent chimney would have been considered in the English Cottage style when the hall was built. The prominent chimney dominates the Monroe Street façade, with its three-dimensional brick ornament. Hill succeeded in combining the many required functions in a carefully detailed, picturesque structure. The building continues to provide meeting space for city and county women's organizations and can be rented for private events. In recognition of the times and its expanded usage, a major renovation in 2007 added a men's restroom.

C-61
409 West Jefferson Street
1924

On March 19, 1924, the *Daily Light* reported that J. A. (Happy) Drummond and J. H. Hutchinson and their families had moved into "Mr. Drummond's attractive new home on West Jefferson." The exterior of this one-story side-gable duplex with Craftsman style details reflects a 1924 date, but the 1904 and 1914 Sanborn maps show a similar footprint for the front wing of the house, which could indicate that part of the early 1900s house remains beneath the later exterior. The design and details of the house emphasize its role as a two-family dwelling, particularly the symmetrical façade with central porch flanked by double windows and the small paired windows where a single central entrance door would normally be found. Surveyor J. H. Hutchinson and his wife rented half of the duplex, while owner James Albert Drummond and his sister Josie lived in the other half.

Born in 1894 in Kansas, James, known as "Happy," came to Waxahachie with his mother and sister when he was still in school. In 1911 he started selling sandwiches from a tiny stand in the alley behind the building on the southeast corner of Franklin and Rogers Streets. (The 1913 city directory listed him as a "peddler.") His personality as well as his hamburgers attracted steady customers, and his stand became a popular meeting place and a town institution that lasted for over forty years, until air-conditioning equipment for the building that faced the square replaced his stand in the alley in the late 1950s. By 1921 he had earned enough from selling hamburgers to purchase the previous house on this lot, and three years later he was able to update and rebuild it into this income-producing property. Although he spent long hours at his stand, Happy also served as a Boy Scout leader and taught Sunday school. When he died in 1968 he left his estate of $25,000 to the Methodist Church for educational grants. His sister Josie became a schoolteacher and shared the duplex with him until her death in 1950. Happy and his hamburger stand were featured in *Life Magazine* in 1952.

C-62
413 and 415 West Jefferson Street
c. late 1880s (413), c. 1890s (415)

Sanborn maps indicate that the one-story L-plan cottage at 413 West Jefferson was moved here sometime between 1898 and November 1904. Since its original location is unknown, its period of construction has been based on its form, proportions, and materials, including the tall, narrow windows with two-over-two lights. William A. Satchell and his wife Anna may have moved the house here after purchasing the lot in January 1904 for $850. William's butcher shop, Satchell & Company, was located at 207 East Main. The Satchells moved to the country after 1913, but kept this house as rental property into the 1930s. The neighboring house at 415 West Jefferson also was moved from another location, arriving here between 1914 and 1922. A one-story side-gable house with shed-roof porch, it represents a common type built for workers' housing in the late nineteenth and early twentieth centuries.

C-63
417 West Jefferson Street
c. 1883

In the 1880s this stretch of West Jefferson and West Franklin contained the homes of several of Waxahachie's most prosperous residents, including businessman Oscar B. Sims, the original owner of this two-story L-plan house. Sims probably built the house soon after purchasing the lot in May 1883. In January 1885 he sold the house to his brother, W. B. Sims, having sold his grocery business in November 1884 to his brother and J. F. Strickland. He planned to leave town and start a cattle ranch in west Texas, but romance appears to have altered, or at least delayed, his plans. A few days after selling his house, the newspaper recounted his unexpected marriage to Jessie Buchanan, and it was July 1890 before it reported that he had moved his family to Claude, in the Texas Panhandle. Oscar was back in Waxahachie three years later, building a new house (**1408 West Main**) and working as superintendent of the new cotton compress. He later worked in the cattle industry, in cotton buying, and in farming. The delicate Italianate details on this house contribute to its air of restrained elegance. The stacked bay windows receive the greatest decorative attention, with paired pilasters separating the bays and bracketed architraves capping them. Similar details are repeated on the porch and at the eaves. Although the presence of a door on the second floor above the entrance suggests that the porch might have been two stories originally, the 1898 Sanborn map shows only a one-story porch matching the current configuration.

C-64
507 West Jefferson Street
c. 1910

The 1886 bird's-eye view of Waxahachie and the 1898 Sanborn map show a two-story L-plan house in this location, similar in appearance to the house at **417 West Jefferson**. Built by insurance agent Harrison F. Parks in the early 1880s, that residence may remain at the core of this much-altered and extended structure. The bay windows are gone, and a pyramidal roof replaced the earlier gables and incorporated an addition to the rear. The changes occurred after 1907, when John Harrison bought the property from Parks's daughter Minnie and her husband R. D. McCombs. By that time, the neighborhood's residential status had declined, and Mr. Harrison's construction of a cotton warehouse in 1907 on the adjoining property to the south only escalated the situation. Harrison's warehouse burned in 1910, and the fire damaged this house as well. The current form and additions to this house probably date to the post-fire repair or rebuilding process. In 1913 Mrs. Rose Johnson ran a boarding house here. Her husband, William, worked as a traveling agent for the Waxahachie Marble and Granite Works.

C-65
510 West Jefferson Street
c. 1912

Carpenter and contractor Joseph H. Meredith and his wife Lucile bought this lot in July 1912 from Mrs. Mattie E. Rowen, who was selling part of the land behind her large house on West Franklin, where two brick apartment buildings stand now. The son of house-mover and real estate investor J. B. Meredith, Joseph was returning to Waxahachie after working in a lumberyard in Hale County, Texas. The present two-story Prairie style house is the result either of the Merediths' renovation of an existing one-story L-plan cottage or new construction. The front porch was partially enclosed at a later date.

C-66
513 West Jefferson Street
c. 1870s

This side gable house probably was moved to this location. Its style and form indicate an 1870s or early 1880s construction date, but the lot was empty in the 1886 bird's-eye view. The move may have been as early as 1887, when the owner of the lot, William A. Calfee, advertised a house for lease, or around 1890, when an *Enter-*

prise reporter commented on the number of houses being moved from their original locations for the expanding business district, saying that "One by one the old landmarks are being moved away to give place to business houses." The house was here by the time of the 1898 Sanborn and was serving as rental property for hardware merchant Calfee and his wife Mary E. (Ellie), who lived a few blocks away at 110 South Hawkins (no longer extant). Side gable houses like this with double or triple cross gables evolved from Gothic Revival designs popularized by A. J. Downing in the 1840s. Similar examples were built across northeast Texas in the 1870s and early 1880s. One with triple gables, built in 1880, remains in Waxahachie at **816 Cantrell**.

C-67
527 West Jefferson Street
1880

Nancy Parks Bullard and her husband George built this one-story cottage soon after she received the land from the estate of her parents, early Waxahachie settlers William W. and Sophia Ann Parks. William and Sophia both died in the 1860s, but the division of their property did not occur until 1880, after all five of their daughters were married. Nancy's sister Sarah (Sadie) Morris received the lot to the east. She and her husband built a one-story L-plan house and lived there with their four children until Sadie's untimely death in 1890. The Thompson family eventually acquired the Morris property, and in 1946 Mrs. Arch F. Thompson donated it to the city for use as a park in memory of her husband and her son, Floyd. The Bullard house probably started as an L-plan similar to the Morrises', but subsequent additions led to the current unusual "pinwheel" plan, which was in place by 1904, the year of the earliest Sanborn map to include this part of West Jefferson. The plan allows multiple porches on all sides of the house to provide shade at all times of the day.

Nancy Bullard's nephew, William A. Spalding, recalled Nancy and George with fondness in his memoir, for he visited them frequently when he was young and they still lived in the country. He described George as primarily a farmer, but also an excellent trader in land and stock. William "never knew him to get the worse in a horse trade but once." The Bullards' three children were born in this house. In 1910, when both Nancy and George were in their sixties, they moved to **305 University** in the recently developed University Park neighborhood.

C-68
600 West Jefferson Street
1889

The projecting front wing of this two-story T-plan house retains its original proportions and tall, narrow windows, but later renovations have altered other aspects of the house's original appearance. In the early 1900s, the current porch arrangement replaced two smaller side porches that did not connect around the front. The large brackets at the eaves and the extension of the east wing date to a later renovation. Oscar F. Parks, who built the house, began his career, as other successful businessmen of the era did, as a clerk in a grocery store. The 1880 Census shows him in Waxahachie, working in that capacity, and aged twenty-two years. He managed to accumulate enough money to invest in property on West Main and West Jefferson Streets and to build this house. By the time he sold this lot in 1889, he was living in Dallas, but the deed includes a reference to the "new dwelling" on the property, "in which I have lately resided." The property bounced back to Oscar when the buyer defaulted in 1891. Two years later Oscar lost it in his turn to creditors. Various owners used the house as rental property until farmer William Stiles acquired it in 1907 and lived here until his death in 1925.

C-69
601 West Jefferson Street
c. 1916

At first glance this appears to be an American Foursquare house of the early 1900s, but the façade is deceiving. Sanborn maps, along with the bay on the west side, and the tall, narrow windows on the sides of the house all indicate an earlier construction date. The house may date to the early 1880s, for Luther K. Allen owned this lot in August 1886 when the *Enterprise* noted that he had moved a residence from Dallas Street to his West End lot. Or Robert W. Beale, deputy clerk in the county clerk's office, may have renovated or replaced that structure soon after purchasing the property in December 1889. The façade and roof were probably updated to their current appearance around 1916, when Archibald F. (Archie) Thompson and his wife May bought the house. The wider windows, hipped dormer, entrance door with flanking windows, and front porch all contributed to the new look. Archie worked in various capacities over the years for his family's business, the D. H. Thompson Grain Company. In 1913 he was listed as a clerk, in 1922 as manager, and in 1924-25 and 1927, bookkeeper. Mrs. Thompson donated the land at 515 West Jefferson to the city in 1946 to be used as a park in memory of her husband and son.

C-70
604 West Jefferson Street
1887, 1922

A 1922 porch and sunroom addition do much to camouflage the 1887 Italianate-style house that remains behind them. Clues to its earlier identity can be seen in the second-floor windows, with their tall, narrow proportions and their asymmetrical placement that reflects a hall and parlor floor plan. A pre-1922 photograph documents the original decorative details, including spindlework on the porch and paired Italianate brackets at the eaves. This was one of several Waxahachie houses built by Oscar F. Parks for speculative sale. Subsequent owners included Mrs. A. L. Redding, a widow; A. B. McKnight, county treasurer; and another widow, Mrs. T. L. Ross. It was Mrs. Ross who in 1922 contracted with W. B. and C. C. Ramsey to add the sun room on the east side and rebuild the front porch as part of a major redo that included a new roof, painting the exterior, and papering the interior.

C-71
607 West Jefferson Street
1910

This handsome Prairie style two-story house, with its broad porch wrapping around the east corner, was built by Laura Parks Spalding when she was in her sixties. Her husband, John H. Spalding, had been killed in 1882 while serving as city marshall, leaving her a widow with four young children. She continued to live in the earlier house that he had built on this lot and managed to hold the family together, partially by taking in boarders. Her struggles inspired her great-grandson Robert D. Benton's film *Places in the Heart*, although many changes were made in the story, including a shift in time to the 1930s. An August 19, 1910 *Enterprise* article confirms the construction date of this house, but a surviving letter from Laura Spalding to her aunt, dated 1913, describes its genesis in greater detail:" . . . we built a new house on the lot where the old house stood and moved the old house back." The earlier house survives at **207 South Hawkins**. Both houses remain in the Spalding family and were featured in the Horton Foote film *1918*.

C-72
106, 108, and 110 South Hawkins Street
c. 1915-19

These three front-gable bungalows with front-gable porches represent a common form used for working-class housing in Waxahachie, as well as much of the rest of the country. In a slight deviation from the usual plan, a small rear wing on the south side of each bungalow provided extra space to the inhabitants and visual interest to the passerby. Over the years, additional changes, including the obvious difference in paint colors, have helped to give each of the identical houses a slightly distinctive appearance. Hardware merchant William A. Calfee's 1886 two-story house once stood here, on the land given by his wife's father, B. F. Hawkins. Calfee died in 1902, and, based on the evidence of Sanborn maps and deeds, his family built the bungalows sometime between 1914 and 1920. Local legend says that materials from the old Calfee house were used in constructing these houses. The 1922 tenants included a cottonseed salesman, a dry goods clerk, and an automobile mechanic.

C-73
200 South Hawkins Street
1899; E. M. Thrash, builder

The overall appearance and details of this two-story house date from 1899, but its unusual, complex plan, which is a departure for the period from the more common modified L-plan, probably derives from the incorporation of the previous dwelling on the site. That one-story cottage of 1887 had, in its turn, incorporated an earlier two-room side-gable house of c. 1880. The 1899 changes included an extension of the first floor as well as the addition of an entire second floor and a third-story tower room. With such major alterations, it is not surprising that the local newspaper evolved in its description of the project as the work progressed. What was noted in August 1899 as a "rebuilding and remodeling" became a "handsome new home" by the time of its completion in October of that year. The third-floor tower room above the front bay was removed in the 1920s due to leakage. Its original finial surmounts the lower, more water-tight roof that replaced it. The eyebrow dormer with its multiple small panes is the only surviving example in Waxahachie of a form associated with Queen Anne and Shingle style houses of the period.

Built by Edward P. (Ed) Hawkins, the house stands on part of the land acquired by his father, B. F. Hawkins, in 1851 and formed part of a line of family houses known as "Hawkins Row." Ed worked for his father as assistant county clerk from 1878 until 1891, when he was appointed county clerk after his father's death. He served in that capacity until 1898, but he also was involved in the abstract business. He bought out the Ellis County Abstract Company in 1895 and was one of the incorporators and directors of the Texas Title Company in 1903.

C-74
206 South Hawkins Street
1891; I. L. Dunn, builder

County Clerk B. F. Hawkins looked after his children well, deeding them property near his homestead and enabling construction of a line of five family residences along South Hawkins that became known as "Hawkins Row." But in February 1891 only four had been built, and his daughter Emma's lot next to his own house remained empty. He wrote his will in that month, evidently in ill health, and instructed that his estate should build her house if he was unable to do so before his death. He died two months later, and estate checks dated in August and September indicate that his wishes were carried out. The house may originally have been smaller, for Hawkins had specified a cost limit of $1,000, and houses of this size usually would have cost at least $1,500 at the time. Emma and her husband, C. A. Arnold, could have made additions as their fortunes improved, or simply added their own funds to those from her father's estate to construct a larger house in 1891. The stepped-back extensions visible on the south side of the house date back at least to 1909, the first year that this portion of Hawkins Street was included in the Sanborn maps. The *Enterprise* of August 1891 confirms the beginning of work on this "neat residence," but, following the custom of the time, the initiative, construction, and ownership are attributed entirely to Mr. Arnold, with no mention of Emma or her father's estate.

Born in 1856 in Atlanta, Georgia, C. A. Arnold arrived in Waxahachie in 1874 and married Emma in 1879. He worked in the drug business, dealt in real estate, and invested in land, but became best known for his music supply business, first with V. H. Shelton, then with B. T. Pettit. When the *Memorial and Biographical History of Ellis County* was published in 1892, the Arnold & Petit store was described as "the only exclusive music house in Ellis County," with a stock that included everything from "a box of resin to a grand piano." A photograph dating from the 1890s and now in the collection of the Ellis County Museum shows the interior of the establishment with Mr. Arnold and Mr. Pettit, as well as two upright but no grand pianos.

C-75
207 South Hawkins Street
c. 1859, 1882

William W. and Sophia Parks built a house on this property soon after their 1856 purchase of sixteen acres east of Hawkins Street and south of Jefferson. According to their grandson William A. Spalding's 1952 memoir, that first structure was replaced in the late 1850s with this two-story I-house. One of Waxahachie's early residents, Parks worked as a land surveyor while also serving as district clerk. He organized a regiment of Texas Cavalry during the Civil War and died in 1862. Sophia died six years later, leaving five unmarried daughters ranging in age from nine to twenty-two. John H. Spalding married the second-oldest Parks daughter Laura in 1868, moving into the Parks family's house and managing the estate's property in addition to working in the furniture business. He later served as county tax collector and marshal, and in 1882 he was killed while trying to make an arrest. His wife and four children stayed on in the house and took in boarders to help make ends meet. William's memoir notes that his father had a new roof put on and ceilings added not long before his death, but a small note in the newspaper's "West End Items" column of May 12, 1882 stated that "Mr. Spaulding's [sic] new house is about completed." This suggests that the renovations may have been major, and is supported in a column of 1887 comparing the relative age of the houses at this intersection, stating that "Mrs. Spalding's house is new, Mr. Calfee's is newer. . . . " (Mr. Calfee's house was built in 1886.) It seems unlikely that a house built in the late 1850s would still be considered "new" in this context. Around 1910, Laura moved this house to its current site, which was at the back of her property, and replaced it with a new house (**607 West Jefferson**). Both remain in the Spalding family today. Much of Horton Foote's movie *1918* was filmed in this house.

C-76
210 South Hawkins Street
Early 1880s, 1903

A Neoclassical two-story full-width portico of 1903 dominates the façade of this imposing house, but a triangular gable emerges above on the right, breaking the symmetry and serving as a reminder of the house's earlier L-plan identity. Parts of an 1850 one-story side-gable house may remain in the current structure, but everything visible on the exterior dates to the 1880s or later. A family photograph of the 1880s shows an Italianate L-plan two-story house with paired brackets under the eaves, a squared bay window, and a one-story porch. In addition to adding a portico deep enough to encompass the projecting L-wing, the 1903 renovation replaced the tall narrow windows with larger, wider ones. Double entrance doors with side lights and transom window were substituted for the single, narrow entrance door.

Benjamin Franklin (B. F.) Hawkins (1828-1891) built his first house on this property soon after assisting with the organization of Ellis County and his election as the first County Clerk in 1850. His thirteen-acre plot included a spring at the bottom of the hill. The spring, the hill, and the street eventually bore his name. Except for ten years after the Civil War, he served as County Clerk for the rest of his life, while also investing in land. B. F. and his wife Mary had six children, and as children and grandchildren began to leave Waxahachie, reunions became yearly events often noted in the newspaper. Son F. L Hawkins and his new wife Kate joined B. F. and Mary in the big house after he obtained his law degree from the University of Texas in Austin in 1889.They remained after B. F.'s death in 1891. F. L.'s progressively more responsible public positions, including prosecuting attorney and county judge, as well as his inheritance, enabled the 1903 updating and renovation. After serving sixteen years as district judge, F. L. was appointed to the State Court of Criminal Appeals in 1921, where he continued for thirty years. Their daughter Christine Hawkins Wilson's 1960 memoir *Life on Hawkins Row* provides an account of life in the house and the neighborhood at the turn of the twentieth century.

C-77
214 South Hawkins Street
1955

This house and its neighbor at 212 South Hawkins serve as a reminder that looks can be deceiving, for there are very few exterior clues that these houses were once part of a 1909 hipped roof bungalow. The relative ease of moving houses for much of the nineteenth and twentieth centuries enabled adaptive reuse years before the term gained prominence in preservation circles. In 1955 the bungalow at 604 Ferris Avenue, which once belonged to blacksmith Will Farley, stood in the way of commercial development. It was sold to W. T. Allen, who had it moved to South Hawkins, cut in half, and transformed into two modest rental houses in March of that year. The splitting of the house necessitated the most noticeable exterior change, for the hipped roof was replaced with gable roofs of a much lower pitch. The *Daily Light* could well have been describing part of the move of Farley's bungalow from Ferris to South Hawkins when it reported on January 28, 1955 that a Century Club program at Davis Hall (Ellis County Woman's Building) on West Jefferson Street was interrupted by a pounding on the door when six of the ladies were asked to move their cars "so the house could have clearance."

C-78
300 South Hawkins Street
Waxahachie City Cemetery

Waxahachie's 25-acre city cemetery includes the 4.16 acres that city founder E. W. Rogers set aside for a burial ground, along with later gifts and purchases of additional land. The first recorded burial occurred in 1852. Rogers conveyed that original tract to the Methodist Church in 1858 to be held in trust "for burial purposes for citizens of the town and its vicinity," but by the mid-1880s, the cemetery lacked supervision and maintenance. Graves could be dug by anyone and located anywhere in the tract, and the local paper reported instances of damage and neglect, as well as complaints of the odor from a nearby slaughterhouse. The women of the city founded the Ladies Cemetery Society in October 1887 to improve the situation and elected Mrs. Mary C. Briggs, daughter of E. W. Rogers, president. The women lobbied city council, enlisting Judge J. W. Ferris to be their spokesman. They eventually succeeded not only in convincing the city to take over control of the cemetery but to purchase an additional 3.5 acres as well. The women also obtained deeds to the city from owners of the adjacent "old fair ground," which was no longer being used. The city extended South Hawkins to the cemetery, and a new entrance was created.

The Cemetery Society did not rest on its laurels, but moved to improve the grounds with regular Decoration Day events and fundraisers. In April 1891, the *Enterprise* noted that the city was having walks laid out and beautifying the grounds. In order to accomplish those improvements, the city appointed English-born landscape gardener A. Gardiner as sexton in June 1891. (The paper consistently misspelled his name "Gardner.") The *Enterprise* noted in April 1892 that Gardiner had "transformed the city cemetery." Gardiner's landscaping work included setting marble curbing on grave lots in 1902 and, in 1907, laying out "graceful drives" and planting trees. The 1896 Phillips and Hawkins map of Waxahachie shows the footprint of the consolidated and expanded cemetery, with a small section closest to the creek labeled "Colored Cemetery." Two private African American cemeteries, the Wakefield and Fraternal cemeteries, were later established in East Waxahachie.

Grave markers in the cemetery include locally carved stones as well as elaborate sculptural monuments and family mausoleums produced elsewhere, including the "elegant monuments" by the Waco firm of J. Gooch & Co. that were recorded in the *Enterprise* in May 1902. In 1901 an imported monument for Judge Ferris stopped rail traffic for a day when the almost six-ton stone crashed through the wagon transporting it from the freight depot and landed square across the Katy railroad track.

Early local makers of tombstones included George Kennedy, E. F. Smith, F. P. Baily, Larkin Douglas, D. F. Goughner, and James Martin (J. M.) Youngblood, who opened his marble yard in 1905. In September 1907 the *Enterprise* noted the rapid growth of Youngblood's firm, with "eight or ten men steadily employed transforming the raw material into monuments and markers. . . ." Youngblood & Co. became the Waxahachie Marble and Granite Company, which continued into the 1980s.

C-79
301 South Hawkins
Paul Richards Park

In 1915 local businessmen formed the Waxahachie Ball Park Association and succeeded in convincing the Detroit Tigers to come to Waxahachie for the 1916 spring training season. They then leased this land from Laura Spalding, and on December 24, 1915, the *Dallas Morning News* reported that the park had been staked off and plans for a grandstand and bleachers had been drawn by "a Dallas architect." The ballpark became known as Jungle Park, "a home of Tigers," and the name stuck even when the Cincinnati Reds replaced the Tigers in spring 1919. Only when a new stadium was built in 1946 did the name change. Paul Richards, who grew up in Waxahachie and drew national attention in the final game of the 1945

World Series playing for the Detroit Tigers, promoted the funding of a new stadium, which was named in his honor. Richards went on to play for the Brooklyn Dodgers, New York Giants, and Philadelphia Athletics, as well as the Tigers, and then began a successful career as a major league manager. Since the ballpark's opening on April 5, 1946, it has served as the home of the Waxahachie High School Indians baseball team. The stadium has been updated over the years, and the current entrance gate was built c. 2006 by Randy and Alex Johnson. Monuments within the park provide historical details about Richards, the ballpark, and Waxahachie baseball. The book *A Story of Paul Richards Park and Waxahachie High School Baseball* by Billy R. Hancock was published in 2008, with funding from the RBI Club.

C-80
1000 West Main Street
1896; A. J. Kibler, builder

In June of 1896, newspaperman James O. Jones and his wife Ellie contracted to pay the Cotton States Building Company $800 for the erection of this house, with A. J. Kibler as builder and contractor. Associated with the *Light* when he built the house, Jones and W. K. Stokes bought the *Daily Record* from C. F. Yeager in 1898, intending to combine the publications to form the *Daily Light*, now Waxahachie's remaining daily newspaper. Jones left Waxahachie in 1899 to publish a paper in Waco and sold the house to lawyer C. M. Supple. Jones may have invested more in building the house than the $800 he paid the Cotton States Building Company, since he sold it to Supple for $2,292.00.

C-81
1001 West Main Street
c. late 1890s

This one-story modified L-plan house probably dates to the mid- to late 1890s, when this portion of West Main, approaching the new West End subdivision, became a popular area for development. An unusual, slightly angled wall is inset beneath the central, pyramidal roof to form part of the generous wraparound porch. That part of the design dates back at least to 1909, when the first Sanborn map to include this lot was published, and it probably was original. The Sanborn maps also let us know that the porch and the side gable wing on the left were extended after 1959. The current decorative ornament in the gable and on the porch frieze are replacements, for photographs from the 1980s show the house lacking any sawn or turned woodwork in those locations. T. J. Cole, manager of the Texas Mortgage Banking Company, may have built the house before selling it in 1901 to J. W. Fraser, a tailor.

C-82
1008 West Main Street
1893; Smith & Myall, architects and builders

This is one of the earliest documented Waxahachie examples of a T-plan house with a porch encircling the front wing of the "T." In July of 1893, Israel and Sallie Mincer contracted to pay W. H. Smith & Thomas W. Myall $1,640 to build a one-story frame house of six rooms, with the plans and specifications "furnished by Smith & Myall as architects." Local contractor W. H. Smith had signed mechanics' liens independently for three houses in 1892 and 1893 before Myall joined him for this house. Myall was an English-born architect who had practiced in Dallas in the late 1880s before joining Smith in Waxahachie. Smith died in April of 1895, and by the time of the 1900 Census, Myall and his family had moved to Cleburne, Texas. Other than the loss of original decorative woodwork in the front gable and the replacement of the gable window, this is a well-preserved example of an early Waxahachie T-plan house.

Polish-born Israel Mincer, a dry goods merchant, had been in Waxahachie at least since 1880, when the Census noted his age as twenty-six. He lived in rental housing before building this house on a lot previously owned by his father-in-law, Ennis merchant L. Levy. Only two years after its construction, the Mincers sold the house to R. K. Erwin, who later became the manager of the first cotton seed oil mill in Waxahachie. Ten years after its construction, the house was still considered notable enough to be described as a "pretty cottage home" when the newspaper reported the New Year's entertainment given by the Erwins. In 1902, Erwin moved his family to a larger two-story house at **412 West Marvin**. Grocer W. J. McDuffie and his wife Don Ella bought the house in 1907 and lived in it until their deaths in the 1930s.

C-83
1009 West Main Street
c. 1891; c. 1919

Physician R. P. Sweatt probably built this one-story modified L-plan house as rental housing soon after purchasing the property in 1891. He was then living with his family in the larger, two-story home at **902 West Main**. He may have lived here briefly around 1895, when the directory lists him on the odd-numbered side of West Main, but by the time of the 1900 Census, he and his wife Ellen were back at 902, along with two daughters and a son-in-law. His family sold this house soon after his death in 1902. T. J. Stonar, who owned a meat market at 109 East Main, bought it in 1919. The square porch supports on brick piers probably date to his time in the house.

C-84
1015 West Main Street
c. 1900; c. 1919

A modified L-plan cottage of c. 1900 forms the core of this house and is visible from the street in the gable-front wing on the right and the steeply pitched roof. Alterations to the porch date from c. 1919, with later additions to the side and rear. Approximately two years after building it, cotton buyer and businessman F. B. Kenner moved with his family to Dallas, but retained ownership of the house. In May of 1904, the *Enterprise* noted the family's return to Waxahachie and their home on West Main. In 1907 they moved to North College Street and sold this house to F. B.'s brother, R. F. Kenner. In 1919 E. V. McElroy bought the house, and the "updated" porch either dates to his ownership or that of A. L. Tune, who bought the house in 1921. Tune, who was listed as a farmer in the 1923 city directory, and his wife, Annie, remained through the 1930s.

C-85
1020 West Main Street
c. 1891

R. J. Moore owned a farm implement business when he and his wife had this house built after purchasing the lot in 1891. Moore's newspaper advertisements included products such as the Black Land Plow, made especially for the "black sticky mud" of Ellis County. Business was good enough to allow the purchase of this elevated lot, away from the bustle of the square and close to the newly developed West End Addition, just across the railroad tracks to the west. The Moores were settled in the house by December 1892, when the *Enterprise* noted a social event at their "beautiful West End home." Sheriff George C. Sweatt purchased the house soon after his second marriage, to Mattie Poindexter, in 1901. In October 1902 the local paper noted that the sheriff was remodeling and enlarging his West End home. The rear wing probably dates to that time. A modified L-plan cottage with a projecting corner entrance, the house displays the asymmetrical façade and steeply pitched roofs characteristic of the Queen Anne style. Other Queen Anne features include the corner brackets on the front bay and the small gable perched on top of the central hipped roof. The decorative woodwork in the front gable appears to be original, but the other gables contain later examples in the same style. Sweatt remained sheriff for many years and was known well beyond Waxahachie. The *Dallas Morning News* covered his funeral in 1921, noting that county offices were closed. Thousands attended the service, including officers from Dallas, Fort Worth, and Corsicana.

C-86
1021 West Main Street
1919

Mary E. Moore and her new husband Stacey had this house built soon after her father, E. F. Owen, gave her the lot in March of 1919. She had grown up in the house across the street, **1022 West Main**, with her widowed father and three sisters. Her husband was the son of hardware merchant Will Moore, who lived a few lots to the west at 1122 West Main (no longer extant). The couple chose an up-to-date bungalow design. The horizontal emphasis typical in bungalows of the period is evident in the wide front porch with its low-pitched roof, but in an interesting twist, the roof of the main façade has a steeper pitch, and the central chimney on the façade provides a contrasting vertical thrust. In August of 1923, Stacey died after an appendicitis operation, at the age of only twenty-five, leaving his wife with one child. Mary later married Charles Conway and left Waxahachie, but she retained ownership of the house for many years, using it for rental income.

C-87
1022 West Main Street
1896-97; J. S. Moad, architect; C. J. Griggs, builder

According to the mechanic's lien of December 1896, Dallas architect J. S. Moad provided the plans for this house, and local contractor C. J. Griggs received $2,500 for the materials and labor to construct it. Moad, in partnership with J. E. Flanders, also designed a house for T. J. Cole at **309 East Marvin** (now significantly altered), as well as Trinity Methodist Church in Dallas, the Shackleford County Courthouse, and the W. A. Strain house in Lancaster. In this relatively small house, Moad pulls multiple elements of the Queen Anne style into delightful play. The asymmetry of the plan is emphasized by the corner porch entrance and the front-facing gable wing projecting from the main, hipped-roofed body of the house. Bay windows project at the front and the side; lacy decorative woodwork abounds; and a complex roof landscape includes three types of dormers, with the most prominent being the polygonal tower emerging above the side bay window. (A recent renovation added a square tower at the peak of the hipped roof.)

Marcus P. Exline had the house built for his bride, Bena Lobdell, of Lobdell, Louisiana. Since it was not quite complete upon their return from the wedding in January of 1897, they stayed a few weeks in a boarding house before moving in. Born in Galveston, Marcus was listed as a "commercial solicitor" in the 1895 Waxahachie city directory, but after moving to Dallas in 1900 he established a printing company and built a five-story building for the M. P. Exline Company in downtown Dallas in 1905. Emerson F. Owen bought this house from the Exlines in 1901. Owen worked for forty-five years as the distributor of the *Dallas Morning News* in Waxahachie. His 1950 obituary noted that he was known as "Owen the Newsman" and carried copies of the paper on his arm whenever he went out. In 1919 he gave his daughter Mary the lot across the street, and she and her new husband built the house that still stands at **1021 West Main**.

C-88
1025 West Main Street
1902; C. J. Griggs, builder

Originally located at 411 West Main Street, this two-story modified L-plan house was built as rental property by S. P. and Willia Skinner on the rear portion of their lot with a substantial 1892 house that faced West Franklin. In order to create two lots and make room for this new house facing West Main, the Skinners removed part of the back wing of the West Franklin house and moved a servant's house from the center to the rear of the West Main lot. When the Skinners sold the West Main property, they reserved the right to separate the northwest room of the servant's house and move it to another location. There is no evidence, however, that they ever availed themselves of this right. Mr. Skinner remained busy with his law practice, business interests, and two terms as a state senator. By 1913 the couple had left Waxahachie to settle in San Antonio. The house was moved to its current location in January 2010, when a large wing was added to the rear.

C-89
1026 West Main Street
c. 1899

Mrs. Louella Sims Siddons bought this lot in March of 1899, and she and her husband J. C. probably built the house soon after. A photograph dating to about 1900 shows it generously ornamented with Queen Anne-style ornament in the gables and on the porch, much like its neighbor at **1022 West Main**. Later owners removed the ornament and "updated" the house, but some of the current design anomalies derive from its original Queen Anne form. The most noticeable of these is the off-center placement of the windows in the prominent front gable. The roof of a front entry porch originally projected from the right side of that gable, filling the current blank space above the door. In addition, the current hipped-roof dormer was once a smaller curved eyebrow dormer. J. C. Siddons sold his drug business in 1901 to B. W. Fears. In 1906, the Siddons sold the house to Edward Forrest Cunningham, who was a banker and son of wealthy landowner and banker George H. Cunningham, who lived at **808 West Main**. Edward died in 1915, at the age of forty-two. His widow Laura probably was responsible for the updating, and she continued to live here until her death in 1949.

C-90
1030 West Main Street
1899

James B. Dunaway bought this lot in May of 1899, and a month later, the *Enterprise* observed that "James Dunaway's handsome new cottage" was nearing completion. A photograph of about 1900 shows a few features that have been lost over the years, including decorative woodwork in all of the gables and an entire gable at the southeast corner. Even so, this one-story modified L-plan cottage retains its basic form and many original details, including the extra-wide front door. In the 1900 Census, James was twenty-six and living here with his wife, Ida Hosford Dunaway, their son, and a servant. Dunaway was working as bookkeeper for the First National Bank when he built the house, but by 1907 he entered the lumber business with Ed Campbell and his brother, O. B. Dunaway. He next managed the Trinity Farm Company. When he resigned that position, his own agricultural holdings were sufficient to support him for the rest of his life. Ida continued to live here after his death in 1939 until just a few years before her own death in 1969, at the age of ninety-five.

C-91
1109 West Main Street
1911; W. W. Walston, builder

When Frank L. Compton and his wife Emma agreed to pay W. W. Walston $2,750 to build this house, the instructions in the mechanic's lien were quite specific. Walston supplied the plans of what was to be a "one story brick house of five rooms, two galleries and a bathroom . . . to be covered with metal shingles . . . walls . . . to be brick and 9 inches thick . . . a modern brick bungalow . . . " Although bungalows tend to be associated with gable roofs and the Craftsman style, like the example down the street at **1210 West Main**, hipped roof examples like this one were built, with the low-pitched roof and wide wraparound porch contributing to the bungalow's essential horizontal emphasis. The Mission style parapet above the dormer was very unusual in Waxahachie, but a popular form in house catalogues and magazines of the time. Although Compton was a contractor, he tended to specialize in brick, concrete, and commercial structures rather than houses. This was one of a series of houses that he built, lived in for a few years, and then sold, beginning with the 1895 brick T-plan cottage at **703 South College Street**. He was familiar with W. W. Walston and his work before selecting him to build this house, for in 1909 he and Walston worked together as contractors of the union passenger railroad depot in Sherman, Texas. Continuing his previous peripatetic pattern, Compton sold this house to D. W. Burleson and moved further out West Main, then to the university area. When he died in 1924 at the age of sixty-five, he and Emma were living at 411 Cynisca, where she was able to remain for several years.

C-92
1121 West Main Street
1899; C. M. Sammons, architect;
C. W. McDuffie & J. D. Bushong, builders

In March of 1899 successful merchant Seaborn Y. (S. Y.) Matthews and his wife Mary signed a mechanic's lien agreeing to pay local contractors McDuffie & Bushong $2,494.50 to construct this substantial modified L-plan house. While living here Matthews continued to expand his chain of dry goods and men's clothing stores. The *Enterprise* noted the opening of a new branch in Waco in 1902, the fourth in Texas. After selling this house to J. B. George in 1905, Matthews moved to Dallas and entered the insurance business. The original mechanic's lien described the house simply as a "one story frame house of six rooms," but it also specified that the plans had been furnished by C. M. Sammons. Born in New York, Sammons lived in Dallas for many years, practicing architecture in the firm Sammons and Toppin. He moved to Waxahachie in the early 1890s and remained until his death in 1907. The house was remodeled in 1924 when George Coleman bought it. After fire damage in 1952, the original porch, which stopped at the east edge of the house, was removed. The current wraparound porch was added in 1999.

C-93
1203 West Main Street
1890-91; Cooperative Building Plan Association, architect

Built by Oscar E. Dunlap, one of the original investors in the West End Addition, this two-story Queen Anne style house was based on a design published in 1887 and 1889 issues of *Shoppell's Modern Houses*, a popular New York magazine that sold house plans by mail. The editor, Robert W. Shoppell, credited the designs to a group of architects called the Cooperative Building Plan Association. In this design the tower with bulbous roof dominates a façade ornamented with a variety of tripartite elements. These include triple windows in the projecting rectangular wing, the three sides of the bay windows on the opposite side, and the three-sided central porch and balcony echoed in the third-floor balcony of the tower. Patterned shingle siding and geometric woodwork decorate the walls and gables, while brackets highlight the eaves and gables, and lacy pierced woodwork trims the porch and balconies. Changes over the years include the removal of a small central dormer and the enclosure and expansion of what was originally a one-story porch on the east side.

Oscar Dunlap's business and social prominence in Waxahachie is evident in the attention that the local newspaper gave to the construction of his new home. The October 17, 1890 issue reported that work had commenced on the foundation, and progress was noted on November 21. The "modern design" of the home was commended on April 17, 1891, and, finally, on May 22 it was announced that the Dunlaps were ready to move into their "elegant" new West End house.

Dunlap had come to Texas in 1867 at the age of eighteen. He studied law after his marriage in 1876 to Ella McDuffie, the stepdaughter of a successful farmer and landowner. Referred to as "Judge" for the rest of his life in deference to his four years as a county judge in the 1880s, he ceased practicing law when he was elected president of Citizens Bank in 1886. He concentrated his energies on the bank and other business and community interests, including the street railroad and the electric company, in addition to his investment in the West End Addition. He served as president of the Texas State Bankers Association and on the executive council of the American Bankers Association. The Dunlaps lived in the house for over forty years. A fascinating account of life in the house, as well as in Waxahachie's African American community, was included in the memoir of Ely Green, the Dunlaps' chauffeur from about 1913 to 1918. (*Ely: Too Black, Too White*, University of Massachusetts Press, 1970.) The petrified wood retaining walls, fences, walks, and steps date to the 1930s, when former mayor, banker, and hardware merchant Burton Prince owned the house. The June 25, 1936 *Daily Light* noted the new, "beautiful rock garden, which construction men declare will be one of the most attractive in this section."

C-94
1206 West Main Street
1924; McCanless & Garvin, builders

Built in 1924 by Thomas W. Burleson with profits from his successful honey business, this house represents a popular variation of a Foursquare house, with a recessed wing to the side containing a sunroom below and sleeping porch above. The *Daily Light* of May 22, 1924 described it as "very attractive and pleasing to lovers of fine homes." Burleson bought his first colony of bees in 1903, but did not quit his job as District Clerk of Ellis County until 1906. He established the T. W. Burleson Honey Company in 1907, keeping his beehives on the large lot behind the house. The business remained in this location until 1936, when it moved to a commercial building just north of the square at 224 North Rogers. Burleson's is now one of the largest honey companies in the country, still headquartered in Waxahachie. Its current facility, 301 Peters Street, was built in 1966. The founder, T. W. Burleson, died in 1944, after being struck by an automobile when walking across Main Street to visit an ailing friend.

C-95
1209 West Main Street
1938; Fin Garvin & Son, builders

In March of 1938 Wood P. and Selma Haynes contracted to pay Fin Garvin & Son the sum of $3,395 to build this house, described in the mechanic's lien as a "seven room and bath frame building." A straightforward front-gable bungalow with sloping porch columns on brick piers, it looks as if it could have been built in the 1920s rather than the late 1930s, when English-style cottages were more popular. Mrs. Haynes was a popular piano and organ teacher in Waxahachie for many years. Born in Waxahachie and sister of the florist W. B. (Bird) Forrest, she studied piano and organ at Southern Methodist University in Dallas and taught in Waxahachie before marrying Wood Haynes. The couple lived in Burleson, Texas, where Haynes owned a grocery and hardware store until coming to Waxahachie in the 1930s. In 1940 the *Daily Light* noted that the Haynes Food Store on East Franklin was growing and increasing its stock. Wood and Selma were still living in this house when she died in 1973 at the age of seventy-three.

C-96
1210 West Main Street
1923; Fin Garvin Jr., builder

This simple front-gable bungalow with wide front gable porch was built for Hilliar Franklin and Ethel Rousseau in 1923, according to plans that they supplied. The mechanic's lien for the house specifies a six-room "bungalow house," including a built-in "Pantry front" inside. The Rousseaus could have acquired the plans from one of the many catalogues of bungalow plans published in this era or ordered them from a magazine. The tapered porch supports above the brick piers are typical of bungalows of the 1920s, but the indentation of the right half of the façade, creating an irregularly shaped porch, is more unusual. Rousseau worked as an abstracter at the Waxahachie Abstract Company. The couple moved here from **411 East Marvin Street**, a house that Hilliar had built in 1906. Fin Garvin also built the bungalow across the street, **1209 West Main**, fifteen years after this one.

C-97
1300 West Main Street
Coca-Cola Bottling Plant
1931

On July 14, 1930, a fire destroyed Waxahachie's previous Coca-Cola Bottling Company plant, located two blocks away from the square, on North College Street. Five months later the company purchased this lot, and in February 1931 the newspaper noted "preliminary work already has been done toward the construction of the new Coca Cola Plant. . . . " Located on the main east-west highway running through town (now US 287 Business), the site combined easy access for trucks with high public visibility. Built before the many Streamline-Deco Coca-Cola Bottling Company buildings of the mid- to late thirties, this one represents a more straightforward, red-brick-industrial approach to design. The bricks were laid in a pattern known as American bond, or common bond, with five courses, or rows, of stretchers to one course of headers. (Headers are bricks laid with their ends toward the face of the wall.) The original building consisted of the two-story structure with one-story warehouse in the rear. In 1950 Coca-Cola remodeled the original building and added a new one-story office wing on the west side. The geometric screen in front of the original entrance was built after Coca-Cola sold the building in 1977.

C-98
1303 West Main Street
1891; E. H. Griffin, builder

G. L. Adkisson, with his carriage business and other interests, was either a very prominent citizen or a good friend of the *Enterprise*'s editor, for the newspaper carried regular notices on the progress of this house. (It also helped that construction occurred at a time of intensive promotion of the West End development.) In January of 1891, Adkisson was "preparing to build a magnificent home. . . ." In Feburary, it was "being built"; in April, it was of "the most modern design"; and in May he "moved into his magnificent new home." The newspaper also noted that E. H. Griffin was superintending construction, but county records indicate that he may have subcontracted part of the carpentry work to M. M. Shelton. The latter gentleman was named in a mechanic's lien of April 1891 in which the lumber firm of Musgraves Brasher & Co. was trying to obtain payment for $62.29 in materials for the Adkisson house. Payment must have been settled, for, as the paper noted, the Adkissons moved in May, and they remained there for over twenty-five years. Photographs from the 1975 survey show decorative woodwork on the porch and balcony that is now gone, but the basic form of the house and many of its Queen Anne-style details remain, including the prominent corner tower and the decorative shingles in the gables and in bands between floors.

C-99
1307 West Main Street
1913

In February of 1913 the *Daily Light* mentioned not only that William A. Briggs was building this "very pretty residence in the West End," but also its substantial cost of $6,000. This is one of three bungalows built around the same time on West Main that resemble each other in style and materials, with the brownish-red brick veneer being the most noticeable shared feature. (The others are at **701** and **814 West Main**.) This example displays the strong horizontal emphasis typical of bungalows in its broad low-pitched roof with exposed rafter ends over a deeply recessed porch. The unusual line of four windows in the gabled dormer reinforces the horizontality. Briggs evidently did well with land and cattle investments, and the *Dallas Morning News* occasionally noted his cattle activities as well as his return from visiting the Chicago Columbian Exposition in 1893. In October of 1895 he received forty-nine railroad cars of cattle from Mineral Wells, Texas, to "winter" them on his property before shipping in the spring. The *Enterprise* noted in December 1902 that his cattle won a second-place award in Chicago at the National Live Stock Show. He and his wife Angie retired to Harlingen in 1929, where their son Emory lived.

C-100
1404 West Main Street
1894; E. H. Griffin, architect and builder

This relatively modest one-story modified L-plan house was built by a man who later amassed a fortune, with national holdings in railroad, bank, telephone, oil, and cotton oil mill stocks as well as land and cattle interests. Marvin E. Singleton was born in 1872 on his family's homestead west of town, land given to his father as a bonus for serving in the Texas War of Independence in 1836. In April of 1894, he contracted to pay E. H. Griffin $1,000 to build what was described as a "one story frame building of five rooms" according to plans supplied by Griffin, who was a successful Waxahachie contractor at the time. Griffin also built the G. L. Adkisson house nearby at **1303 West Main**. His plans for this house may derive from the design for a "Southern Cottage" by Abilene builder J. W. Archer that was published in the April 1893 issue of the journal *National Builder*. Singleton was living here when the 1895 city directory was published, and after he married Susie Clary of Corsicana in 1897 the couple remained for about a year. They leased the house in 1899 when they moved to Fort Worth, where Singleton organized and managed the Fort Worth Cotton Oil Company. Although Singleton later moved to Saint Louis and established substantial business interests there, he maintained ties to Waxahachie that included chairmanship of the Citizens National Bank beginning in 1932. His death in 1938 was noted with a lengthy obituary in the *New York Times*, and his Saint Louis funeral was held in the chapel he had given to Saint John's Methodist Episcopal Church in memory of his wife Susie.

C-101
1408 West Main Street
c. 1893

Delicate ornamental woodwork distinguishes this one-story L-plan cottage, particularly on the gable wing and front porch. Multipaned windows in the squared bay are flanked by pilasters and crowned by pendant brackets and a shingled hood. The elaborate gable ornament includes turned spindles as well as pierced and sawn work. Oscar B. Sims probably built the house soon after his purchase of the lot in April 1893, when he returned to Waxahachie after a few years in Claude, Texas, to become superintendent of the town's new cotton compress. He and his wife Jessie remained in this house over the next thirty years as he became a cotton buyer and farmer. We do not know the builder or designer of this house, but Sims's previous Waxahachie residence, **417 West Jefferson Street**, also displays noteworthy details and ornament.

C-102
1500 West Main Street
c. 1896

W. H. and Annie Fears bought the lot in November of 1895 and probably built this two-story modified L-plan house soon after. Born in Georgia, Fears met his future wife Annie Moore when he moved to Ennis in the early 1880s. His work as a lawyer often took him to the courthouse in Waxahachie, and in 1889 he and Annie were even married in Waxahachie, at the residence of Deputy Sheriff Grizzard, also known as the county jail. After Fears was elected county attorney in 1892, the couple moved to Waxahachie, where they remained except for a brief sojourn in Fort Worth, but they displayed a certain restlessness within Waxahachie, moving periodically. They sold this house to school teacher H. S. Parsons and his wife Ella in 1900. In 1904 the Fears built a smaller house at **205 Oldham** where they finally settled down. J. M. Alderdice, who served in the Texas legislature as a representative and then as a senator, lived in this house longer than either of the previous residents, staying here from 1904 into the 1920s.

The handsome hipped-roof bungalow next door at 1502 West Main was moved to that location around 1955, perhaps from Ferris Avenue, when several homes were replaced by commercial development.

C-103
West End Park
[now Getzendaner Memorial Park]
1889

Although intended by the Waxahachie Investment Company as a selling point for the West End Addition, West End Park, now the Getzendaner Memorial Park, quickly became an integral part of Waxahachie's social, recreational, and cultural life. It continues in that role today. The company set aside twenty-three acres for the park at the southwest corner of the development, next to Waxahachie Creek. They not only planted trees and laid out a curving roadway, but in 1890 they built a pavilion large enough to seat one thousand people. Families, schools, Sunday schools, and social and political organizations all held picnics in the park, and crowds witnessed W. H. Leroy's balloon ascension there in 1891. The pavilion served as the setting for dances, concerts, speeches, and the Ladies Cemetery Association Floral Fair. When the Cumberland Presbyterian Chautauqua began holding their summer assemblies in the park in 1900, it was renamed the Chautauqua Park. The Investment Company deeded the land to the Chautauqua Park Association in 1902, the same year that the 2,500-seat Chautauqua auditorium was built. Although the Chautauqua assemblies and the park remained popular over the next few years, the Park Association ran into financial difficulties. In 1914 banker R. W. Getzendaner and his sister Willia Getzendaner Skinner covered the debts and deeded the land and structures to the City of Waxahachie in memory of their parents, and the park was given its current name. Waxahachie citizens and organizations continued to use and enjoy the park in the ensuing years, and it benefited from periodic upgrades and improvements. An entrance archway (no longer extant) was added in 1920, a year after the city added nine adjoining acres to the park. The park also now provides access to the city's Waxahachie Creek Hike and Bike Trail.

C-104
Chautauqua Auditorium
1902; E. S. Boze, contractor

After the Texas Cumberland Presbyterians voted to transfer their annual Chautauqua assembly from Glen Rose to Waxahachie, visitors flocked to the park beginning in July 1900. By August 1901 a group of local citizens agreed that a larger structure was needed to replace the pavilion built in 1890 by the developers of the West End Addition. The Waxahachie Chautauqua Park Association was formed and announced in May of 1902 that a "new and much more commodious pavilion" would be built that summer. Chautauqua assemblies began in 1874 in Chautauqua, New York, and many independent assemblies across the country, like this one, followed the original model of providing opportunities to the public for education, entertainment, recreation, and religion in a communal outdoor setting.

When the *Enterprise* reported on June 13, 1902, that the contract for Waxahachie's new pavilion had been awarded to local builder E. S. Boze, little time for construction remained before the opening on July 22. Nonetheless, the *Enterprise* reported on July 18 that the new pavilion would be ready in time with "a large force of carpenters at work putting on the embellishments and finishing the interior." Even with last-minute rain, the building opened on schedule, at a cost of $2,750.

Waxahachie's Chautauqua auditorium looks nothing like the New York Chautauqua amphitheater of 1893 or the Texas-Colorado Chautauqua auditorium of 1898 in Boulder, Colorado, though all three featured either open sides or sides that could be opened to cooling breezes and accommodate overflow crowds outside. The designer of Waxahachie's building may have been the contractor E. S. Boze, given the short time allowed for design and building, the absence of any Chautauqua-sponsored standardized plans, and Boze's design abilities evident in other buildings around town and touted in his advertisements. Whoever the designer was, he avoided the oblong forms used in New York and Boulder that had entrances on one end and a stage on the other. Waxahachie's octagonal plan more closely resembles a number of polygonal Texas churches, community halls, and dance halls of the nineteenth century, many from a German tradition like the octagonal Schultzenverein dance hall in Peters of 1900. But the scale of the Waxahachie auditorium overwhelms most of these possible precedents. The broad, steeply sloping sides of its octagonal hipped roof dominate and define the building, with only a hint of ornamentation found in the narrow band of scalloped trim on the eaves. There is no architecturally designated main entrance, but a rectangular appendage on one of the southern sides clearly identifies the location of the stage. Each of the other seven sides has the same pattern of openings—two large entrance "doors" flanked by paired "windows." All of the openings were equipped with panels that slid up and down on ropes and pulleys in an arrangement similar to panels installed on part of Boulder's auditorium in 1899.

The local Chautauqua Park Association may have been too ambitious in their desire for this impressive building, for in 1906 they were unable to complete payments for the construction costs. E. P. Hawkins paid the debt that time, and in 1914 banker R. W. Getzendaner and his sister Willia Getzendaner Skinner covered subsequent debts and deeded the land and structures to the City of Waxahachie as a park in memory of their parents. Even after the Chautauqua assemblies ceased in the early 1930s, the auditorium continued to be used for civic events and school graduations for many years. As use and maintenance decreased, the structure deteriorated. The city closed it in 1971 and considered demolition, but a small group of local citizens including Josephine Ruskin,

Dr. Ford Lane, Steve Chapman, Marvin Singleton Jr., and Forrest and Ola Upshaw worked to encourage funding for restoration and public recognition of the building's significance, including a Texas Historical Marker in 1971 and listing on the National Register of Historic Places in 1974. The restored auditorium was rededicated on July 4, 1975. The Chautauqua Preservation Society, first formed in 1974, was revived in 1999. Board members Kirk Hunter and Maureen Moore helped establish an annual program beginning in 2000 that enables participants to enjoy the Chautauqua experience in the only remaining Texas structure built for that purpose.

C-105
202 North Grand Avenue
1922

This one-story front gable bungalow and two others to the south facing West Main (1314 & 1316), were all built for speculative sale by John G. Russell, manager of the local branch of the H. H. Hardin Lumber Company. Not surprisingly, Russell acquired the building materials from his employer, and the mechanics' liens that he used to secure funding provide documentation of the timing and scale of his investments. He began with this house on October 27, 1922, contracting to pay $2,400 for the materials. On the 28th and the 30th of the same month, he contracted for 1316 and 1314 West Main, respectively. The slightly larger sum of $2,500 for each of those houses is reflected in their larger scale and additional decorative details. The clipped front gables and plan of this bungalow is echoed in 1314 West Main, and was used by Russell again when he built **210 East University** in November 1922. The plans were probably derived from examples provided by the lumber company.

C-106
203 North Grand Avenue
1904; B. F. Sargent, builder

Prominent lawyer Milton B. Templeton did not hesitate in his decision to rebuild when his 1895 residence on this lot burned in March 1904. Within two months of the fire, the *Dallas Morning News* noted that contractors had begun work on Templeton's "handsome home." A few days later the Waxahachie newspaper reported that the new home would be "strictly colonial" and would cost $8,000, a sizable sum at the time. Its style would be considered Neoclassical today, but in early 1900s Waxahachie almost anything with columns was described as "Colonial," and, needless to say, Colonial was the style that any successful, establishment gentleman such as Judge Templeton would want. One-story extensions to the porch originally wrapped around both sides of the house in a manner similar to a 1901 design by mail-order architect George F. Barber that might have served as the inspiration for this one. (The house next door at **209 North Grand** was built from Barber plans in 1895, the same year that Templeton built his first house on this lot.) The newspaper noted that Ennis contractor B. F. Sargent was hired to "look after the work," for this residence, as well as the Chaska house under construction at the same time at **716 West Main**.

Born and educated in Tennessee, Templeton came to Texas in 1878, two years after being admitted to the Tennessee bar. He settled first in Ennis and practiced law, then moved to Waxahachie around 1880 when he was appointed county judge. He was then elected county attorney and served until 1887. He retired to private practice, but retained the honorific "Judge" for the rest of his life. He maintained a busy law practice and argued a case before the State Supreme Court in 1906, but he still found time for business and community activities. He served as a director in such enterprises as the Water-Works Company, the Street Railway Company, the Electric Light Company, and Waxahachie National Bank. When serving as a director of the West End Development Company, he supported the company's West End project by moving here from his previous residence on College Avenue. Templeton moved his family to Dallas around 1909, selling this house to J. Houston Miller, president of Waxahachie National Bank. In 1921 prominent pharmacist Lem C. Curlin bought the property. The owner of two Curlin pharmacies in Waxahachie and a chain of music stores in Ellis County, he died unexpectedly of pneumonia the next year. His wife and four small children remained in the house into the 1930s.

C-107
206 North Grand Avenue
1922; O. B. Bennett, builder

In October 1922, newlyweds A. Dupree and Ethel Davis contracted to pay O. B. Bennett $4,500 to build this "one-story frame house of five rooms, breakfast room, bath room, hall, front porch and rear porch." The basic form of a front-gable bungalow with front gable porch was common in Waxahachie at the time, but this example was unusual in its deeply recessed front porch that provided more room for social activity and leisure. The house also included special features, such as the decorative rows of dentils along the frieze lines of the gables and the triple-window arrangement on the façade, with a wide window closely flanked by two narrower ones. The current porch supports probably are not original. Brick piers surmounted by wood pillars, similar to those at **202 North Grand**, are more likely to have graced this carefully detailed bungalow. Dupree served in the Army Engineers Corps during World War I and taught school in Ellis County before moving to Waxahachie and marrying Mary Ethel Sharp in 1922. His career soon moved into the public realm, and he served as Ellis County school superintendent for six terms. His other governmental positions included county clerk, city councilman, and mayor (1952-56). The family moved from the house in the 1930s, but did not sell it until 1941.

C-108
209 North Grand Avenue
1895; George F. Barber, architect; C. J. Griggs, builder

H. W. Trippet obviously intended to impress the viewer with this residence, and, with the help of mail-order architect George F. Barber, he succeeded. Barber's design used a standard though sizable two-story modified L-plan and incorporated features that made it appear even larger. The prominent corner tower accentuates the height of the house. It emerges from the roof at the attic level and is crowned by an unusually tall, elongated, bulbous roof. At the top of that roof a decorative finial, originally one of a pair, stretches the height even farther. The mass of the house is emphasized by the two-story gallery that extends outward and curves around two sides of the building. The first floor entrance gable projects even beyond the deep porch and is echoed by another gable directly above it. Trippet could have become aware of the architect when his Waxahachie National Bank colleague J. J. Metcalfe used a Barber's catalogue design for his 1894 residence, or perhaps two years earlier when F. P. Powell built a Barber house. Unlike these gentlemen, however, Trippet evidently requested a custom design, for even though the mechanic's lien specified the use of plans by Barber, and many elements and details reflect Barber's works, the house does not match any of his catalogue designs exactly.

Trippet's decision to build the house turned out to be ill-timed and may have contributed to his downfall. The son of successful Waxahachie businessman and dry goods merchant Aaron Trippet, H. W. withdrew from his father's firm in 1887 and moved to Alvarado, Texas, to help establish a new bank. By 1889, the local newspaper noted that he had moved to Weatherford, where he opened a dry goods store. His various enterprises enabled him to return to Waxahachie in 1890, when he became cashier of the new Waxahachie National Bank that his father helped organize. Moving upward, H. W. became president the next year and purchased a house on West Main Street. Continuing his financial ascent, H. W. bought out his father's dry goods business in January 1895. In spite of a national depression that year, he felt optimistic enough to hire C. J. Griggs in November to build this house. Only a year later, however, the dry goods store was in serious trouble. H. W. filed a Chattel Mortgage (equivalent to bankruptcy) in November 1896. His father took back the store, and H. W. scrambled to rebuild his finances and keep his house. He hung on for a few years, but sold the house in 1900, moved to rental housing in Fort Worth, and eventually settled in Oklahoma. The house remained one of Waxahachie's landmarks for many years. W. H. Getzendaner's daughter Willia and her husband S. P. Skinner bought it from Trippet and lived here while S. P. served two terms in the state senate. When they moved to San Antonio in 1910, Willia's brother, Ralph W. Getzendaner, bought it. Willia and Ralph donated the land for Getzendaner Memorial Park, at the south end of Grand Street.

C-109
212 North Grand Avenue
c. 1921

J. R. Mayhew's Waxahachie Nursery Company originally operated on this block. In 1907 the *Enterprise* described it as "one of the best known nurseries in this part of the country." The company's advertisement in the 1913 city directory claimed that "Planting Trees and Flowers Will Make Waxahachie the CITY BEAUTIFUL, Over One Million Trees for the Coming Season." Although tree sales may not have reached one million, the company prospered for several years. By the early 1920s property values in the area had increased, and Mayhew consolidated operations in the block to the north and sold the lots in this block. Mrs. Ida Sheets, wife of nursery foreman E. Owen Sheets, bought this lot in 1920, and the couple had this house built soon after. Although similar in form to the bungalow at **206 North Grand**, which was built around the same time, this house displays a more vertical emphasis, with the roof pitched a bit more steeply.

C-110
301 North Elm Street
The Appliance House
1956

Unique when built in Waxahachie in 1956, this modular building remains unique on the Waxahachie landscape. The simple exposed construction, all-glass walls, shed roof, and minimal signage are characteristics of modern commercial buildings. Perhaps most importantly, its design and placement at the Elm Street curve acknowledged Waxahachie's version of major changes that were taking place in retail marketing everywhere. Pedestrian-oriented shops like those around Courthouse Square were now competing with expansive glass-front showrooms designed and illuminated for viewing from a moving automobile. Big signs were not necessary because the showroom itself was on the street and everything appeared to be for sale!

Property owner Clarence Lander built the structure specifically to lease to Waxahachie businessman and friend Rex Odom for a startup business called The Appliance House. The *Daily Light* gave appreciative attention to the building when it was built but identified neither an architect nor a builder. Within a few years, Odom had almost doubled the size with additions on the north side, but he continued to use a drawing of the original "glass and redwood modernistic building" in advertisements during his thirteen years at this location. Given the date of construction, the building was in all likelihood architect-designed, as most contractors were not, as yet, familiar with buildings of this type. It was possibly an early project of a young Forrest Upshaw, who was from Waxahachie and who, after receiving his architecture degree from the University of Texas in 1951, was practicing on his own in Dallas in 1956. Two years later, he designed the Southland Cotton Oil office building at **106 South Monroe Street**, which was also on property owned by Clarence Lander.

C-111
500 Royal Street
c. 1913

Proclaimed as an "Example of Civic Attractiveness" when it was illustrated in the September 13, 1915, issue of the *Dallas Morning News*, this two-story hipped-roof house was built by florist and nurseryman W. B. (Bird) Forrest. Its red tile roof colorfully highlights the hipped roofs of the square core and rear wing, as well as the broad wraparound porch and the later gable-roof one-story addition. Rusticated concrete blocks form the porch foundation. Although the horizontal emphasis and broad eaves indicate a strong debt to the Prairie style, the house would have been called "Colonial" when it was built, due to its Ionic column capitals and the decorated pediments above the front and side porch entrance bays. As shown in the 1915 newspaper photograph, the second-floor sleeping porch at the southeast corner originally had only screened windows, and canvas awnings protected sleepers from the elements.

By the time he built this house, Forrest was well established in his floral and nursery business, and the extensive greenhouses that enabled his success surrounded his new house. Born and raised in Arkansas, Forrest came to Waxahachie at the age of seventeen. In 1903 he was working as a contractor with H. W. Madson, but late that same year he built a 14 x 16 ft. greenhouse on land east of Ferris Avenue and concentrated on his new business. He purchased this corner of the block from the Ferris Estate in 1905, first building greenhouses and a smaller residence that are shown in a 1912 advertisement in the *Daily Light*. Additional advertisements that year indicated the range of his products, featuring cut flowers in one and announcing over 100,000 tomato plants in another. Forrest acquired more of the block in 1912, probably building this larger house soon after, and completed his ownership of the south half of the block in 1916. When the 1914 Sanborn map was drawn, this house was in place, and the smaller house had been moved to **501 Gibson**. Forrest eventually purchased the rest of the block, and by the time of the 1952 directory his son could proclaim 60,000 square feet in greenhouses on the property. Remnants of the greenhouses remained on the property into the twenty-first century, but are now gone.

C-112
503 Ferris Avenue
1902; E. S. Boze, builder

The *Enterprise* noted that A. D. Thompson was building this "handsome cottage" only a few days after he signed the contract with builder E. S. Boze on August 5, 1902. Boze supplied the plans for the one-story seven-room house and also contracted to repair an existing four-room house on the lot behind this one, which the Thompsons probably intended to use as a rental. A month later the family moved into their new hipped-roof house. They celebrated in early December with an "entertainment" that was mentioned in the paper, but they sold the house in June and appear to have left Waxahachie. Subsequent owners showed more stability, particularly banker J. N. Langsford, who bought the house in 1919, moving from the large family home at **1208 East Marvin** to this smaller, newer home. Langsford's daughter Rilla opened a gift shop in part of the house in 1935 that became a Waxahachie institution. She never married and continued to run the shop in the house, celebrating fifty years of operation in 1985. She died in 1986 at the age of eighty-eight.

C-113
507 Ferris Avenue
1902, 1905

In 1902 the *Enterprise* noted that Thomas A. Ferris, son of J. W. Ferris, was having this "handsome cottage" built. Thomas had no intention of moving out of his recently completed "stately colonial home" (demolished) at the northwest corner of Ferris and McMillan. He used this cottage as a rental property until his son Floyd married Bettye Duke in September 1905. The day before the marriage Thomas deeded the property to Floyd, and a few weeks later the newspaper noted that Floyd was having the cottage "remodeled and improved." The current pyramidal roof and central dormer probably date to the 1905 remodeling. The house now bears new siding and commercial signs, but it retains much of its 1905 form and appearance. Floyd and Bettye kept the house until pharmacist Lemuel C. Curlin purchased it in 1911.

C-114
512 Ferris Avenue
1927-28; H. D. Rankin, builder

On November 28, 1927, Mary and J. S. Brooks signed a contract with H. D. Rankin to build this "seven room and bath brick veneer one-story residence with front and back porches; front porch to have cement floor cement terrace in front and roof to be made of Johns-Manville Asbestos Roofing. . . . " A few months later the local newspaper approved the results in an article summarizing recent improvements around town: "Adding much to the appearance of Ferris avenue, J. S. Brooks has built a brick veneer English-type home that is one of the prettiest ever erected here." It still projects a charming appearance, with its arched leaded-glass front windows balanced by the wide arch of the deep porch on the right, even though blank expanses of parking lots have replaced the bungalows and cottages that once surrounded it. The original cream-colored brick has been painted gray. Brooks and his wife ran a shoe store for many years on the east side of the square. In 1951, a year before Brooks died, the *Daily Light* described it as the "oldest shoe store in the county."

C-115
519 Ferris Avenue
c. 1920

The small second-floor bedroom identifies this front-gable bungalow as an "airplane bungalow." Such bungalows emerged in the early years of the twentieth century, only a few years after the Wright brothers' first flights in 1903. That the small rooms perched on spreading first-floor roofs could be compared to the cockpit over the wings of an early plane indicates the popular fascination with the new world of flight and the eagerness of entrepreneurs and promoters to capitalize on that fascination. Practical considerations also may have contributed to its continued use in Waxahachie and the rest of Texas, for summer nights became much more comfortable in those second-floor bedrooms with multiple windows and cross-ventilation. (Other Waxahachie examples can be seen at **305 Oldham** and **708 West Main**.) Although similar to a design published in *Holland's Magazine* in June 1920, the pitch of the roof here is steeper, losing some of the horizontal emphasis associated with bungalows. Instead of hugging the ground, this bungalow rises vertically through the three ascending gables. Farmer and grocery man J. M. Davis and his wife Ruth lived here through the 1920s.

C-116
609 Ferris Avenue
c. 1905

Mrs. Martha E. Stroud, a widow, probably built this one-story pyramidal house soon after purchasing the lot in August 1905 for $600. She and her daughter Lila were living here in 1907, but they sold it for $3,000 two years later to real estate agent Thomas C. Cole. Four generations of the Burton family later lived in the house, including Ruth Burton, an early proponent of Waxahachie's Gingerbread Trail.

C-117
617 Ferris Avenue
1923; W. W. Walston, builder

In May 1923, L. J. and Irene Lawrence agreed to pay contractor W. W. Walston $6,000 to construct this "two story frame house of seven rooms; two halls and two porches." An early example of the Dutch Colonial style in Waxahachie, its design was probably inspired by illustrations in current magazines or lumberyard catalogues. Three years later, the same design appeared in the 1926 Sears catalogue *Honor Bilt [sic] Modern Homes*. (Sears staff architects often adapted popular designs from other published sources.) L. J. worked as manager of the Southland Cotton Oil Co. on South Rogers Street through the 1920s.

C-118
407 West Parks Street
1921

This front-gable bungalow possesses a more elaborate form than most examples in Waxahachie. Four cross-gable extensions provide variety and depth to the side elevations while adding square footage and light to the interior. (The bungalow across the street at **412 West Parks** shows a simpler, more common example of the form.) In August 1921, Mrs. Cecilia Knowles contracted to pay the William Cameron & Co. $3,000 for the materials to build this "one-story frame bungalo [sic] consisting of six rooms, hall, bath room, breakfast room, front porch and rear porch." As the widow of painter W. D. Knowles, she evidently was familiar enough with the local members of the building trades to arrange separately for the actual construction, without using a mechanic's lien. Her son, Harry, and daughter-in-law Nannie, lived with her. Harry prospered in his work as a cotton buyer, moving the entire family to Dallas in 1924. In 1928 the *Dallas Morning News* reported that he was building a new house in Highland Park. Spanish-American War veteran and Ellis County landowner and farmer Will Keplinger and his wife Lurah lived here for many years after the Knowles family.

C-119
409 West Parks Street
1921

A small group of cotton buyers congregated in this neighborhood in the early 1920s. The first of them, W. C. Biggers, bought this lot in February 1921, and in June of the same year, the *Dallas Morning* News noted the construction of his "residence on Park street" in an article about building activity in Waxahachie. That same month another cotton buyer, L. Parham Martin, contracted with W. W. Walston to build the front-gable bungalow across the street at **412 West Parks**. A few months later, cotton buyer Harry Knowles moved into the bungalow next door at **407**. Biggers was the only one of the three to remain on West Parks into the 1930s. The plan of this side-gable bungalow is somewhat unusual, with only a small entrance porch at the northeast corner and two groups of triple windows filling the remainder of the façade.

C-120
412 West Parks Street
1921; W. W. Walston, builder

A 1921 mechanic's lien records the agreement between cotton buyer L. P. Martin and his wife Alice to pay contractor W. W. Walston $2,290 to build this one-story bungalow "of five rooms, hall, bath room and front and back porches." Plumbing, electrical, painting, and paper hanging were excluded, which accounts for the unusually low price for the time. Perhaps Mr. Martin was handy enough to complete the house himself, or he arranged for others to do the work without mechanics' liens. This version of the popular front-gable bungalow with front-gable porch was distinguished by a wraparound porch that was later enclosed. The design is similar to one published in the January 1921 issue of *Holland's Magazine*.

C-121
502 West Parks Street
1921; W. W. Edwards, builder

The *Dallas Morning News* noted in November 1921 that W. W. Edwards had been awarded the contract to build a "twenty-room apartment building" for Mrs. N. B. Newton at the corner of Highland and Parks. Although this structure appears more modest than we might expect from that description, it does contain four apartments of five rooms each (for a grand total of twenty), and the location fits. (Bryson Street was originally named Hiland [sic].) In addition, an August 1921 deed records the property's purchase by Mrs. Mina E. Newton, a widow, for $2,000. Apartment buildings were a rarity in Waxahachie at the time, and the form of this one echoes the single-family bungalows in the neighborhood. It looks a bit like the big brother of a one-story front-gable bungalow, such as 501 West Parks across the street. During the Depression tenants included an engineer with the WPA, Percy C. Neel, and a surgeon with the Civilian Conservation Corps, Boyd Nibling. In the early 1920s this lot was considered part of the 400 block of West Parks. It was changed to 502 after 1948.

C-122
501 Gibson Street

c. 1906

Originally located a few blocks away at 500 Royal Street, this one-story pyramidal house was built by florist and nurseryman W. B. (Bird) Forrest. The central hipped dormer and symmetrical side dormers are similar to other pyramidal houses built a few years later, including **115 University**, but the porch treatment is different. The separate porch roof emerges just below the house roof rather than being incorporated into an unbroken roofline. A 1912 photograph, included in a local newspaper advertisement, shows this house still on Royal Street, surrounded by greenhouses, but it had been moved by the time of the 1914 Sanborn map. Its new owners were bookkeeper Thomas N. Herring and his wife Docie. They sold it in 1917 to another bookkeeper, David L. Maxwell, and his wife Florence. The Maxwells immigrated to Waxahachie from England in 1910. The Census of that year shows them lodging with James W. Harrison and his wife, Fannie, on West Main Street. Since the Harrisons were very well-to-do, it is likely that the Maxwells were related to or associated with them in some way, perhaps as employees. (Fannie Harrison had grown up in England, and James's father had been born there.) The connection is reinforced in the deed, for James Harrison financed the purchase, and Maxwell committed to repay him. Maxwell worked for many years at Citizens National Bank as a bookkeeper and teller before leaving with his family in 1927 for Monte Vista, Colorado.

C-123
411 Gibson

West Ward School
[now Waxahachie Independent School District Administration Building]

1911; W. W. Walston, contractor

It should come as no surprise that the current Waxahachie Independent School District Administration Building began its life as a school. With its square shape, hipped roof, central bell tower, and red brick exterior, it perfectly fits the stereotype of a "little red schoolhouse," though it is much larger than the one-room schools often associated with that phrase. As Waxahachie began to grow to the west in the late 1890s, the need for a school in the area became evident, and in 1903-04 the trustees leased the former Texas College building, near the west end of Jefferson Street, for that purpose. By 1911 they were able to acquire this site from Thomas A. Ferris and contract with local builder W. W. Walston to build the new school. Only three years later, in June 1914, four rooms were added to the rear of this building.

Mr. Ferris had a good incentive to sell the land to the school board, since the presence of the school would be a major selling point for the new residential area he was developing just to the east. The school soon became associated with the nearby neighborhood, and its name was changed to Ferris Ward School in 1913. The name changed again in 1939, to Ferris Elementary School. In 1974, after sixty-three years of service as a school, the building became the home of the WISD administration offices, and the students were reassigned to the more up-to-date Marvin and Northside schools.

C-124
408 Gibson Street
1921; D. H. Thompson Lumber Co., builder

This front-gable bungalow with front-gable porch represents a popular form of the 1920s, and a smaller-scale version with the same partially recessed front porch can be seen only two houses away, at 404 Gibson Street. A mechanic's lien of January 1921 informs us that J. T. Manning and his wife Bettie contracted to pay D. H. Thompson Lumber Company $1,500 to build the six-room house according to plans supplied by the Mannings. J. T. would have been capable of supervising the construction of his own house, for the city directories list him as a carpenter in the 1920s and a contractor in 1913, but perhaps he was too busy with other work.

C-125
608 Royal Street
1913

Horizontal proportions and lack of historical ornament on this two-story hipped-roof house contribute to its identity as Prairie style today, but it would have been called "Modern" at the time of its construction. That term now refers to a distinctly different and later style, but the straightforward presentation and clean lines of the house retain a modern spirit almost one hundred years later. Window shutters would not have been present originally. Will Howorth and his wife Cora built the house soon after purchasing the property in October 1912. As superintendent of the Waxahachie Cotton Mills, he was able to live almost across the street from his work, while still living on land separate from the mills. Born in England in 1875, Will had grown up in Canada. He moved to Waxahachie when his father, a mill expert, was hired by the new cotton mill in 1900. Will also worked at the mill and, in a few years, was promoted to superintendent. After Will died in 1921, at the age of forty-six, his wife and children remained in the house and built a front-gable bungalow at the back of the lot (404 Gibson Street) as a rental property.

SECTION D

Bullard Heights

Even though the elevation of Bullard Heights has always offered sweeping views across Waxahachie Creek, few photographs have surfaced to illustrate that. One exception is this view taken c. 1910 by a member of the Simpson family. *Courtesy of the Dr. Charles W. Simpson Family and the Ellis County Museum.*

INTRODUCTION

Bullard Heights has always had a distinctly different character from the rest of Waxahachie. For starters, it was located on the south side of Waxahachie Creek, which separated it from the rest of town. But it was, observed the *Enterprise* in October 1889, the elevated, hilly terrain overlooking Waxahachie that gave it a "special prominence."

David Burton Bullard developed Bullard's Addition in the late 1880s and 1890s on part of a 478-acre tract that he and his wife Margaret L. Johnson Bullard bought in April 1868 from the estate of early pioneers Peter and Elizabeth Apperson. Born in 1830 in East Tennessee, Bullard moved to Missouri in 1852 and married Margaret in 1859. The following year, the couple came to Texas, where they settled in Ellis County in 1862 and where Bullard engaged in stock raising, farming, land investments, and general merchandising.

In November 1887, the *Enterprise* reported that Bullard had divided his land south of the creek and sold several pieces of property for $500 each but was reserving two or three acres for a public park. B. R. Moffett, who would build Rosemont, the centerpiece of the development, bought his long narrow Block 30 (the equivalent of five uninterrupted blocks) in May 1892. Less than a month later, Bullard filed the plat for his erratically numbered and sized thirty-block addition. No doubt, the Moffett sale gave a boost to both sales and status for the area.

Rosemont, built by B. R. and Eliza Moffett in 1894, became the centerpiece of Bullard Heights. Photograph c. 1895. *Courtesy Ellis County Museum.*

In this first version of Bullard's Addition, buyers bought a full block or blocks, the most popular blocks being those bordered by Washington (now College) Street on the east side and Dillon Street on the west. Some owners built a residence in a pastoral setting while others used their property exclusively for pasture or farmland, which explains the strong rural character that still exists on the west side of Bullard Heights. Frequently, streets were named for these early buyers who included farmers, ginners, and tradesmen, many of whom were longtime friends or associates of the Bullards.

On April 1, 1895, Bullard filed a revised map of Bullard's Addition that extended the development to include another line of blocks east of College Street to what is now Ellis Street. Unlike the undivided blocks on the 1892 map, the new blocks followed an urban format, each with sixteen long, narrow lots, eight lots to a street side and split by an alley. By late May, the lots were selling, especially those on the east side of College Street facing the newly completed Moffett property.

City Council annexed Bullard Heights at its April 1, 1902, meeting, the *Daily Light* reporting that the move increased the city's population by "about four hundred souls."

David and Margaret Bullard's house was east of the subdivision he created in the late 1880s. The central structure with three Gothic Revival gables dated to the 1860s and had two later additions that are visible in this photograph, taken before the house burned in 1917. *Courtesy Melanie Price Reed.*

In 1911, nine years after Bullard Heights was annexed by Waxahachie, a permanent school was built on Dunaway Street. This photograph from the 1914 *Cotton Boll* high school yearbook shows the original brick walls and roof parapets. *Courtesy Ellis County Museum.*

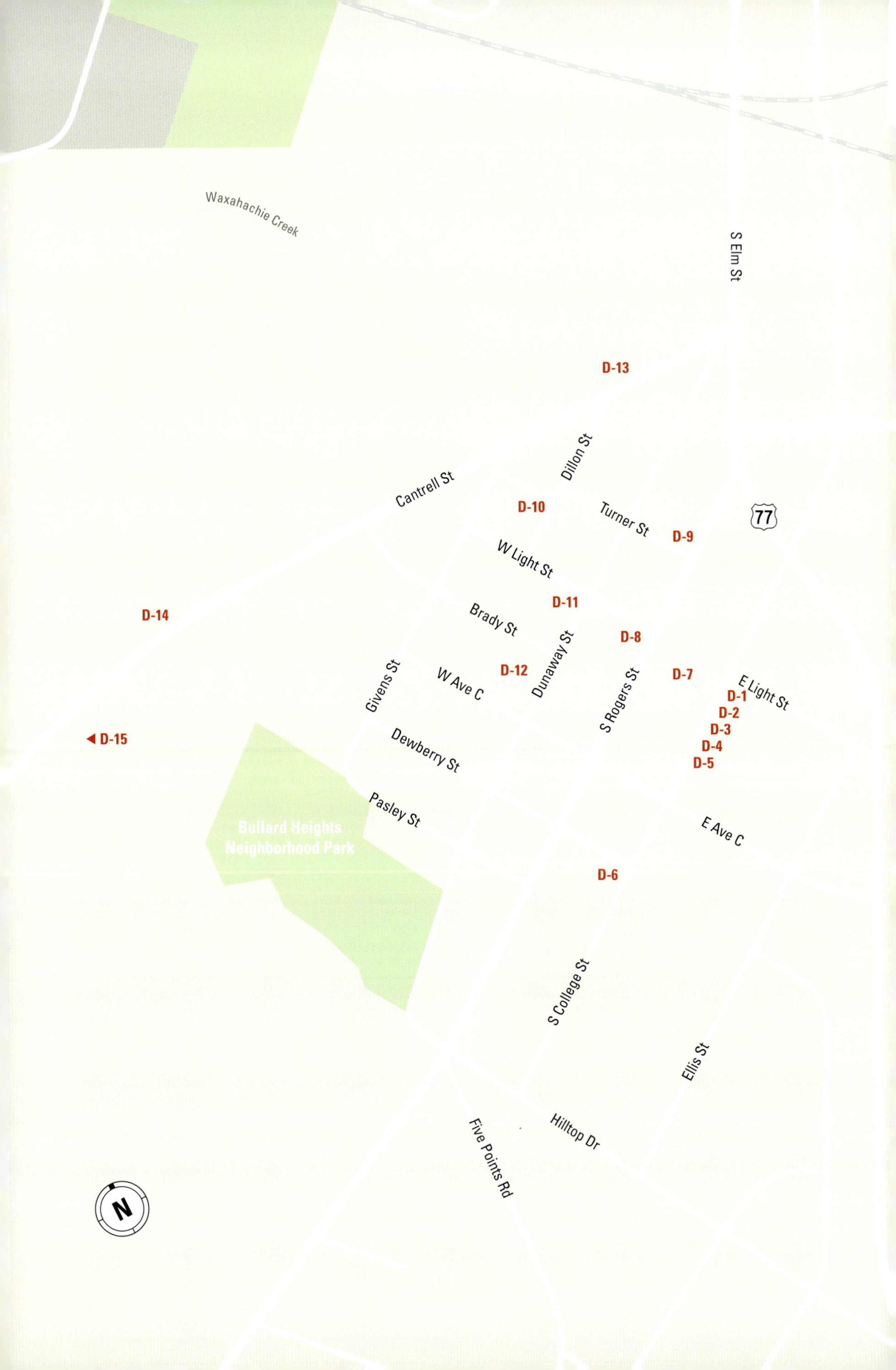
Waxahachie Creek
S Elm St
D-13
Dillon St
Cantrell St
D-10
Turner St
D-9
77
W Light St
D-11
D-14
Brady St
D-8
Dunaway St
D-12
D-7
Givens St
W Ave C
S Rogers St
E Light St
D-1
D-2
D-3
D-4
D-5
D-15
Dewberry St
Pasley St
Bullard Heights
Neighborhood Park
E Ave C
D-6
S College St
Ellis St
Hilltop Dr
Five Points Rd
N

D-1 701 S. College St.

D-2 703 S. College St.

D-3 705 S. College St.

D-4 707 S. College St.

D-5 709 S. College St.

D-6 810 S. College St.

D-7 701 S. Rogers St.
Rosemont

D-8 700 S. Rogers St.

D-9 612 S. Rogers St.

D-10 401 Turner St.

D-11 700 Dunaway St.

D-12 716 Dunaway St.
South Ward School
(later Bullard Heights School)

D-13 500 Cantrell St.
Southland Cotton Oil Co.
Storage Tank

D-14 816 Cantrell St.

D-15 855 Cantrell St.

D-1
701 South College Street

1898; J. W. Stokes, builder

This L-plan cottage is one of five dwellings that comprise the most intact row of small workers' cottages remaining in Waxahachie. This lot on the northwest corner of the 1895 Bullard's Addition sold twice before a house was built. The third time was the charm when "feme sole" (the legal term for a single woman) Sarah Ray bought it for $215 on February 11, 1898. The next day, the sixty-two-year-old, twice-widowed Mrs. Ray signed a $575 contract for J. W. Stokes to build a three-room frame dwelling within forty-five days. The core of the compact and tidy L-plan house has changed little since its construction. The two-bay porch with shed roof retains the original jig-sawn brackets, scalloped frieze, and turned wood posts.

Mrs. Ray and her house have a unique history among Waxahachie buildings. It was a destination point for many people (some travelling a considerable distance) who were terrified for their lives or the lives of their children because Mrs. Ray possessed a madstone, which was believed to cure rabies. Formed from calcium deposits and found in the stomachs of cud-eating animals, such stones were applied to the wound to draw the "poison" out. If it fell off, the victim was considered free of any serious results from the bite. Among accounts reported in the local newspapers, Mrs. Ray's madstone adhered eighty hours to an Ennis boy, sixteen hours and "still sticking" to one adult, and sixty-seven hours to another adult. When Mrs. Ray died in 1915, her estate sold this house. What happened to the madstone is unknown, but one of the stipulations of folk medicine was that a madstone was never to be sold. They were usually passed from father to son; Mrs. Ray's madstone had belonged to her husband.

D-2
703 South College Street
1895-96; C. E. Van Houten, builder

Brick residential structures in nineteenth-century Waxahachie were extremely rare, and relatively small examples like this one even more so. In fact, this is the only recorded example, and there is probably a simple explanation. It was built for a brick mason, Frank L. Compton, and his wife Emma Lee. The Comptons bought their lot in June 1895, and in November contracted with the Cotton States Building Company for C. E. Van Houten to build a cottage for $750. As part of the contract, the Comptons agreed to invest an additional $600 in the building, an amount that made the difference between a frame house and a brick house, with a few other extras as well, including stone sills, brick hood moldings with stone detailing at the windows, and diapered brick work in contrasting colors in the gable end.

This cottage was the Comptons' first real estate investment in Waxahachie. In 1880, twenty-two-year-old Frank Compton was living in Georgia with his family, but by 1883, he was moving westward with a stop in Alabama, where he married Emma Lee Hope and where their two daughters were born in 1884 and 1887. Exactly when the Comptons arrived in Waxahachie is unknown, but both Frank and Emma had carpenter and brick mason relatives already living in Texas. If the Comptons intended for their Bullard Heights cottage to advertise Frank's trade, they were successful because his name—sometimes independently, other times in partnership—began appearing in conjunction with local building projects. In October 1903, the Comptons sold this property and began a series of moves to different houses, all of which they paid other contractors to build but not all of which were built of brick.

D-3
705 South College Street
1896

"Laundryman" William G. Johnson and his wife Zula built this T-plan house in 1896 shortly after buying the lot from E. R. and Laura Griffith. It is the only house in the row of five for which there is no recorded mechanic's or materials lien. Sanborn maps indicated that a porch originally surrounded all three sides of the projecting front wing. According to the 1900 Census, the Johnson household at this location included the couple, their two young children, and Zula's mother and sister. In 1906, the Johnsons sold the property. Eventually they bought the house at **503 North Rogers Street**, and William became manager of the Waxahachie Steam Laundry.

D-4
707 South College Street
1895; C. E. Van Houten, builder

In early November 1895, farmer E. R. Griffith purchased this and the adjoining lot to the north from the Bullards. In less than a month, Griffith and his wife Laura signed a $500 contract with the Cotton States Building Co. of Paris, Texas, to finance "all the materials and fixtures" for

C. E. Van Houten to build this house according to plans and specifications that Van Houten provided. As part of the contract, the Griffiths agreed to invest an additional $275 on improvements "over and above" the $500. The result was a three-room L-plan cottage that the Griffiths used as rental property. In early 1901, Ellis County Constable W. A. Hodge and wife Callie bought the property and lived here until mid-1904. As is true for all the dwellings in the row, multiple appendages were added over the years, and in this house the window openings were altered significantly when the original windows were replaced.

D-5
709 South College Street
1901

The Bullards sold the other four lots in this row for $200 each in 1895, but they did not sell this lot until November 1897, when blacksmith John T. Wilbanks and his wife Nancy bought it for $175. Two days later, the couple purchased $200 in lumber and building materials to build their first house on the lot, with John probably doing most of the work, as he was listed as a "stairs carpenter" in the 1900 Census. The present house, however, dates from fall 1901, the replacement perhaps necessitated by a fire or, more likely in this instance, because the couple wanted a newer house. The *Enterprise* reported on October 18 that Wilbanks was building "a neat cottage" in Bullard Heights, an addition that was "fast coming to the front as a desirable residence place." The Wilbanks moved to Dallas in August 1904 and two years later sold the property. The bay window on the front façade, an unusual feature for a house this size, is original.

D-6
810 South College Street
1909; W. W. Edwards, builder

The pyramidal house with the lattice-enclosed front porch (the lattice a recent addition) was built for Charles and Louise Genter Velte. Both Veltes were German immigrants who met after Charles, an "experienced cabinetmaker," came to Waxahachie from St. Louis in spring 1886. Charles worked for several furniture stores before becoming a traveling furniture salesman. The couple purchased their Bullard Heights property—Block 28—in February 1907, and probably lived in an existing structure before contracting with W. W. Edwards in 1909 to build "in a true, thorough, perfect and workmanlike manner . . . a cottage house of seven rooms, hall and pantry" and a barn. In December 1919, the Veltes, now living in San Antonio, sold the property to produce dealer W. C. Commons and his wife Maggie, who moved from Collin County to Waxahachie. The Commons added an unusual structure to the Bullard Heights landscape when they built an "18 x 30 ft, boxed, stripped with shingle roof" store building on the back side of their property in August 1925. Within the year, however, they sold out and moved on. The store was demolished by a later owner.

D-7
701 South Rogers Street
Rosemont
1894; C. J. Griggs, builder

In the mid-1890s, Waxahachie witnessed a competition (unspoken, of course) among its wealthiest residents to see who would build the city's largest, most extravagant residence. When the *Enterprise* reported on January 4, 1895, that Burt Ringo Moffett (known as B. R.) would soon be moving into "his beautiful house," the paper wondered, "Who will be the next lucky man that will build a $10,000 mansion in Waxahachie?"

B. R. and his wife Eliza Beckley Moffett had bought their eight-and-a-half acre tract on the south side of Waxahachie Creek in May 1892, one month before David Bullard officially filed the Bullard Addition plat. It was a perfect location for the couple. By fall, Moffett's Cotton Mill, built at the foot of the hill, was added to B. R.'s list of industrial enterprises. Exactly two years later, the Moffets began construction of their residence on the crest of the hill—a spectacular site for a residence. Offering the most dramatic view of Waxahachie, it was aligned with the courthouse square, soon to be crowned with a new county courthouse designed by San Antonio-based architect James Riely Gordon.

Tempting as it may be to make the leap (and many have) that Gordon was also the Moffetts' architect, several factors suggest that there was a connection, but one that was more tangential than direct. Gordon kept meticulous office records, the bulk of which are now deposited in the Alexander Architectural Archives at the University of Texas in Austin. The Moffetts' name does not appear in Gordon's client listings, which seems an unlikely oversight had he been their architect. In addition, Gordon never made an on-site visit to Waxahachie, always relying on staff or affiliates like Otto Kroeger to deal with county officials during the months leading up to the start of courthouse construction in March 1895.

On October 12, 1894, the local newspaper announced that the Moffetts' contractor was C. J. Griggs but did not name an architect. Griggs was an experienced contractor who, during the 1890s, built more extravagant Queen Anne residences in Waxahachie than any other builder. In at least one instance (**1022 West Main**), he worked with an architect, but he also used plan-book designs, in three instances published by George F. Barber, but no published design has been found that ties directly to the Moffett house.

Rather, the Moffett house shows strong similarities to the Mrs. W. E. Lowry house in San Antonio that Gordon designed and built circa 1890 (now demolished). Although the Lowry house was a much grander brick structure, its onion-domed porch bay and horseshoe arches show a striking similarity to the Moorish-inspired two-tiered veranda on the Moffetts' Queen Anne house. This suggests that the design was a collaboration between someone from Gordon's San Antonio office (just not Gordon himself), who was in Waxahachie for the courthouse project, and contractor Griggs.

Once the house was completed, many Waxahachians no doubt crossed the creek to get a closer look at the imposing structure—and it was big: twenty rooms, three stories plus basement, and a high-pitched hipped roof with intersecting gables that dramatized its prominence even more. The outbuildings, typical of a Victorian estate, included a greenhouse, carriage house, privy, and barn. Atypical was a two-story mansard-roof tower building, matching the main house in style and detailing, and built to house power equipment for the Bullard Heights subdivision. Landscaping was of special interest to Mrs. Moffett, whose fondness for roses probably inspired the name "Rosemont."

The Moffetts were generous hosts, making Rosemont, from the beginning, an elegant and frequent setting for Waxahachie's socially elite. However, their life here was not without its difficulties—only one of four sons born at Rosemont grew to adulthood. In 1921, Mrs. Moffett died from complications of ptomaine poisoning after which B. R. moved back to Lancaster, their Texas hometown. The property remained vacant until 1930 when it was bought in February by farmer Jasper L. Cox and his wife Amanda, an older couple who lived near Forreston. The 1930 Census, taken in early April, listed two sons and four daughters in their household, all in their twenties and thirties and all "farm laborers." The same six (of fourteen) children were living at Rosemont when Jasper died in 1938; one child lived here until the late 1970s.

Rosemont was in a deteriorating state when Dallasites Keith and Helen Beers bought the property in May 1979. The couple immediately launched a major restoration and preservation project, noting that few structural alterations had been made to the mansion since its construction and that most outbuildings had survived (including the tower). Mr. Beers, a registered builder, acted as general contractor, while Mrs. Beers focused on the interiors and research. The property was listed on the National Register of Historic Places in 1982. Sande and Ron Wilkinson became Rosemont's stewards in 1998 and were living here when Mr. Wilkinson served as Waxahachie's mayor in 2008-10.

D-8
700 South Rogers Street
1894

When James M. and Martha J. Patterson built this modified L-plan one-and-a-half-story house, it was laden with bargeboards, scroll-work brackets, gable-peak finials, tall corbeled chimneys, and decorative porches. In other words, it was a highly embellished Queen Anne cottage that would not be intimidated by a considerably larger and more extravagant soon to-be-built neighbor across the street, the Moffett house. Although the Pattersons' house has lost much of its "gingerbread" over the years, remnants, such as the fish-scale shingles on the gable ends and the window surrounds that combine classical capitals and jig-sawn trim, are still there. (The same windows are found on the house built by James's cousin Tilmon F. Patterson at **612 South Rogers**.) A partial view of the front façade in a circa 1895 photograph shows the clipped dormer on a considerably steeper hipped roof—the change in roof pitch perhaps the result of a fire or changing styles. Most importantly, the house plan with its intersecting multiple gables remains essentially as built and is visible unencumbered on three sides.

The Pattersons built their cottage shortly after acquiring this and the adjacent block to the south in February 1894. Married in 1869, both Pattersons belonged to pioneer Ellis County families. James, born in 1844 in Hempstead County, Arkansas, came to Ellis County with his parents in 1854. Martha was born in Mississippi, the daughter of Judge E. M. Brack and Lucy P. Sims Brack, who moved their family from Mississippi to Dallas County in 1850-51, then to Ellis County in 1859. James was primarily a farmer and owned a sizeable tract of land east of Waxahachie that he began acquiring in the early 1870s. Like many large landholders, he also owned and managed a cotton gin. The Pattersons lived here with their four children until selling the property in 1911. In 1913, it was bought by farmer J. H. Chapman and his wife Mary.

D-9
612 South Rogers Street
1892

When built, this modified L-plan house was one of the first houses to greet those who crossed the creek and continued going up the Rogers Street hill in Bullard's Addition. MKT railroad agent Tilmon F. Patterson and his wife Ollie purchased Block 20 from the Bullards on June 15, 1892, and by July 1, they were building a "neat house," as reported in the *Enterprise*. Unlike most L-plan houses, where the structure runs parallel to the primary street (in this case, South Rogers), the bulk of the Pattersons' house takes advantage of the corner lot and runs parallel to the secondary street, i.e., Turner. Sanborn maps suggest that the house never had the customary back porch, which is unusual for the period. Note the pedimented window surrounds with classical capitals and jig-sawn scallops—they also appear on another Patterson family home at **700 South Rogers**.

In June 1899, saddler and harness maker George F. Plumhoff bought the house. George had migrated from Illinois to Waxahachie and established his own business in 1891, the same year in which his marriage to Augusta Cutler was reported in the *Dallas Morning News*. With the help of two brothers, George's business was so successful that they moved their wholesale and manufacturing departments to Fort Worth in fall 1905, while keeping the retail and repair business in Waxahachie. The hard-working George died at age fifty-two in 1913, his obituary describing him as "a splendid citizen, a progressive business man." His widow and two daughters moved to Dallas and rented this house as well as the tenant house that they had built at 608 South Rogers circa 1910. The daughters sold both properties after their mother died in 1921. Ron Wilkinson, Waxahachie's mayor from 2008-10, lived up the hill in Rosemont (**701 South Rogers**) and adapted this house for use as his law offices.

D-10
401 Turner Street
c. 1895

Although at first glance this appears to be a shotgun house, a closer look reveals a short cross-gable wing in the rear, making the house a T-plan with a very short cross on the T. (It could even be called a "Mini-T.") It is one of Waxahachie's few surviving examples of modest working-class houses that were built with design and decorative elements found in larger, more expensive houses. The high-pitched gables facing the front and the sides feature ornate jig-sawn bargeboards, fish-scale shingles, pent roofs, and boxed eaves. Molded architraves cap the window frames. The porch originally wrapped around the front and north side of the house, which would have obscured the forward thrust of the narrow front gable wing that contributes to the shotgun appearance of the house today. The Sanborn maps indicate that this house first stood a few blocks away at 607 South College but was moved to this location sometime between 1925 and 1959, probably when its original lot was used in routing US Highway 77. The maps also document two other Mini-T's in Waxahachie, at 804 Givens and 717 West Jefferson, but both are now gone.

D-11
700 Dunaway Street
1895, 1898, 2001

Size and placement give this house a strong but baffling presence on the Bullard Heights landscape. Is it an old or a new house? It is both. The house began life as a one-story four-room house built by W. A. Knight for Mrs. Maria Louise Swindall in 1895, the same year that Mrs. Swindall swapped a block that she owned in the neighboring town of Italy for this block in Bullard Heights owned by J. F. Dunaway. Tax and census records suggest that by 1898 Mrs. Swindall had enlarged her house to the two-story modified L-plan house with porches that fronts Dunaway Street. She was obviously accommodating an expanding household that by 1900 included daughter and son-in-law Louella and Crockett Jennings (the county tax collector) and three grandchildren. Louella lost her husband in January 1916 and her mother in March the same year, but she continued living here until selling the property in 1925 and moving to University Addition. The substantial two-story addition extending across the back of the house was built by Chris and Lisette Cole, who bought the property in 2000. The couple learned that one owner, tired of painting the original "gingerbread trim," had removed and burned it in the late 1940s or early 1950s.

When Mrs. Swindall built her house, her neighbor across Light Street was cotton gin owner Farley Brady, whose gin, built in 1887, was a short distance away on the west side of Cantrell Street. Brady's two-story house, built in 1893, and the gin are both gone. The block to Mrs. Swindall's immediate south was used as a pasture until 1911, when South Ward School was built.

D-12
716 Dunaway Street
South Ward School
1911; W. W. Walston, contractor
1917; C. H. Page, architect; W. J. Moore, contractor

Originally called South Ward School, the building was erected in 1911 to serve students in the Bullard Heights Addition and surrounding neighborhood. About one acre of land was purchased for the school from Eugene Dunaway of Italy, Texas, for $350. The contract to build both this school and West Ward School at **411 Gibson** (now WISD administrative offices) was awarded to local contractor W. W. Walston for the sum of $13,725, and with the stipulation that both buildings be completed in time for the start of school in mid-September 1911. A 1914 photograph shows this structure with its original roof parapets and brick walls. (The stucco was added later.) Not surprisingly, since the South and West Ward schools were built at the same time, by the same contractor, they shared similar construction and details, including the arches above their entrance doors. The brick beneath this stucco is probably the same red brick still visible at 411 Gibson. The building originally housed two classrooms. Two more rooms were added to the back in 1917 when the same architect also designed the much larger Waxahachie High School at **600 Second Street** and the Oak Lawn School on the 500 block of Wyatt Street. By the early 1940s, South Ward School became known as Bullard Heights School. It was closed in 1965, and in 1976 the Ellis County Committee for the Aging renovated it for use as a Senior Citizens Center. It served in that capacity until 1989, when the center was moved to a building at **219 Patrick Street**.

This property is now privately owned. The one-story building with a flat roof and a double-door central entrance with half-moon transom lights has suffered recently from lack of maintenance. In 2007, when this photograph was taken, it presented a very prim, self-contained appearance, and the arch above the entrance, highlighted by the painted stucco, remained a simple but effective detail.

D-13
500 Cantrell Street
Southland Cotton Oil Co. Storage Tank
c. 1950s

The Ellis County Courthouse and this 105-foot-high steel cotton seed storage tank have several things in common: both are a commanding presence on the Waxahachie landscape; both are reminders of the role that cotton played in Waxahachie history; and, in their simplest abstract form, they share a similar shape. But whereas the courthouse and surroundings represent the business of cotton trading, this site represents the cotton industry and is one of the last remnants of the cotton mills and gins that populated both sides of Waxahachie Creek. By the late 1880s, any inland community wanting to engage in the fiercely competitive cotton market had to have both a compress to transport cotton more efficiently to the coastal markets and a cotton seed mill to process multiple cotton by-products. Waxahachie built both.

The first cotton seed mill in Waxahachie was the Ellis County Cotton Seed Oil Mill built in 1891 along the Katy tracks at the Hawkins Street crossing. In 1896, the enterprise, now incorporated as the Waxahachie Cotton Oil Co., moved to this site, closer to Waxahachie's industrial activities and where it had room to expand. As shown on the 1898 Sanborn map, it was a sizeable complex split by a Katy track spur. The primary structures on the north side of the tracks were a brick mill (portions of which are there today), a frame hull house, and six iron storage tanks for cotton seed oil. On the south side of the tracks and connected to the mill by an elevated wooden conveyor bridge were the much larger (250 x 80 ft.) one-story frame seed house and a small office that doubled as a weigh station. Even though facilities were enlarged and modernized, the plant layout remained basically the same throughout its history.

In 1914, the mill was sold to the Southland Cotton Oil Company, based in Paris, Texas, and already owner of eight mills in the southeast region, including three in Texas. Southland lost little time modernizing the Waxahachie plant, and by fall 1917 the mill was "housed in a modern brick structure just completed," as illustrated in the souvenir program for the United Confederate Veterans' reunion held in Waxahachie in October. In 1952, Southland became a subsidiary and, a few years later, a division of Houston-based Anderson, Clayton & Co. (ACCO), one of the largest world traders in raw cotton. It was during the 1950s that the huge storage tank was added to the complex.

In 1958, Southland moved its general offices from Paris to a new building at **106 South Monroe** in Waxahachie. The move occurred when cotton production and demand were beginning to wane, due to the Federal acreage reduction program that limited the raw material available to mills and to competition from emerging new products such as synthetic fabrics. Paymaster Oil Co., also a division of ACCO, replaced Southland in the mid-1960s with mill activity gradually shutting down and the property selling in the late 1970s. Many Waxahachie residents say that what they really missed when the mill closed were the "wonderful smells like a bakery or popcorn" that floated through town when the mill was operating. On January 15, 1980, fire destroyed most of the mill buildings, which at the time were leased for storage or manufacturing purposes. The site continues to be the setting for a mix of adaptive uses and activities.

D-14
816 Cantrell Street
1880

In late October 1880, Edwin Malcolm Wise and his wife Mary Jane (Mollie) purchased twenty-four acres about one mile southwest of the courthouse "on the waters of Waxahachie Creek," and they probably built the house soon after. Although family accounts give 1879 as the construction date, the property was not purchased until 1880, and the 1880 Census, which was taken in June of that year, lists the family on Franklin Street. Edwin, who was listed at various times as a carpenter, woodworker, and buggy maker, may well have built the house himself with the help of family members and carpenter colleagues. The form of this side gable house with three cross gables was derived from the Gothic Revival style popularized by A. J. Downing in the 1840s. Similar examples were built across northeast Texas in the 1870s, including the James M. Brent House of 1876, originally near Plano, but now in the Dallas Heritage Village. Two related examples remain in Waxahachie, a smaller-scale triple-gable example at **700 Water**, which also dates to c. 1880, and a double gable at **513 West Jefferson**. The Wise house remained in the family until 2000, when George Wise, Edwin's grandson, sold it to Wes and Diane Collard. Wise family history says that the house originally stood close to the creek, but concerns about the children's health led to moving it close to the road. When Cantrell Street was widened in 1950 the house was moved to its current location, and the previously detached one-story kitchen wing was attached.

D-15
855 Cantrell Street
1890

Sited on one of the highest elevations in the area, this two-story side gable house with an asymmetrical front gable wing enabled its owners to enjoy sweeping views of their property and the surrounding countryside. In 1887, H. A. (Guy) and Ella J. Hilburn Pierce bought the property and a previous residence as part of a 150-acre farm, but in mid-August 1890, that house burned. On August 31, the newspaper noted that they signed a contract for construction of a "splendid two-story house to be built where the former residence stood." Instead of building a hipped roof house with cross-gables, as might have been expected at this date, or even a more conservative I-plan,

L-plan, or T-plan house, the Pierces built what looks like an L-plan with an additional wing extending to the right, beyond the base of the "L." (Perhaps the decision was based on a thrifty reuse of the foundation of the previous house.) The original porch supports and ornamentation have not survived, but the decorative brackets below the eaves remain. Guy and Ella both were born to prominent Ellis County pioneer families. Guy primarily raised cattle and had large landholdings in Ellis and adjoining counties. In the 1880s, Guy partnered with his Hilburn in-laws in raising cattle, and in 1899, the newspaper reported that he and O. B. Sims had shipped in one thousand head of beef from Indian Territory. Guy Pierce committed suicide in 1931, with the newspaper hinting at possible health concerns as the reason. Ella died two years later. The land surrounding the house was sold off over the years, but the house still retains its spectacular view.

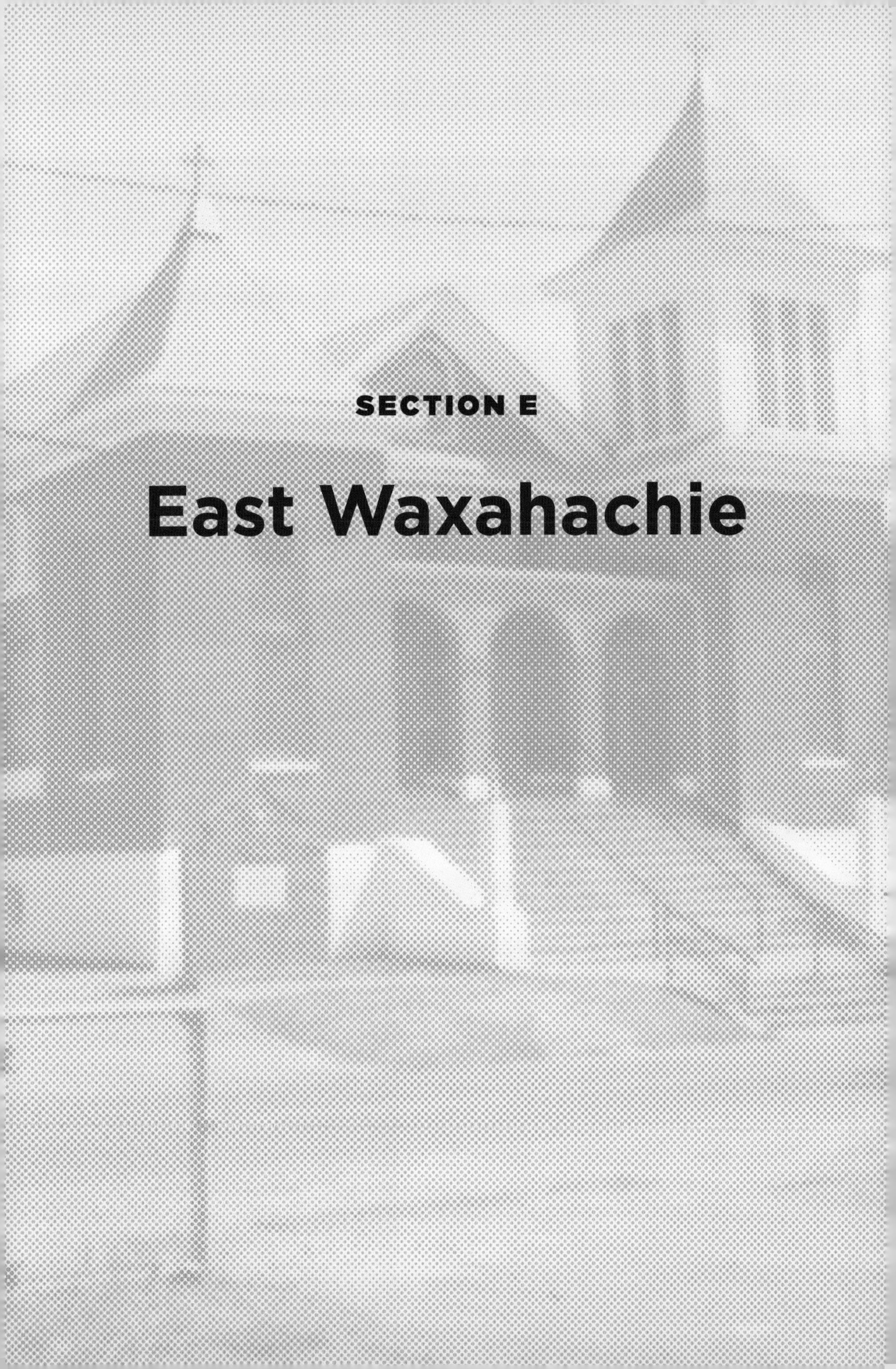

SECTION E

East Waxahachie

Detail of the 1886 bird's-eye view showing East Waxahachie, with East Main Street (now Martin Luther King Jr. Blvd.) running east from Kaufman Street, on the far left of the image, to Aiken Street, which is on the far right. *Courtesy Ellis County Museum.*

INTRODUCTION

The area now known as East Waxahachie, and in previous times as Freedman Town, Freedmen's Town, the East Side, and by an offensive racial epithet, was on E. W. Rogers and A. M. Keen Survey lands, just east of the original forty-block Waxahachie township. It stretched from some of the lowest flood-prone creek land to some of the hilliest on the north side of Waxahachie Creek. Although it was between the town center on the west and sizeable farm tracts on the east, both of which needed an accessible labor source, it was not particularly good real estate—and that probably explains why this is where the black community developed. Following the Civil War, freed slaves in Waxahachie and elsewhere settled where they were allowed to buy land, to rent, or to camp, and usually that was on land that few others, if any but the very poorest, would want. Perhaps several families of free blacks camped along Waxahachie Creek, or E. W. Rogers let them settle on his land up the hill knowing that a black community would evolve. Perhaps Rogers was influenced by his former slave Cyrus Aiken, to whom he sold in 1870 eight and

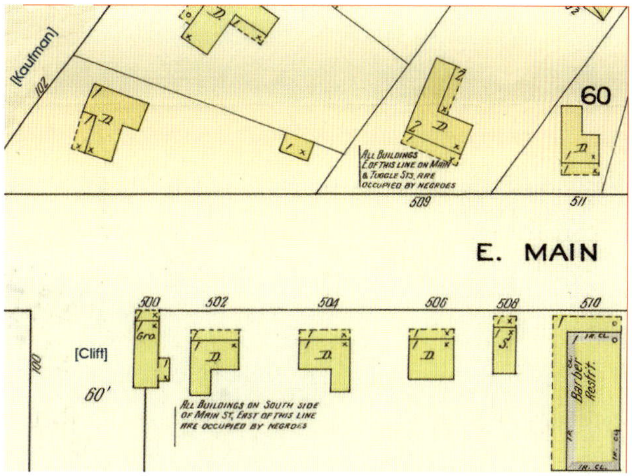

Sanborn map 1914, detail from sheet 4 showing the lines on both sides of East Main Street that indicated where "All Buildings...East of this line are occupied by negroes." Kaufman Street angles into Main from the north, and Clift Street extends to the south from Main. *Courtesy Perry Castaneda Library Map Collection, University of Texas at Austin.*

a half acres of land that became the core of Freedman Town. The sale is important in Waxahachie history not only because it was the largest in-town land tract sold to a free black but also because it essentially determined the East Waxahachie that Waxahachians know today.

If anyone ever questioned that there were two Waxahachies—one white and one black— they need only look at the 1913 city directory and the 1914 Sanborn map, two key documents when researching Waxahachie buildings. In the street listing of the 1913 directory, all but three of the eighty listings from 500 East Main to the far east end of the street, are followed by a "(c)" for "colored." On the 1914 Sanborn map, a vertical line on both sides of East Main Street (now Dr. Martin Luther King Jr. Blvd.), near Clift Street on the south and between Tuggle and Kaufman Streets on the north, marks the point where "All Buildings . . . East of this line are occupied by negroes." Although the lines were not drawn on the street itself, the lines existed in the minds of Waxahachians long before 1913 and 1914.

East Waxahachie poses challenges for an architecture guidebook. Historic images are rare, early buildings are gone, very little is known about the early inhabitants, including the prominent figures, and local newspapers had little interest in reporting East Waxahachie news.

Once again, the 1886 bird's-eye view provides not only the first, but in this case the only aerial view of the area even after photography. The 1886 view shows an East Waxahachie of predominantly small houses developing along Main, Wyatt, and Aiken Streets. By then, many of these houses were owned and occupied by blacks who began buying property in the area around 1870. There were also rental houses, some owned by blacks while others were owned by white investors

East Waxahachie street illustrated in Charles M. Simpson's *Sanitary Survey of Waxahachie, Texas*, 1917, and labeled "A Street in the Poorer Negro Section." *Courtesy National Library of Medicine.*

like Joseph Farley, who developed the cluster of houses on the north side of Main Street, between Aiken Street and the cut to the west. Known as the Farley Block (block 159), the *Enterprise* reported in July 1879 that Farley had contracted E. H. Griffin (also white) to build ten "tenements" for $1,225, enough at the time to build ten box houses, one and two rooms in size. By late fall, most of the houses were completed and occupied "by colored tenants" who paid a $5 or $5.50 monthly rent. By 1886, Farley had sold most of the properties to individuals like former renters Julia Cade and Wesley Phillips.

East Waxahachie residence illustrated in Charles M. Simpson's *Sanitary Survey of Waxahachie, Texas*, 1917, and labeled "A Better Class Negro Home." *Courtesy National Library of Medicine.*

Sanborn maps, extant buildings, and rare documentary images show that over time, East Waxahachians built the same mix of small house types found in other parts of town— rectangular, L-shape, T-shape, and pyramidal cottages, shotgun houses, and bungalows. A substantial number of mechanics' liens were filed for East Waxahachie houses, including some of the smallest. These liens, in which a lumber company or a contractor served as both builder and lender, were the only available way for many blacks to finance home ownership. For present-day researchers, the liens not only disclose the price of a house and offer a comparison to similar structures in other parts of town, they also document that well into the twentieth century, many houses in East Waxahachie were "box" or "boxed" houses, a type of construction now called "box and strip." Using standard dimension lumber and having no foundation, no insulation, and no framing, it was the cheapest, quickest way to build a house, as it was not unlike building a large wooden box. For people with limited resources, box construction made homeownership a possibility; for landlords, it was a way to build cheap rental housing. Although box houses were built in other parts of Waxahachie, proportionately they were far more prevalent on the east side.

Early newspapers are one of the most valuable sources for researching and dating buildings in Waxahachie—but *not* for structures, even major structures, in East Waxahachie. Typical of mainstream town and city newspapers at the time, Waxahachie newspapers reported very little news either about new buildings and development in the black community or about its prominent people and events. Granted, there was probably a limited readership among free blacks immediately after the Civil War, but the absence of news about the black community, except for criminal activities, whether real or imagined, also reflected prejudices of the time. Contemporary articles reporting construction of buildings like the spacious pyramidal house built on East Main Street circa 1906 for farmer and businessman Murry Munchus, and the New Joshua Chapel built in 1918-1919 and designed by William Sydney Pittman, the first black architect to practice in Texas, simply were not written. New residential subdivisions in the neighborhood were not advertised or reported in local papers as were those in other parts of town, the one exception being Oak Lawn Addition in 1905.

Documentary photographs of East Waxahachie are rare for both individual structures and streetscapes but have surfaced in unexpected sources. Three rare photographs of East Waxahachie in the second decade of the twentieth century appear in *A Sanitary Survey of Waxahachie, Texas*, a 1917 paper written by Waxahachie native Charles M. Simpson while a student at Harvard Medical School. (He later became a surgeon at Scott and White Hospital in Temple, Texas.) Simpson's photograph labeled, "A Street in the Poorer Negro Section," shows a streetscape with a range of house types and construction methods, including a side-gable cottage with shed-roof front porch and weatherboard siding; a front-gable cottage with inset corner porch and a shotgun house, both of box construction; and an L-plan cottage with weatherboard siding. Another of his photographs, labeled "A Better Class Negro Home," depicts a relatively new, well-constructed pyramidal cottage that is similar to many middle-class houses built in white Waxahachie neighborhoods during the same era. The third Simpson photograph shows the two-story Oak Lawn School built in the 500 block of Wyatt Street in 1896.

One more historic photograph, taken c. 1915 by an unknown photographer from the second floor of that same Oak Lawn School, recorded the school's student body and faculty and inadvertently offers a glimpse of the Wyatt Street streetscape with a few of its houses in the background. The house directly behind the students was owned by Sam and Mary Loyd at the time. The weatherboard siding of their T-plan cottage, as well as the box-and-strip construction of the back wing, are visible in this side view. When a fire burned the house in 1919, the Loyds replaced it with the pyramidal cottage that remains at **412 Wyatt**.

Readers will note that the format for this section of the guidebook differs from other sections. There is no attempt to present a building-by-building or street-by-street tour through the neighborhood, for which there are several reasons: the paucity of existing research and known resources; the deteriorating condition of many buildings and the demolition of many others; and limitations of the guidebook project itself.

Research has concentrated on selected major sites both extant (such as Joshua Chapel and Penn Park) and demolished (the East Main Street-Freedman Town commercial strip and Oak Lawn School); sites discovered in conversations with residents (Brackens Street development); subjects and sites uncovered in period publications (Farley Block and Oak Lawn Addition); and

Bessie Coleman: Oak Lawn Graduate, Honored Aviator

Bessie Coleman shown on the wheel of a Curtiss JN-4 "Jennie," c. 1924. *National Air and Space Museum, photo NASM92-13721.*

Without doubt, Bessie Coleman's story is the most extraordinary of any Waxahachie resident, black or white. She was born in January 1892, in Atlanta, Texas, but grew up in Waxahachie where her family moved in 1895. After graduating from Oak Lawn School and briefly attending college, she moved to Chicago in 1915 and began her quest to fly. Refused entry by American aviation schools, Bessie traveled to France, first in 1921 to earn her pilot's license and then in 1922 to learn stunt flying. She became a popular performer and lecturer, demanding that blacks and whites attending her shows use the same entrance, which she did when performing in Waxahachie on the Trinity University athletic field on September 26, 1925. Once inside the gate, however, her fans were segregated. Bessie, who said that "the air is the only place free from prejudices," planned to use her earnings to open a flight school for African Americans, but sadly, she died in an accident while practicing for a flight show in Florida in 1926. Her honors came later: among them, a commemorative stamp in the Black Heritage Series of the United States Postal Service in 1995 and an exhibit featuring her story at the Smithsonian National Museum of African American History and Culture that opened in Washington, DC, in 2016.

Oak Lawn School student body c. 1915. The photograph, taken from the school building, also shows houses on Wyatt Street in the background. The Sam and Mary Loyd house is directly behind the students. *Courtesy Ellis County Museum.*

visual impressions (the Wyatt Street cluster of houses). In some instances, research became extensive and led to tangential subjects, as was the case with the nineteenth-century cottage at **500 Dr. Martin Luther King Jr. Boulevard**. The house was initially of interest because it was the most architecturally intact early residence in East Waxahachie. However, research revealed a multi-layered story relating to the history of civil rights in Texas and the nation and, on the local scene, to **Clift's Addition**, an early development offering property ownership to free blacks.

The broad history of East Waxahachie, much less its architectural history, has never been placed in the context of Waxahachie history—a fact that is not unusual for communities like Waxahachie where there was always a distinct division between the white and the black parts of town. Consequently, researching aspects of East Waxahachie history for this guidebook was a rewarding exercise in discovery, but it was also one of frustration—frustrating because the history is there but the buildings are not, and because it is obvious that there is so much more to be discovered. What this suggests, frankly, is that an architecture guidebook, while offering a push, is not the ideal format for pursuing the rich and relevant history of East Waxahachie. But, hopefully, it serves as encouragement for more to come.

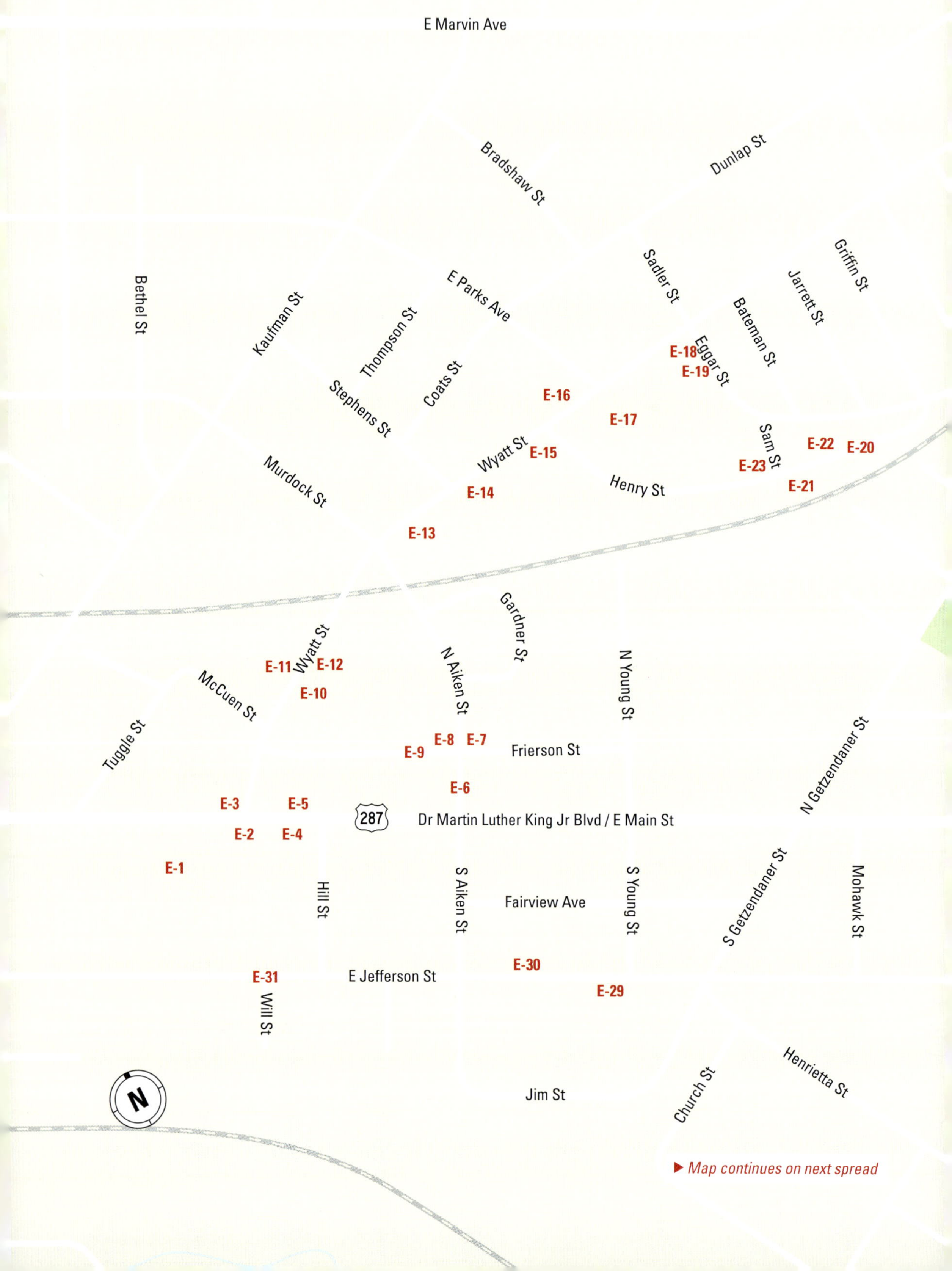

▶ *Map continues on next spread*

E-1 400 block Dr. Martin Luther King Jr. Blvd.
Freedman Memorial Plaza

E-2 Dr. Martin Luther King Jr. Blvd. and Wyatt St.
Site of Freedman Town Business District

E-3 441 Dr. Martin Luther King Jr. Blvd.
Ellis County African American Hall of Fame

E-4 508 Dr. Martin Luther King Jr. Blvd.
Samaria Missionary Baptist Church

E-5 509 Dr. Martin Luther King Jr. Blvd.

E-6 Aiken St.

E-7 110 N. Aiken St.
Joshua Chapel, African Methodist Episcopal Church

E-8 Northwest corner Aiken and Frierson Steets
Site of second African American school

E-9 Frierson St.

E-10 206 Wyatt St.

E-11 211, 213 Wyatt St.

E-12 212 Wyatt St.

E-13 300-314 Wyatt St.
Wyatt St. Shotgun House Historic District

E-14 402 Wyatt St.
Dr. James E. Munchus Office

E-15 412 Wyatt St.

E-16 417 Wyatt St.

E-17 500 block Wyatt St.
Site of Oak Lawn School

E-18 516 Wyatt St.
New Town Drug Store

E-19 207 Eggar St.
Greater New Mt. Zion Missionary Baptist Church

E-20 Henry St., Oak Lawn Addition

E-21 303 Henry St.

E-22 308 Henry St.

E-23 212 Henry St.

◆ *E-24–E-28 on pp. 204-05*

E-29 Fairview Addition

E-30 707 E. Jefferson St.

E-31 Clift's Addition

Map continues from previous spread
Dunlap St
E Ross St
Wyatt St
Leatherwood St
Peters St
Cook St
Munchus St
Burnett St
E-24
Eubank St
N Getzendaner St
E-25
Eggar St
Levi St
Lonzo
Ryburn St
Kinchum St
E-26
Lee Penn Park
E-27
Brackens St
Perry Ave
Graham St
E-28
Dr Martin Luther King Jr Blvd / E Main St
287
Oneida St
E Jefferson St
Flowers St
N
Fraternal-Wakefield Cemetery

◆ E-1-E-23 on pp.202-03

E-24
800 N. Getzendaner St.

E-25
614 N. Getzendaner St.
Turner High School (now Turner High School of Choice)

E-26
404 N. Getzendaner St.
Lee Penn Park

E-27 Brackens St.

E-28 911 Dr. Martin Luther King Jr. Blvd.

◆ E-29-E-31 on pp. 202-03

E-1
400 block
Dr. Martin Luther King Jr. Boulevard, south side
Freedman Memorial Plaza

2007; Dunkin Sims Stoffels, Inc., plaza design; Giles Monument Company with Chuck Beatty, monument design

Dedicated in 2007, Freedman Memorial Plaza pays tribute to "the struggles and lasting contributions" of leaders in Waxahachie's African American community. The plaza centerpiece, a black granite monument, features images of Waxahachie's three black mayors—George Brown (1980-1983), Rutha Waters (1996-1997), and Chuck Beatty (1997-2002)—surrounded by the names of other individuals who have made significant contributions to the city. Design details were chosen for symbolism and meaning: the monument is made of black granite from Africa; the rows on the concrete path symbolize cotton; and the broken chains on the ground represent the end of slavery and emancipation. Beatty, who was elected councilman after serving as mayor, was instrumental in establishing the plaza on land donated by Broderick Sargent in memory of his grandparents, Ira and Myrtle Sargent and Delmar and Gertrude Erskine. Sargent is a former councilman who grew up in East Waxahachie and who, like Beatty, returned to his hometown after retiring from the National Football League.

The plaza and adjacent open space, now a city park, provide a popular setting for special events in the African American community, including annual Emancipation Day celebrations and biannual Oak Lawn High School alumnae reunions, which is when new names are added to the monument. The engraved names represent individuals who, in addition to making significant contributions to the community, were either born or lived in Waxahachie. The life of aviator Bessie Coleman, the first black person in the world to become a licensed pilot, is commemorated on the nearby Official Texas Historical Marker.

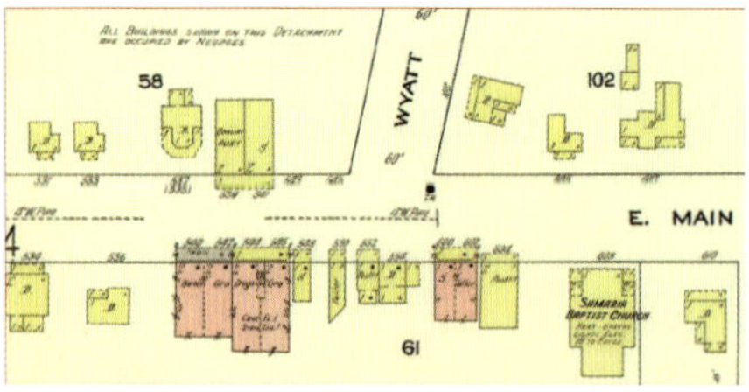

1914 Sanborn map, detail from sheet 14 showing the intersection of East Main and Wyatt Streets. The three pink buildings are brick veneer, while the yellow are wood. Those with a "D" in the center are dwellings; the businesses and church are identified by type. *Courtesy Perry Castaneda Library Map Collection, University of Texas at Austin.*

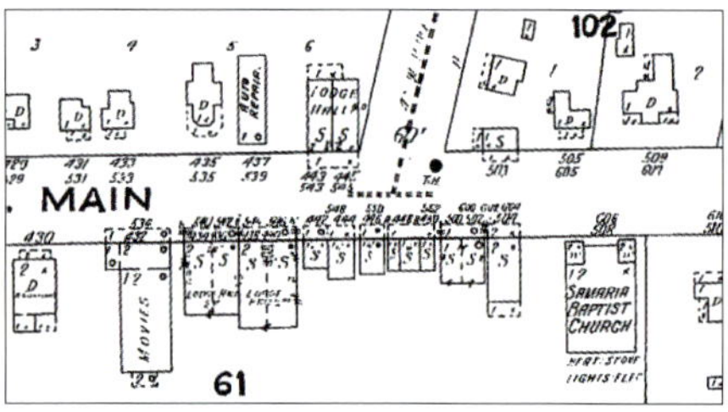

1925 Sanborn map, detail from sheet 12, showing the intersection of East Main and Wyatt Streets with increased commercial density in the years after 1914. *(Used with permission of The Sanborn Library, LLC.)*

500-502 East Main (now Martin Luther King Jr. Blvd.). This 1985 photograph shows the building constructed in 1914 by contractors Richards & Compton for barber William M. Richardson and wife Martha. (Demolished.) *Courtesy Texas Historical Commission National Register Collection, Photograph 1214-17; Portal to Texas History.*

E-2
Intersection Dr. Martin Luther King Jr. Boulevard and Wyatt Street

Site of Freedman Town Business District

From an early date, this intersection marked the major route for movement to and from the eastside of Waxahachie. Although the 1886 bird's-eye view did not show any sign of the commercial row that would soon develop here, it is obvious that this was the logical location for the East Waxahachie business district. It was at this point that Wyatt Street, a primary north-south artery, emptied into Main Street and where, a little to the west of the juncture, a wooden bridge and walkway crossed the creek branch. It was also in the heart of the area known as Freedman Town, a term that was probably used long before it appeared in the local newspaper in the late-1870s.

Early documentary photographs of Freedman Town are nonexistent and once again, as frequently happens in Waxahachie's history, a disaster offers the first description of the commercial district. The *Waxahachie Enterprise* reported that "nearly the entire business portion of the negro settlement on East Main street was wiped out of existence" by a disastrous fire on Monday morning, August 22, 1904. The total loss was about $5,000 for five buildings, all uninsured, on the south side of Main Street. Three one-story frame commercial buildings were destroyed, as were the two-story brick lodge halls of the Odd Fellows and the United Brothers of Friendship, each valued at $2,000 and each housing a first-floor tenant. Among the burned-out black-owned businesses were Will Robinson's barber shop, Will Clark's restaurant, and Willie Sweatt's pool hall. N. D. Grafton, who was white, lost his meat market.

In true post-fire Waxahachie fashion, the African American community rebuilt, and thanks to the Sanborn Insurance Map Company and its maps, we have some idea of how Freedman Town developed and looked into the 1950s. Although the company made its first visit to Waxahachie in 1885, parts of the east side of town were recorded for the first time on the October 1909 map, followed with updates in 1914, 1925, 1932, and 1938.

The 1909 map shows that the Freedman Town commercial row on the south side of Main Street was bounded on the west by the Odd Fellows Lodge Hall, rebuilt in 1905, and on the east by the sizeable frame Samaria Baptist Church. Smaller, mostly one-story frame store buildings were in between. Across the street on the northwest corner was the Knights of Pythias frame lodge hall built in 1904, its members knowing how lucky they were that the fire did not jump the street.

When the Sanborn company returned in November 1914, the cluster of buildings on the south side of the street had grown. The United Brothers' two-story brick lodge hall had been rebuilt, and William and Martha Richardson had replaced their one-story two-unit frame building with a one-story brick version. Businesses now included two each of barber shops, grocers, restaurants, and tailors, and one pool hall, meat market, and druggist. Across the street, the Knights of Pythias, as reported in the newspaper, had moved their frame building a little to the west so they could begin construction of a new brick building on the corner.

More gaps in the row were filled by the time the October 1925 map was drawn. On the western edge was the $6,000 movie house that black businessman Tom Frierson had built in the spring. In July, Frierson signed a lucrative ten-year lease agreement with the same Rockett family that managed theaters in downtown Waxahachie. Originally named the Freedman Theatre, it was called the Lincoln Theatre from sometime in the 1930s until it closed in the early 1940s. During the 1930s, the automobile brought new businesses to the neighborhood, most notably, Rob Cobb's Service Station on the east corner of Wyatt Street. Residents remember a long list of names and businesses that operated in the district, including Henderson Grocery, Hereford Barber Shop, Miss Viola's place (officially the Blue Lantern Café), James Undertaking Company, Jefferson Cleaners, O. K. Tailor Shop, and Evans Shine Parlor, to name a few.

Some businesses lasted for decades and the buildings remained much the same well into the 1950s, but desegregation brought a slow demise to Waxahachie's Freedman Town commercial district, as was true for many African American neighborhood businesses throughout the country. Aside from a few photographs taken of remaining buildings for the 1985 survey, documentary images of the Freedman Town district are rare, and all evidence of the buildings on the south side of Main Street was completely gone by 2008.

E-3
441 Dr. Martin Luther King Jr. Boulevard
Ellis County African American Hall of Fame
1926; W. W. Edwards, contractor

The 1926 Lodge building, now the Ellis County African American Hall of Fame, is the sole survivor of what was East Waxahachie's Main Street business district. When built by Unity Lodge No. 37 of the Colored Knights of Pythias of Waxahachie, it was one of three formidable lodge buildings clustered together at the Wyatt-Main Street intersection. The Knights of Pythias have been at this location at least since February 1904, when the *Enterprise* reported that they were erecting "a large two-story hall" which, according to the 1909 Sanborn map, was frame, unlike the two brick lodge halls across the street. Sometime after the fall 1914 Sanborn map was recorded, the Knights replaced their frame building with a larger brick building which was, in turn, replaced in 1926.

As described in the 1926 mechanic's lien, the lodge contracted W. W. Edwards to build their "Castle Hall" for $10,000. Edwards had been building business and commercial structures in Waxahachie for over twenty years, and probably doubled as project architect, just as the lien, with specifications for materials, measurements, and details, doubled as the blueprint. The plan is a standard lodge hall arrangement with commercial spaces, in this instance three, to be leased on the first floor, and a large open space for lodge meetings on the upper floor. The simple red brick exterior presents a dignified façade, the minimal detailing confined to a corbeled cornice and shaped parapet embedded with the Knights of Pythias emblem. A suspended awning protects the first-floor entrances.

Various businesses rented the first-floor spaces while several lodge groups used the second floor. For many African Americans who grew up in Waxahachie in the 1930s and 1940s, the building is remembered as "the *only* place in town where we could have dances" such as their senior proms. In 1943-44, prominent black businessman

J. Henry James acquired the property for his undertaking business, and in the mid-1950s, he provided offices for a short-lived local branch of the National Negro Business League. The building continued to be used as a funeral home well into the 1990s.

Bethesda Lodge #168, with Grand Master Jamal Rasheed, acquired the property for back taxes and in 2006 transferred ownership to the newly formed Bethesda Education Foundation of Waxahachie, Inc. (BEF), now the Ellis County African American Hall of Fame Foundation, Inc. Listed on the National Register of Historic Places in 1986 and on Preservation Texas's 2011 Most Endangered List, the City of Waxahachie granted Tax Increment Reinvestment Zone funds for a new roof in 2011, after which BEF launched a renovation program with aid from Historic Waxahachie, Inc., the Waxahachie Foundation, the National Trust for Historic Preservation, and others. The museum opened in October 2015. Located on the most visible corner of the busiest intersection in East Waxahachie and with a view toward the Ellis County Courthouse, the 1926 building is of major significance to Waxahachie and the surrounding area.

This photograph of Samaria Missionary Baptist Church and its congregation was probably taken not long after the church was completed in 1915. *Courtesy Ellis County Museum.*

Current view of Samaria Missionary Baptist Church.

E-4
508 Dr. Martin Luther King Jr. Boulevard
Samaria Missionary Baptist Church

1915; J. M. Harris, architect and contractor
1967 remodel; M. D. Barrington, contractor

Samaria Missionary Baptist Church is considered the oldest African American congregation in Waxahachie, the first gathering, according to oral tradition, in 1864 under a tree across the road from the present church building. A young Rev. Gilbert "Dock" Biggins—born c. 1845 in Georgia, a slave in Texas in 1864, and living in Ellis County in the Cummins Creek area in 1870—is recognized as founder of the church.

In August 1880, the Colored Missionary Baptist Church, precursor of the present church, paid Cyrus Aiken $30 cash for the quarter acre of land that became its permanent location. Aiken, a former slave and the largest black landholder in East Waxahachie, was also one of three church trustees to sign the deed. In all likelihood, Aiken had already given the church permission to use the property, as it was the site of a county-wide meeting of "members of the colored Missionary Baptists" reported in the *Enterprise* in March 1879.

At least three church buildings predated this 1915 structure. The rectangular pitched-roof church shown on the 1886 bird's-eye view probably replaced a smaller structure, perhaps even a house, where the congregation first met. On July 31, 1891, the newspaper announced that the "new church is about ready for occupancy," which is likely the building that J. R. Swancy noted was unfinished when beginning his pastorship in February 1893. By December, it was finished and the $600 debt paid. Early in 1898, the church building was once again destroyed by fire. The *Enterprise* reported on February 25 that the congregation had engaged Waxahachie builder E. S. Boze to build a $2,500 church to replace it. Finished in April, that building survived the 1904 East Main Street fire, but is probably the church that burned in February 1915. The following September, church trustees, with membership approval, signed a mechanic's lien for another white contractor, J. M. Harris, to build a $5,840 church according to plans and specifications provided by "architect" Harris. At the signing, the church paid $3,340 in cash with the rest to be paid in five annual $500 payments.

The impressive frame edifice, which survives in photographic form, was a highly individual interpretation of the classic African American twin-towered southern church building. Was it solely Harris's design, or was he guided by Pastor J. S. Simmons and maybe others in the congregation? One suspects that they all wanted their large stained-glass window to be prominently displayed and easily seen by passersby on the roadway that was so close to the building. Harris accomplished this by placing entrances and smaller windows in the side towers and centering the elaborate window on the recessed wall between them. The battlement-like corner caps on the flat-roofed towers are an unusual feature.

Faced with serious structural and maintenance issues in the mid-1960s, the congregation undertook a major remodeling project in 1967. Although significantly altered over the years, Samaria Baptist Church remains an imposing presence and historic reminder on the main thoroughfare of East Waxahachie.

E-5
509 Dr. Martin Luther King Jr. Boulevard
c. 1891; 1912

This small cottage is one of the most important structures not just in East Waxahachie but in all of Waxahachie. It tells the story of the Sweatts, an extraordinary family whose commitment to education began in Waxahachie and led to *Sweatt v. Painter*, one of the most important early cases in the American civil rights movement.

Richard and Sylvia Sweatt, both former slaves and both illiterate, married in Waxahachie in January 1869. Their only child, James Leonard, was born one year later. The first homestead that they bought for $40 cash in January 1877 was a sixth of an acre in Clift's Addition (See **E-31**), located in the flood-prone "valley" near the juncture of Spring Branch and Waxahachie Creek. In mid-November 1883, they moved to higher ground near this property, which they purchased in 1894. Historic records track the Sweatts as they worked, bought and sold property, and saved money throughout this period to ensure an education for James Leonard, their only child.

James Leonard graduated from Prairie View Normal Institute in 1890 and taught several years before moving to Houston where he married, worked for the post office, and became active in the local NAACP chapter. All five of his children who grew to adulthood graduated from Wiley College in Marshall, Texas, and four obtained advanced degrees from out-of-state universities including Columbia University. (Texas's segregated public education system offered no professional schools for blacks.) When the fifth child, Heman, was denied admission to the University of Texas Law School in 1946, the NAACP and Heman began the four-year *Sweatt v. Painter* lawsuit that resulted in a US Supreme Court decision in his favor in June 1950. Central to the *Sweatt v. Painter* decision was the court's determination that the State of Texas could never provide "separate but equal" education opportunities for its black citizens. The ruling set the stage for the 1954 decision of *Brown v. Board of Education of Topeka* that desegregated public education in the United States.

Although Richard and Sylvia did not live to see the many accomplishments and "firsts" of all their grandchildren and subsequent generations, there is no question but the Sweatt family legacy began in Waxahachie. Richard died on December 8, 1926, just two months shy of the Sweatts' fifty-eighth wedding anniversary. Sylvia died in October 1928. In 1936, their son sold the property.

In all probability, the house began life as a three-room L-shaped cottage built by Rev. J. D. Morrow, minister of Samaria Baptist Church, and his wife Priscilla after they bought this lot in 1891. Three years later, blacksmith Richard Sweatt and his wife Sylvia Gibbons Sweatt paid $250 cash and signed a $250 note for the property where they would live for more than thirty years. Like many owners of these small houses, the Sweatts built numerous rear and side additions, their last being the extension and porch added to the west side sometime around 1912. If the house survives, it typifies many houses in East Waxahachie in the late nineteenth-early twentieth centuries—compact and simple in form with touches of decorative detailing.

Most Waxahachians, black and white, are unaware of the connection between the Sweatts, as represented by this house, and what was a monumental decision in the history of American civil rights. For a detailed discussion of the *Sweatt v. Painter* lawsuit, see *Before Brown: Heman Marion Sweatt, Thurgood Marshall, and the Long Road to Justice* by Gary M. Lavergne, University of Texas Press, 2010.

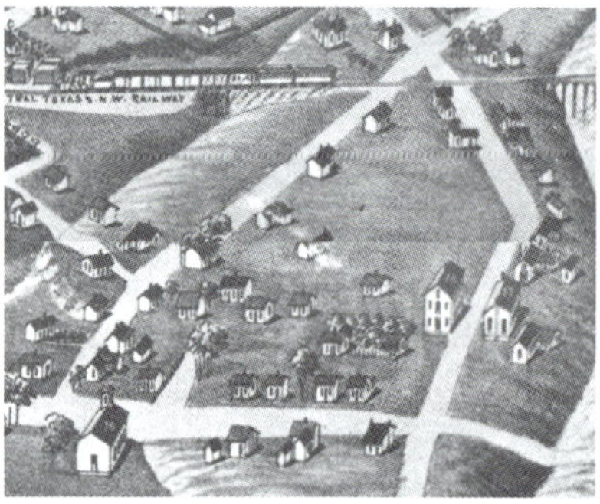

Detail of the 1886 bird's-eye view showing Aiken Street on the right. *Courtesy Ellis County Museum.*

E-6
Aiken Street

Bearing the name of Cyrus Aiken, one of Waxahachie's earliest African American property owners, this street is notable in East Waxahachie history due to the institutional buildings constructed here and to Aiken's role in the community's development. Waxahachie's first two public schools for African Americans stood on this street as has the African Methodist Episcopal Church since 1876. The school buildings are gone, but the AME's Joshua Chapel of 1917-18 survives as an architectural and community landmark.

Cyrus Aiken had an enormous impact on East Waxahachie in the 1870s and 1880s. More is known about Aiken than about most former slaves because when he died on January 13, 1904, in what was thought to be his eighty-sixth year, the local newspaper accorded "one of the best known and most remarkable negroes of the county" a far lengthier obituary than was customary for Waxahachie's African Americans. The obituary, combined with other documents, reveals quite a bit about Aiken, or "Si," as he was called. He was brought from Georgia to Texas in the mid-1850s by Col. Thomas Neel who was, with fifty-two slaves, the second largest slaveholder in Ellis County in 1860. After Neel died in September 1863, Aiken "passed into the possession, or employ" of E. W. Rogers and worked as "hostler and general utility man about the old Rogers hotel" until branching out on his own after the war. It is noteworthy that Neel's widow married W. H. Getzendaner in 1865, which means that Aiken came in contact with the most influential people in town during those early years.

In 1870, Rogers granted Aiken a title bond and in 1873, the deed to eight and a half acres that became prime real estate in East Waxahachie. Aiken added town lots and farmland to his holdings, at one point estimating a yearly income of about $1,500 from his rental properties alone. "Aiken" is an appropriate name for a street in the part of Waxahachie where his name weaves in and out of so many early property transactions. At the time of his death, Aiken's estate was valued at a modest $850, as he had dispersed his holdings to family members over the years. He requested in his will, written in March 1903 and signed with an "X," that not less than $100 be spent for his tombstone. He is buried in what was designated the "Colored" section of the City Cemetery.

This 1918 photograph by Abilene photographer W. A. Lee shows the Joshua Chapel soon after completion. *Courtesy Ellis County Museum.*

E-7
110 North Aiken Street

Joshua Chapel, African Methodist Episcopal Church
1917-18; William Sydney Pittman, architect;
George R. Powell, contractor

Tucked away on Aiken Street is Joshua Chapel, one of Waxahachie's most important buildings. It was designed by William Sydney Pittman (1875-1958), the first African American architect to practice in Texas and, at the time, one of few black architects with their own firm in the United States. Born in Alabama, the son of a laundress who was a former slave and a white man, Pittman earned degrees in architectural and mechanical drawing from Tuskegee Institute (Alabama) in 1897 and an advanced degree from Drexel Institute in Philadelphia in 1900. After returning to Tuskegee to teach and to court his future wife, Portia Washington, professional pianist and daughter of Institute president Booker T. Washington, Pittman established his first independent practice in the Washington, DC, area where, in fall 1906, he won the design competition for the Negro Building at the Jamestown Ter-centennial Exposition. His contract with the US Secretary of the Treasury to supervise construction of the building was the first contract between the Federal government and a black architect. Hoping that a Texas location would lead to more commissions, Pittman moved his family to Dallas in 1912-1913 where he maintained an office until the late 1920s, his practice consisting primarily of churches and institutional buildings in Texas cities and towns including Dallas, Houston, Waco, San Antonio, Fort Worth, and Waxahachie.

The only documentation that ties Pittman to Joshua Chapel is literally carved in stone—on the dated 1917 cornerstone that identifies Pittman as architect and George R. Powell, another African American from Alabama, as contractor. On October 9, 1917, church trustees and Powell signed a mechanic's lien to build "a one story brick veneer house" within three months for $6,000, "according to the plans and specifications thereof agreed upon . . . and furnished by [the church]." Pittman is not named in the lien, suggesting that there was a separate agreement either between Pittman and the church or Pittman and Powell. The exact date of the first service in the new building is uncertain.

Based on early newspaper reports of fires and storms in Waxahachie, Pittman's Joshua Chapel was either the fourth or fifth AME church to be built on the lot that the congregation bought in October 1876 for $25 cash from E. W. Rogers's estate. Although it was not an easy site —sloping on the backside, cramped, and rocky—Pittman designed a formidable church structure typical of the period and commanding of its location on one of the highest points in East Waxahachie. It was "the church on the hill," the bell tower visible (and still visible) from several vantage points, including Courthouse Square, in the city. The three-part Aiken Street façade with a raised central entry flanked by towers is a church type identified with African American Protestant congregations in the South from the 1910s through the 1950s. In contrast to the weighty multilayered front façade, the side elevations are a single plane, each with five tall arched windows that originally encased stained glass windows.

Joshua Chapel AME Church was an established institution in Waxahachie's African American community long before Pittman appeared on the scene. Organized in 1876, the church was named for Rev. Joshua Goins, known as the "father of African Methodism in Texas." Born in Ohio in 1848, Goins served in the Union army, and following the Civil War became a Buffalo Soldier stationed in Fort McKinney, Texas. Honorably discharged in 1870, he began his long career as itinerant minister (one source credits him with organizing 115 AME churches in Texas and adjoining territories), sometime pastor, and church officer. After serving as one of Joshua Chapel's early pastors, Goins maintained his home base in Waxahachie and was buried in the Waxahachie City Cemetery after his death on January 14, 1907.

Local contractor Carroll Davis built an office addition in 1975, and a restoration project was completed in 2004, with Precision Restoration as the general contractor and Colonial Restoration restoring the bell tower. In recognition of its architectural and cultural significance, Joshua Chapel has been designated a Recorded Texas Historic Landmark (1984) and listed on the National Register of Historic Places (1986). On October 22, 2017, the congregation held special services for the "141st Church Anniversary and Mortgage Burning Celebrations."

Detail from the 1886 bird's-eye view showing what would become the intersection of Aiken and Frierson. The two-story building on left was the school. *Courtesy Ellis County Museum.*

E-8
Northwest corner Aiken and Frierson Streets
Site of second African American school

This intersection has major historical significance for Waxahachie—not only because the African Methodist Episcopal Church (AME) has been located here since 1876 and the William Sidney Pittman designed Joshua Chapel since 1917, but also because the second African American public school was located on the northwest corner from 1884-1896.

The history of public education for Waxahachie's African American children began in 1871, when Texas adopted a public school law with the two-fold purpose of providing an education for black children and requiring compulsory attendance for all children. Supported by a state school tax, the law was administered at the county level. To implement the law, Governor Edmund J. Davis appointed Jacob Carl Maria DeGress as the state's first Superintendent of Public Instruction. DeGress's duties included acquiring properties for black schools, and it was for that purpose that he paid E. W. Rogers $194.45 for one and three-fourth acres just south of this site, at the southeast corner of what are now known as Dr. Martin Luther King Jr. Blvd. and Aiken St., on November 3, 1872. The payment money came from "the school fund of the County of Ellis."

The school for Waxahachie's African American children probably opened at that site sometime in 1873, definitely by 1874, but exactly when is difficult to determine in the absence of a local newspaper at the time and limited early records. Ellis County Commissioners Minutes do document that county school funds were mishandled during this period, and that may have caused some delay. In fall 1874, Commissioners' Court named respected educator Thomas B. Criddle the Superintendent of County Schools, a position he held for three years. Criddle was a Missourian who, after serving in the Confederate army, settled in Waxahachie in 1867. Upon receiving his teaching degree from Marvin College, he was instrumental in the organization of Waxahachie's city schools before his county appointment. Criddle's biography in the 1891 *History of Ellis County* and his lengthy obituary, published when he died in October 1917, credit him with laying the foundation for public schools in the county and organizing "the first public school for colored children" in Waxahachie.

The school remained at that location until fall 1884, when revision to the Texas public school law in 1884 brought increased income to the state's schools and with it, changes for both black and white children. In August 1884, Waxahachie's school trustees contracted to acquire the Marvin College campus for development as the public school for white students. On September 20, the trustees bought this lot directly across the street from Joshua Chapel on Aiken Street for $80 "for school purposes," and the site of the first school was sold. The city moved white students from several schools to the new Marvin campus, including pupils from Oak Lawn Academy. The latter, founded in 1879, was located on Madison Street at the corner of Monroe in "the Oak Lawn school house . . . a building 30x40 feet, two stories high," as described in an *Enterprise* article on November 7, 1879. In all probability that building was moved to the Wyatt street location, and the name "Oak Lawn" transported with the building. Moving buildings was not an uncommon practice at the time and was accomplished in various ways, depending on a building's size. Larger structures were moved in sections or dismantled and rebuilt on a new location. The "Colored Free School" shown on this site on the 1886 bird's-eye view can be interpreted as the relocated version of the two-story 30 x 40 ft. school house.

Local newspaper articles published during the twelve years that the African American school was on this site offer small bits of information. The fifth annual commencement of "Oak Lawn Graded School, colored" was held on May 9, 1889, which places the first commencement in spring 1885. In August 1890, the music hall building at the Marvin College site was moved to this location for use as a school room "by the colored people," and in spring 1892, the city council funded "considerable improvement" to the school. Commencement programs and other special events were held at the AME and Baptist churches because there was no assembly hall in the school (nor in any black school in Waxahachie until 1952).

On March 26, 1896, fire destroyed "the negro school house" as well as the church and parsonage across the street. In July, the Waxahachie Public Schools bought a lot on Wyatt Street for $500 and in turn soon sold the Aiken Street lot to Cyrus Aiken for $300, the deed noting two things of importance: 1) that "the Buildings and improvements . . . Known as the Oak Lawn School Building and Grounds and used for Public Free School purposes for colored children" were totally destroyed and that 2) the Trustees were selling this property and applying proceeds to the purchase of "a larger and more suitable lot upon which to erect a new building," that is, the property on Wyatt Street. Aiken immediately sold this lot to Joshua Chapel for $150 cash and a $150 note.

Detail from the 1886 bird's-eye view showing where Frierson Street was cut between Wyatt and Aiken Streets. *Courtesy Ellis County Museum.*

122 Frierson Street, 1985. *Courtesy Texas Historical Commission National Register Collection, Photograph 1162-01; Portal to Texas History.*

E-9
Frierson Street

The one-room side-gable cottage at 122 Frierson that was recorded in the 1985 Texas Historical Commission survey is typical of many that were built on Frierson Street and throughout East Waxahachie, as well as fringe areas of other parts of town. This cottage still stands but is in deteriorating condition. No doubt of box-and-strip construction with horizontal siding added later, these most basic of structures provided inexpensive housing, usually for rental, but sometimes were purchased to be owner occupied. As can be seen in the 1886 bird's-eye view, Frierson Street was then more of a footpath than an actual street, but cottages like this one were placed in a row along the line where the narrow street would eventually be cut.

The street was named for Tom Frierson, a person still remembered by some townspeople, both black and white. Born in Maury County, Tennessee, on July 3, 1871, Thomas Jefferson Frierson migrated to Waxahachie with his family in 1890 and quickly established himself as a "facial upholsterer," as he once advertised. His barber shop was always located in rental property just off the square on the northwest side of Franklin and Jackson Streets. In 1894, he made his first investments in East Waxahachie real estate, including his first homestead on the backside of Block 159 (the Farley Block). Frierson Street did not appear on the 1896 map but had become a street address in time for the 1900 Census. By November 1904, the *Enterprise* reported that Frierson owned nineteen rent houses and was about to build three more (not all on this street).

Older East Waxahachie residents, some of whom say Frierson "could pass for white," remember seeing him in the 1930s driving his horse-drawn buggy (he never drove a car) to collect his monthly rents. Frierson's investments included commercial property on East Main Street (now Dr. Martin Luther King Jr. Boulevard), where he contracted construction of a $3,700 two-story brick store and lodge building in 1914 and the $6,000 Freedman (Lincoln) Theatre in 1925. One can only guess that he aspired to owning property in downtown Waxahachie, where his barbershop was always located, but that was not an option for any African American. At the time of his death on June 29, 1940, the short obituary in the local paper described Frierson as the "well-known negro businessman" who was "proprietor of a barbershop for white patrons for 45 years" and who "owned considerable real estate." His estate inventory listed fifty parcels of real estate with untold numbers of rental houses and also listed the monies he loaned to a host of East Waxahachie residents to purchase property.

E-10
206 Wyatt Street
1929

Wyatt Street has always been a major roadway in East Waxahachie. Its southern tip begins and ends at Main Street (now Dr. Martin Luther King Jr. Boulevard), Waxahachie's primary east-west artery. The naming of the street was probably a nod to Robert M. Wyatt who, after settling in Waxahachie in 1860, served as Ellis County surveyor during the years 1862-1868 and then opened his own real estate and homestead location business. He obviously had an enormous impact on early development throughout the county.

A detailed chain of title for all properties lining Wyatt Street (irrespective of what buildings are now sitting on them) would reveal a great deal not only about East Waxahachie—its development and its residents—but also about *all* of Waxahachie. The first property owners have the familiar names of prominent white families who, in the 1870s, began selling parcels to African Americans. Wyatt Street became a favored residential street in the black community, with many of the residences being owner occupied.

Although the original dwelling house on this property no longer exists, it serves as an example of early land transactions between whites and blacks in East Waxahachie. The story begins in 1872, when Sandy McCuen purchased "One half acre of land" from E. W. Rogers for $65, paying one dollar cash and signing a note for the remaining amount at 10 percent interest. The purchase signaled that McCuen was moving his family to town and leaving the Ellis County farm where they were living at the time of the 1870 Census. When Rogers died in 1874, his estate credited McCuen with paying $13 on his note, and in March 1877, McCuen was given the deed when he paid the balance in full. In the 1880 Census, Sandy was listed as a "job laborer," living at this location with his wife Victoria and their five children.

Many aspects of the couple's early lives are murky, but "the rites of matrimony between Sandy McCuen and Victoria Hines Freedman and woman" are clearly recorded on January 24, 1867, in the Ellis County Freedman's Marriage Book. Sandy's tombstone (his last name spelled McCune) in the Waxahachie City Cemetery documents his birth in 1839 and his death in 1892, the censuses listing Missouri as his birth state. Victoria was born in Tennessee and, given her maiden name, may have been, at one time, a slave of Thomas Hines, Ellis County's largest slaveholder.

In December 1928, widow Victoria McCuen still lived on the property when she sold Wesley and Edna Ford the north quarter acre of the lot for $250. The Fords, both Texas-born, married in 1924 when in their mid-forties (a second marriage for both). They rented a house on Hill Street before purchasing this lot and building their house which, with its generous width, single front gable, and full-width inset porch, was not the typical bungalow house being built in the neighborhood. (At the same time, Victoria McCuen built the more typical double gable bungalow on the south quarter of her lot at 204.) People often assume that houses with side-by-side front doors were built as duplexes, but many, like the Fords' house, were built as a single residence. Actually, the two doors reflect a very practical floor plan: without a hall, the two front rooms, each with an exterior door, gain more useable space and flexibility. Wesley worked as a janitor at Trinity University until the university left Waxahachie in 1942. Edna died in March 1952, and after Wesley's death in December 1955, their heirs sold the property.

E-11
211 and 213 Wyatt Street

211: c. 1890; 1905 addition, C. J. Griggs
213: 1913, J. S. McCanless

As is true for many late nineteenth-century residents in East Waxahachie, little is known about the early life of Samuel and Augusta (Gussie) Montgomery. Census records reveal that both were born in pre-Civil War Georgia, Samuel around 1850, Gussie around 1855, and that their circa 1890 marriage was the second for both. The 1895 city directory lists them on Wyatt Street, probably living in a small house on the 211 Wyatt Street property that they bought for $450 in 1896. However, the 1900 Census finds the Montgomerys living on West Main Street and working as servants in the household of M. P. and Bena Exline. Whether the Montgomerys rented their own house, left it vacant, or built a new one during this period is unknown, but early in 1901 they returned to East Waxahachie when the Exlines moved to Dallas. In March 1905, the Montgomerys contracted C. J. Griggs to add a room and a porch to their "existing two-room house" for $135. Griggs, builder of some of Waxahachie's most elaborate houses in the 1890s, seems an unlikely connection until one learns that he was also the Exlines' contractor when they built their $2,500 house at **1022 Main Street** in 1896-97.

By 1910, the Montgomerys were tenant farmers working land just outside Waxahachie, with Sam listed in the Census as "Farmer" and Augusta as "Farm Labor" on a "Gen[eral] Farm." Their ten-year-old Georgia-born niece Allie Hughes was living with them, but unlike her aunt and uncle, Allie could read and write. In December 1913, the Montgomerys furnished "plans and specifications" to contractor J. S. McCanless to build a one-story, four-room house with hall and two porches for $775 on an adjoining lot they owned (213 Wyatt). McCanless had sixty days to complete the project, a longer than usual construction period for a four-room house, but that may have been a trade-off for hiring one of Waxahachie's busiest contractors. After it was built, the Montgomerys rented their older rectangular cottage and moved to their new house at 213 Wyatt, which was a small version of the hipped roof pyramidal cottage, the most popular house type being constructed (many by McCanless) in Waxahachie at the time. After Sam died in 1917, Augusta continued renting 211 and lived at 213 until her death in 1944. Her brother James Smith lived with her during some of that time.

E-12
212 Wyatt Street

1925; Rockwell Lumber Company

Widowed in 1917, Augusta Montgomery in 1920 bought property with an eighty-foot Wyatt Street frontage across the street from her homestead at **213 Wyatt Street**. The $950 that Augusta paid Tom Frierson, East Waxahachie's wealthiest black landlord, indicates that there was rental housing already on the property. But Augusta did some investing of her own, selling off two parcels before contracting Rockwell Lumber Co. to build this shotgun house for $588.67 on the remaining lot in February 1925. In all likelihood, Augusta's choice of house types was influenced by the row of rental shotgun houses built a few years earlier in what is now the 300 block of Wyatt Street (**300-314 Wyatt**). At the time of her death in 1944, Augusta had a tidy estate that included three houses, two of which she rented, as well as $400 cash in her bank account. She left her personal property to her brother James Smith, who periodically lived with her, and divided her real estate among James, two sisters in Ohio, and two sisters in California.

E-13
300-314 Wyatt Street

Wyatt Street Shotgun House Historic District

1921-25

This eight-house streetscape is unique in Waxahachie. There were—and are—other shotgun houses scattered about town, but nothing like this grouping appears on the Sanborn maps. The row was developed by barbershop porter Norman Broomfield, who bought the corner lot with a 105-foot Wyatt Street frontage in November 1920, and in late 1922 and early 1923 bought the adjoining 116-foot frontage from the heirs of Rev. Joshua Goins. Broomfield took several years to build the row and probably served as his own contractor, as suggested by his $1,064 purchase of building materials from the nearby Waxahachie Lumber Company in March 1921. All eight houses were completed in time to be shown on the October 1925 Sanborn map.

With one exception, the houses are almost identical in their box construction, 14 ft. 6 inches in width, and an exterior appearance with a low-pitched hipped roof and single-bay, inset front porch. The floor plan, one room wide and three rooms deep, is also uniform. The lone exception is the gable roof house at 308 Wyatt, but its scale, materials, porch, and siting are compatible with its neighbors. Although the houses are devoid of embellishment, the squared porch columns and exposed roof rafters are Craftsman details seen on larger bungalow houses built in Waxahachie during this same period. The small rear additions on all the houses date from the early 1940s, when city codes required indoor toilets.

When Broomfield built his row of rental property, the shotgun house was a long-established vernacular house type in the African American culture. Originating in tribal Africa, black slaves introduced it into the Caribbean and eventually into the southern United States.

Following the Civil War, the shotgun house spread to densely populated low-income urban areas throughout the South, where it proved to be a profitable rental housing type for laborers and was built well into the 1930s. Broomfield had little trouble renting his houses. The 1922 directory lists occupants at four addresses in the row; by

1924-25, seven addresses are listed; and in 1927-28, all eight addresses are inhabited. Among the early renters were laborers Willie Tyson and Ora Walker, cotton mill worker Mary Cummins, and garage worker Mesiah Austin. According to the 1930 Census, the monthly rent for each house was $8.

Norman Broomfield was a thirty-four-year-old bachelor when he bought his first property in 1920. His parents Jeff and Maria, along with their children, migrated from Georgia to Texas around 1875-76 and lived in the Ennis area, where Norman was born in 1886. By the mid-1890s, they were living in Waxahachie on McLain Street, which is where Norman resided until marrying Maggie Richardson in December 1931. Broomfield continued working as a barbershop porter as he accumulated property, which, when he died in October 1933, included multiple properties in Waxahachie and one lot in Denton. His widow managed the properties until her death in 1985.

In 1986, the "Wyatt Street Shotgun House Historic District" was listed on the National Register of Historic Places as an important link to "an often overlooked segment of Waxahachie's past . . . lower-class, black housing of the early twentieth century." The relatively unaltered architectural integrity of the row also contributed to the significance of the listing. By the late 1990s, the buildings were in such dire condition that the city pooled resources with the owner and local and state preservation groups to avert demolition. Work began in 2000, and in January 2002, the row was certified as meeting the Secretary of the Interior's "Standards for Rehabilitation" for historic structures. The buildings remain rental property but are now owned by multiple landlords.

E-14
402 Wyatt Street
Dr. James E. Munchus Office
c. 1912; moved post-1953

Dr. James E. Munchus built this one-room office when he returned to Waxahachie after graduating from Meharry Medical School in Nashville, Tennessee, in 1912. Originally tucked in the northeast corner of his parents' property at what is now 606 Dr. Martin Luther King Jr. Boulevard, it was where Dr. Munchus practiced until his death in November 1953, after which the building was moved to this location and converted to residential use with the help of a small rear addition. It is a rare surviving example of what was a common vernacular building type for physicians and lawyers practicing in small towns and in the poorer sections of larger towns.

James's parents, Murry (sometimes Murray) and Lou Munchus, sent two sons to Meharry, which was founded in 1876 and is the oldest African American medical school in the South. James received his pre-medical degree from Lincoln University, established in 1854 in Oxford, Pennsylvania, and the first degree-granting historically black university in the United States. With the exception of a California hiatus in the late 1920s-early 1930s, James's practice was confined to Waxahachie. His older brother George (1887-1952) graduated from Meharry in 1909, and for the greatest part of his career practiced in Fort Worth, where he established the Negro Community Hospital in 1928.

The boys' parents were former slaves born in Alabama—Murry in 1857 and Lou in 1860. They married in Ellis County on September 23, 1878. The couple bought farmland in both Hill and Ellis Counties and lived in Hillsboro before buying their first piece of property in Waxahachie in 1895 and moving to town, which means that both James and George attended Oak Lawn School. Murry was described as one of Ellis County's "respected and well to do black farmers" in a May 1913 article in the *Daily Light.* Will, the oldest Munchus son (1880-1956), lived most of his adult life in Amarillo, where he worked as a hotel porter.

Two other Meharry graduates opened practices in East Waxahachie during these years. Mississippi-born Dr. Charles S. Diggs (1875-1938) arrived in Waxahachie soon after graduating in 1901. Within a few years, he located his residence and a separate one-room office on the northeast corner of Dr. Martin Luther King Jr. Boulevard (MLK) and Tuggle Streets, where he remained until moving to Los Angeles to practice and co-manage an African American hospital in 1922. In his autobiography, Ely Green wrote that his employer, Judge Oscar Dunlap, considered Dr. Diggs "the best doctor in Texas for men." It seems probable that Dr. Diggs was a mentor to the Munchus boys. Dr. Lonnie Clarence Moore (1882-1948) listed Hubbard City (seven miles from Hillsboro) as his hometown when he graduated from Meharry in 1911. He is known to have practiced in Piggot, Clay County, Arkansas, in 1914-15, and in Hillsboro in 1918 before settling in Waxahachie in the early 1920s. His arrival was perhaps coordinated with Dr. Diggs's departure for California. Dr. Moore's office still stands on the northeast corner of MLK and Aiken Street.

E-15
412 Wyatt Street
1919; Dunaway Brothers, builders

In March 1919, Sam and Mary Loyd signed a contract to pay Dunaway Brothers $600 for "lumber and other building material as per price list" to build this residence on the Loyds' homestead. The Loyds were building a new house because of necessity, not choice: their T-plan cottage with back wing, which shows so prominently in a c. 1915 photograph taken from the adjacent Oak Lawn School building, had burned. When rebuilding, the Loyds chose a more up-to-date house form—the pyramidal cottage. Their compact version features a centered front dormer on a gently sloping roof, side-by-side front doors—a wise choice in a large household—and a three-bay porch with squared columns.

In 1900, the Loyds and their four children were living in Grimes County, where thirty-eight-year-old Sam was farming on rented land. The family had moved to Waxahachie by November 1904, when Sam paid $400 for this property. Given the price, there must have been an existing small house that he either replaced or enlarged. At least from 1910-1914, Sam operated a grocery store in a building south of the railroad tracks on Wyatt Street. By 1920, he, along with his nineteen-year-old son Sam, was back to farming, and his four younger children were cotton field laborers. On August 12, 1930, the Loyds' granddaughter Erma Faye Moore Newton was born in the house to the Loyds' only daughter, Blanche (Penny) Loyd Thompson. A 1947 graduate of Oak Lawn High School, Mrs. Newton was well known in Waxahachie as a civil rights and community leader, the Citizens for Progress being one of many local boards on which she served. In the mid-1990s, Mrs. Newton retired after a thirty-year career at the Dallas Veterans Administration Medical Center, during which time she was elected the first black and first female president of the center's chapter of the American Federation of Government Employees. Mrs. Newton, who died in 2016, loved to say that "I've been in the 400 block of Wyatt all my life. I haven't even crossed the street." The Newton family still owns the family home and adjacent properties.

E-16
417 Wyatt Street
1922

This pyramidal cottage incorporated a much earlier house and was one of numerous major alterations and new residences that changed the face of Wyatt Street in the 1920s. The house was long known as "Miss Doll's house," a reference to Mary L. Porter, a popular and diminutive primary grade school teacher at Oak Lawn School from 1917 to the early 1960s. It is located on what was part of a larger lot owned by Mary's parents Sarah and William J. Truelove. Her father was an early teacher and principal at Oak Lawn School when it was located on Aiken Street.

In June 1922, Mary acquired, for a token amount, this part of her father's estate—a lot with a fifty-seven-foot frontage on Wyatt Street and an existing two-room rectangular house with a back ell and partial front porch that was typical of smaller residences built along Wyatt Street in the 1870s and 1880s. Mary and her husband Jesse, who first appeared in the 1910 Census when he was boarding in a neighbor's house and working as a hostler, may have moved to the earlier house after their marriage in September 1914.

On July 1, 1922, the couple signed a $500 materialman's lien for the Waxahachie Lumber Company to furnish lumber and material "to build and construct an addition of one room, one bath room and front porch, new weatherboarding and new roof on entire building, entire house to be painted and new doors and all new windows." Perhaps the Porters were influenced by the house that their neighbors, the Loyds, had built a few years earlier at **412 Wyatt**, because once finished, their remodeled house could pass for another pyramidal cottage with its almost-square shape, three bays, hipped roof, and front porch with squared columns.

Jesse died in the mid-1920s. Mary, who continued teaching at Oak Lawn, rented this house and moved back to her mother's, where she lived until the late 1930s. She was living here when she died in 1967.

Photograph of the second Oak Lawn School, included in Charles M. Simpson's *Sanitary Survey of Waxahachie, Texas*, 1917. *Courtesy National Library of Medicine.*

Oak Lawn School Building, showing the two-story 1919 section on the left and the one-story 1941 addition on the right. It was demolished in 1990. *Courtesy Ellis County Museum.*

E-17
500 block Wyatt Street
Site of Oak Lawn School

When considering community significance, the most important building in East Waxahachie is a building that no longer exists—and that's the Oak Lawn School building, which was the only school for African American children in Waxahachie from spring 1919 through spring 1952. After Turner High School opened in fall 1952, Oak Lawn housed grades one through seven until fall 1961, when grades six and seven were also moved to Turner. Oak Lawn was permanently closed when Waxahachie's school system fully integrated in fall 1970. Several community groups and individuals attempted to adapt the building for other uses but without success. In 1990, the Waxahachie Independent School District demolished the structure. The site and the Oak Lawn name, however, continue to hold strong historic and cultural associations for Waxahachie's black community. The biannual reunions draw graduates mostly from the Waxahachie and Dallas area, but also from greater distances.

Wyatt Street is the third documented site of an African American public school in Waxahachie. The first location was on the southeast corner of Dr. Martin Luther King Jr. Boulevard and Aiken Streets and was established following passage of the 1871 Texas public school law. The second location was on Aiken Street directly across from Joshua Chapel, on a lot acquired by school trustees in fall 1884 (see **E-8**). It was there that the name Oak Lawn became associated with Waxahachie's school for black children. When that building burned on March 26, 1896, the trustees bought this "larger and more suitable lot" on Wyatt Street.

A photograph taken in 1917 shows a two-story frame building labeled "Negro Public School Building" that probably was the first school built on this Wyatt Street site after the building on Aiken Street burned in 1896. The bulky T-shape and two corner porches match the building footprints shown at this location on 1909 and 1914 Sanborn maps. Also visible in the photograph is one of the two single-story rectangular frame buildings used for classrooms—the second one is hidden behind the main building, as are the schoolyard and ravine along the creek branch.

The Oak Lawn School that alumni remember today was one of three major school projects—Oak Lawn was the reluctant third—built in Waxahachie in the years 1917-1919. Following a special bond election in fall 1916, Waxahachie School Trustees commissioned Austin-based C. H. Page & Brother, the most prolific school architects in Texas at the time, to design Waxahachie High School (**600 Second Street**), and a two-room addition to South or Bullard Heights Ward School (**716 Dunaway**). As of March 1918, plans for Oak Lawn School did not go beyond maintenance of the existing frame buildings, even though Principal P. E. Goldthwaite had repeatedly voiced a desperate need for more room and more teachers for the nearly five hundred black students. Finally, in early April, the board voted to ask City Council to hold another bond election to raise funds for erecting "A Substantial Public School Building for the Colored School." It was a request that assumed an urgency when trustees, at the savvy invitation of Oak Lawn's Domestic Service Department, lunched at the school and toured the facilities on May 17. As recorded in their minutes, the trustees "had an informal session in the road" and appointed a committee to draft a resolution requesting city council to hold another bond issue for an "Emergency fund" for the school. Three days later, the council adopted the resolution, the action speaking volumes about the condition of the African American school and also suggesting that few Trustees, if any, had ever visited the site. In early July, the bond election passed.

Already on the scene, architect Charles Page was retained to design the Oak Lawn building, and new Waxahachie resident architect R. W. Mulhausen was hired as project superintendent. Local contractor A. A. Few & Son was awarded the job based on a low bid of $16,988.20. Once started, things moved rapidly. In late August, the frame buildings were moved to make room for the new building. In September, trustees selected a dark brick made by Groesbeck Brick Company of Corsicana, and in November, the contractor was complaining about the difficulties of excavating "in rock." The building was ready for occupancy by mid-April 1919.

Oak Lawn School was typical of the simpler, smaller brick school buildings of the period—a rectangular block with a flat roof and a noticeable absence of ornamentation. The centered, primary entrance was on Wyatt Street. Groupings of five small-paned double-hung windows on both floors of the front façade reflected the interior cross-hall plan that accommodated four large classrooms on each floor. A partial basement included space for the woodworking shop. Upon completion, Oak Lawn was still not large enough for Waxahachie's African American student population plus students who came from outlying areas, which meant that the one-story frame buildings continued to be used as classrooms for primary grades.

Oak Lawn was not enlarged until 1940-1941, when M. Z. Hicks was principal. The *Daily Light* reported on October 16, 1940, that "improvements to Oak Lawn colored school" would soon begin with a one-story six-classroom addition on the west side and the "installation of inside toilet facilities" in a wing on the east side. It was indeed the first time that African American students would not be using what were essentially detached water closets. Construction was under WPA supervision and employed WPA laborers. This was the structure—the original two-story Page building with one-story wings on each side—that served as Oak Lawn School until closing in spring 1970. The building was demolished in 1990.

A monument, built of bricks from the demolished building, incorporates the cornerstones from the original school building and wings. A Texas State Historic Marker also commemorates Oak Lawn School. Since 2008, the City of Waxahachie has owned the property, which now serves as a community park under the auspices of the Parks and Recreation Department.

E-18
516 Wyatt Street
New Town Drug Store
1925; Rockwell Lumber Company

Wilson L., known as "Deacon," and Alice Williams's corner drug store was part of a cluster of small commercial buildings in the New Town business district. Exactly when the term "New Town" surfaced in East Waxahachie's vocabulary is unknown, but the first written reference found thus far is a property deed dated July 1913. Although there are no official boundaries for New Town, it is generally defined as north of the railroad tracks or Oak Lawn School (depending on who you ask), Dunlap Street on the west, Henry Street on the east, and Park School Road on the north.

In all likelihood, New Town began to evolve when Oak Lawn School moved to Wyatt Street in 1896 and developed in earnest with the platting of three residential subdivisions to the north of what is now Eggar Street. Murry Munchus developed two of the subdivisions, which made him the first African American to develop a platted subdivision in East Waxahachie. In 1901, Munchus filed the plat for a thirty-three-lot Munchus Addition, to which he added another ninety-nine lots in 1906. The third subdivision was the thirty-eight-lot New Town Heights Addition filed in 1914, and although no developer was named on the latter plat, individual property sales indicate that J. F. Patterson and D. H. Thompson were involved (both white men).

The 1914 Sanborn map shows that Eggar Street, the cross street at this intersection, had not, as yet, been cut through, but there were groupings of small frame commercial buildings on both sides of Wyatt Street, and the Christian Church and New Mt. Zion Baptist Church were in their present locations. However, by the time the 1925 map appeared, Eggar Street, New Town Drug Store, and a growing number of residences had been added. The Williamses bought their corner lot in February 1924 for $250, and one year later, signed a $450 contract with Rockwell Lumber Company to build their small three-unit vernacular brick commercial structure. The neighborhood considered the brick "a major step up," according to Carroll Davis, longtime East Waxahachie resident.

The Williamses operated their business at this location for forty years. During the first ten years Deacon worked at other jobs, while Alice was the primary storekeeper. The store accommodated the New Town postal station during the 1920s and early 1930s, and in the 1950s, became Williams Grocery and Market. Deacon ventured into politics in spring 1956 when he ran for the Waxahachie Independent School District Board of Trustees, an optimistic and admirable but unsuccessful effort, as it would be another fourteen years (1970) before Waxahachie would fully integrate its schools and twenty-three years (1979) before funeral home owner Edgar Thomas would be appointed to fill an unexpired term and become its first African American board member. Among the businesses in the row over the years were Littlejohn Cleaners in 1939, Wyatt Street Barber Shop in 1955, and New Town Fashion Shop, owned by Eddie and Frances Finley, in 1970. When Deacon Williams died in 1971, he left the building to his wife's nephew, Ezra Waters. The Waters family still owns the property.

E-19
207 Eggar Street
Greater New Mt. Zion Missionary Baptist Church
1927: H. L. Jackson, contractor

This church and the smaller Wyatt Street Christian Church on the corner of Wyatt and Eggar were already established institutions when Deacon and Alice Williams built their drug store on the corner at **516 Wyatt Street**. Mechanics' liens document that both congregations built their first church soon after purchasing their properties, and that the present buildings replaced those original structures. Greater New Mt. Zion Missionary Baptist Church bought four lots in March 1910. None of the lots faced an existing street when the congregation built its first church, nor had Eggar Street been opened when black contractor and church deacon Dave Carroll Sr. built a $1,200 addition and made other improvements to the original church in 1914. The present brick-faced structure was built in fall 1927, when church trustees signed an agreement with Rockwell Lumber Company to furnish as much as $3,500 in lumber and other building materials and Rockwell, in turn, subcontracted H. L. Jackson "to furnish labor and tools." Jackson is listed as contractor on the cornerstone laid on the north façade in 1927. The cornerstone for the 1910 church can be seen on the front façade at sidewalk level between the two stairways.

Wyatt Street Christian Church bought its property fronting Wyatt Street in late 1909, and in 1921 replaced its first church building with the present rectangular structure using lumber and other materials purchased from the Waxahachie Lumber Company. In 1926, the church added a front porch and made interior improvements with building materials purchased from H. H. Hardin Lumber Company. Documents suggest that church members were its builders in both 1921 and 1926.

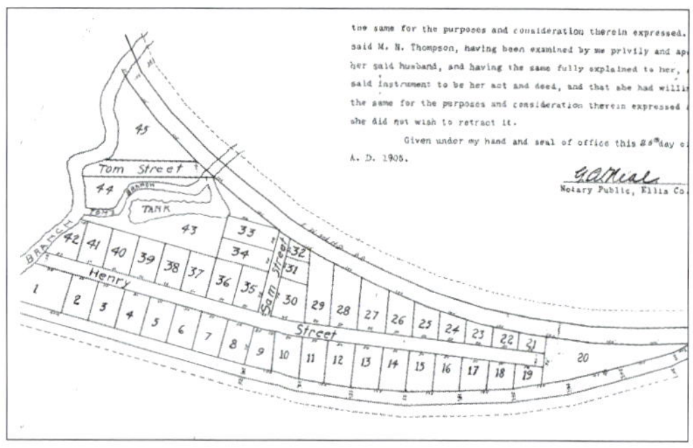

Oak Lawn Addition Plat Map.
Courtesy County Clerk's Office, Ellis County.

E-20
Henry Street, Oak Lawn Addition
Platted 1905

This self-contained and virtually unknown narrow streetscape in East Waxahachie reveals a great deal about land development and building practices as well as social attitudes and shifts in poorer minority neighborhoods during the first half of the twentieth century. Given that very little news appeared in Waxahachie papers about real estate dealings in East Waxahachie, readers must have been surprised to see the "Home for Colored People" advertisement that wealthy white businessman and grain dealer D. H. Thompson placed in the *Enterprise* on September 29, 1905. Thompson offered $25 to $100 lots for sale on several acres of land adjoining Oak Lawn School, a location where "no white man will trouble a good, respectable, law-abiding colored person." He had acquired the horn-shaped piece of property for $300 in January 1905, and three months later, he and his wife Mannette filed the plat for what would be known as Oak Lawn Addition.

The eastern point of the addition was at the convergence of two railroad lines—the Fort Worth and New Orleans Railroad tracks that curved northward and the Houston and Texas Central tracks that defined the southern line of the addition—while the meandering Rock Branch Creek formed the west-side boundary. Into this unorthodox shape, Thompson squeezed forty-five lots, most of them more or less rectangular and most with a fifty-foot frontage on Henry Street, the only street that ran through the addition. Lots on the east and west ends were considerably freer in shape, the upper northwest end being a bizarre arrangement of three lots sharing space with Tom Street, a short "street" that bordered Tom's Branch (an offshoot of Rock Branch Creek) and an uncovered tank, or pond, that collected overflow from the creek and Wyatt Street. The Thompsons named the streets in the addition for their three young boys, Henry, the oldest, Sam, and Tom.

Besides the lots, Thompson also advertised having $300 to $550 houses "ready to move," an offer made, no doubt, in conjunction with his father-in-law, lumberyard owner and builder H. D. Timmons. Most interested buyers, however, could not afford to buy both lot and house, and chose to buy an empty lot or lots and after a period of time, contracted Timmons or another builder or lumberyard to build a house.

By the end of 1907, Thompson had sold at least eleven lots and another twelve by the end of 1913. Mechanics' liens document that during these same years, a substantial number of houses were built. The 1910 Census listed fifteen separate households, twelve of those owner-occupied, on what the census taker called School House Alley, otherwise known as Henry Street. In the 1930 Census, the twenty-five households that are listed correspond to the number of dwellings shown in the addition on the 1925 Sanborn map. City directories and census records document that there was some fluidity in the population, but there were also longtime residents.

Most of the first houses built in Oak Lawn Addition cost less than $300 and were either two-room two-door rectangular houses or three-room L-shaped houses. As described in the liens, most, if not all, were "box" or "boxed" houses. Over the years, many of these early houses were enlarged, altered, and sometimes cobbled together, practices that typify neighborhoods where residents make do with existing materials and limited resources. The houses at **303** and **308 Henry Street** are two examples where owners made adaptations to an original, smaller structure.

Hazel Pruitt remembered that when she moved to the street as a young bride in the late 1940s, there were few empty lots and an active neighborhood. Over the years fires, neglect, limited resources, greater job opportunities elsewhere, and absentee or indifferent landlords—including relatives of people who once lived here as well as public entities, most specifically the Waxahachie Independent School District—have taken their toll on the neighborhood. Mrs. Pruitt also acknowledged another factor that contributed to the change: African Americans and other minorities have far more options now when buying property than they did in 1905 and the 1940s.

E-21
303 Henry Street

Three generations of the Erskin family have lived in three different houses on Henry Street beginning in late 1907 or early 1908. Twenty-year-old day laborer Agene Erskin and his sixteen-year old wife Annie were among Thompson's first buyers, purchasing a lot in 1906 for $52.50. In December 1907, they contracted Timmons Lumber Co. to build a "one story two room box house and porch" for $135.30 at what is now 303 Henry Street. The house assumed an L-shape form in June 1910, when the Erskins again hired Timmons to add "two rooms 12 x 14 each . . . to the house as it now stands," at a cost of $184.15. The house was probably also weatherboarded for the first time. According to the 1920 Census, Annie, now widowed, was raising three sons at this address, and working in the cotton fields alongside her two oldest boys, eight and ten, who also attended school. Annie remarried in the late 1920s; her heirs sold the property after her death in 1947. In the late 1940s, the Erskins' middle son Delmar built a house, now demolished, on another lot on Henry Street, while a third generation Erskin still lives on the street in a family-owned property. (The family name is also spelled Erskine.)

E-22
308 Henry Street
c. 1911; 1958

The three-room house that Ned Pruitt and his wife Hazel rented at 308 Henry Street in 1947 was probably much the same house that lumberman N. J. Thomas sold in 1911 for $375. Mrs. Pruitt remembered an outhouse and that the couple immediately installed a bathroom. After buying the house in July 1956, the Pruitts hired black contractor Jack Livingston in March 1958 to make further improvements, including a "new roof, new siding, complete sheetrock job, repairs to the porch, complete paint job inside and out, new bath and two complete new rooms, all under plans and specifications in the hands of both parties." The house reflects the 1958 rehabilitation and remained Mrs. Pruitt's home until her death in 2014.

E-23
212 Henry Street
1928

As with the rest of Waxahachie, the favored house type built in the Oak Lawn Addition in the late teens and 1920s was the modest double front-gabled bungalow like 212 Henry Street and 204 further down the street. Both were built for an initial $500 by Rockwell Lumber Company. This bungalow (212 Henry) was built in 1928 for farm laborer Lee R. Runnels and his family. Laborer Rueben Cox and his wife Gertrude signed their first contract with Rockwell in fall 1924 for 204 Henry, followed by a second contract for a $300 addition in 1927. Sitting between the two bungalows is 206 Henry Street, the lone pyramidal cottage on the street. Built as a speculation investment in 1917, it was enlarged by owners Gip and Viola Mims in 1928.

The newest house on the street—209 Henry—borrows the form and scale of its older bungalow neighbors and is a Jim Walter Homes Inc. product, as are other more recent infill projects in the addition.

E-24
800 North Getzendaner Street
1953; Boese & Harkrider, architects;
Orts Company, contractors

In April 1952, the Waxahachie Housing Authority announced that preliminary work had begun on "the new Negro housing project" to be located on a site recently annexed into the city limits. Actual construction began in mid-summer on the twenty-two duplex units that were the second phase of a public housing program, the first phase being the larger Patrick Street Apartments complex (**208 Patrick**) built for white tenants, which had been completed in 1951. This project on Getzendaner opened in 1953. The two projects utilized the same plans as well as many of the same contractors and subcontractors. The original flat roofs were later replaced by the current hipped roofs.

E-25
614 North Getzendaner Street
Turner High School
[now Turner High School of Choice]
1952; Wilson & Patterson, architects

1961 classroom wing and cafeteria; Upshaw and Todd, architects

1995 addition; SHW Group Inc., architects

2015 gymnasium rebuilt; Corgan Architects; Gallagher Construction Services, contractor

Opening in fall 1952, Turner High School was built in response to an equal facilities lawsuit against the Waxahachie Independent School District (WISD) that centered around the woefully overcrowded conditions at Oak Lawn School on Wyatt Street. (See **E-17**.) Willia Getzendaner Skinner (only daughter of W. H. and Willia Getzendaner) gave four acres of land for the school, her deed of gift stating that it was "in tender rememberance [sic] of the faithful devotion of Matilda Turner for my mother, Willie Latimer Getzendaner and her family for nearly three-quarters of a century." The WISD Board of Trustees named the school in Matilda Turner's memory at its meeting on May 26, 1952, and in September, the school opened with 127 students in grades eight through twelve. (Oak Lawn still had 408 students.) M. Z. Hicks, who devoted thirty-eight years to educating Waxahachie's African American children, was the first principal and served in that position until retiring in 1965.

When Turner High School was completed, East Waxahachie, for the first (and only) time, could boast having the most modern school building in town. The minimalist budgets that WISD had historically allocated for African American school facilities were a perfect match for the simple, no frills minimalist architecture of early 1950s institutional and educational buildings. Fort Worth architects Wilson & Patterson designed a compact two-block school structure, with the primary entrance façade facing Getzendaner Street. The east side was a long, low one-story classroom block with a generous supply of windows, while the bigger, bulkier solid block on the west side housed the first gymnasium-auditorium built for African American children in Waxahachie, as well as a cafeteria and kitchen. The arrangement allowed the west side to be closed off from the classroom block and used by community organizations for business or social functions.

The 1960s brought change to Turner and the entire WISD school system. Upon completion of a new classroom wing and cafeteria in 1961, grades six and seven were moved from Oak Lawn School to Turner. In the 1965-1966 school year, when WISD began construction of a new campus that would integrate city high school students in fall 1970, Turner students were given the option to transfer to the existing Waxahachie High School. Most chose to stay at Turner, where the last senior class graduated in spring 1970. With total integration of Waxahachie's public schools the following fall, Turner was assigned the new roles of serving as the only middle school for all sixth graders in the system and as temporary offices for WISD administrative staff. Coincidentally, the building also served as the first introduction to East Waxahachie for many white students and their parents.

Demands on Turner facilities and space continued to grow as Waxahachie's population grew. Major renovations were completed in 1985, and in 1995 another one-story classroom block and larger cafeteria were built. By 2010, all the city's sixth graders were dispersed to Howard and Finley Junior High Schools, and Turner was adapted for yet another new role as the Turner Learning Center, which provided facilities for the Waxahachie Challenge Academy, an alternative education program; a day-care facility; and the High School of Choice for nontraditional students, including single parents and working students. In 2015, WISD demolished the original Turner gym—described as "once the pinnacle of integration in Waxahachie," in a July 29, 2015 article in the *Daily Light*—and replaced it with a smaller version.

E-26
404 North Getzendaner Street
Lee Penn Park
1936 (designation date)

East Waxahachie residents had been using and referring to the open area east of the Union Pacific Railroad tracks and across Getzendaner Street as "the park" long before

November 3, 1936, when the city council designated four acres of land given by Mrs. J. Lee Penn for "a colored park . . . to be known as the 'Lee Penn Park.' " Carroll Davis, born in 1921, vividly remembers watching Oak Lawn School play football here in the late 1920s-early 1930s. Mrs. Penn's gift, named in her husband's memory, stipulated that the city supervise and maintain the park and not charge an admission fee.

Over the years, volunteers and service organizations from both the black and the white communities in Waxahachie have been instrumental in making improvements and maintaining the park. In spring 1954 and in response to a proposal from East Waxahachie residents, the city council appointed a five-member Colored Council "to represent any community effort of the colored citizenry." Henry Hereford, who had owned a barber shop on East Main Street since the early 1920s, was appointed mayor. High on the group's first list of requests was maintenance of Penn Park, beginning with the removal of seventeen dead trees. The city followed up by promising to budget sufficient appropriations to maintain not only the park but also "the Colored part of the City Cemetery."

The Regular Fellows Club, composed of leaders in the East Waxahachie community with George Brown serving as president, initiated efforts to build a youth center in the park in spring 1957. Several women's organizations, including the Friendship Social Club, the Royal Art and Charity Club, the Ladies Aid Club, and the Beauticians Club supported the project. Unable to raise the monies to build the new structure for which they had plans, the groups began searching for a building to move. The Buena Vista school board responded and donated a vacated, circa 1925 frame schoolhouse building, which served as the Penn Park Youth Center from late 1957 or early 1958, until it was heavily damaged by fires in 2013. In 2014 it was demolished. For many years, the building was also home to the Rock Solid Boxing Club run by Ernest "Big E" Smith, a former professional boxer and one-time sparring partner of Muhammad Ali.

Spring 1964 saw construction of the Penn Park Little League Baseball Diamond, a project that received citywide support as well as baseballs sent for the summer opening by Paul Richards, who was general manager of the Houston Colt 45s at the time. The swimming pool was added in 1969 and the bath house in 1971.

Prompted by the demolition of the youth center, renovation of Penn Park took place in 2017. The project followed an extensive planning process that involved the city's parks and recreation staff working closely with East Waxahachie citizens in identifying and developing what the community wanted. At the top of the list were a large pavilion and a regulation-size covered basketball court, both of which have been completed.

E-27
Brackens Street

1969-74; The Houseman Inc., builders and developers

Incorporated in 1969 specifically to develop the Brackens Street project, The Houseman Inc. was the first African American contracting firm to build in volume for the East Waxahachie community. The five directors, all tradesmen who lived in East Waxahachie, had worked together on other projects: founder and president, carpenter Carroll Davis; carpenter Clarence Davis; plumbers Russell Owens and M. J. Waters; and painter Willie Cavitt. Several factors influenced Davis's decision to establish the corporation. Waxahachie's black tradesmen and black homeowners had both experienced discrimination—tradesmen in the hiring practices of the local building industry, property owners in the lending practices of local financial institutions. The directors knew that a particular housing market was not being serviced, and Davis was familiar with Federal Housing Administration (FHA) programs for qualifying minorities.

Brackens Street is built on farmland once owned by the Davises' step-grandparents, Tom and Dora Graham. It was first platted as part of a larger Tom Graham Addition in 1949 by Lucille Graham Davis, the Grahams' daughter and the Davises' stepmother. The street name acknowledged Charles and Katie Brackins, African American insurance agents from Dallas who enabled the Graham family to keep their land in an ownership dispute. (Two notes of interest: Brackens with an "e" was the last name of an Ellis County white family with substantial land holdings and was the spelling used on the Grahams' plat and subsequently applied to the street; and Tom Graham was well known as one of, if not *the* best bronco buster in this part of Texas.)

When The Houseman Inc. acquired the property in 1969, nothing had been built on the twenty-four 50 x 125 ft. lots shown fronting Brackens Street on the 1949 plat. Before selling any lots, the corporation adjusted lot widths to seventy-five feet, which in turn reduced the number of properties from twelve to eight on each side of the street. The bulk of the lots sold in 1971, the same year that the city declared Brackens Street a public street. Homeowners-to-be worked with Davis in selecting a house design and plan from FHA-approved pattern books. Interim financing was provided by a local financial institution, but no local lending agency existed at the time that would assume long-term loans for either blacks or whites. Waxahachie resident Bill Spalding and his employer, the Fort Worth Mortgage Company, solved the problem for the Brackens Street project.

Built primarily of brick with some wood components, the Brackens Street houses are modest one-story ranch-style structures, rectangular in shape, with low-pitched or gabled roofs. Most have three bedrooms and two baths, and all have an attached, enclosed garage. What distinguishes Brackens Street today is the oak tree canopy. To meet FHA landscaping requirements, The Houseman Inc. subcontracted tree-farm owner and former East Waxahachie resident Thad Taylor to plant an oak tree in every front yard. Entered and exited from Graham Street, the self-contained space obviously appealed to residents, as many of the houses remained in the same families, often with the same inhabitants, throughout most of the thirty-year loan period.

E-28
911 Dr. Martin Luther King Jr. Boulevard
1919; Waxahachie Lumber Company
1929; Rockwell Lumber Company

If this property seems on the edge of town today, it was *really* on the edge of Waxahachie when Oak Lawn teacher Edward Lee Gibson bought it for $450 from his uncle T. J. Frierson in January 1918. The property had been part of the sizeable Harriett I. Nowlin Estate partitioned in the 1890s, but the area was slow to develop and barely inside city limits. In all likelihood, Frierson bought the property in December 1913—the $600 purchase price indicating an existing structure —specifically to rent to Ed Lee and his bride Harriett Conner. Married in July 1913, the couple's first home was probably on Frierson Street in a house that Ed Lee had bought and shared with his mother before his marriage.

In September 1919, the Gibsons signed a mechanic's lien with the Waxahachie Lumber Company for $550 in "labor and building material . . . to be used in the erection or repair of improvements" on the property. Whether this was to build a new house or to enlarge an existing structure is uncertain. We can be certain, however, that the house we see today is the product of the Gibsons' second lien of May 1929 for $1,080 with the Rockwell Lumber Company. It is an unassuming and unadorned, generously proportioned two-story house, almost square in shape, with a pyramidal roof, attached partial front porch, and single front door and window openings. A circa 1930 photograph shows an exterior that has changed little over the years. (The carport attachment does not deface the building structurally and can be easily removed.)

A graduate of Oak Lawn High School, Prairie View A&M College, and Paul Quinn College, Professor Gibson, as he was often called, taught at Oak Lawn School for many years and was principal of Dunbar School in Forreston, Texas, until his retirement in 1957. The Gibsons raised their children and lived out their lifetimes (he died in 1967, she in 1974) on this property, which remained in the Gibson family until 1988, when they sold it to a principal in the Waxahachie school system. Even though the Gibson house is lacking in architectural detailing, its simplicity and directness lend a dignified presence to the far east side of Waxahachie.

Fairview Addition, corner 700 block of
Dr. Martin Luther King Jr. Blvd. and Young St.

E-29
Fairview Addition
Platted 1911

Filed in the County Clerk's office on October 31, 1911, Fairview Addition encompasses land that the Getzendaner family had assembled in the late nineteenth and early twentieth centuries. The fifty-nine-lot subdivision was developed by Ralph W. Getzendaner, only son of Capt. W. H. Getzendaner, and is another example of a platted neighborhood in East Waxahachie. It is bound by East Main Street on the north, East Jefferson Street on the south, the diagonal Houston and Texas Central Railroad right-of-way on the east, and Givens Street, now South Aiken Street, on the west, and is split east-west by Fairview Avenue and north-south by Young Street. Originally, many lots had a fifty-foot street frontage with a one hundred-foot depth.

As there are no known early photographs of Fairview Addition, we have to depend on a combination of deed records, mechanics' liens, city directories, and the 1925 Sanborn map to get a sense of the people and buildings that populated the subdivision. The consistent sale of lots for $110 and $125 indicates that most lots were vacant land. By the end of 1916, Getzendaner had sold at least thirty lots to nineteen buyers, the latter almost evenly split between homesteaders and speculators; add to those numbers six more lots and three more purchasers by 1925.

The 1925 Sanborn map shows twenty-three residential buildings, twelve of which can be tied to a mechanic's lien between an owner and a contractor, the latter being in every instance but two a local lumberyard. None of the liens involved a building and loan association like those that financed many houses built for Waxahachie's white laborers. Based on construction dates and building shapes on the 1925 Sanborn map, the Fairview residences fit the same description as those built throughout the city's working-class neighborhoods—small bungalows, two and three room rectangular and L-shaped houses, and pyramidal cottages.

Getzendaner began selling lots soon after the plat was filed in fall 1911. His first sale was $265 in mid-December to trustees of the Church of God for two lots on the southwest corner of East Main and Young Streets. The small frame vernacular church building standing on the corner today is probably similar in size and form to the original church.

Among the first lots sold for residential use were those adjacent to the church property. Laborer Thomas J. Collins and his wife Ida M. paid $110 for lot 4 (710 East Main) in February 1912 but did not immediately build. The couple was living across the street when contracting the Waxahachie Lumber Company to build their $675 "improvements" in April 1917. Two doors east, builder J.A. Dewberry, the only white investor in residential properties in the subdivision, bought lot 6 (714 East Main) for $115 in July 1913, built another bungalow-style house, and sold the property to Claborne [sic] and Mozelle Taylor for $800 in September 1914. Taylor was a teamster for the Waxahachie Transportation Company.

African American developer and East Waxahachie resident Tom Frierson bought three Fairview Addition lots in February 1913 and one lot in July 1914, all in the 700 block of East Jefferson and all across the street from his house on the south side of East Jefferson. Frierson built houses on two of the lots before selling them, but buyers of the other two lots built their own dwellings. Eventually, Frierson regained ownership of three of the four properties, as shown in the probate listing of his rental properties at the time of his death in June 1940.

E-30
707 East Jefferson Street
1924; Rockwell Lumber Company, builder

Later investors in the Fairview Addition included widow Mary Ellen Burnett and her school-teacher daughter Willetta Burnett, who bought lot fifty-five on East Jefferson in July 1924. In August, Mrs. Burnett signed an $1100 contract with Rockwell Lumber Company (successor to

Waxahachie Lumber Company) to build the bungalow style house at 707 East Jefferson. Mrs. Burnett was the widow of Robert Burnett, proprietor of the Richardson Hotel on East Main Street, which is where the couple was living when Robert died in 1924. From 1927-28 through 1939, city directories list Mrs. Burnett (her maiden name was Richardson) living at 707 East Jefferson and working as charwoman at the post office. She paid off her house debt in full in 1931.

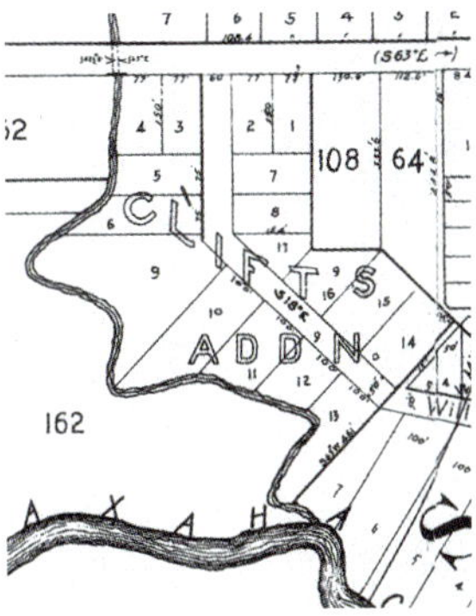

Detail from the 1896 city map showing Clift's Addition. *Courtesy Ellis County Museum.*

1985 photograph of a house, now demolished, that once stood on Will Street in Clift's Addition. *Texas Historical Commission National Register Collection, Photograph 1259-09, Portal to Texas History.*

E-31
Clift's Addition
Platted 1881

Will Street marks the location of Clift's Addition, the first named and platted addition in East Waxahachie. It was filed on November 14, 1881, in the Ellis County Clerk's office by white merchant S. A. Clift, who bought the oddly shaped eight-acre tract in June 1877 and began selling parcels even before officially registering the addition. Located on the south side of East Jefferson Street, the seventeen lots, also oddly shaped, bordered Will Street. The western boundary followed the meandering Spring Branch that flowed into Waxahachie Creek and placed the addition in what was locally referred to as "in the valley," an area that experienced serious flooding well within the memory of some Waxahachians today. Among Clift's early buyers were blacksmith Richard Sweatt, barber Robert Armstrong, and laborer Levi Reagor. Sweatt and his wife Sylvia were typical of the black families who purchased their first property here. In 1877, they bought a sixth of an acre for $40 cash, then bought an abutting lot for another $40 in November 1879 for $4 cash and six $6 notes. Like others, the Sweatts moved to higher ground as soon as they could afford it, buying their first property on East Main Street in 1883 and eventually purchasing the property that is now **509 Dr. Martin Luther King Jr. Blvd**.

Most houses in Clift's Addition, as well as others built along the creek, were one or two rooms, three at most, and all unlikely candidates for survival because of location and construction. One exception was a house that survived long enough to be recorded in the 1985 survey. Raised on posts, the one-and-a-half story, one-room frame dwelling with gable roof, and attached two-bay porch was a rare, intact example of the simplest houses found in Waxahachie's poorest neighborhoods.

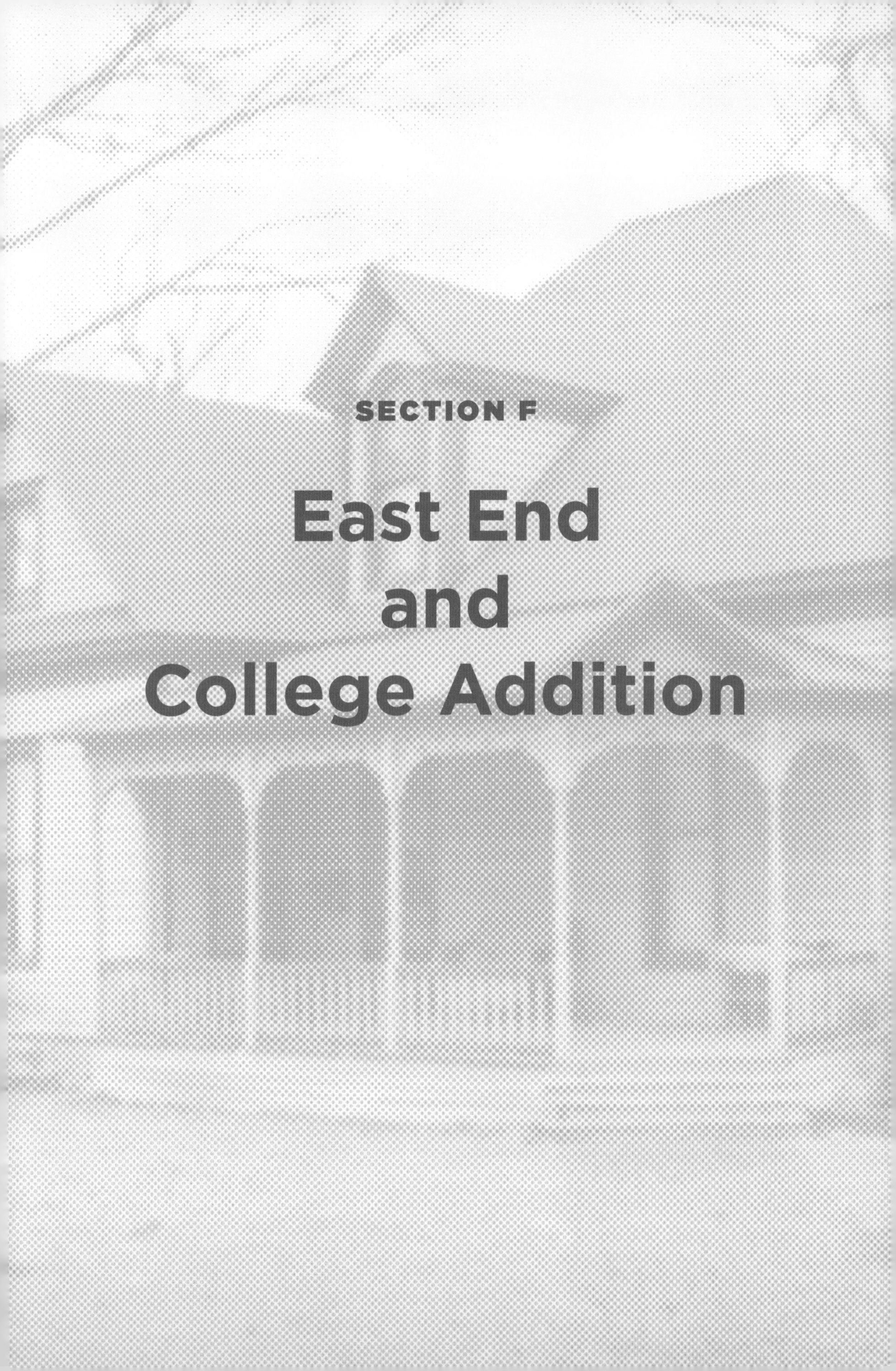

SECTION F

East End and College Addition

Detail from the 1886 Bird's Eye View showing Marvin College and surrounding streets. South College on this map later became East Marvin Avenue. West College became Brown Street. *Courtesy Ellis County Museum.*

INTRODUCTION

Schools and streetcars led to the early development in this section. Marvin College, named for Methodist Bishop Enoch M. Marvin, opened in 1871 and provided the earliest incentive to homebuilders in this area, while the public schools that followed in its place solidified the area's appeal for homeowners and renters. Brown and East Marvin Streets, as well as the blocks north and east of the school grounds, filled with houses. In 1891, streetcars in the form of the mule-drawn Lake Park Street Railway made the land at the eastern end of Marvin Avenue accessible for home sites and profitable for developers.

Although Marvin College itself struggled financially and barely lasted much over ten years, its name remains on the major streets of College and Marvin. "College" also survives in the historic names of multiple streets that continue to confuse anyone delving into early deeds and documents related to the area. The blame for that confusion lies with the unknown person who platted the College Addition that surrounded the Marvin College property. The 1886 bird's-eye view shows *four* College Streets in addition to the College Street we know today. It must have led to complications even then, for by the time of the 1896 Phillips & Hawkins map, South College had become Marvin, West College was Brown, and East College was Briggs. North College lasted longer, only becoming

An early 1880s photograph of the Marvin College campus with students and faculty decoratively arranged on the grounds. The central building with bell tower remained in use as part of the public school until demolished in 1921. *Courtesy Ellis County Museum.*

Built in 1904, the Park Public School building was constructed in front of the old central building of Marvin College. The third floor was removed in 1939. Architects: S. Wemyss Smith & Malcolm Moore. *Courtesy Ellis County Museum.*

Built with WPA and PWA funding in 1939 and sporting a curved Deco entry hall, this Marvin Elementary addition connected to the west side of the previous Park School building. It was demolished in 2000. Architects: LaRoche & Dahl. *Private Collection.*

Ross Street in 1920, when the city council renamed several streets that were originally separate but were later connected to streets with different names. With that 1920 change, order and reason finally settled the remaining College Street confusion, and the street that honored W. J. F. Ross, mayor from 1903 to 1905, became a few blocks longer.

Richard Vickery, one of the developers in the East End, built this house in 1886-87 on a large property outside the city limits facing the extension of East Marvin then named Vickery Street. It still stands at 1104 East Marvin Avenue. *Courtesy Ellis County Museum.*

In 1891, a group of developers with land at the east end of Marvin followed the example of Waxahachie's West End Addition of the late 1880s and joined together to charter a street railway company to provide transportation that would make their land more desirable for potential residents. As had been done in the West End, they also laid out a park, Lake Park, and built a park pavilion. The newspapers carried reports of the new developments to the east, as well as reports of an East-West rivalry (perhaps somewhat manufactured). In September 1891, the *Enterprise* published a poem "East and West Ends" that extolled the virtues of both areas, which was fitting since the author, Mrs. Elizabeth O. Dannelly, lived in the West End, and her oldest son, F. M. Dannelly, lived in the East End. The developers in the East End, however, did not join together to create a single platted addition, as had been done with the West End. The individual landowners platted their own subdivisions, and consequently Marvin Avenue east of Kaufman retains to this day a less unified appearance. Nonetheless, lots were sold and houses were built, including two of Waxahachie's most striking Queen Anne style examples, belonging to investors Richard Vickery (**1104 East Marvin**) and William F. Lewis (**1201 East Marvin**).

Beyond Coleman Street, East Marvin became even more free form as it merged with the surrounding rural countryside. It ends at Hackberry Street, where the rural landscape that many of East Marvin's houses replaced survives, for the moment. The small house at **200 Hackberry** preserves the appearance of a rural homestead with outbuildings, once common on the outskirts of town.

Lumberman William F. Lewis built this house at what is now 1201 East Marvin in 1887, where it still stands. Lewis chose a site across the street from his friend Richard Vickery's house. Both men were involved in developing and promoting property in the East End. Image from *Memorial and Biographical History of Ellis County, Texas (1892). Courtesy Ellis County Museum.*

This photograph shows the house at 501 East Marvin not long after it was built in 1911 for Tax Assessor Wathan G. Reagor and his family. Marvin was not paved at that time. *Courtesy Ellis County Museum.*

▶ *Map continues on next spread*

F-1 207 W. Marvin Ave.

F-2 119 W. Marvin Ave.

F-3 110 Brown St.
Marvin Elementary School

F-4 111 Brown St.

F-5 207 Brown St.

F-6 111 McKenzie St.

F-7 204 Brown St.

F-8 307 Brown St.

F-9 310 Brown St.

F-10 107 E. Ross St.

F-11 113 E. Ross St.

F-12 407 Brown St.

F-13 415 Brown St.

F-14 501 Dunn St.

F-15 501 Brown St.

F-16 505 Brown St.

F-17 521 Brown St.

F-18 609 Brown St.

F-19 617 Brown St.

F-20 618 Brown St.

F-21 802 Brown St.

F-22 206 E. Marvin Ave.

F-23 300 E. Marvin Ave.

F-24 303 E. Marvin Ave.

F-25 304 E. Marvin Ave.

F-26 309 E. Marvin Ave.

F-27 314 E. Marvin Ave.

F-28 317 E. Marvin Ave.

F-29 319 E. Marvin Ave.

F-30 320 E. Marvin Ave.

F-31 323 E. Marvin Ave.

F-32 310 Williams St.

F-33 407 Williams St.

F-34 411 Williams St.

F-35 415 Williams St.

F-36 600 Williams St.

F-37 604 Williams St.

F-38 611 Williams St.

F-39 614 Williams St.

F-40 401 E. Marvin Ave.

F-41 404 E. Marvin Ave.

F-42 411 E. Marvin Ave.

F-43 501 E. Marvin Ave.

F-44 504 E. Marvin Ave.
Saint Joseph Catholic Church (now Saint Joseph Chapel)

F-45 611 E. Marvin Ave.

F-46 613 E. Marvin Ave.

F-47 616 E. Marvin Ave.

F-48 617 E. Marvin Ave.

F-49 621 E. Marvin Ave.

◆ *F-50–F-68 on pp. 236-237*

◀ Map continues from previous spread

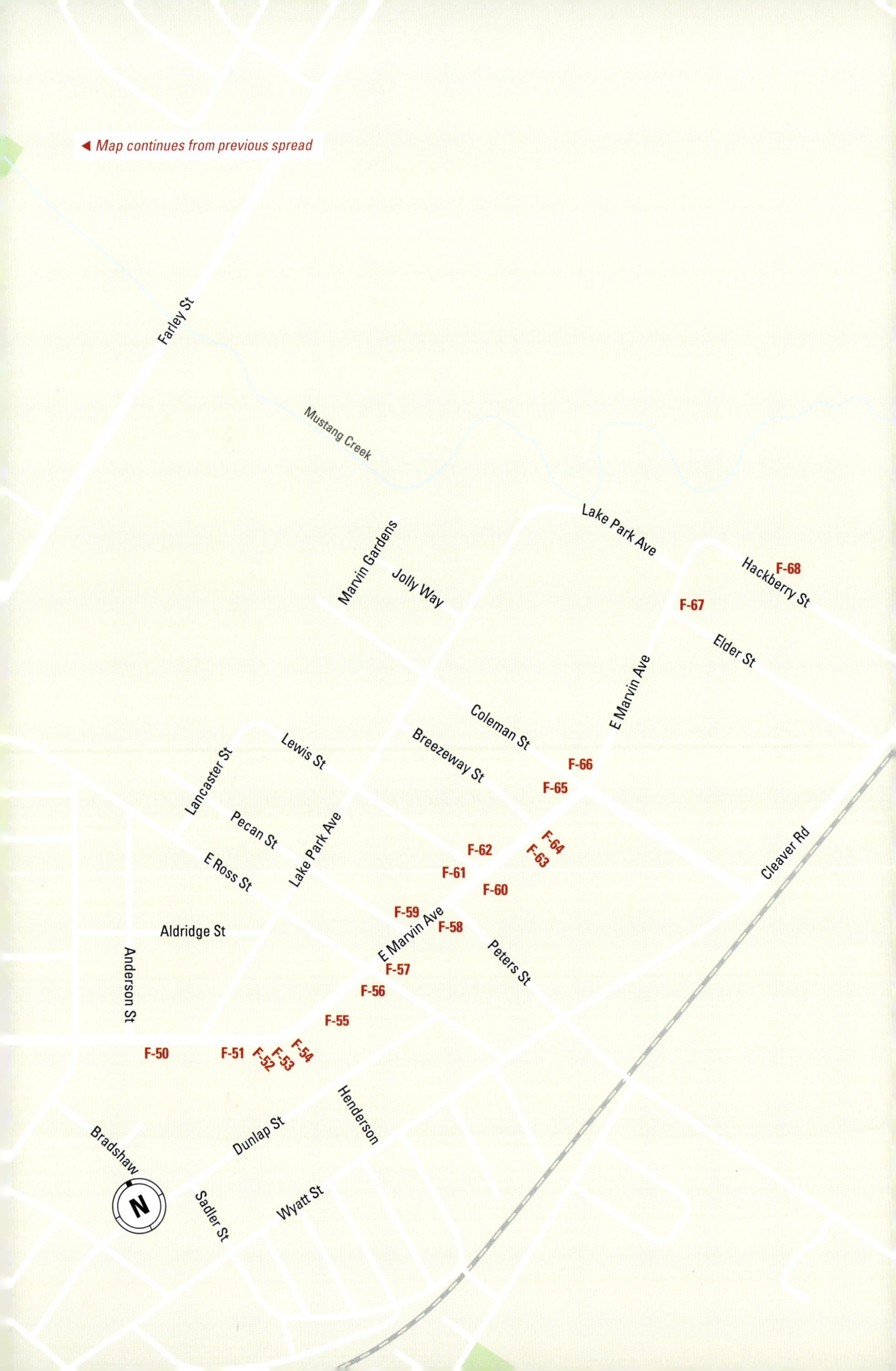

◆ F-1-F-49 on pp. 234-35

F-50 712 E. Marvin Ave.

F-51 806 E. Marvin Ave.

F-52 900 E. Marvin Ave.

F-53 902 E. Marvin Ave.

F-54 904 E. Marvin Ave.

F-55 912 E. Marvin Ave.

F-56 922 E. Marvin Ave.

F-57 1002 E. Marvin Ave.

F-58 1012 E. Marvin Ave.

F-59 1101 E. Marvin Ave.

F-60 1104 E. Marvin Ave.

F-61 1109 E. Marvin Ave.

F-62 1201 E. Marvin Ave.

F-63 1208 E. Marvin Ave.

F-64 1212 E. Marvin Ave.

F-65 1219 E. Marvin Ave.

F-66 1301 E. Marvin Ave.

F-67 1400 E. Marvin Ave.

F-68 200 Hackberry St.

F-1
207 West Marvin Avenue
1905

This compact one-story modified L-plan cottage was built between April 1905, when Thomas J. and Electra Bales bought the full corner lot on Marvin Avenue between Rogers and Monroe, and December 2 of that year, when they sold this small parcel to newlyweds Cole Y. and Clemmie Bailey for $1,500. Bales was a farmer and large landholder in Ellis County, while Cole was Mrs. Bales's son and a salesman in a Waxahachie dry goods store. The couple married in Italy (Texas) in June, so there was apparently a family plan for the property when the Baleses purchased the lot and the "Walker place," the large home of Dr. George Walker that was on the Rogers Street side. When built, the Baileys' house was surrounded by residences in all directions. Now adapted for a non-residential use, the house with its picket fence and manicured lawn holds its own on the eastern edge of the Ferris Avenue commercial strip.

F-2
119 West Marvin Avenue

The 1886 bird's-eye view of Waxahachie shows what appears to be a one-story L-plan house on this lot, which may form the core of this one-story hipped-roof cross-gable house. The narrow two-over-two double-hung windows facing North Rogers are typical of that era, but the wider one-over-one window in the front gable wing more likely dates to the early 1900s, when the house probably assumed its current form in a major redo after G. C. Groce bought it for rental property in 1901. The house behind this one, at 616 North Rogers, also had a hipped roof added over the original L-crossing of the two gable wings around the same time. The intent would have been to make them look like the modified L-plan cottages that were very popular at the time.

F-3
110 Brown Street
Marvin Elementary School
2001; SHW Group, architects;
Charter Builders, Inc., contractors

The present structure, designed by Dallas architects SHW Group, stands on the site of key educational institutions in Waxahachie's history. Marvin College was founded by the Methodist Episcopal Church and named for Bishop Enoch M. Marvin. E. W. Rogers donated the ten-acre site, and the first building, a two-story brick structure surmounted by a bell tower with mansard roof, was constructed in 1870 by E. H. Hoffman for a cost of $22,000. That building, with later appendages and ancillary buildings, along with students and teachers arrayed across the generous front grounds, was captured in a photograph from the early 1880s. Courses were offered for high school, preparatory, and college. As a private church institution, students were charged tuition, and some boarded there. Financial difficulties plagued the school throughout its existence, and in the 1880s, the City of Waxahachie used the buildings as a public school, eventually named Park School.

In 1904, a new three-story public school building was constructed in front of the central section of the old Marvin College and facing College Street, for a cost of $18,643. (S. Wemyss Smith & Malcolm Moore, architects; E. S. Boze and Frank Compton, contractors.) As the number of students grew with the city, the high school students were moved to a new building on Second Street in 1918, and in 1921, the old Marvin College building was demolished. In 1939, a WPA/PWA grant funded construction of a new primary school addition and removal of the third floor of the 1904 building. With a distinctive curved Deco entrance at the southwest corner, the new addition contained ten classrooms and was named Marvin Elementary. All buildings and additions were demolished in 2000 in preparation for the construction of this building. The applied portico (with no entrance) facing West Marvin was intended to recall the columned entrance of the 1904 building, as the projecting cylindrical rooms at the front corners were a nod to the 1939 building's corner entrance.

F-4
111 Brown Street
1902

When Margaret Curlin moved her family into this newly built house late in 1902, it was in a row of substantial houses lining Brown Street and overlooking Park School, Waxahachie's public school. Mrs. Curlin's house had all the characteristics of the two-story Queen Anne style modified L-plan house, with a hipped roof and lower cross gables, steeply pitched roof of irregular shape, front-facing gable, asymmetrical façade, and a one-story partial-width front porch extending along one side. Originally, the house exhibited more decorative detailing than seen today—the patterned shingles on the front gable and the scalloped trim and drop finials on the upper porch are vestiges of that—but it was always restrained.

It was an appropriately respectable and fashionably neutral house for Mrs. Curlin, who may have come to Waxahachie as a newcomer in August 1902, but whose family's credentials and accomplishments immediately placed her in good standing. Born Margaret Emma Calvert in Lovelaceville, Kentucky, her father, Rev. L. N. Calvert, was a descendant of the Baltimore Calverts and minister of the Cumberland Presbyterian Church. She was a student at the Union City (Tennessee) Seminary for four years and, in 1873 at age seventeen, married Union City school superintendent J. V. Curlin. By 1880, the Curlins had moved to Clarksburg, Missouri, where J. V. taught school. The 1900 Census finds the couple and their five children living in Lufkin, Texas, where he is a druggist and the three oldest children, all girls, are teaching school. Mrs. Curlin was left a widow in February 1902. By the end of the year, she had moved her family to Waxahachie, purchased property, built a house, and enrolled her two youngest children in Trinity University. Her obituary in December 1934 noted that they all "became citizens and workers in the business, educational and religious life of Waxahachie." Two daughters are remembered for their contributions in education: Berta Curlin was recognized as "a prominent Texas educator" when she died in 1962; Lottie Curlin Hood is remembered for her work as director of Sims Library.

F-5
207 Brown Street
c. 1885

This house is one of three one-story L-plan dwellings on the south end of Brown—the others being 311 and 412 Brown. All have experienced some alterations in architectural detailing—e.g., replacement windows or doors, porch trim, etc.—but all retain the basic form on the street façade. It can be difficult to date these houses exactly, because the form was extremely popular for a period extending from circa 1875 into the early twentieth century. This house was probably built circa 1885 after T. J. and H. N. Jenkins bought the property (in a sale of multiple tracts), and is the structure that T. J. Jenkins offered for sale on "terms reasonable or [in] exchange for farmland" in September 1887, though it could have been built around 1900 as a rental property with three rooms and a foyer. The house originally stood in the middle of the lot, but was moved to its present spot in 1962 to make room for a new brick neighbor on the south side. Two gable-end additions on the rear combined with unusual angles and corners in the interior center hall are evidence that the house experienced numerous enlargements and changes.

F-6
111 McKenzie Street
1923; A. A. Few & Son, builder

Noah Franklin Vantreese and his wife Cordelia contracted with A. A. Few & Son in August of 1923 to build this "frame Airplane Bungalow house . . . with four rooms below, with bath and front porch and one room above. . . ." It appears that in the ensuing years, part of the front porch was enclosed to provide another room. The Craftsman style design with its staggered three front gables of the porch, house, and second-floor "airplane" bedroom is similar to plan no. 10378 published in a Ye Planry house catalogue of the early 1920s. Noah was born in Tennessee in 1882 and came to Texas with his family in 1897. He learned to drive electric streetcars in Dallas and graduated to Interurban cars after three years. He and his wife were living in Waxahachie on McKenzie Street by the time of the 1920 Census, and evidently liked the location enough to build this house and remain here until Noah's death in 1969. After thirty-four years as motorman of the Texas Electric Interurban Dallas-Waco route, Noah retired on the last day of that interurban service, December 31, 1948.

F-7
204 Brown Street
c. 1913

By the time the 1914 Sanborn maps were published, Waxahachie could boast of having at least two imposing examples of two-story pyramidal houses with two-story wraparound porches. The one that Story E. Fowler built in 1910 at 801 West Main no longer exists, but this one, built by Patrick (Pat) and Lucy Witten, remains a well-preserved example of the relatively uncommon house type. One-story pyramidal houses were popular in Waxahachie at the time, with several examples on Brown Street, including **501 Brown**. The pyramidal roof form that dominates such one-story examples tends to recede in importance here, overpowered by the straightforward geometric repetition of porch supports and balustrades crowned by the triangular dormer gable. The decorative details that stand out in one-story examples, including the entrance door with sidelights and patterned shingles on the porch and the dormer gable, can be found here, but you have to look closely. This house is all about the porches, and the luxury of that extensive, protected outdoor living space. The July 1910 *Enterprise* notice about Mr. Fowler's new house made sure to mention the unusual 150 feet of "double story galleries," which covered the front and east side of the house. Mr. Witten surpassed even that extravagance when his porches wrapped around three sides of his house—front, south side, and back.

The exact construction date of this house is uncertain, but it was built sometime between January 1909, when the Wittens bought the lot with a one-story house, and 1914, when the Sanborn maps recorded the footprint of the new house. One possibility is 1913, when the city directory lists the family residing around the corner on McKenzie Street, where they might have moved while the new house was being built. Born in 1868, and a lifetime resident of Ellis County, Pat Witten was a prominent farmer and stockman. He and his wife remained in their grand home until they died—Pat in 1950 and Lucy in 1964.

F-8
307 Brown Street
1902; D. D. Pittman, contractor

In February 1895, tax collector R. H. Connally and his wife Josephine bought this property for $1,300, an amount that indicates a house was on the lot—the same house where the Connallys and seven of their eight children were living in 1900. On March 14, 1902, the *Enterprise* reported that Connally (now a banker) had moved his family to another house in the neighborhood, "torn out and moved away" his old residence, and was building an eight-room, two-story house "with all modern improvements, including electric lighting, hot and cold water baths and sanitary conveniences." As a "believer in home industries," he was using only local talent to design and build the house and, "as far as practical," all Texas materials in its construction. By April 11, when the residence "was rapidly nearing completion," contractor D. D. Pittman gave the reporter a tour of the house which was "built after the French style of architecture, the porches being finished in Colonial style."

The design for the house, in all probability, started with plans and elevations that the Connallys saw in a publication such as *Farm and Ranch*, published by the Texas Farm and Ranch Publishing Company of Dallas. In fact, the design for a slightly larger and very similar house that appeared in the March 23, 1901, issue seems a likely source. The Connallys would have directly contacted E. H. Silven, the Dallas architect for all the *Farm and Ranch* published plans, who in turn would have worked with the couple and contractor Pittman to finalize the design. The newspaper also reported that Jolesch & Chaska, a local dry goods emporium, was chosen from a number of competing firms from other cities to furnish "the carpets, mattings, curtains, etc."

The Connallys sold the property in 1909 and moved to a smaller house at **209 Williams Street**. In 1912, druggist and manager of the Waxahachie Medicine Company

John S. Herring and his wife Lenora bought the house and lived here with their four children until 1922, after which it became rental property and was subjected over the years to major interior and exterior alterations, including removal of the tower. Its return to single family use began in 1987, and subsequent renovations included reconstruction of the tower.

The L-plan house next door, at 311 Brown, was probably built by attorney O. H. Chapman and his wife Loretta shortly after acquiring the lot for $350 in March 1895. The Chapmans declared this to be their homestead in October 1903, but by 1907 they were renting it and living at another address. In 1910 they sold the property to John D. and Elizabeth Keys, both of whom were from old Waxahachie families. Elizabeth's paternal grandparents were William and Elizabeth Payne, who settled in Waxahachie in 1873 on "the old Payne homestead" at **111 Williams**. According to John's 1942 obituary, his parents moved from Arkansas to Waxahachie in 1869, when he was three months old. In 1908, John became a partner in Shive & Keys, the "fuel and feed" business that sold coal, wood, and feed from its sizeable complex located on the south end of downtown at **441 South College**.

F-9
310 Brown Street
1905-06

House painter Colbey C. Elkin and his family moved to Waxahachie sometime between June 1900, when they were residents of nearby Italy, and fall 1905, when they bought this lot in November for $300. It is another instance of "buy and build," because in July 1906, the Elkins sold this newly constructed house for $2,100, which gave them the cash to start their trek through the local housing market. Although similar in basic form to other pyramidal cottages with a partial porch, the L-shape porch on this house is more typical of the earlier modified L-plan house type. The Elkin house has other details of note including the fluted Doric porch columns, an entrance door with sidelights (rather than just a single door), and the contrasting use of narrow 117/121 siding on the main façade with wider siding to define the wainscoting, porch railing, and entablature. The dormer is the only centered element on the façade. The house had seven owners from 1906 to 1923, when Paul R. Bird, manager of the Waxahachie Abstract Company, bought it and lived here until selling the property in 1944.

F-10
107 East Ross Street
1902; W. B. (Bird) Forrest, builder

This house originally stood around the corner, facing Brown Street. Farmer J. H. Gregory built it in September 1902, when he moved into town from the Howard community to enable his children to attend Waxahachie's schools. The newspapers noted his purchase and contract for construction of a "six-room cottage" only days after Gregory purchased the property on September 4, 1902. On October 17, the *Enterprise* reported that local builder Bird Forrest completed Gregory's cottage. The distinctive polygonal dormer projecting from the center of the steep hipped roof may have been inspired by a design by mail-order architect George F. Barber that was published in the February 1901 issue of Barber's magazine *American Homes*.

Three years after building this house, Gregory sold it to another farmer, George Washington Stout, and built a new home on West Marvin for his family. Stout and his wife stayed here until their deaths. When he died in 1931 at the age of eighty-three, the paper reported that he was one of the oldest natives in Ellis County, but also made a point of noting that he spent much time with his "many friends" and was "always jolly and enjoying their companionship." In 1947, owner Exline Martin, a civil engineer, moved the house to its current location facing East Ross on the back of his lot, in order to build a new brick duplex for himself. The Martins then used this house as rental property. When Exline died in 1966, the *Dallas Morning News* noted that he had served as Ellis County's engineer and surveyor since 1937.

F-11
113 East Ross Street
c. 1893

Elijah S. (E. S.) Boze was one of Waxahachie's most prolific builders of the late nineteenth and early twentieth centuries, and, although there is no documentation that he built this house, he appears to have lived here longer than in any other house in town, and his family remained here after he moved to Oklahoma sometime after 1913. He first appears at this location in a 1902 *Daily Light* directory of telephone listings. That the cross street at this corner bears his name probably reflects his ownership of multiple lots in the area. The modified L-plan form of the house and other details would indicate a construction date of sometime in the 1890s, but since the jig sawn porch ornaments are the same as many of those on the 1893 Ed Williams house at **412 West Marvin**, the more specific estimate of c. 1893 is possible.

Boze arrived in Waxahachie in the early 1890s and built homes, commercial buildings, and institutional buildings in town and beyond. Although he does not appear to have studied architecture or apprenticed with an architect, he supplied designs for many of his projects and advertised as an "architect and builder" in the newspaper and in the 1907 city directory. He may have designed the outstanding 1902 Chautauqua building (**C-104**) in Getzendaner Memorial Park, and he definitely was responsible for its construction. Several of the houses that he built have survived, as has the Sims-Thomson Garage (**300 West Main**), but the Methodist Church on College Street and the Park School on West Marvin were demolished. His departure from town may have been connected to bankruptcy. In 1916 some of his property on this block was auctioned off by his trustee. The bankruptcy could have resulted from overextending on his construction projects, or some of his investments may have gone bad. (He was a major investor in the Waxahachie Cement Stone Manufacturing Company, which entered bankruptcy around this time.) By the time of the 1920 Census he was living in Ardmore, Oklahoma, while his wife Maggie was still in Waxahachie at this house, and listing herself as a widow. The separation remained permanent, and he remarried, though she did not.

F-12
407 Brown Street
1903; W. B. (Bird) Forrest and H. W. Madson, builders

Two weeks after buying this lot in February 1903, Lon Eagle and his wife Mary Ellen (Nelle) Pryor Eagle contracted with W. B. (Bird) Forrest and H. W. Madson to build, in two months, a five-room frame house "with hall, and porches," for $1,100. Forrest provided the plans and specifications for the modified L-plan dwelling. The central hipped roof is almost indiscernible from the street façade, making it easy to mistake the house for an L-plan. The recessed, second front-facing gable rising above the attached porch is not a common feature on this house type in Waxahachie. When the Eagles divorced in 1909, Nelle took back her maiden name and assumed the house note. In 1910, she sold the house for $1,400 to Effie Middleton, another "feme sole" (as they were referred to in legal documents), and it became rental property.

F-13
415 Brown Street
1903; William L. Callens, builder

Of the many modified L-plan cottages built in Waxahachie, this house is among the elite grouping with corner towers and Queen Anne embellishments. Built in

1903, it was one of several real estate investments made by farmer and carpenter Will Callens when he moved with his wife Bessie and young son from their Red Oak Creek farm to Waxahachie at the end of 1902. Callens's first purchase was a house just one block to the north, where the family lived while he was building this house and probably working other jobs. In April 1906, the *Enterprise* reported that Callens had "recently swapped" houses with T. S. Middleton, the deeds disclosing that the deal also included a monetary exchange.

As with the Callenses, it was Waxahachie schools that enticed the Middletons to move into town in 1903. Middleton gave up farming around 1910 and pursued other trades, including retail grocer and owner of the downtown "Pop Corn Stand." After he died in 1936 at age seventy-eight, his widow Nettie lived here another twenty years. Probably sometime during the 1960s, the house was partitioned into two apartments and used as rental property. When George and Susan Susat bought the property in 1986, there were still two kitchens in the house. The house retains many of its original features such as the finial-topped tower, fish-scale shingles on the gable ends, wood sash double-hung windows with 1/1 lights, and dentiling under the porch and tower eaves. The small window on the porch façade provides light for the narrow tower staircase tucked in the corner of the entrance hall. During their renovation, the Susats discovered two inscriptions of note: a shipping label dated 1903 on the back of a mantel and an attic board inscribed "3/28/17 Sewell Electric" in pencil, the latter indicating improvements made by the Middletons.

F-14
501 Dunn Street
1904; S. J. Erwin, architect and builder

As part of the Williams Addition, platted in 1890, the west side of Dunn Street between Marvin and Sycamore is characterized by smaller square blocks and more frequent cross streets than on the east side of the street. Contractor and builder Stonewall Jackson (S. J.) Erwin built this one-story L-plan house in 1904, a year after moving with his family to Waxahachie from Dallas. The house itself became an advertisement of his abilities, and the *Daily Light* aided his publicity when it mentioned his "quite an attractive home" in June 1904. Like many local builders, he sold this house not long after he built it and moved on to another. In all likelihood, Erwin drew the plans for this house, with its up-to-date pediment above the entrance bay of the porch and simple Doric columns. The steeply pitched hipped roof of a rear wing continues the slope of the main side-gable roof. Erwin was never able to work exclusively as an architect, but he frequently advertised his abilities as a designer, as well as a builder, in the *Daily Light*. Additional examples of his design work that were recorded in local mechanics' liens included **301 East University**, built in 1904, and **218 Virginia**, built in 1915. His 1927 obituary ignored his many building projects and described him solely as an architect.

Deed records indicate that the small L-plan house across the street to the south (415 Dunn) probably was built around 1894 by J. H. Grimes. In 1904, J. Osgood Ray and his family were living there, and according to the *Daily Light*, their property included "one of the prettiest orchards, berry patch and flower gardens in that section of the city."

F-15
501 Brown Street
1911

In April 1911, J. P. and Angie Fleming bought all of Lot 1 in this block on the northern edge of Waxahachie. They split the lot in half and sold the corner half to his seventy-three-year old widowed mother, Susan A. Fleming, who built one of the most fashionable moderately sized house types at the time—the pyramidal house. Mrs. Fleming's residence, which remains one of the most intact examples of the type in Waxahachie, displays all the defining characteristics: hipped roof, square shape, balanced façade, single entrance door with transom and sidelights, columned front porch, and centered "Waxahachie dormer." Mrs. Fleming lived in her house until 1919, when she sold it to retired farmer J. V. Brown and moved to Dallas, where she lived with a son until she died at age ninety in 1928.

F-16
505 Brown Street
1923; W. B. and C. C. Ramsey, builders

In April 1923 and one year after purchasing the lot, bookkeeper Charley Middleton and his wife Mildred contracted W. B. and C. C. Ramsey to build this one-story bungalow with wide, low-slung double gables for $5,500. As described in the mechanic's lien, the plan was a typical five-room bungalow—the five rooms being living and dining rooms, kitchen, and two bedrooms—plus a bathroom, hall, breakfast room, and sleeping and front porches that were also specified in the lien. Adding to the cost were not-so-typical features for a small bungalow: the brick veneer and porte cochère, and a pergola that has disappeared. The latter shaded the triple windows and would have been covered, as was the style, with vines planted by the Middletons. The couple sold the house in 1937.

F-17
521 Brown Street
c. 1905

The orientation of this curious little house with its narrow end fronting the primary street and a minimal L-shaped porch on the southeast corner is more typical of houses built on long, narrow lots in denser urban settings. With an alleyway on the south and open space on the north, it is easier to see the complicated hipped and cross-gabled roofing system as well as the back wing that was common to most small houses.

From 1895 through 1900, this property changed owners four times before being purchased for $800 by farmer John McElroy and his wife Leila in December 1900. The amount indicates that the McElroys started with a smaller house that they replaced or rebuilt around 1905, a date based on the similarity of this house to other houses built during the years 1904-1906. The McElroys raised their family here, which at the time of the 1910 Census included six children, ages two to sixteen. John died seven years later. In fall 1933, all six children joined their mother in contracting builder O. B. Bennett to make improvements to their childhood home that included leveling, reroofing, painting two coats both inside and out, repairing the front porch, repapering all the rooms, and building kitchen cabinets. It was a worthwhile investment—Mrs. McElroy lived here until she died in 1949.

F-18
609 Brown Street
1911; A. N. Guthrie, builder

In 1900, twenty-two-year old John C. Verheyden was living and working, along with four siblings, on his parents' farm in Ellis County. One year later, he married Lottie Della Steele. By April 1910, when the Census was taken, he was farming and living on rented land with his wife and two young sons. But by summer 1911, the Verheydens had joined the stream of farm families moving into town, John advertising in late July in the *Daily Light* that he had purchased the Page tailoring and pressing shop on College Street and with Mr. Page's help would guarantee the shop's work.

The couple bought this lot on November 2, and four days later, contracted for $2,000 with A. N. Guthrie to build their first town residence according to plans and specifications that they provided, which means they probably had selected it from a plan book. Once finished—in thirty days—their six-room pyramidal cottage joined other examples of the popular house type already along the street. John Verheyden either did not like the tailoring business or was not successful, for he sold this house eighteen months later and by 1918 was listed once again as a farmer. In 1920, Richmond Garrett, a retired farmer, purchased the property. Waxahachians still identify the house with the Garrett family.

F-19
617 Brown Street
1905; E. S. Boze, builder

The story of this house and its neighbor at 615 Brown actually begins on East Marvin where, in 1900, Sarah Wilkins, her husband marble dealer Carson Wilkins, and their one-year-old daughter were living with her parents, tombstone salesman John T. Robinson and his wife Martha. Among the Robinsons' real estate investments was this corner lot, which they sold to the Wilkinses in March 1905. The young couple immediately contracted with E. S. Boze, one of the town's busiest builders, to build this modified L-plan dwelling. With its interior brick chimney, L-shaped porch, turned porch columns, and one-over-one sash windows, it is one of the most intact small, unadorned examples of the house type in town. It is also one of the few Waxahachie houses covered with narrow 117/121 siding.

In 1906, the Robinsons bought the vacant lot on the south side of their daughter's residence and built a similar house. In 1908 the Wilkinses sold their house and moved back to East Marvin, but five years later, they bought 615 Brown from Sarah's parents, who had left Waxahachie. In 1916 the Wilkinses signed a $500 contract for H. D. Rankin "to make improvements" to 615 Brown, which meant it was given its distinctive bungalow appearance with the double front gables, projecting porch gable, and tapered, paneled columns planted on brick supports. The L-shaped porch is a clue to its earlier house form. The Wilkins family remained at 615 Brown, and Carson worked at the Waxahachie Marble and Granite Co. for decades.

F-20
618 Brown Street
c. 1913

At first glance, it is obvious that *something*, in addition to its generous proportions, separates this pyramidal cottage from other similar houses in Waxahachie. That something is the roof. It is steeper and higher than roofs on other pyramidal cottages, a feature accentuated further by the vertically seamed tin roof presently on the building. Otherwise, the pyramidal cottage that widow Cora Webb built shortly after buying this property in June 1913 is a typical example with its "Waxahachie dormer," inset porch, and single entrance door with sidelights. The house is most identified with Mrs. Webb's son, photographer James Massie Webb, who opened his Webb Studio in downtown Waxahachie in 1916. "Massie," as he was known, photographed the town and its residents for decades; many remember his taking their annual school pictures through the early 1960s. He lived here until his death in 1969.

F-21
802 Brown Street
1899

When insurance agent Charles A. Kirksey bought this property in April 1896, it included 110 acres, along with a house and multiple farm buildings, on the northern outskirts of town. For many years it was believed that this house was built in 1893, as documented in an 1893 mechanic's lien. However, several obscure news items found not long ago in the *Waxahachie Enterprise* reveal that Kirksey and his wife Myra actually built this house in 1899, suggesting that the earlier house may have burned or that the Kirkseys simply wanted a newer house. On September 22, the paper reported that Kirksey let the contract for "a handsome two-story residence on the city end of his farm on north Brown," and by October 13 his "suburban palace is being pushed to completion." A Kirksey family photograph taken in the early 1900s shows the house surrounded by farmland. The landscape has totally changed in the ensuing years, but the house remains amazingly intact.

Although the simple porch columns and balustrade look forward to Colonial Revival styles gaining popularity at the time, the patterned shingles in the front and side gables and the scroll-sawn and turned decoration at the corner eaves of the three-sided bays represent the Queen Anne style that was on its way out. In addition to the front and side cross-gables of a standard modified L-plan house, two more gables extend from the hipped central roof.

In 1905, the Kirkseys sold eighty acres that included the house. Gradually, a series of sales whittled the property to just five acres when it was bought by F. O. and LaVena Weldon in 1937. The Weldons undertook modernizing the dilapidated house and remaining farm structures. Mrs. Weldon is remembered today for what was, at the time, a unique organic garden she planted in the late 1950s. When lawyer-son Fred and his wife Betty became owners in 1986, their multi-year restoration project of the house to its late nineteenth-century character reflected the national shift in attitude from modernization to preservation of historic buildings.

F-22
206 East Marvin Avenue
1894

For over forty-five years, this small, unpretentious L-plan house was home to the Reymuller family. Both F. P. Reymuller and wife Jeanette were brought to America by Prussian-born parents who settled in St. Louis, which is where the couple married in January 1865, the same month that F. P. entered the Union army. In spring 1876, the Reymullers, now parents of a son and two daughters, followed the call to "come to Texas" and migrated to Waxahachie, where F. P. advertised as a "house and sign painter" in the *Enterprise*. The Reymullers bought this lot for $100 in November 1882 and built the house where they lived while F. P. plied his "artistic brush" to the town's buildings and signs well into the 1890s. Son W. B., known as Bismarck, joined the business, which received frequent praise in the local newspaper, including the March 30, 1894, note that F. P. "had moved into his new residence on Marvin Avenue." Late in 1898, Bismarck opened a paint and wallpaper store at the corner of College and Water Streets which, after his father's death in 1905, he moved to the west side of the square and advertised as the "exclusive dealer" in wallpapers, paints, oils, glass, etc. The store remained a business icon until Bismarck's death in 1935. Bismarck, like his sisters, never married and always lived at this address (sometimes with boarders). All three siblings died between 1935 and 1939. The Marvin Avenue façade of the Reymullers' 1894 house has changed little over the years. Multiple rear additions have been kept in scale with the original one-story structure.

F-23
300 East Marvin Avenue
1896; D. A. Cook & Co., builder

The year 1896 was an eventful year for twenty-five-year-old Norman Jett Thomas, bookkeeper for the M. T. Jones Lumber Company. In late May, the *Enterprise* reported that Jett (as he was called) and his bride Ada had returned from their bridal tour through southwest Texas and Mexico, and were living in a boarding house on College Street. On June 19, the couple purchased this corner property and on August 13, contracted D. A. Cook & Co. to build, for $2,000, a one-story six-room frame house and a two-story barn within forty-five days. The tapered square porch columns are not original and may have been an attempt to "update" the façade circa 1906. In addition to his getting married and building a stylish hipped roof cross-gable cottage, 1896 was important for Jett professionally. After buying the shares of bankrupt lumberyard stockholder William F. Lewis, Jett was named manager of the M. T. Jones Waxahachie office in the fall. Eight years later, he parlayed that investment into ownership of the newly named Waxahachie Lumber Company when M. T. Jones sold out. In 1908, the Thomases sold this house. The family of John E. and Lulu McWhorter, owners of the Waxahachie Steam Laundry, resided here from 1913 through the late 1920s.

F-24
303 East Marvin Avenue
1933; Fin Garvin, builder

In 2012, when new owners Sam and Laura Beth Anderson began renovating their picturesque "cottage of English influence" at 303 East Marvin, they found artifacts and recycled materials that helped piece together the history of the house. The most important find was a wall board signed "Fin Garvin April 14, 1933 Contractor." Garvin was an active Waxahachie builder who worked in Waxahachie from the 1920s through the 1950s. The date with Garvin's signature coincided with a December 15, 1932 deed in which owner and banker J. Scott Rutherford transferred the property to his wife Katie Marchbanks Rutherford, who invested $3,650 from her own estate "in a dwelling house to be erected on said premises." When Scott's father, realtor M. D. Rutherford, bought the property in 1919, a large c. 1885 Victorian house was on the site which, when built, was just to the east of Marvin College. It was that structure that the younger Rutherfords replaced with this modest Tudor Revival cottage. The asymmetrical massing, steeply pitched front facing gable, small entry porch, and paired multiple-pane windows are typical of the style that was popular during the 1920s and the 1930s. Notable interior features include a wood ceiling in the living room and a signed Batchelder fireplace, the tiles produced in the California studio of Ernest A. Batchelder, a leader in the American Arts and Crafts Movement.

F-25
304 East Marvin Avenue
1900

Separated by four years in construction dates, this house and its neighbor at **300 East Marvin** share the same basic house form—a hipped-roof cross-gable cottage with partial porch. Although both houses have experienced alterations such as synthetic siding and window replacements, the similarities and differences between the original structures are still obvious. This house, with its clipped gable dormer, sunburst motif and shingles in the gable end, jig-sawn corner brackets on the front-projecting wing, and turned wood porch supports, is the most elaborately detailed. Bank cashier William E. Hipp was apparently planning ahead when he acquired the first piece of this property in 1897. Two years later, on May 3, 1899, he married Jennie Cole, daughter of real estate agent T. J. Cole, who lived at **309 East Marvin** in what was then an imposing Victorian residence. Exactly one year later, the *Enterprise* reported that Will Hipp's new home—"one of the prettiest cottages in the city"— would soon be ready for occupancy. The young couple had only to move across the street because, according to the June 1900 Census, they were living in her parents' household along with three brothers and three sisters. The Hipps lived here for only a few years before selling the property in October 1905 to Prof. Walter L. Acker, superintendent of Waxahachie's public schools from 1898 to 1909. Prof. Acker, who was active in the Waxahachie Masonic Lodge, combined his Masonic and educational interests when he became superintendent of the Masonic Orphans Home and School in Fort Worth in 1914.

The square hipped-roof one-story house next door at 308 East Marvin was built in 1910 for another daughter of T. J. Cole, Davella Cole Carothers. After she married insurance agent Sam Carothers in 1906, they lived across the street, at **309 East Marvin**, with her parents, until the elder Coles purchased this lot for them in December 1909, and the house was built. By 1920, the Carothers had moved to Dallas, and their East Marvin house was owned by another insurance and real estate agent, John V. Singleton, and his wife Pauline Bauder. In the mid-1930s, the Singletons moved to Austin, then to Houston, but, like many Waxahachie natives who left, they asked to be returned to their hometown for burial in the City Cemetery—she in 1949 and he in 1971.

F-26
309 East Marvin Avenue
1917 or early 1920s

Although this house appears to be a Craftsman style bungalow, parts of a two-story 1895 house remain behind the broad expanse of the side gable roof and the inset front porch. Some of the alterations may date to either 1917 or the early 1920s, according to previous owners, when a fire may have damaged the second story of the house. (Neither the local papers or mechanics' liens have documented the fire or a redo during that period.) The Sanborn maps continue to show a wraparound porch only on the right side through 1959, which would indicate that the current porch that stretches across the entire façade was built after that date. The 1895 house was built for real estate agent T. J. Cole and his wife Emma by local builder E. H. Griffin according to plans by Dallas architects Flanders & Moad, probably in a Queen Anne style. The interior still features many original details and proportions, but few hints remain visible on the exterior.

When the Coles's daughter Jennie married banker William E. Hipp in 1899, the couple lived here until their house across the street (**304 East Marvin**) was completed the next year. When Jennie died in 1910, Will and their four young children moved back in with the Coles for a couple of years until Will built a bungalow next door (311 East Marvin) for his family. The following year, Will left banking for the new field of automobile sales and did very well after becoming the local Buick dealer in 1914. He and his family transferred back to the familiar, bigger house in 1917, after Emma Cole died and T. J. moved to Dallas. When the children were grown, Will married Maude Patrick in 1923 and moved into the large Patrick family house (**233 Patrick**), but this house remained in the family with his son Tom W. and wife Lucie living here. Will moved back here with them when Maude died in 1934, and remained until his death in 1948. The house remained in the Hipp family until the 1970s, but it was divided into three apartments. Jim and Becky Kaufman purchased it in 1976 and restored it to a single-family dwelling.

F-27
314 East Marvin Avenue
1911; J. R. McCanless, builder
1938; O. B. Bennett, builder

Married on October 16, 1911, Lynn and Grace Chastain Lasswell moved into their new house sometime in 1912. Lynn's parents, who lived on the adjacent corner lot, had given the property to Lynn one week before his marriage. Originally, the younger Lasswells' house was a near duplicate of the corner house across the street at **323 East Marvin**. Lynn moved from banking to insurance in 1929, and both he and Grace were prominent in civic affairs. By June 1938, the couple was ready for a larger, more up-to-date residence, but rather than moving to a newer part of town where many of their contemporaries lived, the Lasswells chose to remain on East Marvin and hired one of Waxahachie's busiest contractors, O. B. Bennett, to remodel the residence with both interior and exterior alterations and additions. The corner porch with its low-slung roofline is a remnant of the earlier façade. The house remained in the Lasswell family until 1999. Across the street at 311 East Marvin, E. M. and Dessa Clayton similarly updated their house soon after purchasing it in 1938.

F-28
317 East Marvin Avenue
1892; Barnes & McDuffie, builders

Dry goods merchant George H. Alderman and his wife Emma acquired this lot and the one to the east in January 1887, shortly after they moved to Waxahachie. Apparently, there was a house on the property, as the *Enterprise* reported in August that George was "remodeling" and "adding valuable improvements" to his residence. In February 1892, that house burned, and the following August the couple contracted Barnes & McDuffie to build a "one story frame house" for $1,500 on the west lot. With its late-nineteenth-century massing and exceptional detailing, this house is one of the best local examples of the modified L-plan house, the most popular regional house type of the period. Local newspapers document that the Aldermans loved to entertain and did so frequently. According to the 1910 Census, George was an insurance agent (he pursued several businesses) and both daughters worked—Rosa was a cashier in a dry goods store, and Henry taught school. (Her name was spelled "Henri" on some documents, but "Henry" was carved into her tombstone.) On July 7, 1913, George died unexpectedly at age fifty-nine. Three weeks later, his widow and two daughters signed an agreement to build a two-story house for $1,800 on the east lot, **319 East Marvin**.

F-29
319 East Marvin Avenue
1913; Dunaway Brothers, builders

Only three weeks after George H. Alderman, owner of **317 East Marvin** next door, died in 1913, his wife and two daughters began construction of a new house on this lot, which the family already owned. Their reasons were probably more than just wanting a more up-to-date, fashionable residence. Building a larger, two-story house enabled them to take in lodgers, not an unusual income-producing arrangement for widows at the time. In 1920, there were five people renting rooms: a chiropractor, his wife and small child, and a minister and his wife, who was a teacher. The newspaper articles document that running a boarding house did not curtail the Alderman women's tradition of frequent and gracious entertaining. They remained in the house until they died—Mrs. Alderman in 1941, Rosa in 1978, and Henry in 1981. The Alderman estate gave a collection of family photographs, china, and other items to the Ellis County Museum.

F-30
320 East Marvin Avenue
1899

On September 22, 1899, the *Enterprise* reported that Ellis County Clerk Allen Lasswell was about to begin building a "beautiful home" on the large lot at the corner of East College (now East Marvin) and Williams Streets. It was the second house that Lasswell and his wife Annie built since moving from Bosque County to Waxahachie in 1889, when they were in their late twenties. Much had transpired for the Lasswells during those interim ten years: Allen worked for an abstract company before becoming a "regularly installed deputy county clerk" by April 1891; in fall 1890, they bought two lots and built their first house just north of this location on Williams Street. Their second son was born in 1892; in late 1895, they bought this property; and in 1899, not only did they build this house, but Allen was elected county clerk. Allen then served as Waxahachie's mayor in 1908-1911. After his death in 1923, the property was bought by Mrs. J. H. Chapman. With its steeply pitched center hipped roof, tall chimneys, decorative trim, and gracious corner setting, the modified L-plan house made an appropriate statement for a couple with the Lasswells' status and ambitions in Waxahachie at the turn of the century. The most unusual detail is the pedimented entry bay that addresses both streets from the cut-away porch corner. A circa 1908 photograph shows that decorative trim has been lost in the gables, but it also illustrates that Hector and Jan Jimenez preserved the essence of the house in their renovation.

F-31
323 East Marvin Avenue
1911; W. W. Edwards, builder

Noah W. Pierce, owner of two downtown barber shops (one in the Rogers Hotel), bought this property on April 19, 1911. Five weeks later, N. W. and his wife Katie contracted W. W. Edwards to build in sixty days a five-room frame house "with hall and two porches and shingle roof" for $2,104. The H. D. Timmons Lumberyard provided the house plan and specifications, all building materials, and financing. A deed of trust between the lumberyard and the couple specified that the Pierces would pay off their loan by June 15, 1913, and they did. The house is a typical hipped-roof pyramidal house with several distinguishing features: the intersecting back gable extension on the east façade, the generous L-shaped porch, and the slightly larger proportions than many similar houses have.

Fortunately, the Pierces were settled in their new house by November 12, 1911, when N. W.'s Hotel Barber Shop was destroyed in the Rogers Hotel fire. N. W. temporarily relocated that shop while continuing to operate his second shop on the square. He was granted the coveted lease for the barber shop in the new Rogers Hotel, which he opened in spring 1913. Come September 1914, the Pierces sold this house to Carroll and Mabel Todd and moved farther out on East Marvin. The Todds lived here until 1929, a period that included the years 1917 to 1923, when Carroll served as Waxahachie mayor. After three intervening owners, Tanya and Kent Brewer bought the property in 2006. They were guided in their restoration by documentary photographs dating from the early twentieth century that clearly show both street façades.

F-32
310 Williams Street
c. 1895; c. 1905, moved to this location

With "her sole and separate money," Mrs. Addie F. Robinson of Reagor Springs was the first person to buy lots in the newly platted Getzendaner Addition on October 12, 1905. The date is significant because in mid-September, Mrs. Robinson had filed for divorce from her husband, farmer and stockman Madison Doyle Robinson, in the Ellis County District Court. Whatever the difficulties were, this T-plan cottage was either built or moved to Mrs. Robinson's property at the corner of Williams and Rousseau Streets in time to appear on the 1909 Sanborn map. (It seems likely that she had the house moved, because post-1900 is late for a T-plan cottage to be built in Waxahachie.) Notwithstanding the divorce filing, in the 1910 Census the Robinsons are living in the same household in Reagor Springs, a small community five miles southeast of the county seat. Like many families who owned farmland in Ellis County, they also maintained property in Waxahachie that served as both a rental and a sometime residence, a choice often determined by educational opportunities in the larger town. The Robinsons were never listed at this address in any census or city directory but declared the property to be their homestead in 1912, suggesting that they lived here when their only child was high school and college age. When Mr. and Mrs. Robinson permanently moved to Waxahachie in 1934, they lived on North College Street.

F-33
407 Williams Street
1926; W. B. Ramsey, builder

Replacement houses were constantly under construction in Waxahachie, but few mechanics' liens were specific about what was demolished and what was built on a given property. The lien for this house is an exception. On June 30, 1926, H. T. Ramsey and his wife Lola bought the property, which included an existing house, and on August 19 they signed a mechanic's lien with his brother, builder W. B. Ramsey. W. B. agreed to "the tearing down of a five room house, two porches and bathroom and building new, using the old material in house torn down, a one story frame residence, consisting of five rooms, hall, bath and front porch, closets and etc. Most of the material in the new house to be new, using only of the old lumber that is good and sound." Construction was underway when H. T. and Lola sold the property to R. D. Oliver, an employee of the Waxahachie Dye & Hat Works, and his wife Lola [yes, another Lola] in mid-September. Once completed, the Olivers' double front-gabled bungalow was a common form in town, though the clipped gables gave it an extra stylish touch shared by only a few others, including **210 East University**. The Oliver family did not sell the house until 1978.

F-34
411 Williams Street
c. 1900

Waxahachie's early neighborhoods, both black and white, were full of three-room L-plan houses. It was a popular small-house form built for mill housing and rental property. It was also built by owners with limited income, and for some, served as starter housing. Although most house carpenters of the late nineteenth and early twentieth centuries did not need a plan to build these structures, plan books of the period published multiple variations of the form. Over the years, many of these three-room houses were enlarged—frequently beyond recognition—or demolished. It is still easy, however, to find these compact little L-plan houses with their front-facing gables along Waxahachie streets.

F-35
415 Williams Street
c. 1880s; 1909

The c. 1880s date for the core of this house coincides with development of this area as part of the Marvin College tract. Unfortunately, multiple sales and vaguely worded documents do not provide specifics, but the steeply pitched gable roof, one-and-a-half story square shape, and two single-door front entrances that were still evident in a 1985 photograph are characteristics of an early building.

In March 1907, laborer J. C. Reagor acquired the property. The city directory of that year listed J. C., his wife Bettie, and sons Frank and Lynn at this location. Two years later, in May 1909, the *Daily Light* reported that J. C. was "having some valuable improvements made to his residence in the way of new galleries and additional rooms." That is the house footprint that appeared with a full-width front gallery on the 1914 Sanborn map, the first to record this area. (The wraparound portion of the porch was built after 1984.) The Reagors were still living here when, with their six grown children and their families, they celebrated their sixty-fourth wedding anniversary in late February 1928. J. C. died the following year.

F-36
600 Williams Street
1907

The exceptionally steep pitch of the hipped roof distinguishes this one-story modified L-plan house from other Waxahachie houses of the same type. In December 1905, mail carrier Will Yager and his bride of ten months, Edna Nycum Yager, paid $225 for this lot in Cerf's Addition. Atypical for Waxahachie, the couple did not build immediately but continued living on Kaufman Street, where they were listed in the 1907 directory. They apparently started construction on this house sometime in 1907, because a mechanic's lien dated August 7 specifies that $850 of lumber and materials be delivered to this lot "now occupied" by the Yagers "for erections, repairs and improvements." The lien was between the couple and Will's widowed mother, Mrs. Sarah V. Yager. While the financial arrangement between family members was not unusual, finding it recorded in the county deed books is. The *Daily Light* reported on September 4 that the Yagers had just completed their "handsome cottage." The lien was paid off in March 1911. In 1949, still living at this address, Will retired after forty-eight years as a postal employee.

F-37
604 Williams Street
1915; W. I. Bagley, builder

In June 1912, Will Yager paid $250 for the still undeveloped lot next door to his house at **600 Williams**. Two years later, in May 1914, he sold the lot for $400 to H. N. Naylor, with the stipulation that he "erect a house to cost not less than $2,000 . . . within a period of six months." Apparently, Naylor, who was manager of the Southwestern Telegraph & Telephone Co., and his wife Blanche began construction immediately but encountered difficulties. On July 23, they signed a contract for $674 with builder W. I. Bagley to "complete the present unfinished building, now standing upon said premises" and to "secure . . . the material and labor necessary to complete the building in its present haulted [sic] condition." The document included a bill specifying interior and exterior details such as cabinetry, painting, paper-hanging, "grading up yard," and sidewalk and curb cement work.

The *Daily Light* reported on June 26, 1915, that Edith Naylor was hostess of "a delightful porch party" on "the veranda of the new bungalow" that her parents had just built on Williams Street. One wonders if the party extended to the second-story gable-end balcony, which is the most unusual feature of the house. The Naylors sold the property for $3,250 in 1916. Subsequent owners and residents included the families of physician Dr. W. B. Jackson and of D. E. Dahlgren, publisher and owner of the *Ellis County Free Press* newspaper.

F-38
611 Williams Street
1902; Ed Thrash, architect;
W. S. DeBerry and W. A. Knight, builders

This modified L-plan cottage is the second house that V. H. and Katie Shelton built on this corner. The first, built immediately after Katie's father gave her the property in October 1889, burned in December 1899. (Fire was a fear of all homeowners but probably even more fearful for those who lived on the edge of town.) Rather than immediately rebuild, the Sheltons and their six children, ages three to fifteen, moved to a rent house on East Marvin. It was not until June 10, 1902, that the couple signed a mechanic's lien with W. S. DeBerry and W. A. Knight to build a one-story six-room house for $1,200.

The mechanic's lien was more demanding than most for residential structures in Waxahachie. It identified the architect—Ed Thrash, who drew the plans and specifications—and specified that the contractors had fifteen days (yes, fifteen days!) to build the house to Thrash's "perfect satisfaction and approval." Failure to do so meant a forfeiture of $10.00 for each day, while any changes to the contract had to be agreed upon to avoid a penalty. Originally, there might have been a smaller dormer or no dormer at all; the triple-window dormer is a later alteration. What distinguishes the house today is its placement and setback on the generous corner lot.

In 1886 Shelton and his partner C. A. Arnold opened a drug and stationery store to which they added a music store and music hall in 1887. After the partnership dissolved in 1890, Shelton shifted to the dry goods business and became one of the most aggressive (and successful) advertisers in the local paper. The Sheltons were interested in developing the town's cultural activities, as seen in the opening of the music hall as well as in an early attempt to open a library at the Arnold & Shelton drug store and, most particularly, in building and opening an opera house on South College in 1902, which may explain the couple's delay in rebuilding their own house. Shelton died in 1924, and his wife Katie died ten years later. This property remained in the Shelton family until 1983.

F-39
614 Williams Street

1924; A. A. and J. A. Few, builders

In February 1924, Tarrant County residents Traxie and T. D. Harrison contracted A. A. and J. A. Few to build for $4,000 a house and separate garage on a lot owned by Traxie's family since 1908. The design for the five-room frame bungalow with "breakfast room, hall, front and back porches" was ideal for a corner lot. The L-shaped porch and intersecting gable roofs—the higher gable end fronting Williams Street and the lower gable end oriented to Ross—address the corner and create a presence on both streets. The first tenant was Hans R. F. Helland, who had grown up a few blocks away at **201 Williams**.

F-40
401 East Marvin Avenue

1923; Bertram C. Hill, architect; Ramsey Brothers, builders

With its four sharply defined Craftsman style gables in syncopated succession floating above the Colonial Revival entrance and dark brick walls and columns, this house stands out on the East Marvin streetscape and displays the architect's ability to blend eclectic elements into an effective whole. The design also hints that the clients were more interested in a distinctive rather than a flashy or imposing house. The *Daily Light* of September 21, 1923, recognized the extra care and expense involved in the design and construction, indicating that the house would be "one of the finest in the city," and that the "plastered walls, tile floors in the bath, kitchen and porch make the home very substantial." English-born architect Bertram C. Hill worked in New York, Boston, and St. Louis before moving to Dallas around 1905 and working for other firms until establishing his own firm in 1921. Although now known for his substantial Dallas houses on Swiss Avenue and in Highland Park, he shows his talents here on a smaller scale. He designed several other Waxahachie buildings in the 1920s and 1930s, including the 1925 Woman's Building (**407 West Jefferson**), the 1924 Anderson residence (**712 West Main**), and the 1935 Y. C. Carlisle residence (**600 Sycamore**).

Huntsville native Duncan Douglas (D. D.) Eastham and his wife, Bryan native Jennie Howell, contracted with Waxahachie's Ramsey Brothers to build the house. Eastham attended Southwestern University at Georgetown and the University of Virginia before moving back to Texas to manage his family's and his own substantial land holdings. Married in 1906, the couple lived in Italy (Texas), then around 1917 moved to Waxahachie, where they rented a house (also on East Marvin). They bought these two lots in 1919 but remained renters until building their multi-gabled bungalow, where they stayed throughout their lifetimes. D. D. died in 1943 and Jennie in 1960.

F-41
404 East Marvin Avenue
c. 1928

Mrs. A. F. (Minnie) Dahnke and her son Earl moved to Waxahachie from the country near Boyce in 1928, when she was seventy-one and he was forty-four. (Her husband had died in 1911.) Another son, the dentist C. A. Dahnke, was already living with his family on West Jefferson Street in Waxahachie. Minnie and Earl lived across the street at 407 East Marvin before building this one-story brick veneer house on property she had owned for some time. The arched entrance porch and front chimney were considered in the English Cottage style at the time, but the neat, clean lines and uniform brick exterior would have given a greater sense of modern efficiency than Old World charm, and that could well have been exactly what Minnie was looking for after forty-eight years in the country. Similar elements were incorporated in a 1935 house at **707 Sycamore,** though the siding was wood rather than brick. Minnie continued to live here until her death in 1948 at the age of ninety-one.

F-42
411 East Marvin Avenue
1906

Hilliar Frank Rousseau, an abstracter and a bachelor, probably built this house soon after purchasing lot four in the Getzendaner Addition in February 1906. Hilliar's parents, Mabel and C. C. Rousseau, were the first occupants of the house. Married in 1913, Hilliar and his wife Ethel were living here when they sold the property in 1924. The house was given a major face-lift in a recent renovation.

F-43
501 East Marvin Avenue
1911

Tax assessor Wathan G. Reagor and his wife Maggie built this house shortly after buying the lot in February 1911. The *Daily Light* reported on March 25 that the Reagors' house, now completed, was one of fourteen houses built or under construction in the city since the beginning of the year. It was a period of "considerable building activity," in contrast to 1910, when only fourteen houses were built all year. The Reagors built Waxahachie's most popular house type at the time—the pyramidal house with a front dormer. The hipped roof dormer with curved sides was also a popular feature in Waxahachie houses. A photograph taken shortly after completion shows that there were minor alterations to the house over the years (the front steps originally were wooden and there were no shutters) and that it originally fronted a rutted, muddy Marvin Avenue. The Reagors were one of those Waxahachie couples who built and sold houses on a regular basis. On September 3, 1913, they sold this property to saddler Ed Plumhoff who, one month later, married Ellis County native Mamie Walker. Born in Elkton, Illinois, in 1898 Ed came to Waxahachie, where he operated a saddle shop for thirty years, then a hardware store and shoe shop for another twenty years. Mamie had attended Marvin College and taught music in Waxahachie and Forreston. The couple lived their forty-two years of married life in this house.

F-44
504 East Marvin Avenue
Saint Joseph Catholic Church
[now Saint Joseph Chapel]
1954; James N. MacCammon, architect

The flat brick façade of this front-gable church designed by Dallas architect James N. MacCammon is broken by a projecting three-bay entrance porch and a vertical stone masonry section above the central door. That section encompasses two tall vertical stained glass windows, composed of smaller horizontal sections stacked above one another, and a statue of Saint Joseph in a niche above the windows. Instead of a steeple, the central stone masonry section projects slightly above the gable's peak to form an octagonal plinth for a small cross. A narrow stone masonry band outlines the roof, with three angled projections on each side that echo the corners of the central masonry section. MacCammon, who studied architecture at George Washington University, is known for his mid-twentieth-century shopping centers and office buildings, including the Meadows Building on North Central Expressway in Dallas. In a very different vein, Saint Joseph's effectively blends modern simplicity with restrained but recognizable traditional forms and elements.

St. Joseph Parish was established and built its first church in Waxahachie in 1874. Four Irish stonemasons and plasterers who had moved to Waxahachie to work on the courthouse volunteered to build the small brick structure (26 ft x 56 ft) on College Street, north of the square. John Solon, whose house still stands at **617 Solon Road**, was one of the stonemasons. In 1892 the College Street property was sold, and a new wood frame church was built on this East Marvin property. By 1953 the parish had one hundred families, and plans were made for this larger church, which was completed in late 1954. Fifty years later, with over two thousand families, the parish began planning a larger structure, and construction began in 2015. Designed by Waxahachie architect Hugo Monsanto, it stands near the corner of East Marvin and Kaufman Street.

F-45
611 East Marvin Avenue
1899; Robert L. Ingram, builder

This modified L-plan house originally stood at 410 North College Street, where it was built for Eliza Gammon, widow of livery stable owner Pryor L. Gammon. On July 31, 1899, Eliza contracted Robert L. Ingram to build and complete the house by October 1 for $2,430. Ingram met the deadline ahead of schedule, as the *Enterprise* reported on September 15 that Mrs. Gammon "is now at home at her elegant new cottage." Around 1990, the property was donated to the Central Presbyterian Church, which, in turn, gave the house in 2014 to contractor Brad Yates, who moved it to this location.

F-46
613 East Marvin Avenue
1917; W. W. Walston, builder

Although this two-story Prairie style house has received alterations and a very visible second-floor addition on the east side in recent years, the front section with its stepped-back entrance porch retains the basic footprint visible on the 1925 Sanborn map. Tax Assessor Lem Wray and his wife Jessie Mae were living on West University when they contracted with W. W. Walston to build a two-story "frame house of nine rooms" for $2,300, with plans furnished by the Wrays. Lem and Jessie Mae sold the house only two years later and moved two more times before settling down at **113 Williams**. Well-known chiropractor Dr. Frederick Reglin and his family were here by 1924 and remained into the 1960s. Born in Newark,

New Jersey, in 1879, Dr. Reglin received early training in music before earning his chiropractic degree in Iowa in 1919. He maintained his office in this house for many years. The house still had only nine rooms in 1973, when it was advertised for sale in the *Daily Light*.

F-47
616 East Marvin Avenue
1914; W. W. Walston, builder

Walter Plumhoff, owner of a shoe repair shop, bought this lot in November 1913, just two months after his brother Ed (a saddler) bought the house across the street at **501 East Marvin**. On January 31, 1914, Walter and his wife Mae contracted W. W. Walston to build a six-room house with two halls and two porches within ninety days for $1,987. This simple house is distinguished by its broad front-facing gable end. The Plumhoffs celebrated their golden wedding anniversary in this house in 1957. Walter's obituary in 1959 noted that he had operated his shop for forty-six years before his retirement.

F-48
617 East Marvin Avenue
1905; Conway-Leeper Co., builders

The May 23, 1905, mechanic's lien between homeowners Thomas P. and Willie Vinson Whipple and Conway-Leeper Co., a local lumberyard that also provided building services, is a typical building agreement of the period. For $1,250, Conway-Leeper agreed to "construct and complete" within sixty days and "in a workmanlike manner," a "one-story house of five rooms; hall and bath room, frame dwelling," according to plans and specifications provided by the Whipples. The Whipples chose to build a tidy, modified L-plan cottage, a popular form since the 1890s. An early photograph shows that the curved porch never had a balustrade or railing, which was typical of many Waxahachie houses. The Whipples built their house in Strickland's Addition on a three-lot parcel given Tom by his stepfather J. C. Fears, a prominent citizen and physician. Tom earned distinction in his own right as a lawyer who studied in the office of Judge O. E. Dunlap, served as prosecuting attorney for Ellis County, and practiced law for nearly half a century. When the Whipples moved into their new house, they had one child. By 1916, there were three children, which, no doubt, was one of the reasons they decided to build a bigger house on their adjacent property at **621 East Marvin**.

F-49
621 East Marvin
1916; H. W. Madson, builder

Like many other Waxahachie couples whose families and fortunes grew, Tom and Willie Whipple built a bigger house to replace their smaller 1905 cottage at **617 East Marvin**. But unlike many of their contemporaries, they resisted moving to the West End, and instead built this imposing eight-room residence on property adjoining their cottage in the East End. As a result, their house made a far greater visual statement on the East Marvin landscape than it would have made on a street in the West End.

On August 23, 1916, the *Daily Light* reported that construction began that day on the foundation of the Whipples' house. To be built of hollow tile with brick veneer on the first floor and stucco on the second story, Tom boasted that it would be "practically fireproof throughout" with its plastered room partitions (walls) and composition fireproof roof. No mention was made of its architectural qualities, which reflected the progressive Prairie style with its sedate horizontality, bulk, and minimal decoration. What a contrast to the hyperactive Victorian houses built by Whipple counterparts twenty years earlier! No architect's name has surfaced in connection with the house, although the same 1916 article stated that local contractor H. W. Madson "will supervise the construction work." The design may have been provided by an architect or taken from a catalogue of house plans.

F-50
712 East Marvin Avenue
1891

Widow Julia A. Smith probably built this U-plan house shortly after her son, County Judge James C. Smith, and his wife Lena gave her half an acre out of six acres that they bought in March 1891. The U-plan house—a Victorian modification of the L-plan dwelling but built in far fewer numbers—featured projecting, balanced wings and a centered, recessed entry porch. After two interim owners, one of Waxahachie's local celebrities, Captain E. P. Anderson, purchased the property in June 1907. Born in 1842 in South Carolina, Anderson was known for his Civil War record, most specifically for organizing and commanding an independent company of cavalry scouts that he attached to General Nathan Bedford Forrest's forces. After the war, Anderson studied law at the University of Virginia, and around 1870 came to Waxahachie, where he practiced law, invested in land and stock, and married Elizabeth (Lizzie) Watson, daughter of Colonel Ben W. Watson of the Nineteenth Texas Cavalry. The Andersons' permanent residency in the house was delayed. When their daughter Mary died in October 1907, they rented this house and moved to Brown Street to live with their widowed son-in-law Robert J. Gammon and his two young children until Gammon remarried in 1912. Captain Anderson died in this house in 1923, his obituary describing the couple as "fine examples of the old southern aristocracy, both being highly educated and refined." The family sold the property after Mrs. Anderson's death in 1941. Sadly, the original porch ornamentation, including turned posts, decorative spindlework, and jigsawn brackets, were only recently lost in a renovation.

Next door at 716 East Marvin is a modified L-plan house that was built in 1905 by another Civil War veteran, Colonel Boling Felty Marchbanks, and his wife Lida B. Hall Marchbanks. Marchbanks practiced law in Ellis County and died in the house at age ninety-two in 1932. The shingled tower, decorative front-gable sunburst, and two-story rear addition post-date the 1985 survey.

This c. 1900 photograph shows 806 East Marvin with the original porch and gable decorative ornaments. *Courtesy Ellis County Museum.*

F-51
806 East Marvin Avenue
1893

The Sanborn maps indicate that this house originally stood on the lot next door to the west, now the site of the Calvary Baptist Church. The move may have occurred when the church bought the property in 1953. Benjamin Thomas Pettit built the one-story T-plan residence soon after marrying Maria Zollner of Rockwall, Texas, on June 11, 1893. The *Enterprise* noted on December 29 that his new residence was "ready for occupancy." One of Waxahachie's many modest T-plan houses built in the 1890s, this one is distinguished by the canted bay of the front gable wing. A circa 1896 photograph of the house, in the collection of the Ellis County Museum, shows the original turned and sawn decorative porch and gable ornaments that are now gone. Benjamin and Maria stand to the left, with their daughter Lena standing on the "pretty picket fence" that the April 24, 1896 *Enterprise* reported Pettit had built. Born in Alabama in 1865, Pettit was raised in Wills Point, Texas, and was living in Terrell in 1889 when the *Enterprise* reported that he would be in town for twenty days, taking orders for landscape work. He evidently liked the town, for he opened a nursery here in 1890 and continued to do landscape work as well, with prominent merchant Ed Chaska being one of his clients that year. He also joined C. A. Arnold's piano and sheet music business as a partner the same year, and continued in the music business when he and Maria moved to Dallas around 1900. Pettit was the southwestern representative for the Estey Pipe Organ Company when he died in Dallas in 1936.

F-52
900 East Marvin Avenue
1904

Over the years, as lots were subdivided and sold along East Marvin, different architectural styles and periods appeared along the streetscape, as exemplified by this house and its neighbor, **902 East Marvin**, which were built on the lot located at the bend where, originally, East Marvin became Vickery Street. Built exactly ten years apart, these two houses are modest, straightforward examples of their house types. The oddly shaped lot that extended back to Dunlap Street remained vacant until it was bought in June 1904 by tailor J. S. Perrin and his wife Willie who, in all likelihood, immediately built this modified L-plan frame dwelling on the west side of the lot. They referred to the property as the homestead "upon which we live" when selling it in 1907 to W. W. and Elizabeth Edwards. Although the Edwards family were contractors by trade and owned the property until 1964, they obviously refrained from making major alterations, as the house is close to its original configuration. They did, however, sell the east half of their lot in 1914, and the bungalow at 902 East Marvin was built by the new owners.

F-53
902 East Marvin Avenue
1914; Dunaway Bros., builders

On June 2, 1914, carpenter Edward Fogg and his wife Mary bought this lot from W. W. and Elizabeth Edwards and, two days later, contracted with Dunaway Bros. to construct, for $1,000, this low-slung, front-gabled bungalow. The house was completed in time to appear on the October 1914 Sanborn map. The Fogg and the Edwards families remained neighbors until the former sold their house in spring 1929. The modified L-plan house across the street at 901 East Marvin was given an unusual orientation, facing the curve of the street, when moved to that location sometime after the 1959 Sanborn map.

F-54
904 East Marvin Avenue
1910; Walter N. Kidd, builder

After buying this property on July 27, 1910, cotton farmer Walter N. Kidd and his wife Bettie (both twenty-five years old), wasted little time in building their house. In early August, the Waxahachie Lumber Co. delivered $850-worth of lumber and material to the Kidds' address "to be used . . . for the erection, repairs and improvements on our Homestead." Walter probably built the house with the help of four brothers who lived in the Waxahachie area and perhaps some help from hired tradesmen. The square, hipped roof cottage that the Kidds built exhibited all the elements of the popular form, with its balanced three-bay front façade, attached porch, single door entrance with sidelights, and "Waxahachie dormer." The Kidds sold the house in 1917 and moved to Dallas, where Walter worked as a salesman for an oil company. The original porch supports would have been simple round columns with no decorative ornament, as can be seen on a very similar house (built in 1911) at **501 East Marvin**. The Victorian porch details are later embellishments added when the house was on the 1969 Gingerbread Trail.

F-55
912 East Marvin Avenue
c. 1893

This is one of the few U-plan cottages in Waxahachie. Besides its unusual shape, the exuberant decorative ornament, distinctive paint job, and landscaped setting make it one of the most notable (and noticeable) cottages on the east side. William J. Owen and his wife Eliza Ferrel Owen bought this property in April 1893 for $257. No mechanic's lien or newspaper article has surfaced to provide a specific building date, but its similarity to other East Marvin houses built during 1892-1893 suggests that the couple built the house soon after purchasing the property. The Owens were among the many who were investing in Waxahachie's exploding real estate market when they built the house as rental property. They resided on Oldham Avenue through the 1890s, with the 1900 Census listing William's occupation as "rent collector."

On April 11, 1901, the couple sold this property to grocer William B. Moore and his wife Connie, a dressmaker, for $1,000, the *Enterprise* reporting that the Moores had bought "Bable Owens house." (Perhaps "Bable" was a nickname based on Moore's middle name Barton.) The Moores did not immediately move to East Marvin, for the newspaper reported in late February that they entertained at their Kaufman Street residence. Perhaps they rented this house for a time or made changes before moving in. They were definitely living here by 1907 and remained here until their deaths—Connie in 1937, and William in 1942. A series of owners followed the Moores. There were changes to the house over the years, including multiple alterations and additions evident on the backside. One undocumented account stated that the Moores added the front half to what was originally a three-room house, but the similarity of this house to **712 East Marvin**, clearly visible in 1985 survey photographs, is another rationale for dating this house 1893. The 1985 photographs also show that neither house had decorative detailing in the gables then, but they did share the same decorative porch details.

F-56
922 East Marvin Avenue
1896; E. S. Boze, builder

In late April 1896, the *Enterprise* reported that John R. Shelton "is erecting a pretty one-story residence in East End." That residence was this typical modified L-plan cottage, financed by The Cotton States Building Company of Paris, Texas, and built by E. S. Boze for $1,000. John was seventy years old when he and his wife Virginia built the house and moved from Selma, Arkansas, to Waxahachie to join their son, merchant V. H. Shelton. Father and son were business partners in both Selma and Waxahachie. After Virginia died in 1909, John moved to **611 Williams Street** to live with V. H. and his family.

F-57
1002 East Marvin Avenue
1893; F. M. Dannelly, architect and owner; A. J. Kibler, builder

Although the detailing and decorative ornament have been altered, the basic form of this quirky cross-gable cottage is evident and worth noting. The unusual number of porch angles, roof gables, and peaks shows a close similarity to the house at **1020 West Main**. Contractor A. J. Kibler built this house for $2,100 immediately after F. M. and Nettie L. Dannelly bought the property on December 6, 1893. The mechanic's lien, dated December 12, stipulated that Kibler had two months to complete the house according to plans and specifications furnished by Dannelly "as architect." Dannelly had operated a drug business in Waxahachie in the early 1880s, then studied medicine and practiced in Celeste, Texas, before moving to Dallas in the late 1880s to become a "manufacturing druggist." He continued to maintain ties and pursue real estate investments, including this house, in Waxahachie.

Dannelly's mother, Elizabeth O. Dannelly, who lived in the West End, wrote "East and West Ends," a poem that praised the virtues of both areas. In September 1895, the Dannellys sold the property to James W. and Kezia Couch, who typify many Ellis County farmers and landholders who, in the late nineteenth century, continued farming but moved their families into town. The Couches and daughter Jennie, one of their seven surviving children (there were eleven), are listed at this location in the 1900 Census. Both parents died in 1902, leaving an estate of several large tracts of farmland and this property, appraised at $3,000. When their executor and son, R. N., became owner of the property, he also moved into town. R. N.'s 1918 obituary noted that he was seventy-one years old, a Confederate veteran, and father of seven children by his second wife and three by his first. Active pallbearers at his funeral included Judge O. E. Dunlap, J. N. Langsford, R.W. Getzendaner, and George Coleman, an indication that he was a major landholder.

F-58
1012 East Marvin Avenue
1911-12

After purchasing this lot from Richard Vickery in November 1911, widow Thula McDonald built this house and moved her family from their Limestone County farm to Waxahachie in 1912. Mrs. McDonald's pyramidal house with hipped roof, balanced façade, and "Waxahachie dormer" was very much in style. This particular version, with a front porch splayed to the side, takes full advantage of the corner lot and gives the residence a strong horizontality. The 1913 directory lists Mrs. McDonald and three sons, two of whom are farmers and one a student, at this address. Another son, J. E., became well-known (infamous in some circles) as a Texas legislator and highly controversial Commissioner of Agriculture for nearly twenty years.

F-59
1101 East Marvin Avenue
1923

This house once stood at 705 Brown Street but was moved to this location when the Ferris Heights Methodist Church expanded its parking lot. On November 6, 1923, Ernest C. Ledwell and his wife Minnie contracted to pay the H. H. Hardin Lumber Company $2,000 for the lumber and other materials to build this "one-story frame house with shingle roof, of five rooms, front porch and back porch." Ledwell could have built the house himself with the help of his family or hired a carpenter to do the work. The couple probably selected the design from house plan catalogues available at the lumberyard or through popular magazines. When he built the house, Ledwell was working at the local Supreme Ice Cream Factory run by his father G. W. Ledwell, and he later became the owner. Minnie and Ernest remained in the house until their deaths in 1968 and 1969, respectively. The house was featured in the 1984 movie *Places in the Heart*, directed by Robert Benton, where it was used as the beauty shop and home of the main character's sister.

F-60
1104 East Marvin Avenue
1886-87

By the time Richard Vickery bought the property for this house in 1886, he had become one of Waxahachie's most successful businessmen. Born in 1850, the son of a farmer in Devonshire, England, Vickery immigrated to America in 1869, first to Michigan, then to Ellis County. Successful restaurant and bakery businesses provided the cash to begin investing in real estate. By 1886, he was able to retire from "mercantile life" and enter upon his "prosperous career as a capitalist," in the wording of his biographical sketch in the 1892 *Memorial and Biographical History of Ellis County*. In choosing a large lot outside the city limits, with room for an orchard and gardens, he was emulating Justus W. Ferris and John C. Gibson, whose estates west of town were prominently recorded in the 1886 bird's-eye view of Waxahachie, but no longer exist.

To build this house he probably turned to his good friend William F. Lewis, manager of the local M. T. Jones Lumber Company, who built his own house across the street from Vickery at **1201 East Marvin**. Lewis evidently closely read the trade magazine *Carpentry and Building*, for both his house and Vickery's were inspired by designs published in that publication. Although two-story L-plan houses could be found on many town lots and farms in the area, the corner tower and decorative detailing made this house stand out when built, and they still do so today. The spindlework gable ornament was based on a design by Kansas architect Frank J. Grodavent, while the polygonal tower was probably inspired by one in a design by J. R. Church of Rochester, New York. Both designs were published in the January 1886 issue of *Carpentry and Building*. The location of the tower at the end of the long gable wing distinguishes the design. (It was more common to place towers at the junction of the two wings.) Neither of the *Carpentry and Building* designs, however, included the ornate brackets that were liberally placed beneath the eaves on both levels. Their presence both here and on Lewis's house across the street may indicate a personal preference on Lewis's part as well as availability from the lumber yard that he managed. By merging these design sources and decorative elements into one of Waxahachie's finest homes of the 1880s, Lewis demonstrated his friendship with Vickery during a period when both men were rising stars in Waxahachie's elite. Vickery met with continued success, expanding his interests to Fort Worth and moving there in 1901.

F-61
1109 East Marvin Avenue
1926; A. A. Few & Son, builders

In January 1926, Carl Trentham and his wife Eva took the auspicious step of contracting with A. A. Few & Son to build this "seven room Aeroplane Bungalow dwelling" as well as a "double garage boxed and stripped with composition roof and eighteen feet square." The cross-gable bungalow with the smaller second story that defines it as an airplane bungalow was in the latest style, with tapered wood porch supports on brick bases and decorative corner brackets under the eaves. Unfortunately, the couple was unable to enjoy their new home together for long. Only seven months later, on August 24, records indicate that either because of financial problems or the couple separating, Carl transferred the property to Eva, along with the debt of $4,031 still due to A. A. Few. Eva was also given "all household furniture, fixtures and personal property of every kind except one ivory bed room suite, one gas range, one rug, and one Hudson coach automobile," which sounds like separate households might have been planned. Carl needed the automobile for his job as an agent for the Texas Company, predecessor of Texaco. Only a year later, the *Daily Light* reported Carl's death after an illness of six weeks. In September of 1928 it reported that Eva was living in Dallas.

F-62
1201 East Marvin Avenue
1887

One of Waxahachie's most striking nineteenth-century houses, this Queen Anne style confection stands in the center of its generous lot like a meticulously decorated wedding cake. The profusion of delicate ornament and the unusual form of the house inevitably lead to thoughts of cakes and pastry. Built at a time when L-plan and I-plan houses lined the town's streets, no letter can describe this plan. Alternating rectangular, curved, and polygonal wings or bays extend from a hipped-roof core, forming an odd, asymmetrical, almost pinwheel plan. A walkway and the pedimented corner of the porch appear to lead to an entrance, but instead dead-end into a window. One must make a sharp left to find the entrance door tucked into the side of one of the bays.

A design in the magazine *Carpentry and Building* evidently inspired lumberman and investor William F. Lewis as he planned his new house across the street from his friend Richard H. Vickery. Architects Gould & Angell of Providence, Rhode Island, designed the distinctive plan, which was published in January 1883. There's little doubt that Lewis was deeply involved in the design and construction of the house. As manager of a lumberyard, he would have advised and assisted local home owners and builders, and his biography in an 1892 history of Ellis County mentions the he had erected one of the schoolhouses where he taught before moving to Waxahachie. Lewis made only a few minor changes to the published plan, but used very different exterior ornamentation, probably reflecting the materials available through his suppliers as well as his personal preferences. He demonstrated his satisfaction and pride in the result by paying to have a full-page photograph of the house included along with his biography in the local history, where other businessmen included their portraits. This also served as an advertisement. That black-and-white photograph shows us that the original color scheme varied horizontally, with the wood siding of the first floor a dark color and the fish-scale shingles of the second floor a light color, capped by the dark shingles of the roof.

As a native of Nelsonville, Ohio, who taught school before moving to Texas in the late 1870s and finding success in business, Lewis built the house at a time when his fortunes were rising. He was one of the founding stockholders of the M. T. Jones Lumber Company and managed the local yard. He also invested in the local street railway, served as its vice president, and served as vice president of the Waxahachie Building and Real Estate Association as well. His rapid rise soon reversed, perhaps in part due to the national depression of 1895. Lewis filed for bankruptcy in 1896, lost the house, and left town. When the *Enterprise* noted his death in 1901, it mentioned his "appetite for drink," which also could have contributed to his financial problems. Charles W. Gibson, a banker, farmer, and investor, bought the house in 1898.

F-63
1208 East Marvin Avenue
1892; A. J. Kibler, builder

A. J. Kibler was one of Waxahachie's premier builders in the 1890s. This two-story modified L-plan house is one of many imposing residences that Kibler built for an aspiring clientele—in this instance, insurance agent Samuel Pierce (known as S. P. or Sam) Langsford and his wife Laura E. Shepherd. Married in Millican, Brazos County, Texas, in September 1866, S. P. and Laura were living in

Waxahachie one year later when the first of their eleven children was born. S. P.'s parents had been living in Waxahachie since 1861, and in the 1870 Census S. P. and his father each owned property worth $3,000 on the east side of town, where S. P. operated his blacksmith shop and his father was a "real estate agent." By 1880 S. P. had become a farm machinery dealer, and in 1892 he formed an insurance agency in partnership with J. W. Phillips.

This house was already under construction on September 29, 1892, when the Langsfords contracted with the Ellis County Building and Savings Association to finance the project. The contract specified Kibler as "builder and contractor [to] perform the wood and brick work" on the "two-story dwelling house consisting of three large rooms, kitchen, stair hall, and six feet hall down stairs and three large rooms and one small room, bathroom and six feet hall up stairs." More subdued than many large dwellings built in Waxahachie during the 1880s and the 1890s, the Langsfords' house is, nevertheless, a formidable and stately presence in the East End.

Widowed in 1904, S. P. lived here until his death in 1911, at which time the Langsfords' oldest child, J. N. Langsford, moved his family from their cottage at **1301 East Marvin** to this larger house. In January 1919, Charlie and Edda Davis bought the property and moved from farm to town with six (of seven) children. Davis continued farming until he died in 1944, and Mrs. Davis lived in the house until her death in April 1969, fifty years after her family moved to the East End. The Davis family sold the property in 1971.

F-64
1212 East Marvin Avenue
1892; W. H. Smith, builder

The decorative porch detailing, fan brackets, and gable shingles on Mrs. Meta Hawkins's modified L-plan cottage resemble those on other neighborhood residences of the same type and era. One year after buying her East End property, Mrs. Hawkins signed a lumber lien for $350 in August 1892 that specified lumber dealer H. D. Timmons as supplier and W. H. Smith as builder. No doubt Mrs. Hawkins knew something about Waxahachie's building industry, as she was the second wife and widow of house and sign painter W. A. Hawkins, who had worked in Waxahachie from the late 1850s until his death in 1889. On October 14, 1892, the *Enterprise* noted that Mrs. Hawkins had moved into her "neat, new cottage" with her children, ages eight and fourteen. Sadly, Mrs. Hawkins died the following February. In 1902, her heirs sold the property to teacher Gray B. Winn, who was principal and superintendent of the Waxahachie school system from 1909 to 1935. Winn's early years of service were considered an especially formative period for the schools. Still at this address when he died in September 1941, Winn was eulogized by the *Daily Light* for his "valued life."

F-65
1219 East Marvin
1903; c. 1911 or c. 1923

Although not original to the house, the extended two-story entry bay makes this façade one of the most striking and curious in Waxahachie. On May 20, 1903, the *Daily Light* reported that George Coleman was about to begin construction of a residence "on the beautiful corner lot just east of his mother's house." Exactly three months later, the "handsome new cottage" was "almost done." Looking at the house today, it is possible to see the original structure: It was a one-and-a-half-story dwelling with a modified L-plan, hipped roof, twin front-facing gables framing the primary entrance area, and a one-story full-width front porch that curved around to the east side. The original house probably resembled **603 Highland**, with one of the front gables above a projecting bay. In this case the projecting bay was on the left, and even though the gables were regularized somewhat in the later redo, the left gable still projects slightly more than the one on the right. The central hipped-roof porch extension with two-story Doric columns may have been inserted sometime around 1911. George's mother Juliette died in 1910, after which there was some shifting of family property on East Marvin, with George adding another lot to the two he already owned. It would have been a logical time to make changes to the 1903 house. The extension also might date to c. 1923, when grocer J. W. Cole bought the property. The second-floor porch, which probably originally was a sleeping porch, was enclosed at a later date.

The Colemans were a prominent pioneer family, George's parents James W. and Juliette Coleman migrating from Kentucky to Texas sometime between George's birth in March 1870 and the birth of the next of seven boys in September 1872. Widowed in 1887, Juliette moved from farm to town "to school her children" and bought property in the developing East End along Vickery Street, which until May 1890 was not in the city limits. In 1901, George married Maude Boaz in Fort Worth and the couple lived with Juliette until their own house was completed in 1903. In 1906, Juliette gave them the property. Like all the surviving Coleman boys, George worked in banking and real estate; specifically, he was president of the Texas Title & Loan Company and the State Bank and Trust Company. One would expect it to be easy to document all aspects of a house associated with such a prominent family as the Colemans—but this property is proof that that is not always the case. The Sanborn maps never extended this far on East Marvin, nor were any newspaper references or official documents found that date the front extension.

F-66
1301 East Marvin
1893; W. H. Smith, builder

The Langsford family can be counted among those who made major contributions to the early development of the East End. Insurance agent S. P. Langsford and his wife Laura built their substantial two-story house at **1208 East Marvin** in fall 1892. The following spring their oldest son, bank clerk J. N. Langsford, and his wife Rilla contracted with W. H. Smith on April 11 to build this more modest "one-story Cottage dwelling house" less than a block away. The mechanic's lien provides a very exacting description of the five-room cottage with "Bath Room, 4 closets, & Hall and back & front galleries One fire place & chimney & 3 flues to be built during dry weather and of dry material." Beginning construction on April 13, Smith would supply all "material and fixtures" and collect his $1,350 payment upon completing the house, which he did on May 20, less than six weeks after construction began. The Langsfords' cottage is one of the best and most intact examples of the modified L-plan house type remaining in Waxahachie. The corner location offers an excellent view of the decorative turned and jig-sawn ornament of the porch and the side gable, as well as the two entrance doors. The Langsfords and their growing family lived here until moving to **1208 East Marvin** in 1911, after both of J. N.'s parents had died. They sold their cottage in 1913.

A few lots to the east, 1333 East Marvin has received major alterations over the years and is now hidden by trees, but the man who built it in 1892 was one of Waxahachie's most unusual residents at the time, and he perfectly represents the in-between status of this stretch of Marvin. Known as "the cowboy preacher," S. W. Wesley had been captured by the Commanches as a child and later returned to "civilization." He lived a restless life, and although he used Waxahachie as a home base for about twenty years, he pursued varied careers that included traveling as an evangelist as well as working as a lawyer and a chiropractor.

F-67
1400 East Marvin Avenue
1892; Hilliard M. Beauchamp, probable builder

This modified L-plan house with slender boxed columns and the absence of any trim (except for the conservative decorative shingles in the gables) was built by Hilliard and Ellen Beauchamp in 1892. It was built on a fourteen-acre parcel that Ellen purchased in 1892 as "her own Separate property." The sellers were William F. and Lavena Lewis, William F. acting both for himself and as a trustee for the M. T. Jones Lumber Company. On May 19, the Beauchamps signed a lumber lien for M. T. Jones to deliver $520 of "good merchantable goods" for the "immediate construction" of this residence. Among the lengthy listing of materials are measurements and quantities for windows, doors (including one "Fancy" door), cypress shingles, flooring, crown molding, and native pine "burl" siding. Within two years after the house was built, the Beauchamps were divorced and William F. Lewis was bankrupt, but the lumber company remained in good financial standing. Over the years, the fourteen-acre tract was divided and subdivided many times, but (amazingly) alterations to the house were confined to enlarging the back wing. Well into the twentieth century, subsequent owners of the house were farmers and stockmen. These included Nash stockman Joe Meharg, who bought parts of this tract in January 1904, in what the *Daily Light* called "another big land deal." Meharg, known as one of the county's prominent horsemen, and his wife Maggie lived here until his death in 1916. Hungarian-born Julian and Elizabeth Zsohar moved into the house with their children in 1950 and continued to live here for almost fifty years. Julian retired from Tom Thumb groceries in 1967 and became a full-time artist and teacher. Their son Zoltan's book *Surviving Through Faith* (2001) recounts his parents' lives in Hungary, escape to Austria in 1945, and arrival in Waxahachie as refugees sponsored by the Central Presbyterian Church.

F-68
200 Hackberry Street
1901; J. S. McCanless, builder

Odell and Sarah DeVaughan built their vernacular farmhouse in 1901 on a thirteen-acre tract that DeVaughan had bought from Richard Vickery in 1890. Born in 1856, Odell came from a farm family (rather than a mercantile family) that originated in Coosa County, Alabama. By the mid-1870s, the family had moved to Independence County, Arkansas, where Odell (the oldest of four boys) married Sarah Josephine Griffin, daughter of the county judge, in 1884. By the late 1880s the DeVaughan family, parents and children together, had moved once again to another location to farm—this time to Ellis County, Texas.

On December 13, 1901, the *Enterprise* reported that Odell, "good citizen of the East End," was "building a nice cottage on the plot he owns." Odell and Sarah had contracted J. S. McCanless on December 2 to furnish for $450 "all material and Labor . . . to erect, construct and complete, except painting and papering . . . one framed house, shingle roof, with two rooms 16 by 16 feet each, with a hall 6 by 16 feet, two closets and one porch 6 by 30 feet. . . ." Given how quickly houses were built, chances are that the DeVaughans were in their new house by Christmas.

The house that they built is the one-story, three-bay rectangular structure with gable-end roof, attached porch, and centered front gable that is visible to the street today. Over time, numerous rear additions expanded the house well beyond the original two rooms and center hall. Multiple farm buildings completed the complex. Sarah died in 1941; Odell remained "remarkably active" until his death at age eighty-seven on March 17, 1946.

When the DeVaughans built their house, it was on the eastern edge of Waxahachie's town limits. At least for the time being, the property still gives a sense of the landscape of farm houses and farmland that surrounded the town in 1901.

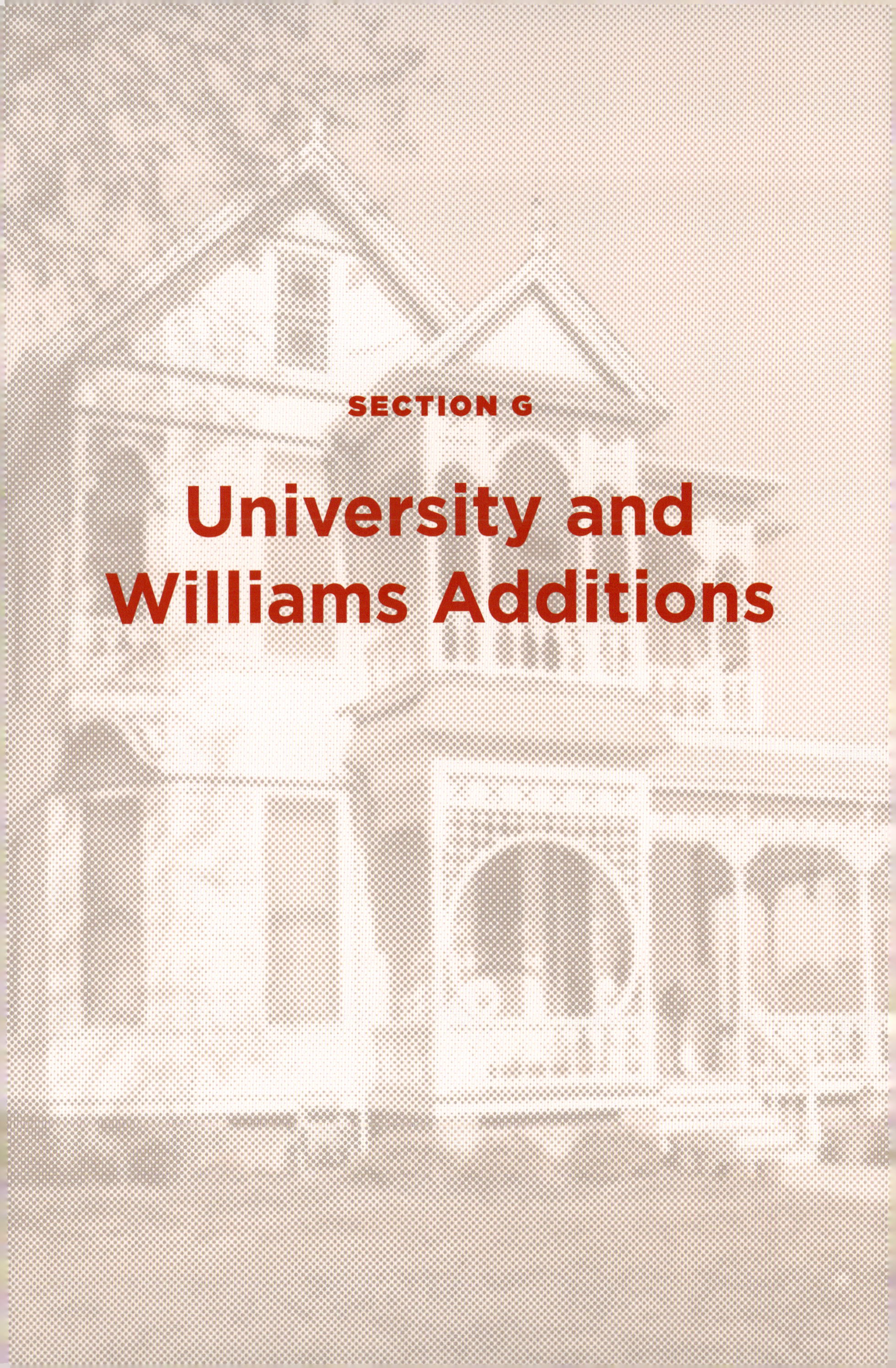

SECTION G

University and Williams Additions

Photograph taken c. 1910 from the Trinity University main building that shows the eastern edge of the University Addition. Sycamore Street is in the foreground, and the houses face East University Avenue. The house on the left is 330 East University. The undeveloped area to the east would become the Trinity Heights and Hilcrest Additions. *Courtesy of the Dr. Charles W. Simpson Family and the Ellis County Museum.*

INTRODUCTION

Development in this section began in 1890, saw a significant spike when Trinity University moved its campus here in 1902, and continued when the new high school building opened on Second Street in 1918. The Depression greatly slowed construction, but some of Waxahachie's most noteworthy homes built in the 1930s can be found here, along with an upper-end development of the 1950s and 1960s. In addition to its educational and religious buildings, a wide variety of residential styles await the visitor, including Queen Anne, Colonial Revival, Neoclassical, Prairie, Craftsman, Tudor, Spanish Revival, and Mid-Century Modern. The houses range in size from modest one-story cottages and bungalows to substantial two-story houses designed to impress.

In March of 1890, John Williams, probably spurred by the success of the West End Addition, decided to create a development of his own north of town. A prominent Waxahachie businessman, banker, and former mayor, Williams named the development after himself rather than a cardinal direction, and gave his name to its central avenue as well, even though the street was a continuation of Ferris Avenue. (By the time of the 1922 city map, Williams Avenue had been renamed Ferris Avenue.) Dunn Street and Bryson (then called Hiland) formed the east and west borders of the subdivision. John Williams wasted

House built in 1893 by Ed Williams, son of the Williams Addition developer, John G. Williams. The house still stands at 412 West Marvin, but the gazebo is gone. *Courtesy Ellis County Museum.*

no time in building a fine residence for himself (on Williams Avenue, of course). That house, described in the paper as a "most elegant structure" that was designed by "one of the best architects in the state," is gone. However, the house built soon after his father's death in 1893 by Ed Williams, John's son, remains one of the best surviving houses of the Williams Addition, and a Waxahachie treasure.

Of far more importance to Waxahachie's growth than the Williams Addition was Trinity University's decision in 1901 to move its campus to Waxahachie. A committee appointed by the mayor and chaired by W. H. Getzendaner proposed the winning offer when the Presbyterian college, then located in the east Texas community of Tehuacana, decided to move to a more populous, and prosperous, location. Waxahachie's bid provided ten acres for the campus and $80,000 in cash partially funded by platting one hundred acres of pasture land around the proposed campus as the University Addition and selling the lots at around $200 each to civic-minded residents, who also stood to make a profit if they resold after the university was built. To provide easy access to downtown, the street railway was extended to the campus. Waxahachie's population was boosted with Trinity students and faculty as well as by families from the surrounding country moving to town to enable their children to attend Trinity while living at home.

Just to the west of the University Addition, lots on Highland and Grand Avenues began to sell, and to the east, the Trinity Heights Addition was opened in 1914. When the high school was built in 1918 on land between Trinity Heights and the Williams Addition, the Hilcrest Addition (including Harbin, Gibson, and Bryson [originally Penn] Streets) began to see house construction also. The lots in these post-1900 subdivisions display a regularity and consistency not possible in the older parts of town, and the houses likewise reflect that planning. Larger houses were erected on the larger lots on West Marvin and Sycamore, while smaller bungalows and cottages occupy the smaller lots on the north/south streets.

Photograph taken from the Trinity main building looking south down University Avenue, c. 1910. The two-story house closest to the camera is 321 University and the one beyond is 305 University. Streetcar tracks were laid on University in 1913. *Courtesy of the Dr. Charles W. Simpson Family and the Ellis County Museum.*

View looking north up University Avenue to the Trinity University main building, 1914. The streetcar tracks laid in 1913 are visible in the center of the street. The first house on the right is 108 University, and the second on the left is 115 University. *Courtesy of the Dr. Charles W. Simpson Family and the Ellis County Museum.*

This c. 1931 view of the Trinity University campus shows the landscaping and maturing trees, with the main building on the right and the women's dormitory, Drane Hall, in the distance, from a Chamber of Commerce brochure *Waxahachie: Queen City of the Cotton Belt. Private collection.*

In the 1920s and 30s, architectural eclecticism found fertile ground on Sycamore Street. Merchants, doctors, and other successful citizens built substantial architect-designed homes on generous lots, even during the difficult years of the Depression. In November 1935 the *Dallas Morning News* even published a feature on the "Residential Building Boom at Waxahachie," illustrated with pictures of four houses, three of which were on Sycamore.

Sycamore's 1930s "building boom" was not repeated to the north on Overhill Drive. Oscar H. Chapman built his impressive Georgian Revival home there in 1929, but only two other houses were built on the street in the 1930s, and those were for his daughters. After Chapman's land was incorporated into the city limits in 1951, building picked up, and the wide lots were perfect for sprawling ranch-style homes built by new corporate managers moving to town.

Waxahachie continued to expand over the years and convert former farm lands to housing developments. On Solon Road, new development now surrounds the once-rural home of stone mason, builder, and farmer John Solon. He built it in the early 1890s, around the same time that John Williams was building his home in the Williams Addition. Both men were making statements with their grand homes. Fortunately, Solon's stone house survived with its distinctive red sandstone horseshoe arch in honor of his Irish heritage.

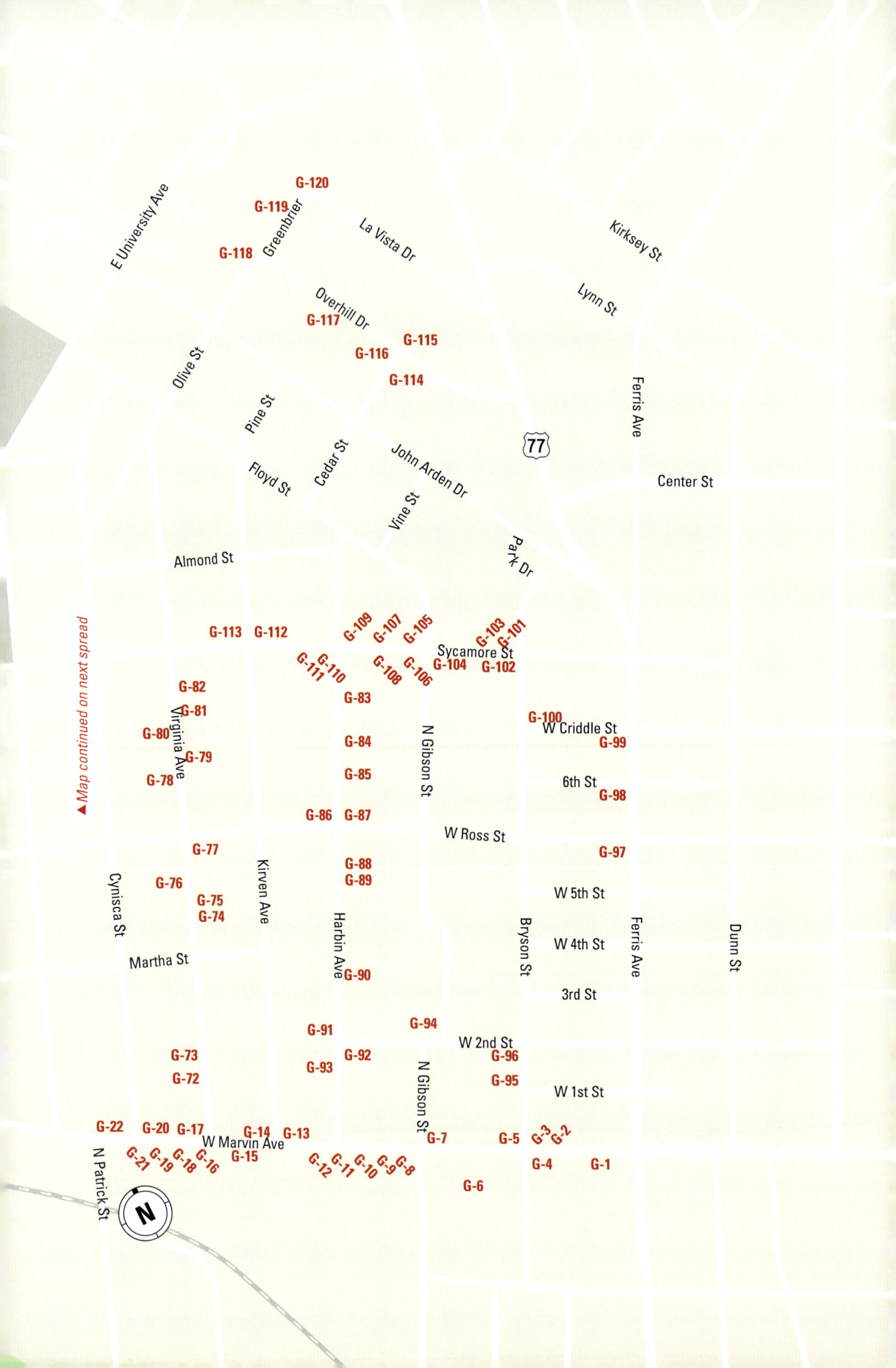

▲Map continued on next spread

G-1 405 W. Marvin Ave.

G-2 412 W. Marvin Ave.

G-3 414 W. Marvin Ave.

G-4 415 W. Marvin Ave.

G-5 502 W. Marvin Ave.

G-6 505 W. Marvin Ave.
First United Methodist Church

G-7 514 W. Marvin Ave.

G-8 603 W. Marvin Ave.

G-9 607 W. Marvin Ave.

G-10 611 W. Marvin Ave.

G-11 615 W. Marvin Ave.

G-12 707 W. Marvin Ave.

G-13 708 W. Marvin Ave.

G-14 804 W. Marvin Ave.

G-15 807 W. Marvin Ave.

G-16 901 W. Marvin Ave.

G-17 902 W. Marvin Ave.

G-18 905 W. Marvin Ave.

G-19 909 W. Marvin Ave.

G-20 910 W. Marvin Ave.

G-21 913 W. Marvin Ave.

G-22 1004 W. Marvin Ave.

◆ G-23-G-71 on pp. 274-75

G-72 111 Virginia Ave.

G-73 115 Virginia Ave.

G-74 206 Virginia Ave.

G-75 208 Virginia Ave.

G-76 213 Virginia Ave.

G-77 218 Virginia Ave.

G-78 307 Virginia Ave.

G-79 312 Virginia Ave.

G-80 317 Virginia Ave.

G-81 322 Virginia Ave.

G-82 326 Virginia Ave.

G-83 330 Harbin Ave.

G-84 324 Harbin Ave.

G-85 316 Harbin Ave.

G-86 313 Harbin Ave.

G-87 310 Harbin Ave.

G-88 306 Harbin Ave.

G-89 304 Harbin Ave.

G-90 208 Harbin Ave.

G-91 201 Harbin Ave.

G-92 104 Harbin Ave.

G-93 103 Harbin Ave.

G-94 600 W. Second St.
Waxahachie High School (now STEAM Elementary School)

G-95 201 Bryson St.

G-96 205 Bryson St.

G-97 913 Ferris Ave.

G-98 1007 Ferris Ave.

G-99 1015 Ferris Ave.

G-100 900 Bryson St.

G-101 500 Sycamore St.

G-102 501 Sycamore St.

G-103 504 Sycamore St.

G-104 513 Sycamore St.

G-105 600 Sycamore St.

G-106 601 Sycamore St.

G-107 606 Sycamore St.

G-108 607 Sycamore St.

G-109 610 Sycamore St.

G-110 701 Sycamore St.

G-111 707 Sycamore St.

G-112 710 Sycamore St.

G-113 800 Sycamore St.

G-114 119 Overhill Dr.

G-115 120 Overhill Dr.

G-116 201 Overhill Dr.

G-117 205 Overhill Dr.

G-118 311 Olive St.

G-119 103 Greenbrier St.

G-120 105 Greenbrier St.

◆ G-121 on pp. 274-75

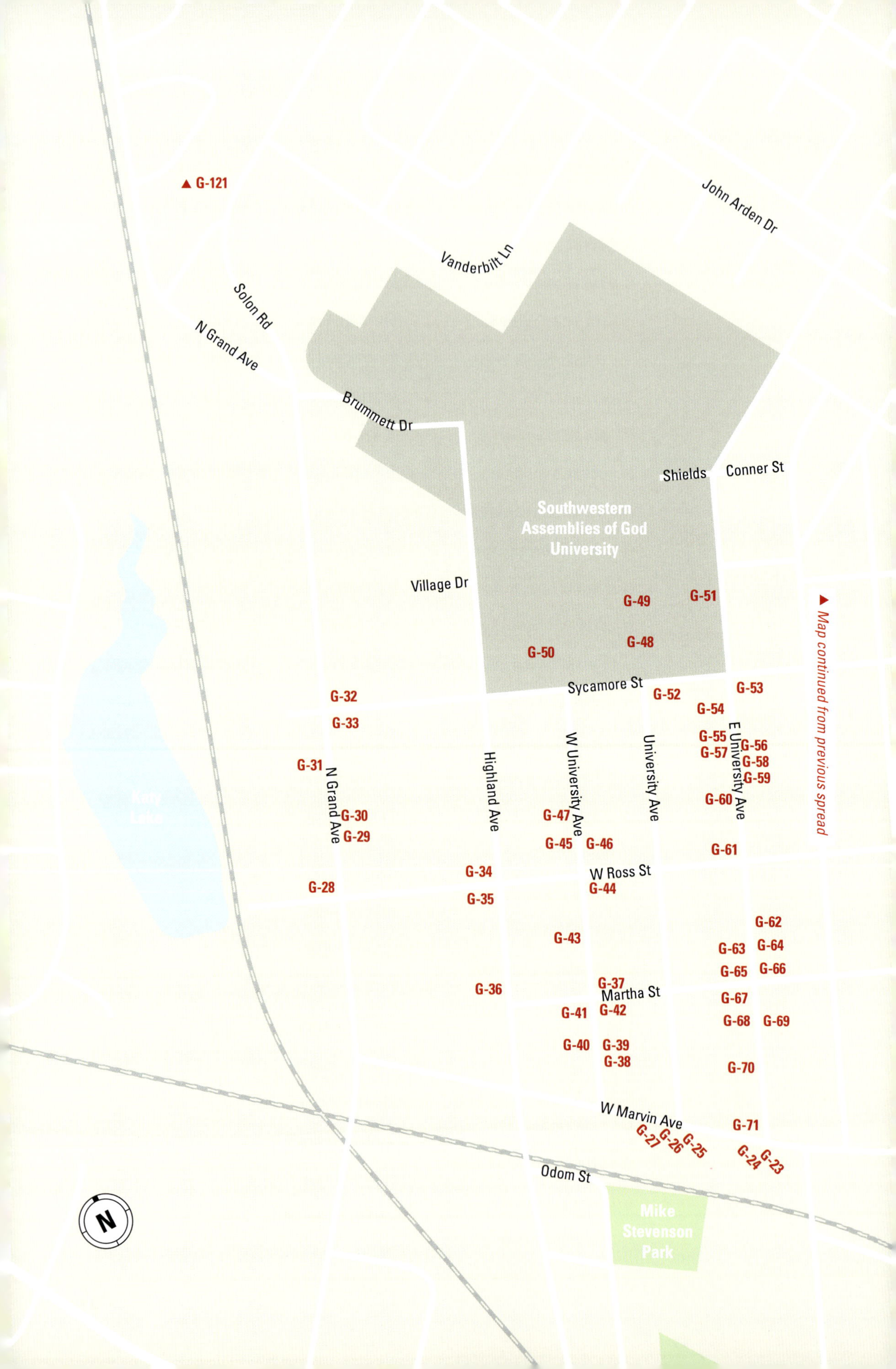

▲ G-121
John Arden Dr
Vanderbilt Ln
Solon Rd
N Grand Ave
Brummett Dr
Shields
Conner St
Southwestern Assemblies of God University
Village Dr
G-49
G-51
G-48
G-50
Sycamore St
G-52
G-53
G-54
G-32
G-33
G-31
N Grand Ave
Highland Ave
W University Ave
University Ave
E University Ave
G-55
G-56
G-57
G-58
G-59
G-60
G-30
G-29
G-47
G-45
G-46
G-61
G-34
W Ross St
G-28
G-35
G-44
G-62
G-43
G-63
G-64
G-65
G-66
G-36
G-37
Martha St
G-67
G-41
G-42
G-68
G-69
G-40
G-39
G-38
G-70
W Marvin Ave
G-71
G-27
G-26
G-25
G-24
G-23
Odom St
Mike Stevenson Park
N
▲ Map continued from previous spread

◆ *G-1-G-22 on pp. 272-73*

G-23 1107 W. Marvin Ave.

G-24 1111 W. Marvin Ave.

G-25 1119 W. Marvin Ave.

G-26 1201 W. Marvin Ave.

G-27 1203 W. Marvin Ave.

G-28 501 N. Grand Ave.

G-29 508 N. Grand Ave.

G-30 512 N. Grand Ave.

G-31 521 N. Grand Ave.

G-32 1424 Sycamore St.

G-33 1423 Sycamore St.

G-34 603 Highland Ave.

G-35 523 Highland Ave.

G-36 511 Highland Ave.

G-37 1210 Martha St.

G-38 108 University Ave.

G-39 114 University Ave.

G-40 115 University Ave.

G-41 119 University Ave.

G-42 120 University Ave.

G-43 207 University Ave.

G-44 218 University Ave.

G-45 305 University Ave.

G-46 306 University Ave.

G-47 309 University Ave.

G-48 1200 Sycamore St.
Trinity University Campus (Southwestern Assemblies of God University)

G-49
Trinity University Main Building (now Farmer Administration Building)

G-50
Drane Hall (Now M. E. Collins Hall)

G-51
P. C. Nelson Memorial Library

G-52
1103-1115 Sycamore

G-53
330 E. University Ave.

G-54
327 E. University Ave.

G-55
321 E. University Ave.

G-56
318 E. University Ave.

G-57
317 E. University Ave.

G-58
314 E. University Ave.

G-59
312 E. University Ave.

G-60
309 E. University Ave.

G-61
301 E. University

G-62
210 E. University Ave.

G-63
205 E. University Ave.

G-64
204 E. University Ave.

G-65
201 E. University Ave.

G-66
200 E. University Ave.

G-67
123 E. University Ave.

G-68
119 E. University Ave.

G-69
116 E. University Ave.

G-70
107 E. University Ave.

G-71
103 E. University Ave.

◆ *G-72-G-120 on pp. 272-73*

G-121
617 Solon Road

G-1
405 West Marvin Avenue
1912; H. D. Rankin, builder

The *Daily Light* noted in March 1912 that John Ratchford was having this "ten-room house" erected, with H. D. Rankin in charge of the work. John Ratchford evidently possessed both technical and management skills, for he was listed as a machinist in the 1907 directory and manager of the People's Gin in the 1913 directory. The 1920 Census shows him still working as manager of a gin only a few months before his death that same year. His widow, Kate Naughton Ratchford, continued living in the house and evidently managed the family's farm properties. The *Dallas Morning News* in August 1939 noted her success with an experimental flax crop, planted in an effort to discover new crops for the area, which was still suffering from the Depression-era collapse of the cotton market. A 2007 renovation altered the original façade of this two-story hipped roof house by adding a central dormer and the center second-floor window.

G-2
412 West Marvin Avenue
1893; C. J. Griggs, builder

One of Waxahachie's treasures, this Queen Anne-style house presents an impressive array of turned and sawn ornament. Porch, balcony, and gable ornaments generously adorn every corner of the structure with a lacy filigree. Built by grocery merchant Ed Williams for his new wife Ella, the house was based on the F. P. Powell house, built the previous year on a lot just across the street. The Powell house exactly duplicated (in reverse) design number 56 published in George F. Barber's 1891 mail-order catalogue *Cottage Souvenir No. 2*. Since Ed's house was built just a few feet away, it is not surprising that a few changes were made. No documentation remains to tell us if Williams requested the changes from his contractor, C. J. Griggs, or from the architect. Although the basic plan of the house remained the same, the decision to leave out the crowning central tower of the Powell house and to use more sawn than turned ornament on the porches and gables transformed the appearance of the Williams house. The addition of two clipped-gable dormers on the east side also contributed to its distinctive appearance. Mechanics' liens inform us that the basic building materials came from a local lumberyard, but the ornamental pieces, as well as the doors and other millwork, were acquired from a Dallas company, Buell & Connelly. The "big city" source supplied high quality, finely-detailed, stylish components. Similar delicate scrolls and pierced patterns at the porch cornices were described as "cornice drapery" in a trade catalogue of the period, and the aptness of the term is clear here. Approximately a year later, this house design was duplicated again, though with additional variations in the ornament, a few miles north of town by William Hosford.

The house stands in the Williams Addition, platted by Ed's father, John G. Williams, in 1890. Ed built on the block just west of his father's house (no longer extant), but, interestingly, waited until after his father's death to do so. The reason probably rests in the convention of the time that houses were built for families, rather than single persons. Single men and women tended to live either with their parents, other relations, or in boarding houses. A marriage often provided the justification for building a new house, when the means were available. Only a month after his father's death, Ed had both the means and the marriage. While the timing of the wedding may have been coincidental, it is also possible that Ed had hesitated to marry his chosen lady for fear of parental disapproval. His bride Ella was a widow, one year older than Ed, with a thirteen-year-old son. John G.'s opinion of Ella remains a mystery, but documents tell us that he gave each of his children, including Ed, $5,000 not long before his death on January 19, 1893. One month later, the *Enterprise* noted both Ed's marriage to Mrs. Ella Anderson and his plans to begin work on a "fine residence" in the Williams Addition.

Construction of the house may have gone smoothly, but despite Ed's $5,000 inheritance, payment did not.

In October of 1893, both lumber suppliers and the contractor filed liens on the house in order to guarantee payment of the amounts still owed. Ed was able to clear those debts by 1895, but in 1902, he sold his show place and built a smaller house on West Jefferson. The new owner, R. K. Erwin, had built the first cottonseed oil mill in Waxahachie and become a successful businessman. After Erwin's death in 1929, his son Frank moved his family, including son Frank Jr., into the house. As Chairman of the University of Texas Board of Regents in the 1960s, Frank Jr. wielded great power and stirred up a fair amount of controversy.

G-3
414 West Marvin Avenue

1916; W. W. Edwards, builder

This delightful bungalow, with its cascading front and side gable roofs, forms a striking contrast to the larger, more ornate house next door at **412 West Marvin**. The horizontal emphasis, low pitched roofs, and projecting rafter ends are typical of the early twentieth-century Craftsman style bungalows, just as the house at 412 embodies the vertical emphasis and decorative woodwork of the late-nineteenth-century Queen Anne style. The first owner of this house, Joe R. Erwin, had lived at 412 with his parents, R. K. and Mary Erwin, before attending the University of Texas in Austin and the University of California, Berkeley. When newly married, he and his wife Katie boarded at a house on South Elm Street, but in August of 1916 they contracted with W. W. Edwards for the materials to build this bungalow next door to his parents. The bungalows he would have seen while at Berkeley may have influenced his design choice. In September 1916, the *Daily Light* noted that Joe's "California bungalow" was under construction, with an expected cost of $4,000. Joe was associated with the El-Co Creamery before he switched to the automobile business and became president and general manager of the Waxahachie Nash Company. When Joe and Katie left Waxahachie in the early 1920s, they sold the house to E. Stewart Moore and his wife Monette. Stewart had flown with the 169th Aero Squadron in World War I before returning to work in his father's hardware store, eventually becoming its proprietor.

G-4
415 West Marvin Avenue

1906; Sanguinet & Staats, architects;
J. S. McCanless, builder

One of six "palatial homes" illustrated in the 1910 publication *Waxahachie Illustrated*, this two-story, hipped-roof house helped to bring the Prairie style to Waxahachie. The 1910 photograph shows a Mission-style parapet and intertwining circular ornamentation on the balcony railing that were lost when the central balcony was enclosed. The 1910 photograph also indicates that the second-floor shingle siding was painted a darker color than the first-floor clapboards, enhancing the horizontal emphasis so integral to the style. Designed by the Fort Worth architectural firm Sanguinet & Staats before it became known for steel-framed skyscrapers, the house demonstrates the architects' unique interpretation of national styles in domestic architecture.

Lee Penn built this house in 1906, the year after his father, well-to-do businessman G. J. Penn, died. After returning from college in 1889, Lee began his career as bookkeeper and secretary of the Waxahachie Milling Company and then ventured into the grocery business. By the time he built this house, he and his brother Charles were both successful cotton buyers. (Charles built a house next door at 411 West Marvin, now demolished, and, after Lee died, moved to a much grander house at **603 West Marvin**.)

Lee's wife Gertrude evidently loved to entertain here. In July of 1906, the *Enterprise* noted her party to celebrate the move into this house and included accounts in later years of events at her "beautiful" and "spacious" home. In order to fund these entertainments and their daughter's education at Randolph Macon College, Lee continued to work as a cotton buyer while also becoming involved in other enterprises. At his death in 1920, he was president of the Texas Electric Railway, the regional interurban railway system. A special rail car brought Dallas businessmen to his funeral. His wife Gertrude continued to live in the house and commissioned the same architects in 1921 to design "alterations and additions" that included a screened sleeping porch and updating many of the decorative details from Prairie style to Neoclassical. She sold the house in 1935 to Frank O. Martin, sales representative for the L. W. Singer Publishing Company of New York, who lived here with his family until his retirement in 1948. W. H. Getzendaner, grandson of Captain W. H. Getzendaner, and his wife Betty then acquired the property.

G-5
502 West Marvin Avenue

1924; Krohne & Brasher, builders

The house now located at **205 Bryson** first stood at this location. In 1892, Fines P. and Myrtle Powell owned the entire block and built their house on this corner, across the street from the fashionable new Williams Addition. When they moved to Amarillo in 1904, they took advantage of the increased land value of their block to divide it into three parts, selling the east third, including their two-story house, to George W. and Jennie Callens. George, a farmer, had previously lived in the country, but moved to this lot in town when he married his second wife, Jennie. By the early 1920s, with G. W. in his early sixties, the Callens were ready for a smaller, more modern home. They moved the original house to the back of the lot, facing Bryson, and in 1924 built this one-story side-gable brick veneer bungalow on the 65 x 210 ft. corner plot. They then sold the old house and the remainder of the property. Their new bungalow was uncompromisingly modern—all straight lines and no decorative flourishes—a stark contrast to their previous Queen Anne-style house. Although it was smaller in size, its brick veneer siding indicated a significant investment and promised greater solidity. A hint of the Craftsman style was displayed in the patterned shingled surfaces of the prominent porch gables and exposed rafters. The generous porch provided ample seating space and exposure on two sides.

G-6
505 West Marvin Avenue

First United Methodist Church

1950-55; A. George King & Associates, architects; Dolph Construction Co., contractor

The dominant central entrance tower anchors this large-scale church complex built in a restrained 1950s version of the Gothic Revival style. Architect A. George King took full advantage of the spacious full-block site by angling the two main wings from the tower toward the corners of the lot. The resulting wide "V" visually funnels visitors to the central entrance and helps to enliven the long façade. The design acknowledges the importance of the automobile by providing a rear entrance from the parking lot into the same main entrance hall. King was born in Corsicana, Texas, in 1906 and graduated from Rice Institute in Houston with an architecture degree in 1928. He was working for W. G. Clarkson when design work for this building began but established his own practice in 1952 and listed the church as his in the 1962 *American Architects Directory*. His most famous building, the theater Casa Mañana in Fort Worth (1958), incorporated a geodesic dome.

Waxahachie's Methodist congregation erected their first building in 1852 near the courthouse square. When that building was destroyed by fire, they shared a building with the Presbyterians and Baptists before constructing their own brick church on North College Street in 1893. Fire destroyed that structure in 1904, but a replacement was quickly built and remained in use until June of 1950. The congregation moved a war-surplus building to the new site on West Marvin Avenue and met there while the east wing was under construction. Dedication of the east education wing occurred on May 18, 1952. Construction of the sanctuary wing began two years later, with its formal opening on May 1, 1955.

G-7
514 West Marvin Avenue
c. 1904

J. T. Couch bought this lot in September 1904 and probably built the modified L-plan house soon after. He listed his occupation in the 1910 Census as farmer, but he appears to have invested in residential real estate as well, owning lots in both the University Addition and Park Hill Addition. He sold this house to farmer B. C. King in January of 1907 for $4,550, and two months later the newspaper noted that Couch had a new residence under construction (**1107 West Marvin**). This cottage merges Queen Anne style asymmetry with Colonial Revival elements that include classical porch columns and a pediment above the entrance. The wraparound porch on the right has been filled in. The strong triangular shape of the pyramidal roof is echoed in the triangular gable above the central dormer, the triangular dormer to its left, and the triangular pediment above the entrance section of the porch.

G-8
603 West Marvin Avenue
1913; C. D. Hill, architect;
W. W. Walston, builder

On February 16, 1913, the *Daily Light* noted that "E. C. McCartney is building a handsome, modern residence on Marvin Avenue which will cost approximately $14,000. It will have steam heat and all other modern conveniences and will be ready for occupancy in March." Two months later another article declared it "the handsomest house between Dallas and Waco," and the cost estimate had risen to $18,000. The architect, C. D. Hill, had designed the Rogers Hotel on the square the previous year. Known for his 1914 Beaux-Arts Dallas City Hall and Highland Park houses in Tudor and Colonial Revival styles, Hill here demonstrated his proficiency in the Prairie style. The many light-colored decorative elements almost pop out in contrast to the dark brown brick and the red tile roof. Most noticeable are the geometric patterned window muntins and the large-scale brackets at the eaves joined at their bases by a horizontal trim band that also outlines the tops of the windows. On the front porch and porte cochère, similar brackets and trim lines are superimposed over the concrete caps of the pillars to create an interesting geometric pattern as well.

The house became a showplace in the town, featured on a 1914 color postcard and illustrated in the *Dallas Morning News* in 1915. McCartney, whose success was based in real estate and substantial agricultural holdings, was in his early forties when he built the house for his sizable family, composed of his wife Myrtle, four daughters, and one son. Marital difficulties may have led to the sale of the house in 1920, or financial difficulties may have caused both, but E. C. and Myrtle were living at separate, and more modest, addresses in the 1922 city directory. When cotton buyer and farmer Charles L. Penn bought the property from the McCartneys for the very substantial sum of $30,000, the deed specified the inclusion of "the set of dining room furniture." Penn's family continued to live in the house after his death in 1941.

G-9
607 West Marvin Avenue
1928

Parts of a 1906 modified L-plan cottage lie behind (or within) this charming 1928 remodel. On the same day in April of 1906 that James C. (Jack) Lumpkins bought this lot, the *Enterprise* noted that he was having a "modern five-room cottage erected." The house's footprint on the Sanborn maps indicate that it probably looked very similar to the house next door at **611 West Marvin**, built by his law partner John McRae the same year. Lumpkins, who had been brought to Waxahachie as a young child in 1874, opened a law office in 1900 after obtaining a law degree at the University of Texas Law School. He served as County Judge for several years, as well as city attorney, vice president of the Texas Title & Loan Co., and elder in the First Presbyterian Church.

The house was enlarged and altered over the years as three generations of the Lumpkins family resided in it, but the most visible change was made by the original owners in 1928. In that year the *Daily Light* reported on August 23 that "Judge and Mrs. Jack Lumpkins have remodeled their homeplace for the last twenty years by erecting a large English home on West Marvin. Located on a large lot, this place with every convenience is one of the most attractive in Waxahachie." The "English" façade visible from the street hides the asymmetrical footprint of the older, remodeled home.

G-10
611 West Marvin Avenue
1907

Lawyer and assistant county attorney John D. McRae bought this lot on the same day in April of 1906 that his law partner J. C. Lumpkins bought the lot next door (**607 West Marvin**). Without delay, they both built similar modified L-plan cottages with wraparound porches. (Additions to the Lumpkins house in 1928 greatly altered its modified L-plan form.) Three years earlier, in October of 1903, McRae and Miss Mattie Graham had surprised their friends with an unannounced marriage. Not quite an elopement, they were married by Waxahachie's Presbyterian minister, J. C. Smith, in the parlor of the Oriental Hotel in Dallas, and they moved in with the bride's parents upon their return. The McRaes moved to Eastland, Texas, in 1919 and sold the house to farmer William M. Samford. William shared his home with his eighty-three-year-old mother as well as with his widowed brother-in-law and two nieces. He probably updated the house soon after the purchase, for the current porch supports date from the 1920s. The original supports would have been slender classical columns, similar to those on the cottage at **514 West Marvin**. Colonial Revival elements that have survived include the ornamented triangular pediment above the entrance of the porch and the entrance door with sidelights.

G-11
615 West Marvin Avenue
c. 1953; Forrest Upshaw, architect

Former state representative and teacher Rae Files Still built this house soon after she and her husband purchased the property in 1953. She had represented Waxahachie in the state legislature for ten years (1941-1951), and played a significant part in the 1949 passage of the major educational reform legislation that became known as the Gilmer-Aikin Laws. Her work as a teacher at Waxahachie High School provided practical background for her interest in education legislation, and she served as chair of the House Education Committee. Her husband, Forest A. Still, managed the Rockwell Lumber Company on Ferris Avenue. Architect Forrest Upshaw had grown up in Waxahachie and studied with Mrs. Still in high school but was practicing in Dallas when she commissioned the design. An unusual example of early 1950s modernism in Waxahachie, the windowless street façade gives little indication of the house's size or light-filled interior. It opens up on the west side, with wide expanses of glass overlooking a small creek.

G-12
707 West Marvin Avenue
1913; H. D. Rankin, builder

In February of 1913, the *Daily Light* reported that "J. O. Ray has commenced the erection of a pretty home on Marvin avenue that will cost approximately $3,000." The large triple-window gable dormer dominates the façade of this side-gable bungalow with wraparound porch. (The porte cochère with room above is a later addition.) The strong horizontal emphasis of the roof and porch, along with the shingle siding of the dormer, are characteristic of many bungalows of the time. The triangular pediment above the porch entrance is reminiscent of earlier Colonial Revival cottages but is filled with the same shingle pattern as the dormer and reasserts the central focus of the dormer and entrance. Joseph Ray had been listed as a merchant in the 1895 directory and the 1900 Census, but by the time he built this house, at age fifty-two, he gave his occupation as farmer, indicating he had sufficient rural property with tenants or laborers to finance the construction of this substantial middle-class town dwelling. The Rays lived at several different Waxahachie addresses between 1895 and 1913, but they never moved again after settling in this house. Joseph died in 1932, and Dora continued to live here until her death at age ninety-four in 1958. Swede McDaniel, a Waxahachie High School football coach, then bought the house, living here until his death. In the mid 1970s, John and Lynette Compton renovated the house.

G-13
708 West Marvin Avenue
1913

In February of 1913, this two-story hipped-roof house was nearing completion as the bungalow across the street at **707 West Marvin** was commencing. Although both display the horizontal emphasis typical of the time, this one had none of the other's Colonial Revival elements. The rafter ends that are visible under the eaves were often used in two-story Prairie style houses like this one, as well as in Craftsman bungalows. The current porch columns probably replaced square porch supports. Five identical windows, rather than the usual four, stretch across the second-floor façade, but the later addition of narrow dark-green shutters detracts from the rhythm of the original configuration. The recessed side extension originally would have had a sun room beneath a second story sleeping porch, a frequent feature in houses through the 1920s.

When Warren G. and Pearl Lomax built the house, Warren was working as an agent for the Southland Life Insurance Company. Born in South Carolina, he had come to Texas at the age of seventeen, settling in Waxahachie a few years later. Working first as a druggist, he became an insurance agent at the age of forty-nine. Four years later, he and Pearl were able to build this substantial house, noted in the newspaper as costing $4,000. In the late 1920s, their youngest daughter, Josephine, studied music in New York City, where she met C. C. Luhnow, a graduate of the Columbia University School of Journalism. They married in 1929 and settled in New York after their honeymoon in Europe. (He became editor of the publication *Trusts and Estates* in 1933.)

G-14
804 West Marvin Avenue
1960; Smith and Ekblad, architects;
Leslie Lowry and Phillip N. Jeffers, contractors

A 1924 two-story brick house designed by Bertram C. Hill stood on this lot until the afternoon of December 31, 1959, when dripping wax from a candle on top of a television started a fire that gutted the structure. The owners Jack B. and Frances Eastham wasted little time in planning a replacement. In July 1960, they signed a mechanic's lien with Lowry and Jeffers to pay $50,000 for the construction of this red brick ranch dwelling with a cross-hipped roof. The quality of interior and exterior materials and workmanship is indicated by the list of subcontractors and specifications included as part the mechanic's lien. Clear-grain paneling was to be approved by the owner, cabinets and doors were to be mill-made, and the kitchen was to have "at least one breadboard."

Jack Eastham graduated from Southern Methodist University Law School, owned agricultural land in Ellis County, and served as director of the Ellis County Farm Bureau and president of the school board. When young, he lived at **401 East Marvin** with his parents, while his future wife and her family lived at this address in the 1924 house that burned in 1959. As of 2018, the architectural firm that designed this house was continuing to design luxury homes in Dallas as Smith, Ekblad and Associates, Inc.

G-15
807 West Marvin Avenue
1911; W. W. Walston, builder

Three months after purchasing the lot in May of 1911, George P. Mizell and his wife Mary contracted with W. W. Walston to build this "one-story frame house of six rooms, hall and porches," at a cost of $2,547. The mechanic's lien notes that the plans were supplied by the Mizells rather than the builder. The horizontal emphasis typical of bungalows of the period is evident in the wide, deeply recessed wraparound porch and the triple windows banded together on the first floor and in the dormer. The convex-curved sides of this "Waxahachie dormer" are unusually narrow. The original entrance has been altered.

Born in Alabama, Mizell came to Waxahachie as a young man and for more than fifty years was a partner in the Mizell-Peters Insurance Company. He was a charter member of the Rotary Club, member of the school board, and a city alderman. He also was a deputy grand chancellor of the Knights of Pythias.

The bungalow next door at 811 West Marvin Avenue was built c. 1910 by Jack R. Hood and his wife Lottie when he was working as secretary of the Waxahachie Abstract Company. Jack later became president of the abstract company while also running an insurance agency. After Jack's untimely death in a railway accident in 1928, Lottie and her two children moved in with her family at **111 Brown Street**. She became head librarian at the Sims Library and served as an officer in the Texas Library Association. The porch has been partially enclosed and new siding added.

G-16
901 West Marvin Avenue
c. 1905-06

In 1905, J. E. Coleman and his brother created a small subdivision of only ten lots, including this one, on the south side of Marvin, east of Patrick Street. They sold most of the lots without houses, but when R. Lee Ingram bought this lot in October 1905, the price of $3,750 indicated the presence of a house. Ingram was a contractor, and he may have added a second story to a one-story cottage, which would explain the unbalanced placement of the entrance door and first floor windows. This is one of a small group of two-story hipped-roof houses with full-height, full-width entrance porches, and the only one of those with asymmetrical first floor windows. (The house at **103 East University**, two blocks away, shows a more typical symmetrical arrangement.) When W. Bass Williams bought the house in August of 1906, the newspaper noted that this "prominent citizen of the Nash community" would be moving to Waxahachie in the fall and placing his children in school. The 1910 Census recorded four children in the Williams household along with the fifty-six-year-old Bass and his wife Mary. Businessman and farmer Norman J. Thomas lived here with his family from 1919 until 1924, when he built a new house at **1004 West Marvin**.

G-17
902 West Marvin Avenue
c. 1917

Built for insurance agent E. F. Phillips and his wife Minnie, this two-story hipped-roof Prairie style house soon changed hands when Berta and P. A. Chapman Jr. purchased it in 1922. They continued to reside here even after Chapman inherited a share of his father's substantial estate in 1924, which included a 35,000 acre ranch in South Texas, part of the original King Ranch. He died in Corpus Christi in 1939 while on a business trip to the ranch. Berta continued to live here into the 1950s. The original porch was located in the center of the façade, emphasizing the symmetry of the facade. The asymmetrically placed replacement is in the style of the 1920s. The brick pillar on the southeast corner of the lot marked the entrance to the Trinity Heights subdivision, platted in 1914, and developed by R. W. Getzendaner and T. H. Harbin.

G-18
905 West Marvin Avenue
c. 1919

Dr. L. H. Graham, who lived next door at **909 West Marvin**, deeded this property to his daughter Bessie in December 1918. This one-story bungalow was probably built soon after, following a design by architect R. E. Sutherland that was published in the September 1918 issue of *Holland's Magazine*, a general interest magazine for the Southwest that regularly featured house designs during the first decades of the twentieth century. The broad overhanging eaves and stepped curving porch supports were described in the magazine as being "on Japanese lines." Bessie lived here through the late 1920s with her husband, Clyde Dennis, co-owner of the Dennis-Trippet men's clothing store on the west side of the courthouse square. Dr. William C. Tenery, physician-in-charge of the Waxahachie Sanatorium, lived here in the 1930s with his wife Leona. Tenery's key role in the city's medical care was recognized in 1965 when the hospital (now part of the Baylor Scott & White Health system) was named in his honor. His son, Dr. Robert Mayo Tenery, and his wife Barbara lived here for a few years after WWII, before moving to **819 West Main Street**. In 2009, their son, Dr. Rob Tenery, published *Dr. Mayo's Boy*, a memoir and account of Waxahachie's changing health care through the careers of his father and grandfather.

G-19
909 West Marvin Avenue
1909

Physician L. H. Graham and his wife Nora bought this lot from developer J. E. Coleman in December of 1908, and three months later the *Enterprise* noted that their new house was complete. The family moved to Waxahachie from the small community of Boyce, only a few miles away. Given the fact that two of three daughters were in their teens at the time, the move might well have been intended to provide them with access to better education or a larger social circle. The new house certainly provided generous rooms for entertaining, and it was close to Trinity University. Within a few years, the oldest daughter Bessie married Waxahachie merchant Clyde Dennis, and Dr. Graham deeded her the lot next door (**905 West Marvin**). After Dr. Graham's death in 1939, Nora stayed in this house, even though Bessie and Clyde had moved to Dallas and no longer lived next door.

Although the *Enterprise* described it as "one of the latest type of bungalows," the house would not be described as a bungalow today. Responding to the popularity of the new house type at the time, newspapers, as well as other media and individuals, tended to refer to any stylish, new house of one or one-and-a-half stories as a bungalow. In this case the Colonial Revival pedimented entrance and the relatively steep pitch of the triangular gable that dominate the façade provide a vertical emphasis not associated with bungalows. (The horizontal proportions and lines typical of bungalows can be seen just next door at **913 West Marvin**, built around the same time.) The Grahams' house displays curved convex gable walls framing the triple windows above the entrance. Similar curved walls, usually in dormers, are found in Waxahachie houses of all types built around this time, including bungalows. Whether we call it a bungalow or not, this house presents a striking, well-proportioned façade that effectively blends strong geometric symmetry and restrained decorative details. John and Ruth Quarles liked the design so much that they copied it in the home they built at **301 Kaufman** soon after the Grahams moved into their new house.

G-20
910 West Marvin Avenue
1908; H. W. Madson, builder

This two-story hipped-roof Prairie style house looked dramatically different in 1908 when H. W. Madson built it for Frank and Mary Oldham. A two-story porch stretched across the entire façade, and a small balcony graced the central second-floor window, as in the house a block away at **103 East University**. A few years after Cary and Ella Bell Wilson bought the house in 1916 they modernized the home's appearance by replacing the original two-story porch with a one-story Prairie style porch. They also replaced a Palladian dormer with the current hipped-roof dormer and added large decorative paired brackets beneath the eaves of the house and porch. In 1953, most of that second porch was removed, but the current porch essentially recreates the 1923 design. The Wilsons' daughter Agnes and her husband Dr. Ernest M. Thomson lived here after her parents died. Dr. Thomson's optometry equipment and business sign are in the collection of the Ellis County Museum.

The lot was part of forty-seven acres that Mary Oldham had inherited from her mother, Cynisca Williams. Her father John Williams had owned a substantial amount of property in the area, part of which he developed as the Williams Addition a few blocks to the east. (Mary's brother Ed built the house at **412 West Marvin**.) Following in her father's footsteps, Mary, along with her husband Frank, platted a subdivision in 1913 on her inherited property, naming it the Oldham Addition. By 1914, however, the Oldhams had sold most of the subdivision to R. W. Getzendaner and T. H. Harbin, who renamed it Trinity Heights Addition.

G-21
913 West Marvin Avenue
c. 1908

James M. Callens and his wife Elizabeth built this hipped-roof bungalow sometime after purchasing the property in March 1908. The front projecting wing is reminiscent of earlier L-plan cottages, but the horizontal emphasis of the low-pitched hipped roofs and the bands of triple windows firmly characterize it as a bungalow. It closely resembles a plan in the 1908 house catalogue *Radford's Artistic Bungalows*, published in Chicago. Based on that design and other similar ones of the period, it is likely that the porch supports originally were square pillars. James, an established farmer from a few miles away in the Red Oak area, may have moved to town in order to take a position as a road construction foreman, for that was his occupation when the 1910 Census was taken. He selected a lot close to his brothers Will and George, who lived at 1101 and **502 West Marvin**, respectively; both of them had also moved to town from the Red Oak area only a few years previously. In 1913, however, James sold this house and moved back to the country, once again giving his occupation as "farmer" in the 1920 Census.

G-22
1004 West Marvin Avenue
1924; Bertram C. Hill, architect;
H. D. Rankin, builder

British-born Dallas architect Bertram C. Hill designed two houses for prosperous Waxahachie residents in 1924—this one for Norman J. Thomas and his wife Ada, in a straightforward Colonial Revival style, and a larger brick house at **712 West Main** for William D. Anderson in an English Cottage style. Hill continued to work with Waxahachie clients in the 1920s and 1930s, demonstrating his proficiency in eclectic designs. This example displays the pedimented entrance porch, symmetrical façade, and side gable roof typical of the Colonial Revival. The slightly projecting roof over first floor windows hints at the profile of a gambrel roof without actually impinging upon the basic rectangular block of the house. Thomas built the house at the height of his career, at the age of fifty-three. He started in the retail lumber business but later invested in other enterprises and in land. In 1908, he was one of five men who formed the Waxahachie Hot Wells Natatorium Company. By the 1920 Census, he listed himself as a farmer. He paid contractor H. D. Rankin $8,000, a substantial sum at the time, to construct this ten-room house, though that was small compared to the $25,000 that William Anderson is reported to have paid the contractor for his Bertram Hill house on West Main. Thomas liked this one well enough to remain here until his death.

G-23
1107 West Marvin Avenue
1907

This two-story hipped-roof house dates to March 1907, when the newspaper noted that work was "progressing nicely" on James T. Couch's West Marvin house. Couch had bought the lot in 1906 but did not start construction here until he sold his house at **514 West Marvin** in January 1907. The vertical emphasis of the current full-height entry porch was originally balanced by a one-story porch that stretched across the entire façade and wrapped around the east side. That original porch configuration closely matched the one that remains at **716 Water Street**. Couch gave his occupation as a farmer, but he invested in residential real estate as well. He also managed to turn a profit by building and selling his own residences. He sold this house for $6,000 three years after building it, having previously sold his earlier house in 1907 for $4,550, also after a three-year tenure. Another farmer, E. T. Gillean, lived here in the early 1920s with his wife Ida and son Edgar, who worked at Curlin's Pharmacy. By the time Mr. and Mrs. J. C. Howle bought the house in the early 1970s, the interior had been divided into multiple apartments while the exterior was deteriorating and the front porch crumbling. They restored the original floor plan, removed the crumbling one-story porch, and replaced the missing front door with a taller antique cypress door they found in Galveston.

G-24
1111 West Marvin Avenue
c. 1913

Roy A. Callens was in his early twenties when he built this modest front-gable bungalow a few lots down from his uncle's bungalow at **913 West Marvin**. It replaced an earlier house that burned in 1913. Roy had previously farmed near Red Oak, but by 1912 he had ventured into real estate, offering Ellis County farm homes in the *Dallas Morning News*. Waxhahachie's 1913 directory gives his occupation as a driver for S. P. Spalding's furniture company. He and his wife later moved to Dallas, where he worked for the Texas Farm Bureau Cotton Association. Subsequent owners included W. D. Woodroof, who operated a dry goods store on South Rogers, and Trinity University chemistry professor J. B. Ford, who lived here with his wife from 1923 until his death in 1939.

G-25
1119 West Marvin Avenue
1914

Della Dalton bought the property in May 1913, the year after her husband William died at the age of forty-six, and the *Daily Light* indicated that she would begin her new home "soon." But it was not until June of 1914 that the *Dallas Morning News* noted she had begun construction of her residence on West Marvin. Della and William had lived for several years above their millinery shop on the square, and she continued to live there until she built this two-story hipped-roof Prairie style house. (The porch may have been altered.) A resourceful woman, Mrs. Dalton continued to run the shop while also renting rooms in the house that she built large enough for that purpose. Her advertisement in the 1915 *Daily Light* stated, "Beautifully furnished rooms, in private home; all modern conveniences; in cool University addition." World War I brought more difficulties to her life. While her son was fighting in France, his wife died in New York. Mrs. Dalton arranged to bury her remains in Waxahachie. Although injured in the war, her son returned safely. The 1920 Census shows both Mrs. Dalton and her son in Dallas, with Mrs. Dalton running a boarding house with six roomers and two servants. She sold this house to lawyer J. Lea Gammon and his wife Quincy in 1918. Gammon practiced law in addition to his interests as a director of the Enterprise Publishing Company and the Texas Electric Railway Company. He also served as president of the school board. Quincy died in 1928, but J. Lea remained in the house into the 1950s.

G-26
1201 West Marvin Avenue
1913

With its full-width front porch and central gable dormer, this bungalow resembles the one built at **108 University** a couple of years earlier, as well as designs in many popular magazines and catalogues of the period. Decorative details are limited to the rhythmic punctuation of the exposed rafter ends under the eaves of the porch roof and triangular knee braces at the dormer roof. The porch supports have been rebuilt in the style of the period. The deed records, local newspapers, and Sanborn maps provide documentation that confirms a construction date of 1913, but leaves the builder somewhat in question. Homer Chapman bought this lot and the one to its west for $1,000 in December 1912, and sold only this lot two months later to A. L. Connally for $3,500. That increase in price normally would indicate that a house had been built on the property by Chapman during those two months. The *Daily Light*, however, reported Connally's purchase a few days later and indicated that he would "immediately commence the erection of a fine residence," which implies that Chapman had not built a house. The Sanborn map of November 1914 shows a house with this footprint on this lot. Either Connally expanded an existing house, or Chapman made an excellent profit on his initial investment. Connally, who invested in real estate, only kept the property for a few months, and it continued to change hands with some frequency during its early years. Educator B. F. Crews, who had run unsuccessfully for the US Congress in 1916, bought the house in 1919. In 1921, he left his position as principal of the Central Ward School to become an internal revenue collector. Railroad conductor S. J. Bennett bought the house from Crews in 1924 and lived here with his family until 1926.

G-27
1203 West Marvin Avenue
1914; A. N. Guthrie, builder

In a 1914 mechanic's lien Edward A. DuBose Jr. agreed to pay A. N. Guthrie $2,100 to build this "six room frame shingle roof dwelling." Though modest in size, the side-gable bungalow with front-gable porch resembled up-to-date examples illustrated in magazines and catalogues of the period. Although the low-pitched roof and wide band of clapboards at the base of the porch gable present the horizontal emphasis typical of bungalows, the narrow vertical boards ornamenting the front gable and the porch supports create an interesting interplay of vertical and horizontal that is emphasized with the current contrasting paint colors. Edward built this bungalow at the age of twenty-six, a year after his father died. His father had been one of Waxahachie's major businessmen, mayor for several years, and manager of the cotton mill. After studying in the textile department of Texas A&M, DuBose Jr. returned to Waxahachie and joined his father at the mill in the position of assistant manager. He probably built this house for rental income and continued to live with his mother on College Street. He sold the house in 1919, and in the 1920 Census is listed with his mother, along with his wife and two young children, at the family home on College Street, though he left Waxahachie soon after. In the 1930 Census he appears in San Antonio, working as manager of a cotton mill.

Another "Junior" bought this bungalow in 1924. George P. Bullard Jr. and his wife had been living nearby with his parents at **305 University** when the 1920 Census was taken, but the death of his father in 1922 led to the sale of that house and George Jr.'s move to West Marvin. Like DuBose and many other Waxahachie residents, Bullard also was involved in the cotton industry, working as a weigher at the National Compress Company.

G-28
501 North Grand Avenue
1895

Bookkeeper Worth C. Rockett and his wife Anna built this two-story modified L-plan house soon after purchasing the land from the West End Development Company in 1895. The design responds to the corner lot with a small second-story balcony above a one-story rectangular bay that is enfolded by a one-story curving porch. Towers often served a similar function when owners wanted to elaborate on a modified L-plan, and the house at **1303 West Main** provides a nearby example of a corner-tower variation. Worth and Anna lived in the house until the early 1920s, when they moved to a bungalow on East University.

G-29
508 North Grand Avenue
1896; C. M. Sammons, builder

Lawyer Charles M. Sherrod and his wife Helen contracted with C. M. Sammons to build this one-story L-plan house in November of 1896, not long after they arrived in Waxahachie. They agreed to pay Sammons $1,000 for a "one-story frame house of four rooms and a hall" with plans furnished by the owners. The lien also specified that the Sherrods would be supplying some of the materials. The *Enterprise* had announced in September of that year that Sherrod would be forming a partnership with M. W. McKnight. Sherrod encountered financial difficulties, however, and in July of 1899 he was forced to deed this house to the National Building and Loan Association, which had purchased the lien from the builder Sammons. Sherrod and his family returned to their home state of Alabama. Two years later teacher James B. Baker bought the property, and he and his wife Mattie lived here into the 1920s.

G-30
512 North Grand Avenue
1896; E. H. Griffin, builder

Real estate developer and contractor E. H. Griffin invested primarily in Waxahachie's East End, but in building this one-story modified L-plan cottage, he ventured beyond his familiar territory into the portion of the West End subdivision north of the railroad tracks known as Arlington Heights. He obtained funding for the construction in February 1896 from the Southern Home Building & Loan Association, and in April of that year the local newspaper reported that J. Will Gilliam had rented E. H. Griffin's "new cottage in Arlington Heights." Griffin sold the house two years later, and it passed through a series of owner-landlords until Mrs. Julia E. King bought it in 1911. The widow of furniture store proprietor and undertaker J. Thomas King, Julia lived in the house rather than renting it to others. The house may have been based on Design No. 9 in George F. Barber's *Cottage Souvenir No. 2*, although the window openings and decorative details were simplified.

G-31
521 North Grand Avenue
1903

Morrison S. Payne purchased the property in September 1903, and three months later the *Enterprise* noted his move into the recently completed "handsome house." The one-and-a-half-story modified L-plan cottage still presents a handsome appearance, with its two gable wings nicely balancing the polygonal entrance and tower. A Confederate veteran and prosperous farmer, Payne moved to Waxahachie from the nearby community of Red Oak, along with his wife Elizabeth and two youngest children, then in their late teens. He remained here until his death in 1936 at the age of ninety-one. His youngest daughter Hattie never married and continued to live in the house into the 1950s.

G-32
1424 Sycamore Street
c. 1902

Although Mrs. Mary Amonette McClellan bought the lot in 1895, she waited several years before building, probably until Trinity University's arrival. The child of early Waxahachie settlers Mr. and Mrs. Andrew C. McCartney, Mary married ginner W. W. McClellan in 1877 and bore six children before his death in 1893. As a widow in her thirties, with four children still at home, Mary began investing in property, with this lot one of many that she purchased. (She gave her occupation for the 1900 Census as "landlord.") With a son and two daughters in their teens when Trinity announced its move to Waxahachie, Mary might have been influenced by this lot's location near the campus in her decision to build. The builder is not known, but the basic form of this two-story modified L-plan house is similar to at least two other examples in Waxahachie (**305 University** and **607 North Rogers**). Mary died in the house in 1927, having previously deeded it to two of her daughters "with love and affection" in 1925.

G-33
1423 Sycamore Street
1903

The gable and roof pattern of this one-story modified L-plan cottage represents a popular variation of the form also found at **300 East Marvin** (1896) and **1030 West Main** (1899). The original porch balustrade is now gone, but much remains of the "handsome new home" owned by Young Taylor that was noted in the November 13, 1903, issue of the *Enterprise*. The newspaper previously reported in May 1902 that Taylor was considering the move from Weatherford to Waxahachie for his children to enter Trinity. The family probably never lived in this house, since Young sold the newly completed house less than three months after buying the lot. They did, however, buy a similar cottage at **523 Highland**, three blocks away, in January 1904, and lived there until Young's untimely death the following year at the age of fifty-two. In 1913 Robert S. Watkins moved here and remained until his death in 1930. Identified in his obituary as a "native pioneer ranchman and benefactor of Christian education," Mr. Watkins included Trinity University in his donations. The gymnasium on the campus was named in memory of his father, Richard O. Watkins, who was the first Presbyterian minister to be ordained in the Republic of Texas.

G-34
603 Highland Avenue
1903; S. E. McElroy, builder

When P. A. Chapman decided to move to Waxahachie and build this modified L-plan house, the local newspapers noticed, as well they should have. The *Enterprise* reported in October 30, 1903, that Chapman's residence was nearing completion and in a later article described it as "elegant." Born in Missouri, Chapman had moved to Texas with his parents in 1850, and he lived in the Ovilla area (eleven miles north of Waxahachie) until he had this house built. Chapman already had substantial land holdings when he moved, and he continued to expand his business interests, finding additional success in banking and oil. He probably decided on the Waxahachie move and this specific neighborhood because of Trinity University's relocation here. (In the 1900 Census, seven of his eight children were under twenty years old.) In 1916 Chapman had a substantial brick residence built at **903 West Main** and deeded this house to his son, P. A. Chapman, Jr. When P. A. Jr. "moved up" in his turn to the house at **902 West Marvin**, farmer F. F. Farrar bought this house.

Rather than using a Waxahachie builder for this house, Chapman selected S. E. McElroy from Midlothian, whom he probably already knew. The unknown designer created a pleasing pattern of triangular gables against the flat-topped pyramidal roof, and the geometric shapes predominate in the absence of any decorative gable ornaments. (No surviving spindlework or ornament is evident in the 1985 survey photograph.) The house was neglected for many years before a recent renovation.

G-35
523 Highland Avenue
1902

Wiley J. Barksdale brought his family from Oklahoma to join his brother George in settling in Waxahachie. He bought two lots in May 1902 from George's block of land and built this house. (The brothers were next-door neighbors, but intervening houses were constructed later.) The newspaper noted on July 4 that both men were in town "superintending" construction of their houses, and on July 25 that Wiley's family had arrived in town. According to the newspaper, Wiley moved to East Texas in 1904 when he sold the house to Young Taylor, but he resumed residence after Young died in 1905 and his widow, Tennessee, deeded the property back to him. The brothers and their families evidently maintained cordial relations, for they continued to live next to each other through the rest of the decade, and the newspaper reported their joint trip to San Antonio's flower carnival in 1907. In 1912 Wiley sold the house to farmer Sid Farrar.

This modified L-plan cottage has Queen Anne style proportions, massing, and details, but a few of the details, including the Ionic porch column capitals, represent the Colonial Revival style that was gaining in popularity at the time. The smooth curve of the porch roof visually joins the two projecting gable bays. The additional corner bay window to the left of the entrance adds an interesting touch of complexity.

G-36
511 Highland Avenue
1902

Although platted in the late 1880s as the part of the West End Addition, the lots on Highland Avenue remained empty until March of 1902, when construction began on Trinity University nearby. That same month, the *Enterprise* noted that East Texas lumberman George I. Barksdale intended to move his family to Waxahachie and enroll his children in Trinity. He was back in the paper again the next month, when he purchased most of this block and announced his intention to build a "magnificent" residence. By the time construction was actually underway, the newspaper's description was downgraded to the term used more frequently for new houses, "handsome." The newspaper also noted that both George and his brother Wiley J. were building houses on the block. George's became 511 and Wiley's, 523. The two houses embody different plans and styles. This symmetrical side-gable house with an unusually wide central front gable dormer may have been the inspiration for a similar house built six years later at **707 West Marvin**. The horizontal emphasis of the side-gable roof and full-width front porch as well as the lack of ornament are representative of many early bungalows, while the triangular entrance pediment is reminiscent of the Colonial Revival style, also popular at the time.

G-37
1210 Martha Street
1925; Ye Planry Corp., architect;
A. A. Few & Son, builders

When real estate agent Porter L. Williams ventured into speculative building with the construction of this one-story front-gable bungalow, he knew the neighborhood well, having lived two blocks away at **200 East University** for several years. He may have intended to rent the property, or he may have had trouble selling it, for it was two years before he sold it to Mrs. Fannie Bell Elliott, widow of J. S. Elliott. He barely covered the construction costs of $5,250 with the sales price of $6,000. Mrs. Elliott also knew the neighborhood, having previously resided in Trinity University's women's dormitory, Beeson Hall, while working as its superintendent. The design, including the triple windows on the façade and prominent dentils across the porch and front gables, exactly matches one published in a Ye Planry catalogue of the early 1920s. The additional side-gable section of the porch acknowledges the lot's corner location and would permit an approach from either street, were the fence not there.

G-38
108 University Avenue
1911; Andrew N. Guthrie, builder

Builder and contractor Andrew N. Guthrie and his wife Gertrude bought this lot in May of 1911, and on July 28 the *Daily Light* reported that they had moved into their new home. Actually, in the paper's usual fashion, only the male Guthrie was mentioned as "occupying his new residence on University Avenue," but his wife and two children probably joined him. As a busy local builder, Andrew would have been well aware of the variety of bungalow designs popular at the time. For his own house, he built an up-to-date side-gable bungalow with central dormer, similar to examples in magazines and catalogues. Another example of the type was built a few lots away (**1201 West Marvin**) two years later. Many of its original Craftsman style bungalow elements have been altered over the years, most notably the windows, but the broad expanse of the roof and the wide porch still present the horizontal emphasis typical of bungalows. The dormer roof is unusual in projecting significantly beyond the windows, a feature repeated above the windows in the side gables. Andrew and his wife were in their late twenties when they moved into the house with their two children, having previously lived a few blocks away on Highland. Andrew's family evidently helped with his business, for the 1910 Census shows that both his father and brother-in-law were living in the household and working as house carpenters. In 1920, Andrew and his wife moved to Dallas, where he continued to work as a contractor for another thirty years. Grocer James M. Chapman and his wife Mary bought the house in 1922 for their growing family. By the time of the 1930 Census, they had eight children living here with them.

G-39
114 University Avenue
1921

Albert E. Moore, manager of the local branch of the Cameron Lumber Company, bought this lot in July of 1921 and built the side-gable Colonial Revival style bungalow soon after. It was probably based on a design from a house plan catalogue available at his own lumberyard. The small curved entrance porch surmounted by a classical balustrade forms the most distinctive feature of the house, as well as serving as an early example of the national trend toward smaller front porches. Moore was listed in the 1922 city directory as living here, but he sold the house on January 30 of that year to Maggie Simmons, and her descendants remember her saying it was "built for her." She could have selected the design from the lumber company's catalogue and commissioned Moore to construct the house. Maggie was the widow of G. B. Simmons and daughter of Bullard Heights founder D. B. Bullard. She and her two teenaged daughters moved in soon after the purchase. According to Maggie Simmons's granddaughter, Hilda Chapman, the house became a popular gathering place when the daughters reached college age, for Mrs. Simmons allowed dancing, which was forbidden on the Trinity campus. Younger daughter Lena married James H. Harbin, son of developer T. H. Harbin. After a few years in Harlingen, the couple returned to Waxahachie and raised their family in this house, adding a second-floor room in the attic space in 1946.

G-40
115 University Avenue
1910-11; J. S. McCanless, builder

In December 1910, James A. Posey and his wife, Berta, contracted to pay J. S. McCanless $2,280 to build this "one story frame house" with "six rooms and bath room, two porches and a hall" according to plans supplied by the Poseys. In this pyramidal house the entrance door and the hipped-roof dormer directly above serve as the central focus of a powerfully symmetrical façade. The symmetry is only strengthened by the profiles of the flanking side dormers. The absence of ornament contributes to a straightforward composition of triangular forms and rectangles, with curved lines banished even from the porch supports. The Poseys might have obtained their plans from a mail-order catalogue such as *Artistic Homes* published by Herbert C. Chivers in 1910, which includes several similar designs. Posey was the superintendent of the Farmers Gin & Milling Company, as well as an investor in real estate. Berta, his second wife, also ventured into real estate, purchasing in her own name another lot in the University Addition in 1912, as well as the house on West Main where they moved after selling this one to William T. and Emma Harris. William Harris was born in Canada, but lived for many years in West, Texas (near Waco), where he was elected their first mayor and served as a director of the West National Bank, as an officer in the West Cotton Textile Mills, and business manager of the *West Times*. He retired to Waxahachie at the age of fifty-nine for his two sons to attend Trinity University. His son David became a professor at Stanford University. Emma continued to live in the house after William's death in 1938.

G-41
119 University Avenue
c. 1911

Real estate agent James. T. Sullivan and his wife Rebecca bought this lot in July of 1911 and probably built this side-gable bungalow with gable dormer soon after. Another example of the type was built around the same time at **108 University**. Here, the wider dormer dominates the façade, and the house and dormer roofs are more steeply pitched than those at 108. Sullivan visited Waxahachie in 1889 as a representative of the Texas Building & Loan Association, and moved his family to town a few months later, first living in a house on North Rogers.

He became an early investor in the University Addition, buying his first lot in 1903. His firm advertised University-area property as its specialty in a 1905 issue of the *Enterprise*. By 1907, he and Rebecca were living in the area, for the *Enterprise* noted their daughter's wedding in their "University Heights" home. After having occupied multiple Waxahachie houses over the years, the Sullivans finally settled in this house. Rebecca remained after James's death, being listed here in the city directories through 1939.

G-42
120 University Avenue
c. 1922

This front-gable bungalow and the one at **208 Virginia** are closely related in design. Both possess a similar front-gable entrance porch, placed asymmetrically against the façade with a roof pitch much lower than that of the main roof. They also have wraparound porches leading to secondary entrance doors. In this example, the front gable of the porch is wider, and a porte cochère extends from the side porch. Thomas B. Simms, who taught education at Trinity University, bought this corner lot from W. T. Harris in June of 1922. (Harris lived in the bungalow across the street at **115 University**.) Simms probably had the house built soon after buying the property, for he and his family are listed at this address in the 1924-25 directory. Born in Tennessee, Simms came to Trinity in 1918 after serving as president of two small colleges in Kentucky and as superintendent of public schools in Oklahoma and Texas. He taught at Trinity for twenty years, and his obituary mentions his keen interest in sports and chairmanship of the Trinity athletics committee. He and his wife lived here until he died in 1941, at the age of sixty-six.

G-43
207 University Avenue
1913

The *Daily Light* noted on February 16, 1913, that Sidney C. Turner had nearly finished this "very handsome and comfortable residence on University Avenue, which will cost a little over $4,000." The broad, sloping roof of the side-gable Craftsman bungalow incorporates a full-width front porch and is broken only by an unusually flat shed dormer. Two other examples of the type survive in Waxahachie, and both have higher, more prominent dormers (**218 Virginia** and **814 West Main**). The horizontal multilight windows flanking the entrance door are also unusual. Similar designs in bungalow books and magazines of the period, along with the Waxahachie examples, indicate that the porch originally would have had thicker square supports and a balustrade or solid railing that would have visually balanced the massive flat expanse of roof. Turner managed the G. H. McFaddin & Brothers firm of cotton dealers.

G-44
218 University Avenue
c. 1922

Tax records indicate that Dr. Will Marion Jenkins had this substantial brick-veneer bungalow built for his family around 1922. Although the use of brick veneer indicated a more substantial and expensive house than many of its neighbors, the design of this bungalow de-emphasizes its size. The second-story side-gable section recedes behind the dominant cascading three front gables. The placement of the porte cochère towards the rear also contributes to the first impression of a smaller house, compatible in scale to its neighbors. The house next door (212 University) includes a similar two-story section behind a simpler, smaller-scale front gable. Jenkins, who obtained his medical degree at Vanderbilt University, came from a family of doctors. Not only his father, but all six of his brothers also practiced medicine. His brother, F. Hop Jenkins, also lived and worked in Waxahachie. Will died only five years after building this house, at the age of fifty-six, while working on his farm south of Waxahachie, in Hill County. His wife Sudie continued to live in the house for many years after his death.

G-45
305 University Avenue
1902

One of the earliest houses built in the University Addition, this handsome two-story modified L-plan frame house was built during the summer of 1902 by cotton buyer and landowner R. K. Erwin. Born in Tennessee, Erwin came to Texas in 1875 at the age of seventeen. He farmed and ran a cotton gin in Mount Pleasant, a few miles from Waxahachie, before moving to Waxahachie to manage the Farmers Alliance warehouse. Erwin next managed the first cottonseed oil mill in Waxahachie, from which he resigned in 1901 to have more time for other business interests, including cotton buying. He joined the leading businessmen of Waxahachie in purchasing lots in the new University Addition for development, but he was among the first to build on his. In June 1902 the newspaper noted that Erwin was building this house to be occupied by Young Taylor, who was returning to Ellis County to educate his children at Trinity. After the Taylors bought a house nearby on Highland Street in 1904, Erwin sold the property to contractor and farmer R. H. Dearing. Another farmer, George P. Bullard, then in his sixties, and his wife Nannie bought the house in 1910. When the Bullards filed a Designation of Homestead for this property in 1912, they described the improvements as "one two story, nine room frame house, one good barn, servants house, chicken house, and wood and coal house and smoke house." The number of outbuildings may reflect the rural character of the neighborhood at this time, but this was a transitional period when many people in town still kept horses and chickens on their property. A 1912 photograph of this house in the *Daily Light* shows a line of trees planted between the street and the house as well as a glimpse of one of the outbuildings. In 1923, a year after George died, their daughter Mary W. Bullard sold the house to Ed L. Evans, field manager of Shamrock Oil Company, and his wife Hattie. Their youngest child, Ernest Burke Evans, was a 1939 graduate of Waxahachie High School and became a distinguished orthopedic surgeon and Chief of the Division of Orthopedics at the University of Texas Medical Branch in Galveston.

G-46
306 University Avenue
c. 1917

This modest bungalow served as the home of Trinity University President Dr. John H. Burma for the twelve years he held that position. It had been built by cotton buyer and real estate investor Robert H. Smellage sometime after he bought the property in February 1916 for $750 and before he sold it to C. M. Hall in March 1918 for $2,775. A front-gable bungalow with full-width front porch, it displays Craftsman details that include square porch supports and knee braces in the front gable. Rectangular bay windows on both sides of the house add variety to the plan. The narrow drop siding used on the house was becoming more common during this period. Burma and his wife Manetta bought the house a few months after moving to Waxahachie in 1921. Born in Iowa, Dr. Burma came to Trinity from a position as vice president of the University of Dubuque, Iowa, but he had spent time in Texas before that, serving as pastor of the Second Presbyterian Church of Dallas. He presided over Trinity in good times and bad. During the prosperous period of the 1920s the endowment increased, enrollment doubled, the gymnasium was constructed, and the University was admitted to the Southern Association of Colleges. The Depression, however, led to a drop in enrollment and increasing operating deficits. Dr. Burma resigned the presidency in 1933 to become Pastor of the Central Presbyterian Church in Sherman, where he remained until his death in 1938.

G-47
309 University Avenue
1922; Ramsey Brothers, builders

Physician Fred R. Adamson built this cross-gable brick-veneer bungalow almost two years after he purchased the lot in August of 1920. The brick piers and square porch supports with sloping sides were frequently used in bungalows of the 1920s. The size and complexity of the house are somewhat disguised from the street view by the wraparound porch and the size of the porch gable. The house's brick veneer, however, clearly indicated a more substantial investment than most of the frame bungalows in the area. The *Daily Light* noted on May 23, 1922, that excavation had commenced, and on June 15 that the framework was nearly complete. It also named the brick contractor, H. H. Richards, in addition to the Ramsey Brothers, the general contractors. In his mid-forties at the time of the purchase, Dr. Adamson came to Waxahachie from Teague, Texas. Ten years later, he and his wife Pearl moved to Abilene, selling the house to Ona Plummer, a single schoolteacher. Ona had graduated from Trinity in 1917 and earned an MA from the University of Texas in Austin. She and her sister, Laura Sue Plummer, also a teacher, lived here until the mid-1970s.

G-48
1200 Sycamore Street
Trinity University Campus
[now Southwestern Assemblies of God University]

Waxahachie citizens had good reason for celebrating with a "jollification meeting" after successfully winning the bid as the new home for Trinity University in June 1901. Previously located in the small, isolated east Texas community of Tehucana, the Presbyterian school had been losing enrollment and struggling to survive. When the Texas Synod made the decision to advertise for bids from Texas cities interested in supporting a move, Waxahachie citizens quickly formed a committee, chaired by W. H. Getzendaner, to locate a site for the campus and obtain the financial support necessary for a successful bid. The committee settled on 110 acres, primarily pasture land, less than a mile northwest of the square. Setting aside ten acres for the campus, they came up with the novel idea of raising funds by platting the remainder of the land as a subdivision, named University Addition, and selling lots for $200 each. With all sales contingent upon Trinity's acceptance of the bid, the plan enabled residents of relatively modest means to support the proposal and potentially profit from increased land values resulting from the university's relocation. Trinity's locating committee chose Waxahachie's bid, valued at $80,000, over Itasca and Corsicana, citing Waxahachie's "desirable site . . . the accessibility of the town, the enthusiasm of the citizens, and the handsome cash consideration. . . ."

The campus plan benefited from its integration with the plan of the adjacent University Addition. The neighborhood's central street, University Avenue, terminated at the central axis of the campus, where a walkway continued to the main building. When architects were hired to design the main building, they also drew two flanking dormitory buildings in the same Gothic style, forming a cross axis. The one on the west was built in 1902 as Prendergast Hall, but has been replaced. Trinity later built a woman's dormitory at the southwest corner of the campus, which still survives, and a gymnasium behind the main building, which was demolished. Although the university's initial years in Waxahachie saw drought, floods, and administrative upheaval, it eventually grew and prospered. In 1928 the American Council on Education named it one of only five accredited colleges and universities in Texas. Unfortunately, the Depression years of the 1930s dealt serious blows to enrollment and financial support, which precipitated another change in location. Trinity moved to San Antonio in 1942. The Southwestern Bible Institute, later to become the Southwestern Assemblies of God University, bought the campus in 1943.

Well-known alumni who spent time on this campus include internationally acclaimed theater director and educator Paul Baker, who graduated from Trinity in 1932, and rock-and-roll pioneer Jerry Lee Lewis, who attended the Southwestern Bible Institute in 1950, but, according to legend, was expelled after playing a boogie-woogie version of *My God Is Real* in a school assembly.

G-49

Trinity University Main Building [now Farmer Administration Building]

1902; Hubbell & Greene, architects; Dennis Mahoney, contractor

This three-story Collegiate-Gothic style building, with eighty-four-foot tower, still dominates the campus, over one hundred years after its construction. Built of brick with white terra cotta and cast-stone trim, it contained classrooms, laboratories, library, offices, and a chapel that seated six hundred, as well as women's and men's gymnasiums in the raised basement. Early descriptions of the building refer to its gray brick, which now appears more beige than gray. The slightly projecting east and west bays and central tower provide depth and variety to the façade, while the octagonal stair tower on the southeast corner of the main tower gives an interesting element of asymmetry. Bands of brick and cast-stone masonry at the level of the raised basement provide a strong horizontal base. Simple cream-colored hood moldings highlight the narrow lancet windows in the stair tower and join the third-floor window groupings. Most of the decorative ornament is concentrated on the central tower, including the crenellations at the top, horizontal band at the roofline, and cast-metal balcony above the entrance. The original wood entrance doors have been replaced with glass and aluminum, but the decorative surround survives, with terra cotta leaves and vines entwined around the construction date of "AD 1901." The wood window frames have been replaced with aluminum, and the chapel in the rear has been extended.

The selection of a Gothic style followed a precedent found in campuses across the country in the late nineteenth century that would continue through the 1930s. Architect Ralph Adams Cram became one of its major proponents, citing connections to "the old ideals and sound methods of the English colleges." Since the Gothic Revival style was also strongly associated with church architecture, its use here would have been considered even more appropriate, given the religious affiliation of the school.

Dallas architects James P. Hubbell and Herbert Miller Greene designed the building barely a year after forming their partnership in 1900. They also designed a number of major Dallas buildings in a variety of styles, including the Kingman Texas Implement Company Building (1902), First Church of Christ Scientist (1910), Scottish Rite Cathedral (1913), Parkland Hospital in Oak Lawn (1913), and the Nieman-Marcus Building (1914). After they dissolved their partnership in 1917, they both produced academic work. Hubbell designed high school buildings for Dangerfield and Hillsboro. In 1922, Greene was appointed University Architect for the University of Texas, where he designed ten buildings. Although the contractor Dennis Mahoney lived in Waxahachie, he had a statewide reputation and practice. In addition to Trinity, his university work included the east wing of the Main Building at the University of Texas (1899), a dormitory at Texas A&M (1899), and the main building of the Girls' Industrial College (later Texas Women's University) at Denton (1902). He evidently approved of Hubbell & Greene's architectural work for Trinity, since he had them design his own house (**604 West Main**) two years later.

G-50

Drane Hall [now M. E. Collins Hall]

1911-12; C. D. Hill, architect;
Fred A. Jones Construction Co.;
South wing 1923; Christie & Dolph Co., contractor

This two-story dormitory with raised basement looks very different from the main administration building, although it was built only ten years later. The two buildings share the same brick, but no effort was made to use the same Gothic style for the dormitory. The Prairie style predominates here, although a few classical elements are provided as visual punctuation points. Classical triangular pediments cap the secondary entrance doors at the interior corners of the entrance court; a classical wreath crowns the central tablet bearing the name "Woman's Building," and a balustrade edges the entire roof. Though classical in inspiration, the balustrade ends up reinforcing the strong horizontal emphasis of the building's proportions that is typical of the Prairie style. The original wood entrance doors and window frames have been replaced with aluminum, and the entrance stairs have been altered. Architect C. D. Hill worked for the Fort Worth architects Sanguinet & Staats before opening his own firm in Dallas in 1907. This was his first project in Waxahachie, to be followed by the Rogers Hotel (1912) and the E. C. McCartney House (1913), both of which were also in the Prairie style. He used the Gothic Revival style when he returned to town in 1917 for the Central Presbyterian Church. His Dallas buildings included a grand city hall and several major churches. Successful completion of the Trinity project evidently served as a good recommendation for the contractor as well. Only a few months later, Fred A. Jones Co. was awarded the contract to build the administration building of the new Southern Methodist University in Dallas.

The original women's dormitory, Prendergast Hall, built to the west of the main building in 1902, was inadequate for the demand by 1910, when the Trustees began planning erection of a larger, modern facility. Waxahachie citizens, represented by the Commercial Club, supported the effort by pledging $25,000 to match $50,000 raised by the trustees. When that amount proved insufficient for a fireproof building of the desired size, the decision was made to build in phases. Construction on the central and north wings began in August 1911. In May 1912 the *Dallas Morning News* noted the formal opening of "this magnificent building." In addition to its handsome exterior, the many modern comforts merited praise, including hot and cold water in every room, forty candlepower tungsten lighting with wall switches, and steam heat. The raised basement housed a large kitchen, dining room, and recreational facilities. Fundraising difficulties and World War I delayed construction of the south wing until 1923.

G-51

P. C. Nelson Memorial Library

1960; Noftsger-Lawrence and Associates, architects;
James T. Taylor & Sons, contractors

The Southwestern Bible Institute moved to this campus in 1943, but other than replacing a fire-damaged men's dormitory in 1954, they did not undertake a major construction project until 1960, when they built the Nelson Memorial Library. Not surprisingly, given the era and the new institution, the administration decided to break with the Gothic and Prairie style precedents in building the library, but they kept within the existing campus plan and placed it on the same horizontal axis with the administration building. The library was named after P. C. Nelson, who had founded the Southwestern Bible School in Enid, Oklahoma, in 1927, which later merged with two other Bible schools to form the Southwestern Bible Institute. The school's name was changed to Southwestern Assemblies of God College in 1954 and Southwestern Assemblies of God University in 1994. Oklahoma architect B. Gaylord Noftsger practiced on his own in the 1920s and 1930s, designing Art Deco buildings that included the Fort Worth Public Market and the Warehouse Market Building in Tulsa. In 1941, he established a partnership with William Martin Lawrence, and they designed projects in a variety of styles including the Mid-century Modern style of the Nelson Library. The school also used the firm to plan the 1967 renovation of the administration building. The library's original massing remains intact, but the overall exterior color scheme has been altered, particularly on the panels of aggregate stone and concrete to the right of the entrance, which originally were a uniform color. The poured concrete stairway with aluminum rails, visible through the glass entrance walls, remains a well-detailed feature of the building. At the building's dedication on November 1, 1960, librarian Pearl Ellis was credited with playing "an important role in the plans for the new modern design."

G-52
1103-1115 Sycamore

Although the current buildings probably date from post-World War II, commercial activity on this lot goes back to before August 1916, when O. H. and Helen Hood sold the property to W. C. Wallis, "including all the fixtures in a store building . . . and also one steam clothes press." Even with a prime location directly across from the Trinity University campus, ownership and tenants changed frequently. The 1925 Sanborn map shows two frame commercial buildings occupying only the west half of the lot. The larger one, on the corner, contained two shops, while the smaller contained one. In the 1927 city directory, they were occupied by a barber shop, a grocery, and a pharmacy. By 1948, the entire lot facing Sycamore had been filled with shops, including a washateria, cleaners, shoe shop, barber shop, lunch room, and two groceries.

G-53
330 East University Avenue
1903-04

Although its original windows and siding have been replaced, this modified L-plan house retains its basic form. An early photograph shows that it never possessed any decorative turned or sawn ornament on the porch or in the gables. In contrast to the simplicity of the façade, a complex hipped roof with multiple cross gables presents a series of intersecting slopes and angles that is partially hidden by surrounding trees. The property's location across the street from the Trinity University campus led to its early development and use. Isaac A. Looney, a teacher in Hillsboro, Texas, built the house for his son, Trinity University professor B. E. Looney, soon after purchasing the lot in October of 1903. A year later, the *Enterprise* noted that B. E., "an energetic, ambitious young man" and "experienced chemist," had bought an interest in the Herring Drug Company (later the Waxahachie Medicine Company) and planned to give up teaching. Things did not work out quite as planned, for in the 1910 Census he was living in Abilene, teaching again. Since there was a severe shortage of on-campus student housing at the time, Mrs. M. F. Simms, a widow, probably rented rooms to Trinity students after buying the house in August of 1904. She in turn sold it in 1907 to a widow who rented it to yet another widow, Mrs. J. G. Anderson, who was listed in the 1910 Census as keeping a boarding house.

G-54
327 East University Avenue
1924; A. A. Few & Son, builders

R. E. Poulter, who worked for the Texas and Brazos Valley Railroad at the time, bought this lot in January of 1924, and by May 22 the *Daily Light* noted that his "pretty home" was just completed. The front-gable bungalow with a wide front-gable porch displays many characteristics of the Craftsman style, including exposed rafter tails under the eaves, triangular knee braces in both gables, and tapered square porch supports resting on brick piers. Poulter and his family lived here through the Depression, when Poulter worked in various law enforcement jobs—he was a deputy sheriff in 1932, assistant jailor in 1936, and city policeman by 1939. On Christmas Day of 1932, Poulter participated in a sensational car chase with gunfire across Ellis County that made the *Dallas Morning News*. A keg of "Christmas liquor" was confiscated, and the driver was committed to the county jail. Next door to the south (323 East University) is another variation on a front-gable bungalow with front-gable porch, but with an intervening side-gable section. It was built or moved to the lot sometime after 1925 by Titus H. Williams, a taxi driver, who had previously worked as a house mover.

G-55
321 East University Avenue
1913

Motion pictures provided the means for Paris Q. Rockett and his wife Minnie to build this substantial Prairie style house. In May of 1913 the newspaper noted that construction of their two-story house had begun, at a cost of $4,500. The Rocketts contributed to a small building boom in the area, for the paper reported that their house was the third residence to be started on East University in "the last few weeks." The strong horizontal emphasis of the hipped roof, wide dormer, and wraparound porch, along with the absence of ornament, are typical Prairie style elements. Although this house is almost identical in form and proportions to its neighbor at **317**, its details are more representative of the Prairie style, with paired straight porch supports, rather than Colonial Revival columns.

Born in 1872 near the community of Rockett that bore his family's name, Paris was an early motion picture entrepreneur. He was president of the Waxahachie Amusement Company from 1912 through 1927 and also had interests in theaters in the nearby towns of Italy, Ferris, and Midlothian. His business interests moved beyond entertainment when he and his wife founded the Hillcrest Burial Park to the west of Waxahachie in 1927. Minnie continued to live in the house after his death in 1944.

G-56
318 East University Avenue
1922; W. W. Edwards, builder

Samuel Sylvester (Vester) Andrews contracted to pay W. W. Edwards $5,500 to build this side-gable Craftsman style bungalow, specifying that it should include six rooms with "hall, bath room, breakfast room, closets, and front and back porches." The front-gable porch and dormer emerging from the larger side-gable roof echo a pattern published in several bungalow books of the period. This particular variation may have been based on a plan book produced in Dallas by R. M. Williamson for lumberyards. Craftsman details include the sloping square porch supports on brick piers, exposed rafter ends under the eaves, decorative knee braces in the front gables, and the geometric pattern of the muntins on the upper sash of the windows. Vester, aged twenty-eight at the time of construction, built the house across the street from his father, J. Thomas Andrews (**317 East University**), and brought his bride, Edith, to the house. Two daughters eventually grew up here. Samuel worked at his father's cotton gin, but during the Depression he found work as a traveling salesman. Along with many others he must have experienced reduced income during the 1930s, but he was able to keep the house by extending the mechanic's lien and his payments. Vester and Edith remained in the house into the 1950s.

G-57
317 East University Avenue
1910; E. S. Boze, builder

This two-story hipped-roof house merges the Prairie style with Colonial Revival elements. Although the overall effect is symmetrical and solid, the mixture of styles and variations in its plan create an interesting tension. The horizontal emphasis of the wide front porch that stretches across the façade and around the south corner is broken by the low-pitched pediment marking the entrance. The simple rectangular form of the house is complicated in the rear by slightly projecting hipped-roof extensions on either side. An early photograph shows that the original wood clapboard siding, now replaced, bore a contrasting paint scheme that would have contributed even more to the awareness of the various design elements. At least three colors were used, with the second floor the darkest, a lighter color for the first floor, and a white or cream trim. Prominent local builder and probable designer E. S. Boze built the house for J. Thomas Andrews, whose previous house burned in March of 1910. The fire made the *Dallas Morning News*, which noted that "the boys of Trinity University organized a bucket brigade and saved other buildings from burning."

Andrews was manager of the People's Gin Company and a city alderman. By 1924 he and his son Vester, who lived across the street at **318 East University**, owned their own gin. Andrews was one of the founders of the Texas State Ginners Association and was chair of the organization's executive committee when he died in 1940. In his younger days, before joining the ranks of substantial homeowners, his marriage to Bettie McQueen received special notice in the local paper, for it was held in a buggy!

G-58
314 East University Avenue
1924; W. B. Ramsey, builder

Farmer John Wesley Byrum and his wife Mamie bought the property in February of 1924 and ten days later contracted to pay W. B. Ramsey $4,045 to build this "frame dwelling house" with "5 rooms, bath room, hall, breakfast room, and front and rear porch." Front-gable bungalows with front-gable porches, like this one, with varying degrees of ornament, were a common form during this period. This porch originally wrapped around the south corner of the house, but the south portion was enclosed at a later date. The Byrum family lived here through the early 1930s, when they moved a few blocks away to the 300 block of Cynisca Street. Low crop prices during the Depression may have led to their move, for they sold this house to the owner of their lien for the amount they owed, plus ten dollars.

G-59
312 East University Avenue
1912

Presbyterian minister Finis E. Lawler and his wife Nellie built this side-gable bungalow soon after buying the lots in 1912. The horizontal emphasis typical of bungalows is reinforced here by the porch, which stretches across the full façade and turns to include a recessed side entrance. The prominent hipped-roof dormer has curved sides similar to several other examples in Waxahachie. In addition to its large size in proportion to the house, this dormer is unusual in the staggered shingle pattern of the sides. The Lawlers lived in the house until Finis died in 1923 at the age of seventy-three. His wife Nellie then moved to Dallas and rented the house well into the 1930s.

G-60
309 East University Avenue
c. 1880s or early 1890s

The tall, narrow windows and the L-plan form help to date this house to the 1880s or early 1890s. The porch originally would have extended across more of the façade. The house probably was moved to this location by Trinity University classics professor James M. Gordon and his wife Alice soon after they purchased the land in June 1902. The *Daily Light* noted on June 5 that Professor Gordon "came in this morning from Tehuacana to look out a location." Two days later he and Alice bought the lot. When Gordon received a sabbatical to study at the University of Chicago during the 1907-08 school year, he and Alice sold the house. They must have liked the neighborhood, however, for, upon their return, they purchased the bungalow across the street at 308 East University. Gordon later served as dean of faculty at Trinity and as president of the University of Tulsa. Other Trinity faculty members who lived in this house over the years included Jesse B. Ford in 1913 and Edward P. Childs in the 1920s. Childs moved from Cumberland University in Lebanon, Tennessee, to assume the post of Trinity's dean in 1920. He remained in that position and in this house into the 1930s.

G-61
301 East University
1904; S. J. Erwin, architect and builder

Presbyterian minister H. H. Burkes contracted with local builder S. J. Erwin in August of 1904 to construct this "one story frame house of 9 rooms," with plans supplied by Erwin. The large number of rooms indicates that the attic space may have been utilized, and the large dormer in the hipped roof may date to the original construction. The modified L-plan and high-pitched roof were similar to many Waxahachie houses of the late nineteenth and early twentieth centuries, including **330 East University** at the northeast end of this block. The original porch trim probably included "colonial" details and classical columns popular at the time, but turned ornament similar to the current trim might have been used. H. H. and his wife Mollie sold the house in 1908. Another preacher, J. Elmer Ferguson, lived here by the time of the 1910 Census, along with his wife and a roomer, Trinity professor H. L. Williamson.

G-62
210 East University Avenue
1922

John G. Russell, manager of the Waxahachie branch of the H. H. Hardin Lumber Company, bought this lot and the one next door at 208 East University in November of 1922. Five days later he signed a mechanic's lien with his firm to purchase $2,500 in building materials to construct a six-room "frame house" on the 208 lot. Eleven days after that he contracted for another $2,500 in building materials for this slightly smaller bungalow of five rooms. His speculative building proved successful, for in May of 1923 Mrs. Loula V. Gunn bought this house for $4,353, and in early June, S. L. Todd Jr. bought the house next door. Mrs. Gunn's husband William was a court reporter, and the couple continued to live here through 1936. Russell was one of several small-scale speculative builders in the university area, including the previous Hardin Lumber manager, J. M. Buxton, who built **322 Virginia**. Russell's two front-gable bungalows with front-gable porches are just south of three other variations of the same form by different builders. This one is distinguished by its clipped front gables and rows of dentils along the frieze lines of the gables. It closely resembles a design from a plan book produced for lumberyards by R. M. Williamson of Dallas.

G-63
205 East University Avenue
1911; W. W. Walston, builder

Although modest in size, this Craftsman style bungalow displays fine detailing and a relatively complex plan. The gable roofs of the porch and front wing dominate the façade, hiding the hipped-roof body of the house from the front, but not from an angle view. The deep porch wrapping around the south corner, the rectangular bay window in front, the angular bay on the south side, and, most noticeably, the staggered shingle pattern on the porch, front gable, and foundation walls all contribute to a lively, textured effect. The decorative variety would have been even more evident in the original color scheme, noted on the back of an early photograph—dark green foundation walls and gables contrasted with cream walls. Although the low pitch of the porch roof is unusual in Waxahachie, it can be found in magazines and bungalow catalogues of the period. In those examples, however, the pitch of the main roof echoes that of the porch, whereas here, the pitches of the main roofs are much steeper. According to the mechanic's lien, Roy Connally and his wife Clara supplied the plans to contractor W. W. Walston, who built several other Waxahachie bungalows. Roy was active in promoting Waxahachie's growth, working as secretary of the Waxahachie Commercial Club, later the Chamber of Commerce. He and his wife Clara lived here for over forty years.

G-64
204 East University Avenue
1912; W. J. Moore, builder

In March of 1912, J. F. and Mabel Barker agreed to pay local builder W. J. Moore $2,000 for the construction of this "one story frame house of seven rooms (bungalow)" according to plans supplied by the Barkers. Since J. F. managed the H. D. Timmons Lumber Company, he might have obtained the plans from catalogues at the lumberyard, or Mabel might have acquired them from a *Ladies Home Journal* catalogue. *Journal Bungalows* of 1910 included a design by Frank M. Tyler that displays the basic plan and proportions of the Barkers' house, as well as similar porch details. Whatever the source, the Barkers knew enough of the increasingly popular bungalow house type to select a stylish example and to specify the term "bungalow" in their contract with the builder. The design they selected features a hipped roof with prominent gable front porch to one side of the façade. The shingle cladding of the sloping foundation walls echo the *Ladies Home Journal* source, as does the decorative "X" pattern in the cut-away section of the porch's solid balustrade. The dentil detailing in the porch gable is currently highlighted in a contrasting color.

After only three years, the Barkers sold their new house. It passed through several owners before W. S. Cantrell and his wife bought it in 1921. Cantrell owned a transfer company and garage on S. Rogers Street.

G-65
201 East University Avenue
1905; R. L. Ingram, builder

A mechanic's lien records that contractor R. L. Ingram built this two-story hipped-roof house according to plans supplied by the owner, physician John S. Berry. Berry might have acquired the plans from mail-order architect George F. Barber. A similar design by Barber appeared in the 1905 edition of his catalogue *Modern Dwellings*, as well as in the March 1905 issue of *Keith's Magazine on Home Building*. The perfect symmetry of the façade is emphasized by the two prominent front-gable triangular dormers flanking the smaller central hipped-roof dormer. The 1910 Census indicates that Dr. Berry was a widower, living in the house with his eighty-one-year-old mother and twenty-four-year-old son Wilmer. Black servants Lizzie and Paul Johns lived in a small servants' house in the backyard. During the 1920s and early 1930s, dentist Clarence C. Cooke and his family lived here, having moved from the house they built at **400 Oldham**, but they returned to Oldham after 1936.

G-66
200 East University Avenue
c. 1917

Real estate agent Porter L. Williams built this bungalow a few years after his marriage to Willa McKay in 1914. They were living here by the time of the 1918 telephone directory, and a 1917 penny found behind a bedroom baseboard suggests that year as a possibility. The couple raised two sons in the house and lived here for over forty years. Williams built many homes for speculative sale during the 1920s, with a 1924 article in the *Daily Light* stating that "twelve new residences have been erected by him the past few years, now occupied by permanent citizens." The broad porch wrapping around the side forms one of the dominant features of the house, along with the prominent central dormer with its unusual stacked triple-window pattern. The body of the house recedes so deeply beneath the strong horizontal line of the porch roof that it makes the asymmetry of the door and windows less noticeable. The triple windows on the right side of the façade also help to provide a visual balance to the asymmetrical composition. Craftsman style details include the exposed rafter tails under the porch and dormer roofs and the square porch supports resting on brick piers.

G-67
123 East University Avenue
1907; E. S. Boze, builder

This unusual early bungalow was built by contractor E. S. Boze for George C. Dillon in 1907. Although the tiny front porch suggests that it might have been larger originally, the 1914 Sanborn map shows the current minimal corner indentation. An article on bungalows in the September 1905 issue of *Architectural Record* could have influenced this design. The hipped-roof dormer and the projecting triple window of the façade are both distinctive elements that were illustrated in the article. The small but pronounced Ionic column capital at the porch corner serves as a lone reminder of the Colonial Revival style also popular at the time. The convex-curved sides of the dormer resemble several other Waxahachie examples. Three years after building the house Dillon sold it to John T. Williams and his wife Lillian Beatrice for $2,700. After venturing into several disparate occupations over the years, John, who had previously lived at **209 Williams** and on Water Street, appears to have settled down for a while with this move. He and Lillian remained in the house until 1927, and he restricted his jobs to two, concurrently, real estate agent and insurance salesman.

G-68
119 East University Avenue
1917

John Thomas Williams lived next door at **123 East University**, but in December 1916 he bought this lot and a few days later made arrangements to move the old R. A. Davis house, which had been damaged by fire, from West Jefferson and Monroe Streets (where the Woman's Building is now) to this location. The large two-story house had been used as a boarding house after Mr. Davis died, and it is likely that Williams planned for it to serve the same purpose in its new location, only a few blocks from the university. After repairing, renovating, and possibly extending the house, he sold it to J. I. Williams for $5,500, who sold it eight months later to Robert McCombs and his wife Minnie for $5,000. Since an older house formed the core of this one, its projecting front wing and asymmetrical plan differ from most Prairie style houses, but the removal of all Victorian decorative ornament and the creation of a full-width front porch help the house to fit comfortably with its Prairie style neighbors. McCombs was in the insurance business and also served as an alderman on the City Council. His concern for the community was evident early in his career through the local Charity Relief Association. In January of 1897, the *Dallas Morning News* published a short article about McCombs and others distributing quilts to Waxahachie's needy. Minnie continued to live in the house after McCombs's death in 1920 at the age of sixty, but by 1931 she had moved to Dallas.

G-69
116 East University Avenue
1923; Krohne & Brasher, builders

This unusual variation of an airplane bungalow was based on a design from a catalogue published by Dallas entrepreneur R. M. Williamson, who produced house-plan books for retail lumber companies to promote lumber sales. The exposed rafter ends and decorative roof beams are typical of Craftsmen-style bungalows of the period. Waxahachie widow Mary Ralston, or her daughter Sadie, who lived with her, probably saw this design at the local branch of the H. H. Hardin Lumber Company. A 1923 mechanic's lien documents the purchase of lumber for this house from the Hardin company. Although Mrs. Ralston signed the lien, her daughter was very involved in the design decisions, according to the *Daily Light*, which complimented the "airplane home" and noted that "Mrs. Ralston, Sadie, and Krohne have put forth effort to make it attractive." The original porch supports would have been square or tapered pillars, thicker than the current slender columns, and, if the Williamson plan was followed exactly, they would have been brick. The carport is a later addition. Born in Scranton, Pennsylvania, in 1864, Mrs. Ralston had lived in Waxahachie since her childhood. She invested in university-area property for several years before moving into her own house in the neighborhood. She and Sadie, a teacher, lived here together until Mary's death in 1941.

G-70
107 East University Avenue
1912; J. S. McCanless, builder

In the 1912 mechanic's lien for this house, J. S. McCanless agreed to build a one-story frame house of six rooms in the "bungalow style" to cost $2,350. The complex hipped roof extends over the full-width front porch and dominates the façade, providing the broad horizontal emphasis typical of early bungalows. The hipped-roof dormer with its convex-curved sides represents a type found on many Waxahachie houses. Grocer Frank D. Rogers evidently built this house as an investment, for the 1913 city directory shows it was rented by a Trinity University professor, Frank P. Cheak, and his wife Mary, while Rogers was listed as boarding at 401 East Franklin. Rogers sold the house in 1914 to T. W. Bounds for $3,750. Only a year after McCanless constructed this house he built the two-story house across the street (114 East University) with a similar dormer, now altered. In 1919, that house became the home of William A. Baker and his family, including son Paul, who became nationally recognized as a theater director and educator.

G-71
103 East University Avenue
1906

This two-story house would have been considered "Colonial" when it was built, due to its full height porch, reminiscent of Mount Vernon. But, typical of many residences of this period, it actually combines elements from a variety of styles. The hipped-roof front dormer and overall massing reflect the Prairie style of the early twentieth century; the band of decorative shingles between the first and second floors recalls the earlier Queen Anne style; and the Ionic columns and small balcony above the entrance represent the Classical Revival. A low balustrade might have connected the porch columns originally. Banker William E. Hipp and wife Jennie built the house in 1906 after their second child was born, moving across town from **304 East Marvin**. In 1909 William left banking for the new field of automobile sales, having secured the Buick dealership. After Jennie died in 1910, William sold the house and moved with his four young children to Jennie's parents' house at **309 East Marvin**. In the 1920s, R. E. Moore owned this house. He owned and operated the Moore Furniture Company, located two blocks south of the courthouse square.

G-72
111 Virginia Avenue
1914

George O. Patten bought this lot in May of 1913, when it was part of the Oldham Addition, a three-block subdivision filed by Frank and Mary Oldham in March of 1913. (The Oldhams lived next door at **910 West Marvin**.) The generous lot size reflects the original Oldham plat. The remaining lots were reduced in size a year later, when a group of local investors bought the Oldham Addition, minus the Oldhams' and the Pattens' homesteads. They combined it with adjacent land to the east and created Trinity Heights Addition, which developed slowly until the boom years of the 1920s. The June 25, 1914 newspaper noted that plans for Mr. Patten's residence were being drawn. This hipped-roof bungalow, with its "Waxahachie dormer," was probably built soon after. Sanborn maps indicate that originally a porch stretched across the entire façade and continued around the corner to the south side. (It probably looked very similar to **107 East University**.) Patten managed the National Compress for sixteen years, but he committed suicide in 1921, presumably for business reasons. His wife and three children sold the house a few months later to farmer E. L. Bailey.

G-73
115 Virginia Avenue
c. 1918

Willie Fern Kennedy, a teacher at the West End Ward School, bought this lot in 1914 but continued to live with her parents on North Monroe until her marriage to Talmadge Edward Newton in 1916. The couple built this bungalow on her property soon afterward. The unusual interlocking front gables may have been modeled after a design published in the 1910 edition of Henry L. Wilson's *Bungalow Book,* a catalogue of mail-order house plans. The floor plan is different and the roof pitch is slightly steeper in the Newtons' house, but the gable pattern duplicates Wilson's. The strong symmetry of the gables is reinforced by the trees flanking the entrance. Later changes include an addition and partial porch enclosure on the south side. Talmadge was proficient enough in his real estate and insurance work for the local Woodmen of the World lodge to appoint him financial secretary in 1916. The organization eventually provided a career for him with positions as state manager for North Carolina and assistant field manager at the Woodmen headquarters in Omaha, Nebraska. Upon retirement in 1952, he returned to Waxahachie.

G-74
206 Virginia Avenue
c. 1920

This bungalow with its wide, low-pitched porch roof was built c. 1920 by Stephen Marvin Rudolph and his wife Eula Grace. Rudolph and his brother W. K. owned the Rudolph Furniture Company on East Main when the bungalow was built, but by 1924 they were running the Rudolph Walker Funeral Home on West Franklin Street. In the 1930s the firm's name changed to Rudolph Brothers, and it became one of the principal funeral homes in the city. Around the same time, Marvin and his wife moved into the firm's building on West Franklin, and Mrs. Lou Smith, a widow, took up residence in this house.

The bungalow's very low-pitched gable roofs were unusual in Waxahachie, but the design is reminiscent of earlier bungalows published in magazines and catalogues around 1910-15, including the 1914 catalogue by the Dallas architectural firm Ye Planry. Distinctive original details include the multipaned windows surrounding the large central front window, the decorative half-timbering in the front gable, and the smaller-scale geometric decorative work and dentils on the porch gable. The current porch columns probably replaced original sloping square supports.

G-75
208 Virginia Avenue
1921; H. D. Rankin, builder

Norman M. Jones, manager of the Rockwell Lumber Company, had this front-gable bungalow built for his wife and two daughters eight months after purchasing the lot. The relatively simple rectangular form of the house is somewhat masked by the generous wraparound porch, with its front-gable roof over the entrance joined to a side-gable roof for the corner extension. The window and door pattern of the façade reinforces the asymmetry of the wraparound porch. The sloping supports on brick piers are typical of the period. Norman was active in the Chamber of Commerce, serving on its board of directors in 1930, but he died in 1932 at the age of thirty-eight. Tax collector John C. Mallory and his family lived here through the rest of the 1930s.

G-76
213 Virginia Avenue
1915; W. W. Edwards, builder; 1928

William M. Kelley and his wife Maude may have intended to use this one-story side-gable house as a student boarding house when they contracted with W. W. Edwards, for the mechanic's lien specified a plan, supplied by the Kelleys, of 1,848 square feet with eleven rooms. The 1925 Sanborn map shows that the house was one-and-a-half stories at the time, and, given the footprint of the house on the map, that half story probably entailed a central shed dormer in the front, similar to the one in the bungalow on the corner across the street at **218 Virginia**. William taught in Ellis County public schools for many years, and his daughter Mattie followed in his profession. His son Powell became city tax assessor and collector in the 1930s. The Kellys sold the house to farmer J. H. Quaite in 1920. In January 1928, on the day the Quaites were planning to move back to their farm, a fire seriously damaged the rear portion of the house. J. C. Culbertson bought and rescued the house and, according to the *Daily Light*, showed "what can be accomplished when time, money and thought are employed." The article continued, "Mr. Culbertson now has a pretty place with plenty of trees, shrubs and lawn and has made an excellent home." Many of the trees survive to this day.

G-77
218 Virginia Avenue
1915; S. J. Erwin, architect;
J. S. McCanless, builder

In March of 1915, Neal and Dora Harden contracted to pay J. S. McCanless $3,100 to build this bungalow with plans supplied by local architect and builder S. J. Erwin. The mechanic's lien described the dwelling as a one-story frame "bungalow house" of six rooms with hall and porches. Side-gable bungalows with shed-roof dormers such as this one regularly appeared in catalogues of bungalow plans of the period, but were rare in Waxahachie. (Only two other examples survive, at **207 University** and **814 West Main**.) A version with the side gable extended to form a porte cochère, as seen here, was published in the May 1912 issue of *The Craftsman*, the magazine of the American Arts and Crafts movement. If Erwin used that design as his model, he made several changes, increasing the height of the dormer window and extending the porch to the full width of the house. Sanborn maps indicate the original porte cochère on the south and an extension of the porch around the north corner. Both were enclosed at a later date. The current porch supports probably are not original. Most bungalows of this type had straight or tapered square porch supports. Neal Harden was a bookkeeper with the National Compress Company. The next owner, C. A. Miller, also worked in the cotton industry as manager of a cotton gin. He and his wife Minnie bought the house in 1923 and continued to live here through the 1930s.

G-78
307 Virginia Avenue

1920; R. E. Sutherland, architect; John H. Dalton, builder

This one-story side-gable bungalow stands out from its neighbors with its unusual conical porch roof flanked by trellises. All these elements appeared in a design by Dallas architect R. E. Sutherland that was published in the July 1918 issue of *Holland's Magazine*, as well as a similar design in a later plan book produced by Dallas businessman R. M. Williamson for use in retail lumberyards. In July 1920 civil engineer Hans R. F. Helland and his wife Frances agreed to pay John H. Dalton $7,197 to build this five-room house with sleeping porch. The contract serves as evidence of the growing importance of the automobile to the town's middle class, for a garage and concrete driveway were included in the price. The Hellands probably intended to live in the house, for Hans had recently been appointed Waxahachie's city engineer, and they were renting a house on Patrick Street when the 1920 Census was taken. Hans had grown up in Waxahachie, son of Norwegian-born railroad general manager and civil engineer Hans E. H. Helland, and his brother Erling and sister Marie still lived here. Hans followed his father into the field of engineering, studying at the University of Texas in Austin and in Europe, working in Paris when WWI began, and in the US as the City of Austin's assistant engineer before he returned to Waxahachie. The Hellands sold their new house in late 1921 when Hans pursued other positions, but they returned to Waxahachie again in 1924 when Hans accepted the position of assistant county engineer. Being more cautious this time they rented a house on Williams Street, in the neighborhood where Hans had spent part of his childhood. Renting turned out to be wise. After a few years the family returned to San Antonio where Hans worked in partnership with his father.

G-79
312 Virginia Avenue

1921; William A. Spalding, builder

In a memoir written for his family, William A. Spalding mentions buying this lot and building the "nice six room residence" when he returned to Waxahachie after twenty years of valuation and survey work for various railroads in Arkansas, Texas, California, and Missouri. Born in 1869, Spalding had grown up in Waxahachie and earned a civil engineering degree at the University of Texas at Austin. Fresh from the university in June of 1896, he was awarded the job of preparing the Phillips & Hawkins official map of Waxahachie, which remains an invaluable primary resource in any study of the city's history and growth. It depicts the new West End and Williams Additions, as well as the large undeveloped area in the northwest part of the city that would become the logical spot for Trinity University when Waxahachie made its bid for the school in 1901. By the time Spalding returned in 1921, the area south of the campus had developed into a strong middle-class neighborhood, but a number of lots were still available for building.

In September of 1921 Spalding signed a mechanic's lien to pay the William Cameron Lumber Company $2,250 for the materials to build this "one-story bungalow." The front gable of the porch roof echoes that of the body of the house but emerges from a contrasting side gable. That side-gable section gives the house an appearance of greater width from the street, as well as the horizontal emphasis usually found in bungalows. (A similar gable pattern was used nearby at **322 Virginia**.) The design closely matches one by R. E. Sutherland that was published in the October 1918 issue of *Holland's Magazine*, but a similar design might have been available in plan books available at the lumber company. After years of moving around the country, the Spalding family settled into this house to stay. William then built two other houses that he was able to sell for a "small profit," according to his memoir. He served as county highway engineer from 1923 to 1932 and county engineer for the Works Progress Administration from 1935 to 1941. In his later years, Spalding became the unofficial historian of Waxahachie and wrote articles about his work with the railroads as well as the memoir of his life and family that mentions the construction of this house.

G-80
317 Virginia Avenue
1936; W. D. Brasher, builder

In July of 1936 salesman Oscar H. Pitts and his wife Addie contracted to pay W. D. Brasher $3,700 to build this "one story brick veneer house of six rooms" according to plans furnished by the Pitts. They lived here through the rest of the decade, hosting daughter Nitabell's wedding in the house in 1939. The Pitts evidently acquired the plans through the popular Dallas-based periodical *Holland's Magazine*, for the Tudor Revival cottage exactly matches a plan in *Holland's House Plan Book*, published around 1935. The publication asserted that the home's "splendid exterior features . . . will cause it to stand out among its neighbors as a home of charm and distinction." The house does stand out in its neighborhood of frame bungalows, with its brick veneer and Tudor Revival style. Tudor Revival features include the front chimney, the prominent steep cross gables projecting from the side-gabled body of the house, and the arched openings for the entrance and front porch. The most distinctive feature is the incorporation of irregularly shaped stones of contrasting color into the light-colored brick of the chimney and punctuating the corners of the house, chimney, and entrance bay. (A similar treatment can be found on the house at **313 Harbin**.) Along with the leaded-glass windows on either side of the chimney, the stonework was meant to recall English construction of an earlier era. Although the stonework is too minimal to convey a true old-world feel, the combination of front gables, arches, and chimney form a pleasing example of Tudor Revival on a small scale. The rear extension is a later addition.

G-81
322 Virginia Avenue
1922; A. J. Moore, builder

This bungalow's similarity to **312 Virginia** is most evident in the gable pattern of two front gables emerging from a side gable. The houses are not exact duplicates, however. Here the triple window pattern is repeated on both sides of the façade, and, since the entrance portion of the façade recedes and the door does not face the street, the symmetry of the windows is emphasized. (Re-siding may have altered trim details in the gables and at the windows.) Even with the differences, the house probably was modeled on 312, since it was built only a year later and within a few feet of its predecessor. John Mack Buxton, manager of the local branch of the H. H. Hardin Lumber Company, and his wife Gussie contracted to pay A. J. Moore $4,850 to build what was described concisely as a "Six Room Frame House, with Bath and Breakfast Room and front and back porches." The mechanic's lien does not mention the source of the plans, but the house matches a design in a catalogue produced by Ye Planry of Dallas, a firm that often supplied catalogues to retail lumberyards. Buxton sold the house a few months after its completion, probably to take a job in a Dallas County lumberyard. By 1924 J. T. Bruce, a farmer, and his wife Susie had bought the house, moving their family to Waxahachie from the nearby Forreston area when their three children were school age. Son William attended Trinity University, achieving the honor roll in 1928, and later worked as a civil engineer for the Texas Highway Department. J. T. and Susie moved back to the country in the 1930s after their children were grown.

G-82
326 Virginia Avenue
1922; F. W. Howard, builder

This modest bungalow's design and details indicate that it was probably built according to plans from a catalogue. Craftsman style details include the brackets under the eaves and the decorative shingles in the front porch gable. In April 1922, auto mechanic J. T. Mays and his wife Nannie signed a mechanic's lien to purchase lumber and other building materials for the house from the H. H. Hardin Lumber Company. According to the newspaper, the "five-room bungalow" was "under the handiwork of F. W. Howard." Although the mechanic's lien did not mention a plan source for the house, it could easily have come from a lumber company book of house plans. The specific plan for this house has not been discovered, but another house built with H. H. Hardin lumber, **116 East University**, was built according to a lumberyard plan book produced by R. M. Williamson. The Mays only stayed in the house (and Waxahachie) a few years, selling it in 1926 to John C. Holland. John, a barber who switched to styling ladies' hair during the Depression, and his wife Ura remained here into the 1950s.

G-83
330 Harbin Avenue
1924; W. B. Ramsey, builder

Real estate investor Hugh T. Ramsey built this side-gable bungalow, along with several other houses in the neighborhood, with the help of his contractor brother W. B. Ramsey. Family support and trust evidently had its limits, for the brothers sealed most of their deals with very official mechanics' liens filed at the courthouse. In this case, Hugh agreed to pay W. B. $5,500 to construct this "frame dwelling house consisting of six rooms, breakfast room, hall, bath room, front and rear porch." The clipped gables and tapered square porch supports resting on brick piers are typical of many 1920s bungalows. Cooper Curry, who invested in real estate along with running Claud's Lunch Room, bought the house from Ramsey and sold it after a few months to Edgar H. McElroy and his wife Myrtle. Edgar, a native of Ferris, began as a printer's assistant in 1913 at the *Daily Light* and rose to managing editor in eleven years. After twenty-two years at the *Daily Light* he was appointed Waxahachie's postmaster in 1935 and remained in that position for twenty-eight years. Four McElroy sons and a daughter grew up in the house.

G-84
324 Harbin Avenue
c. 1924

M. Howard Gibson bought this lot from T. H. Harbin and the other developers of the Hilcrest subdivision in 1924, not long after marrying Louise Wright. Their cross-gable bungalow was one of the first houses built on the street, and they continued to live here through 1948. Gibson was a farmer and a cotton ginner, eventually owning the Valentine Gin Company and the Gibson Grain Company on South Rogers. Mrs. Gibson actively participated in Waxahachie women's clubs and was elected to several offices in the Texas Federation of Women's Clubs. At first glance the house appears to be a simple front-gable bungalow with projecting front-gable porch, but closer examination reveals greater complexity. A strong horizontal emphasis results from the relatively low pitch of the gables and the extension of the side gable to the north. The regular pattern of dentils across the tie beams at the bases of the gables also reinforces the horizontal emphasis.

G-85
316 Harbin Avenue
1925

Real estate investor Hugh T. Ramsey built several of the houses on this block, including this side-gable bungalow, which originally had a recessed corner-entrance porch. Although there is not a mechanic's lien, Hugh probably used his brother W. B. Ramsey as contractor, as he did for most of his other houses. Six months after purchasing the property, he sold the completed bungalow to Roy F. and Nona Mahaney for $6,000. Roy operated Mahaney's Service Station at the corner of Elm and Main. The Mahaney family later moved to Pittsburgh, Pennsylvania, where Roy became state manager of the Woodmen of the World in Pennsylvania. Also in 1925, Hugh T. Ramsey contracted his brother W. B. Ramsey to build the brick cottage two lots to the south at 312 Harbin, but the Sanborn maps indicate that the entrance and front room are later additions.

G-86
313 Harbin Avenue
1936; W. D. Brasher, builder

Two days after purchasing the lot, Lee J. Douglas and his wife Madie signed a mechanic's lien with contractor W. D. Brasher to build this Tudor-Revival style cottage. Lee demonstrated flexibility in his occupation over the years, operating the Douglas Cleaners in 1936, the Douglas Furniture Company in 1939, and working as a salesman in 1948, but he remained in his residence into the 1950s. The steeply pitched front-gable entrance porch and the large front chimney are typical of the Tudor Revival, but the most distinctive feature of the house is the presence of irregularly shaped stones incorporated in the brick veneer. The dark color of the stones and their odd shapes stand out sharply from the light-colored brick walls. The stone work was meant to be reminiscent of early English masonry, though the treatment could never be mistaken for the real thing. A similar mix of stones with brick veneer can be found at 309 Harbin, across the street to the south, but one has to look closely to spot the stones due to the uniform tone of a coat of paint. That house was built in 1935 by contractor O. B. Bennett for Arthur E. Curry of Curry's Pharmacy and Trinity Pharmacy. Another example, without camouflaging paint, can be found at **317 Virginia**, just a few blocks away. It also was built by W. D. Brasher.

G-87
310 Harbin Avenue
1927; W. B. Ramsey & C. C. Ramsey, builders

Built in 1927, this one-story cross-gable and hipped-roof house presents another variation on the English Cottage style—this time in brick veneer. In an August 23, 1928 *Daily Light* article summarizing recent construction, the newspaper described it as "one of the most attractive homes in the city on Harbin street," though the "most attractive" accolade was not uncommon in the paper. Arches abound, over the door and all the windows except for the one on the south side of the façade, which is not original. Sanborn maps indicate that the original corner porch was later enclosed. The multi-paned windows beneath the gable and to the left of the door, as well as the small diamond-paned window to the right, constitute some of the "English cottage" elements. The bricks in basket-weave bond in the front gables also contribute to the English feel. The construction of this house provides another example of an entrepreneurial lumber company employee, but with a slight feminist twist. Fred Primm, assistant manager of the local branch of the Cameron

Lumber Company, owned the property with his wife, but both the property deed and the mechanic's lien name Mrs. Virginia Primm first, before her husband, in complete contrast to the usual arrangement on contracts. This probably indicated Virginia's active involvement in the enterprise, perhaps financially, but no additional documentation clarifies her contribution. She also may have been involved in the landscaping. The local paper seldom mentioned such things, but the same *Daily Light* article that complimented the house also noted that it was "located on a high lot, the terrace having a pretty lawn and bordered with many shrubs." The Primms may have lived in the house briefly, but they sold it in November 1928 to John H. Hamlin, a sixty-year-old cotton buyer from Forreston, Texas, and his wife Lucy.

G-88
306 Harbin Avenue
1926; A. A. Few & Son, builders

On March 15, 1926 Earnest A. Barnes and his wife Nona signed a mechanic's lien instructing local builder A. A. Few and Son to construct a "six room frame shingle roof dwelling house, with bath, hall, breakfast nook, two front entrance porches and back porch and boxed and stripped garage." In a clear break from the bungalows being built in the area at the time (like the one next door at **304 Harbin**), Earnest and Nona opted for an English Cottage style. It was one of the first of several eclectic English-oriented houses that were built on Harbin. The unusual asymmetrical entrance porches with their arched openings contribute to the vaguely Tudor appearance, as well as the paired leaded-glass windows by the north entrance. Barnes owned the Barnes Auto Top Company on Water Street, near the square. Only a few years after building the house, the family moved to San Antonio.

G-89
304 Harbin Avenue
1925; W. B. Ramsey, builder

The recessed corner entrance porch of this bungalow is marked by a front gable roof that is echoed by another front gable crowning the side gable between them. (Similar roof patterns can be found nearby at **312** and **322 Virginia**.) Hugh T. Ramsey, a small-scale real estate investor, built the bungalow, along with several others in the area, with the help of his contractor brothers W. B. and Cal. A September 1925 mechanic's lien records Hugh's contract to pay W. B. $7,500 to construct this one-story frame residence of seven rooms with a front and rear porch. W. B. and Cal served as contractors for several major Waxahachie buildings in the 1920s, including the Woman's Building (**407 West Jefferson**) and Trinity University's gymnasium. Hugh's investment in this house proved successful, for he sold it upon completion to Joe W. Garvin, chief engineer of the Waxahachie Ice Works for many years. Garvin lived here with his wife Lynn and two daughters.

G-90
208 Harbin Avenue
1938; Christensen & Christensen, architects;
Fin Garvin and Son, builders

This frame cottage is an early example of the Minimal Traditional style that would become common in suburban developments during the years just before and after World War II. As in this house, the style includes features typical of 1930s Tudor Revival cottages in a simplified form, such as the dominant front gable projecting from the main body of the house and the large front chimney. Most of the Tudor details, such as leaded windows or a decorative surface treatment, are omitted, and the roofs usually have a lower pitch. Moreland Herring and his wife Lucille bought the lot in March of 1938 and in May contracted with local builders Fin Garvin & Son to build this "frame residence, containing five rooms, Breakfast Room, bath, hall and porches, and a garage of the size 10' x 18', concrete walks and gravel driveway." A previous owner indicated that Dallas architects Christensen & Christensen designed the house. Moreland Herring was active in the Dallas Little Theater and Waxahachie's Civic Players in the early 1930s. He had his own printing business when he built this house, but he soon began a long career as a photographer. In 1948 he bought the two-story house at **417 West Main** to convert into a combination studio and residence.

G-91
201 Harbin Avenue
1926; H. D. Rankin, builder

This brick veneer Tudor Revival style cottage retains much of its 1920s charm, even with significant enlargements over the years. The front gable and the side-gable roof behind it were raised to accommodate a large second-floor addition, perhaps in a 1967 remodeling. The original house, as described in the 1926 mechanic's lien, was a "six-room, shingle roof, brick-veneered residence, with breakfast room, bath room, hall, and closets, with cement terrace and front porch." A "combination garage and servants room," 16 x 20 ft., was included in the $8,000 cost. The July 12, 1926 *Daily Light* described it as "typical of the old English architecture," and credited H. D. Rankin as builder and Doc Coleman for the "splendid brick work." Railroad agent John C. Kennedy bought the lot in May 1924 but waited two years before contracting with H. D. Rankin for construction of the house. He lived here with his second wife, Lucile, who ran Kennedy's Millinery at 109 South College. In 1929 they sold the house to J. E. and Kate Cooper, who remained here at least through 1948, with their son and his wife living less than a block away on Kirven Street.

G-92
104 Harbin Avenue
1924; Lloyd L. McNair, architect; Krohne & Brasher, builders

This symmetrical front-gable bungalow features a front porch roof that emerges with the same pitch just below the level of the main roof. Later re-siding altered the porch supports and details. The architect, Lloyd. L. McNair, practiced briefly in Waxahachie in the 1920s before moving to Dallas and becoming a building supervisor for Southwestern Bell Company. Mrs. Mary Burnett bought the lot from developer T. H. Harbin in February of 1924, and the house was built soon after, one of the first to be built in the Hilcrest [sic] Addition. The property was deeded to Mary alone, and she was the sole client noted on the architect's blueprints, but she and her husband, Charles P. Burnett, both lived in the house, along with their three children. Charles worked as assistant cashier at Citizens National Bank for many years and also served as secretary of the local I.O.O.F. Lodge. Mary continued to live in the house after he died in 1935.

G-93
103 Harbin Avenue
1934; O. B. Bennett, builder

William D. Coleman, manager of the local branch of the Cameron Lumber Company, and his wife Clara signed a mechanic's lien on July 26, 1934, agreeing to pay O. B. Bennett $2,200 to build this cross-gable residence of "six rooms, bath, hall, and breakfast room." A *Daily Light* article of August 8, 1934, described the house as "English-style" and gave the original color scheme as "white siding, with green composition roof." Depression-era building costs are evident in the low price, which also included construction of a garage. (In the mid-1920s a house of the same size and materials would have cost twice as much.) The most distinctive element of the design is the steeply pitched front gable with one side continuing down to form a wing wall. The arched gate opening in the wing wall was meant to recall English cottage garden entries. (A similar gate opening illustrated in a 1929 Sears house catalogue was described as providing a "touch of English architecture.") Even in this period of limited construction due to the Depression, William was able to follow the example of earlier lumber company managers, building and selling houses as a sideline. The Colemans lived here for less than a year before selling it at a profit to District Attorney Lynn B. Griffith and his wife Dorothy.

G-94
600 West Second Street
Waxahachie High School
[now STEAM Elementary School]
1918; C. H. Page & Brother, architects; Caddo Construction Company, contractor

Austin architect Charles H. Page, who specialized in school designs, began planning this building for the school board in 1916, but local disputes regarding the selection of the site delayed the start of construction until February 1917. The building opened to students in September 1918. The two-story structure was designed in a restrained Prairie style and constructed of reinforced concrete with beige brick facing and light-colored stone bands above the basement level and beneath the roof parapet to give a horizontal emphasis. The façade is punctuated with a slightly projecting entrance bay with prominent staircase and projecting classroom bays on each side. The first floor housed the superintendent's office, principal's office, library study hall, and seven recitation rooms. The second floor had four classrooms, science laboratories, and a study hall, while the basement contained rooms for domestic science and manual training, a cafeteria, kitchen, heating plant, and toilets. By the 1930s, the building was overcrowded, and a WPA/PWA grant enabled the construction of the gymnasium wing to the north of the building that was designed by Dallas architects La Roche and Dahl. In 1961, a one-story science wing designed by Dallas architects Upshaw & Todd was added to the west of the main building.

The school became a junior high in 1970 when a new high school opened on Highway 77 North. It subsequently served as an elementary school, the Global High School for students following a STEM curriculum, and now the STEAM Elementary School. With each change, the buildings have undergone remodeling.

G-95
201 Bryson Street
1924; Jesse G. Oakley, builder

This one-story brick-veneer cross-gable bungalow presents clean, straight lines and flat surfaces on the walls and porch supports. Textural Craftsman details emerge above the brick, in the shingled gables and the protruding, trellis-like joists beneath the porch gable. Originally the joists probably continued beyond the porch roof to the brick pillar by the driveway to form a true trellis. The design probably came from a lumberyard plan book. Jesse G. Oakley bought the lot on June 23, 1924, and the next day signed a mechanic's lien with Fort Worth lumber company owner H. H. Hardin for the materials to build a "one story, six room, hall and bath, brick veneered, bungalow house, with front and rear porch, said front porch to be of concrete, said house to have reinforced concrete foundation and shingle roof." The lien amount of $3,500 covered lumber and building materials only. Jesse likely managed the construction himself, for the 1923-24 city directory lists his occupation as building contractor. He sold the house to physician R. H. Looney, who lived here until his death in 1949. His widow Annie remained into the 1950s. After building this house, Jesse bought the lot next door (203 Bryson) in December 1924 and signed another mechanic's lien with H. H. Hardin. Jesse's career as a Waxahachie builder was a short one, however. By 1926, he was living in Wichita Falls, and was still there when the 1930 Census gave his occupation as superintendent of a filling station.

205 Bryson St. on original West Marvin site before 1924 remodel.

G-96
205 Bryson Street
1892; George F. Barber, architect; W. H. Smith, builder; 1924

Waxahachie lawyer Fines P. Powell built this two-story modified L-plan house for his new wife Myrtle using plans from Knoxville architect George F. Barber's house catalogue *Cottage Souvenir No. 2* (1891). It originally stood about one hundred feet to the south, facing West Marvin, on what was then a four-acre lot just west of the Williams Addition. On September 23, 1892, Powell signed a mechanic's lien with W. H. Smith to build a "two story dwelling house consisting of four rooms on the lower floor and three rooms on the upper floor." The house was one of Barber's most distinctive and popular designs, with Moorish arches on the second-floor balcony and a polygonal cupola above interrupting the front-gable roof. Farmer George W. Callens and his wife Jennie bought the house in 1904 but by December 1923 they were ready for a smaller, more modern home. They moved this one to its current location and built the bungalow at **502 West Marvin**. On May 22, 1924, the *Daily Light* noted that this house was being remodeled, with A. J. Moore "doing the work," which would have included adding the current porch and removing the tower. A few exterior details from the original design remain, including multi-paned windows and the unusual front bay window with another small bay emerging from its side.

G-97
913 Ferris Avenue
c. 1908

Farmer James B. Naughton probably built this two-story hipped-roof house soon after purchasing the property in 1908. This end of Ferris was still named Williams Avenue at that time and bisected the Williams Addition, platted in 1890. The Naughton house was one of the first to be built at the northern end of the street. The house is transitional in nature, with an L-plan similar to many farm houses of the late nineteenth century, but presenting the clean lines and absence of ornament more typical of the era in which it was built. In addition, the low-pitched hipped roof encompasses the full house and its porches, as found in many Prairie-style or Foursquare houses of the period. The sleeping porch and porte cochère on the south side were probably added in the 1920s. The house remained in the Naughton family until 2010.

G-98
1007 Ferris Avenue
1919

The first-floor windows of this two-story Prairie style hipped-roof house would originally have echoed the placement and details of those remaining on the second floor, and the space below the sleeping porch on the south would have been open as a porch or porte cochère. Even with these changes and the later addition of window shutters on the second floor, the strong horizontal emphasis of the Prairie style remains. Farmer George L. Green built the substantial dwelling not long after purchasing the property in 1918.

G-99
1015 Ferris Avenue
1912-13; H. D. Rankin, builder

Sumner Franklin (S. F.) Chapman and his wife Lillian bought this property in July 1912, and in February 1913 the local newspaper reported that they had moved into their "handsome residence" on what was then called Williams Avenue. Born near Ovilla, Texas, Chapman studied at Trinity University, Texas A&M, and the University of Missouri before teaching school and then serving as superintendent of schools at Ovilla. He evidently left the field of education for more remunerative endeavors, for in 1907 he was living in Waxahachie and working in the insurance business. The 1913 directory shows him as "loan man" for his brother, O. H. Chapman. By 1922, he had enough rural property to list himself solely as a farmer. This two-story hipped-roof Prairie style house resembles others built in Waxahachie around the same time, including **321 East University** and **319 East Marvin**. The horizontal emphasis of the wraparound porch and hipped roof are representative of the Prairie style, as are the geometric inverted-cross elements on the brick porch supports.

G-100
900 Bryson Street
1870s; early 1880s

Oscar Lander moved this one-and-a-half story L-plan house from 302 Water Street in the 1940s when his brother Clarence built a service station on that lot. The Gothic Revival gable dormer on the right side of the façade indicates that the house originally may have been an 1870s side gable with symmetrical dormers, similar to the example at **513 West Jefferson**. By the time of the 1886 bird's-eye view, the current L-plan was present, which indicates that the projecting gable L-wing on the left might have been part of an 1880s expansion and update. The shingle siding is later, as is the small central dormer. The 1895 directory lists Minna B. Woodlief, the widow of jeweler J. C. Woodlief, living in the house. J. C. had been active in city politics, serving as president of the board of aldermen in 1889 and appointed to a committee to revise the city ordinances in 1890.

G-101
500 Sycamore Street
1938; Christensen & Christensen, architects; O. B. Bennett, contractor

Eclecticism thrived on Sycamore Street in the 1920s and 30s. Merchants, doctors, and professionals proclaimed their success through substantial architect-designed homes on generous lots, even during the difficult years of the Depression. This 1930s homage to Mount Vernon represents Waxahachie's best example of a design type popular throughout the country. (Models also could have been found close to home, in Dallas's Highland Park.) The slender square pillars of the full-façade porch frame the large 6-over-6 windows and the prominent entrance door with flanking pilasters crowned by a scrolled pediment. The sentry-like Mediterranean cypress trees emphasize the symmetry of the façade, distracting the viewer from the one-story extension on the west. A mechanic's lien documents that Floyd W. Casebolt and his wife Fay paid O. B. Bennett $5,470 to build this "two story frame residence consisting of living room, dining room, kitchen and breakfast room on first floor and three bedrooms and bath upstairs, stair hall, front porch and garage." The Christensen brothers designed several other houses on the street, including 510, **606**, **610**, and 700 Sycamore.

Floyd Casebolt had moved to Waxahachie in 1920, after graduating from the University of Missouri's School of Journalism. He worked in various capacities at the Enterprise Publishing Company, which published the *Daily Light*, eventually becoming general manager and editor. In a manner fitting for a newspaper editor, Floyd worked to promote Waxahachie through positions in the Chamber of Commerce and the Lions Club, and he used his new house as an opportunity to promote local home construction and FHA loans. He gave the house and the firms involved in its construction ample coverage in the newspaper, identifying it only as the "FHA Demonstration Home." Upon completion in October 1938, the house was open to the public for three days before the Casebolts moved in. In 1948, when C. C. Woodson of Brownwood, Texas, purchased the majority interest in the Enterprise Publishing Company, Floyd sold his interest in the publishing company and moved to Ennis to become editor of the *Ennis Daily News*.

G-102
501 Sycamore Street
1931; O. B. Bennett, builder

The size and materials of this two-story cross-gable house indicate the prosperity of its owner, but its Tudor Revival style is more restrained than a flamboyant example of the style built around the same time only a block away at **601 Sycamore**. Here, most of the Tudor elements are focused on the first floor, including the uncoursed stonework of the porch and chimney base and the arched openings of the porch and the entrance door. Clothing merchant Joe Cohn and his wife Lillie built it after their more modest one-story frame house on Virginia Street burned. The *Daily Light* was a bit premature when it reported in December 1930 that construction of Joe's "attractive new home" would probably begin within a month. The Cohns did not sign the mechanic's lien contract with local contractor O. B. Bennett until April 13, 1931. Joe, born in Brenham, Texas, ran a men's clothing store on South Rogers Street. Lillie was the daughter of prosperous merchant Henry Cerf, who had moved from Waxahachie to New York City in 1906.

G-103
504 Sycamore Street
1938; Charles Stevens Dilbeck, architect;
Fin Garvin, builder

Homer P. McCartney and his wife Mollie commissioned Dallas architect Charles Dilbeck to design this French Eclectic style house after seeing his very similar house in Dallas's Highland Park (4144 Shenandoah). The Waxahachie house almost duplicates the earlier design. The same cylindrical tower, with a tiny angular balcony jutting improbably from the curving wall and roof, serves as the central focus of these fieldstone and brick residences. Dilbeck designed several French "farmhouses" utilizing similar elements, but this one and its model were particularly successful, as their long, steeply pitched gable roofs help to unite the many lovingly assembled eclectic details. He lavished particular attention on a wide variety of window forms and materials, with generous use of timber framing and diamond-shaped panes. The façade advances and recedes beneath the roof, providing small shadowed porches with rustic timber supports. Dilbeck used towers as a stair hall in most of his Dallas examples, but in this case he inserted a small powder room in the space. Homer McCartney was a successful farmer, who was working for the International Harvester Company when he built this house. The varied eclectic details were expensive to build, and the mechanic's lien records that the McCartneys paid Fin Garvin the substantial sum (for the time) of $6,500 to build this "six room shingle roof dwelling-house."

G-104
513 Sycamore Street
1940; Albert H. Teipel, architect;
W. D. Brasher, builder

Joaquin and Frances Ray signed a mechanic's lien in May 1940 for local contractor W. D. Brasher to build this "six room frame residence with a 2 car garage and servants quarters attached by a roofed arcade." The *Daily Light* noted on July 31, 1940, that the Rays had moved into their "attractive Cape Cod residence." Joaquin, who went by "J," probably was named after the American poet Joaquin Miller. He lived with his parents at **707 West Marvin** before marrying Frances Caldwell in 1927 at the age of thirty-eight. He worked at the Waxahachie Cotton Oil Company, Lone Star Gas Company, and the Enterprise Publishing Company before his marriage, but in his 1976 obituary he was listed simply as a retired farmer. An April 14, 1940 *Dallas Morning News* article reported that architect Albert H. Teipel's house for the Rays was due to start construction soon. Born in Kentucky, with an architecture degree from Cornell University, Teipel moved to Dallas in 1920. Soon after designing the Rays' house, he designed a Monterrey style fire station for Love Field in Dallas.

G-105
600 Sycamore Street
1935; Bertram C. Hill, architect; W. D. Brasher, builder

In the full spirit of the Eclectic era, this Spanish Eclectic style house was designed by a British-born and trained architect who practiced in New York, Boston, and St. Louis before moving to Dallas in 1918. Known for his large houses in the Colonial and Italian Renaissance styles in Dallas and Highland Park, Bertram Hill demonstrated here that he could work with facility in the Spanish vocabulary as well. Using a full gamut of Spanish elements, including the cross-gable tile roof, stucco on brick walls, arched entryway, and decorative ironwork, he still managed an overall effect of restraint and balance. Even the relatively ornate triple window grouping to the right of the entrance avoids dominating the façade. Hill lavished them with decorative details, including masonry framing, spiral column mullions, and leaded glass, but by making them slightly smaller in scale and by repeating the arches from the windows on the left, he maintained a balanced façade. This was the largest of four houses illustrated in a *Dallas Morning News* article of November, 10, 1935, that lauded a Waxahachie building boom, notable at this point in the Depression—"nine new homes of the better type . . . complete or under construction." (Workmen were still applying finishing touches on this house in the photograph.) Alabama-born Young C. (Y. C.) Carlisle moved to Waxahachie in 1925 after living in Waco and McGregor, Texas. His successful Chevrolet dealership, which continues to this day, enabled Y. C. and his wife Hulda Maud to build this substantial house, which remained in the family until 2008.

G-106
601 Sycamore Street
1931; Marion Fooshee, architect;
O. B. Bennett, builder

This exuberant two-story cross-gable Tudor Revival house displays both the architect's skill and his client's financial success. The Texas-born architect, Marion Fooshee, grew up in Dallas and worked with J. G. Thomson before opening his own office in 1918. James Cheek, also from Dallas but educated at the University of Texas, joined Fooshee the next year. Although best known for their Spanish-Mediterranean style Highland Park Village shopping center (1931-1947), Fooshee and Cheek had achieved a successful residential practice by the late 1920s, designing houses in a variety of eclectic styles. Here, Fooshee incorporates a full range of carefully reproduced medieval English architectural elements, with the most prominent being the wide masonry entrance archway, the double-shaft chimney, and the large-scale oriole window in the front gable. (A couple of years earlier, the firm had included a similar window above the entrance door of 4305 Lorraine Avenue, in Highland Park.) The steep, long slopes of the two staggered front gables make the derivation of the English architectural term "catslide roof" quite clear. Particularly with the right gable and its extension over the arched entrance of the wing wall, one can envision a cartoon-like cat with all four feet pressed fiercely against the shingles sliding against his will down the slope.

As manager of the Trinity Farm Construction Company, J. D. Kirven handled major dam- and levee-building projects throughout the region. Managing the multi-million-dollar Trinity River levee project in Dallas from 1928 to 1931 probably helped him finance the construction of this showplace during the early years of the Depression. Later in the 1930s Kirven joined in the establishment of the George Black Company, which handled farm properties.

G-107
606 Sycamore Street

1935; Christensen & Christensen, architects; Fin Garvin, builder

Although the timber window heads and slightly extended shed-roof over the entrance door indicate an eclectic design approach, with French farmhouse elements, this cross-gable one-and-a-half story house evades a straightforward stylistic classification. The long dormer, with its oddly spaced, though symmetrically arranged windows is unusual, and the large multi-paned arched window in the front gable would never have been found in a rustic farmhouse. When the *Dallas Morning News* included a photograph of it under construction in November 1935, the caption described it simply as a "new brick veneer." The fact that it was "new" and built of substantial (and relatively expensive) brick at this point in the Depression was noteworthy and a welcome development in a community heavily dependent on a struggling rural economy. Salesmanship, rather than farming, financed its construction. The 1930 Census recorded Ed Waltman renting a house on University Avenue, but by 1935 his work as a traveling salesman enabled him and his wife Mattie to obtain plans from Dallas architects Christensen & Christensen and pay Fin Garvin $5,150 to build this home alongside the other showplaces on Sycamore. Christensen & Christensen also designed the Art Deco 1936 band shell at Fair Park in Dallas with theater architect W. Scott Dunne. Additional examples of their eclectic houses can be found in Dallas's Lakewood neighborhood.

G-108
607 Sycamore Street

1924; R. L. Lowry, builder

Dr. John B. Jenkins and his wife Kathleen built this Tudor Revival-style brick, stucco, and clapboard two-story residence only four years after moving to Waxahachie. It originally stood isolated on the end of the block and helped to establish this stretch of Sycamore as a prime location for larger-scale stylish new homes in the 1920s and 30s. The steeply pitched front gables and prominent chimney on the façade proclaim the English antecedents of the style, as does the partially enclosed front porch, more suited to a northern than a Texas climate. Compared to a later example of the style just to the east at **601 Sycamore**, the Jenkins house looks simpler and more rustic. Similar designs in house catalogues and magazines of the time were referred to as "English Cottage style," and the less formal approach implied by the word "cottage" is evident here. Although not highly ornamented, the house reflects a cohesive, well-detailed design. Born in Texas, Dr. Jenkins attended the University of Texas in Austin before earning his medical degree at Vanderbilt in 1915. He practiced in Waxahachie from 1920 until his death in 1954. Kathleen continued to live in the house until her death in 1988. When the Jenkins's son Joe, born in 1925, retired from a successful career in social work for an Illinois nonprofit organization, he moved back to Waxahachie and to his childhood home with his wife Jan. Joe served as mayor of his hometown from May 2000 through 2010.

G-109
610 Sycamore Street
1937-38; Christensen & Christensen, architects; O. B. Bennett and Fin Garvin, builders

Lynn B. Gardenhire and his wife Mildred began construction of this brick-veneer house in 1937, and the large "G" still visible on the wide chimney remains as evidence of their ownership. The one-story side-gable portion of the house, with an open-truss shed-roof entrance porch, parallels the street and joins a two-story hipped-roof wing perpendicular to the street. The wall dormers in the two-story wing and the brick stringcourses recall Texas Regional work popularized by David R. Williams. Although Mildred's father founded Waxahachie's Cheeves Brothers clothing store in 1896, she grew up in Temple and graduated from St. Mary's school in Dallas in 1929 before marrying Lynn Gardenhire in Oklahoma in 1931. The couple could have become familiar with the Christensen brothers' work in Dallas, where they lived before moving to Waxahachie in the mid-1930s for Lynn to manage the local Cheeves store, but the connection could have been even closer to home. The Christensens designed the house next door, **606 Sycamore**, in 1935.

G-110
701 Sycamore Street
1926; Cal Ramsey, builder

The local newspaper noted the construction of this "lovely nine room Dutch colonial dwelling" in August 1926. Along with the Jenkins house at **607 Sycamore**, it helped to establish this end of Sycamore as a site for prosperous Waxahachie homeowners attracted by large lots and eclectic revival-style homes. The gambrel-roof side wing originally included an open porch at the ground level, equipped with a porch swing, and a sleeping porch above. Examination of the brick on the east side of the wing reveals how the porch openings were later filled in. Early photographs show that the distinctive belcast gambrel roof (curved at the eaves) and shed dormers were original.

Waxahachie native Edward Pryor Gammon was in his forties and was a bookkeeper for the Penn Cotton Company when he had the house built for his wife Kathleen and two children. When the Depression hit, Edward worked various jobs and struggled to keep the house until he found stable employment with Waxahachie's branch of the Texas Employment Commission. He remained in the house until his death in 1958.

G-111
707 Sycamore Street
1935; H. D. Rankin, builder

In November 1935 the *Dallas Morning News* published a photograph of this house and three others newly constructed in Waxahachie with the heading "Residential Building Boom at Waxahachie." The accompanying text identified this as the "Model Home" of Mr. and Mrs. Romney Rudolph, "credited with starting the boom." New home construction was rare at this point in the Depression, so it is not surprising that the *Daily Light* recorded these projects also. It noted on May 7 that contractor H. D. Rankin had begun construction of the "model home," which would be "open for inspection from time to time." Rudolph had signed a mechanic's lien nine days earlier, agreeing to pay Rankin $3,500 to build this "newly constructed house . . . of two bedrooms, one kitchen, one breakfast room, one dining room, one bath room, one living room," plus a garage, concrete terrace porch, sidewalks, and gravel driveway. Although small in scale, with little ornamentation, it presented a minimal Tudor

Revival style through the diamond-pane leaded glass window, double stack chimney, and steep gables of the entrance porch and front cross gable. Romney, son of one of the founders of the Rudolph Brothers Funeral Home, succeeded his father as president soon after returning from World War II. Romney's wife, Willette, took over as head of the firm after his untimely death at the age of forty-eight in 1954.

G-112
710 Sycamore Street

1951; E. Davis Wilcox, architect;
O. B. Bennett, builder

On April 8, 1951, the *Daily Light* reported that contractor O. B. Bennett would be starting construction of a "two-story brick and frame residence" designed by Tyler architect Dave Wilcox for Mrs. Mary Ellen Marchman. Mrs. Marchman's parents, John D. and Roberta C. Kirven, had used the same contractor twenty years earlier to build their Tudor Revival home at **601 Sycamore**, when she was a teenager. Wilcox earned an architecture degree at Georgia Tech in 1935, subsequently studying at Yale and the Ecole des Beaux-Arts in Fontainebleau, France before starting his practice in Tyler. In this Monterrey style house he designed a long, two-story side-gable main structure enlivened by a projecting one-story living room wing on one side of the entrance and a five-bay second-story balcony on the other. Mrs. Marchman was appointed head librarian of the Sims Library in 1977 and served in that position for several years.

G-113
800 Sycamore Street

1938

This Tudor Revival side-gable house is one of the few examples in Waxahachie with masonry veneer covering the entire wall surface, rather than serving as trim or accent. Dark brown bricks outline the doors, windows, and arched vents, and form a decorative arch and banding on the chimney. Although the shorter height of the three windows on the right of the façade suggests a later alteration, the pattern of the stonework abutting the stone sill and the brick infill indicate that they may be original—perhaps an alteration from the original plan made during construction.

Given its location within blocks of what was then the Trinity University campus, it is not surprising that the house was built by a Trinity professor, Jerome L. Kerby. It is surprising, however, that a professor could afford to build such a substantial house during the Depression, but his subject expertise as a professor of economics and business administration might have assisted him in acquiring the needed funds. A job as head of the Business Administration Department of Sul Ross State College took Jerome and his wife Alice to Alpine, Texas, only two years after the house was completed.

G-114
119 Overhill Drive

1954; E. A. Sibley, architect and contractor

When Conrad Martin and his wife Helen contracted with E. A. Sibley in September 1954 to build this "two-story, brick veneer residence with attached garage," it was the first structure on this part of Overhill Drive. It clearly embodied the new design aesthetic of the 1950s, in stark contrast to the 1929 red brick Georgian Revival house just to the north across Cedar St. at **201 Overhill**. The Martins' house sported low-pitched cross-gabled roofs with wide overhangs, narrow Roman brick veneer on the first floor, and shingle siding in the gables and as the second-floor siding. The presence of a second floor is unusual for a Ranch style house, but since it is smaller than the first floor and set back, the low lines of the front and side gable wings predominate. Sibley may well have served as architect as well as contractor of this house, for he had designed the house built at 211 Overhill in April 1954, and the *Dallas Morning News* featured houses designed by him in the 1950s and 60s in French and Colonial styles as well as Ranch. Conrad Martin started Martin Florists in 1938, and while continuing to run that business also became involved in real estate and other investments. At the time of his death in 1966 he was president of Jo Jan Electronics Company of Dallas. It is not surprising that the First Methodist Church's new 1957 parsonage was built next door to Conrad at 115 Overhill, for he served on their board of trustees and building committee for many years.

G-115
120 Overhill Drive

1958; Robert Davies, architect;
M. F. Davenport, contractor

As the staff of the Southland Cotton Oil Company planned the 1958 move of their headquarters from Paris, Texas, to Waxahachie, the general manager, Robert L. Horton, and his wife Tommye Jo signed a contract in September 1957 with M. F. Davenport to build this house. The company headquarters building at **106 South Monroe** was uncompromisingly Modern in style, but Horton and his wife chose a more conventional, though tasteful, Ranch style for their dwelling. Dallas architect Robert Davies supplied the plans. He provided the typical expansive horizontal spread of an upscale example of the type, but slight projections of the entrance porch and the southeastern side, with their corresponding low-pitched roofs, provide a subtle modulation in the façade.

G-116
201 Overhill Drive

1929; William Brown Fowler, of Coburn & Fowler, architect;
Burt Building Co., builder

This handsome two-story hipped-roof Georgian Revival house stood in splendid isolation outside the city limits when constructed in 1929. Completed just before the stock market crash of October 1929, the house provided an impressive physical confirmation of Oscar H. Chapman's long and successful career. Although born and raised in Ellis County, Oscar obtained his BA from Trinity University in 1893, when it was still in Tehuacana, and a law degree from Cumberland University in Lebanon, Kentucky. He returned to Texas to marry Loretta Lancaster in 1895 and settled in Waxahachie. He served as county attorney, but left that position to practice real estate law. His business interests included real estate investment and loans. A loyal Trinity University supporter, he served as a trustee and as treasurer. If Chapman originally planned to develop his twenty-acre plot for similar substantial, architect-designed revival-style residences to join his, the stock market crash and ensuing Great Depression would have slowed progress in that direction. In 1933 and 1934, he deeded land to each of his two married daughters, Allyne Keplinger and Ruth Estes. With their houses at the north end, Overhill Drive remained a Chapman family enclave through the 1940s. (The north end of Overhill has since been renamed. The current addresses of the daughters' houses are **311 Olive Street** and **103 Greenbrier**.)

The Chapmans selected Dallas architect William Brown Fowler, of the firm Coburn & Fowler, to design their dream house. A graduate of Texas A&M College in 1913, Fowler was associated with the firm of Herbert M. Greene before establishing his own firm with Douglas F. Coburn in 1928. He worked with Greene on the Scottish Rite Cathedral at El Paso and buildings at the University of Texas at Austin and the UT Medical Branch in Galveston. His later work in the 1930s included the Museum of Fine Arts and the Museum of Natural History at the Dallas Fair Park and the General Electric exhibition building at the New York World's Fair. In the Chapman house, he was able to display his proficiency in finely detailed domestic eclectic design. By placing the elaborate pedimented entrance off center, Fowler introduced a single, but powerful element of asymmetry in an otherwise strictly symmetrical façade. The off-center entrance may have been chosen to allow the formal living room to extend across two-thirds of the house's width, but it also acknowledged the primacy of the automobile. Guests, or residents, arriving through the porte cochère could enter into the same grand entrance hall as those who passed through the official entrance door. The house is complemented by a similarly styled and detailed garage with servant's quarters above.

G-117
205 Overhill Drive
1951; O. B. Bennett, builder

Overhill Drive began its transformation from a private family enclave to an upscale modern subdivision in 1951, when the Chapman property was annexed by the city. Only three houses stood in the neighborhood at that time, O. H. Chapman's 1929 house next door to this one, and the residences of two of his daughters at **311 Olive** (1933) and **103 Greenbrier** (1941). John and Helen Murchison's 1951 modest one-story Minimal Traditional style house became the first home built in that year of transition. Murchison moved to Waxahachie from Paris, Texas, to manage the local Texas Power & Light office, and he was the first new executive in town to choose the Chapman Addition for his home. He would be followed by R. L. Richardson, president of Southome Furniture Industries, who built 209 Overhill later in 1951, and Southland Cotton Oil Company manager Robert Horton, who built **120 Overhill** in 1958. When Waxahachie native Tom Curlin was promoted to the position of manager of the local Tyler Fixture Company plant in 1952, he also began to plan for a house on Overhill. In July 1953, he contracted with the same builder that the Murchisons had used, O. B. Bennett, to construct a house next door at 203 Overhill, but he chose to build a more up-to-date Ranch house.

G-118
311 Olive Street
1933; Bertram C. Hill, architect

Architect Bertram C. Hill was already familiar with Waxahachie by the time he designed this house in 1933, having designed Davis Hall (**407 West Jefferson**) in 1925 and residences at **401 East Marvin**, **1004 West Marvin**, and **712 West Main** in the 1920s. He would follow this house two years later with the Carlisle house at **600 Sycamore**. An established Dallas architect, proficient in a variety of styles, Hill designed a neat, nicely proportioned version of a side-gable Neoclassical style cottage that became popular in the late 1920s. It would have been called Colonial when it was built, due to the full-façade porch with flat roof edged by a balustrade, which echoes the larger version at Mount Vernon. (The dormers were added later, as were extensions to the rear and west side.)

Hill's clients were banker Pickens A. Keplinger and his wife Allyne. The Texas General Contractors Association's May 1933 *Bulletin* listed the one-story 60 x 40 ft. frame house as prospective work, with plans by Hill and P. A. Keplinger as client. Allyne's father O. H. Chapman deeded them the property, close to his home at **201 Overhill**, in September 1933. (This street was considered part of Overhill until 1955, when its name was changed to Olive Street.) The recently married couple had been living on Farley Street earlier in 1933 when twenty-two-year-old Allyne was knifed by a former girlfriend of her husband. The throat wounds were not dangerous, according to the *Daily Light*, but the timing of the new house might be related to that incident.

G-119
103 Greenbrier Street
1941; Norman W. Crittenden, architect

This sizable lot of 1.4 acres was deeded to Ruth Estes by her father, Oscar H. Chapman, who lived nearby at **201 Overhill**. On May 10, 1939, the house that they had built here was struck by lightning and suffered fire damage. They repaired the damage, but in 1941 commissioned Dallas architect Norman W. Crittenden to design this two-story brick-veneer side-gable house. Crittenden earned his degree in architecture from the University of Texas at Austin before practicing in Dallas. During World War II he worked as a facilities engineer at North American Aviation, Inc., where he met his future business partner J. Murrell Bennett. Just before the outbreak of the war, however, the Estes house gave him the opportunity to use his residential design skills in a Neoclassical style. The full-height gable-roof entrance porch and large front door crowned by a broken pediment combine to form an imposing façade. The deep setback from the street was unusual in Waxahachie at the time, as was the landscaped circular drive, proclaiming that visitors to this house would arrive by automobile, rather than on foot. When Ted and Ruth built the house, only two other houses stood nearby, her father's (**201 Overhill**) and her sister's (**311 Olive**).

G-120
105 Greenbrier Street
1956; J. A. Zollicoffer & Associates, architects

This expansive Contemporary style house broke with the Ranch style pattern established on nearby Overhill Drive in the 1950s. Architect J. A. Zollicoffer took advantage of the large site at the curving intersection of Greenbrier and LaVista to give the house a deep setback and place the U-shaped house at an angle to the driveway, which splits to the right for the family entrance and carport and to the left for the public entrance and parking. As described in the *Daily Light* of August 12, 1956, the house was "contemporary in design and, with a detached guesthouse and bath house, forms a 'U' around a kidney-shaped swimming pool." Waxahachie had nothing else quite like it at the time, and not surprisingly, the owners were newcomers to town. J. J. (Jim) Larkin Jr., executive vice president of the Larkin Packer Company, built the house soon after the oil field equipment manufacturing company, based in St. Louis, Missouri, opened a plant in Waxahachie. A few years later, in 1963, the same architect designed a more conventional ranch house at 113 Overhill for Nathan and Peggy Blair.

G-121
617 Solon Road
c. 1890-94

John Solon's two-story stone house stands out among Waxahachie's nineteenth-century residences for more reasons than the unusual horseshoe-shaped red sandstone arch that he intended as a tribute to his Irish heritage. Solon's choice of stone masonry construction ensured that his house would be unique in Waxahachie. The stone was transported by rail from the Millsap quarries, west of Fort Worth. The local newspaper noted the arrival of the stone in June 1890 for Solon's "substantial residence," to cost about $6,000. By the time of construction, his income primarily came from farming and stock-raising enterprises, but Solon had been a major stone mason and contractor in Waxahachie since the mid-1870s. He was responsible for many of the first stone and brick buildings on the square, as well as the stone work for the 1886 county records office and the construction of the 1888 county jail. It is not surprising therefore that he chose to build his own house in stone. The L-plan form of the house was more typical of the 1880s, when Solon was working as a contractor, than of the early 1890s, when Queen Anne style, modified L-plan houses were gaining in popularity. The tall, narrow windows also would have been considered somewhat old-fashioned at the time of construction, as larger, wider windows were becoming more available. The porch trim, however, was quite up-to-date, with several elements matching those used in the Ed Williams House of 1893 (**412 West Marvin**). Even if the plan was old-fashioned, no one could deny the obvious care and substantial resources lavished on the house, or the flamboyance expressed in the huge red sandstone horseshoe arch. Although the house was located in the country, two miles out of town, it was well known and often referred to as the "Stone House," rather than the Irish name "Killaiden" that Solon himself had given it. Solon's niece continued to live in the house into the 1970s, but Waxahachie's expansion eventually surrounded the once isolated, grand house.

Appendix I:
Looking At Waxahachie Houses:
A Guide To Types

The following house types appear frequently in this guide and in Waxahachie. House types refer to form or shape, whereas styles encompass the arrangement of building elements and decorative details as well as form. Building types and styles are not mutually exclusive—bungalows can be in a Craftsman or a Spanish Revival style, and modified L-plan houses can display Queen Anne or Classical style details.

Side-Gable Cottage
112 Kaufman Street
c. 1912

A side-gable cottage is a one-story house, one room deep, usually two rooms wide, with the ends of the gable roof facing the sides of the lot.

Shotgun House
212 Wyatt Street
c. 1912

A Shotgun is a narrow house, one room wide and two or three rooms deep. The narrow end of the house and entrance face the street. Roofs are either gabled or hipped.

I-House
207 South Hawkins Street
c. 1859, 1882

An I-House is a two-story house, one room deep, usually with a central hall and a full-width porch of one or two stories.

L-Plan House

207 Brown Street

c. 1885

The L-plan house is a one- or two-story house identified by its L-shaped footprint. The most distinctive feature from the street view is its front-projecting wing extending from the side-gabled main building mass.

Modified L-Plan House

305 University Avenue

1902

A modified L-plan house is one or two stories and consists of a hipped-roof central mass with projecting gable-roof wings to the front and side. Popular in the late nineteenth and early twentieth centuries, these houses often included Queen Anne or Classical Revival ornamentation on the porch and gables.

T-Plan House

1008 West Main Street

1893

In a T-plan house, a front-gable wing projects from the center of a side-gable mass. There also may be a wing projecting to the rear, but the T-form visible from the street identifies the type.

Pyramidal Cottages

219 and 221 North Hawkins Street

A pyramidal cottage is a small square house with a hipped roof of four equal sides that form a pyramid.

Pyramidal House

115 University

1911

A rectangular (rather than square) house with a hipped roof may be called pyramidal if the roof is steeply pitched and appears to be pyramidal from the street. These larger houses are sometimes called Massed Plan Pyramidals.

Bungalow

312 Virginia

1921

Bungalows are houses of one or one-and-a-half stories with wide overhanging eaves and an emphasis on horizontal lines and proportions. They are usually built closer to the ground than nineteenth-century houses. The roofs may be gables or hipped, but their pitch is lower than most nineteenth-century houses and early twentieth-century pyramidals.

Appendix II: "Waxahachie Ts"

T-plan houses, with a front-gable wing projecting from the center of a side-gable mass, became popular in Waxahachie in the late nineteenth century. Several survive, but the Sanborn maps document that many others have been lost. A T-plan house design was even titled "Waxahachie Cottage" in a catalogue of house plans that St. Louis architect Herbert C. Chivers published in 1901. Chivers named many of his plans after American towns, and he could have arbitrarily pulled the names out of an atlas, but, given the prevalence of T-plans in Waxahachie, it is entirely possible that his use of the town's name for a T-plan design was inspired by a visit here.

The popularity of the T-plan in Waxahachie probably was due primarily to two characteristics, the first of which was a practical one. The perpendicular orientation of the house to the street required less land than many houses where the plan ran parallel to the street. With its projecting front gable, bay front, and receding sides shaded by an attached porch with decorative trim, the Waxahachie cottage enabled some of the same decorative flourishes found on larger, more flamboyant Queen Anne style houses.

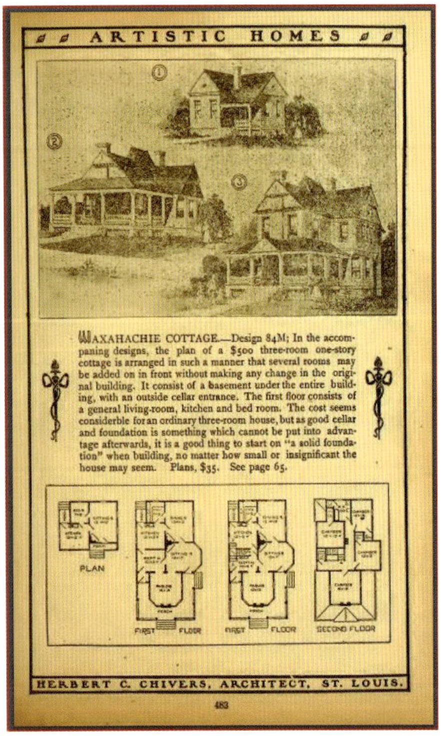
ARTISTIC HOMES

WAXAHACHIE COTTAGE.—Design 84M; In the accompaning designs, the plan of a $500 three-room one-story cottage is arranged in such a manner that several rooms may be added on in front without making any change in the original building. It consist of a basement under the entire building, with an outside cellar entrance. The first floor consists of a general living-room, kitchen and bed room. The cost seems considerble for an ordinary three-room house, but as good cellar and foundation is something which cannot be put into advantage afterwards, it is a good thing to start on "a solid foundation" when building, no matter how small or insignificant the house may seem. Plans, $35. See page 65.

PLAN FIRST FLOOR FIRST FLOOR SECOND FLOOR

HERBERT C. CHIVERS, ARCHITECT, ST. LOUIS.

483

Designs for T-plan houses titled "Waxahachie Cottage" by St. Louis architect Herbert Chivers in his catalogue *Artistic Homes*, 1903 edition.

515 North Rogers Street
c. 1893

217 Williams Street
c. 1895

310 Williams Street
c. 1893

Appendix III: "Waxahachie Dormers"

During the first two decades of the twentieth century, Waxahachie builders favored a distinctive type of dormer with convex shingled sides, or jambs, curving out from the windows. Most of the dormers have hipped roofs, but their convex shingled sides might have been inspired by the 1904 gable-roofed dormer at 716 West Main Street, designed by architect H. A. Overbeck. These dormers may not be unique or original to Waxahachie, but on the evidence of the surviving examples, Waxahachie residents certainly claimed them as their own. A few examples are shown below, but many others can be found along Waxahachie's streets.

716 West Main Street
1904

310 Brown Street
1905-06

501 Brown Street
1911

807 West Marvin
1911

107 East University Avenue
1912

111 Virginia
1914

SELECTED BIBLIOGRAPHY

Bird's-eye views

Morse, D. D. *Bird's Eye View of Waxahachie, County Seat of Ellis Co. Tex. 1876.* Chicago: Chas. Shober & Co. Prop's Chicago Lith. Co., 1876.

Wellge, Henry. *Waxahachie, Tex. County Seat of Ellis County. 1886.* Milwaukee: Norris Wellge & Co., 1886.

Government and institutional records

Ellis County Clerk's Office: deeds; mechanics' liens; probate, death, marriage, and Commissioners' Court records

Ellis County District Clerk's Office: District Court records

Ellis County Tax Rolls, 1850-1910 (on microfilm at the Sims Library, Waxahachie)

Waxahachie City Secretary's Office: City Council minutes

Waxahachie Independent School District Superintendent's Office: School Board minutes

United States Bureau of the Census. U. S. Population Census. 1850-1940.

Maps

Phillips & Hawkins Official Map of the City of Waxahachie, Texas. St. Louis: Geo. D. Barnard & Co., 1896.

Texas Title & Loan Company. *Official Map of the City of Waxahachie, Texas.* 1922.

Waxahachie Abstract Company. *Official Map of the City of Waxahachie, Texas.* 1946.

Sanborn Fire Insurance Maps

- Waxahachie Sanborn maps for the following dates are accessible through the Proquest *Digital Sanborn Maps 1867-1970* database: Mar. 1885; July 1890; Apr. 1893; Oct. 1898; Nov. 1904; Oct. 1909; Nov. 1914; Oct. 1925; Oct. 1925 – June 1959.
- Waxahachie Sanborn maps (in color) for the following years are accessible online at no charge through the Perry Castaneda Library, University of Texas at Austin. http://legacy.lib.utexas.edu/maps/sanborn/w.html. 1885, 1890, 1893, 1898, 1904, 1909, 1914.

Newspapers

Waxahachie Daily Light

- 1898+ on microfilm at the Sims Library, Waxahachie.
- 1902-1916 searchable at no charge through the *Portal to Texas History* (www.texashistory.unt.edu)
- Many (but not all) issues from 1902-1977 are accessible online through www.newspapers.com.

Waxahachie Enterprise

- 1876-1934 on microfilm at the Sims Library, Waxahachie.

Dallas Morning News

- 1885-1985 accessible online at libraries through www.NewsBank.com.

Waxahachie Directories

The Ellis County Museum holds the most extensive collection of Waxahachie directories in original or photocopied form, but the collections of the Sims Library and the Texas State Library were also consulted. Directories for the following years were utilized. Those with an asterisk include an index by street address.

1895* (only a transcribed index of this directory is available), 1907, 1913*, 1918, 1922*, 1924-1925*, 1927-1928*, 1936, 1939*, 1942*, 1948*, 1952*, 1955*, and 1958*. Later directories were also consulted for buildings in the downtown area.

The *Waxahachie Daily Light* on May 8, 1902 (page 3), published a list of residents with telephones, giving their names and addresses.

Two churches published directories of their members, with addresses, in the early 1900s.

Directory of the First Cumberland Presbyterian Church. Waxahachie, 1903.

Directory First Baptist Church, Waxahachie, Texas. Waxahachie: The Ladies Aid Society, First Baptist Church, [circa 1904-1906].

Historic Resource Surveys and National Register Nominations

Copies of the following surveys and forms, along with a set of slides and photographic contact sheets, can be consulted in the Ellis County Museum.

Hardy, Heck, Moore, Inc. for Historic Waxahachie, Inc. *Historical Resources of Waxahachie, Texas: A Comprehensive Survey and National Register of Historic Places Nomination."* Austin, TX.: Hardy, Heck, Moore, Inc., 1985. http://www.waxahachie.com/document_center/heritage/Historic%20Resource%20Survey%201985%20Full%20Report.pdf.

Hardy, Heck, Moore, Inc. for Historic Waxahachie, Inc. *Historic Resources of Waxahachie, Texas (Partial Inventory of Architectural and Historic Properties): National Register of Historic Places Inventory—Nomination Form.* Austin, TX: Hardy, Heck, Moore, Inc., 1985.

The following Historic District Nominations were also created as part of the 1985 survey and nomination process:

North Rogers Street Historic District: National Register of Historic Places Inventory—Nomination Form. 1986. https://atlas.thc.state.tx.us/NR/pdfs/86002465/86002465.pdf.

Oldham Avenue Historic District: National Register of Historic Places Inventory—Nomination Form. 1986. https://atlas.thc.state.tx.us/NR/pdfs/86002461/86002461.pdf.

West End Historic District: National Register of Historic Places Inventory—Nomination Form. 1986. https://atlas.thc.state.tx.us/NR/pdfs/86002474/86002474.pdf.

Wyatt Street Shotgun House Historic District: National Register of Historic Places Inventory—Nomination Form. 1986. https://atlas.thc.state.tx.us/NR/pdfs/86002463/86002463.pdf.

Hardy, Heck, Moore, Inc. for Historic Waxahachie, Inc. *City of Waxahachie: Waxahachie Historic Resources Survey Update: Final Report, August 2004.* Austin, TX: Hardy, Heck, Moore, Inc., 2004. http://www.waxahachie.com/document_center/heritage/Historic%20Resource%20Survey%202004%20Full%20Report.pdf.

Hardy, Heck, Moore, Inc. for Historic Waxahachie, Inc. *City of Waxahachie Survey Update of 2016: Survey Area One—Downtown, November 2016*. Austin, TX: Hardy, Heck, Moore, Inc., 2016. https://drive.google.com/file/d/0B6D-ClVLYHCM-Nm1XYzRyU1Q4YzA/view.

Texas Historical Commission. *Ellis County Courthouse Historic District Survey.* Austin, TX: Texas Historical Commission, 1974.

Texas Historical Commission. *Ellis County Courthouse Historic District: National Register of Historic Places Inventory—Nomination Form*. Austin, TX: Texas Historical Commission, 1975. https://atlas.thc.state.tx.us/NR/pdfs/75001971/75001971.pdf.

Texas Historical Commission. *THC Historic Resources Survey Collection.* Accessible online through the Portal to Texas History. (Includes almost 200 black-and-white photographs taken in 1974-75 of buildings in Waxahachie as part of the historic resources survey.) https://texashistory.unt.edu/explore/collections/THCHS/.

Texas Historical Commission. *THC National Register Slide Collection*. Accessible online through the Portal to Texas History. (Includes over 1,500 color slides taken in 1985 of Waxahachie buildings as part of the National Register nomination process.) https://texashistory.unt.edu/explore/collections/THCNR/.

Ellis County Museum Files

Over the years, the museum staff members and volunteers have compiled files about various buildings in Waxahachie, including paper files of miscellaneous clippings and articles, and digital files of historic images.

Books, Articles, and Websites

Alter, Kevin, ed. *Dance Halls of Central Texas*. Austin, TX: School of Architecture, University of Texas at Austin, 2005.

Ancestry. https://www.ancestry.com/.

Beasley, Ellen, and Stephen Fox. *Galveston Architecture Guidebook*. Houston, TX: Rice University Press, 1996.

Brown, Anita. "Waxahachie." *Main Street Matters: A Monthly Publication of the Texas Main Street Program*. (May 2018). https://www.thc.texas.gov/public/upload/MS%20Matters%20may_0.pdf.

Brun-Ozuna, Barbara. "Marshall Robert Sanguinet." *Legacies* 9 (Fall 1977): 10-12. https://texashistory.unt.edu/ark:/67531/metapth35107/m1/12/.

Bucher, William W. *Dictionary of Building Preservation*. New York: Preservation Press, 1996.

Bruce, William C. *High School Buildings*. Milwaukee: Bruce Publishing Co., 1919.

Chapman, Steve. *The Presbyterian Church-USA and Waxahachie.* Typescript of sermon presented at Central Presbyterian Church, May 3, 1981.

Childers, Sam. "William Sidney Pittman." *Legacies* 9 (Fall 1977): 21-23. https://texashistory.unt.edu/ark:/67531/metapth35107/m1/23/.

Culbertson, Margaret. *Texas Houses Built by the Book: The Use of Published Designs 1850-1925*. College Station: Texas A & M University Press, 1999.

Davis, Ellis A., and Edwin H. Grobe. *The New Encyclopedia of Texas*. Dallas, TX: Texas Development Bureau, 1934.

Dawson, Carol and Roger Allen Polson. *Miles and Miles of Texas: 100 Years of the Texas Highway Department.* College Station, TX: Texas A&M University Press, 2016.

Dexter, W. W. *Texas: Imperial State of America with Her Diadem of Cities*. St. Louis: Sam'l F. Myerson Printing Company, 1904.

Donnelly, Mary Louise. *St. Joseph's Catholic Community, Waxahachie, Texas: Our Parish's 125 Years, 1874-1999*. Ennis, Tex.: M. L. Donnelly, 1999.

Ellis County Museum, Inc. *Ellis County: A Photo History*. Dallas, TX: Printed by Taylor Publishing Company, 1993.

Ellis County History: The Basic 1892 Book (with the Presidents Section Deleted: with Additional Biographies). Waxahachie, TX: Ellis County Museum, 1972.

Ellis County History Workshop. *History of Ellis County*. Waco, TX.: Texian Press, 1972.

Eriksen, Kathryn E., and Laurie J. Wilson. *Waxahachie*. Charleston, SC: Arcadia Publishing, 2009.

Everett, Donald E. *Trinity University: A Record of One Hundred Years*. San Antonio: Trinity University Press, 1968.

FamilySearch. https://www.familysearch.org.

Felty, Margaret. *Central Presbyterian Church of Waxahachie, Texas*. Paper written for the class Historiography 5339, University of Texas at Arlington, January 13, 1972.

Felty, Margaret. *Waxahachie, 1850-1900: A Kaleidoscopic History*. Master's thesis, University of Texas at Arlington, 1975.

Find A Grave. https://www.findagrave.com/.

Fox, Stephen, Gerald Moorhead, and Barrie S. Bradley. *Houston Architectural Guide*. Houston, TX: AIA Houston, 2012.

Fuller, Larry Paul, ed. *The American Institute of Architects Guide to Dallas Architecture: With Regional Highlights*. [New York]: McGraw-Hill Construction Information Group, 1999.

Gottfried, Herbert and Jan Jennings. *American Vernacular Buildings and Interiors, 1870-1960*. New York: W.W. Norton and Co., 2009.

Green, Ely, and Elizabeth N. Chitty. *Ely: Too Black, Too White*. Amherst, MA: University of Massachusetts Press, 1970.

Handbook of Texas Online. Texas State Historical Association. https://tshaonline.org/handbook/search

Hancock, Billy Ray. *A Look at Downtown Waxahachie about a Century Ago, 1911-1914*. Waxahachie, TX: College Street Printing Co., 2016.

Hancock, Billy R. *Story of Paul Richards Park and Waxahachie High School Baseball*. Waxahachie, TX., 2008.

Harris, Cyril M. *Dictionary of Architecture & Construction*. New York, NY: McGraw-Hill, 2006.

Hazel, Michael V. "They called it Chautauqua." *Legacies* 8 (Spring 1996): 26-32.

Henry, Jay C. *Architecture in Texas: 1895-1945*. Austin, TX: University of Texas Press, 2010.

A History of Waxahachie, Texas and Citizens National Bank. Waxahachie, TX: Citizens National Bank, 1969. (Title on cover: *Your History and Ours, a Tribute to Waxahachie and Ellis County by Citizens National Bank On This, Our 100th Birthday.*)

Jakle, John A. and Keith A. Sculle. *The Garage: Automobility and Building Innovation in America's Early Auto Age*. Knoxville: The University of Tennessee Press, 2013.

Kylar, Mark Wesley. *The Historical Development of the Public School System in Waxahachie, Texas: Exploring a Local Dialect in the Grammar of Schooling*. PhD dissertation, University of Texas at Austin, 2010.

Lancaster, Clay. *The American Bungalow, 1880-1930*. New York: Abbeville Press, 1985.

Lavergne, Gary M. *Before Brown: Heman Marion Sweatt, Thurgood Marshall, and the Long Road to Justice*. Austin, TX: University of Texas Press, 2010.

McAlester, Virginia, Suzanne P. Matty, Steve Clicque, A. L. McAlester, Lauren Jarrett, and Juan Rodriguez-Arnaiz. *A Field Guide to American Houses: The Definitive Guide to Identifying and Understanding America's Domestic Architecture*. Second edition. NY: Alfred A. Knopf, 2013.

McAlester, Virginia, Willis Winters, and Steve Clicque. *Great American Suburbs: Homes of the Park Cities, Dallas, Texas*. New York: Abbeville, 2008.

McDonald, William L. *Dallas Rediscovered: A Photographic Chronicle of Urban Expansion 1870-1925*. Dallas, TX: Dallas Historical Society, 1978.

Meister, Chris. *James Riely Gordon: His Courthouses and Other Public Architecture*. Lubbock, TX: Texas Tech Press, 2011.

A Memorial and Biographical History of Ellis County, Texas. Chicago: Lewis Publishing Company, 1892.

Miller, Douglas K. "The Salt Lake County Rotary Jail." *Utah Historical Quarterly* 75, no. 4 (Fall 2007): 322-341. https://issuu.com/utah10/docs/uhq_volume75_2007_number4.

Parsons, Jim, and David Bush. *DFW Deco: Modernistic Architecture of North Texas.* Fort Worth, TX: TCU Press, 2017.

Phillips, Steven J. *Old-House Dictionary: An Illustrated Guide to American Domestic Architecture (1600-1940).* New York: John Wiley & Sons, 1996.

Portal to Texas History. https://texashistory.unt.edu/.

Quimby, Marcel. "Lang and Witchell: Shaping the Dallas Skyline." *Legacies* 9 (Fall 1997): 13-20. https://texashistory.unt.edu/ark:/67531/metapth35107/m1/15/.

Roark, Carol. "Make Lots of Little Plans: The R. M. Williamson House Plan Books." *Legacies* 9, no. 2 (Fall 1997): 24-29. https://texashistory.unt.edu/ark:/67531/metapth35107/m1/26/?q=roark%20williamson.

Russell, Tim. *Fill'er Up! The Great American Gas Station.* (reprint) New York: Crestline, 2013. First published by Voyageur Press, 2007.

Simpson, Charles Moffett. *A Sanitary Survey of Waxahachie, Texas.* Boston: Harvard Medical School, 1917. (Copy in the National Library of Medicine.)

Some Work from the Office of Sanguinet & Staats Successors to: Messer Sanguinet and Messer Architects Fort Worth, Tex. Fort Worth, Texas, 1896. (Photocopy in the biographical ephemera files of the Amon Carter Museum Library and Archives.)

Spalding, William A., Sr. *Recollections of a Long Life: By a Native Texan.* Typescript, Waxahachie, July 1, 1952.

Spears, Timothy B. *100 Years on the Road: The Traveling Salesman in American Culture.* New Haven: Yale University Press, 1994.

Stevenson, Katherine C., and H. W. Jandl. *Houses by Mail: A Guide to Houses from Sears, Roebuck, and Company.* Washington, DC: Preservation Press, 1996.

Stott, Kelly M. M. *Waxahachie: Where Cotton Reigned King.* Charleston, SC: Arcadia Publishing, 2002.

Swanson, Marilyn. "Charles Dilbeck: A One-of-a-Kind Architect." *Legacies* 9, no. 2 (Fall 1997): 39-46.

Tenery, Rob. *Dr. Mayo's Boy: A Century of American Medicine.* Dallas, TX: Brown Books Pub. Group, 2009.

Texas Genealogical Records, Ellis County. Volumes 1-22. Waxahachie, TX: Daughters of the American Revolution Rebecca Boyce Chapter, 1954-1968. Accessible online through the *Portal to Texas History.* https://texashistory.unt.edu/search/?fq=str_title_serial:%22Texas%20Genealogical%20Records%2C%20Ellis%20County%22.

Texas General Contractors Association. *TGCA Monthly Bulletin.* (Accessed at the Houston Metropolitan Research Center, Houston Public Library.)

This Was Ellis County: An Historical Perspective. Waxahachie, TX: College Street Printing Company, [no date]. (Reprint of the Waxahachie High School student publication that was issued annually for the years 1977-1981.)

Valentine, Maggie. *The Show Starts on the Sidewalk: An Architectural History of the Movie Theatre.* New Haven: Yale University Press, 1994.

Walton, John Brooks. *The Architecture of Charles Stevens Dilbeck.* Tulsa, OK: JBW Publications, 2006.

Waxahachie Chautauqua Preservation Society. "Explore Chautauqua History: Waxahachie, Texas, North America." Accessed July 17, 2018. https://www.waxahachiechautauqua.org/history-new.

Waxahachie Illustrated. Southern Print. Co., 1910.

"Waxahachie: The Thriving Capital of a Rich County." *The Republican* (St. Louis), Dec. 14, 1887, 8.

Weldon, Fred. *Carved Ornament of the Ellis County Courthouse.* Ellis County Museum, 1995.

Wilson, Christine Hawkins. *Life on Hawkins Row.* Houston, TX: Phil Wilson, 1960.

Wilson, Laurie J. and Peggy Holland Rankin. *Railroading in Ellis County.* Charleston, SC: Arcadia Publishing, 2010.

Yinger, Edgar, ed. *The Campus Sketchbook: Trinity University, Waxahachie, Texas, 1930-1931*. Waxahachie: Bayless, 1931.

Zsohar, Zoltan, and Elizabeth Zsohar. *Surviving through Faith: A True Story of a Refugee Family's Hope, Faith, Love, Devotion and Determination*. Dallas, TX: Brown Books Pub Group, 2001.

The following plan books, catalogues, and periodicals included house designs that were possible design sources for Waxahachie houses.

American Homes. Knoxville, TN, 1895-1904.

Barber, George F. *Cottage Souvenir Number Two*. Reprint of the 1892 edition with new introduction by Michael Tomlan. Watkins Glen, NY: American Life Foundation, 1982.

Carpentry and Building. New York. 1879-1909.

Chivers, Herbert C. *Artistic Homes*. St. Louis: Herbert C. Chivers, 1903. https://archive.org/details/artistichomesoochiv.

Chivers, Herbert C. *1000 Turn-of-the-Century Houses: With Illustrations and Floor Plans*. New York: Dover Publications, 2007. (Reprint of 1910 edition of *Artistic Homes*, by Herbert C. Chivers.)

Craftsman. Edited by Gustav Stickley. Eastwood, NY. 1901-16.

Farm and Ranch. Dallas, TX. 1901-02.

Fifty House Plans Designed for Home Builders in the Southwest. Dallas, TX: Associated Architects, 1910.

Holland's House Plan Book. Dallas, TX: Holland's Magazine, 1935.

Holland's House Plans. (Title on cover: *Distinctive Southern Homes*) Dallas: Holland's Magazine, 1936. https://archive.org/details/HollandsMagazine.

Holland's Magazine, Dallas, TX. 1905-36.

Keith's Magazine on Homebuilding, Minneapolis, MN. 1899-1931.

Ladies Home Journal. *Journal Bungalows*. Philadelphia, PA: Curtis, 1916.

Radford's Artistic Bungalows. Chicago: Radford Architectural Col, 1908.

Scientific American, Architects' and Builders' Edition. New York: Munn & Co., 1885-94.

Stickley, Gustav. *Craftsman Bungalows: 59 Homes from "The Craftsman."* New York: Dover Publications, 1998. (Selection of thirty-six articles published from 1903 through 1916 in the periodical *The Craftsman*.)

Stickley, Gustav. *Craftsman Homes: Architecture and Furnishings of the American Arts and Crafts Movement*. New York: Dover Publications, 1979. (Reprint of the second edition of *Craftsman Homes*, published in 1909.)

Stickley, Gustav. *More Craftsman Homes*. Mineola, NY: Dover Publications, 1982. (Reprint of 1912 edition published by Craftsman Publishing.)

Williamson, R. M. *A series of plan books produced for sale to retail lumber dealers*. Held in the R. M. Williamson Collection (MA 92-11), Texas/Dallas History & Archives, Dallas Public Library.

Ye Planry Architects. *Better Homes*. Dallas, TX: Ye Planry Corp., [192-?].

Ye Planry Beautiful Homes. Dallas: Ye Planry Company, 1914.

Ye Planry Bungalows. Los Angeles: Ye Planry Company, 1908.

Illustration Credits

Cover: Shannon Simpson
Back cover: Margaret Culbertson

Maps by Jim Parsons

p. 5: Ellis County Museum
p. 6: Ellis County Museum
p. 7: Courtesy of the Dr. Charles W. Simpson Family and the Ellis County Museum
p. 8-9, top: Private collection
p. 8, bottom: Private collection
p. 14: Ellis County Museum
p. 15, top: Ellis County Museum
p. 15, bottom: Webb Gallery Collection
p. 16: Ellis County Museum
p. 17: Ellis County Museum
p. 26, A-8: Ellis County Museum
p. 34, A-19: Ellis County Museum
p. 40, A-32, top: Ellis County Museum
p. 70: Ellis County Museum
p. 71, top & bottom: Ellis County Museum
p. 72: Private collection
p. 73, top & bottom: Ellis County Museum
p. 74: Ellis County Museum
p. 89, B-21, top: Ellis County Museum
p. 112, B-71, top: Ellis County Museum
p. 116: Ellis County Museum
p. 117, top: Private collection
p. 117, bottom left and right: Ellis County Museum
p. 118, top: Ellis County Museum
p. 118, bottom: Private collection
p. 119: Ellis County Museum
p. 120, top: Ellis County Museum
p. 120, bottom: Courtesy of the Dr. Charles W. Simpson Family and the Ellis County Museum
p. 182: Courtesy of the Dr. Charles W. Simpson Family and the Ellis County Museum
p. 183, top and bottom right: Ellis County Museum
p. 183, bottom left: Courtesy Melanie Price Reed
p. 196: Ellis County Museum
p. 197: Perry Castaneda Library Map Collection, University of Texas at Austin
p. 198, top and bottom: National Library of Medicine
p. 199: National Air and Space Museum, photo NASM92-13721
p. 201: Ellis County Museum
p. 206, top: Perry Castaneda Library Map Collection, University of Texas at Austin
p. 206, middle: Used with permission of The Sanborn Library, LLC.
p. 206, bottom: Texas Historical Commission National Register Collection, Photograph 1214-17; Portal to Texas History
p. 208, E-4, top: Ellis County Museum
p. 210, E-6: Ellis County Museum
p. 210, E-7, top: Ellis County Museum
p. 211, E-8: Ellis County Museum

p. 213, E-9, top: Ellis County Museum
p. 213, E-9, bottom: Texas Historical Commission National Register Collection, Photograph 1162-01, Portal to Texas History
p. 218, E-17, top: National Library of Medicine
p. 218, E-17, bottom: Ellis County Museum
p. 220, E-20, top: Ellis County Clerk's Office
p. 227, E-31, top: Ellis County Museum
p. 227, E-31, bottom: Texas Historical Commission National Register Collection, Photograph 1259-09; Portal to Texas History
p. 230: Ellis County Museum
p. 231, top & middle: Ellis County Museum
p. 231, bottom: Private collection
p. 232: Ellis County Museum
p. 233, top & bottom: Ellis County Museum
p. 257, F-51, top: Ellis County Museum
p. 268: Courtesy of the Dr. Charles W. Simpson Family and the Ellis County Museum
p. 269: Ellis County Museum
p. 270, top & bottom: Courtesy of the Dr. Charles W. Simpson Family and the Ellis County Museum
p. 271: Private collection
p. 315, G-96, top: Ellis County Museum
p. 330: University of Connecticut Libraries

Current photographs in entries taken by Ellen Beasley and Margaret Culbertson.
Ellen Beasley:
A-07, A-10, A-11, A-12, A-13, A-14, A-15, A-16, A-18, A-20, A-22, A-23, A-24, A-25, A-26, A-28, A-29, A-30, A-31, A-33, A-34, A-37, A-38, A-41, A-42, A-43, A-46, A-48, A-49, A-50, A-52, A-53, A-54, A-55, A-56, A-57, A-59, A-60, A-61, A-62, A-63, A-64, A-69, , B-02, B-03, B-06, B-08, B-09, B-11, B-12, B-13, B-14, B-15, B-16, B-17, B-18, B-19, B-20, B-30, B-35, B-37, B-38, B-39, B-43, B-45, B-46, B-58, B-59, B-60, B-65, C-001, C-002, C-003, C-004, C-005, C-006, C-007, C-009, C-011, C-012, C-013, C-014, C-015, C-019, C-021, C-022, C-023, C-024, C-025, C-028, C-029, C-031, C-032, C-033, C-034, C-036, C-039, C-040, C-041, C-042, C-043, C-050, C-051, C-052, C-053, C-055, C-056, C-061, C-063, C-064, C-068, C-071, C-072, C-073, C-077, C-081, C-083, C-086, C-087, C-090, C-091, C-092, C-095, C-096, C-098, C-099, C-102, C-106, C-108, C-111, C-120, C-121, C-123, C-124, C-125, D-01, D-07, D-11, D-12, D-13, D-14, E-05, E-07, E-10, E-12, E-13, E-14, E-15, E-16, E-18, E-19, E-20, E-21, E-22, E-23, E-28, F-01, F-03, F-05, F-12, F-21, F-22, F-24, F-49, F-55, F-57, F-60, F-63, F-65, F-68, G-003, G-05, G-006, G-008, G-009, G-010, G-011, G-012, G-015, G-018, G-019, G-020, G-021, G-023, G-024, G-025, G-026, G-027, G-028, G-031, G-037, G-038, G-039, G-040, G-041, G-042, G-043, G-044 ,G-046, G-049, G-050, G-053, G-054, G-055, G-056, G-057, G-058, G-059, G-061, G-62, G-063, G-066, G-068, G-070, G-071, G-072, G-073, G-074, G-078, G-080, G-082, G-083, G-, 85, G-088, G-089, G-090, G-091, G-092, G-095, G-102, G-106, G-108, G-109, G-116, G-120, G-121

Margaret Culbertson:
p. vi, A-01, A-02, A-03, A-04, A-05, A-06, A-09, A-17, A-21, A-27, A-32, A-35, A-36, A-39, A-40, A-44, A-45, A-47, A-51, A-58, A-65, A-66, A-67, A-68, B-01, B-04, B-05, B-07, B-10, B-21, B-22, B-23, B-24, B-25, B-26, B-27, B-28, B-29, B-31, B-32, B-33, B-34, B-36, B-40, B-41, B-42, B-44, B-47, B-48, B-49, B-50, B-51, B-52, B-53, B-54, B-55, B-56, B-57, B-61, B-62, B-63, B- 64, B-66, B-67, B-68, B-69, B-70, B-71, B-72, C-002, C-008, C-010, C-016, C-017, C-018, C-020, C-026, C-027, C-030, C-035, C-037, C-038, C-044, C-045, C-046, C-047, C-048, C-054, C-057, C-058, C-059, C-060, C-062, C-065, C-066, C-067, C-069, C-070, C-074, C-075, C-076, C-078, C-079, C-080, C-082, C-084, C-085, C-088, C-089, C-093, C-094, C-097, C-100, C-101, C-103, C-104, C-105, C-107, C-109, C-110, C-112, C-113, C-114, C-115, C-116, C-117, C-118, C-119, C-122, D-02, D-03, D-04, D-05, D-06, D-08, D-09, D-10, D-15, E-01, E-03, E-04, E-11, E-24, E-25, E-26, E-27, E-30, F-02, F-04, F-06, F-07, F-08, F-09, F-10, F-11, F-13, F-14, F-15, F-16, F-17, F-18, F-19, F-20, F-23, F-25, F-26, F-27, F-28, F-29, F-30, F-31, F-32, F-33, F-34, F-35, F-36, F-37, F-38, F-30, F-40, F-41, F-42, F-43, F-44, F-45, F-46, F-47, F-48, F-50, F-51, F-52, F-53, F-54, F-56, F-58, F-59, F-61, F-62, F-64, F-66, F-67, G-001, G-002, G-004, G-007, G-13, G-014, G-016, G-017, G-022, G-029, G-030, G-032, G-033, G-034, G-035, G-036, G-045, G-47, G-048, G-051, G-052, G-060, G-064, G-065, G-067, G-069, G-075, G-076, G-077, G-079, G-081, G-084, G-086, G-087, G-093, G-094, G-096, G-097, G-098, G-099, G-100, G-101, G-103, G-104, G-105, G-107, G-110, G-111, G-112, G-113, G-114, G-115, G-117, G-118, G-119

Street Address Index

(Address followed by page numbers.)

General Index

ABOUT THE AUTHORS

MARGARET CULBERTSON is the director of the Powell Library, Bayou Bend Collection and Gardens, Museum of Fine Arts, Houston, and project director of Bayou Bend's William J. Hill Texas Artisans & Artists Archive. Her most recent book is *Texas Houses Built by the Book: The Use of Published Designs, 1850-1925.*

ELLEN BEASLEY is a preservationist and historian whose publications include *The Alleys and Back Buildings of Galveston: An Architectural and Social History.* She is also the coauthor of the *Galveston Architecture Guidebook.*